AF478253

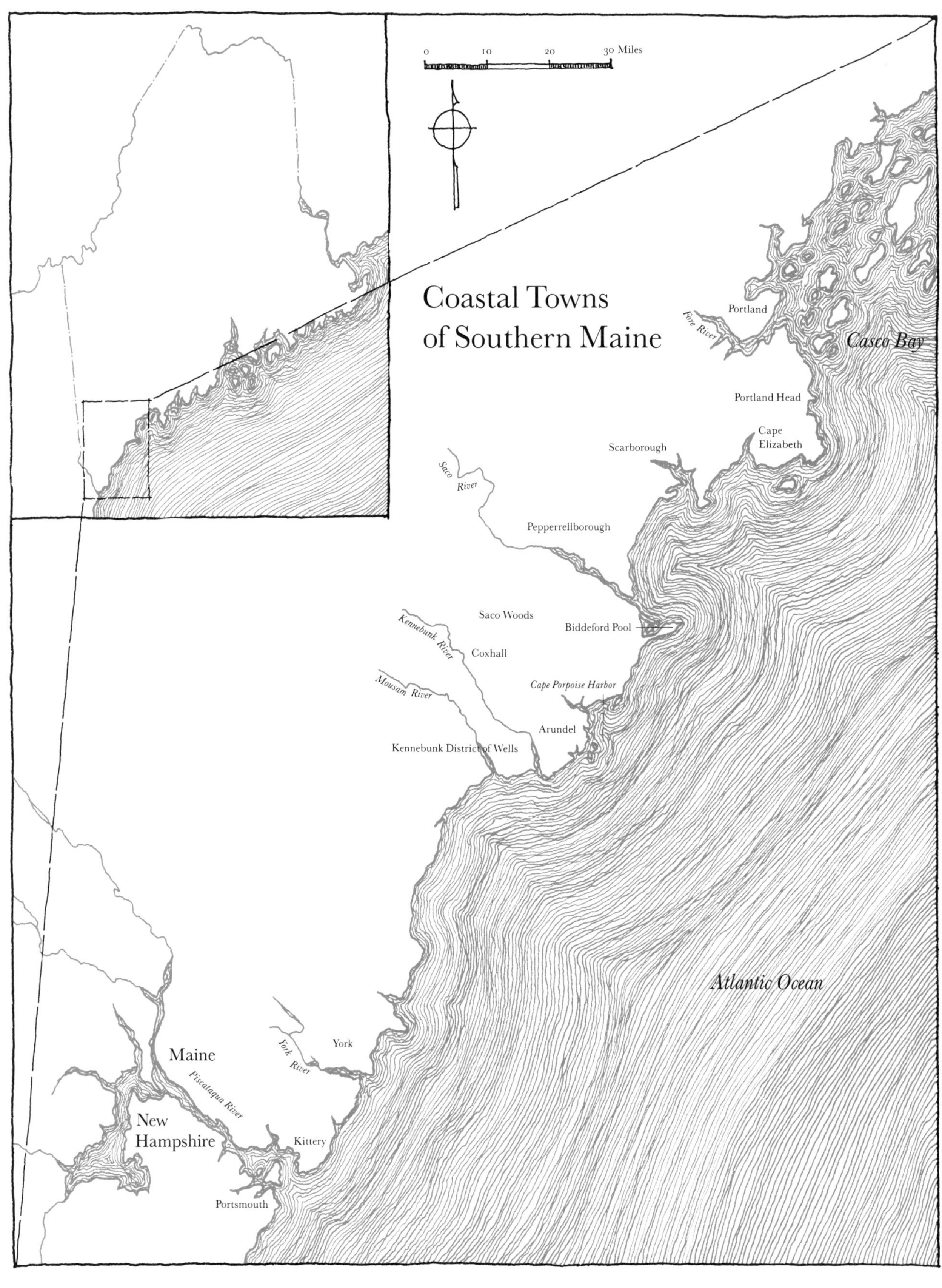

Coastal Towns
of Southern Maine
0 10 20 30 Miles
Casco Bay
Portland
Fore River
Portland Head
Cape Elizabeth
Scarborough
Saco River
Pepperrellborough
Saco Woods
Biddeford Pool
Kennebunk River
Coxhall
Cape Porpoise Harbor
Mousam River
Arundel
Kennebunk District of Wells
Atlantic Ocean
Maine
New Hampshire
York
York River
Piscataqua River
Kittery
Portsmouth

Agreeable Situations

Society, Commerce, and Art in Southern Maine, 1780–1830

Edited by Laura Fecych Sprague

Essays by Joyce Butler, Richard M. Candee,
Laura Fecych Sprague, and Laurel Thatcher Ulrich

The Brick Store Museum · Kennebunk · Maine

Distributed by Northeastern University Press · Boston

This catalogue has been made possible by a grant from the National Endowment for the Humanities, a federal agency.

Cover: Lemuel Moody, *Signals at Portland Lighthouse*, 1807 (cat. 5)
Collection Maine Historical Society

Library of Congress Cataloging-in-Publication Data

Agreeable Situations.

    Catalog of selected objects from the Brick Store Museum et al.
    Bibliography: p. 277
    Includes index.
    1. Material culture–Maine–Catalogs.   2. Art,
American–Maine–Catalogs.   3. Art, Modern–19th
century–Maine–Catalogs.   4. Maine–Commerce–History–
19th century.   5. Maine–Social life and customs.
I. Sprague, Laura Fecych, 1954–
II. Butler, Joyce.   III. Brick Store Museum.
F24.A34 1987   709'.74'07401419   87–5143
ISBN (clothbound) 0–9617576–0–4; (paperback) 0–9617576–1–2

Contents

Foreword

In recent years the state of Maine has experienced a surge of growth that has inspired articles in national publications reporting on the "livability" of our state. While this attention seems a new phenomenon, Maine's advantages have been long recognized. During the federal period such well-traveled figures as Timothy Dwight, the Duke de la Rochefoucault-Liancourt, and Anne Royall extolled the agreeable situations to be found here. This fascinating volume celebrates the quality of life in the region through an examination of Maine's historical collections. The contents are devoted to the permanent holdings of four southern Maine historical institutions: The Brick Store Museum in Kennebunk, Maine Historical Society in Portland, Old York Historical Society in York, and York Institute Museum in Saco. The vast majority of the objects in these collections have been previously overlooked; this publication helps to determine the contributions they make to the study of American fine and decorative arts, and life in the early Republic.

The history of these institutions reflects an early and continuing awareness by Maine people of the importance of their state's history. The Maine Historical Society, the fourth oldest historical society in the nation, was founded in 1822, only two years after statehood was achieved. Among the founders were Governor Albion K. Parris, Bowdoin College president William Allen, Stephen Longfellow (cat. 43), Judge Prentiss Mellen (cat. 30), and other leading citizens of the new state. Initially housed in quarters at Bowdoin College, then at temporary locations, the Society found a permanent home in Portland when in 1901 Anne Longfellow Pierce gave the Wadsworth-Longfellow house and its contents to the Society with the stipulation that it build a library to house its collection of research materials. Today the Society maintains the Wadsworth-Longfellow house, an important fine and decorative arts collection, the state's largest historical library, and a highly significant manuscript collection.

The York Institute Museum was organized in Saco in 1867. That same year George Addison Emery established one of the state's earliest art collections at the Institute when he presented the Brewster portraits of his great-great-grandparents, Thomas and Elizabeth Cutts (cat. 33). With the John S. Locke Collection, bequeathed to the Institute by Almira Locke McArthur in 1950, the museum's holdings of decorative arts increased dramatically. Objects from the Cleaves family link this organization with The Brick Store Museum.

The Old York Historical Society traces its roots to 1900 when, at the height of the colonial revival movement, William Dean Howells, a novelist, editor of the *Atlantic Monthly*, and York Harbor summer resident, spearheaded the preservation of the Old York Gaol built in 1720. In the ensuing years, the Old Gaol Museum and Old York Historical and Improvement Society acquired additional eighteenth- and nineteenth-century properties to house ever-growing collections. A merger with the Society for the Preservation of Historic Landmarks in York County in 1984 led to the establishment of today's Old York Historical Society.

The Brick Store Museum in Kennebunk was founded in 1936 by Edith Cleaves Barry, a descendant of Maine's Lord and Cleaves families. Beginning with one room in the 1825 store of Miss Barry's great-grandfather, the museum has grown to include four historic commercial buildings and the 1805 Taylor-Barry house. Many of the objects illustrated in this volume are derived from the collection of the great antiquary William E. Barry.

Agreeable Situations fills a gap in Maine's published history, and, as never before, shows that Maine people enjoyed a surprising level of accomplishment and affluence during the federal period. It draws attention to the rich and relatively untapped resources available in southern Maine for scholars interested in the social, cultural, and economic history of the new Republic. As a catalogue, as a research tool, as a series of interpretations, this volume offers a challenge to researchers, who have long mined the historical riches of southern New England, to look north beyond the Piscataqua River to Maine. Rarely has such a vein of new ore been struck.

Earle G. Shettleworth, Jr., Director,
Maine Historic Preservation Commission

Preface

The period 1780–1830 is the first in Maine history from which a large number of objects have survived. Many families prospered as the economy grew, and their domestic and personal possessions reveal an increased standard of living that matched that in other regions of federal America. Although a wealth of material has been available, the study of federal Maine has been largely neglected. Since its founding in 1968, the Maine State Museum has made great strides in the exhibition and publication of Maine-made objects, some of which date to this period. In addition, catalogues of fine and decorative arts of national importance have included objects with histories in federal Maine. With *Agreeable Situations*, however, for the first time a large and related group of the fine and decorative arts of Maine has been published. The objects not only have individual significance, but as a group they also vividly illustrate and contribute to the interpretation of economic and social history in the District of Maine. As a result, our understanding of Maine's role in the growth of the nation is enhanced.

Agreeable Situations is the product of a recent series of related studies of federal Maine. It had its beginnings in 1983 when James S. Leamon, professor of history, Bates College, Lewiston, Maine, and Eldridge H. Pendleton, director of the Old Gaol Museum (now Old York Historical Society), approached me with the idea of an inventory of Maine decorative arts of the federal period. This inventory was to be one of many projects undertaken as part of "Maine at Statehood: The Forgotten Years, 1780–1820," a year-long, statewide project conducted by the Maine Humanities Council and funded by a Chairman's Award from the National Endowment for the Humanities. The purpose of the project was to encourage the study of life in Maine in the forty years after the Revolution, marking its transition from a District of Massachusetts to statehood.

As inventory co-directors Eldridge Pendleton and I, with the assistance of Carolyn S. Parsons and Kevin D. Murphy, searched historical organizations, museums, and libraries throughout the state for objects owned by Maine families during the late eighteenth and early nineteenth centuries. Although artifacts in major collections outside of

Maine were included, the objects in Maine's own repositories were the basis of our work because they were virtually unknown. The resulting archive of catalogue worksheets, photographs, and supporting materials is now housed at the Maine State Museum, Augusta, as part of the newly formed Center for the Study of Maine Material Culture.

A subsequent project entailed an examination of the extensive manuscript holdings of the Maine Historical Society in order to document the decorative arts and their use in the District of Maine. A small traveling interpretative exhibition entitled "'Neatness, Comfort, and Independence': Life in Federal Maine," funded by a grant from the Maine Humanities Council and the National Endowment for the Humanities, was prepared from the results of the inventory and this documentary research.

In January 1984 Sandra S. Armentrout, director of The Brick Store Museum, brought a grant announcement from the National Endowment for the Humanities to my attention with the offer to sponsor an application. The NEH sought applications for funds for the research and publication of catalogues interpreting permanent collections. Publications could focus on an entire collection or portions of it. To select a part of the collection of any single Maine historical institution, based on the research we had completed, would have reduced the project from one of national interest to one of regional concern, thus putting it outside of the Endowment's mandate. The proposal we submitted called for a catalogue of the federal-period collections of four institutions, to be published in conjunction with historical essays that would serve as a source for the study of American culture.

The collections of The Brick Store Museum, Maine Historical Society, Old York Historical Society, and York Institute Museum are the focus of *Agreeable Situations* for several reasons. They are among the oldest collections in the state, and concentrated as they are in the southern counties, they complement one another. The objects selected are among the most important in the collections; nearly all were saved by descendants of the original owners—merchants, shipbuilders, and lawyers—and form the core of each institution's respective collections. Through their provenance, the collections document the richness of life along the southern Maine coast, yet with few exceptions, the objects have never before been published. Efforts were made to present the range of objects found in these institutions, but it was not possible to include all the different media. In this volume, five essays are presented on town history and maritime trade, architecture, the arrangement and decoration of interiors, the patronage of artists and craftsmen, and women's lives. Following each essay is a section of catalogue entries arranged thematically; we hope any inconvenience this arrangement may cause will be compensated for by a more informative and stimulating combination of ideas and objects.

This catalogue expands our understanding of ideas presented during the Maine at Statehood project by focusing on objects and what they reveal of cultural, social, and economic history. Because of its role as a catalogue of the permanent collections, and not as a comprehensive publication on life in federal Maine, the reader who would like to learn more about this period is referred to the forthcoming publication of the Maine of Statehood symposium papers, Charles E. Clark and James S. Leamon, eds., *Maine in the Early Republic, 1783–1820: From Revolution to Statehood.*

Agreeable Situations, a period reference to Maine society, is not only an apt title for this project but it also describes my experience in working with so many dedicated people. The collaboration of Joyce Butler, Richard Candee, Laurel Ulrich, and the catalogue contributors enriched the essays and entries and often helped assure accuracy. The catalogue has benefited immeasurably by the high standards of scholarship of our two project advisors, Edward S. Cooke, Jr., assistant curator, Department of American Decorative Arts and Sculpture, Museum of Fine Arts, Boston, and Arlene Palmer Schwind, museum consultant of Yarmouth, Maine. Their approach to American material culture helped shape the contents of the book. At many times we relied not only on their experience to help us interpret our raw research materials but also upon their skills to transform ideas into clearly written prose. We are also indebted to Mr. and Mrs. Dean A. Fales, Jr., decorative arts authors and consultants; Jane C. Nylander, director, Strawbery Banke, Portsmouth, New Hampshire; and Richard C. Nylander, curator, Society for the Preservation of New England Antiquities, Boston, who read and critiqued drafts and brought many pertinent references to our attention.

For their contributions in the areas of Maine architecture, fine arts, and the decorative arts, we are grateful to Earle G. Shettleworth, Jr., director, Maine Historic Preservation Commission, Augusta; William David Barry, Portland historian; and Edwin A. Churchill, chief curator, Maine State Museum, Augusta.

The directors of the four institutions and their staffs were always helpful, facilitating many aspects of the research and book production. At The Brick Store Museum, we would like to thank Sandra S. Armentrout, director, who with grace and humor eased project administration; Ellen Byrne, administrative assistant; Joyce Butler, curator of manuscripts, who shared her extensive research into the Wadsworth-Longfellow family, thus adding greatly to this catalogue; Kathryn A. Hussey, assistant registrar, who performed miracles when preparing the costumes for photography; and Mary Lord Kline, registrar. Our thanks are extended to the staff of the Maine Historical Society: Neal W. Allen, Jr., former acting director; Thomas L. Gaffney, curator of manuscripts; Elizabeth S. Hamill, museum curator; Margaret J. McCain, librarian; Elizabeth J. Miller, executive director; Cynthia J. Murphy, staff assistant; and Stephen T. Seames, manuscript assistant. At Old York Historical Society, Peter W. Cook, director; Debra Cunningham, librarian; Sharron Drew, interpreter; Kerry O'Brien, former curator; Juliet H. Mofford, educator; Ann Reiss Cole, architectural historian; and Karen Temple, librarian, all kindly assisted at various stages of the project. We are grateful to Christine Bertsch, reference librarian; Audrey Milne, senior curator; Kerry O'Brien, curator of collections; Maureen Oppenheim-Golub, reference librarian; and Stephen Podgajny, executive director, at the York Institute Museum and Dyer Library.

We owe a debt of gratitude to the following individuals who assisted us in our research: Mr. and Mrs. Earl F. Adams, Mr. and Mrs. Theodore Blaisdell, Alfred Coulombe, Bev Davis, Mrs. Benjamin Flayderman, Norman Flayderman, Natalie Rogers Green, Theodore E. Jewett, Rick Litchfield, Mrs. R. A. Page, Weston Pease, Father Leo Polselli, Mr. and Mrs. William C. Pierce, Mrs. John A. Rogers, Barbara Storer, Mr. and Mrs. Trevor Wilkie, Mark Willett, Michael Willett, and Mr. and Mrs. S. Thompson Viele.

Other research assistance was ably provided by Kathleen Catalano, curator, Longfellow National Historic Site, Cambridge; James Cheevers, senior curator, United States Naval Academy Museum, Annapolis; Lorna Condon, associate librarian, Society for the Preservation of New England Antiquities; James Garvin, curator, New Hampshire Historical Society, Concord; Arthur Gerrier, researcher, Greater Portland Landmarks, Portland; Dorothy Healy, curator, Maine Women Writers Collection, Westbrook College, Portland; Brock Jobe, chief curator, Society for the Preservation of New England Antiquities; William B. Jordan, professor of history, Westbrook College; Edith McCauley, special collections librarian, Portland Public Library; Robert Mussey, chief furniture conservator, Society for the Preservation of New England Antiquities; Barbara Redjinski, registrar, Portland Museum of Art; Ellie Reichlin, director of archives, Society for the Preservation of New England Antiquities; and Katharine J. Watson, director, Bowdoin College Museum of Art.

R. Bruce Hoadley of the University of Massachusetts,

Amherst, visited Maine on a crisp autumn weekend to microanalyze the woods used in the furniture. His findings made important contributions to the entries. All the photographs in the catalogue are the work of David Bohl, Society for the Preservation of New England Antiquities, who with skill, flexibility, and good humor endured a variety of trying studio conditions. With the counsel of Thomas C. Hubka, Scott Benson expertly drew the floor plans, elevations, and maps. In addition to contributing entries, Kevin D. Murphy devoted many summer hours to making manuscript revisions. In its final stages, the manuscript was greatly improved by Gerald W. R. Ward, whose experience and copy editing skills helped ensure a professional editorial standard. Catherine Waters, with sensitivity to the subject matter, good judgement, and an adept eye not only designed the book but also supervised all the stages of its production. At Meriden-Stinehour Press, Paul Hoffmann skillfully oversaw the typesetting and binding and Sue Medlicott brought her expertise to the task of supervising the printing. Robert J. Hennessey, the halftone photographer has taken great care to enhance the photographic information. We are thankful to Margaret York who assisted in proofreading the galleys.

In his unofficial role as assistant project director, Seth Sprague contributed large, and much appreciated, quantities of patience, constructive criticism, and encouragement.

Our thanks are graciously extended to Karen Bowden, executive director of the Maine Humanities Council during the Maine at Statehood project, who supported the decorative arts inventory and encouraged its funding, and to Dorothy Schwartz, who followed Ms. Bowden as director and subsequently encouraged the Maine Historical Society's "'Neatness, Comfort, and Independence'" project which proved to be an important research phase.

Finally, we would like to thank the National Endowment for the Humanities for the grant that made this publication possible and the Phineas W. Sprague Memorial Foundation, Mrs. Millard S. Peabody, and Mr. and Mrs. William C. Pierce for their generous additional funding.

Laura Fecych Sprague

Contributors to the Catalogue

L F S
Laura Fecych Sprague
Project Director
The Brick Store Museum

Joyce Butler
Curator of Manuscripts
The Brick Store Museum

Richard M. Candee
Professor, American and New England Studies Program
Boston University

Laurel Thatcher Ulrich
Assistant Professor of History
University of New Hampshire

S S A
Sandra Siver Armentrout
Director
The Brick Store Museum

A A E
A. Abigail Ewing
Curator
Bangor Historical Society

K D M
Kevin D. Murphy
Research Associate
The Brick Store Museum

K A O
Kerry A. O'Brien
Curator of Collections
York Institute Museum

C S P
Carolyn S. Parsons
Registrar
Strawbery Banke

Notes to the Catalogue

Each of the 175 catalogue entries in this volume includes a heading giving detailed information on the object's maker, form, place of manufacture and date, materials, signature or maker's mark (if any), dimensions, collection, and credit line. If the maker of a decorative arts object is unknown, the first line of the heading has been silently omitted. In the case of paintings and other pictorial arts, unknown authorship is so indicated. Each artist's and maker's vital dates are listed, when known, or the known working dates (w.) are given. If the name of a wood is given in italics, it indicates that the species has been identified by microanalysis. Signatures or marks by the artist, maker, or manufacturer are listed. Inscriptions, where appropriate, are mentioned in the commentary. Height (H), length (L), width (W), and depth (D) are overall measurements, unless otherwise noted. Diameter (Diam.) is an overall measurement if listed as the only dimension; if given as a secondary measurement, it denotes the rim diameter unless otherwise noted. Costume measurements are as follows: height (H) is the greatest point of the article or overall height at center back; length (L) denotes the measurement of the skirt with front and back noted if there is a train; the location of the circumference (Circum.) is noted; waist dimensions are noted as original or altered, if known. Full fabric width (W) is noted when appropriate. Throughout, dimensions are given in inches, followed by metric measurements in centimeters enclosed in parentheses. Each catalogue entry is followed by the initials of the author or authors. For these and other abbreviations, consult the list of contributors to the catalogue and the list of abbreviations. Short titles used in the essay and entry notes are listed in full in the selected bibliography. Essay footnotes follow their respective essays.

Generally, probate records for York County, and deeds for York and Cumberland counties, are cited with the volume number followed by the page number or numbers. In some instances, the docket number is cited instead. Cumberland County probate records for this period were destroyed by fire.

Frequently cited newspapers published in Maine include the *Eastern Argus* and *Portland Gazette*, both in Portland; *The Weekly Visiter, Annals of the Times*, and *Kennebunk Gazette* are Kennebunk newspapers.

Objects at The Brick Store Museum from the estate of William E. Barry were either given during the museum's founding (1936–1940), or were bequeathed in 1969 by Edith Cleaves Barry and Julia Barry Bodman, William's heirs and only remaining descendants. Although Julia Barry Bodman died in 1971, it was through the bequest at the time of Edith's death in 1969 that the collection came to the museum. The credit line has been simplified to stress the preservation by William E. Barry of his family's collection (much of which was located in the Taylor-Barry house).

Abbreviations

BSM
The Brick Store Museum, Kennebunk, Maine

CCRD
Cumberland County Registry of Deeds, Portland, Maine

LNHS
National Park Service, Longfellow National Historic Site, Cambridge, Massachusetts

MEHS
Maine Historical Society, Portland, Maine

OYHS
Old York Historical Society, York, Maine

SPNEA
Society for the Preservation of New England Antiquities, Boston, Massachusetts

YCRD
York County Registry of Deeds, Alfred, Maine

YCRP
York County Registry of Probate, Alfred, Maine

YIS
York Institute Museum, Saco, Maine

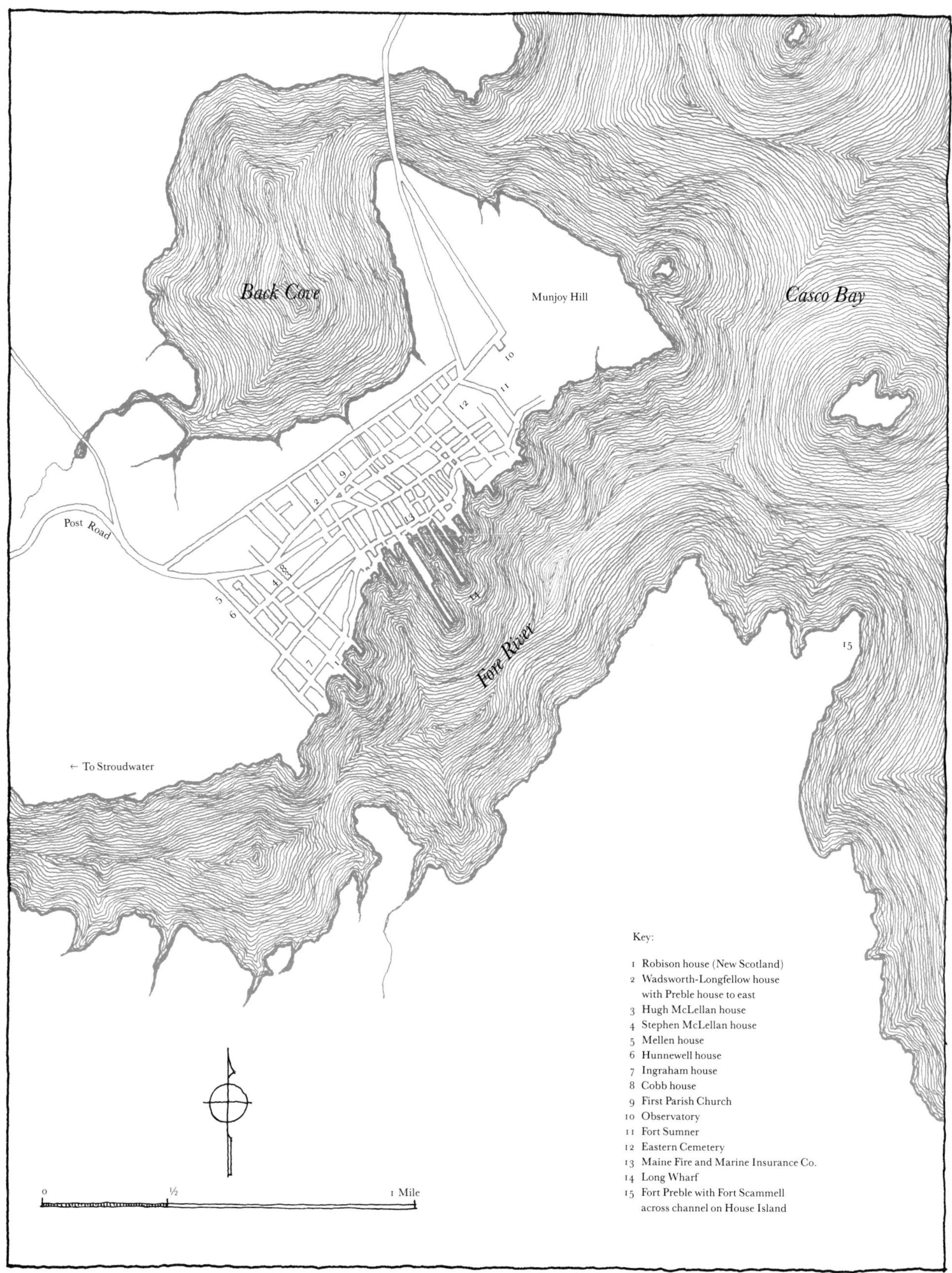

Fig. 1.1 Map of Portland (Falmouth Neck until 1786). Drawing, Scott Benson.

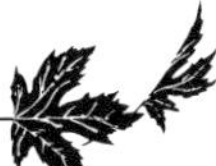

Chapter 1

Rising Like a Phoenix:
Commerce in Southern Maine, 1775–1830

Joyce Butler

The morning of October 18, 1775, was clear and pleasant on Falmouth Neck in the District of Maine where the thriving town of Falmouth was situated. Although much of Falmouth was still undeveloped forest and swamp, its center was an attractive village on the peninsula's gentle southern slope above the Fore River. Dwelling houses and stores were interspersed with two churches and other public buildings along picturesquely named streets that here and there passed on stone bridges over brooks that flowed from ponds and alder swamps through the town to the river. Although most of the buildings were of modest size and unpainted, prosperity was evident in a handful of houses of two-and-one-half stories or with brick ends. Along the waterfront, eighteen wharves bearing the names of the more important local merchants and shipmasters extended into the river. It was from these wharves that the town's shipping carried on the commercial ventures that had turned Falmouth from a struggling frontier settlement into a busy and important seaport (fig. 1.1).

Until the onset of America's war for independence at the battle of Lexington and Concord, just six months earlier, locally owned ships had been engaged in the lucrative West Indies trade, carrying lumber, wood products, and dried fish to the islands of the Caribbean that were owned by England, France, and other European countries. A fleet of deep water fishing vessels also operated out of Falmouth, and the harbor was visited regularly by mast ships from England and large merchant vessels from Europe and America's principal seaports.

On that bright October morning when there was no wind to turn the windmill that stood off Back Street or to rustle the leaves in the orchards and small woods scattered through the town, four armed British ships stood in a line in the river. Their guns were pointed at Falmouth. They had come to bring the war to the District of Maine. At exactly 9:40 a.m. they opened fire, beginning a day-long bombardment that left three-quarters of the town a smouldering ruin (fig. 1.2). More than 400 buildings were destroyed, including 136 dwelling houses, as well as the "handsome new court-house, the Episcopalian church, the town-house, the

custom-house, a fire engine, nearly new, together with barns and almost every store and warehouse in town, all the wharves but one or two short ones, and all the vessels in the harbor but two, which the enemy took away with them."[1]

At the end of that frightening, sad day, when at last the guns fell silent under the pall of smoke that hung over the Neck, Falmouth had lost more than her buildings, her wharves and shipping, and her inhabitants (for the people had fled to the surrounding countryside and most would not return until the Revolution was over). The destruction of Falmouth effectively ended fifty years of business enterprise and its resulting prosperity. The town was plunged back into its own history. Its center was as desolate and uninhabited as it had been in 1720 when Samuel Moody, one of a handful of inhabitants who had dared to return following the third Indian war, had built a house on India Street fronting the beach, which had been for many years the principal house in the town.[2]

News of the brutal destruction of Falmouth spread rapidly, producing "universal indignation and horrour." Even the British ministry found the first reports of the incident hard to believe. Thomas Oxnard, a Falmouth Loyalist living in exile in London, upon hearing the news, wrote in his journal, "Oh, my poor heart, how can I support the tidings; my tenderest connections driven to the extremes of poverty and distress. . . . I spent a most melancholy day."[3]

In southern Maine's other coastal villages, the news produced more than depression. South of Falmouth on the Saco River, the people of Pepperrellborough and Biddeford, who must have heard the firing of the guns and seen the pall of smoke (and whose settlements narrowly escaped the same fate), as well as the inhabitants of nearby Arundel and Wells, with its developing Kennebunk district, must have feared for their own safety.[4] Farther south, at York, merchant Jonathan Sayward wrote in his journal on October 24, "for severall Days past all hath been uprore and Confusion since Falmouth is burnt, and Portsmouth [New Hampshire] expects the fleet to Destroy [it]."[5]

Merchants and mariners all along the southern Maine coast must have felt shock and dismay at the loss of the commercial center Falmouth had represented. Although naval offices were located in every seaport "for the entering and clearing of all . . . vessels trading to and from it," the only collection district in Maine was located at Falmouth. Moreover, the use of Falmouth by vessels from Europe and America's southern ports would have provided markets and imports of significance even to merchants south of Falmouth, who were close to the large shipping centers of New Hampshire and Massachusetts proper.[6]

In 1775 no other coastal town in southern Maine, where the largest percentage of the District's population lived, had matched Falmouth's commercial success and its attendant town development, even though all had been established as long or longer than Falmouth, all had access to the supplies of lumber and fish that were the basis of Falmouth's shipping economy, and most had been settled by enterprising men who with varying degrees of success had brought their towns into the lucrative merchant marine trade.[7] Qualifying to a degree as an exception was York, whose importance and growth during the seventeenth and eighteenth centuries was reflected in its substantial colonial houses and its position as shiretown of York County. York, however, had achieved the pinnacle of her development, while Falmouth was just beginning to reach for hers.

Falmouth's Advantage

Falmouth's advantage over her sister towns lay in her choice situation on the protected, deep-water, ice-free harbor of Casco Bay and the Fore River. From the earliest days of settlement Falmouth's inhabitants had realized the importance of their harbor. In an age when the communication and commerce of Maine, indeed the American colonies, depended on the ocean, Falmouth's settlers did not have to contend with the topographical disadvantages and uncertainties that beset those of the Saco River settlements, Arundel, Wells, and even York.[8]

On the Saco River the earliest settlement had been at its mouth where two spits of land create a natural pool or harbor for vessels (today's Biddeford Pool). The presence four miles inland of a forty-two-foot drop in the level of the river presented an even more appealing location for settlement. As the Reverend Jonathan Coggswell of Saco noted in 1815, "It is no exaggeration to say, there is probably not a better place in the world for all kinds of mills and factories."[9] Coggswell can be forgiven his chauvinism, for he had seen impressive utilization of the fall's waterpower. However, another contemporary observer noted, "the Saco River was not well fitted for vessels of a large draft."[10] Millowners at the falls were plagued by the need to raft at least part of their cargoes of lumber down river to be loaded on vessels that could not get over a troublesome bar near the river's mouth if fully loaded at the falls. Another disadvantage for merchants and mariners at the falls was the ice that closed the river to navigation for three or four months a year. It was rare for ice to close Falmouth's harbor.[11]

Nevertheless, on the eve of the Revolution a lumbering industry that since 1772 had been drawing its raw material

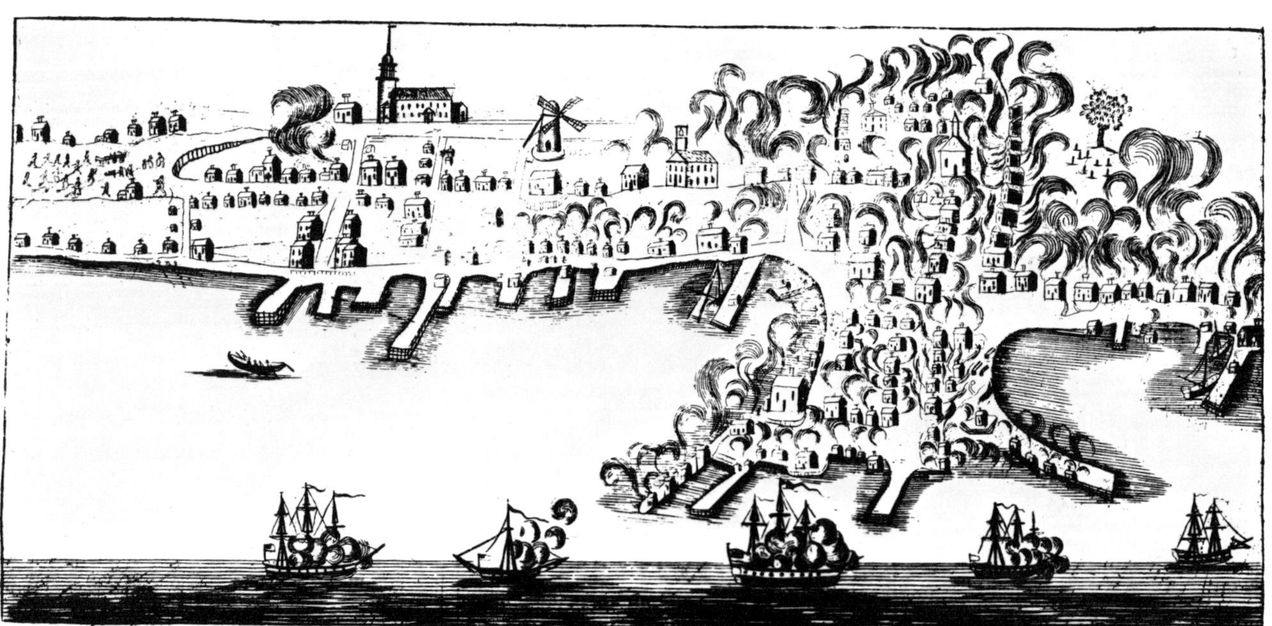

Fig. 1.2 *The Town of Falmouth, Burnt by Captain Moet, October 18, 1775.* From James Murray, *An Impartial History of the War in America* (Boston, 1782). Courtesy, American Antiquarian Society.

from inland as far away as Fryeburg was in full swing at the falls, and men like Thomas Cutts were already making their fortunes. Although there was still a busy settlement at Biddeford Pool, villages had begun to grow up at the falls on both sides of the river. Pepperrellborough, which had taken its name from the largest landowner in the town, Kittery's Sir William Pepperrell, and Biddeford were in the process of overcoming what had been in essence a false start at Biddeford Pool and finding their town centers at the Saco falls (fig. 1.3).

Uncertainty of place and purpose had also marked the history of Arundel on the shore of the Kennebunk River and the neighboring Kennebunk district of Wells. Arundel had begun as Cape Porpus with the homes of its inhabitants clustered at Cape Porpus harbor. Although the center of the town had grown away from the Cape, it had moved into the outlying farming areas rather than toward the river. Few if any vessels were owned in the town. In 1775 Arundel was still essentially a frontier town, its inhabitants living in simple houses, traveling to the Saco River settlements for a doctor, battling wolves in the woods, eking out a living as farmers (fig. 1.4). The war would make poorer a town that was already called "Poor Arundel."[12]

On the other side of the Kennebunk River, the people who lived in the section of Wells that was called Kennebunk (and would eventually after a long struggle for independence from its parent town become the Town of Kennebunk) were making better use of that river and the Mousam River on the Kennebunk district's southern border. Although sawmills and shipyards had been active on the Mousam since the earliest days of settlement, in 1755 the district's coasting trade had been moved from the Mousam to the mouth of the Kennebunk River. In 1766 a small vessel was built on the Kennebunk upriver at The Landing where a village had grown up around the district's church. But in 1775, although shipbuilding and the milling of lumber were pursued by Kennebunk's businessmen, shipping and trade were not. The vessels built in yards on both rivers were commissioned by merchants from Boston, Salem, and Newburyport. As Kennebunk's first historian noted, "None of the men of wealth in Kennebunk would listen to the suggestion of investing in navigation."[13]

Perhaps they were influenced by the difficulties both rivers presented to shipping. The Mousam's circuitous course and a sand bar at its mouth probably had influenced coasting vessels that came to load lumber to shift their operations to the Kennebunk River. But even on the Kennebunk there were difficulties because it was "a barred harbor, there being only about two feet of water at its entrance at low water," and due to the river's peculiarity of "requiring a foul weather wind to sail out of it."[14] Kennebunk had yet to experience the prosperity of Falmouth or York.

York, despite what seems to be a cohesive and productive

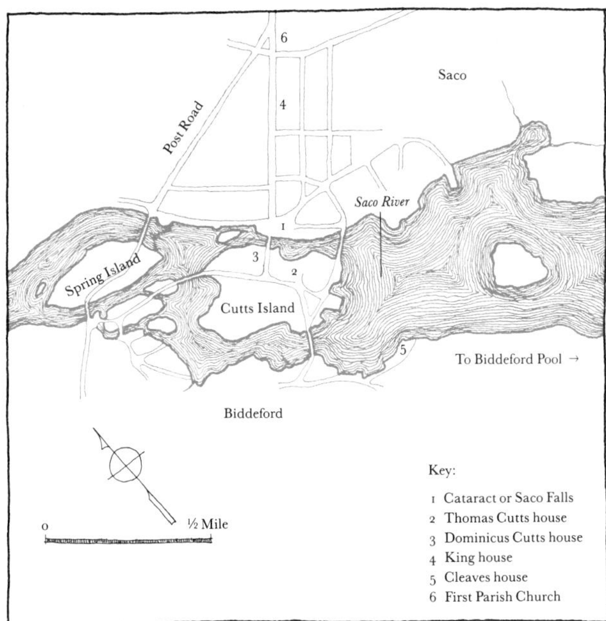

Fig. 1.3 Map of Pepperrellborough (Saco and Biddeford). Drawing, Scott Benson.

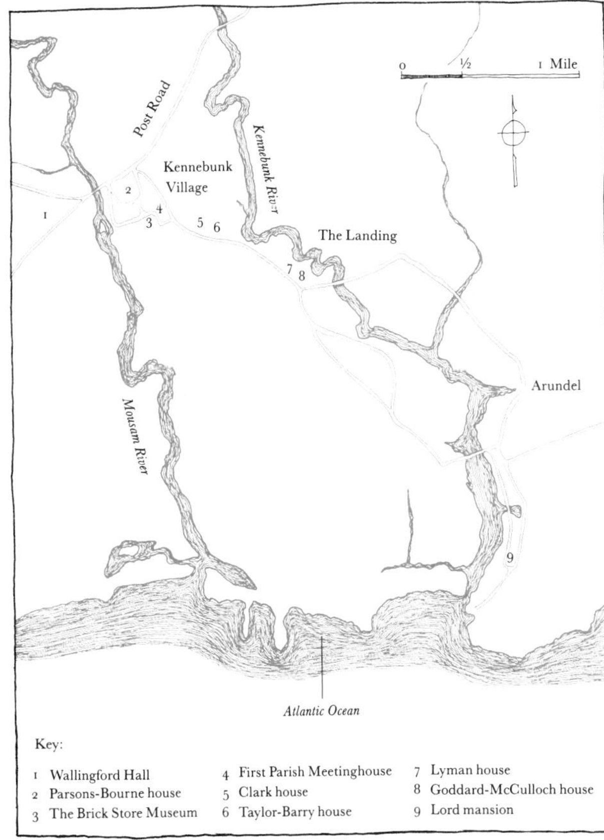

Fig. 1.4 Map of the Kennebunk District of Wells (Kennebunk) and Arundel (Kennebunkport). Drawing, Scott Benson.

historical development, also had problems. In 1794 the Honorable David Sewall described York as "a maritime place" but said of the York River, which provided the principal harbor, "[while] vessels of two or three hundred tons burthen may enter . . . the entrance being narrow and crooked, renders it rather difficult of access to strangers."[15] At the start of the Revolution, between twenty and thirty York vessels were employed in the West Indies and coastal trade, and there were men—Jonathan Sayward and Edward Emerson—who had made money in shipping. During the war most of those ships and many of the York men who sailed them were lost, and the town would never achieve again the same level of maritime activity.[16] Although there were different reasons for this, the difficult nature of the town's harbor was certainly a factor (fig. 1.5).

The war brought immediate, crippling devastation to Falmouth. Before it was over it would bring the progress of all of Maine's seacoast towns and maritime industry to a standstill. At the end of the war most of the District's merchant fleet had been seized or destroyed by the British, as had the approximately sixty vessels that had been engaged in deep-sea fishing. Worse yet was the loss of the men who had sailed the ships; many had been killed, many maimed.[17]

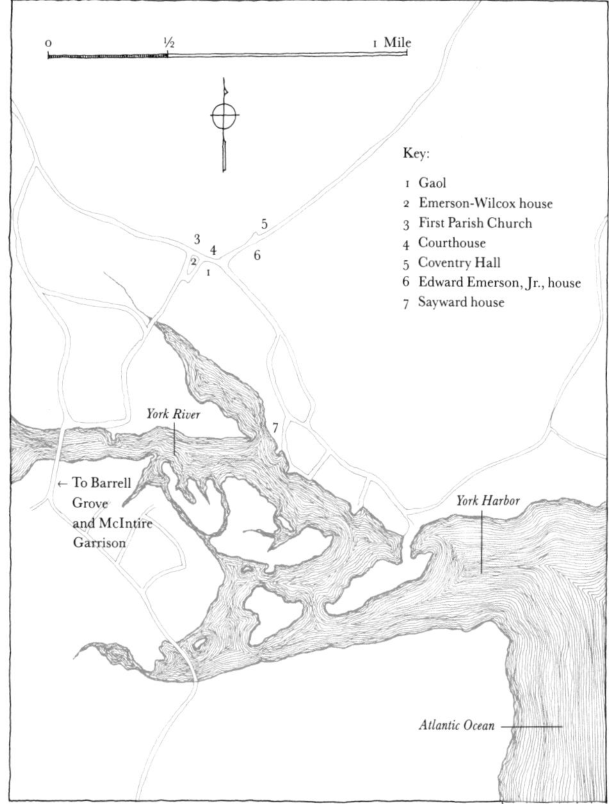

Fig. 1.5 Map of York. Drawing, Scott Benson.

The economy of Maine, whose inhabitants lived for the most part on the coast, depended on her maritime enterprise. Historically, with their backs to virtually trackless forest, Maine's settlers had looked to the sea as their "highway" to the rest of the world. Shipbuilding and shipping were the key to the District's economy, indeed to its very existence. The harvesting of timber and building of ships to carry lumber, masts, spars, shooks, and other wood products to waiting markets took precedence over all other work. Even cultivation of the land was of secondary importance so that southern corn for making bread and other basic foodstuffs were imported.[18]

If lumber was Maine's greatest natural resource, fish was her second, and there was a seemingly endless demand for both products in the West Indies and to a lesser degree in Europe. In Maine, as in all the American colonies, there was a need for the sugar, molasses, and rum of the islands and for Europe's manufactured goods. Because Europe, which provided a limited market for Maine's fish and lumber, wanted the islands' sugar products and coffee, a "triangle trade" had developed, following well-defined sea lanes. Lumber and dried fish were carried from Maine to the West Indies. The products of the islands, which Maine vessels exported to American ports, were then carried to Europe and exchanged for the manufactured goods that were wanted in the American colonies.[19]

Brigs, sloops, and schooners carried on the West Indies trade and the coastal shipping that brought native corn and cotton from America's southern colonies, as well as European goods, from major ports like Boston to Maine's smaller ports (fig. 1.6). These vessels, which ranged in capacity from 50 to 200 tons, required smaller crews because of their design, rigging, and size, and were better suited for use in barred, difficult harbors like those on the York, Kennebunk, and Saco rivers. They were also, "being of moderate draft," better able to ply the trade routes and island harbors of the Great Bahama Bank. *Ships*, however, which ranged in size from 200 tons upwards, were safer on longer, transatlantic voyages. These stockily built, square-rigged vessels were designed for cargo capacity in preference to speed.[20] Variations on these basic trade routes and the types of vessels that plied them were dictated by the enterprise of the mariners involved and the nature of their home ports.

Before the Revolution the largest percentage of American-owned shipping was brigs, sloops, and schooners, which were engaged in the lucrative West Indies trade. This was especially true in Maine, with its preponderance of small harbors. Of the southern Maine ports encompassed by this study, the only one that was used by more large than small vessels was Falmouth.[21]

Dependent as they were on the maritime trades to bring

within their reach the bare necessities as well as the amenities of life, Maine people felt severely the depredations to shipping wrought by the business of war. It was a poor and struggling populace who heard at last that the war was over.

Peace and the Beginning of Prosperity

On March 31, 1783, the Reverend Samuel Deane of Falmouth wrote in his diary, "Mr. Fosdick got home with news of peace."[22] Nathaniel Fosdick, a merchant, had been to Boston where he had heard the news of the signing in Paris of the treaty that acknowledged American independence. Peace had been foreshadowed by the defeat of Cornwallis at Yorktown on October 19, 1781, six years after the burning of Falmouth. Although during those six long years one or two shops had been opened in Falmouth and one or two houses built, at the end of the war the center of Falmouth was still a ruin marked by blackened, naked chimneys. Within another year, however, the Reverend Thomas Smith wrote in his journal, "Strangers, traders, and others crowd in among us surprisingly," and the Reverend Samuel Deane noted in his, "General Wadsworth and Mr. Goodwin arrived in Capt. Cooper."[23] General Peleg Wadsworth, a war hero, brought his family from Plymouth, Massachusetts, and before the year was out had built a barn and store on Back Street (today's Congress Street). Within a few months, construction of his dwelling, Falmouth's first brick house, had begun (see Chapter 3 and fig. 3.7). Goodwin, a Plymouth ropemaker, would start a ropewalk on Spring Street. Falmouth's rejuvenation had begun.

Maine's population had increased dramatically during the war, for many had looked upon the District as a haven. It experienced another, even more extraordinary, surge in growth immediately after the war.[24] With its undeveloped land, resources, and commercial potential, Maine represented "opportunity" to veterans eager to reap the rewards of their war service, to bright young men ready to launch careers in law and politics, and to ambitious European as well as American businessmen. But they began their quest for personal betterment at a difficult time. Although it is true, as one Maine historian has written, that at the end of the war the District "embarked on her first period of sustained growth and development," it is also true that immediately after the war all of New England entered into a great depression.[25] With America's paper currency depreciated to two cents on the dollar and little hard money available, many lacked the means to rejuvenate old businesses or begin new.[26] Only those with ample resources or the possibility of gaining credit in England were able to take quick advantage of the peace.

There were, of course, such men. Thomas Cutts of Pepperrellborough and Thomas Robison of Falmouth are examples. Cutts, who came to the Saco River from Kittery in

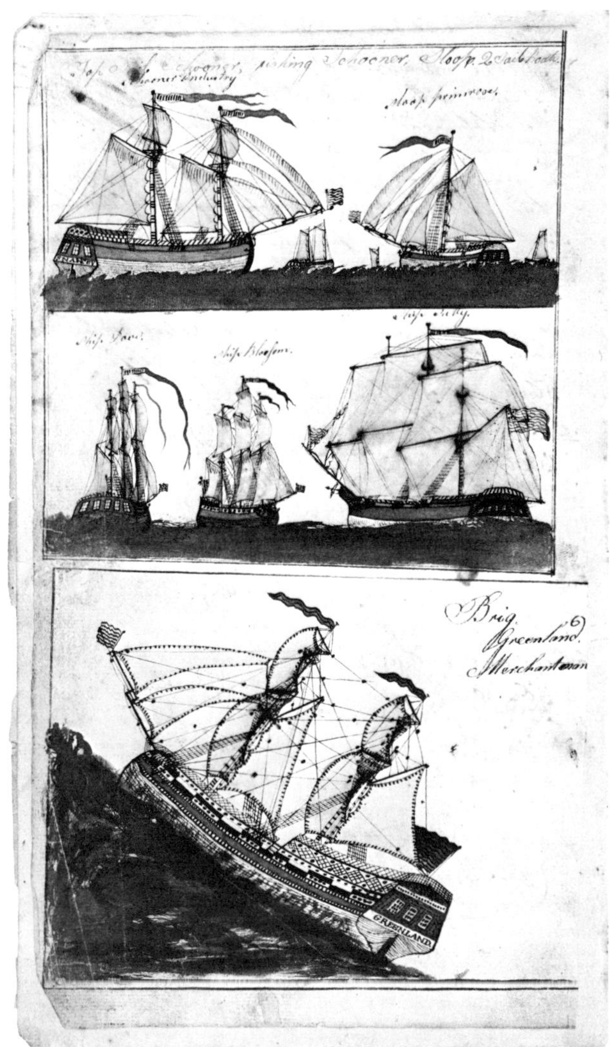

Fig. 1.6 Unidentified artist, *Top Sail Schooner, Fishing schooner, Sloop. 2 Sail Boats. Schooner Industry, Sloop Primrose, Ship Dove, Ship Blossom, Ship Sally, Brig Greenland. Merchantman*, York County, Maine, 1803–1833. Watercolor and pen and ink on paper; H 11¹³⁄₁₆ (30.0), W 6¹¹⁄₁₆ (17.0). From Ammi Quint account book. Maine Historical Society.

1758 with capital of $100, took advantage of the river and its resources to parlay that modest investment into a profitable lumbering, shipbuilding, shipping, and trading business. Cutts was able to remain solvent through the war when the main source of his and everyone else's income was cut off. By 1782, before the official peace had been declared, he had the financial resources to build a new mansion house for his family (see Chapter 3 and fig. 3.6).[27] Resuming his business activities after the war was not a problem for Thomas Cutts.

Thomas Robison, a Scotsman who had lived in Falmouth before the war with a younger brother, returned with his family in 1782 to "Carry on trade, the distillery Business, Shipbuilding etc." A fur trader on the Great Lakes, he had served in the British army during the Revolution, and following that service had lived for a time in England. It was through business and family contacts that he was able to raise the money to build his distillery and vessels that would take Maine lumber and fish to the West Indies and return with the molasses necessary to make rum. Writing from Falmouth on March 14, 1784, to the firm of Phyn and Ellice in London to advise them that he had drawn on them "for one thousand pounds Sterling, in favour of Samuel Brick Esq. [of Boston]," Robison noted that his new "Distilhouse and Warehouse" and a wharf would cost about £4,000 sterling. "It is most peoples oppinion," he wrote, "that We will do exceeding Well. There is no Distilhouse here at present and Very few (if any) who are able to set one up" (cat. 38).[28]

Robison had chosen his new business enterprise well. Rum was such an important part of the average diet that supplying it to the poor was considered an allowable expense. Those with the wherewithal stocked it in their homes as they did flour and molasses. Shop and tavern keepers sold it by the glass and kept a "grog score" in their ledgers for frequent customers. Itemized bills for the building of a house, a ship, or even a church included a figure for rum (or brandy or some other "spiritous liquor"). Workmen readily accepted rum as part payment of their wages. Drinking rum was a way of life, and large quantities had to be imported into Maine because of a scarcity of orchards and therefore of cider, the countryman's substitute.[29]

Robison got not only his capital from England, but also the four stills and other equipment for his "distilhouse." These were shipped into Newburyport, Massachusetts, and from there brought at Robison's risk (that is, uninsured) by coasting vessel to Falmouth.[30] Such arrangements indicate the undeveloped nature of business affairs in newly independent America.

There were enterprising men eager to remedy that situation, but England took steps to cut them off from the one business route that would do that quickly: West Indies trade. In 1783, even as English and French ships vied to import goods into the impoverished United States, the British government decreed that henceforth only British vessels owned and manned by British subjects could trade in and out of the British West Indies. Similar restrictions were placed on the importation of American products into English ports. France, Spain, and Holland followed suit, and with Barbary pirates in the Mediterranean suddenly preying on the fledgling country's shipping, all the familiar trade routes were barred to American ships (cat. 1).

The "United States of America" were united in name only. There was, in practice, no central government to negotiate a way out of this impasse. The government that had been formed under the Articles of Confederation was too weak to override the regional differences of the states or to command respect from established governments. The years between 1783 and 1789, when America's first federal government was at last organized under the Constitution, "were years of struggle and discouragement for the American merchant marine."[31]

But the affairs of individuals often seem to belie the broader view of history. Such was the case in the District of Maine during this crucial period. The inhabitants of Falmouth, the Saco and Kennebunk river towns, and York began immediately to work their way from poverty and depression to economic stability. In Falmouth, "as soon as the war was over, trade started at once into full activity," bolstered by the capital brought into town by "a number of enterprising persons" like Robison.[32] The Saco River also attracted its share of enterprising men, and shipbuilding and the shipping of lumber were pursued once more at Pepperrellborough and Biddeford.

In Arundel, Thomas Wiswell and Ephraim Perkins and his sons built wharves and warehouses on the Kennebunk River and sent the first vessels into the West Indies trade. The people of Arundel were beginning at last to recognize that the seat of their prosperity lay on the banks of the Kennebunk River. In Kennebunk, even before the war was over, Tobias Lord, Jr., a native of Arundel, returned from his war service and built a small house and store on the bank of the Mousam where he began a shipbuilding and shipping business. The traders and shipbuilders Theodore Lyman and John Bourne had settled at The Landing, on the Kennebunk River.

In York, although Jonathan Sayward and Edward Emerson did not elect to return to their pre-war shipping activities, other York men began to build new ships to sail to the islands. On March 25, 1785, seventy-year-old Jonathan Sayward wrote in his journal, "Capt Millar in a new Briganti[ne] saild out of York from Randals Wharfe." On Thanksgiving Day, 1787, Sayward noted, "Thirteen sail of vessels at anchor. I never saw so many before."[33] All of these men, like so many others free of the encumbrances of war, turned their attention to personal interests and found ways to overcome the shortage of money and the obstacles to trade.

Although the lack of a reliable currency retarded postwar growth, an absence of cash was not new. The familiar, time-honored barter system continued to be relied upon.

An important infusion of cash into Maine's economy came as a result of shipbuilding. Still-affluent merchants, both local and outside the District, supplied commissions to Maine's shipbuilders. The Salem-owned *Maria*, for example, was built in Falmouth (fig. 1.7). Fishermen also found ways to replace the vessels and equipment they had lost, and began once more to bring fish to market, for the treaty that had ended the war had "secured to [them] their immemorial right to take fish anywhere in the sea where they 'used any time heretofore to fish.'"[34]

Gradually but inexorably vessels were returned to the seas despite the depression and European restrictions against trade. Coastal trade was not shut off, and even the West Indies, where the real profits lay, were still open to those who were not afraid to take a chance.

On September 25, 1784, George Shand, a merchant at St. Georges on the island of Granada, wrote to Thomas Robison and his partner William Edgar as follows:

If Mess[rs]. Robison & Edgar send any vessels to this country; . . . send them loaded with red oak staves; white D[itto] & heading Boards and plank ranging timber of yellow pine different dimensions and a few good Shingles . . . , also send 15 or 20 quintals Dumb fish packd in Boxes of a quintal each . . . the vessels to come into St. Georges under an English flag, with the Instructions you already know.[35]

Those instructions were conveyed to Captain Joshua Preble by Robison and Edgar in a long letter dated at Falmouth on January 3, 1785. Preble was

to proceed for St Georges in the Island of Grenada on your arrival [at] the Harbour you will hoist an English Jack. . . . immediately go on shore & deliver your letters to Mr Shand . . . if possible before you are boarded by the Kings Boats—if they should come you must tell them your are from St Andrews in Novascotia that your Vessell was built there & owned in Grenada by Mr George Shand if they insist on seeing your papers you will inform them there is no Custom house in St Andrews & the severity of the season would not admit of your getting them from St Johns or any other port of Novascotia at the time when you Saild, but that Mr Shand will give them the Necessary proofs.[36]

The three-page letter continues, advising Captain Preble in detail what to do "if you obtain admission." Circumventing attempts to keep them out of the West Indies trade was risky for American merchants and mariners, but the islands' great need for lumber and the willingness of merchants there to take risks to get it encouraged the Yankees in their own eagerness to end the economic depression of the war years. Trade went forward.

It was during this period that England's attempt to shut America out of familiar trade routes led Americans to search for new markets (cats. 20–21). In May 1785 Salem's *Empress of China* arrived in New York from Canton with a rich cargo. The China trade had begun. But it was a "luxury trade," requiring large outlays of capital that few could afford. Although many of the ships entered in this trade were built in Maine, not until 1796 with the launching of *The Portland*, which was named for her home port, would an East Indiaman owned and manned by men from southern Maine take part in the fabulous China trade. Only one other locally owned East Indiaman is known to have operated out of Portland but not until after 1815.[37]

The fragmentary shipping records that have survived show that in the postwar years the merchants and mariners of southern Maine went seeking their fortunes in the fisheries and the coasting and West Indies trades. Of the almost fifty clearances reported by York's naval office between October 1785 and July 1786 only one (for France) fell outside coastal or Caribbean routes. The same pattern of trade was true for Falmouth vessels during this period.[38]

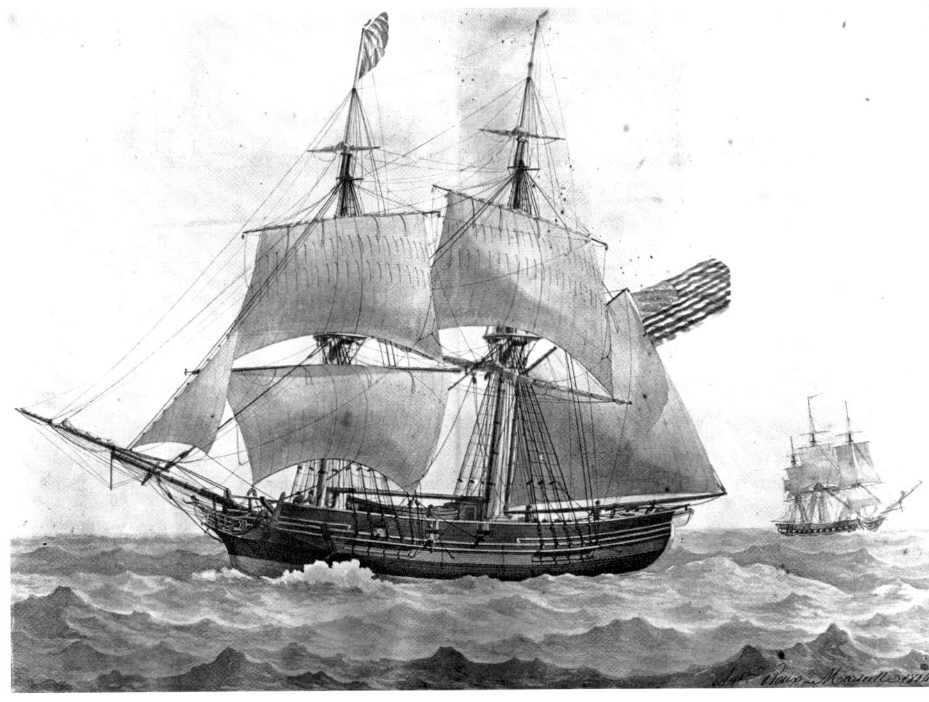

Fig. 1.7 Antoine Roux, brig *Maria*, Marseilles, France, 1804. Watercolor on paper; H 15 (38.1), W 19¾ (50.2). Courtesy, Peabody Museum of Salem: Photo, Mark Sexton.

Based upon this trade, Falmouth was flourishing. On July 4, 1786, the settlement on Falmouth Neck became Portland, a town separate from other Fore River–Casco Bay communities. Advocates for the separation had wanted it for three years, but the division had been held back because of the desolate condition of the Neck after the war. In 1786, however, there was no longer any need to wait. For three years thirty to forty dwelling houses, plus other buildings, had been built annually. Falmouth had a new courthouse, Robison's distillery, warehouses, and wharves. Efforts had begun to have a lighthouse built for the harbor (cat. 5). The inhabitants had re-established their library, and Benjamin Titcomb, a Falmouth native, had begun publication of Maine's first newspaper. It was probably not long after Falmouth's metamorphosis to Portland that some optimistic merchant commissioned an earthenware pitcher bearing a print of a brig and the legend "May the commerce of Portland flourish forever."[39]

One wonders if that pitcher qualified as one of the European-made "articles of luxury and extravagance" that were a concern to American legislators and businessmen in the years following the war. With the merchant ships of England and France competing for the American market for manufactured goods, attempts were made on a local and state level to charge impost duties on their cargoes. In 1785 Falmouth instructed the town's representative to the Massachusetts General Court to urge passage of laws that would regulate the importation of "foreign luxuries, geegaws, and trifles" and "encourage our agriculture, manufactures, and fishery." "Geegaws and trifles" were not the only concern. When Thomas Robison had returned to Falmouth, he had ordered "12 of the best common chairs and a good dressing glass" from his Boston agent.[40] Such orders for basic necessities would have to be directed locally if craftsmen like cabinetmaker Ebenezer Davis, who moved to Portland's Free Street in 1786, were to prosper.

The Golden Age of Commerce

Not until 1789, with the formation of America's first real government, were steps taken that would effectively increase her merchant marine's chances for economic success and growth. The first Congress moved quickly to enact legislation to protect American commerce and shipping and the cod fisheries, and to establish customs districts. High duties on foreign-owned and built vessels using American ports gave American mariners and merchants a competitive advantage in the carrying trades. A new "Coasting Law" required a coasting vessel sailing along the Atlantic coast to enter and clear its passage both going and coming at a customshouse in each state except those contiguous with its home state. This legislation has been blamed for the collapse of the District of Maine's first effort to gain separation from

Massachusetts, but in general Congress's action brought positive results. It launched the "Golden Age" of America's maritime commerce; between 1789 and the embargo year of 1807 the growth of America's shipping was "without parallel in the history of the commercial world."[41]

In southern Maine, customs districts and ports of entry were declared for York, Biddeford and Pepperrellborough, and Portland and Falmouth. These designations were based on pre-war shipping activity. Arundel and Wells, with its Mousam and Kennebunk river villages, were included in the Saco River customs district. They would soon demonstrate, however, a need for their own district. By 1795 the tonnage owned in Wells alone was larger than that of Biddeford or Pepperrellborough. By 1800 the shipbuilders, merchants, and mariners of Arundel and Wells had received favorable action from Congress on their petition for the creation of a "Port and District of Kennebunk."[42]

The center of Wells's prosperity was at Kennebunk. Mills and shipbuilding on the Mousam River had encouraged the growth of a village center along the post road that connected southern Maine's villages (today's Route 1). But another even more prosperous village had grown up at The Landing on the Kennebunk River. Here postwar shipyards provided the business opportunity that by 1790 caused Tobias Lord to move his shipbuilding operation from the Mousam River. At The Landing he built a fine three-story house on the bank of the Kennebunk not far from the site of his yard. The days of shipbuilding were numbered on the Mousam, where efforts to reroute the mouth of the river finally would fail in 1794. The usefulness of the Kennebunk River for shipbuilding and shipping was assured in 1793 with the building at its mouth of Perch-rock Wharf "for the double purpose of covering [a bad rock] and keeping the channel, [which shifted around it with every storm], in one place."[43]

The Landing shipyards brought into Kennebunk and Arundel a steady flow of shipbuilders—carpenters; riggers; mast, block, sail, and rope makers—as well as blacksmiths; and mariners to sail the new vessels. These in turn stimulated an influx of doctors, lawyers, traders, joiners, masons, shoemakers, tailors, cabinetmakers, and potters.

Although these newcomers were from many areas, a significant number were from York. As they had since the mid-eighteenth century, York men with ambition migrated to southern Maine towns that offered more opportunity. The advanced state of its own development, which meant most of its prime land and business opportunities were already spoken for, gave York the same role as long-developed towns in Massachusetts proper whose younger sons and ambitious men came into the District of Maine to "escape their dwarfed horizons . . . and remake their lives."[44]

One of Kennebunk's most successful businessmen was Theodore Lyman, son of the Reverend Isaac Lyman of York.

He came to Kennebunk as a young man before the Revolution and became a clerk in the store of Waldo Emerson, a successful trader. Waldo, a brother of Edward Emerson, was also a York man. Following Waldo's sudden death at the age of thirty-eight, and shortly thereafter of his wife, Lyman married their only surviving child, fourteen-year-old Sarah Emerson. Upon her death in 1784, Lyman was left sole heir of his father-in-law's estate. His fortune, or at least the basis of it, was made. He built at Kennebunk Landing a fine new house that by local standards was judged "fit for a noble man" (fig. 3.2).[45] Lyman married a Salem woman and, with capital raised through building and entering vessels in the West Indies and coastal trade, was ready to seek more profitable business opportunities. Without doubt the vessels of light tonnage that were being built on the Kennebunk River, which were suited mainly for coastal and West Indies trade, did not measure up to Lyman's ambition. In 1790 he moved to Boston where he would truly make his fortune with ships that he entered in the East India trade.

Lyman did not abandon his business enterprises in Kennebunk. With the assistance of another York man, Dr. Oliver Keating, his shipping and trading operations at Kennebunk Landing continued. Keating married Lyman's sister, lived in his house, oversaw the building of numerous vessels for him by John Bourne, and conducted Lyman's local trading operations. Keating's account books reveal that in exchange for boards, top timbers, oak plank, staves, and hoops as well as veal, butter, cloth, and other country produce supplied by local farmers, he provided imported goods—salt, rum, tea, molasses, chintz, indigo, tobacco, and corn.[46] Such goods were for the most part brought in by coasters from Boston rather than directly from their port of origin.

In December 1791 Keating credited the sloop *Experiment* with three crates of dishes (which included 180 sets of cups and saucers), candlesticks and candlemolds, nail slammers, brass locks, curry combs, chamber pots, pudding pans, snuff boxes, account books, hymnals and bibles, felt hats, spice, bags and bales of cotton, and other items.[47] Raw materials and foodstuffs such as cotton and corn were of American production, while the manufactured goods, at this early date, had been imported from European ports. These were supplemented by "West India goods." In this way every need could be met. The lumber and country produce the farmers bartered for their more exotic needs was exported to the West Indies or to ports like Boston where demand was high and local supplies were exhausted or insufficient.

The Lyman-Keating operation did not rely on strictly local farmers as suppliers and customers. Farmers from all parts of York County brought their boards and timbers to Kennebunk Landing for sale to shipbuilders or to merchants like Keating for export. The Landing road was crowded with teams and the river with gundalows that carried the lumber downriver to be loaded on vessels at its mouth. Indeed, it was from this activity that The Landing, where these supplies were "landed" on the river's bank, got its name.[48]

Lyman and Keating did not leave it to chance that they would secure their share of this trade. In 1792 York's Timothy Lyman, Theodore's brother, with the advice and probably the financial backing of his brother and Dr. Keating, opened a store in Coxhall, an inland town bordering Kennebunk. (In 1803 Coxhall would be renamed Lyman "in honor of Theodore . . . of Boston.") Less than two weeks after he had stocked his store with goods bought in Boston, Timothy was sending teams loaded with boards and staves to Kennebunk. For supplying the lumber or simply hauling it to Kennebunk Landing, Timothy provided farmers like Heber Kimball with rum, corn, molasses, "1 pen knife, 1 Handle bowl, cut nails," and various other staples and "sundries."[49]

There was money to be made from such trade, and in Kennebunk as in other seacoast towns everyone "who could muster a little money [went] into the West India business." Doctors, such as Keating, Thatcher Goddard, and Jacob Fisher, who could not make a living practicing medicine, turned to shipping. Farmers like Nahum Morrill "fell in with the current" and built or bought shares in a vessel. Arundel's Captain Israel Wildes, who made regular runs to the "Westindias," made his living from the trade not only as a shipmaster. While he was at sea his wife, Elizabeth, sold molasses and other West Indies goods from their home.[50]

Lyman and Keating's coastal and local trade was only a small part of their shipping network. While a good living could be made from the trade, the surviving business records of Maine shipowners and merchants reveal again and again that those who made the most money were involved in international or "foreign" trade. Men like the McLellans of Portland, Thomas Cutts of Saco, and Theodore Lyman sent their Maine-built ships from Boston and other major American ports to European markets and beyond. They left carrying America's raw materials—oak, birch, beech, pine, boards, masts, staves, tar, turpentine, corn, and cotton—and brought back manufactured goods—"Printed tea cups, best blue and china glaze, and Cream colored" dishes; "Striped rugs and Kidder minster Bordered" carpets; yard goods of "Drab Plain, Mock Crimson, Blue milked Serges, and Claret and Brown Half thicks"; Dutch cheese, and French wine, as well as the "Deaths head buttons, snuff boxes, needles, shawls, thread, Brass ink pots, men's knit ribbed hose, ink powder, and silks handkerchiefs" that would be brought by coasters from Boston to Maine ports.[51]

The Anglo-French War and the Neutral Carrying Trade

The decade that saw America's merchant marine protected at last by a strong government also brought peril on the high seas that went beyond the natural danger of wind and wave. A Charter Party, or shipping agreement, was drawn up on April 10, 1795, for the 320–ton ship *Minerva*, Thomas Cutts, Jr., of Saco, master. After detailing the cargo of pork, "flower," and corn to be taken in at Norfolk, Virginia, for delivery to Bordeaux, France, the document concludes, "and thus to end the intended voyage excepting always against the dangers of the Seas, Robber Pirates, restraint of Princes and Rulers, and all unavoidable accidents and calamities."[52]

In the spring of 1793 word reached America that England and France had gone to war. The United States claimed neutrality, putting her merchant marine in the position of being the world's largest neutral carrier fleet. Once again the triangle trade and the forbidden transatlantic "long haul" were open to American vessels. France was eager to buy American flour and sugar from the British islands, and found American "bottoms" useful in their coastal trade. England, which like France was concentrating its seapower on the war, found Americans the chief purchasers of its manufactured goods and convenient for carrying its trade to hostile ports. As a result of the Anglo-French war, Americans were drawn into transatlantic trade in a way they hadn't been since before the Revolution. Although trade was still chiefly with the Caribbean Islands, commerce with the continent increased dramatically, and it was American vessels that brought to American ports Europe's manufactured goods.[53] American merchants and mariners rushed to take advantage of the opportunity to reap enormous profits.

As the war dragged on and conditions and loyalties shifted, the "Princes and Rulers" of England and France became unwilling to let the Americans enjoy their windfall; both countries "used and abused the United States" during what was to be more than twenty years of war. Particularly in the Caribbean, but also on transatlantic trips, American ships were chased, boarded, and seized by the crews of English and French warships and privateers. Such vessels were usually "condemned" by British or French magistrates, which meant they and their cargoes became the property of their captors and their governments. The English were not content to seize just American vessels; American seamen were impressed into the British navy on the slightest pretext.[54] There were added dangers in the Mediterranean, where corsairs of the Barbary states, particularly Algiers, were also preying on American vessels and their crews (cat. 1). Algerian "Robber Pirates" sold their captives into slavery.

The United States Congress, outraged at the seizure in February 1794 of forty American vessels at Martinique by a British fleet, within a month had passed legislation to establish an American navy that would provide some protection to America's unarmed merchant vessels. Congress also imposed a sixty-day embargo on American shipping while Chief Justice John Jay sailed for England to negotiate a treaty to end the trouble. The hope was that if England's depredations could be controlled by treaty, France would follow suit. The Jay Treaty provided some relief, although it still legislated against the forbidden "long haul" and did nothing about the British practice of search and impressment. Americans got around its provisions against carrying West Indies goods to Europe by bringing such cargoes into American ports and then re-exporting them. This practice of "breaking the voyage" angered the British, while the French, when they learned about the Jay Treaty, considered themselves betrayed and increased their seizures of America's shipping.[55]

Between 1793 and 1803, when the Louisiana Purchase treaty with France called for the end of French seizures of American vessels, more than two thousand were taken. Many were from Maine ports. Portland lost thirty, for a value of $354,967; Saco's Thomas Cutts alone suffered losses of $90,000; Kennebunk lost twenty-three vessels. Marine insurance was not yet common. As a result, these losses impeded the growth of a developing town like Kennebunk, and brought ruin to newly established shipowners.[56] Thomas Cutts survived his losses, but York's Edward Emerson, Jr., did not.

In 1786, on his twenty-first birthday, Edward Emerson, Jr., had bought a small lot in York Village, opposite the Town House, upon which to build a store. Also, following in his father's footsteps, he bought a share in a brig. It was the beginning of business activities that by 1795 would make him a wealthy merchant and shipowner. He exported fish, lumber, and livestock to the West Indies, importing West India goods and, from Boston, supplies for his store. With his vessels going north to Maine's Penobscot River for lumber, it made good sense to open a store in Bangor, which he did with his brother Bulkeley.

It is not known exactly how many vessels Emerson owned, but by 1802 he had lost four to the French valued at a total of $50,000. On October 13, 1803, Emerson was found dead of a gunshot wound in his counting-room. Although his chief biographer claims the loss of his vessels caused Emerson more depression and worry than crippling financial loss, there seems little doubt that the French piracy led to his suicide.[57]

Thomas Robison is another Maine shipowner whose maritime losses during this period brought him financial ruin. In 1796, not far from Amsterdam, his ship *Eliza* was seized by the British frigate *Unicorn* and taken to London. Although after three years Robison was able to recover his ship, its cargo was condemned. Within a year Robison's commercial property in Portland (although not "New Scotland," the mansion where he had "lived in an expensive style") was for sale (cat. 38).[58]

Advertisements for Robison's real estate described Portland as a "flourishing place." Even as men like Emerson and Robison were being ruined by their maritime losses, merchant princes and wealthy shipmasters were being created. Profits made in the neutral carrying trade far outstripped the losses. In Maine the federal-period mansions and townscapes that elicit admiration and stir the imagination were being created (Chapter 2). Although in York architectural gains were modest, in Kennebunk and Arundel there was money to build many fine houses. Kennebunk's new mansions were dispersed throughout the growing town, but in Arundel they were clustered in its new and handsome river village.

On the Saco River the money was going into mills, bridges, wharves, and vessels in response to the burgeoning lumbering industry. By 1795 "congestion on the water front was so great" that steps were taken to regulate how long loads of lumber could be "piled at the lower landing between the upper and lower wharves" before they were taken away. At the turn of the century, with seventeen sawmills in operation in the vicinity of the falls, exports of lumber required the services of twenty surveyors of lumber and five of logs, six measurers of wood and bark, and others for staves, shingles, and clapboards.[59] Daniel Cleaves, who had come to Biddeford just ten years before with a modest amount of capital to invest, was buying wharves, mills, and real estate.

In 1797 when Timothy Dwight, New England's observant traveler, passed through Saco (as Pepperrellborough was popularly called and would be legally named in 1805) he "saw little in this settlement which could be called agreeable." Saco was a "busy, bustling place," but a lumbering town with poorly placed houses. Saco's failure to develop a cohesive center was due in part to the large amount of land still owned by Sir William Pepperrell's heirs. On January 9, 1798, the selectmen petitioned the General Court in Boston to have the soon-to-be-sold Pepperrell land laid out in numerous small lots rather than to allow it to be sold in one or two large parcels. Asking also for a grant of fifty acres for the use of the ministry, the selectmen declared that both measures would contribute to the growth of the town. When Dwight passed through Saco again in 1807 he declared it "almost entirely changed," with handsome houses and, standing on the Pepperrell land granted to the town, a church superior in style to any other in the District of Maine.[60]

Portland was growing in all ways. Houses, stores, public buildings, bridges, even aqueducts to bring spring water into the town were being built. When Timothy Dwight visited Portland in 1797 he confided to his journal, "No American town is more entirely commercial." This was reflected in the incorporation during this period of Maine's first bank, the Portland Bank; Maine's first marine insurance company; and the Portland Marine Society, an educational and charitable association. With the number of locally owned merchant and fishing vessels continuing to grow, Portland was one of the "most busy and thriving towns in the Union."[61]

Yet Portland was also agreeable. Dwight concurred with the judgment of the Duke de la Rochefoucault who, after his visit in 1797, wrote, "This town of Portland may be reckoned handsome."[62] A more intimate view of its fine new homes with their comfortable furnishings and striking surroundings, the agreeable social life of the inhabitants, the busy streets and harbor, as well as the blight brought to favorite landscapes by development, is presented in the diary of Boston's Abigail May who came in 1796 to visit with her aunt, Mrs. John Frothingham.

Miss May arrived by packet at Portland's Union Wharf "as the bells were ringing one on Fryday," July 3. By Monday she was comfortably settled in her aunt's home and engaged in a round of tea parties, musical evenings, and "rambles" (or walks), often in the company of Peleg Wadsworth's charming daughters. On one visit to Bramhall's Hill she felt "quite sad to see what depridations have been committed on our favorite trees. Nearly half of them are cut down." Yet, for the most part all was so wonderful in Portland that toward the end of her visit she wrote in her journal: "If I were a princess instead of Abby May I could not receive more attention. They live in elegant stile. The greatest luxuries and dainties are prepared—and every species of enjoyment is at our command."[63]

The basis of Portland's prosperity was, as always, her maritime commerce. By the turn of the century, more than seventy ships of various burthens were owned by Portland men. Most still plied the West Indies trade routes, exporting the usual lumber and wood products (including easily dismantled and reassembled house frames), fish, country produce, and a list of livestock to which had been added horses. The returns book of Portland customshouse measurer Nicholas Blasdell, with entries from 1804 through 1807, lists slightly more than one hundred entries of vessels returning with cargoes of West India goods or European salt, coal, hemp and cordage, nails and spikes, window glass, and wine. More than half of the total entries were for West Indies goods.[64]

Yet as important as the West Indies trade was, locally owned vessels did go to Europe, either directly from Portland, or by way of the "long haul" triangle, or from major seaports such as Boston, Philadelphia, and New York. The various McLellans and Asa Clapp (fig. 1.8), who established himself as a merchant in Portland in 1796, were especially active in European trade. Clapp encompassed in his trading activities all the possibilities. Besides the usual exports and imports to the customary Caribbean ports, Clapp imported molasses from Cuba, mahogany from Honduras, and sugar from

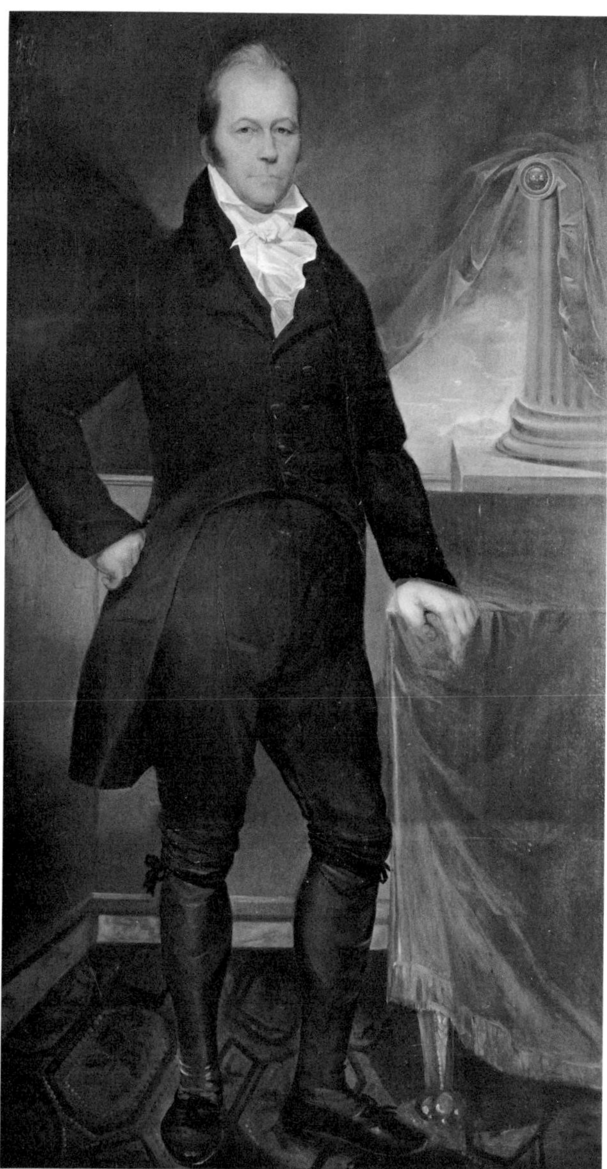

Fig. 1.8 John Wesley Jarvis, *Asa Clapp* (1762–1848), New York City, 1808–1810. Oil on panel; H 75½ (191.8), W 40½ (102.9). Elvehjem Museum of Art, University of Wisconsin-Madison, Gift of Monte Appel.

Brazil. His coasters brought to Portland baled cotton, rice, and tobacco from southern ports like Charleston, and fine flour from Philadelphia, Boston, and Alexandria, Virginia. They carried logwood, country produce, wine, and brandy to Boston. The wines probably came in from Europe on Clapp ships, as did glassware from Hamburg, and down and feather beds, hemp, iron, and duck from Russia. Some of the hemp was supplied to local ropewalks, whose coils and rigging were then purchased by Clapp for export, and some was sold to shipbuilders and owners in Saco and Kennebunk.[65] But other Clapp ships, carrying cargoes from Europe, went directly into major ports like Boston.

Portland's handicap as a port was her inability to utilize the cargoes brought in by local vessels. As the Duke de la Rochefoucault observed in 1795, "Portland [and vicinity] are not equal to the consumption of the cargos which the ships import . . . ; these are generally carried to Boston . . . the principal mart for foreign commodities." In 1801 one merchant, William Brown, did bring $50,000 worth of English fabrics into Portland and had surprising success selling them from his store, but such enterprise and results were rare.[66]

Because most Portland ships took the bulk of their cargoes to Boston or other large ports for sale, affluent Portlanders did their shopping outside of Maine. In 1800 before moving into his fine new Portland mansion, Captain Enoch Preble went to Boston to buy its furnishings. His "Memorandum of Furniture Purchased in Boston" includes not only "1 Sofha, 1 Sett India China, 3 Damask table cloths, 4 Pr. brass candlesticks, table breakfast, [and] table dining," but all the kitchen equipment down to the simplest pot and fireplace shovel. During succeeding years, on voyages to England, Captain Preble supplemented all of this by buying a pair of topaz earrings, a mahogany knife box, a silver pencil case, six prints of wild beasts, a pair of pistols, an ivory nutmeg grater, and other luxury household items and personal "sundries." Preble also had his portrait painted and his miniature taken.[67]

By the turn of the nineteenth century, Portland could lay claim to a number of cabinetmakers, silversmiths, decorative and portrait painters, carvers, and even an architect or two.[68] Support for such craftsmen seems to have come more from Portland's rising professional class and the modestly affluent than from her nabobs. Stephen Longfellow, a young lawyer who married Peleg Wadsworth's daughter in 1804, bought some of his furniture from the local Radford brothers. Eliphalet Smith and his wife, Ann, who kept a dry-goods store on Fish Street, also patronized local craftsmen and artists. Although they traveled to Boston at least twice a year to select goods for their store, like any wise business family they bought for their personal needs locally. On January 1, 1806, Ann Smith wrote in her diary, "Mr. Brewster has this day finished a Miniature likeness of my good husband." In March she purchased of "Joseph Lovis a gold Sitting to my good man's miniature for which he charges 18 dollars" (see cat. 30). During the winter she "looked at Mr. Goddar[d]s Glasses" and "called to see Mr. Radford's cabinet work." In her diary for Saturday, May 8, she wrote, "Purchased a pair of looking Glasses [at] Mr. Goddards for which I was fool enough to give 60 dollars."[69]

The Smiths' Boston trips seem to have been reserved for shopping for their store. Both made the twice-yearly trips to Boston, together or individually, even as they shared running their store. On a buying trip in the fall of 1807 Ann Smith spent more than $400 on imported yard goods, fourteen dozen silk gloves, and other goods. Her husband sent the money for these purchases to her by mail almost daily, in small amounts, perhaps as he collected it over the counter at home. Ann sent her purchases back to Portland by a coasting vessel, returning herself by stage.[70] With stops at New buryport, Portsmouth, Kennebunk, and Saco or Scarborough to eat and sleep, the trip could be made in a comfortable two days.

Between her visits to wholesalers, Ann Smith found time to have a dress and broadcloth coat made for herself. Shortly after her return home she confided to her diary, "Mrs. Hall called to see my coat—intends to have one made like it." There was prestige in owning a Boston-made or at least Boston-styled coat. This was without doubt one of the reasons why Maine's "well-to-do, mobile, and highly fashion conscious" residents bought household and personal goods in Boston or New York even when they became available at home.[71]

Not all Maine residents were well-to-do. In the spring of 1804, while traveling to Boston, a shaft on Ann Smith's hired chaise broke. They had just passed through the Saco woods (between Biddeford and Arundel) and were, as Ann wrote,

at a distance from any house. My good man half crippled with the rheumatism . . . held the horse while I went in quest of assistance. The first house I came to was a miserable one with the windowsall broken, the inhabitants the picture of poverty and wretchedness. I . . . asked if they would help me to a cod line or rope or help in any way to splice the broken limb so we could go on to Jefferds [tavern in Kennebunk]. The poor man looked at me with a vacant stare, his face covered with rum boils, his frame feeble and emaciated [and] said he had not anything that would do.

The Embargo and War of 1812

If Ann Smith noted the face of poverty because it was rare for her to see it, that would soon change. Poverty and failure would soon become common, even in Portland. In the winter of 1807 as she sat writing into her diary a celebration of her comfortable home and good fortune, economic collapse was imminent. Even as Ann enumerated her material blessings— "a pleasant parlor with fine windows, a view of the harbour, . . . a good fire, a clean hearth, money in my pocket, the house well stored"—President Thomas Jefferson was running out of patience with English and French seizures of America's shipping. On December 22, 1807, Jefferson's "Long Embargo," which lasted for fourteen months, was put into effect by Congress. American vessels were forbidden to clear from an American port for a foreign destination. The American government hoped to show England and Napoleon how much they needed neutral carriers. Instead they showed Americans how dependent they were on their merchant marine.

When Portlanders heard about the Embargo, they might have wished for another champion like their own Commodore Edward Preble. In 1798 seizures by the Mediterranean's Barbary pirates had caused the owners of Portland's only East Indiaman, *The Portland*, to outfit her with guns before sending her on her second voyage.[72] But by 1807 the problem with the Barbary States was being successfully handled due in part to Preble's 1804 bombardment of Tripoli. Another Portland man, Lieutenant Henry Wadsworth, Peleg's son, died a heroic death in that battle. Those events had been on the minds of Portland residents in the spring of 1807 when the panoramic painting of Preble's bombardment of Tripoli by noted marine painter Michele Felice Cornè was exhibited at Union Hall, and again in August when Edward Preble died at his home (cat. 1).

Earlier that year timber had been cut on Pike's Hill in Windham and floated down the Presumpscot River to Portland to be used in the building of an observatory (cats. 7–8). The eighty-two-foot-high octagonal tower, in which a good English telescope was installed, was to enable Portland's shipowners and merchants to know when their vessels were entering port. The house flag of the owner of a returning vessel was flown from the observatory to alert him to its return. But few flags were flown during the next fourteen months. In 1806, $342,909 was collected in duties on imports at Portland's customs house, but in 1808 only $37,633 was taken in.[73]

The Reverend Samuel Deane of Portland wrote in his diary on January 29, 1808, "Soup charity begun." A free soup kitchen had been set up for the destitute.[74] A month earlier another Portland minister, Edward Payson, who was afraid the Embargo would ruin the morals of the people, had described conditions in a letter to his father.

A large number of the most wealthy merchants have already failed, and numbers more are daily following, so that we are threatened with universal bankruptcy. Two failures alone have thrown at least three hundred persons, besides sailors, out of employ. . . . The poorhouse is already full. . . . All confidence is lost; no man will trust his neighbor. . . . I cannot describe . . . the distress we are in.[75]

The Reverend William Bentley of Salem felt Portland's troubles could not be blamed on the Embargo. "We have terrible news from Portland," he wrote on January 2, 1808. "The Numerous failures of some unprincipled adventurers in business, by their protested bills have occasioned a general gloom upon that dissipated but infant settlement of Speculators. This is not attributed to the Embargo but to the desperate plans of some projectors with whom P[ortland] abounds."[76] There were certainly Portland speculators who had overextended themselves, but it was the Embargo, the Non-Intercourse Act of 1809, and the subsequent War of 1812 that delivered the coup de grace that ruined Portland merchants like the McLellans and York's Bulkeley Emerson (who in the face of his losses, like his brother Edward, committed suicide), closed the Portland Bank, and turned the busy wharves of southern Maine into grassy platforms.

The Embargo was repealed during the last week of Jefferson's presidency, but President James Madison's Congress replaced it with the Non-Intercourse Act, which forbade trade with Britain and France. In response, American vessels developed trade with Spain, Portugal, North Sea ports, and Russia. But despite these efforts to keep out of their way, between 1807 and 1812 the French confiscated more than five hundred American vessels, the English almost four hundred.[77] In late June 1812, news reached New England that Congress had declared war on Britain. Congress intended that the War of 1812, whose slogan was "Free Trade and Sailor's Rights," would gain for Americans once and for all freedom of the seas. Even so "Mr. Madison's war" was not popular in New England where, despite their losses and humiliations, merchants were profiting in neutral trade.

During the summer of 1812, as news of the war gradually spread across the sea lanes of the world, American vessels ran for home where United States Navy ships, like the *Enterprise*, which patroled the coast of Maine, were keeping the British from blockading our ports, and forts and fortifications were deterring the enemy from entering Maine's harbors (cats. 12–13).[78] On September 23, Solomon Coit of Arundel brought the 193–ton brig *Advance* into the Kennebunk River from Liverpool. Her arrival must have occasioned great interest not only because she had made a dangerous run for her home port, but because of her cargo. The *Advance* was the only vessel of record ever to bring into the river a full cargo of European manufactured goods — crates of earthenware, umbrellas, trunks, leather gloves, silks, muslins, calicos, jewelry, and French iron pots. The vessels that made regular trips in and out of the Kennebunk River were West Indiamen that brought in sugar, molasses, coffee, and thousands of gallons of rum.[79] The *Advance* had been built in 1807 for Tobias Lord, Jr., and part of her cargo was assigned to Lord. Of her eight other consignees, only one, Hugh McCulloch, was local. Ordinarily the *Advance* would have gone into Boston to deliver the bulk of her cargo, but in September 1812 her prudent master's concern was to get her to her home port as quickly as possible.

One other locally owned vessel, the 242–ton bark *American*, also made a run for home from Liverpool, arriving in the Kennebunk River on October 2. Hers was the last arrival recorded at the Kennebunk customshouse until May 1815. The *American* was owned by Nathaniel Lord, Tobias's son, for whom she had been built on the river the year before. Although she brought in 115 crates of earthenware, the bulk of her cargo was 233 tons of duty-free salt. With the profits made on that cargo, Nathaniel would hire joiners to build for him Arundel's most impressive house.[80]

Nathaniel Lord was not the only Arundel man to take advantage of the lull in trading activity and the availability of skilled labor to build himself a new house. During the war several fine houses were built in Arundel's river village, where up to the beginning of the war house lots had sold for more than $7,000 an acre. Arundel's first bank was also built, one of only two brick buildings in the village (the other being a small schoolhouse). With a new road laid out to Kennebunk, and the road to Saco shortened and improved, a post office was established in Arundel for the first time and a stage carrying the mail and passengers ran through the village. Similar improvements took place in Kennebunk, Biddeford, Saco, and Portland, where Asa Clapp, who had made loans to the United States government to prosecute the war, took advantage of the quiet business climate to have his house reshingled and repaired.[81]

Historians have painted a gloomy picture of Maine's maritime activity during the Embargo and War of 1812. Much has been written about grass-covered wharves, vessels "laid up to decay" (wearing on their mastheads the inverted tar pots that were dubbed "Madison's night caps"), stifled commerce, and unemployed seamen, but that seems to be only part of the story, particularly during the early years of the war. Shipping was not entirely idle. While privateers, vessels outfitted or newly built to prey on English ships that were trading with Canada and the West Indies, were operating out of most Maine ports, other armed merchantmen, carrying letters of marque, which licensed them to take "prizes as a by-product of normal trading voyages," continued trading.[82] Fishing and the coasting trade continued also, providing employment for some unemployed mariners. Carrying licenses testifying to their United States citizenship and the peaceful intent of their voyage, such men ran the risk of capture by prowling British warships.[83]

The diary of Biddeford millowner, Samuel Merrill, records the arrival on May 27, 1813, of his schooner *Hiram* from New York. "Brot one thousand bushels of corn and eight barrels of flower. Also brought on freight nearly 500 Barrels of flower for Eastport." In July Merrill noted, "Capt. Israel Lassell arived, also Capt Noah Cole. They sailed in February or March last for some of the West India islands but they were seized and their vessel condemned, and returned home as passengers." On July 19 Merrill observed, "There are a large number of waggons bound on to New York ladened with English goods."[84]

As the war progressed it became more difficult to get a coaster safely to port. In response Maine's merchants transported their goods by wagon. As news of vessels had been published in local newspapers, so too was news of the four-horse teams that ran regularly to Boston. James Remich, editor of Kennebunk's *Weekly Visiter*, published such news under the heading "Horse-marine List." Remich utilized his "horse marine" column to bring his readers some humor in a worrisome time. On October 9, 1813, he wrote,

"Departed from this place, 7th inst., the fast sailing wagon, Rattler, Lt. Jefferds, for Boston with dry goods, etc." And in November:

Arrived November 6, at noon, two horse cutters, "Timothy Pickering" and "Quincy Cannon Ball," Commodore Delande, from Portland for Boston. Spoke on passage sixteen ox schooners from Bath for Boston, cargo, tin plate; all well. Also saw on Scarborough turnpike a suspicious looking cutter, which we escaped by superior sailing.[85]

John and Charles Fox of Portland, merchants and shipowners, who from their store and warehouse on Central Wharf imported and exported hardware and building supplies (nails, linseed oil, white lead ground in oil, varnish, and turpentine) and naval stores (oakum, Russia and Ravens duck, blue and red buntings, and cabooses, or deck cook houses), managed to keep their business going during the war. On June 30, 1814, Samuel Thomas of Waldoboro wrote that he was sending them lead and nails on board the *Mary*. "The master of the boat is a skillful, prudent man and acquainted with inland navigation," wrote Thomas, adding, "Hopeing you may receive the things safe." In July the Fox brothers received word that an order of compasses was still on board a ship in Boston that had "never sailed."[86]

Since April British ships had been lying off Portland boarding merchantmen.[87] With Napoleon defeated at last, the British were now free to concentrate their naval strength on the war with America. On June 16 the British ship *Bulwark* had come into Biddeford Pool and destroyed or seized three of Thomas Cutts's vessels. The next day she

appeared off Arundel. The populace, no doubt remembering the destruction of Falmouth in 1775, moved their dismantled shipping farther up the river, sent their furniture and valuables inland, and removed the money from the bank.[88] Not since the sea battle in September 1813 just north of Portland between the United States schooner *Enterprise* and the British brig *Boxer* had the war been brought home to so many in southern Maine (cats. 13–15). But although that September the British occupied Castine, Maine, by mid-February news of the Treaty of Ghent, which ended the war, reached southern Maine.

Peace and the Era of Reciprocity

On February 18, 1815, the Fox brothers' Norfolk, Virginia, supplier was writing, "Peace having returned . . . we have the pleasure of seeing Merchant Vessels enter our harbor. At present there are verry few here and we have a large Stock of Produce on hand." The rush to reactivate dismantled shipping was on up and down the Maine coast where some vessels were literally embedded in ice. Some were past saving, but new vessels were being built. At Kennebunk Landing the schooner *Washington* was launched and registered at the customshouse on March 27. She was the first of twenty-four vessels, including the brig *Favorite*, to be built in Kennebunk before the year had ended (fig. 1.9).[89]

The War of 1812 did not gain for American shipping the freedom of the seas for which it had been fought. Rather, it led to what is now known as the Era of Reciprocity, another

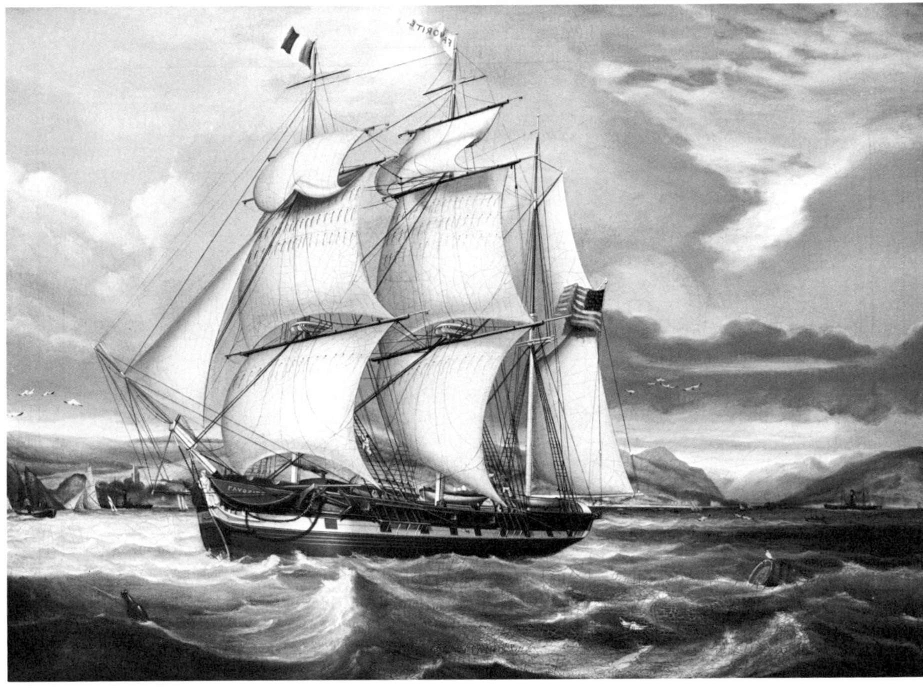

Fig. 1.9 Unidentified artist, brig *Favorite*, probably American, ca. 1830. Oil on canvas; H 25 (63.5), W 35⅝ (90.5). The Brick Store Museum.

decade and a half of struggle, particularly with England, America's greatest competitor for the world's merchant-marine trade. The 1816 Reciprocity Act permitted vessels of other countries to bring their national goods into American ports on the same basis that American vessels were received in their country's ports. It was a flawed treaty. It did not prevent the British from once again closing their West Indies ports to America's shipping, with the effect that while English vessels could bring their manufactured goods into American ports, American vessels not only lost that carrying trade, but the lucrative West Indies trade as well. Various reciprocity agreements would be reached during the next fifteen years in an attempt to achieve a fair balance of trade, but in general the years between the end of the war and 1830 were poor ones for America's merchant marine.[90]

On January 1, 1808, just as the disastrous effects of the Embargo were beginning to be felt in the city, the Grandmaster of Portland's Masonic lodge had proposed a toast to the city. "The town of Portland," he proclaimed. "She once rose like a Phoenix from the ashes! May she soon rise from her present embarrassments."[91] In later years Portland would adopt the phoenix as her symbol. So too that legendary bird could serve as a symbol of the course of commerce in federal-period Maine. Once again in the years following the War of 1812, as they had following the Revolution, the Undeclared War with France, and the Embargo, the merchants of Maine consolidated their losses and began again to build their businesses.

The year 1816 was not a propitious one in which to begin. Unusual weather conditions brought a crippling frost in each of the twelve months, retarding Maine's now important agricultural output. This in turn gave impetus to the so-called "Ohio fever," the migration to western lands that drained the New England states of many of their promising young men, and by 1820 was reflected in a significant deficit in Maine's population. Nevertheless, by 1820, when Maine at last achieved her independence from Massachusetts and became a state, Maine took the lead as the country's preeminent shipbuilding state.[92]

The need of American merchants for new vessels reflected their stubborn ability to stay involved in international trade despite the legal restrictions of the period. Trade with Cuba for sugar products had replaced the lost markets of the British West Indies, and a "cotton triangle" trade had begun to develop from America's Gulf ports to Europe.[93] Ironically, just as the Barbary pirates were finally subdued, the new trade routes laid American vessels open to attacks from another breed of vicious pirates, those of the Caribbean.

Coastal trade was also flourishing. In 1817 the United States had closed its coastwise trade to all foreign-built vessels, launching America's second golden age of domestic trade. One overview of New England shipping during the period states, "Coastal shipping involved a far greater number of vessels, captains, and crews than did the more spectacular foreign voyages." This regional condition is reflected only in part by figures for the percentage of vessels from southern Maine's ports that were *registered* for foreign trade or *enrolled* (or licensed) for domestic trade or fishing in the years after the war. Moses Greenleaf's 1829 *Survey of The State of Maine*, which encompasses 1827, shows Saco and York, where the chief exports were lumber and country produce to Boston and other American ports, with more vessels enrolled than registered. Portland, however, registered more than twice as many vessels as she enrolled. In Kennebunk the percentage of registered vessels was even higher, but those figures are deceptive.[94]

The figures for Portland are not surprising. Once again her deep-water port and marketing position in Maine were bringing her a variety of shipping business. Records for the late 1820s show imports of manufactured goods, raw materials, and produce from Boston and other Massachusetts ports, New York, Philadelphia, and America's southern ports. From the West Indies (mostly islands owned by countries other than England), Cuba, and South American ports, registered vessels brought in the usual West India goods as well as mahogany, hides, and ivory. From Africa came ivory, goat skins and other hides, salt, wine, camwood, and gold. Wine was brought in from the Canary Islands, but from the European continent, except for iron, hemp, feather beds, and duck from Russia, only salt, coal, passengers, and ballast came into Portland. Eastport, Maine, and other down east ports provided lumber, fish, imported salt and grindstones, and, in one instance, "Irish passengers."

Portland vessels exported the usual lumber and wood products and, after 1815, sugar boxes for the Havana market; fish; country produce and livestock; raw materials such as whale oil and produce; manufactured goods that had been brought to Portland from other American ports; and foreign goods that had been brought in by local registered vessels as well as coasters. Portland merchants also exported goods that could have been manufactured in the city: cigars, shoes, bricks, furniture, boats, looking glasses, soap, and bread.[95]

The large percentage of registered vessels in Kennebunk is deceptive, probably reflecting more the number of vessels *owned* by Kennebunk and Arundel men than the number that operated out of the Kennebunk River. While Kennebunk vessels continued to bring in sugar, coffee, and rum from the Caribbean, and a handful of small coasters and fishing boats came regularly in and out of the river, the economy of the area was based on its shipbuilding industry. By 1820, when Kennebunk at last became a town in its own right and Arundel, with its larger population whose average individual wealth was second only to that of Portland, was petitioning the new legislature to be renamed Kennebunk Port, seven shipyards were flourishing at Kennebunk Landing.[96]

The shipping activities of Kennebunkport's Daniel W.

Lord, son of Nathaniel and grandson of Tobias, are typical of a developing trend for merchants and shipowners of the Kennebunks. By the 1820s many were registering their Kennebunk-built vessels in Boston, which means Boston was their home port. Shipping opportunities in Boston far outstripped those in the Kennebunks. Although D. W. Lord registered his vessels in Kennebunk, he operated them out of Portland and Boston, and other major ports.

Lord began his business career in 1817 by opening a store. By 1821 he owned shares in four vessels, and was already choosing to run them in and out of Boston rather than the Kennebunk River. In 1824, while his brig *Union* was coming and going out of Portland harbor, Lord sent his new brig *Commodore Preble* to New Orleans to enter the cotton triangle trade. Four years later the *Commodore Preble* brought a load of salt from the island of Sardinia to Kennebunkport, but only succeeded in getting in over the bar at the river's mouth after waiting there "a few days" for a tide high enough to float her in. In 1830 when the *Union* appeared off the Kennebunk bar from Liverpool with a load of salt, Lord "went out in a boat and took some money from her and sent her to Boston with the salt." Later that year Lord moved to Boston for the winter to run his shipping business. Lord, like earlier Maine shipowners with ambition, recognized that the opportunity to make substantial money lay beyond his doorstep in the wider world of commerce.[97]

Manufacturing and a New Era of Commerce

The years that marked D. W. Lord's rise in business were transitional ones in Maine. Although the new state's commerce was still dependent on her shipping, agriculture and manufacturing were now contributing to the economy. In his survey, Greenleaf estimated that only a little more than ten thousand Maine men were employed in vessels, including those working in Maine's substantial fishing fleet. On the other hand, five-sixths of Maine's inhabitants were primarily employed in agriculture. Greenleaf estimated that approximately $250,000 worth of agricultural produce was exported from Maine in 1826. But the industry that was to bring Maine into a new era of commerce was manufacturing.[98]

Maine people, who had been "manufacturing" vessels and the masts, shooks, staves, and clapboards they exported since the earliest days of settlement, also had ventured into other areas of manufacturing before the War of 1812. It had begun as a "home industry." Before the war, Portland's Fox brothers had supplied the blacksmith Samuel Kingsley, who lived in the inland town of Turner, with iron. From the iron Kingsley made scrapers, flesh forks, caulkers' meaking irons, ladles, and hammers, which the brothers sold from their Portland store and exported to Boston. In exchange for this service they supplied Kingsley with tea, coffee, and other imported goods.[99]

In 1810 Saco's Daniel Cleaves and John Scammon signed articles of agreement for a partnership that included not only "the Art or Trade of Merchandize" but the "manufacturing [of leaf tobacco] into Pigtail and Fig tobacco and Segars." The agreement noted that they owned "two tobacco Presses and all their apparatus for carrying on the Manufactory of tobacco." While these tobacco products were probably made for local consumption, as were shoes, hats, bricks, and other necessary items, by the mid-1820s such locally made goods were being exported from Portland to island ports like the Swedish-held West Indian island of "St. Bartholomew's."[100]

Portland drew such manufactures from surprisingly distant inland towns: Limerick, Bakerstown, Poland, and Minot, and even from New Hampshire and Vermont.[101] Her role as an entrepôt for a cross section of the inland towns of northern New England would increase after 1820 as the Maine Legislature granted more and more charters for canals.

The making of cloth was probably the largest home industry. Like all frontier women, Maine women had made cloth for their families' clothes. Sheep were raised for their wool and cotton was imported from southern ports. Most towns had carding and fulling mills for preparing the wool and finishing the cloth. Arundel's Elizabeth Wildes, and others like her, would develop her spinning and weaving into a flourishing home industry. Widowed and the mother of three children, in 1794 she married the Kennebunk Landing shipbuilder, John Bourne, who had six children. Together they would have six more offspring. No doubt to help with the support of this large family, or perhaps just through the work patterns required to keep them clothed, Eliza turned an interest and facility for spinning and weaving into a home industry. Using three looms, Eliza and her daughters wove various kinds of cloth and cotton counterpanes, which in one year alone earned them almost five hundred dollars. Greenleaf recognized cotton cloth, whose manufacture was "conducted chiefly in private families," as one of Maine's most important manufactures (cat. 139).[102]

Some cotton yarn was manufactured in factories. In 1811 a cotton factory had been built in York. Abigail Emerson, widow of Edward Emerson, Jr., had invested in it, hoping, as had its other backers, that the factory "would bring prosperity to York." That hope was not to be realized. The factory failed, and by 1817, with the selectmen looking for a less expensive way to care for the town's poor, York's role as an important town in southern Maine was coming to an end.[103]

It was also in 1811 that Saco's Thomas Cutts and a partner, Josiah Calef, built an "Iron works" on Cutts Island in the Saco River. Nails were manufactured from iron imported in Cutts's vessels. Kennebunk had had its own iron works. In 1774, in anticipation of the decreased availability of imported iron that the Revolution would cause, a factory was built on an island in the Mousam River to manufacture iron from ore brought in from surrounding areas. The iron produced was suitable for the manufacture of axes, plows, chains, and similar farm tools. The iron works continued in operation for almost twenty years, until improved commerce, which allowed the importation of iron objects of a superior quality, dictated its demise.[104]

Saco's iron works was gone by 1825, four years after Cutts's death, when a Boston-based company purchased most of Cutts Island and built a seven-story, wooden cotton factory. By 1829 five hundred employees (four hundred of whom lived in tenements on the island) worked in the factory. Although this successful enterprise would burn in the winter of 1830, the leading men of Saco and Biddeford had seen their future. The towns' long and successful venture in manufacturing had begun (see cat. 39).[105]

But despite the rise of manufacturing in Maine, by the mid-to-late 1820s the inhabitants of the state were still depending on other states and foreign imports for many of their manufactured goods. In 1824, when D. W. Lord married a Saco woman, they went to Boston to buy new furnishings for the mansion house he had inherited from his father. Like Portland's Enoch Preble, who twenty-four years before had done his nuptial shopping in Boston, Lord bought a full complement of household goods—looking glasses, yellow chairs, bedsteads, bureaus, Pembroke tables, a mahogany couch, silver, fluted decanters, tumblers, "wines," and Britannia teapots—whatever was needed to set up housekeeping. While some of these goods were not available in Maine, many were. But although Lord, and others of his class in southern Maine, had chosen to have his portrait painted by Maine's John Brewster, there was prestige in shopping in Boston, New York, or Philadelphia.[106]

In 1829 Moses Greenleaf had expressed the hope that Maine's manufacturing imbalance would shift in the future and Maine people would take advantage of their waterpower and other facilities to "produce every important manufacture, which may be required for their own consumption, or be advantageously exchanged by means of their commerce with other States and countries."[107] Although he did not address himself to the phenomenon of out-of-state shopping, Greenleaf must have recognized its appeal even as we recognize that it was the making of money, not goods, that furnished the homes and created the agreeable ambience of federal-period Maine.

1 Willis, *History*, 521. For a more detailed account of the destruction of Falmouth, see 515–522, and "Letter from Reverend Jacob Bailey In 1775, Describing the Destruction of Falmouth, Maine," *Collections of the Maine Historical Society* 5 (1857):439–450.

2 Willis, *History*, 320–321.

3 Dwight, *Travels*, 2:116. Charles E. Clark, *Maine: A Bicentennial History* (New York: W. W. Norton, 1977), 67. Thomas Oxnard, journal 2, November 25, 1775, to March 27, 1776, MEHS.

4 Vice Admiral Graves, commander of the port of Boston and of the Royal Navy's North American squadron, had included Saco, as the Saco River settlements were generally known, in his list of Maine seaports to be burned. Donald A. Yerxa, *The Burning of Falmouth: A Case Study in British Imperial Pacification* (Portland: Maine Historical Society, 1975), 125.

5 Jonathan Sayward, journals, 1760–1799, American Antiquarian Society, Worcester, Mass.

6 For the history of Maine's naval offices and Falmouth's collection district, see Willis, *History*, 458–460. Official records of shipping activity from Maine ports before the Revolution and during the early decades of the nineteenth century are either nonexistent or fragmentary. For that reason it is difficult to comment accurately and authoritatively on that vital aspect of Maine life.

7 Willis, *History*, 35, sets 1628 as the date of "first occupation of any part of Falmouth by a European." On the Saco River, settlement was first made (at what would be called variously Winter Harbor, Biddeford, Pepperrellborough, and Saco) by Richard Vines, who had wintered at the mouth of the river in 1616, sometime between 1624 and 1630. Bradbury, *History*, 19, and Folsom, *History*, 30. Both Bradbury and Folsom believed that Cape Porpus, as Arundel was originally called, was settled as early as Saco. Bourne, *History*, 3, states, "We have no definite knowledge of [this town's] occupation by civilized man prior to 1640, though there are facts . . . which seem to indicate very clearly that some persons had previously had a fixed habitation here." York was founded by Edward Godfrey in 1630. Banks, *History*, 1:41.

8 Other villages were developed along the shores of the bay and the Fore River, but Falmouth Neck provided the prime location for the area's principal settlement. Willis, *History*, 440, called the Neck the "parent stock which sent out its branches to the remote portions of the territory." Two Casco Bay–Fore River settlements that flourished for a time were Stroudwater and Cape Elizabeth. For a discussion of Stroudwater's importance as a center for the eighteenth-century mast trade, see Barry, *Tate House*, 7–9. For Cape Elizabeth's importance as a commercial center before the Revolution, see Willis, *History*, 457–458. Fairburn, *Merchant Sail*, 1:490.

9 Rev. Jonathan Coggswell, "A Topographical and Historical Sketch of Saco, County of York, District of Maine, August 1815," *Collections of the Massachusetts Historical Society*, 2d ser., 4(1816):186.

10 Bourne, *History*, 530.

11 On November 9, 1806, Samuel Merrill of Biddeford wrote in his diary, "Capt. Samuel Hartley went over the bar and into the Pool for to finish his loading"; Samuel Merrill, diary, 1799–1844, McArthur Library, Biddeford, Me. One Saco historian notes that "oldtimers had great indoor sport in the shops and taverns guessing the date when the ice would go out in the spring"; Fairfield, *Sands*, 35–36. In January 1826 Daniel W. Lord noted that Portland harbor was frozen, "a rare occurance"; Daniel W. Lord, journal, 27, MEHS.

12 A resident returning from a visit to Plymouth in 1774 "came to Biddeford by water," evidently intending to travel by land from there to Arundel; Bradbury, *History*, 164–165, 177.

13 Bourne, *History*, 571. Bourne decried the dearth of information available to him concerning the early commerce of Wells and Kennebunk, but for an account of what is known see chapter 35 of his *History*.

14 See Bradbury, *History*, 211, for the reference to the river's barred harbor, and for the second quotation, "from an old merchant at the Port," see Remich, *History*, 167. Modern sailboat enthusiasts who use the river have no trouble understanding the reference to a "foul weather" or northerly wind. Because the Kennebunk River runs due south it is necessary to tack in order to leave the river against a southerly or "fair weather" wind. The masters of nineteenth-century merchant vessels would not have had the space necessary to tack into the wind and therefore would have had to wait for a northerly wind to leave the river.

15 Sewall, "Topographical Description of York," 3:6–7.

16 Dwight, *Travels*, 2:140. See also Laurie Carpenter, *Shipping in York*

Prior to 1875, Bulletin no. 6, Historic Programs and Awards Program (York, Me.: Society for the Preservation of Historic Landmarks in York County, Inc., 1972).

17 For a brief discussion of the effects of the Revolution on Maine's maritime enterprises see Rowe, *Maritime History*, 60–61. See also Fairburn, *Merchant Sail*, 1:476, which describes "American independence [as] dearly bought on the seas" with the "loss of a thousand merchant ships," near "depletion" of her "seafaring population," and obliteration of her deep-sea fisheries. For the statistics on Maine's fishing fleet before the Revolution see Greenleaf, *Survey*, 254.

18 Willis, *History*, 449–450.

19 For a more thorough explanation of the triangle trade, see Fairburn, *Merchant Sail*, 2:1128.

20 Rowe, *Maritime History*, 102. Albion and Pope, *Sea Lanes*, 18-21. The authors discuss in detail the design, rigging, crew size, maneuverability, and use of the various types of vessels. They note that a 250–ton ship has a capacity of approximately 25,000 cubic feet. (It should be noted that Albion and Pope have not presented the whole picture. Barks and brigs of larger size were also used on transatlantic voyages.) The distinction between ships and smaller vessels was an important one that rested on size as well as rigging. That is not always understood by twentieth-century historians. Rowe, *Maritime History*, 64, writes, "Even as late as 1787 there was not a single vessel owned in Portland." This is probably a misreading of Willis, who wrote, "In 1787 there was not a ship owned in town" (*History*, 560). Willis, who gives ample documentation elsewhere in his history for local ownership of small vessels in 1787, was probably referring to "ships" as defined above.

21 Albion, *Sea Lanes*, 27–28. Fairburn, *Merchant Sail*, 1: 477, states, "Before the Revolution, colonial trade to the British West Indies amounted to about eighteen million dollars a year." Willis, *History*, 455–456.

22 Willis, *Journals*, 351.

23 Willis, *History*, 550n, and Willis, *Journals*, 356.

24 Greenleaf, *Survey*, 135–136.

25 Ronald F. Banks, *Maine Becomes a State: The Movement to Separate Maine from Massachusetts, 1785–1820* (Somersworth, N. H.: New Hampshire Publishing Company, 1973), 5.

26 William Graham Sumner, *A History of American Currency* (1847; reprint, New York: Augustus M. Kelley, 1968), 46–49.

27 For more complete details, see Folsom, *History*, 260–262.

28 Agreement between Thomas Robison and William Edgar, December 1783; Thomas Robison to Phyn and Ellice, March 14, 1784, Robison Papers, MEHS.

29 For supplying rum to the poor, see Bourne, *History*, 682–683. A list of Robison's disbursements of rum from his distillery between December 1784 and April 1785 consists largely of the names of individuals, only some of whom were traders (Robison Papers, MEHS). John Quinby of Falmouth's Stroudwater section, whose papers are at MEHS, kept "grog scores" in a ledger between 1781 and 1784. In his "Memorandum Book," which is with the Preble Family Papers at MEHS, Edward Preble of Falmouth listed $4 for brandy for the workmen who repaired his house in 1805. Tristram Scammon of Saco, whose business papers are at Harvard University's Baker Library, listed rum among the "supplies" needed for building the schooner *Sally*, and in 1805 Joseph Leland billed the proprietors of Saco's First Parish Congregational Church for rum consumed during the building of their new meetinghouse (archives of the First Parish Congregational Church, Saco, Maine). Noting all of this, we do not need to be told in Willis, *History*, 781, that until "the genius of temperance" prevailed, "nothing could be done . . . but the men must be goaded on by the stimulus of rum." This statement is borne out by item six in the list of grievances put forth in 1786 by those agitating for Maine's statehood. Rum, the separationists argued, upon which the tax was high, had to be imported into Maine in large quantities "to meet the legitimate expectations of working people" because of the scarcity of orchards and therefore cider in the District (Banks, *Maine Becomes a State*, 16).

30 Phyn and Ellice, London, to Robison and Edgar, Falmouth, April 5, 1784, Robison Papers, MEHS.

31 Fairburn, *Merchant Sail*, 1:481–482.

32 Willis, *History*, 555.

33 Sayward, journals, American Antiquarian Society.

34 Salem's William "Billy" Gray, who has been called the "greatest [American] shipowner-merchant of his day," registered the 1784 Kennebunk-built schooner *Freedom* at Salem in 1789 (Fairburn, *Merchant Sail*, 1:549, 560). Although we do not know if Gray commissioned the *Freedom* (he could have acquired her later), we do know that twenty-seven of his ships were Maine-built (Rowe, *Maritime History*, 67), a number of these by Kennebunk builders like Tobias Lord, who received financial backing from Gray. Charles Edward Lord, *The Ancestors and Descendants of Lieutenant Tobias Lord* (Privately printed, 1913), 173. Rowe, *Maritime History*, 267.

35 "Memorandum Geo. Shand . . . , Grenada, September 25th 1784," Robison Papers, MEHS.

36 "Instructions for Captain Joshua Preble, 3 January 1785," Robison Papers, MEHS.

37 Albion, *Sea Lanes*, 66. Rowe, *Maritime History*, 67–70. Portland's second East Indiaman, also named *The Portland*, was entered into the trade by Asa Clapp and Matthew Cobb "soon after the end of the war of 1812"; William Goold, "East Indiamen," William Goold, Scrapbook, 42, 59, MEHS. It is interesting to note that on August 25, 1800, Theodore Lyman and others signed articles of agreement with Captain Dixey Wildes of Arundel to take the Kennebunk-built ship *Atahualpa* on a trading voyage from Boston to the northwest for furs and from there to Canton for "teas and nankins." Photocopies of this and other papers relating to the voyage are in BSM. The originals are owned by the Columbia River Maritime Museum in Astoria, Oregon. The *Atahualpa's* career has been called "one of the classics of the old China trade" (Rowe, *Maritime History*, 69).

38 For York's naval office reports, see Baxter, *Documentary History*, 21:125–126, 183–185, 232–233. For Falmouth's records see Willis, *History*, 558–560.

39 Barry and Holverson, "The Revolutionary McLellans," 83. The pitcher is owned by the museum.

40 Willis, *History*, 558. Thomas Robison to Robert Jenkins, Boston, January 26, 1784, Robison Papers, MEHS.

41 Fairburn, *Merchant Sail*, 1:491. For an explanation of the Coastal Law and its effect on Maine's separation movement, see Banks, *Maine Becomes a State*, 35.

42 Remich, *History*, 172–174. The shipping figures for 1795 encompassed all of Wells, including tonnage owned and operated from the Webhannet River; however, the largest number of ships were owned on the Kennebunk River. The supremacy and importance of the town's Kennebunk district is reflected in the name of the new customs district.

43 Bradbury, *History*, 181.

44 One York man who played a significant role in another southern Maine town was Jedediah Preble, who settled in Falmouth about 1748 and founded one of the town's most influential families. Another was Falmouth's Stephen Longfellow, a schoolteacher, who came in 1768, enjoyed a distinguished career as a politician and legislator, and founded another of Portland's important families. York's Joseph Ingraham, a silversmith, who also came in 1768, was a successful, community-spirited businessman, and built the first house after the 1775 destruction of Falmouth. Pepperrellborough's post–Revolutionary War surveyor, Moses Banks, and Biddeford's lawyer George Thacher were York men. Arundel's Simon Nowell came from York about 1800 and became one of the town's most prosperous merchants, shipowners, and tavern keepers. Many of Arundel's post–Revolutionary War mariners, joiners, and blacksmiths were from York. Kennebunk's John Mitchell migrated from York in 1740. He built the first substantial house near the mouth of the Kennebunk River as well as its first wharf where the river's first vessel was built in 1755. Kennebunk's influential Sewall family came from York about 1815. In his topographical description of York, David Sewall noted that although farming was the principal occupation of the inhabitants, two-thirds of the town's

soil was too poor to grow anything. Although York was also a "maritime place," opportunities for new business in shipping were limited as York's supply of lumber had long since been cut off for export. What remained was "not now more than a sufficiency for the inhabitants." This assessment is borne out by the journals of Jonathan Sayward, which in the 1790s frequently note the departure of York vessels for Maine's Penobscot River region for a "Load of Boards to carry to W[est] Indies" (August 14, 1795). Robert Gross, in his lecture "Rural Life in Early New England," delivered at Saco's Dyer Library in June 1984, described the similar "dwarfed horizons" in many Massachusetts towns, which led to the flow of immigration to Maine that from 1770 to 1790 increased its population "almost fivefold."

45 On July 27, 1785, Jonathan Sayward wrote, "my wife and I went to Kennebunk to visit Mr Theodore Lyman & his sister Lucy and to see his seat[.] it is fit for a noble man & I have seen nothing like it in this County and scar[ce]ly any where" (journal, American Antiquarian Society).

46 Oliver Keating and Company, account book, 1791–1793, BSM.

47 Oliver Keating and Company, account book, 1791–1795, ships accounts, BSM.

48 Bourne, *History*, 529–530, credits Kennebunk with being "the center of business for the county," taking precedence over Pepperrellborough and Biddeford.

49 *Atlas of York County, Maine* (Philadelphia, Pa.: Sanford, Everts & Co., 1872), 80. Timothy Lyman, diary, February 28, 1793, OYHS. Timothy Lyman, general store ledger, Coxhall, Me., 1794, OYHS.

50 Bourne, *History*, 759. In her diary Elizabeth Wildes noted not only the arrivals and departures of her husband to the "Westindias," but those of other local shipmasters. She also recorded transactions for West Indies and other goods, as November 7, 1789, "Cap Hubbard and two strangers came here after some wine," and November 24, 1791, "Sailours came here after molloses." Israel Wildes may have been master of a Lyman vessel. Elizabeth's diary reflects a close connection between the two men. Invariably Israel went to see "Mr. Lymon" in Kennebunk, and in Boston after Lyman's move there, before leaving on his regular four- and five-month-long trips to the islands. Elizabeth Perkins Wildes, diary, 1789–1793, MEHS.

51 Thomas Cutts, Jr., book of invoices, 1790–1793, MEHS.

52 Thomas Cutts, Jr., book of invoices, 1792–1796, MEHS.

53 The projected "long haul" voyage made from Portland in 1806 by a ship owned by Saco's Daniel Cleaves and his partner Jonathan Tucker was typical. From Portland wood products and fish were carried to Jamaica. There rum, coffee, and sugar products were loaded. These were to be carried to Ireland. From Ireland the ship was to go to the Isle of May for salt, which would be carried to Boston. Cleaves and Tucker, account with [Captain] Loving Tarbox, 1806–1807, Cleaves Family Papers, Dyer Library, Saco, Maine. Albion, *Sea Lanes*, 68, 76.

54 Fairburn, *Merchant Sail*, 1:572–574. Rowe, *Maritime History*, 72–78.

55 An explanation of the intricacies of maritime history between 1794 and the Embargo of 1807 that led to the War of 1812, a period that encompassed England and France's Napoleonic Wars and America's Undeclared War and Neutral Profits Era, requires more space than can be allowed here. For a more detailed discussion, see Rowe, *Maritime History*, 62–80, and Fairburn, *Merchant Sail*, 1:572–611.

56 Rowe, *Maritime History*, 74. Bourne, *History*, 577ff.

57 Edward Emerson and Martha Payne Emerson, "The Emerson Family of York, Maine" (manuscript, OYHS), 119–129. This account includes the story that Emerson, having lost all but one of his vessels, sent her out with instructions to the master to "hoist the flag on entering the harbor if the voyage had been successful. When the vessel was signalled, Mr. Emerson went into his counting-room to watch for her, and when he saw the union down he shot himself. The cruise had been successful, but the Captain had forgotten his orders."

58 Willis, *History*, 840. Documents concerning the seizure of the *Eliza* are included in the Robison Papers, MEHS. Robison's loss of

another ship ten years earlier may have contributed to his financial decline. On August 15, 1790, the ship *Eagle*, outfitted as a slaver, sailed from Portland harbor for the coast of Africa. By some means her activities were discovered and her master, Robison, and her other owners were fined for outfitting the ship as a slaver in the first place and for transporting slaves to the West Indies. United States District Court, Maine, records, 1789–1802, 1:36, National Archives–Boston Branch, Waltham, Mass. Another Maine slave ship, a brig owned by Joseph Emerson of Scarborough, a brother to York's Edward Emerson, Jr., was seized by the British in the West Indies in 1793. For details, see Sayward, journal, June 10, 1793, American Antiquarian Society. The history of the *Eagle* and the Emerson slaver are of interest because of what they tell us of their owners' business affairs and because they shed light on the seldom cited involvement of Maine vessels in the slave trade.

59 Fairfield, *Sands*, 23.

60 Dwight, *Travels*, 2:154. Cleaves Family Papers, Dyer Library.

61 Dwight, *Travels*, 2:114. Willis, *History*, 557.

62 As cited in Willis, *History*, 576.

63 Abigail May, journal, 1796, MEHS.

64 Country produce and chickens, pigs, sheep, and cows for export to the islands were supplied by local, New Hampshire, and even Vermont farmers (Dwight, *Travels*, 2:141). Horses were exported from Portland for the first time in 1802 when Josiah Paine contracted to bring the mail from Boston daily. In searching the countryside for the large number of horses he would need, Paine discovered an ample supply and bought some for shipment to the West Indies. William Goold, "Portland's Past Commerce," William Goold, Scrapbook, 43. In 1792 Thomas Robison, writing to his partner about their West Indies trade, lists house frames as one of the local products wanted in the islands (Robison to Edgar, July 16, 1792, Robison Papers, MEHS). Charles Peirce of Portland's Stroudwater section, who ran a store and owned shares in various West Indiamen, also shipped house frames to the West Indies, buying them from local farmers (Charles Peirce Papers, MEHS). District of Portland and Falmouth, measurer's return book, no. 1, 1804–1807, Massachusetts Historical Society, Boston.

65 Asa Clapp, ledgers and accounts, 1796–1815, MEHS.

66 Willis, *History*, 577. Barry and Holverson, "The Revolutionary McLellans," 37. In 1820 when Arthur McLellan "sold a full cargo of English goods" in Portland, it was still an unusual event, causing the local press to hope McLellan's daring and success would influence other merchants to do the same. William David Barry, *A Vignetted History of Portland Business, 1632–1982* (New York: Newcomen Society in North America, 1982), 12, and *Eastern Argus* (May 2, 1820).

67 Captain Enoch Preble, expense book, 1800–1804, MEHS.

68 Barry and Holverson, "The Revolutionary McLellans," 59–62. See also Churchill, "Crafts in Transition," 300.

69 This and all other quotations are from Ann Bryant Smith, diary, 1806–1807, MEHS. A typescript of another portion of her diary can be found with manuscript 67–2675, MEHS.

70 On September 15, shortly after her husband had been to Boston to buy goods, she noted, "Had goods come to the wharf, but could not get them in. Every one was engaged at General muster."

71 Churchill, "Crafts in Transition," 306.

72 William Goold, "East Indiamen," William Goold, Scrapbook, 59.

73 Letter, n.d., William Goold, Scrapbook, 98. Dwight, *Travels*, 2:114.

74 Willis, *Journals*, 393.

75 Cummings, *Memoir of Edward Payson*, 142–143. The following March Payson wrote to his mother, "The embargo . . . will be detrimental to the morals of the people here. They have now nothing to do but saunter about, . . . and I fear they will lose all habits of industry and sobriety." (152).

76 Bentley, *Diary*, 3:336.

77 Fairburn, *Merchant Sail*, 2:758, 759. Banks, *Maine Becomes a State*, 58.

78 Albion, *Sea Lanes*, 112. In Portland, Forts Scammell and Preble, whose construction had been ordered by Congress in 1807, guarded the harbor (cat. 12). In Arundel a fortification was raised on high ground at the mouth of the Kennebunk River. The

deterrent such measures provided to the British is perhaps illustrated by the losses suffered at the mouth of the unfortified Saco River by Thomas Cutts, Jr. (Folsom, *History*, 309n).

79 District of Kennebunk, Kennebunk imports, impost book, 1800–1867, MEHS.

80 For details of the building and ownership of the *Advance* and the *American*, see S. E. Bryant, comp., *District of Kennebunk: A List of Vessels Built, From 1800–1878* (Kennebunk, Me., 1874). Tradition has long asserted that Nathaniel Lord built his mansion with "profits from a salt shipment, the last before the British blockade halted commerce." See "The Captain Lord Mansion: An Abbreviated History," an advertising brochure for the Captain Lord Mansion Inn, Kennebunkport, 1982. The entry in the Kennebunk impost book for October 2, 1812, seems to confirm that local legend. Nathaniel's son, Daniel Walker Lord, noted that workmen "Commenced building the three story house we now live in" in April 1814, completing it the following October; Daniel W. Lord, journal, 3, MEHS.

81 Bradbury, *History*, 188–189. "A Sketch of the Life of the Hon. Asa Clapp," *The Merchants' Magazine* 19, no. 4 (October 1848):397. Among Clapp's papers at the MEHS is an agreement with Joseph Watson, signed on April 29, 1814, for the shingling of the back roof of Clapp's dwelling house and various other repairs.

82 Albion, *Sea Lanes*, 24–25. Rowe, *Shipbuilding Days in Casco Bay*, 26, notes that, "Within a week of June 26 when Congress authorized issuing letters of marque and reprisal, the Collector at Portland had issued several." Privateers also operated out of the Saco and Kennebunk rivers, and York.

83 During the war, Theodore Wells of Wells earned his living fishing and carrying wood to Boston on a coaster as well as by farming and teaching school. Theodore Wells, *Narrative of the Life and Adventures of Capt. Theodore Wells* (Biddeford, Me.: John E. Butler & Co., 1874), 74. For coasting and fishing licenses, see Portland, Maine, Custom House, oaths and registry of vessels at Portland, Maine, April-June, 1813, Massachusetts Historical Society.

84 Samuel Merrill, diary, McArthur Library.

85 Remich, *History*, 260–261.

86 John Fox Papers, 1811–1831, MEHS.

87 On April 5, 1813, Charles Fox wrote to another brother, "The British government Schooner Bream has been close in with our light-house this morning, a fisherman informs me he saw her board a Schooner from the Westward bound downn to the eastward."

88 Bourne, *History*, 603.

89 John Fox Papers, MEHS. Wells, *Life*, 81. Bryant, *List*, 3.

90 For a more complete discussion of the Reciprocity Era, see Fairburn, *Merchant Sail*, 2:927ff.

91 *Eastern Argus* (January 20, 1808). This was not the first time the legendary phoenix had been evoked as a symbol of the town. The following acrostic appeared in the *Falmouth Gazette* (February 5, 1785): "From th' ashes of the old, a town appears, / And Phoenix like, her plumy head she rears, / Long may she flourish, be from war secure / Made rich by commerce and agriculture / O're all her foes triumphant; be content / Under our happy form of govern-ment; / Till (what not doubt will be her prosp'rous fate) / Herself's the mistress of a rising State."

92 Greenleaf, *Survey*, 134. William Willis, "Introductory Address Before The Maine Historical Society, February 2, 1855, At Augusta," *Collections of the Maine Historical Society* 4(1856):25.

93 Trade with the British West Indies was never entirely stopped. It was carried on as an indirect trade through the islands of other nations to the British-owned islands. William Avery Baker, *A Maritime History of Bath, Maine, and the Kennebec River Region*, 2 vols. (Bath, Me.: Marine Research Society of Bath, 1973), 1:221.

94 Robert G. Albion et al., *New England and the Sea* (Middletown, Conn.: Wesleyan University Press, 1972), 124–125. See also Forrest R. Holdcamper, "Registers, Enrollments and Licenses in the National Archives," *American Neptune* 1 (1941):276. For 1825, Greenleaf, *Survey*, 225, gives Portland tonnage registered for foreign trade of over 30,000 and enrolled tonnage of about 12,000. Kennebunk's registered tonnage for the same year was about 7,500,

95 Port of Portland, exports and imports, ca. 1827–1830, Massachusetts Historical Society. An interesting analysis of Maine's maritime commerce, which can be applied to Portland, can be found in Greenleaf, *Survey*. Greenleaf indicates the difficulty of determining the extent of foreign trade percentages because of shipping patterns.

96 In 1820 Kennebunk's population was 2,145, Arundel's 2,498. For Arundel's position as the second wealthiest town in the state, see Greenleaf, *Survey*, 456–457.

97 All information about Lord and his business activities has been taken from his journal, MEHS.

98 Greenleaf, *Survey*, 255, 217, 213. Greenleaf placed Maine's fishing fleet at one-fifth of the country's total.

99 John Fox Papers, MEHS.

100 Cleaves Family Papers, Dyer Library. For the export of such goods from Portland, see Port of Portland, exports and imports, ca. 1827–1830, Massachusetts Historical Society.

101 In his "An Account of Limerick," *Collections of the Maine Historical Society* 1(1831; reprint, 1865):331, Charles Freeman notes that furniture, shoes, hats, and leather were made in Limerick in such quantities "as to be sent abroad into other parts of the country" and "carried away to market," Portland being Limerick's principal market town. William Ladd, in his "Annals of Bakerstown, Poland, and Minot," *Collections of the Maine Historical Society* 2(1847; reprint, 1902):130, lists lumber products including "sugar boxes for the Havana market," and furniture; leather and leather goods—shoes, saddles, and harness; wagons; ploughs; "Leghorn straw and chip hats and bonnets," and other articles as items made for sale in Portland, the "nearest market town."

102 In 1803 and 1809 Kennebunk traders were advertising cotton for sale in the *Weekly Visiter*. Remich, *History*, 221. Greenleaf, *Survey*, 277–278.

103 Emerson, "The Emerson Family," 180. Town of York, warrant for town meeting "for the purpose of devising a cheaper mode . . . for maintaining the poor," OYHS. In 1833 the County Court was moved from York to Alfred, and with the coming of the railroad in the 1840s, which bypassed York, the town was effectively cutoff from the mainstream of events in York County. *Atlas of York County, Maine*, 114.

104 Bourne, *History*, 503–504, 619. In the 1780s Luigi Castiglioni "went to see the ironworks, which is had from a rich mine in these parts. This mine is the kind called muddy (or sludge), in which the metal is found in the state of ocre [?] This is drawn from low land about seven miles from Kennebung, and the mineral is reddish, friable and abundant. It is covered with a great quantity of carbon, and reduced to a shapeless mass of metal, which is then beaten with a hammer into a long bar of fifty or sixty pounds in weight, which is obtained from five to six Bushels of mineral, of which each has about fifty pounds in weight. They make at least four bars a day, and they consume great quantities of carbon, because the furnace is uncovered, and the heat spreads everywhere. The iron is good quality, and it is made into utensils, and farm implements, that before were brought from England"; Luigi Castiglioni, *Stati Uniti Dell' America Settentrionale fatto negli anni 1785, 1786, e 1787*, 2 vols. (Milano, 1790), 1:72–73. Jean K. Cadogan kindly translated this passage.

105 For more details about the Saco cotton factory, see Folsom, *History*, 306.

106 D. W. Lord, journal, 21, MEHS. With Lord's journal is a small notebook of expenditures, which lists his 1824 purchases, and a few receipts for same. In his journal Lord noted that he had had his portrait painted by Brewster in July 1821. Kennebunk's John and Eliza Bourne and the Cutts of Saco also hired Brewster; see cats. 28–30, 33–37.

107 Greenleaf, *Survey*, 286.

I

Attributed to Michele Felice Cornè (1752–1845)
Bombardment of Tripoli
Salem or Boston, Massachusetts, ca. 1805
Oil on canvas
H 36¹¹⁄₁₆ (80.5); W 48¹⁄₁₆ (122.0)
Maine Historical Society;
Gift of Alice Preble Anderson, 1917
Color plate on page 41

This painting is one of three large oil pictures known that depicts the American naval attack on the city of Tripoli in 1804. It descended in the family of Commodore Edward Preble, who is believed to have commissioned it upon his return from the Mediterranean. Although this picture is not signed, and no correspondence has been found between Preble and Cornè, its family history and other sources survive to aid in its documentation.[1]

As commander of the American fleet in the Mediterranean, Edward Preble played a crucial role in the successful conclusion of the war against the Barbary States. For centuries, four North African states had controlled shipping in the Mediterranean through piracy, ransom, and bribery. Once it became an independent nation, the United States was also expected to buy immunity from interference with its maritime trade. The United States had concluded a peace treaty with Tripoli in 1796 at the tremendous cost of $56,000, with an additional sum due on the arrival of the American consul in Tripoli in 1799, a payment the Treasury could not afford. Payment was not made and in 1801, under the leadership of President Jefferson, Congress sent a squadron from its fledgling navy to protect the interests of American shipping. In 1801, when the United States commmenced a naval blockade, the Pasha of Tripoli declared war. The other North African states followed his lead. Preble was sent as the commodore of the squadron in the summer of 1803. The presence of the American fleet and its persistent harassment of the African ports finally led to a settlement; Preble returned to the United States in February 1805.[2]

On March 3, 1805, Congress passed a resolution to honor Edward Preble with a gold medal. A profile portrait of Preble by Rembrandt Peale may have served as the source for the decoration on the obverse of the medal; a design remained to be chosen for the reverse. It is the correspondence relating to this medal that sheds light on the Cornè paintings. On June 15, 1805, Preble wrote to the navy agent in Philadelphia, "I have a painting of the first attack, six feet long by four wide—it is the only one I have at present, but it shall be sent to you if the engraver wishes it." He noted in a letter to the secretary of the navy in July that this large picture cost $50. A *Bombardment of Tripoli* of this size, signed by Cornè and dated 1805, was presented by Preble to the

navy office in Washington in February 1806.[3] Preble is thought to have commissioned the painting illustrated here for his personal use because it remained in his family until 1917 when it was presented by Preble's granddaughter to the Maine Historical Society.

Preble may have advised Cornè because the composition conforms to Preble's perceptions of the conflict, as described in his official dispatches. The scene depicts the high point of the campaign. From right center foreground to left are ships of the American fleet including the *Constitution* (the "flagship" from which Preble directed the blockade and bombardment), *Vixen*, *Syren*, *Argus*, *Nautilus*, and *Enterprise*. The castle of the Pasha is visible in the center of the composition with the fortified city of Tripoli extending from his headquarters to the right.[4]

Michele Felice Cornè, a native of the Kingdom of Naples, emigrated to Massachusetts in 1800 on board a ship owned by Elias Hasket Derby, Jr., of Salem. He remained in Salem for several years where he earned a living as a painter. His work ranged from highly refined ship portraits in oils and watercolors to frescoed wall decorations. Cornè left Salem by 1807, and possibly earlier, because the latest paintings done in Salem are dated 1805. His name appears in the 1810 Boston city directory. Cornè could have met Preble in Salem or Boston since Preble had naval and personal business in both places. Among Cornè's ship portraits is a watercolor dated 1803 of the *Charles* of Boston, owned in part by Edward Preble; it may explain his acquaintance with Cornè.[5]

Although this painting was a specially commissioned work, its subject reached a wide American audience. In April 1807, a ten-foot high by sixty-foot wide panorama of the Bombardment of Tripoli was exhibited at Portland's Union Hall. According to the local newspaper, the panorama "was executed in a masterly stile by the celebrated Italian artist Mr. Corne." Intended as an exhibition piece, this

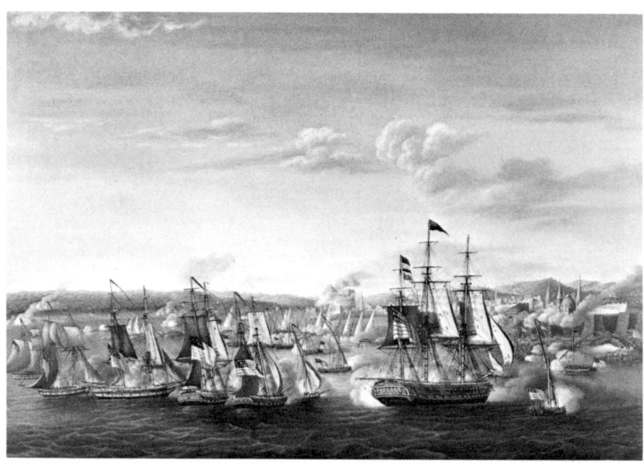

Cat. 1

panorama had been on view in Salem in January 1807, before its Portland appearance, and in May was exhibited in Providence.[6] Painted on canvas, it could be rolled easily for transportation. It was probably painted quickly in tempera colors and did not survive.

Corně's *Bombardment of Tripoli* was copied by engravers. The prints were in turn adapted by English potters for decoration of ceramics made for the American market (cat. 2).[7]

Many of the ships in Preble's squadron returned to the United States to perform other duties. During the War of 1812, the *Enterprise* engaged HM brig *Boxer*, capturing her off the coast of Maine (see cats. 13–15). Many years after his execution of the Tripolitan battle, Corně again depicted current naval engagements.[8] Engraved versions of these pictures were published in early histories of the War of 1812, notably in the *Naval Monument* published by Abel Bowen of Boston in 1816. LFS

1 The second painting is in the collection of the United States Naval Academy Museum, Annapolis, Maryland, (hereafter USNAM); the third is at the Rhode Island Historical Society. Two related watercolors are at USNAM; see *Michele Felice Corně 1752–1845, Versatile Neapolitan Painter* (Salem, Mass.: Peabody Museum of Salem, 1972), 17. I would like to thank James W. Cheevers, senior curator, USNAM, for kindly sharing his knowledge of Corně's work.
2 Christopher McKee, *Edward Preble, A Naval Biography* (Annapolis, Md.: Naval Institute Press, 1972), 86–87, 91–92; see chapters 7 and 8 for a detailed description of these events.
3 Edward Preble to George Harrison, June 15, 1805, and Edward Preble to Secretary of the Navy, July 10, 1805, cited in George Henry Preble, comp., "Correspondence Relating to the Preble Medal," *American Journal of Numismatics* 6, no. 3 (January 1872): 50–51; N. Morris to Edward Preble, February 16, 1806, Edward Preble Papers, Manuscripts Division, Library of Congress.
4 McKee, *Edward Preble*, 264–265.
5 Barry A. Greenlaw, "Michele Felice Corně" (M.A. thesis, University of Delaware, 1962), 11, 21, 99.
6 *Eastern Argus* (April 9, 1807) and Greenlaw, "Corně," 118–119.
7 For a transfer-print of this design, see McCauley, *Liverpool Transfer Designs*, plate 5.
8 *Michele Felice Corně, Versatile Neapolitan Painter*, 18–20.

2

Herculaneum Pottery (1796–1840)
Pitcher
Liverpool, England, 1805–1807
Creamware with transfer-printing in black
Marked (in transfer-printing below the spout)
"Herculaneum Pottery, Liverpool"
H 8 (20.3)
Maine Historical Society
Gift of Fritz H. Jordan, 1916

"Comre Prebble has done gallantly before Tripoli," wrote Peleg Wadsworth in December 1804. Pitchers bearing the likeness of Edward Preble and a view of the attack on Tripoli

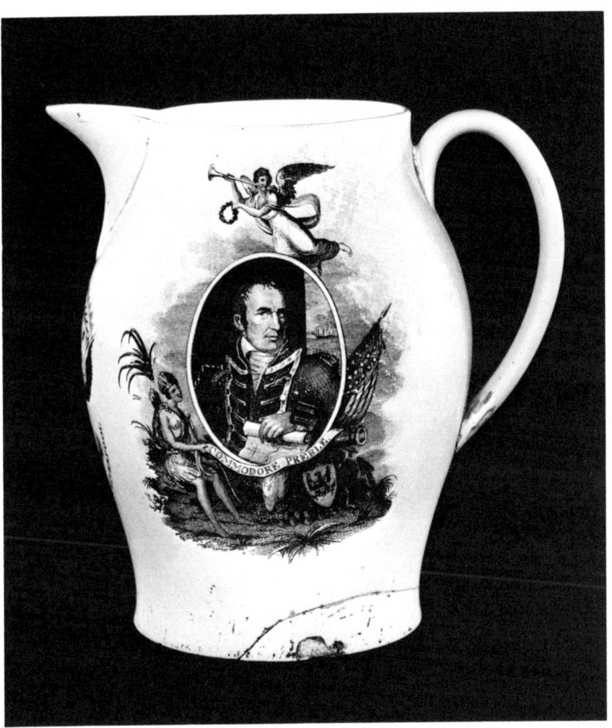

Cat. 2

were made in England expressly for the American market. These pitchers would have been very saleable in Maine, where many public events were held in conjunction with Preble's return to Maine from the Mediterranean.[1]

The original source for the likeness of Preble was an oil portrait. It was popularized through prints, from which an engraver at the pottery must have adapted this design. He enclosed the oval portrait in a cartouche with symbolic American emblems.[2] On the reverse is a transfer-print of Preble's August 3, 1804, attack on Tripoli. One of Michele Felice Corně's paintings of the attack served as the source for this decoration (see cat. 1).

Henry Wadsworth, Peleg's son, accompanied Preble in the Mediterranean. He visited Algiers and followed Preble on his diplomatic rounds. A chart of Tripoli harbor and a sketch of the town executed by Henry have survived in the family papers; he probably sent them to his sister, Zilpah Longfellow. He lost his life September 4, 1804, when a torpedo boat he and others manned to destroy the Tripolitan fleet exploded. His father wrote on learning of his son's death nearly five months later, "I knew the Temper of Henry & the feelings of a soldier. . . . his determination to earn a Character & make himself a Name, gave me great apprehension that I should see his face no more, long before the News arrived of the Catastrophe. He has indeed made himself a Name of which his parents Friends & Family may be proud, tho they deeply regret the price."[3] LFS

1 Peleg Wadsworth to Charles Wadsworth, December 5, 1804,
  Wadsworth Papers, MEHS. A public dinner was held on Preble's
  return to Portland; see *Eastern Argus* (October 18, 1805). For other
  events, see Jordan Newspaper Index, Portland Public Library. This
  pitcher and the others at MEHS included in this volume are also
  discussed in Sprague, "Liverpool-type Pitchers."
2 The portrait, now in the collection of the United States Naval
  Academy Museum (USNAM), Annapolis, Maryland, has been
  attributed to Rembrandt Peale. However, the documentation for a
  Peale portrait refers only to a profile portrait. Research undertaken by
  James Cheevers, senior curator, USNAM, may show that the oil
  portrait was painted by a Neapolitan artist while Preble was waiting
  in Naples during the summer of 1804. Nelson, "Transfer-printed
  Creamware," 97.
3 Henry Wadsworth, journal, Wadsworth-Longfellow Papers, LNHS.
  Peleg Wadsworth to Charles Wadsworth, January 29, 1805,
  Wadsworth Papers, MEHS.

3

Herculaneum Pottery (1796–1840)
Pitcher
Liverpool, England, 1805–1807
Creamware with transfer-printing in black
and hand enamel-painting in red and black
Marked (on bottom) "HERCULANEUM"
H 10½ (26.7)
Maine Historical Society
Bequest of Alice Preble Tucker (DeHaas) Carpender,
1923

Of the Liverpool-type pitchers with special decorations for
Maine residents that have been identified, five feature
polychrome coats of arms enamel-painted within blank
transfer-printed shields.[1] They are far more unusual than the
watercolor or oil-on-panel coats of arms painted by New
England artists (cats. 75–76).

In 1780 Joseph Edmundson published his *Complete Body
of Heraldry* in London. This book is one of several that
heraldry painters used as a source for their designs. From
this group of hand-decorated pitchers, it appears that the
china painters at the English potteries used it as well.
Anyone could order this type of decoration and the factory
decorators were obliging.

Such was the case when an order came to produce a
special pitcher for the new American hero, Commodore
Edward Preble. This pitcher made personally for him is
decorated on one side with "The Arms of Preble," according
to the accompanying inscription. There are no arms for the
name Preble listed in Edmundson's source book but the
decorator, apparently not wishing to disappoint his famous
customer, may merely have turned the page and found the
arms of Prescott which he adapted for Preble. The enameller
excluded the ermine field, replacing it with a simple red field.
He maintained the chevron and black horizontal line with
two leopard's heads above. Three doves, not included in the

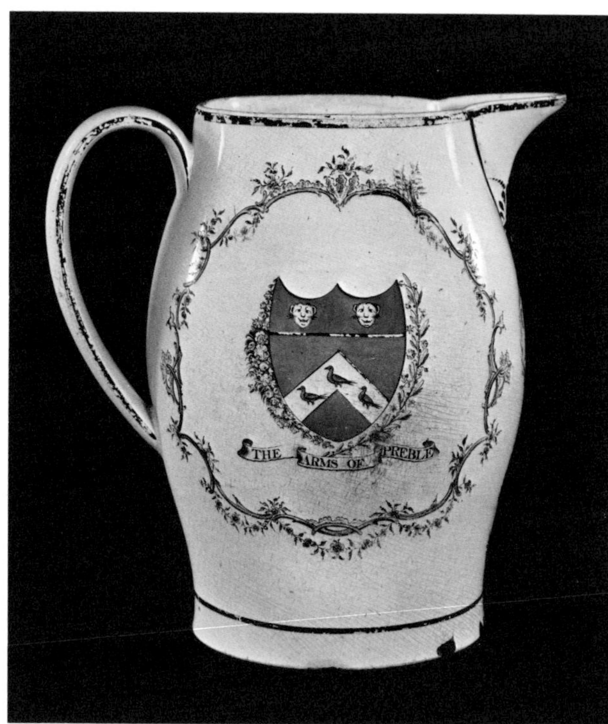

Cat. 3

Prescott arms, were added to the chevron in the Preble
adaptation.[2]

"Commodore E, Preble" is inscribed under the spout.
The reverse displays the transfer-printed scene of the "Attack
of Tripoli"; this is the same scene that decorates the reverse
of the pitcher bearing Preble's likeness (cat. 2). It must date
between Preble's return to the United States in 1805 and his
untimely death in 1807. It was presented to the Maine
Historical Society by a great-granddaughter with a number
of other Preble-owned objects.[3] This marked pitcher is an
important key for dating and attributing this type of decoration (see cat. 4).

The Preble pitcher and others captured the attention
early on of antiquarian William Willis, who described them
in 1862: "Mr. Noyes brought a pitcher which belonged to
Abigail Cobham, with her coat of arms upon it. . . . I
mentioned it to Mr. Davies & he produced two which his
father procured from Liverpool . . . he said there were many
such articles sent for to Liverpool by Portland people, Com.
Preble & others. Two were brought over by Capt. Stone."[4]

LFS

1 In addition to Preble and Curtis (cat. 4), a third pitcher with
  hand-painted arms at MEHS features the Cobham arms. The
  Deering arms decorate a pitcher in a private collection; see Sprague,
  "Liverpool-type Pitchers"; the Elder arms pitcher is at the Peabody
  Museum of Salem.
2 I am indebted to Martha Gandy Fales for her assistance with the

research of heraldic sources. Two other important sources for arms known to have been used by American heraldry painters are John Guillim's *Display of Heraldry* and Samuel Kent's *The Banner Display'd* (see cat. 144). Preble is not listed in either source nor do the arms depicted on this pitcher correspond with those recorded by Charles K. Bolton in *Bolton's American Armory* (Boston: F. W. Faxon, Co., 1927), 135.

3 See cat. 1. Other objects at MEHS include a silk sash and a gold brooch given by Preble to his wife Mary; MEHS also owns family manuscript materials. Preble-owned objects are also at the United States Naval Academy Museum, Annapolis.

4 William Willis, diary, February 27, 1862, Portland Public Library. Earle Shettleworth kindly brought this to my attention.

4

Attributed to Herculaneum Pottery (1796–1840)
Pitcher
Liverpool, England, 1805–1812
Creamware with hand-painted decoration in blue, yellow, and black, and transfer-printing in black
H 10⅜ (26.4)
Maine Historical Society
Gift of Calvin Crocker, 1956

The arms of Curtis enamel-painted on the obverse of this pitcher match those listed for that name in Joseph Edmundson, *Complete Body of Heraldry* (London, 1780). There is

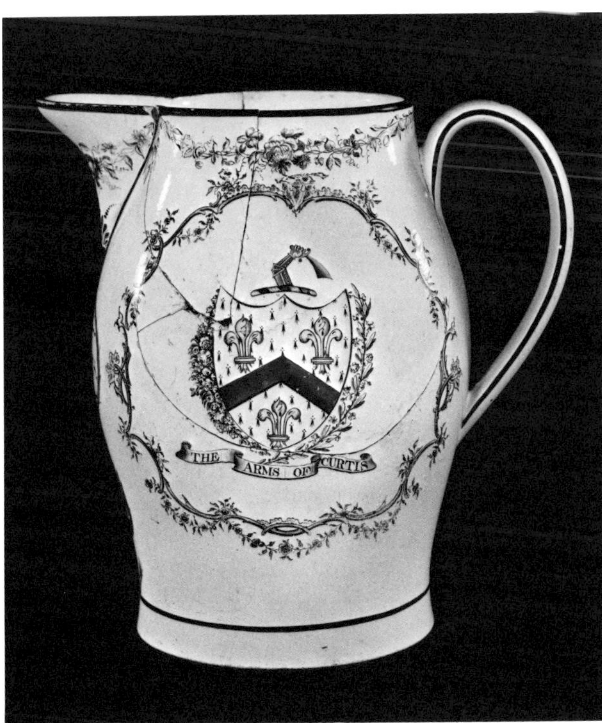

Cat. 4

an ermine field, and a blue chevron that divides three yellow fleur-de-lis. The transfer-printed cartouche around the coat of arms and the wreath surrounding the inscribed name under the spout are identical to the marked Preble pitcher (cat. 3). These similar features suggest that this unmarked pitcher is also a product of the Herculaneum Pottery.

Captain John Curtis (d. 1812) was the commander of the *Dart*, a Portland privateer.[1] Of his successful runs capturing British vessels, the most famous was the capture on August 31, 1812, of the brig *Dianna* from London bound to Quebec. According to Portland historian William Goold, its cargo of 212 puncheons of rum was celebrated "for its peculiar flavor [more] than any cargo of spirits landed in the country." As late as the 1840s, "Old Dart Rum was retailed in Portland from 'the original casks' at fancy prices, but some of them had undoubtedly been refilled several times."[2]

Although the celebrity of the *Dart* and her rum survived the century, the schooner with all hands was lost at sea within the year. Her "faulty construction" was named as the probable cause. According to the information Goold gathered, she did not appear to be a desirable vessel to sail. Her three masts were jointed above the deck so they could be dropped like those on a canal boat. Goold suggested that the jointed masts, low gunwhale, and long sweeps or curve of the ship's timbers may have made her less visible to the enemy, but these features may have also made her less seaworthy.[3]

According to one of her logbooks that survives at the Maine Historical Society, Curtis spent several days recruiting crew members, totaling forty-six sailors on one run. This large number was necessary in order to provide crew for prize vessels.

This pitcher descended in the Curtis family of Gorham, Maine, and was presented to the Maine Historical Society by Curtis's great-great-grandson.   LFS

1 Hugh D. McLellan, *History of Gorham* (1903; reprint, Somersworth, N.H.: New England History Press, 1980), 156–157.
2 William Goold, Scrapbook, 3–4.
3 William Goold, Scrapbook, 4.

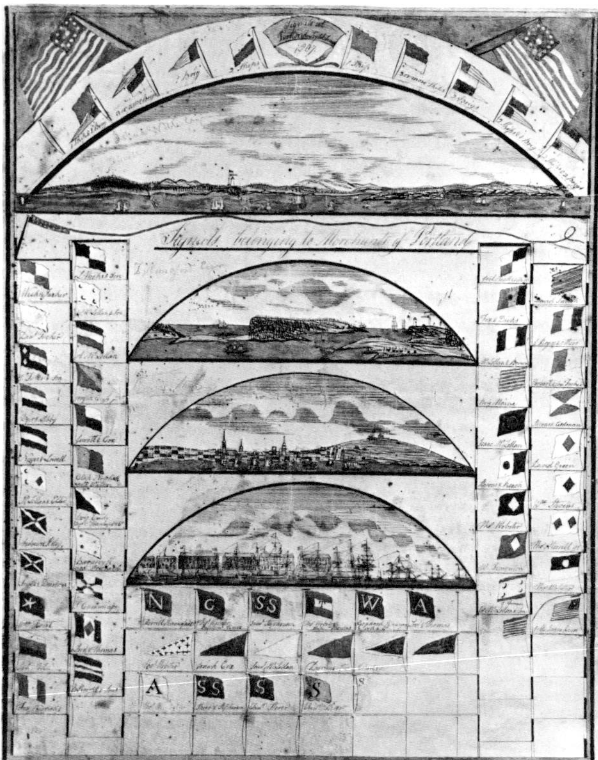

Cat. 5

5

Lemuel Moody (1761–1846)
*Signals at / Portland Lighthouse / 1807 /
Signals belonging to Merchants of Portland*
Portland, Maine, 1807
Watercolor and pen and ink on paper
H 20⁹⁄₁₆ (62.2); W 16½ (41.9) sight
Maine Historical Society;
Gift of the heirs of E. M. York, Jr., 1966
Color plate on page 42

The signal flags of Portland merchants registered at the
Portland Head Lighthouse on Cape Elizabeth are the subject
of this watercolor drawing by Lemuel Moody. Although not
signed by him, the drawing descended in Moody's family
and has always been regarded as his work; it was given to the
Maine Historical Society along with charts and drawings
known to be by him. A master navigator, Moody advertised
that he would teach others the "art of Navigation, use of
Charts, etc."[1]

Dated 1807, this drawing with its snowy landscape
pre-dates the summertime building of the observatory tower.
It and the *Signals at Portland Observatory* (cat. 8) document the

interest in rapid communications concerning shipping in
and out of Portland harbor. In four telescoping scenes, the
central lunettes depict views from Cape Elizabeth to the
Portland waterfront. They are of great interest because few
sources have survived from this period to document Portland's landscape, townscape, and waterfront. Within the
largest lunette at the top is a view of Cape Elizabeth,
Portland Head, and the islands of Casco Bay from the sea.
The next scene has advanced closer to the lighthouse and the
islands; Cushing's Island figures prominently with ships
entering the harbor. In the third lunette, Portland is viewed
from the south side of the harbor. On Munjoy Hill, a large
flag flies from Fort Sumner, but the observatory tower has
not yet been built. The fourth and lowest lunette focuses on
the waterfront with a detailed view of the warehouses and
ships at numerous wharves.

The lunettes are bordered at the top by nine signals for
ships and brigs, and on the side and bottom by rows of
merchants' flags. These include the houses of Weeks and
Tucker, Stevens and Codman, Joseph Holt Ingraham, Lord
and Thomas, and Joseph McLellan and Son.

On October 22, 1783, the Massachusetts legislature
passed a bill that required vessels entering a port to pay a
separate duty to help maintain the state's five lighthouses.
With no lighthouse off their coast, Cumberland County
residents did not see great benefit in this tax. Seventy Maine
ship-owners and masters petitioned the General Court in
Boston for a lighthouse. The demands were met with great
resistance; the Court claimed that the Commonwealth's
depressed economic conditions did not allow for large
expenditures on behalf of Maine. It was not until after
Congress passed legislation in 1789 for additional lighthouses
that these grievances were finally resolved. Of the lighthouses
built at this time, Portland Head is one of four that survive
today.[2]

The seventy-two-foot tower was completed in 1790 and
its fifteen-foot-high lantern was first lit on January 10, 1791.
Modifications in the design in 1813 resulted in a new ten-foot
octagonal lantern, the cage of which was "glassed with the
best double glass of the Boston Glass House Manufacture."[3]

Fort Sumner, another prominent landmark during the
federal period, is visible on Munjoy Hill. Begun in 1794 as
part of the government's "first system" of defense, it was
designed by Stephen Rochefontaine, a Frenchman who had
served in the Continental Army. As Secretary of War, Henry
Knox supplied this military engineer with instructions of the
size and number of armaments for a series of forts to be built
along New England's coast.[4] Like other fortifications, Fort
Sumner was built on the site of a Revolutionary War fort and
was an earthen breastwork with block house and powder
magazine. During his travels through Maine in 1795, the
Duke de la Rochefoucault stopped at Fort Sumner while it
was under construction and reported on "a fortification,

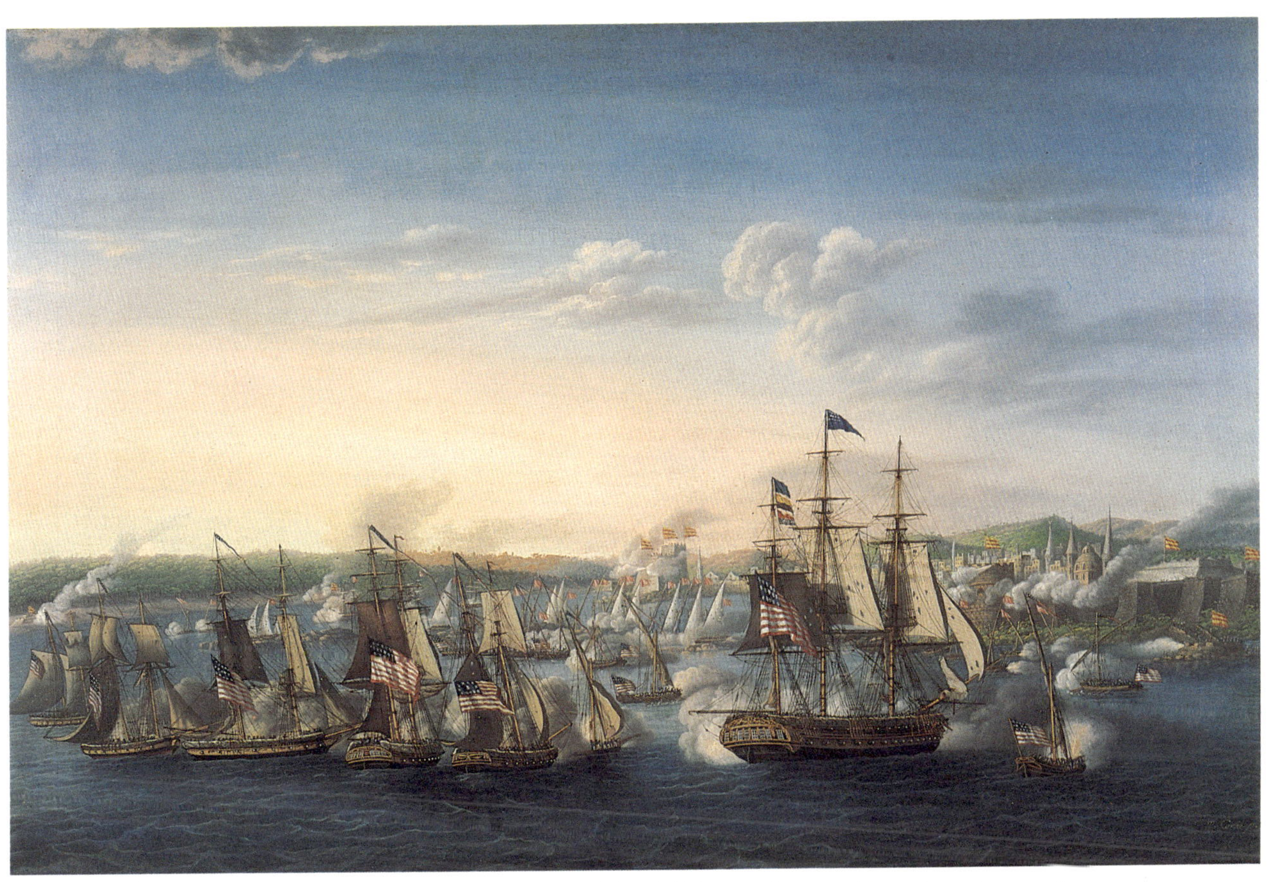

Cat. 1 Attributed to Michele Felice Cornè, *Bombardment of Tripoli*, Salem or Boston, Massachusetts, ca. 1805.

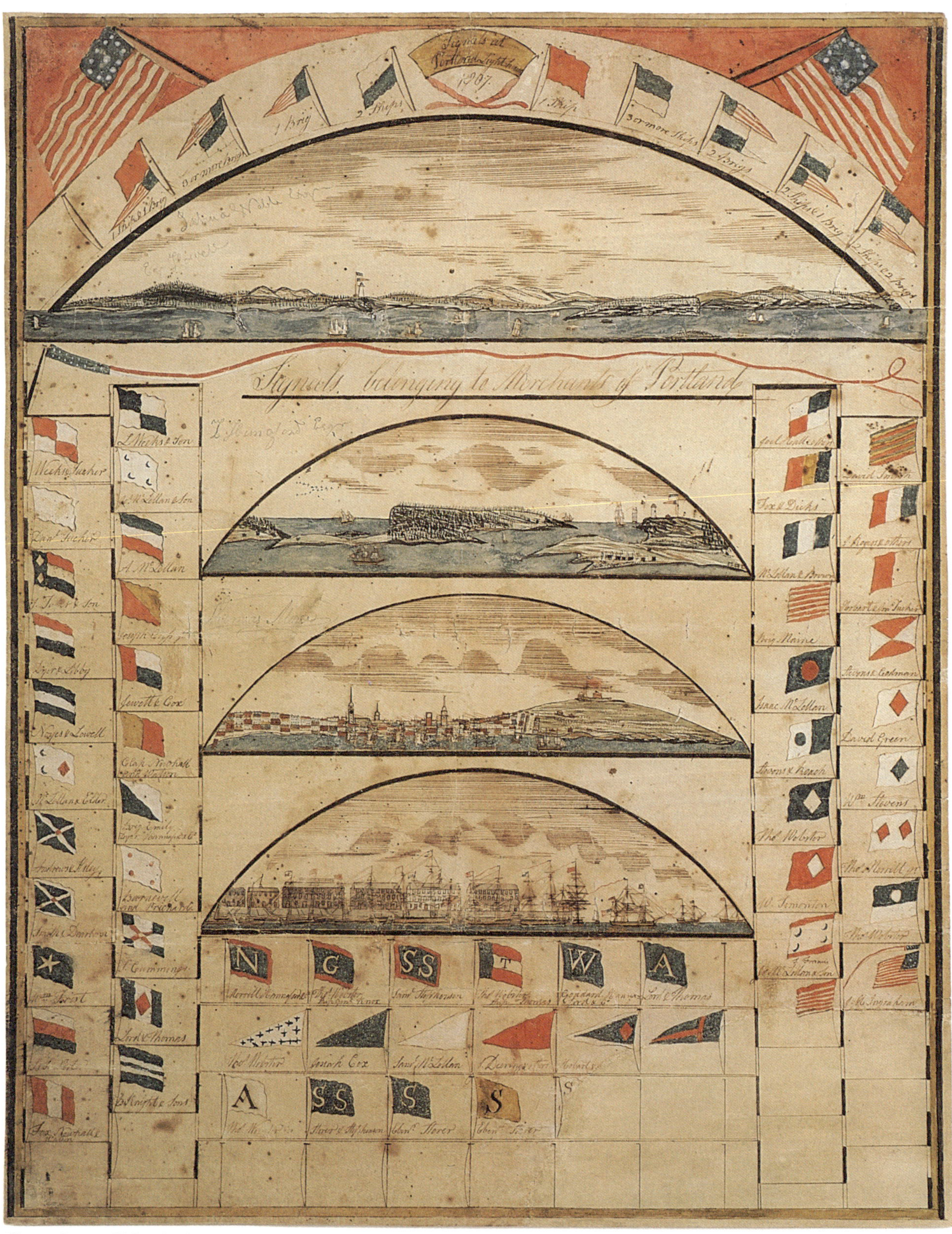

Cat. 5 Lemuel Moody, *Signals at Portland Lighthouse*, Portland, Maine, 1807.

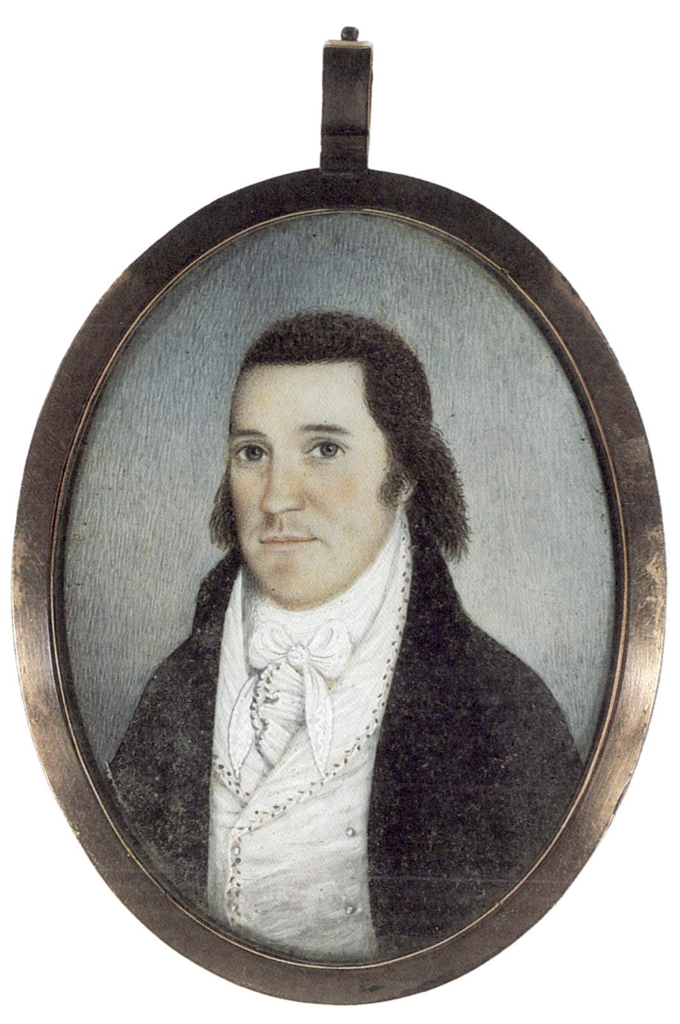

Cat. 30 Attributed to John Brewster, Jr., *Prentiss Mellen*, Saco
or Portland, Maine, 1800–1810.

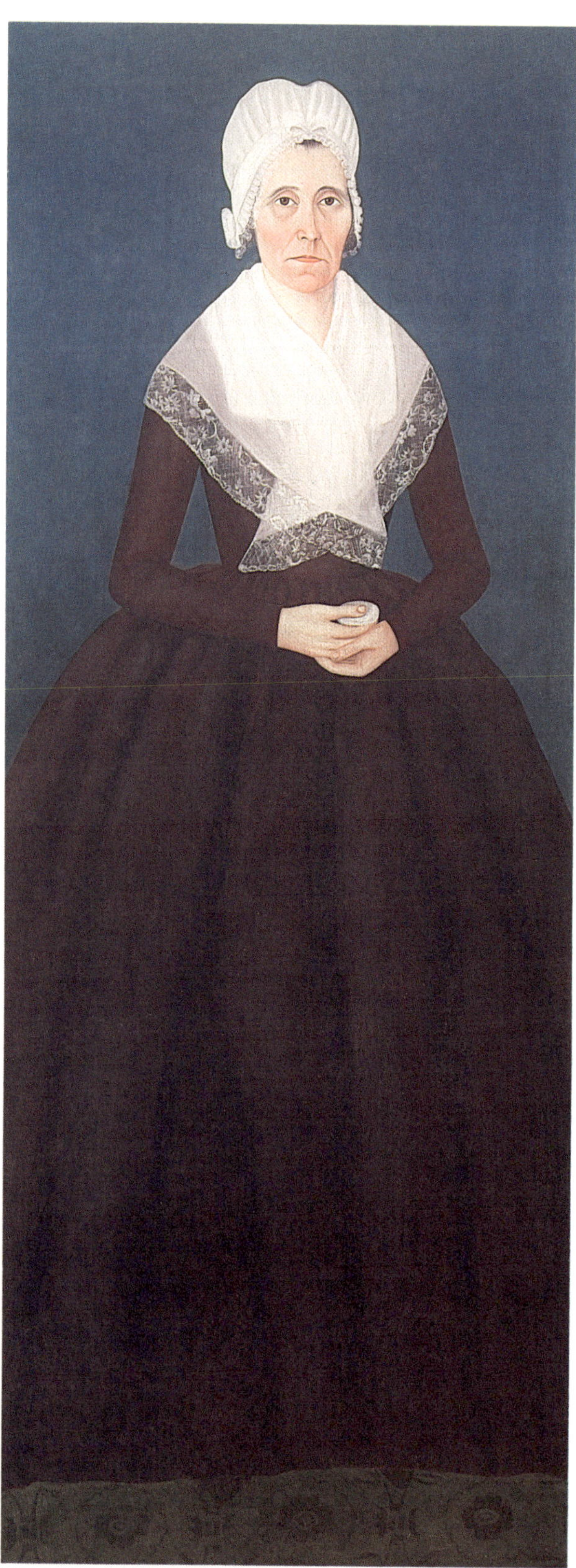

Cat. 33 Attributed to John Brewster, Jr., *Elizabeth Scamman Cutts*, Saco, Maine, 1800–1801.

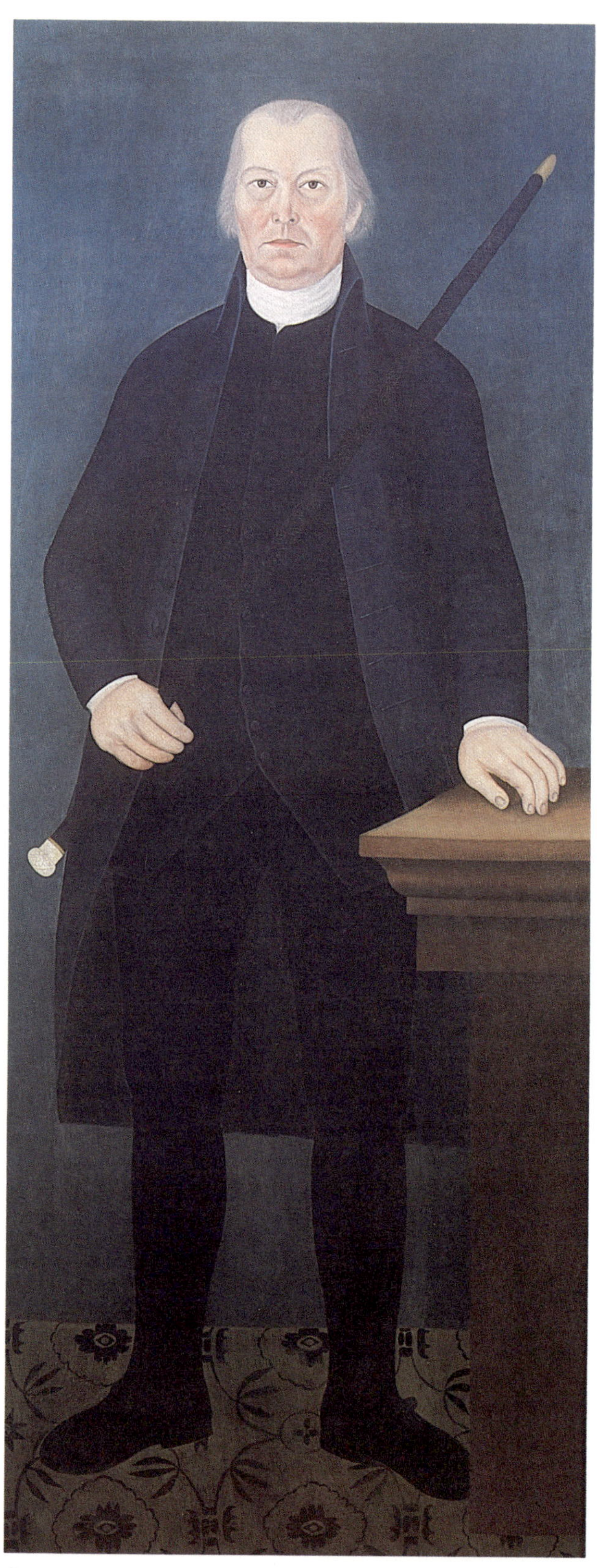

Cat. 33 Attributed to John Brewster, Jr., *Colonel Thomas Cutts*, Saco, Maine, 1800–1801.

which they expect to command the town, and to render it at least secure from the invasion of enemies."[5] It was the only fort protecting Portland until Forts Preble and Scammell were begun in 1808 (cat. 12).

There are numerous pencil inscriptions on this watercolor including "Joshua Webb, Esq.," "Esqr. Howels," "L. Hanaford, Esq.," and "Thomas Morse," which date to the late nineteenth century.   LFS

1 See n. 1 for cat. 8; *Portland Gazette* (November 9, 1807) as cited in Nathan Goold, "Old Observatory," Post Scrapbook, 12 vols., 3:195, MEHS.
2 Peter Dow Bachelder, *Lighthouses of Casco Bay* (Portland, Me.: Breakwater Press, 1975), 1–6.
3 Willis, *History*, 570; Bachelder, *Lighthouses*, 5. Kenneth M. Wilson notes that Boston Glass Manufactory was known for the high quality of its glass in *New England Glass and Glassmaking* (New York: Thomas Y. Crowell Co., 1972), 77. A glass lens from a lighthouse survives at MEHS.
4 Kenneth E. Thompson, Jr., "Federal Fort Construction in Essex County, 1794–1809," *Essex Institute Historical Collections* 121, no. 4 (October 1985): 247–249.
5 Willis, *History*, 576.

6

Eliphalet Grover (1778–1855)
Covered box
York, Maine, ca. 1832
Pine with mahogany, cherry, and maple veneer
H 5½ (14.0); W 7⅝ (19.4); D 6½ (16.5)
Old York Historical Society
Gift of the Reverend Frank E. Sewall, 1900

Eliphalet Grover filled his idle hours as keeper of a remote York lighthouse by fashioning small objects of wood. His finest known production is this hinged pine box veneered with cherry, mahogany, and maple. Each side of the box is embellished with carefully cut human profiles; Grover painted the details of facial features, hair, military uniforms, and drawn swords. The corners of the cover are veneered with maple quarter-circles, each decorated with painted eagles and shields. The box and cover are lined with ecclesiastical passages from a New York newspaper dated 1832.[1]

Captain Grover was a mariner born in 1778. He and his wife Susanna had three children: Jeremiah, born 1802; Eliphalet, Jr., born 1814; and Samuel.[2] In 1816 Grover assumed custody of Boon Island Light, a post he held until his dismissal in 1839 for destruction of a government buoy and other misconduct. It seems that the captain had an entrepreneurial spirit and through the years sold parts of his whale oil shipments, delivered from Portland by the United States government to fuel the light. Grover maintained his innocence; his log entry for May 10, 1839, reads: "turned off

Boon Island after serving as lighthouse keeper for 22 years, 10 months, 20 days without cause."[3] In 1841 he took charge of the Whaleback Lighthouse in Portsmouth, New Hampshire. He died at York in 1855.

Situated nine miles off the coast of York Beach, Boon Island is a jagged ledge approximately one-third of a mile wide. The island is only fourteen feet above sea level with no vegetation. The surrounding shoals caused numerous shipwrecks throughout the eighteenth century, and in 1799 the first beacon was installed on the island. Stormy seas and the low land level cost the government four lighthouses on Boon Island until 1852, when a granite tower was constructed. This beacon still operates today. During their tenure on this barren island, Eliphalet Grover and his family maintained the light, repaired the dwelling house and seventy-foot tower, braved foul weather, and made frequent trips to the mainland, where Grover owned property and a house.

In 1834 Captain Grover presented York's First Parish Church with a bass viol he made for use in the choir. He made an elaborately carved cane in 1844.[4] Another small box with geometric veneer that Grover made has been in the Old York Historical Society as long as this box. The Society also owns a violin labeled: "Made on Boon Island by Capt. Eliphalet Grover 1821." The neck of the fiddle is topped with a carved head of a woman. Grover's son Samuel also made a violin of a smaller size in 1834. It, too, sports a carved and painted woman's face on the fiddlehead. Young Grover also sketched the island and lighthouse in the 1830s.[5]   KAO

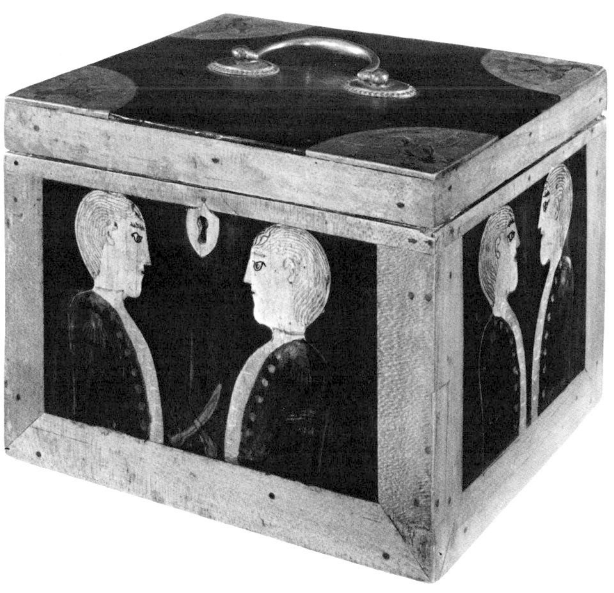

Cat. 6

1 The current brass handle, resembling the damaged original, is a replacement fitted to the box in 1982.
2 George Ernst, "Grover Family Genealogy" (typescript, OYHS).
3 Eliphalet Grover, log books, 1817–1828, 1832–1841, OYHS.
4 First Parish Records, York, Maine, June 7, 1834; Ronald Langille, "A Boon Island Lighthouse Keeper" (typescript, OYHS). The cane is at OYHS.
5 The Eliphalet Grover violin has been at OYHS since 1900; the Samuel Grover fiddle since 1935. The drawing was lent to OYHS in 1900, but its present location is unknown.

7

Probably Herculaneum Pottery (1796–1840)
Pitcher
Liverpool, England, ca. 1807
Creamware with hand-enamel painting in red, blue, yellow, and black, and transfer-printing in black
H 9 (22.9)
Maine Historical Society
Bequest of Charlotte A. Felton, 1920

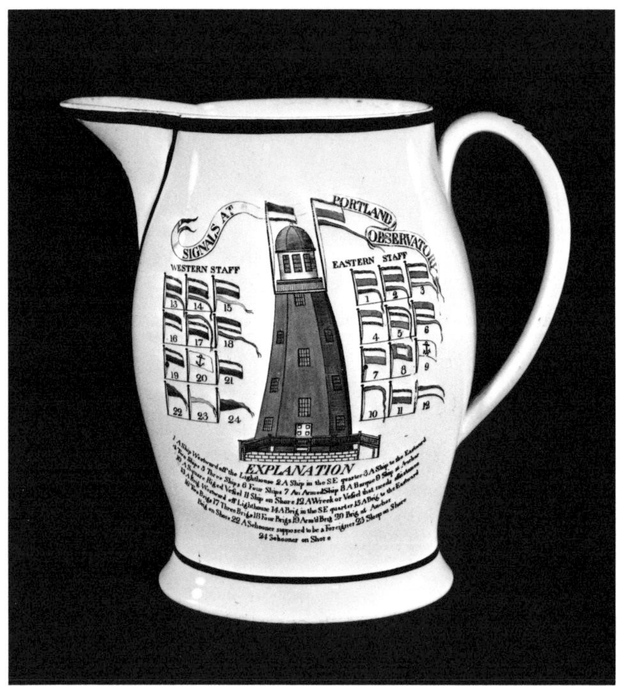

Cat. 7

Pitchers depicting the "Signals at Portland Observatory" are among the best known and most highly prized of the Liverpool-type pitchers made for the American market. Of all the federal-period structures in Portland, none is a greater tribute to the success of the maritime trade than the observatory tower. Built during the summer of 1807, it was the inspiration of Lemuel Moody, a retired sea captain. For him, the observatory was a way to remain active in the trade. Intended to aid the maritime community, the observatory also delighted the public, who responded as though "it was a new influenza."[1]

To raise money for its construction, Moody solicited subscriptions from merchants and mariners in Portland. The eighty-two-foot octagonal tower on Munjoy Hill provided a view over Cape Elizabeth and the islands of Casco Bay. On observing ships while they were still well offshore, Moody hoisted signal flags on staffs outside the cupola. These alerted owners and merchants who could then prepare their wharves and warehouses for the ships' arrival. The flags depicted here signal type of vessel, number of vessels, and location offshore; they differ from the merchants' house flags which identify the vessels by owner (cat. 5).[2]

A new telescope that Moody had just imported from England was the key to his system. It created quite a stir in Portland. One rather humorous account noted that one visitor was so overwhelmed upon viewing the world through the telescope that he imagined seeing the brasses on his sideboard and handles on his writing desk. The same article also discussed why the observatory was painted red. There was speculation among the critics that the tower would blow over in a good strong wind unless it were built of brick. The proprietors, not wanting to be accused of unpatriotic

disregard of the pine, pride of the American forest and of the Maine forest in particular, decided to please as many people as possible. They "made the fabric of wood and gave it the air and similitude of Brick."[3]

Observing ships was a pastime for some; the Reverend William Bentley had a favored spot on Salem Harbor to review activities. Moody, however, took his work seriously. His notebooks record the changes in the signals during the War of 1812, when he added special flags for enemy ships and privateers. He observed the naval engagement between the USS *Enterprise* and the British *Boxer* off Seguin Island, more than twenty-six miles away, and reported what he saw through his glass to anxious citizens on the ground.[4]

Moody built a house at the foot of the tower and added a dance hall and bowling alley. Munjoy Hill soon became one of Portland's popular recreational areas and for many travelers the observatory was a required stop. The well-traveled Timothy Dwight recorded, "It is the only work of the kind, so far as my knowledge extends, in the United States. From the elevation there is a noble prospect of the interior, particularly of Mount Washington, rising at the distance of seventy miles . . . with a sublimity which mocks description." In 1817, when President Monroe stopped here one evening, "the Observatory was illuminated, and a handsome display of fireworks was exhibited." The Portland Rifle Club entertained the Boston Rifle Rangers near the observatory in 1829, an activity recorded by the artist Charles Codman.[5] Ironically, the observatory as a symbol of success was built just prior to Portland's economic collapse brought on by the Embargo of 1807.

Riding on the wave of public enthusiasm, Moody is said to have ordered seventy-five of these commemorative pitchers with views of his observatory. Twelve have been accounted for in public and private collections, and two others may be known through written references. Many appear to have been saved because of the decoration; fewer survive with family or historical associations. The second observatory pitcher at the Maine Historical Society was owned by Portland captain William Webb; one at the Portland Museum of Art belonged to James Deering of Portland.[6]   LFS

1 *Eastern Argus* (September 24, 1807).
2 A watercolor drawing of house flags of Salem merchants is published in *Marine Drawings and Paintings in the Peabody Museum* (Salem, Mass.: Peabody Museum of Salem, 1968), 500.
3 *Eastern Argus* (September 24, 1807).
4 Two of Moody's signal books are at MEHS; Nathan Goold, "Old Observatory," Post Scrapbook, 12 vols., 3: 196–197, MEHS.
5 Dwight, *Travels*, 2:142; Ayer, *Diary*, 224. Two Codman pictures of the Portland Rifle Club entertaining the Boston Rifle Rangers are known, one in the Brooklyn Museum and a second in the Museum of Art, Rhode Island School of Design. Another event that took place near the observatory was recorded in 1837 by Daniel C. Colesworthy in his engraving of a *View of the Whig Pavilion at Mount-Joy.* This print survives in the City of Portland's Spring Street Fire Museum.
6 Isabel T. Ray, "Old Pitcher of Capt. Moody's Observatory here," *Portland Sunday Telegram* (March 17, 1940). In addition to those discussed here, one observatory pitcher is in each of the following collections: Maine Maritime Museum, Bath; Peabody Museum of Salem; Pocumtuck Valley Memorial Association, Deerfield, Mass.; Royal Pavilion, Art Gallery and Museum, Brighton, England; Smithsonian Institution; The Henry Francis du Pont Winterthur Museum; and the Victoria and Albert Museum, London. Two are held privately. The second MEHS pitcher was the gift of G. C. Scott, 1915.

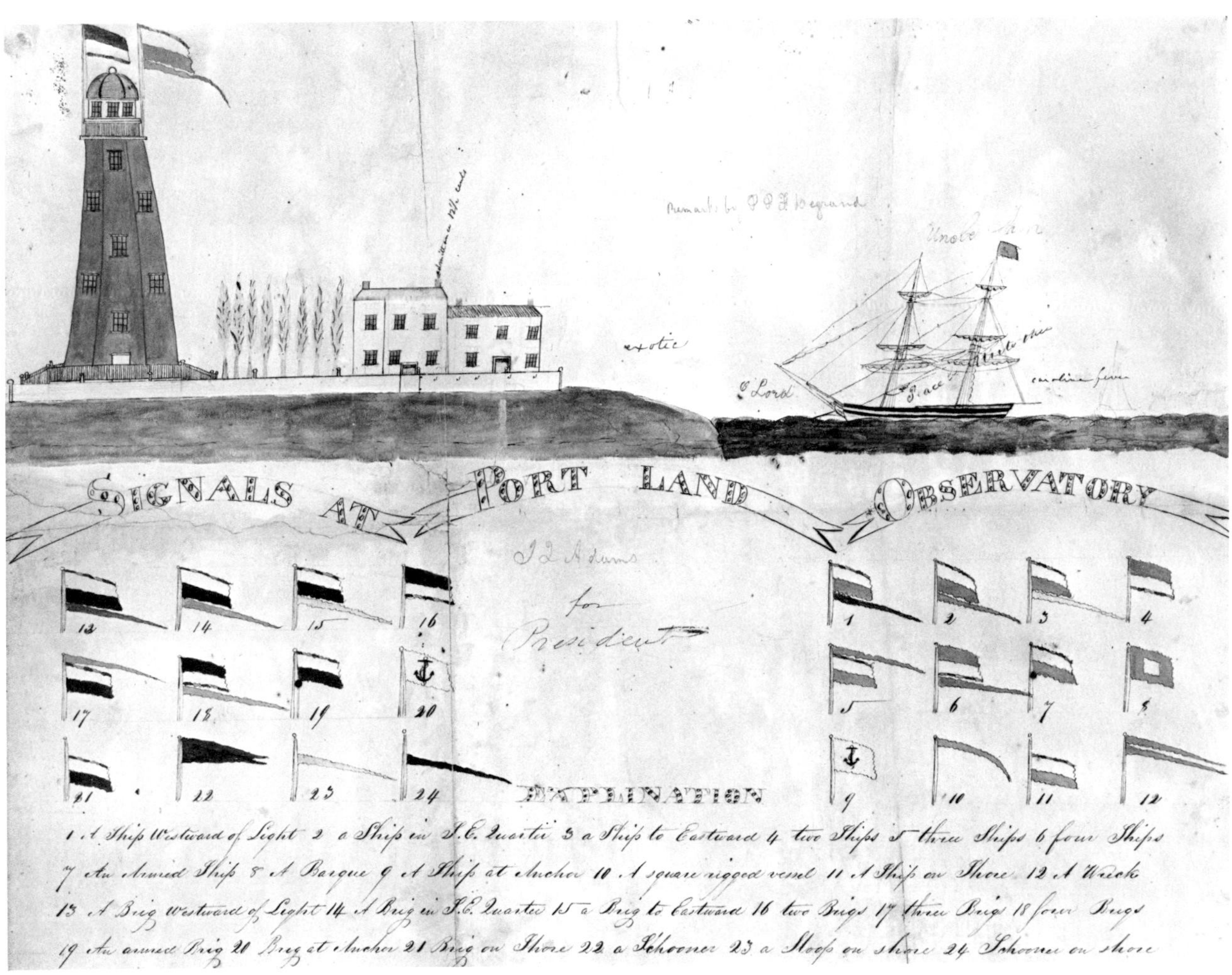

Cat. 8

8

Attributed to Lemuel Moody (1761–1846)
Signals at Portland Observatory
Portland, Maine, ca. 1807
Watercolor and pen and ink on paper
H 17 (43.2); W 21⅞ (55.6)
Maine Historical Society

This watercolor drawing depicts the same signal flags that decorate a Liverpool-type pitcher made for the American market (cat. 7). When orders were placed in England for special decorations, Americans often supplied a drawing or engraving that served as a design source. These would be copied or adapted by the decorators at the factory.

Portland Observatory proprietor Lemuel Moody was a known draftsman (cat. 5). Charts of Portland and Winter Harbor (Biddeford Pool) that descended in his family also were drawn by him.[1] Therefore, it would not be surprising to find him drafting this sketch to be used in his promotional scheme for the new structure. Sent to Liverpool in care of a captain, this drawing may have been the source for the design on the creamware pitchers.

Because the decoration on the pitchers was transfer-printed, a copper plate was required. The engraver of the plate chose those elements of the design that he could fit into the available space. In addition to the tower, flags, and "explanation," which were reproduced on the pitchers, this drawing includes Lemuel Moody's house, Lombardy poplars, and a ship anchored in the bay. The large central space, perhaps reserved for a special inscription, has been left vacant. Numerous pencil and ink annotations, including "admission is 12½ cents" (referring to Moody's charge for visitors to use the telescope) and "John Quincy Adams for President," have been inscribed on the sheet. LFS

1 Lemuel Moody's charts of Wood Island and Winter Harbor (ca. 1814) and Portland Harbor (June 1814) were given to MEHS in 1966 by the heirs of E. M. York, Jr. The MEHS received his ca. 1826 portrait by Henry Cheever Pratt in 1966, a gift of Howard E. York III.

9

James Akin (1773–1846)
Portland Marine Society Certificate
Portland, Maine, ca. 1807
Engraving
Inscribed "J Akin Sculp. Portland Marine Society"
H 10⅞₆ (26.8); W 14⅞ (37.8)
Maine Historical Society
Gift of the heirs of E. M. York, Jr., 1966

When the Portland Marine Society was established in 1796, two-thirds of its members were active or retired commanders of vessels and the remaining third were seamen. The society held regular meetings, collected dues, and assisted widows of captains and mariners as well as impoverished or disabled sailors.[1]

About 1807 James Akin engraved this membership certificate for the Portland Marine Society. Although it is possible that he also designed the certificate, he may have only copied a prepared drawing.

Composed of scenes in oval and rectangular foliate cartouches, the design relates closely to the Boston Marine Society membership certificate engraved in 1789 by Joseph Callender. In both examples, Neptune presides over the six scenes below him. Four of the six vignettes depict similar subjects: a shipwreck, a ship passing a lighthouse, a hospital, and a townscape from the harbor. The inclusion of the 1807 observatory in the townscape reveals that the designer was familiar with current building construction in Portland. However, the hospital with a man on crutches, depicted in the same placement as the Marine Hospital in the Boston Marine Society certificate, is not known to have existed in Portland at this time. The United States Marine Hospital was established in 1803 in Charlestown, Massachusetts, due in large part to the efforts of the Boston Marine Society, and there may have been discussion of a similar institution in Portland. However, until the 1850s when a hospital was built, sick or disabled sailors boarded with private families and the Portland Marine Society contributed to their support.[2] The scenes of shipbuilding and a ship in a storm were selected from another source.

This certificate, one of several known, was presented to Lemuel Moody, the Portland Observatory proprietor who was voted in as the society's third member in 1807.[3] When the certificate became badly discolored, another engraving was applied over the first. The central reserve was cut out so that the inscription to Moody could be read. The second certificate, however, obscures the society seal attached below the inscription.

James Akin, an engraver from Philadelphia who worked briefly in Salem and Newburyport, had Portland clients in addition to the Portland Marine Society (cat. 129). Akin also engraved the title page for an arithmetic book published by G. Goold in Portland in 1803. Two years later, Goold published and advertised Akin's *Perpetual Almanack*.[4] AAE

1 *Laws of the Marine Society, Instituted at Portland, and Incorporated by the General Court. February 1796* (Portland: Baker and George, 1798).
2 Earle G. Shettleworth, Jr., "U.S. Seamen Had to Pay 20¢ A Month To Get Hospital Care," *Portland Evening Express* (August 2, 1967). For an illustration of the Boston Marine Society certificate, see *The Decorative Arts and Paintings of the Colonies and New Republic, 1740–1820* (Boston: Childs Gallery, 1976).
3 Moody kept the accounts of the Portland Marine Society between 1837–1846. Other certificates at MEHS belonged to Moses Freeman

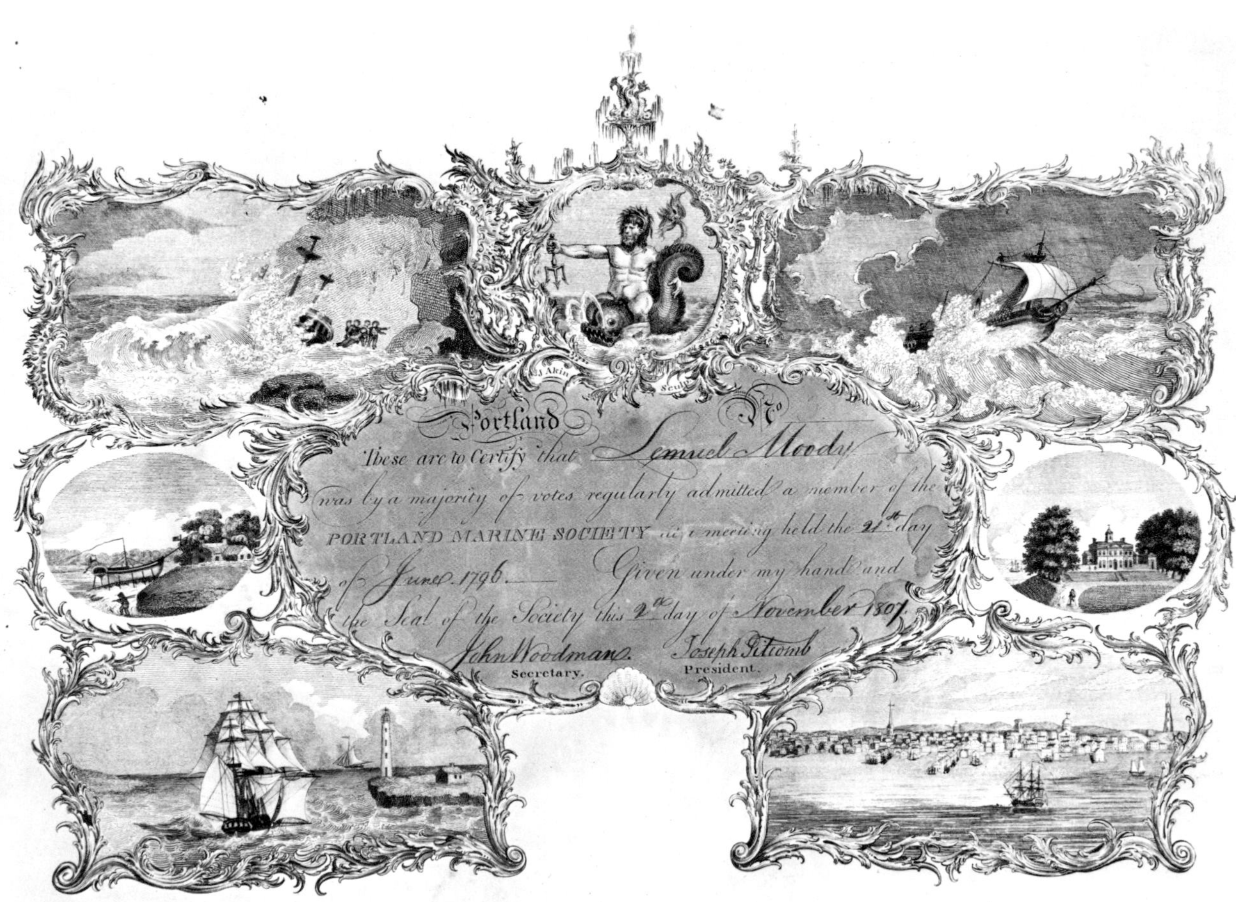

Cat. 9

and William Sweetsir. Photographs of Reuben G. York's 1826 certificate and Enoch Preble's, dated 1808, are at MEHS.

4 Maureen O'Brien Quimby, "The Political Art of James Akin," *Winterthur Portfolio* 7, ed. Ian M. G. Quimby (Charlottesville: University Press of Virginia for the Henry Francis du Pont Winterthur Museum, 1972), 109, 88, and *Eastern Argus* (February 1, 1805). For more on Akin's work in New England, see Lewis C. Rubenstein, "James Akin in Newburyport," *Essex Institute Historical Collections* 102, no. 4 (October 1966): 285–298.

10

Attributed to Herculaneum Pottery (1796–1840)
Pitcher
Liverpool, England, 1796–1805
Creamware with hand-painted decoration in brown, green, red, blue, and black, and transfer-printing in black
H 12¼ (31.1)
Maine Historical Society
Gift of Mary A. Kotzschmar and children, 1920

As early as 1784, John Thorlo piloted a sloop called the *Falmouth Packet* on coastal trips between Portland and Boston. When the town's name changed to Portland in 1786, the packet's name changed as well. In 1796 Captain Thorlo was appointed by the government to carry the American and British commissioners down east in order to negotiate the dispute over the eastern boundary. The *Portland Packet* is painted on Captain Thorlo's large pitcher. The hand-painted decoration makes this pitcher unique, but another example is known that bears a similar design. Marked by the Herculaneum Pottery, the second pitcher depicts the *Orizimbo* of Baltimore and is embellished with a similar scrolled border. In both cases, a watercolor or pen and ink drawing was sent to the factory decorators, who copied the special designs onto creamware.[1]

Thorlo was considered the best pilot in town and served as the first president of the Portland Marine Society (cat. 9). It was Thorlo who was sent to aid the *Grand Turk* of Salem when she was in distress off Portland Head in the winter of 1798. One of Elias Hasket Derby's ships, the *Grand Turk* was

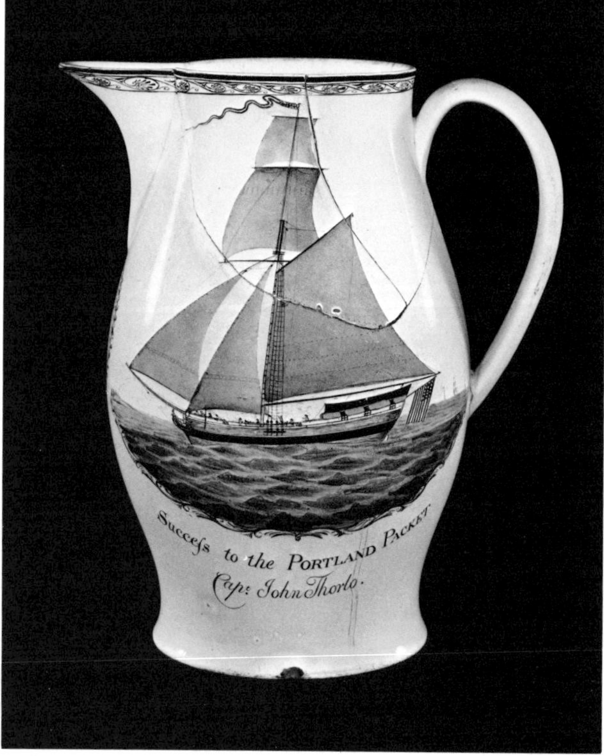

Cat. 10

on her return from India when she had "at last reached Portland." She was "carried by ice upon the shore, & has bilged."[2] Part of the cargo was lost. Events surrounding this disaster were reported in the Boston *Centinel* and nineteenth-century Portland citizens recollected that the porcelains washed out of the hold and cases of silks floated into Portland harbor where they were "secured by covetous people and secreted."[3]

Thorlo's shipping enterprises extended to interests on shore. He was involved with merchants in the construction of a new wharf in 1793.[4] Captain Thorlo was an officer of the Portland Masonic lodge, an activity which explains the Masonic emblems transfer-printed on the reverse. Since Thorlo died in 1805, the pitcher can be dated before that year. The pitcher came to the Maine Historical Society by way of Stephen Waite and his daughters. LFS

1 Nelson, "Transfer-printed Creamware," 114–115.
2 Bentley, *Diary*, 2:252.
3 *Centinel* (Boston) (January 6, 1798), as reprinted in William Goold, Scrapbook, 59.
4 CCRD; 19:525.

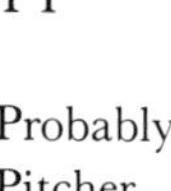

I I

Probably Herculaneum Pottery (1796–1840)
Pitcher
Liverpool, England, ca. 1800
Creamware with enamel-painting
and transfer-printing in black
H 10½ (26.7)
Maine Historical Society
Gift of Mary Scott Conroy, 1965

With its hand-painted portrait of Hannah Robinson and nine of her thirteen children, this pitcher is unique among American market creamwares. It was made for Hannah and Joshua Robinson of Portland and Cape Elizabeth, Maine. Although the source for the portrait is not known, a notice placed in the *Portland Gazette* provides a clue. Artist John Roberts advertised during his stay in Portland that he "paints family groups."[1] Perhaps an itinerant artist such as Roberts was responsible for a sketch that was sent to England. Working from such a drawing, the decorator filled the transfer-printed cartouche with the elements of the composition. The painting on the pitcher is presented as a portrait in a frame.

Far more typical of creamware decoration is the transfer-printed likeness of a man on the reverse. Although it is inscribed "Joshua Robinson," the identical portrait is recorded on other pitchers with the names of "President Monroe" and "Philip Crandall," another Portland resident. But the subject is none of these men and is thought to be a fictitious image, which may have encouraged its indiscriminate use at the factory. Joshua Robinson, a ship's captain, commanded the brig *Ranger*, and is known to have transported cargoes of creamware from Liverpool.[2]

The distinctive painting relates to a pitcher at the Peabody Museum of Salem owned by one of Joshua Robinson's colleagues, Jeremiah Berry (cat. 11.1). Cumberland County deeds confirm that Jeremiah Berry was in the blockmaking business in Portland. He is portrayed in his shop toasting successful trade while one assistant pours from a baluster-shaped pitcher and another remains diligently at work. At first glance, these personalized scenes painted in black within a transfer-printed cartouche appear quite similar. Upon a closer examination, however, differences are evident. The decorator of the Berry pitcher appears to have copied what he saw directly onto the pitcher. He did not take into consideration that the drawing had a horizontal axis and that the space for it was vertical. As a result, the cartouche does not become the successful framing device found on the Robinson pitcher. LFS

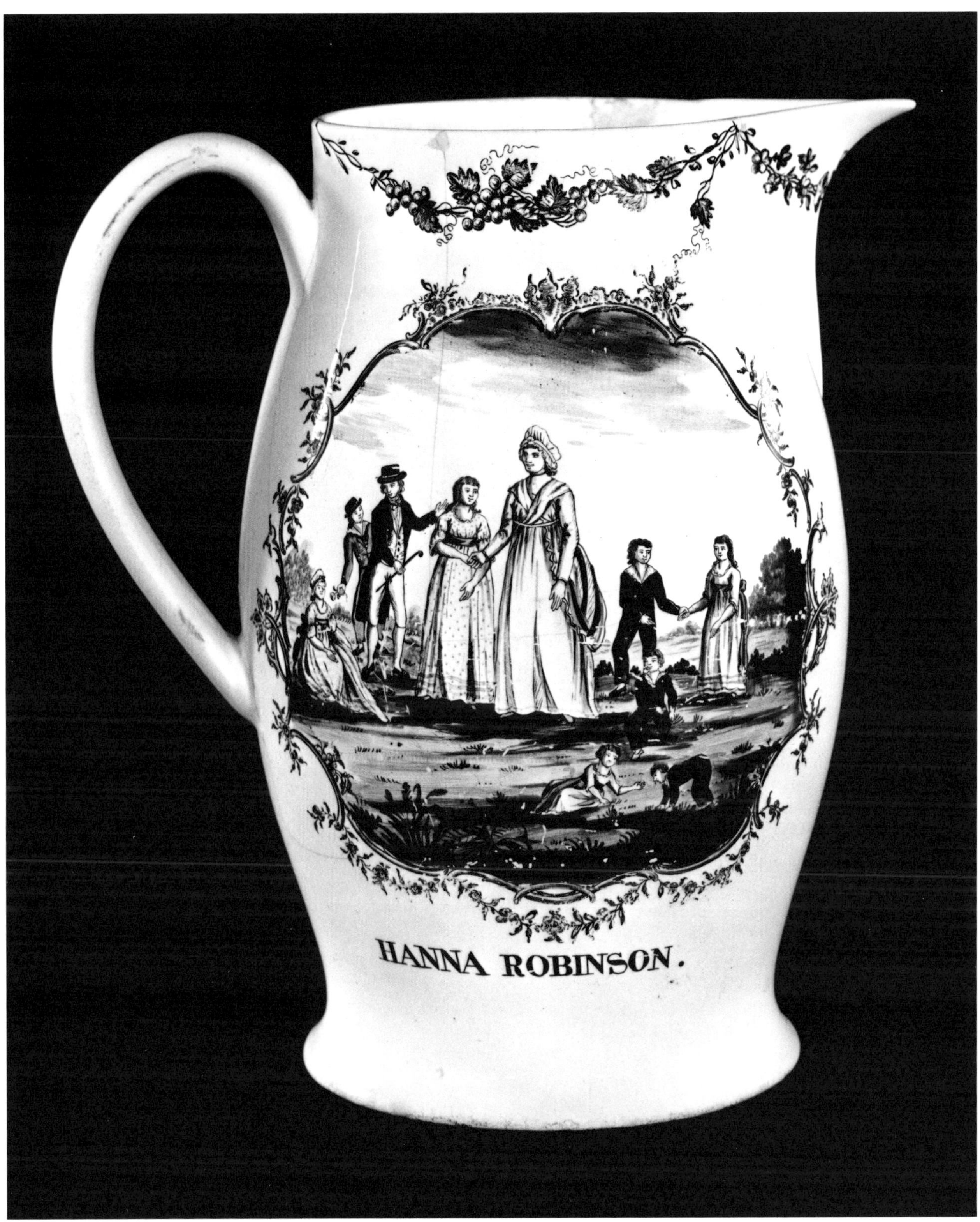

Cat. 11

1 *Portland Gazette* (March 14, 1803).
2 McCauley, *Liverpool Transfer Designs*, 43. For this likeness see Sprague, "Liverpool-type Pitchers," fig. 9. Wendy Wick, letter to author, June 15, 1982. Invoice, September 25, 1789, Robison Papers, MEHS.

Cat. 11.1 Probably Herculaneum Pottery (1796–1840), pitcher, Liverpool, England, ca. 1800. Creamware with enamel-painting and transfer-printing in black; H 12⅜ (31.4). Peabody Museum of Salem: Photo, Mark Sexton.

12

Unidentified artist
*View of Portland Harbor, Cushing's Island
and Fort Scammell from Fort Preble*
Probably Portland, Maine, 1853–1862
Oil on canvas
H 10½ (26.7); W 15 (38.1)
Maine Historical Society
Gift of Mrs. Sylvester Judd Beach

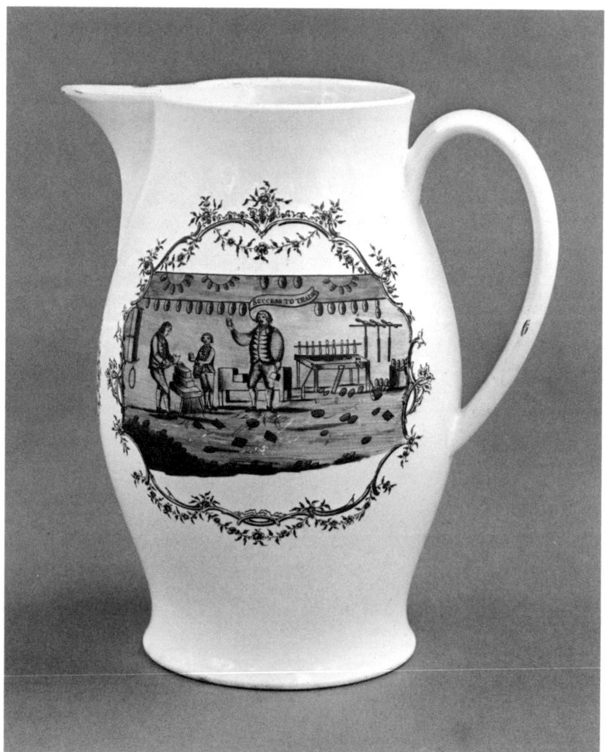

Cat. 11.1

Forts Scammell and Preble, named for Alexander Scammell, a Revolutionary War hero, and Commodore Edward Preble, were constructed in Portland as part of America's "Second System" of defenses, work instituted by Congress in 1807.[1] Until these forts were completed, Fort Sumner on Munjoy Hill, built in 1794, was Portland's only defense against a seaborne enemy (see cat. 5). Completed by 1812, Forts Scammell and Preble were constructed as part of a comprehensive defense system for the town. This view of Fort Scammell on House Island, to the left, is taken from Fort Preble on Spring Point in South Portland. Although dating after the 1853 construction of Ottawa House, a summer resort on Cushing's (formerly Bang's) Island, this painting documents the appearance of both forts before they were enlarged beginning in 1862.[2]

The construction of both structures was superintended by Alexander Parris in 1808 and 1809. His work for the late Commodore Preble undoubtedly helped him secure this post. Parris's drawings for a blockhouse like Fort Scammell's may indicate that he actually designed some of the quarters there and at Fort Preble.[3] Fort Preble was finished with white-washed brick, visible here at Fort Scammell.

When Anne Royall visited Fort Preble in 1828 she found "only two or three shabby men, though the fort is well situated and strongly built. Why government pays men who do not attend to their duty, remains for it to say."[4] Perhaps she did not know that the major purpose of such defenses was their physical presence, discouraging enemies from even the attempt at bombardment or invasion during time of war.

Portland was threatened by the British in 1813, but with its forts and streets full of soldiers, it was unharmed.

The lack of such protection at Winter Harbor (Biddeford Pool), a large sheltered area for shipbuilding at the mouth of the Saco River, was keenly felt when it was bombarded on June 16, 1804. The bombardment destroyed ships of Thomas Cutts, Jr. (cat. 34).[5]

Before and after the end of the War of 1812, visits to the forts provided a form of recreation for Maine citizens. In the summer of 1796, Abigail May reported that she had never visited Fort Sumner, "that fashionable resort."[6] On July 4, 1818, Ann King of Bath wrote to her sister from Portland about a trip to Fort Scammell:

O, what a divine sail, and the fort too and scenery — all look'd too grand & sublime for reality, two shells were fir'd, while we stood on the ramparts watching their course throu the air until they exploded and were skatterd in the water. we saw their smoke ten minutes sailing along the horizon. some lemonade and nice cake was our feast and after wandering romantically oer the Island were hurried into the boat by the heavy clouds threatening "Hale & Electrick shocks" your favorite propensitys: but have patience and these scenes which I but just touch upon shall be descanted at large when I return.[7]

In contrast to this romantic recollection, a more realistic impression of the intended purpose of fortifications is Henry

Wadsworth Longfellow's comment that Fort Sumner "was
one of the terrors of my childhood."[8]   LFS

1 Robert L. Bradley, *The Forts of Maine, 1607–1945: An Archaeological and
  Historical Survey* (Augusta: Maine Historic Preservation Commission
  and the Maine Bureau of Parks and Recreation, 1981), 25; Fort
  Edgecomb survives in Lincoln County and is the best preserved
  "Second System" fort in Maine.
2 Edward H. Elwell, *Portland and Vicinity* (Portland, Me.: Loring, Short
  & Harmon, and W. S. Jones, 1876), 87–88, 91–92. Bradley, *Forts*, 34.
3 Edward Preble's Washington connections also secured jobs for
  shipwrights in the Portland area. The Navy Secretary asked Preble to
  oversee the construction of gunboats for the Department. Preble
  subcontracted the work out to Portland shipwrights; see agreements,
  July 1, 1805, vol. 15, Edward Preble Papers, Manuscripts Division,
  Library of Congress. Zimmer, "Parris," 133–138.
4 Royall, *Black Book*, 215.
5 Owen, *Old Times in Saco*, 110.
6 Abigail May, diary, MEHS.
7 Ann King to her sister, July 4, 1819, Hale-King Papers, Special
  Collections, Bowdoin College Library.
8 Samuel Longfellow, ed., *Final Memorials of Henry Wadsworth Longfellow*
  (Boston: Ticknor and Co., 1887), 20–21.

13

Pitcher
England, probably Staffordshire, 1815–1825
Earthenware with transfer-printed decoration
and lustre glaze
Marked (in transfer-printing below the scene)
"Bentley Wear & Bourne, Engravers & Printers Shelton,
Staffordshire"
H 4⅜ (11.1)
Maine Historical Society

Objects depicting successful United States naval engagements against the British had widespread appeal in America.
Following the close of the War of 1812, and British losses
notwithstanding, the English potters hastened to provide the
American market with wares featuring American heroes and
their honorable achievements. While many battles took

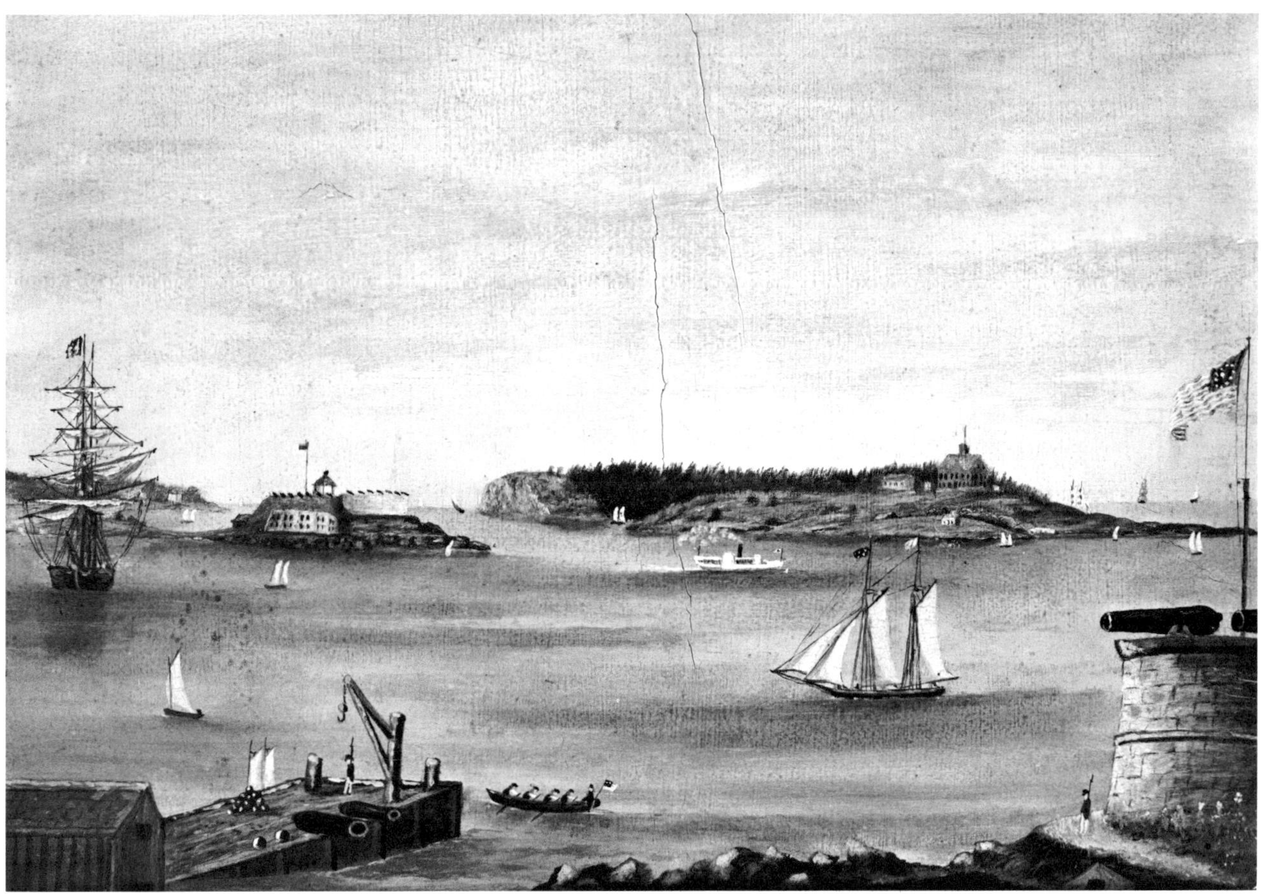

Cat. 12

place on the Great Lakes and Lake Champlain, one famous engagement occurred off the coast of Maine. This pitcher commemorated the capture of the British *Boxer* by the USS *Enterprise* on September 5, 1813.

Many British-made objects decorated with scenes of heroic events of this type were sold in America, and earthenwares with this design may have been among the "naval and military, Laurence and other Pitchers" advertised for sale in Portland in 1816. This small pitcher is highlighted with pink lustre; the reverse is decorated with a transfer-printed scene of the *United States* and *Macedonia*.[1]

The victorious *Enterprise* brought the badly damaged *Boxer* into Portland Harbor. British casualties were heavy and the youthful commanders of both vessels, William Blyth and William Burrows, were mortally wounded. Portland citizens planned elaborate funeral arrangements for the commanders of the two ships. The procession included a military escort, public officials, officers, and crews of both ships. It paraded throughout the town before reaching the final destination, the Eastern Cemetery on Munjoy Hill.[2]

The engagement and the deaths of the captains continued to interest Americans during the nineteenth century. In 1825 "a large Painting by Corne, of the SEA-FIGHT between the Enterprise and the Boxer, 12 feet square" was exhibited in Portland. In 1829, sixteen years after the event, Charlemagne Tower noted his visit to the burying ground and "the graves of the captains. . . . Their monuments are plain marble slabs with suitable inscriptions." Henry Wadsworth Longfellow included a verse about the battle in his poem "My Lost Youth," published in 1877, and *The Graves of The Captains* was painted in 1876 by Charles F. Kimball.[3]   L F S

1 *Portland Gazette* (September 17, 1816). This reference would suggest earlier availability than the 1817 date given and discussed in Nelson, "Transfer-printed Creamware," 102–104. See 108–109 for the James Lawrence ("Laurence") transfer-design. For an illustration of the reverse print, see McCauley, *Liverpool Transfer Designs*, plate 26.
2 *Funeral Arrangements* (September 7, 1813), broadside, Peabody Museum of Salem.
3 *Eastern Argus* (May 5, 1825); Morris, "Tower," 47. The Kimball painting is at MEHS.

14

Bottle
England, ca. 1813
Blown green glass
Marked (in molded seal on neck) "G [broad arrow] R"
H 9⁷⁄₁₆ (24.0); Diam. bottom 4⁷⁄₁₆ (11.3);
Diam. seal 1⁵⁄₁₆ (3.3)
Maine Historical Society
Gift of Harriet Cammett Shaw

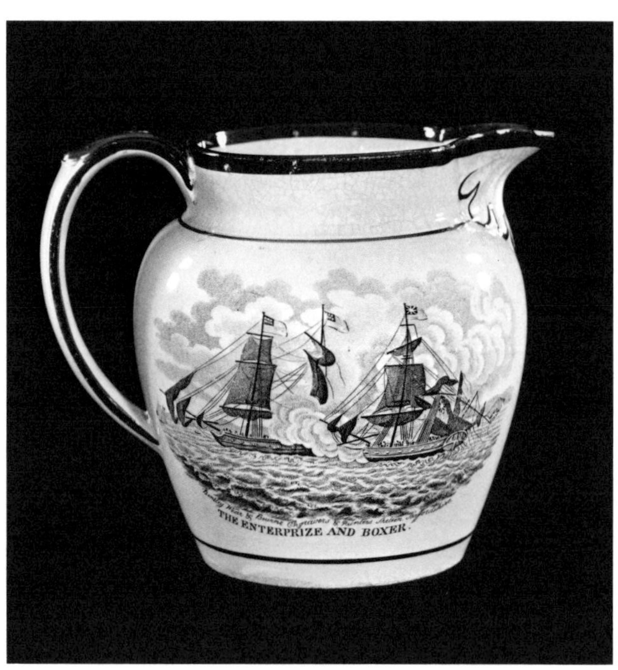

Cat. 13

Following the capture of the British brig *Boxer* during the War of 1812, the ship was brought into Portland harbor where she was sold at a marshal's sale on November 12, 1813. Thomas Merrill, Jr., a Portland merchant, purchased the ship, part of her armament and "many articles of her inventory" for $5,600.[1] This bottle was presented to the Maine Historical Society by his granddaughter.

Applied at the base of the neck of this bottle is a seal molded with the letters G R divided by a broad arrow. The initials stand for *George Rex* and the broad arrow is a symbol of the Royal Navy.[2] The broad arrow was used in Maine during the colonial period to mark mast trees as royal property. G R seals with or without a broad arrow or crown are found on other military items such as firearms, buttons, and blankets (cat. 15). They indicate British military or naval ownership.

Round green glass bottles are most often associated with the storage and service of wines and liquor. The seal on this bottle, however, indicates a different purpose. Medicine was one of the only types of materials among the official naval stores on board the *Boxer* that would have been suitable for a container of this size, a nearly two-quart capacity. This bottle resembles large jars used to store pharmaceuticals, and was probably used for that purpose. Its dark green color would have been a useful feature for those substances sensitive to light.[3]

Seals had been used since the seventeenth century to mark bottles as one's personal property. Bottles dating to the early eighteenth century are known with the seals of Maine men, including Nicholas Brown, a colonist at Pemaquid, and Andrew Frost and John Frost of Eliot.[4] While seal bottles from Maine families of the federal period have not come to light, this bottle illustrates the continued presence of the seal bottle tradition.   LFS

1 Fritz H. Jordan, "Letter accompanying the gift of a photograph of the brig 'Boxer,'" *Collections and Proceedings of the Maine Historical Society*, 2d ser., 1 (1890): 175.
2 Another bottle like this one with a G R seal and a *Boxer* history survives at the Baxter House Museum in Gorham.
3 Olive E. Jones and E. Ann Smith, *Glass of the British Military, 1755–1820* (Ottawa: Parks Canada, 1985), 90, 95.
4 Sprague, "Glass in Maine," 4. The Brown seal was among the artifacts excavated at Colonial Pemaquid, Maine State Bureau of Parks and Recreation.

15

Blanket (detail)
England, ca. 1813
Wool
Marked (in one corner) "G [broad arrow] R"
L 91¾ (233.0); W 67 ⅜ (172.1)
Maine Historical Society
Gift of S.C. Boyd

This blanket was among the stores of a British brig, *Peter Waldo*, captured off the coast of Maine during the War of 1812. It is rare to find such blankets since as naval equipment they were subjected to heavy use and often ultimately discarded. Therefore, it is of even greater interest that this is one of four in the Maine Historical Society. Another has a *Peter Waldo* history; two are associated with the *Boxer*.[1] The G R seal with broad arrow seen on a glass bottle (cat. 14) is repeated here to designate the property of the Royal Navy. This brown-printed mark is the most legible of the four.

   With its thick, fleecy nap, the blanket itself is typical of those produced in Witney, Oxfordshire, England. They were used in England and were also important exports to America. The brown woven double stripe marked the place where the length was to be torn, thus assuring a correct measurement.[2] Above the stripes is a short stripe or "point" which indicated the size of the blanket. This blanket was commercially made on a fly-shuttle loom, eliminating center seams in the fabric and producing a fabric more than 5½-feet in width (see cat. 139). The fulling process has made the blanket very dense; the unfinished ends of the blanket do not appear to have raveled.   LFS

1 The National Maritime Museum in London has no G R blankets of this period in its collection. R. P. Prentice, letter to author, August 27, 1985.
2 Jane C. Nylander, "Rose Blanket," in *The Great River*, 381.

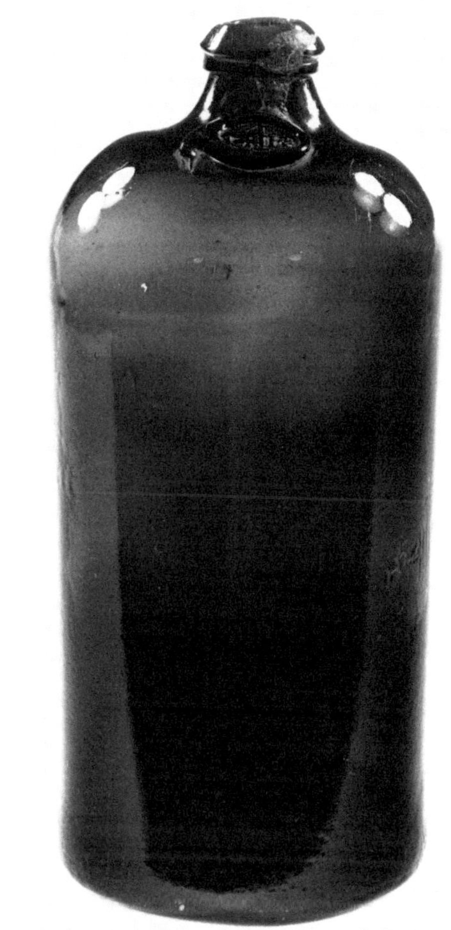

Cat. 14

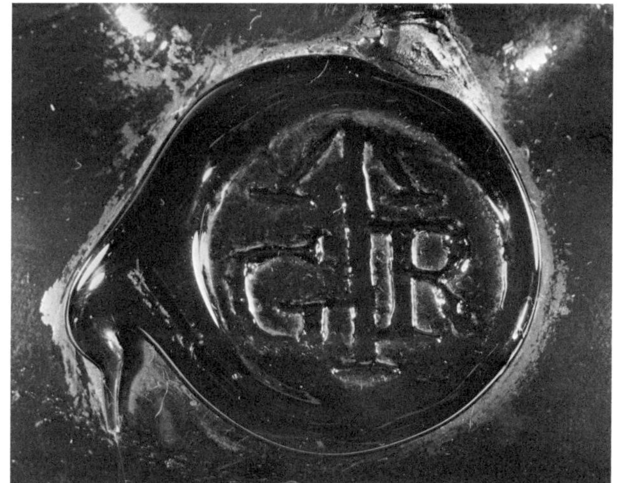

Cat. 14 detail

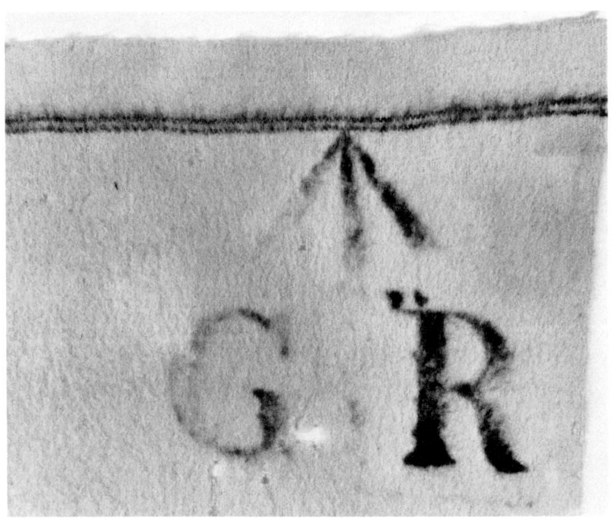

Cat. 15

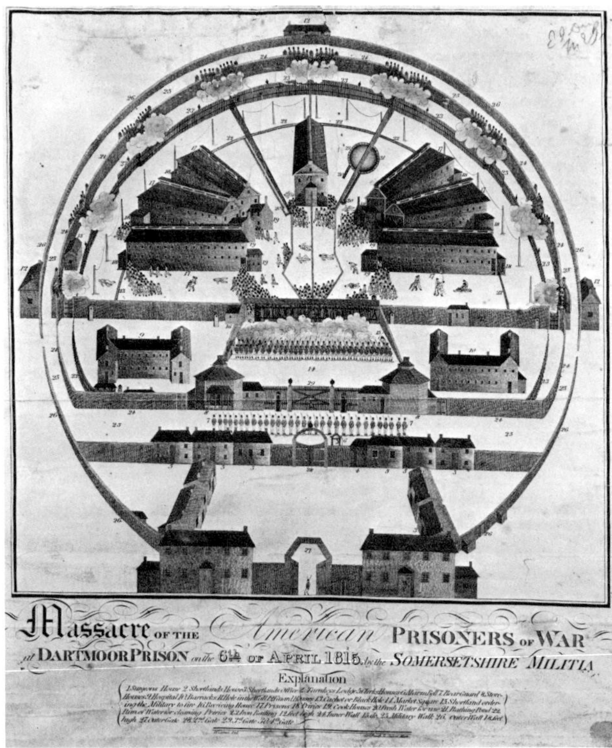

Cat. 16

16

George G. Smith (d. ca. 1858)
*Massacre of the American Prisoners of War at Dartmoor Prison
on the 6th of April 1815, by the Somershire Militia*
Engraving
Inscribed "W. Carnes Del." and "G. G. Smith Sc.
Salem Mass."
H 13½ (34.2); W 11¹³⁄₁₆ (28.4)
The Brick Store Museum; Gift of Essex Institute
probably through Howard Corning, 1956

The 1815 massacre at Dartmoor Prison provoked indignation and anger among Americans. That same year George
G. Smith of Salem engraved this view of the incident at the
prison. A copy of the print, to which colors were added, held
special significance for Kennebunk and Portland residents in
the nineteenth century.

When Congress passed the Embargo Act of 1807,
shipping was halted, but privateering proved a lucrative
(though risky) alternative for numerous seafaring men.
Kennebunk's Captain Daniel Nason sailed with James
Fairfield and other ship captains engaged in privateering
until the British seized his ship *Macdonough*. Nason, Fairfield,
and the others had been captured shortly after their departure from the Kennebunk River. They were held in Dartmoor
prison where Captain Jo Weeks and other Portland men
were incarcerated.[1] In the April 6, 1815, massacre, the
British, fearing insurrection among the prisoners who had
just learned of the American victory over the British, opened
fire on prisoners, killing eight and wounding at least forty-five
others. James Fairfield wrote to his wife Lois, "Fortunately,

none of our Kennebunkers fell Victims to British cruelties on
that never to be forgotten day."[2]

Fairfield and Weeks returned home safely, but the
memory of the massacre lingered in the nation, feeding the
imaginations of many with both horror and fascination. Ten
years after the episode, the Portland Museum in Haymarket
Row advertised curiosities and paintings for people to view.
Among the attractions was "a room fitted for the purpose, a
complete model of the celebrated DARTMOOR PRISON, where
so many *American Sailors* suffered in the late War."[3] AAE

1 William Goold, Scrapbook, 9.
2 Martha Gandy Fales,"Saga of a Shipmaster's Portrait," *Down East* 27,
  no. 9 (April 1981): 16.
3 *Eastern Argus* (May 5, 1825).

17

Possibly by Meyer Nathan Levy
Spoon
Copenhagen, Denmark, 1807
Silver
Marked (on back of handle) with four hallmarks

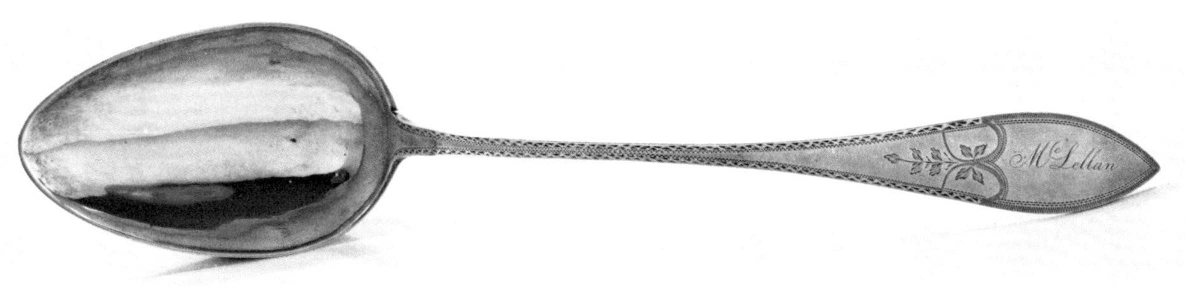

Cat. 17

L 15³⁄₁₆ (38.6); w bowl 2³⁄₈ (6.0)
Maine Historical Society; Gift of Harriet McLellan

This serving spoon was probably owned by William McLellan, Jr., of Portland. The family's shipping business took him to Leningrad and other ports on the Baltic. Copenhagen was one of the ports of call and shipping news printed in the local newspapers indicated that Portland ships often docked there.[1] The fact that captains and crew disembarked and made personal purchases is vividly illustrated by this large spoon. It bears the inscription "McLellan" on the handle and the date "1807" is engraved on the reverse. Assay marks of town, year, month, and assayer confirm the spoon's place and date of manufacture as Copenhagen in July 1807. Although the maker's mark is unclear, the style of the spoon and its engraving is very similar to a fish slice or cake spoon made in 1805 by silversmith Meyer Nathan Levy of Copenhagen.[2]   AAE

1   *Eastern Argus* (November 5, 1807; December 17, 1807; and September 17, 1807). McLellan family silver purchased in London survives at the Portland Museum of Art; see Churchill, "Crafts in Transition," 306–307 and n32.
2   Seymour B. Wyler, *The Book of Old Silver* (New York: Crown Publishers, 1937), 436, and Gudmund Boesen and Chr. A. Bøje, *Old Danish Silver* (Copenhagen, 1949), fig. 490. Martha Gandy Fales kindly brought this latter source to my attention.

18

Plate
Yorkshire or Staffordshire, England, 1775–1785
Creamware
Diam. 8 (20.3)
Maine Historical Society; Wadsworth-Longfellow House

Ownership of creamware plates of this type in Maine is well documented by many sources. The rim with its molded featheredged decoration is further ornamented by a pierced border. A basket and stand owned by Jonathan Sayward in York carries the same design and perhaps represents the "neat open workd Fruit Baskets & St[an]ds" ordered by a Portland merchant in 1784.[1]

It is generally accepted that creamware replaced white salt-glazed stoneware and delftware in the years following the Revolution. There is evidence, however, to indicate that delftware continued to be used in Maine in the federal period along with the most fashionable products. Although Fabre and Dunn, merchants in Portland, advertised "Liverpool and Queen's ware" in the *Falmouth Gazette and Weekly Advertiser* on October 22, 1785, in the following issue Joseph Parsons advertised delftware that had "just arrived." Probate inventories document the shift from delftware to creamwares and green- and blue-edged tablewares during the 1780s and 1790s.   LFS

1   The Sayward basket and stand is in the Sayward-Wheeler house, York, Maine, SPNEA; invoice, Thomas Wilkinson to Phyn and Ellice on account of Robison and Edgar, London, April 22, 1784, Robison Papers, MEHS.

19

Herculaneum Pottery (1796–1840)
Plate
Liverpool, England, 1796–1810
Creamware with green enameled edge
Marked (on bottom) "HERCULANEUM"
Diam. 8 (20.3)
Maine Historical Society; Wadsworth-Longfellow House

Shipped on board the brig *Ranger* for the account of Robison
and McLellan of Portland in 1789 were ten crates of earthenware. Crate 5 contained a large quantity of blue-edged ware:
eight sizes of dishes; salad dishes and baking dishes ranging
from eight to eighteen inches along with twifflers; flat and
soup plates; tureens, stands, and spoons; butter tubs; salts,
mustards, and peppers; and mugs, leaves, and sauce boats.
Crate 6 was "a Crate contain.g same as No. 5 only green
instead [of] blue Edge." The price was the same.[1] Although
shipped from Liverpool, these earthenwares on the *Ranger*
originated at potteries in Staffordshire.

Liverpool's own Herculaneum Pottery represents
another major source of blue- and green-edged wares
shipped to the United States. This plate from Liverpool is an
example of a twiffler, a plate used in dining, of the size
between a dinner and muffin plate. Other creamwares of
Herculaneum manufacture are known with Maine histories,
representing the vast trade carried on by Maine merchants.[2]

LFS

1 Invoice, September 25, 1789, Robison Papers, MEHS.
2 In addition to the pitchers discussed in this catalogue, there is a soup
plate with a McLellan family history at the Baxter House Museum in
Gorham.

20

Soup plate (one of five)
China, 1770–1790
Hard-paste porcelain with underglaze blue decoration
H 1⅛ (2.8); Diam. 9³⁄₁₆ (23.3)
York Institute Museum
Bequest of Almira Locke McArthur, 1950

Porcelains with underglaze blue decoration were staple
Chinese export wares. The hand-painted Chinese landscape
scene on this soup plate is a particularly good example of a
type of decoration that had widespread appeal and was in
great demand in America. Underglaze blue wares were the
least expensive of the China trade porcelains and surpassed
in quantity any other type of export ware. Probate inventories sometimes describe Chinese export porcelains of this
type as "Nankeen" after the Chinese port of Nanking which
was involved in the shipment of the wares.[1] These were the
Chinese designs that so influenced English potters, who
copied them for their painted or printed wares or made their
own designs based on elements of the composition.

When a Portland merchant ordered "Cups & Saucers

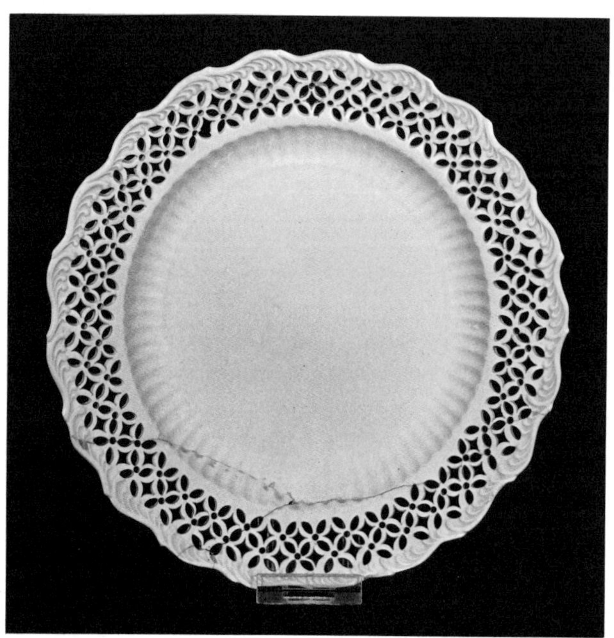

Cat. 18

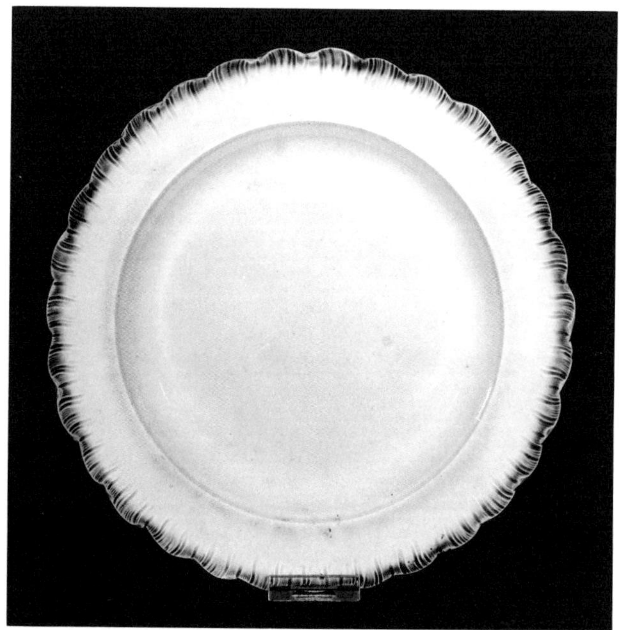

Cat. 19

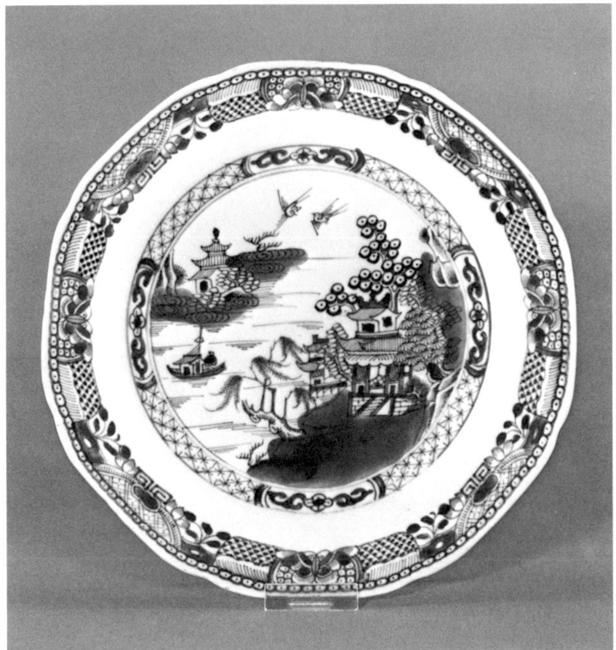

Cat. 20

blue & white that was large" that were unavailable, his Boston agent, Robert Jenkins, replied, "I have put you to a Shilling or two more Expense, and got Burnt China." By "burnt china," he meant with the colors "burned in," or fired on over the glaze. Vessels with overglaze enamel decoration required a second firing and increased the cost (cat. 21). These soup plates were probably part of a large table service.[2] L F S

1 Jean McClure Mudge, *Chinese Export Porcelain for the American Trade 1785–1835* (Newark, Del.: University of Delaware Press, 1962), 54–55, 139.
2 Robert Jenkins to Thomas Robison, January 22, 1784, Robison Papers, MEHS. Arlene Palmer Schwind, "The Ceramic Imports of Frederick Rhinelander, New York Loyalist," *Winterthur Portfolio* 19, no. 1 (Spring 1984): 23–24. Five 9″ plates and two 6⁵⁄₁₆″ plates also survive at YIS.

21

Coffee and tea set (selections)
China, 1790–1810
Hard-paste porcelain with enamel decoration and gilt
H coffeepot 9⅛ (23.2); H teapot 5⁵⁄₁₆ (13.5);
H sugar bowl 4¹⁵⁄₁₆ (12.5); H coffee cup 2³⁄₁₆ (5.5);
H teacup 1¾ (4.5); H saucer 1¼ (3.2)
Old York Historical Society
Gift of Mrs. Malcolm Freeman
in memory of her mother, Mrs. William Neal, 1972

A surprising number of costly Chinese porcelains were exported to Maine during the colonial period and are well documented.[1] This service is typical of China trade porcelains shipped to New England during the federal period. The drum-shaped teapots were fashioned after silver ones, and the tall coffeepot, often referred to today as the "lighthouse" shape, became popular at this time. Probate inventories contain frequent references to "chaney" and "India china," period terms for Oriental wares.

These porcelains are part of a large double service from the Moody and Varrell families of York.[2] A double teaset usually contained 24 cups, 12 teacups, and 12 coffee cups. They were combined with only 12 saucers, since only tea or coffee would have been consumed at a particular time.[3] These porcelains are painted with a landscape scene in sepia enamels and gilt. Porcelains decorated with a similar landscape scene in a medallion, also in sepia, were owned by Zilpah and Stephen Longfellow in Portland. The Longfellow porcelains are said to have been given as wedding gifts in 1804.

Some of the most highly valued, personalized designs of Chinese export porcelains were originally made for residents of Maine. In 1790 Henry Knox of Thomaston received a large service from his friend Samuel Shaw, the supercargo on board the first American ship to China. The Knox porcelains are decorated with the Insignia of the Order of the Society of the Cincinnati, of which Knox was a founding member.[4] The Vaughans in Hallowell owned porcelains bearing their heraldic arms.[5] While these services are of particular importance because of the rarity of their decoration, most other documented examples for Maine have simple designs.[6] The double service at the Sayward-Wheeler house on the York River is ornamented only with a simple gilt border and sprig. L F S

1 Mid-eighteenth-century porcelains at the Sayward-Wheeler house include two important sets, one with Imari decoration and the other with polychrome enamels of a boy and buffalo; see Nylander, "Sayward House," 571. Batavia-type porcelains, those with floral reserves and a brown glaze, were owned by the Tate family of Stroudwater (now at Tate House, National Society of Colonial Dames of America in Maine) and by Parson Thomas Smith of Portland and

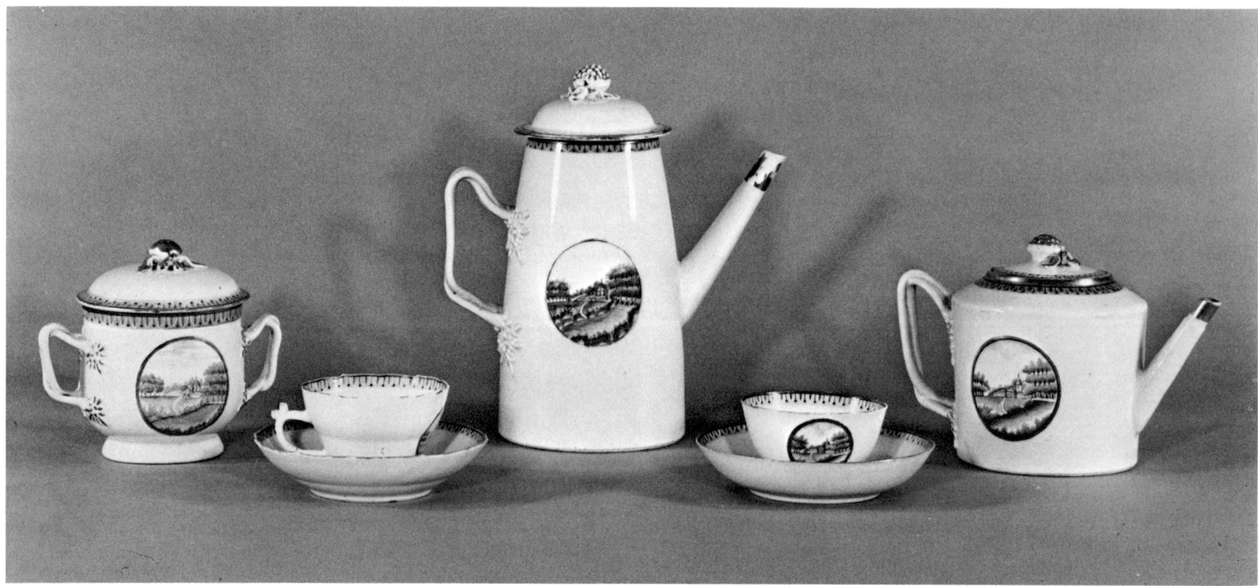

Cat. 21

Windham, Maine. Batavia-type porcelains were painted on the dummy board owned by Smith's second wife; see Martha Gandy Fales, "Two Early New England Dummy Boards," *Antiques* 120, no. 6 (December 1981): 1423.

2 The other half of the set was stolen from the family home before it was given to OYHS in 1972. The coffeepot has traces of gilt initials "WCC."

3 Jean McClure Mudge, *Chinese Export Porcelain for the American Trade, 1785–1835* (Newark, Del.: University of Delaware Press, 1962), 128–129.

4 See John Quentin Feller's documentation of the Knox porcelains in "Collector's Notes," *Antiques* 125, no. 4 (April 1984): 907–908. Knox's chocolate pot from the set, previously unrecorded, is in the collection of Montpelier, Maine State Bureau of Parks and Recreation, Thomaston, Me.

5 The porcelains are in the Abbott Collection, Special Collections, Bowdoin College Library.

6 Other examples from the four collections include part of a dinner service from the Stephen Cummings family of Portland and a small bowl from the Jordan family with underglaze blue decoration that has been overpainted with enamels or "clobbered" at MEHS, and miscellaneous famille rose examples at BSM, YIS, and OYHS.

22

Tea set (selections)
England, 1805–1810
Porcelain with hand-painted silver lustre decoration
Marked (on bottom of four objects) "x"
and "4" (in red enamel)
H teapot 6½ (16.5); H tray ¹¹⁄₁₆ (1.8);
H creamer 3⅜ (8.6); H teacup 2⅛ (5.4);
H saucer 1⅛ (2.9)
The Brick Store Museum; Jane Lord Burbank estate
through Edith Cleaves Barry, 1945

"Upon a table under the [looking] glass, Cornelia found a set of old-fashioned china, though the tea-pot would not receive more than two cups of water at a time, it was filled with joy, by the delighted Cornelia." Novelist Sarah Wood's description of a domestic scene in *Tales of the Night* (1827) vividly conveys the value placed on tea and tea equipage.[1] Even though tea was widely available during the federal period, tea drinking maintained its high place as a ritual in social entertainments.

Decorated with delicate hand-painted sprigs in silver lustre, this teapot illustrates a form modeled after oval silver shapes. Portland merchant Charles Blanchard's stock of tea sets included "best and common . . . silver shape, oval and round."[2] In addition to the shapes, the lustre itself was inspired by expensive silver vessels.

While this type of decoration was called "silver lustre" during the period, silver metal was not actually used in the process. A solution containing platinum was prepared for the decoration. Once fired in a low temperature kiln, a thin lustrous metallic coating was produced. Vessels covered entirely in lustre appealed to those who wanted silver but could not afford the real thing. This tea set represents one style of decoration within a tremendous range available. Copper lustre and pink lustre, made from different solutions containing gold, were also produced; pink lustre highlighted many transfer-printed pitchers made for the American market (cat. 13).

Though less expensive than silver, lustreware was only as durable as its ceramic body. One example that did not fare well was mentioned in a letter Ann King wrote to her sister Caroline in Saco, along with a recipe for its repair. "Have sent you a peice of lime . . . tell Mamma to mix lime and the white of an egg very thick with a little flower and water to join broken crockery particularly that silver pitcher I broke." [3]

Although English porcelains with histories in eighteenth-century Maine are very rare, an interest in English porcelain manufactories is documented by the travel journals of Edward Oxnard. A Loyalist who fled to England during the Revolution, Oxnard attempted to visit the Chelsea porcelain factory but "was turned away." In 1777 he was given a tour of the porcelain works in Worcester and he detailed the manufacturing process in his journal. [4]

English porcelains became more widely available during the federal period. Two important services survive in the Colonel Black house in Ellsworth. One set contains both tea and coffee cups, not uncommon in large services. Decorated with finely transfer-printed Chinese landscape scenes and gilded grape-leaf borders, it is perhaps the product of the Miles Mason factory. All the pieces in the second service have been decorated with hand-painted landscape scenes in polychrome enamels. These extraordinary survivals are thought to have been sent from England as wedding gifts to the Blacks in 1802. [5]   LFS

1 Wood, *Tales*, 15.
2 *Portland Gazette* (February 27, 1816).
3 [Ann King] to Caroline King, [July] 1817, Erving-King Family Papers, New-York Historical Society.
4 Edward Oxnard, journals, MEHS.
5 Other English tea services with Maine histories include a set of Worcester porcelain owned by the Kavanaugh family at the Maine State Museum, and examples of bat-printed porcelains at LNHS, and the Colonel Black house in Ellsworth. Other miscellaneous pieces of various description survive in the collections discussed in this catalogue.

23

Coffee and tea set (selections)
Probably England, possibly United States, 1805–1815
Porcelain with orange enamel decoration
H coffeepot 8⁷⁄₁₆ (21.4); H creamer 3¹¹⁄₁₆ (9.3);
H coffee cup 2¾ (6.9); H tea cup 2⅛ (5.4);
H saucer 1⅛ (2.8); H bowl 2⁷⁄₁₆ (6.2); H bowl 3³⁄₁₆ (8.0)
York Institute Museum
Bequest of Almira Locke McArthur, 1950

These porcelain wares are part of what was once a large service with a coffee pot, also used to serve chocolate, and a teapot, along with cups and saucers, a sugar bowl and creamer, waste bowls, and cake plates. Unlike the low shapes of teapots, the coffee or chocolate pots were tall. Curved-sided cups, with or without handles, were used for tea, while handled straight-sided cups or cans were used to serve coffee. This service retains examples of both cups and cans, indicating that the original service included a teapot and other pieces that are now lost. This set is said to have belonged to Daniel and Sarah Cleaves of Biddeford, Maine.

Coffee and tea sets were available in a great range of form and decoration. Some designs were derived from silver and reflect the neoclassical style. Manufacturing techniques in highly organized porcelain works conformed to a standard. Molds were used so that the same shapes could be made efficiently in great quantity. The shape of the creamer, coffee cans, and saucers illustrated here is seen in English porcelain of this period, but the construction of the coffee pot makes this service unusual. Tall vessels could easily be molded or

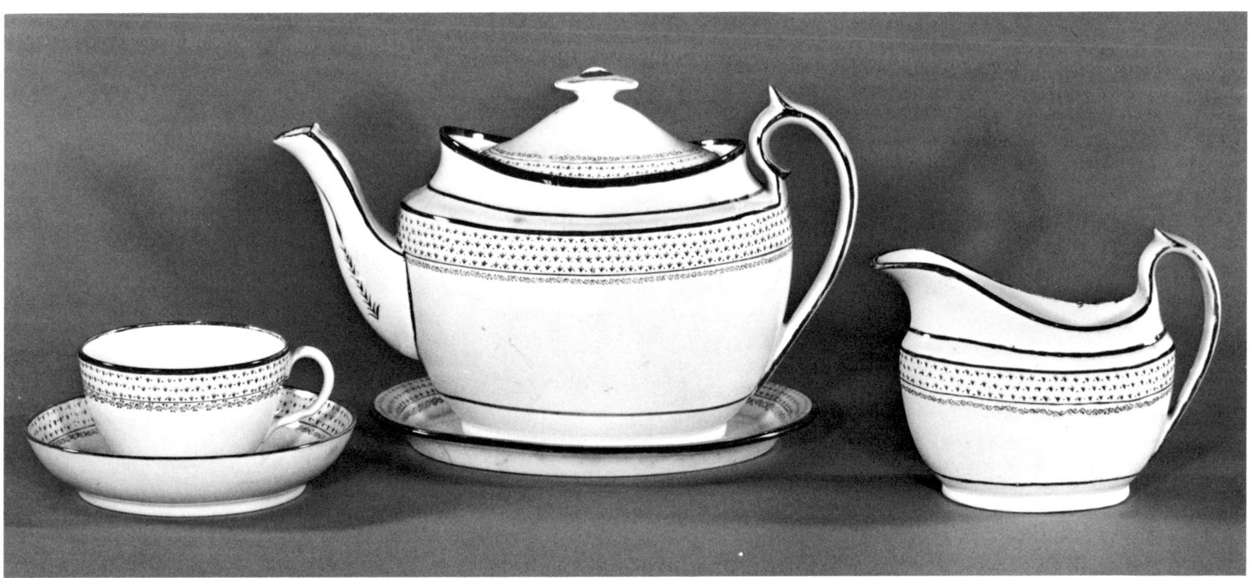

Cat. 22

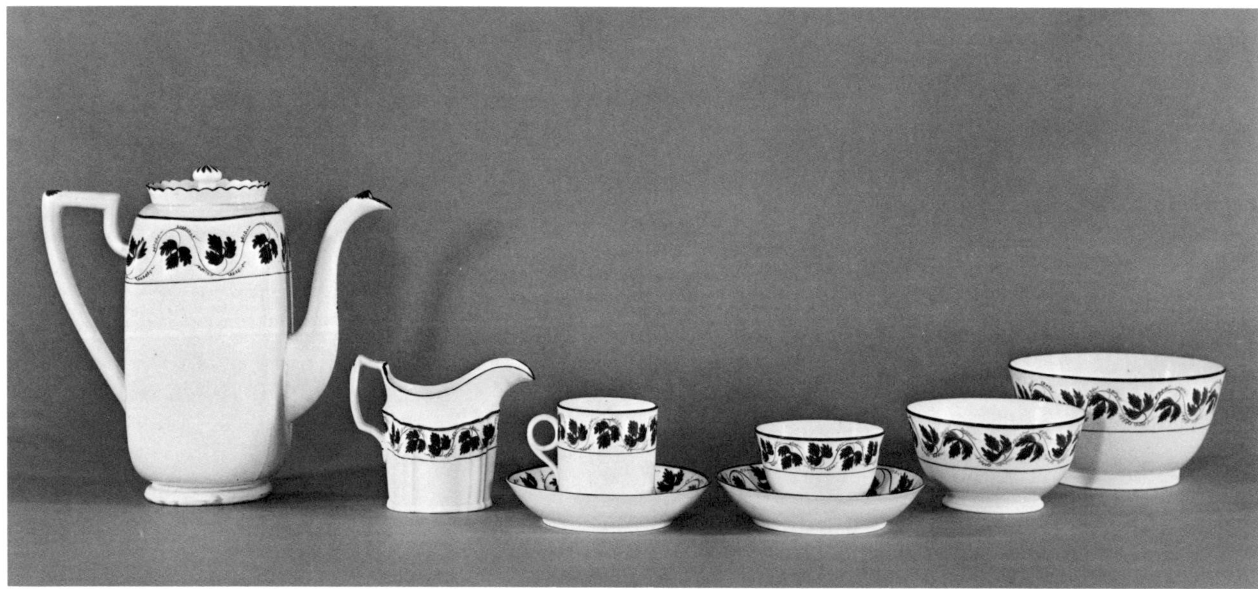

Cat. 23

turned on a wheel. Instead, the maker of this coffee pot employed the rarely seen slab technique, rolling out a large thick rectangular piece and applying it to a circular base. The grape-leaf border in orange enamel was a popular motif. The design is very similar to that decorating a tea set in the Portsmouth (New Hampshire) Historical Society. Features of its construction also merit close scutiny. The inconsistencies suggest that these objects may have been produced by a factory in an experimental stage. While an English porcelain works is a logical source, a fledging American factory is also a possibility.

American attempts at porcelain manufacture date to the colonial period when Bonnin and Morris established a factory in Philadelphia in 1770. Unable to compete with English wares, they closed within two years. There was a particularly strong interest in establishing American manufactories during the War of 1812, when trade with British firms was severed. In New England, the discovery in the late eighteenth century of porcelain clay in Vermont spurred attempts in 1812 to try "to manufacture ware from the Porcelain earth found at Monkton."[1] No wares from this factory, however, are known. Efforts to establish a porcelain works in Maine around 1815 have recently been brought to light.

"We are told that in the district of Maine there is established a manufactory of fine porcelain, which turns out large quantities of ware, which good judges are not able to distinguish from the best *Liverpool ware*. It is to Messrs. *King* and *Wingate*, we are told that the public are principally indebted (under the embargo) for this beneficial establish-

ment."[2] Without the aid of Christian names or other documents, the identification of King and Wingate has not been confirmed. They are thought to be William King of Bath and Joseph F. Wingate of Bath and Portland, who carried on joint entrepreneurial endeavors. William King shared this concern for the development of domestic manufactures with his brother, Rufus, who was instrumental in the passage by Congress of a navigation act in 1818 to protect American commerce.[3] In 1811 Wingate wrote to William King, "I enclose you a copy of a communication . . . penned by me a few days since. . . . I hope you will confess the principal correct. So little having been said in the newspapers respecting the importance of domestic manufactures I wish if possible to bring the matter into discussion."[4] A preliminary investigation of incorporation records and other documents has revealed no additional clues to the possible location of the King and Wingate manufactory, if it was in fact ever in operation. Further research is required before an American porcelain factory in Maine can be documented.

In addition to tea, coffee and chocolate enjoyed great popularity in federal America. On several mornings, Ann Smith of Portland prepared a chocolate drink at breakfast and on a mid-afternoon visit to Broad's Tavern she found a large party taking coffee. Coffee was also served at evening entertainment as late as 9 or 10 o'clock. Ann Smith's diary provides insights into early nineteenth-century brewing, which she recorded as "burning some coffee" and "parched coffee in a new machine for the purpose." Parson Thomas Smith's diary is full of references to chocolate which he purchased often and in great quantity.[5]   LFS

1 John Murry to Abijah Bigelow, Middlebury, Vt., January 30, 1812, Joseph Downs Manuscript and Microfilm Collection, Winterthur Museum Library, and *The Boston Mechanic, and Journal of the Useful Arts and Sciences*, vol. 4 (Boston: Light & Stearns, 1835), 180–181. Gary Stradling brought these references to my attention.
2 *Supplement to Niles' Register, Niles' Weekly Register* 9 (September 1815 – March 1816): 185. Arlene Palmer Schwind brought this reference to my attention.
3 Robert Ernst, *Rufus King, American Federalist* (Chapel Hill: University of North Carolina Press, 1968), 353–354
4 "King Family History" (manuscript, YIS), 185.
5 Ann Smith, diary, MEHS; for an example of Thomas Smith's chocolate purchases, see Willis, *Journals*, 208.

24

Tumbler (one of three)
Probably Bohemia, 1780–1815
Colorless non-lead glass, blown, cut, and engraved
H 3⅚ (8.4); Diam. 2⅜ (6.0)
York Institute Museum
Bequest of Almira Locke McArthur, 1950

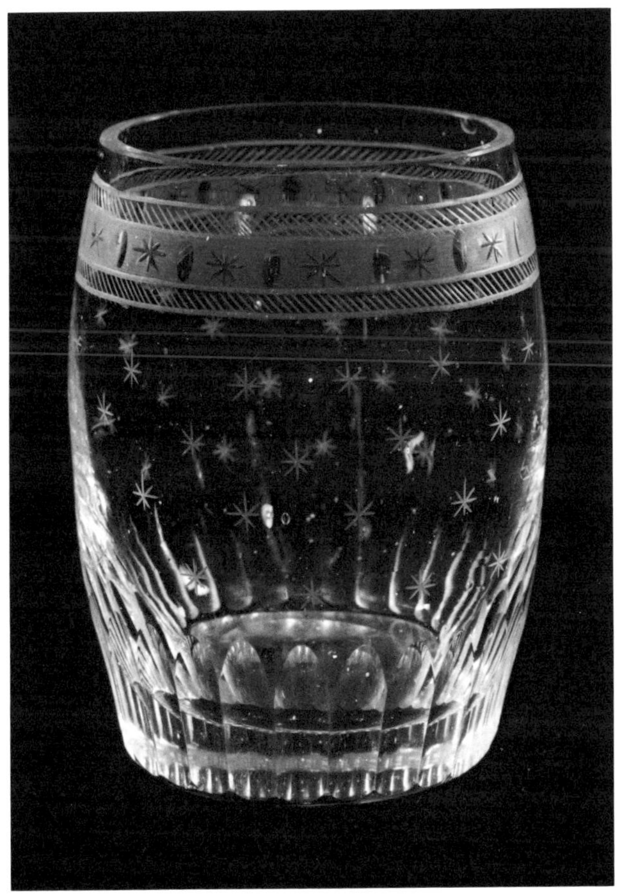

Cat. 24

The "fluted, ground bottom, barrel flint tumblers" advertised in the *Eastern Argus* on March 14, 1811, may have been similar to these, possibly bought by Daniel Cleaves of Biddeford. At his death in 1818, appraisers listed "12 barrel flint tumblers" valued at a total of $3.[1]

Bohemia, now part of Czechoslovakia, had long been a glassmaking center. Manufacturers there excelled in cut and engraved decoration. Neoclassical styles popularized by the English and Irish glassmakers were emulated by the Bohemian factories. During the federal period, the Continental glasshouses exported glass made of a non-lead or soda formula. Soda glass, often of a cloudy appearance, was usually not of the high quality of the English lead glass.

A trade catalogue of a Bohemian glasshouse that exported goods to America described a similar type of non-lead glass tumbler: "cut glass-gilt; with stars; barrel-shaped-with stars."[2] This type of glass was often decorated in gilt, a decoration easily lost by wear.

This glass is one of two with similar decoration at the York Institute. A third glass descended through another family line to William E. Barry and is in The Brick Store Museum. LFS

1 YCRP; 26: 544.
2 "Gardiner's Island Glass Catalogues," cited in Dwight P. Lanmon, "The Baltimore Glass Trade, 1780–1820," *Winterthur Portfolio 5*, ed. Ian M. G. Quimby (Charlottesville: University Press of Virginia for the Henry Francis du Pont Winterthur Museum, 1969), 36.

25

Cann
Probably Bohemia, 1785–1820
Opaque white glass, blown, enameled, and gilt
H 5½ (14.0); Diam. 3¼ (8.3)
York Institute Museum
Bequest of Almira Locke McArthur, 1950

A few federal-period household inventories in Maine included tablewares of "glass china." This eighteenth-century term describes a glass substance made to look like china, that is, opaque white glass. References described "glass china muggs" and one "set glass china teacups and saucers."[1]

While teapots, tea cups, and saucers are known to have been made of opaque white glass, mugs and canns (curved-sided mugs) are forms more commonly found. Bohemian factories often decorated these wares expressly for their markets. This cann, with its eagle and inscription, was obviously designed for American consumption. Other examples with polychrome enamel-painting of Continental origin are painted in close imitation of the desirable Chinese

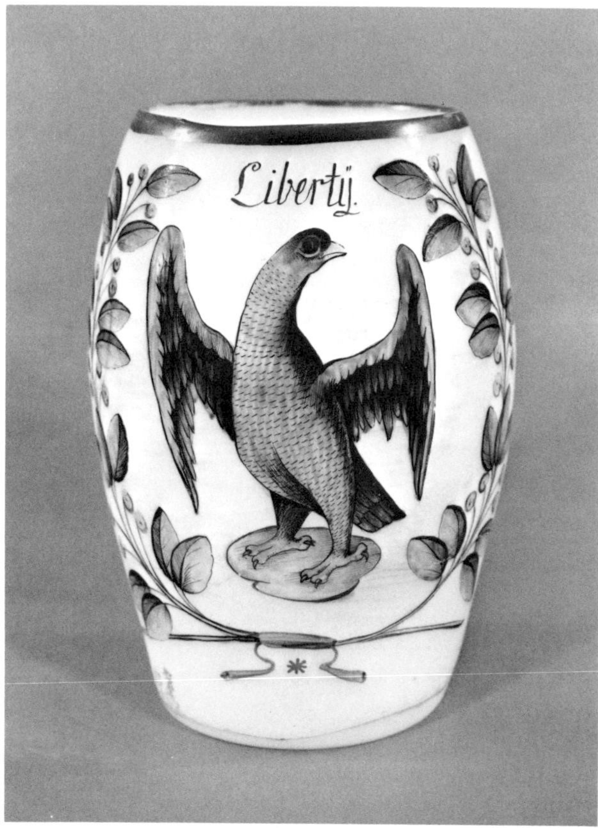

Cat. 25

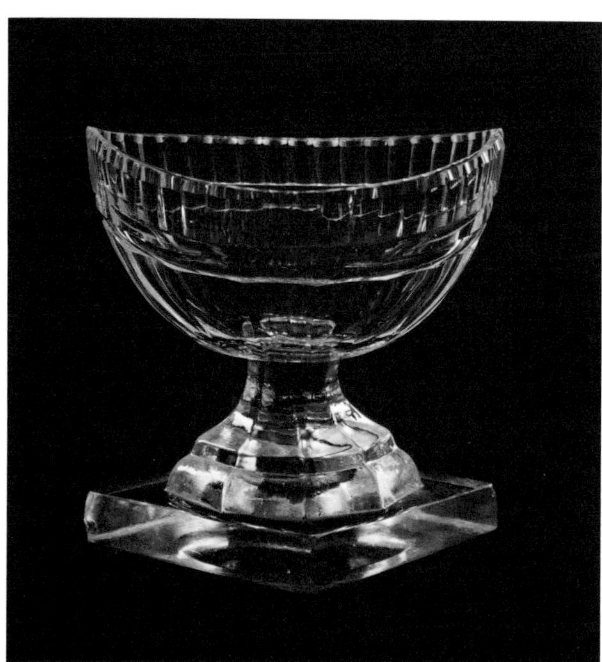

Cat. 26

export porcelains. A trade catalogue of a Bohemian glass-house recorded this type of drinking glass in the entries for "mugs and cans . . . white; . . . with eagle."[2] LFS

1 Lincoln County Registry of Probate (hereafter LCRP); 4: 248. The "glass teapot" recorded in this estate could be of opaque white glass. See also LCRP; 5:186; for other examples with Maine histories, see Sprague, "Glass in Maine," 5.
2 "Gardiner's Island Glass Catalogues," cited in Dwight P. Lanmon, "The Baltimore Glass Trade, 1780–1820," *Winterthur Portfolio 5*, ed. Ian M. G. Quimby (Charlottesville: University Press of Virginia for the Henry Francis du Pont Winterthur Museum, 1969), 36.

26

Salt (one of three)
England or Ireland, 1780–1800
Colorless lead glass, blown, and cut
H 3³⁄₁₆ (8.0); W 3⁷⁄₁₆ (8.7)
York Institute Museum
Bequest of Almira Locke McArthur, 1950

As part of the British colonial empire, Americans used predominantly English wares or European goods imported by British shipping. At the conclusion of the Revolutionary War, Americans, with great vigor, launched free trade directly with Continental and other markets. Despite the war, Americans turned to the established English and Irish manufactories for quantities of glass. Detailed information in account books, probate court inventories, and newspaper advertisements describe the wares imported and used in Maine. They aid in the identification of the great variety of forms and sizes available.[1]

Among the common forms in tablewares were tumblers, wine and other drinking vessels, salt cellars, decanters, cruets, pitchers, mugs, dishes, and "sallad" bowls. The English and Irish products, made of lead glass, were predominantly colorless, and often embellished with cut and engraved decoration. Many federal-period examples, such as these salts, survive in Maine collections.

Oval boat-shaped salt cellars on diamond-cut feet exemplify the highly decorative tablewares used in Maine. English cut glass was shipped to America from the 1760s. Although it would have been available to Maine residents through the Boston market, its appearance in the source materials at this early date is rare. There is greater evidence of cut glass in Maine households between 1780 and 1800.

In 1784 Thomas Robison imported to Maine cut glass wares through his London agents. The number sent indicates the glass was intended for his personal use in his new house overlooking Portland harbor. Included in this early account were "3 pair fine cutt glass salts" costing five shillings a pair. They may have been similar to these salts with a Saco provenance. LFS

1 For a discussion of glass imported to Maine in the colonial and federal periods, see Sprague, "Glass in Maine."
2 Invoice, Thomas Wilkinson to Phyn and Ellice, London, April 22, 1784, Robison Papers, MEHS.

27

Possibly South Boston Flint Glass Works (1812–1827)
Decanter (one of a pair)
Boston, Massachusetts, 1813–1827
Colorless lead glass, blown, with molded stopper
H 9 (22.8); Diam. bottom 3⅜ (8.6)
The Brick Store Museum; William D. Barry estate
through Edith Cleaves Barry

Although there were about a dozen glasshouses erected in colonial America, they were generally unable to compete technically or financially with European firms. This condition resulted in the importation of tremendous quantities of foreign glass. Ports of export specified in manuscript sources included Liverpool and Bristol, England; Belfast, Ireland; and Hamburg, Germany.[1] Other glass was described as "Spanish" and "Dutch." By the early nineteenth century, however, glasshouses in New England began to compete in this brisk trade.

The advertisement for tablewares in B. C. Atwood's Portland shop from "the Boston Glass Manufactory" in November 1813 signaled the factory's competition in the trade. The Boston Glass Manufactory was the parent company through which the South Boston factory products were sold.[2]

"Ringed neck" decanters of this type are documented to Maine households through a variety of sources. They were advertised in Atwood's shop, when he announced he carried tumblers from the "Boston Glass Factory." A decanter of similar shape is depicted in a cut of tablewares from a newspaper advertisement in Portland.[3]

This shape remained in use for many years. In 1829, Dexter Brewer, the Stroudwater gatekeeper for the Cumberland and Oxford Canal, recorded in his shop inventory "88 ring neck decanters" in quart, pint, and half-pint capacity; the capacity illustrated here is one pint.[4] The applied and tooled rings on the neck improved one's hold of the vessel.

LFS

1 For a Maine merchant's observations on the glass factories in Bristol and trade during the Revolution, see Laura F. Sprague, "Bottles and Beefstakes in Bristol," *Glass Club Bulletin*, no. 147 (Fall 1985): 12–13.
2 *Portland Gazette* (November 29, 1813). Kenneth M. Wilson, *New England Glass and Glassmaking* (New York: Thomas Y. Crowell, Co., 1972), 200.
3 See *Portland Gazette* (December 26, 1815).
4 Dexter Brewer, account book, 1823–1849, Baker Library, Harvard University (photocopy, MEHS).

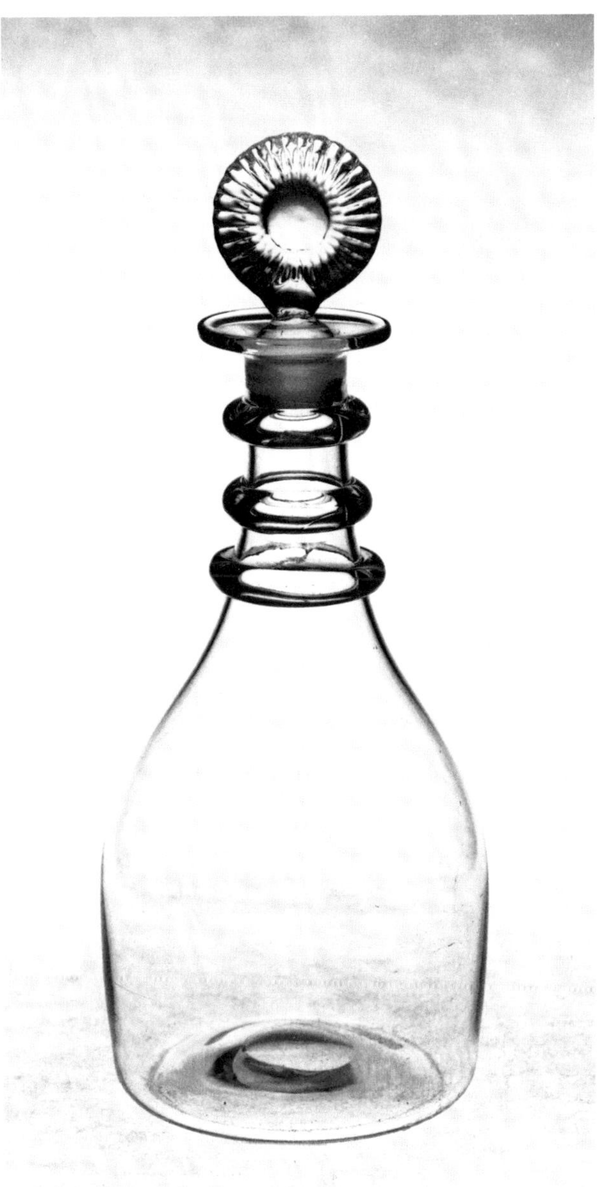

Cat. 27

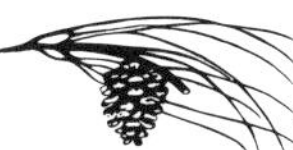

"The Appearance of Enterprise and Improvement": Architecture and the Coastal Elite of Southern Maine

Richard M. Candee

The changing physical appearance of southern Maine's older coastal towns in the decades following the American Revolution was the product of a region-wide building boom. A steady population increase and the revival of an energetic maritime economy stimulated the creation of new town centers. Traveling south from Portland in the 1790s one visitor noted:

The nearer you approach Boston, so much the more does the whole country appear to assume an air of business and industry. Not a creek but ships are building in it; not a river's mouth so small, but merchants companies are there in possession of ships; No situation where a mill could stand, on which there has not been a mill erected. Falmouth, Pepperellborough, Saco, Biddeford, Kennebunk, Berwick, carry on a trade far superior to that at the small towns through which I had passed on my way hither.[1]

During the next quarter century the villages of York, the Kennebunks, and Saco vied with newer inland settlements for primacy in York County. Portland's growth from the ashes of Falmouth occurred at a scale best compared to other urban seaports like Salem and Newburyport in Massachusetts or Portsmouth, New Hampshire. Each of these saw the construction of new brick commercial cores and stylish residences. These southern Maine coastal towns acted as market towns for the agricultural produce of the surrounding hinterlands, mixed maritime trade with shipbuilding, and profited from lumbering the District's timber-rich interior. Here, too, were the first governmental and administrative centers, shiretowns whose courts protected the investments of the mercantile elite, recorded land sales, and resolved disputes.

This essay focuses on the architecture of Portland and the York County coast in the context of the District of Maine's development.[2] It explores the impact of population growth on the creation or rebuilding of town centers, and the key role of the builder-architects in the visual transformation of their communities. Vernacular building for the larger population is ignored here in order to concentrate on the elite's domestic architecture as a useful index of the relative wealth in each town during the early republic. Employing a new architectural vocabulary that confirms their owners' position in society, these homes became outward symbols of individual enterprise and public improvement that marked their towns' prosperity.

Population Growth and Town Building

Not all towns of the southern coast were affected equally by the District's rapid population growth nor did they increase at the same rate in the decades between the Revolution and statehood. In the 1790s Judge David Sewall estimated that the ancient town of York had experienced a net population loss during the eighteenth century. The relatively stable population it achieved in the decades after 1800 (chart 1) did not reverse the effects of exporting both its capital and its talent. Timothy Dwight, visiting the town in 1807, felt "York wears a strong appearance of stillness and solitude. The houses, with few exceptions, together with the outbuildings, and fences, have in a peculiar degree, an air of antiquity."[3]

Perhaps to counter the impact of a static population, York protected its position as county shire against competition from both Kennebunk and Saco. The last major addition to the York County jail, originally built in 1720, was made in 1799 for a

Chart 1
Rate of Population Growth, 1790–1820

Town	1790	1800		1810		1820	
	pop.	*pop.*	*rate*	*pop.*	*rate*	*pop.*	*rate*
York	2900	2799	−4%	3065	10%	3224	5%
Wells	3070	3712	6%	4496	20%	2660	
Kennebunk*						2145	
Arundel	1802	1908	6%	2382	25%	2478	4%
Saco	1018	1846	80%	2494	30%	2532	1.5%
Portland	2240	3822	65%	7371	90%	8581	12%

*set off from Wells, 1820

Source: U.S. Census Abstracts

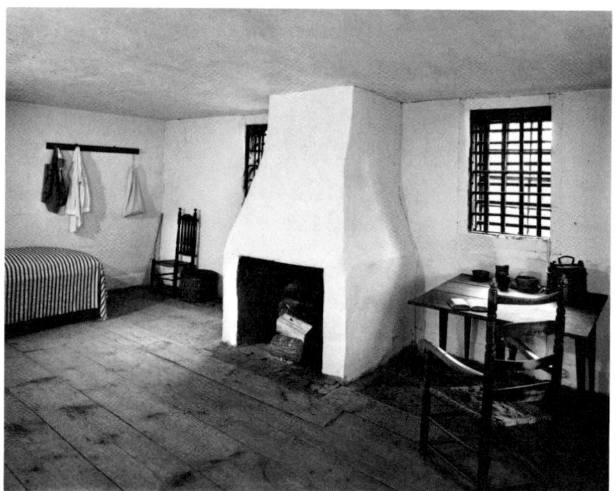

Fig. 2.1 Debtor's cell, Old Gaol, York, Maine, built 1799. Photograph, 1984. Old York Historical Society: Photo, Douglas Armsden.

improved in its building, and in its business." Ignatz Hülswitt, a German traveler arriving in Kennebunkport in 1820, saw "a small, entirely new town, scarely 40 years old. It has 200 homes, built very delicately of wood painted with the most vivid oil paints." Anne Royall predicted in 1828 that Saco would become "one of the most flourishing towns in the state." She noted the town was a port of entry and contained "a bank, an academy, and a population of about 2500 inhabitants" as well as large new textile mills soon to "go into operation."[6] Almost without exception, writers who sketched these coastal towns of Maine described their appearance in terms of "enterprise" and "improvement." Meetinghouses and mansions were visible symbols of an energetic economy and village growth.

Differing rates of population growth between 1790 and 1820, however, had specific consequences for the number and types of buildings in these towns. York had few large new homes built near its central meetinghouse. Already well-housed in older eighteenth-century buildings scattered over its land area, its successful merchants or lawyers were more apt to add to existing buildings rather than to build anew. Pepperrellborough's population almost doubled between 1790 and 1800, when the state sold the confiscated lands of Sir William Pepperrell. With newly available building lots, Saco's excess capital from the lumber trade was transformed into a local building boom as the population grew another 30 percent over the previous decade. Between these extremes, Wells and Arundel experienced only modest growth until the first decade of the new century. From the evidence of surviving buildings, most of their growth centered in the villages of the Kennebunks. The economic impact of the War of 1812, however, brought double-digit growth to a halt and led to a marked decline in building along the York County coast. With a few notable exceptions, new construction did not revive until after the District separated from Massachusetts.

Throughout these decades Portland was in the midst of

debtors' prison (fig. 2.1). Soon thereafter William Frost, the register of deeds, led an unsuccessful campaign to enlarge the courthouse in York, so "Gentlemen, Parties, Witnesses, and Spectators may be accomodated with a seat," and court officials "may be comfortable when there confined in tryal . . . without suffocation."[4] His efforts met greater success in 1811 when the "ancient building" holding the courts was described as having "from its size and decayed situation, become inconvenient." The county appropriated $500, the town of York voted another $600, and the leading citizens of York and Kittery added private funds or materials to finish a new frame 40' by 50', two stories high, located opposite the jail and a few feet from the old court.[5]

High rates of population growth in Wells's village of Kennebunk, in Arundel's Kennebunkport, and in Saco (originally called Pepperrellborough) brought these towns to nearly equal size during these years. Dwight, on his 1807 visit to Wells, found its second parish village "materially

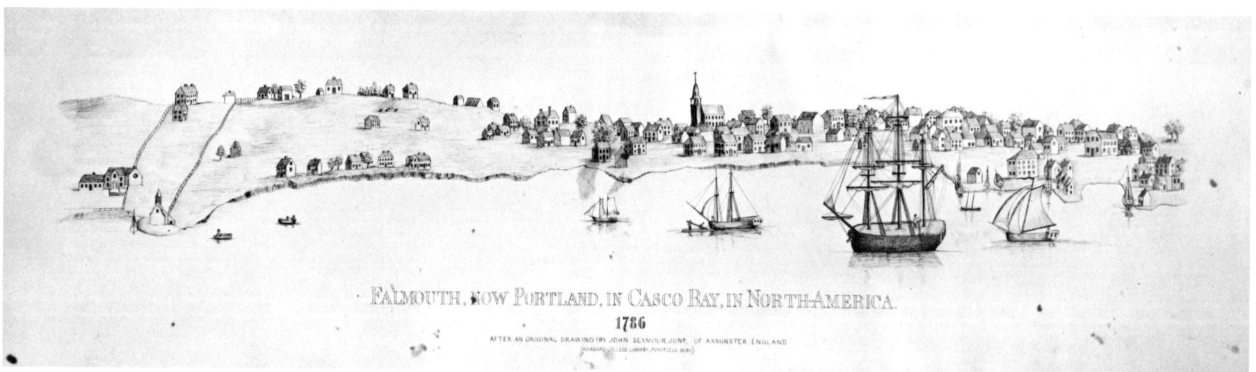

Fig. 2.2 *Falmouth, now Portland, in Casco Bay, in North America, 1786.* Print after a drawing by John Seymour, Jr. H 12½ (31.8), W 15¾ (40.0). Maine Historical Society.

Chart 2
Buildings Erected in Portland, 1784–1809

Building Type	1784–1786	1791–1795	1796–1800	1801–1805	1805–1809
Dwelling houses	90	62	114	158	53
additions to houses	0	11	46	12	13
Barns and stables	0	31	53	24	0
Shops	0	37	24	24	2
additions to shops	0	5	10	2	0
Stores	0	29	33	31	0
barns/shops/stores (combined)	0	0	7	40	3
Schools	0	0	3	1	0
Public buildings	0	0	2	1	0
Ropewalk / bank	0	0	0	2	0

Source: Willis, *Journals*

an almost continuous building boom. Beginning with a post-Revolutionary population almost as large as York, it nearly quadrupled its population by 1820 and became the leading port city in the District. By 1792 the 130 homes lost to the earlier fire had been replaced and another 200 added (fig. 2.2). Dwight found in 1797 that "the houses are new" and "many of them make a good appearance." A decade later, he wrote, "No place, in our route, hitherto, could for its improvements be compared to Portland. We found buildings extended quite to the cove, doubled in their number and still more increased in their appearance. Few towns in New England are equally beautiful and brilliant."[7]

The diaries of the Reverend Samuel Deane, the town's Congregational minister (cat. 29), detailed the number and types of construction in Portland from 1784 to 1809 (see chart 2). While not complete, these statistics provide a measure of the city's reconstruction during the early federal era unmatched for any other community.[8] New homes, like that of Thomas Robison, were laid out on large lots with gardens and outbuildings (cat. 38). After the immediate postwar replacement of the 1780s, Portland saw a healthy increase of new building every year until the Embargo began in December 1807. In spite of the economic collapse immediately following the Embargo, the city's population nearly doubled in the decade between 1800 and 1810. Moreover, in the following decade Portland experienced a further population increase of some 12 percent despite its slow economic recovery. This was more than double the rate of the more stable towns to the south. When Anne Royall visited Portland in the 1820s, she described it as "the handsomest town in the U. States." What made it so, were not only the city's fine public buildings but also, in her view, "the dwelling houses [which] are decidedly the handsomest of any town in the Union."[9]

Men and Women of Property, 1815–1816

The interrelationship of York County families, whose federal-era possessions survive in the decorative arts collections of local museums, suggests the existence of a small economic and social elite. So do the relatively small number of high-style federal dwellings in these coastal towns. Portland's later fires destroyed much of its pre-1820 architecture; what evidence survives needs to be placed in a larger context. The builders of these structures must be studied with an eye to their place in the social order.

The mid-1810s provide a convenient point at which to examine local economic stratification. By that time, those who were wealthy enough to acquire land for a new home could have done so. Moreover, state tax records exist for York County in 1816 and local tax assessments survive for Portland in 1815. Each provides a list of the local hierarchy, measured by property, after the economic shakeout following the Embargo and war.

In the five York County towns, there were 1,774 taxpayers assessed in 1816; only 33 individuals paid more than $11 in taxes. This small group, roughly 2 percent of the whole for these towns, paid more than 20 percent of the total tax. Valuations on their lands and buildings ranged from $5,000 to over $30,000 in the unique case of Thomas Cutts's personal holdings. At the opposite end of the social scale were the 994 people (over 55 percent of the total population) who paid less than $2 in tax. George Emery of Wells, assessed four cents in taxes for two empty acres of land, was perhaps the lowest taxpayer. Farmhouses of this majority of ratepayers were geographically scattered throughout their towns and generally seen by visitors as ill-kept. One-story Cape Cod homes were described as "poor cabins," while even larger farms "portray extreme poverty; and not a few of them have boards hung out, on which are uncouth inscriptions offering *"spiritous liquors for sale"* (cat. 40).[10]

For Portland in 1815, with about 1,200 resident and nonresident property owners, taxes totaled $15,403.31 in assessments. Roughly 20 percent of the population paid more than $15 in local property tax, while the highest 2 percent (24 taxpayers) paid over $68 each but accounted for one-quarter of the total revenue. Of this small group of individuals or businesses, three men were each assessed over $400 in taxes (although one later had his abated to $395). Below these three merchants, the next assessment was less than $200.

Thus, in the small coastal towns as well as in Portland, there were a few extremely wealthy property holders who paid nearly one-quarter of their towns' taxes. If any families were likely to have participated in the building activity of the preceding decades, theoretically, they would have been from this group. Research should prove they each owned expensive new federal-style homes in their communities. Where this does not prove true, as in York, it may define underlying conditions required for the introduction of new architectural styles and help clarify our ideas about those who need to express their position in society through building.

Chart 3 identifies thirty-three members of this York County elite with the number of acres, houses, and outbuildings for which each was taxed by this 1816 state assessment. What is immediately clear from this data is that most owned two or three dwellings, some in more than one town. Only about one-third of this group owned merely one home and just three people had but a single barn or other secondary structure on their land. For the wealthiest of the coastal towns, and probably many more in the top 10 percent of the tax list, property was an investment. Land was not just held, it was acquired to be developed, leased, or (in the case of stores, wharves, and other commercial sites) managed in partnership.

Little is known about early rental property in southern Maine, and less about the relationship between wealthy landholders and their tenants. It is clear, however, that many village houses were let to those who could not afford to own. William Frost of York, while not in the top 2 percent of the 1816 list, was among the highest 10 percent. In 1810 he leased to one James Hart a "Certain tenement and House Lot" with a barn, a well, and necessary house in York Village. Hart agreed to pay Frost $25 that year, to fix a broken window, and promised not to break other windows or damage the floors and partitions in the house. Daniel Cleaves, who owned several farms (as well as a dozen business properties in partnership with others), rented Lemuel McCorrison a Biddeford farm in 1809 for $45 a year and gave him nine days rights to use the so-called bog grist mill that year. Likewise, Captain Seth Storer had not only his own house, but also an outlying farm in Saco. At the time of his death a few years later his holdings had increased to include his own 19-acre homestead with 2 barns and a shed, 3 rented houses, part of a store, several lots of land, and 168 acres on the Buxton road with a house and barn occupied by a tenant farmer.[11]

The tax lists for these highest York, Wells, Arundel, and Saco taxpayers suggest some surprising conclusions. York had the greatest number (ten) in this top 2 percent, although none of these had land and buildings individually assessed over $10,000 in value. Saco had six men in this group with two also owning property on the Biddeford side of the river. Colonel Thomas Cutts tops the list with 5 houses, 14 out-buildings, and 1,640 acres in his own name and nearly as many in partnerships. Daniel Cleaves was a distant second

with more property in partnerships than he held in his own name.

York's most prosperous families were the most dispersed, with at least half occupying outlying farms; only three homes in the village center near the town meetinghouse or the river harbor were owned by those shown in chart 3. In both York and Wells many dwellings of the wealthiest families were earlier eighteenth-century homes, although several were remodeled and enlarged during this era. On the other hand, all the homes of this elite group located in Kennebunkport and Saco, and most of those in Wells (Kennebunk), were new products of the population and building boom that created their village centers.

The building of large and substantial new homes among a small mercantile elite was even more evident in Portland. With few pre-Revolutionary buildings surviving the fire of 1775 and its population almost doubling every ten years, the city attracted some twenty known architect-builders to provide the new residential, commercial, and public buildings it needed. A comparable list of the highest taxpayers in Portland (chart 4) is supplemented, from other sources, by the date and location of the individual's residence and the name of any associated architect or builder.

Unlike the state assessment of the smaller coastal towns, the Portland list did not differentiate multiple properties under single ownership. For example, Asa Clapp's and Matthew Cobb's taxes must have included vast property holdings besides their own houses, wharves, stores, and distilleries. Well-known federal-era homes, like that built for Sheriff Richard Hunnewell, cannot be identified in the tax list. Matthew Cobb held the mortgage on that house in 1812 before foreclosing in 1816. In fact, nearly all the houses designed by the city's most talented young architect, Alexander Parris, were owned by this small group or still held and leased by banks after failures caused by the Embargo and war.

These mansions, as described by Anne Royall, were "high, large, exactly square" and of bright red brick, terraced or set out on large lots, with "four fronts, that is windows and doors on all sides."[12] The three-story homes, like those of the newest style built for federal-era merchant princes of Boston and Salem, were nearly square blocks beneath low hipped roofs with decorative balustrades. This form was soon to be copied by local builders in other coastal towns, supplanting the house types first favored by members of southern Maine's elite before 1800.

Post-Revolutionary Homes
of the Coastal Elite, 1789–1800

Several of the largest houses in Maine built immediately after the Revolution were two-story, gambrel-roofed buildings with dormer windows lighting a finished attic, classically

Name	Town	Acres	Houses	Outbuildings	Value	Tax
Capt. Thomas Cutts	Saco	1386	3	10	$24,304.	$53.47
Capt. T. Cutts	Biddeford	254	2	4	5,219.	11.48
Capt. T. Cutts and 21 partners	Saco	1025	12	12½	20,984.	44.75
Daniel Cleaves	Biddeford	241+	2	3	6,614.	14.55
Daniel Cleaves and 11 partners	Saco	286	11	11	12,089.	30.00
Daniel Cleaves and 3 partners	Biddeford	90	3	3	1,779.	3.39
Joseph Storer, Esq.	Wells	631	3	9	12,525.	27.56
Mrs. Nathaniel Lord	Arundel	1+	3	5	12,225.	26.90
Tobias Lord	Arundel	1+	3	6	10,642.	23.42
Eliphelet Perkins	Arundel/Wells	22	3	3	9,567.	21.05
Micum McIntire heirs	York	452	3	3	7,804.	17.17
Mrs. Edward Emerson	York	191	2	3	7,750.	17.05
William Jefferds	Wells	356	2	10	7,740.	17.03
Capt. Seth Storer	Saco	55	2	6	7,525.	16.56
Foxwell Cutts, Esq.	Saco	19	1	3	7,525.	16.55
Capt. Daniel Walker	Arundel	113	2	5	7,256.	15.97
John U. Parsons	Wells	50+	2	3	7,047.	15.51
Maj. Simon Nowell	Arundel	3+	3½	4	7,009.	15.42
Hon. Cyrus King	Saco	19	2	3	6,880.	15.14
Isaac Lyman, Esq.	York	142	2	5	6,485.	14.27
Samuel McIntire	York	238	1	2⅔	6,450.	14.19
Daniel Sewall	York/Wells	18	1	2	6,250.	13.79
Thomas G. Thornton	Saco	54+	1	4	6,152.	13.54
Col. Moses Lyman	York	100	1	1	6,127.	13.48
Samuel Preble	York	260	1	1	6,020.	13.25
Joseph Leland, Esq.	Saco	12+	2	3	5,027.	12.82
Nahum Morrell	Wells	387+	2	6	5,822.	12.81
Capt. Joseph Perkins	Arundel	241+	2	3	5,643.	12.42
Hugh McCullock	Arundel/Wells	166+	6	8	6,471.	13.54
Isaac Kimball	Wells	155	1	3½	5,380.	11.84
Samuel Sewall, Esq.	York	200	1	4	5,375.	11.83
John Barrell	York	208	1	4	5,160.	11.35
Elijah Blaisdell	York	152	1	3	5,160.	11.35
Michael Wise	Wells	145	2	6	5,138.	11.30
Capt. Jos. Hatch	Wells	109	2	4	5,052.	11.12
Hon. David Sewall	York	125	1	1	5,052.	11.12
Jacob Wildes, Esq.	Arundel	164	1	3	5,047.	11.11

Source: Massachusetts Assessments, 1816

ornamented front doorways and windows, and often a large gambrel ell in the rear. Their Georgian "double pile" plan, with a central hallway separating two rooms on either side and each pair of rooms divided by a large chimney, was adopted by many leading New England families. Such forms were common in Salem, Newburyport, and Portsmouth as homes of the urban gentry, as well as among the rural elite of the Connecticut Valley, throughout the mid-eighteenth century.[13] Sparhawk Hall, built by Sir William Pepperrell in 1742 for the wedding of his daughter to Nathaniel Sparhawk, near his own home (itself a large gambrel-roofed mansion) at Kittery Point, Maine, was a classic example of this type (fig. 2.3).

When Thomas Cutts built his new dwelling house in

Chart 4
Top 2 Percent of Taxpayers, Portland, Maine, 1815

Name	Tax*	House date	Address and/or designer
Asa Clapp	$469.49	1794	corner Elm and Congress streets, Alexander Parris (remodeled 1804)
Matthew Cobb	438.48	1801	corner High and Free streets, Alexander Parris
Arthur McLellen	402.48	1800	corner Portland and High streets
William Widgery, Esq.	196.72	1797	
Benjamin Welles	166.12		
Ralph Cross	147.44	1792	brick house, Fore Street
Robert Boyd	142.32	1804	Alexander Parris
Isaac Ilsley	122.48	1802	brick house, Spring Street
Harry Smith & Co.	118.76		
Joseph Cross	117.36		
James Deering (non-res.)	116.48	1804	barn, Alexander Parris, 1805
Thomas Brown	114.80		
John Hobart	112.12	1793	Fore Street
William Chadwick	105.84		
Edward Porter	105.20		
Reuben Marlen	102.52		
Israel Richardson	100.60		
Thomas Robison	92.60	1784	Park Street
Widow Mary Preble	89.40	1806–7	Congress Street, Alexander Parris
Cotton B. Brooks	82.80		
Samuel Trask	75.00		
Joseph Pope	70.52		
Prentiss Mellen, Esq.	68.72	1807	State Street, Thomas Eaton
Thomas Beck	68.60		

Source: 1815 Portland tax assessment

1782 (figs. 2.8.1 and 3.6), it was remarkably similar to the earlier Sparhawk Hall. Having served Pepperrell as a clerk, Cutts (cat. 33) came to Saco in 1758 as a trader. He amassed a fortune in the timber trade during the next twenty-five years, wealth which he expressed in his new mansion on Indian (later Factory) Island. Built by four brothers named Moody, Cutts's mansion echoed Sparhawk Hall in its large scale, central-hall plan, and five asymmetrically placed front window bays. Both facades had triangular first-floor window pediments and a fine broken-scroll pediment with a central plinth over the center door, features repeated in the dormers above. The second-floor windows of the facade were undecorated; like those at Sparhawk Hall, they ran nearly to the cornice. The Cutts mansion substituted quoins for Sparhawk's corner pilasters, as had the builders of the 1760 mansion for Sir William Pepperrell's widow at Kittery. The choice of such a home, like the heraldic coats of arms made for leading families (cats. 73–74, 142) in the years immediately following the Revolution, suggests the role Cutts saw for himself in Pepperrellborough.

Theodore Lyman's house at Kennebunk Landing (1784) was a smaller version of the same type (fig. 3.2). It was one of several gambrel houses on the central-hall plan built in the Kennebunks during the first decade after the end of the Revolution. Similar examples (fig. 2.2) could also be found in Portland. These post-colonial Georgian mansions continued traditional symbols of class and wealth into the landscape of the early republic.

Such elaborate post-colonial Georgian mansions were apparently unknown in York. The central-chimney house appears to have been nearly ubiquitous there throughout the eighteenth century, even among the most affluent yeomen and merchants.[14] When more rooms were needed, most York homes were redesigned by additions. The heirs of Micum McIntire, the most affluent family in York, continued to live in rural Scotland parish. Jeremiah McIntire inherited the 1710 McIntire log garrison in 1815 and may have built the two-story lateral extension at one end (fig. 2.4). More commonly, extension of a central-chimney house was made at right angles to the main block. Joseph Sayward had built such an L-shaped house about 1720, joining the whole under a pitched roof angled at the front by a hipped corner (fig. 3.4). It later became the home of Judge Jonathan Sayward, one of York's eighteenth-century leaders.

As the Pepperrells set the style for other local squires, perhaps Sayward set a similar standard in York. There are a number of York houses composed of one-room-deep, central-chimney cores to which a rear ell was later added. The resulting form, approached from its hipped corner, gave the appearance of a large, square, Georgian-plan block. One of the most interesting of these, Barrell Grove, was listed in the 1816 tax assessment of John Barrell, Judge Jonathan Sayward's grandson.

Barrell Grove (fig. 2.5) took its name from Nathaniel Barrell (cat. 32), the eccentric and controversial Boston and Portsmouth merchant who became Jonathan Sayward's son-in-law. Sayward bought the farm in 1760 (about the time he remodeled his late father's house) and the Barrells resided here during the Revolution as Nathaniel's own property was confiscated on account of his Tory leanings. When Judge Sayward died in 1797 he left the farm to his daughter Sarah, and on her death, to his grandson, John Barrell. Nathaniel and Sarah Barrell had eleven children, of whom Sally Sayward Barrell, the novelist later known as Madam Wood, was the eldest (fig. 5.2).[15] To hold this large family, a new ell with its own pedimented entrance was added to the old farmhouse by the 1770s (fig. 2.6). By 1816, two more outbuildings, in addition to the older barn and cider house, had been constructed.

The additive quality of Barrell Grove can be seen in the building histories of several prominent homes near the York meetinghouse. The old house occupied by Edward Emerson, Sr. (fig. 2.7), at the corner of Lindsay Road opposite the county jail, was enlarged in this way, creating a second facade on York Street across from the courthouse. The house served as a tavern and stage stop between Portsmouth and Portland from 1784 to 1826, first under the Emersons, then, after 1816, under jailkeeper David Wilcox. Wilcox served as postmaster from 1821 to 1829, so he added another ell to the west end of the house for the post office. Nearly a dozen other L-shaped homes survive in and around York Village. Some, like the Matthew Lindsay tavern, were enlargements of earlier homes; others were newly built in variations on this plan after the 1790s. Squire Alexander McIntire, collector of customs, built a home about 1812 that was "considered a noble structure, and inferior to none in this town, except Judge David Sewall's."[16]

Nor was York unique in its preference for this type of housing. A most striking post-colonial central-chimney house originally, constructed with a two-story ell and its own end chimney, was that at Kennebunk Landing occupied in 1816 by the shipbuilder Hugh McCulloch (fig. 3.3). Built by Thatcher Goddard soon after the Revolution, it continued the Georgian vocabulary in the use of the pedimented dormer windows in a high hipped roof.[17] The greater convenience of this plan led others to transform older, smaller homes in this way. Blacksmith James Kimball's Kennebunk home, built about 1763, had an ell added for a larger new parlor and straight-run staircase in the early nineteenth century. Likewise, the mid-eighteenth-century home of Colonel Joseph Storer, who died in the Revolution, was improved by his son Joseph. The new ell and side entrance, two-story pilasters, and balustrade hiding the low roofline, may have been added by the time of Joseph Storer's marriage in 1808; it long remained the home of Kennebunk's highest taxpayer.[18]

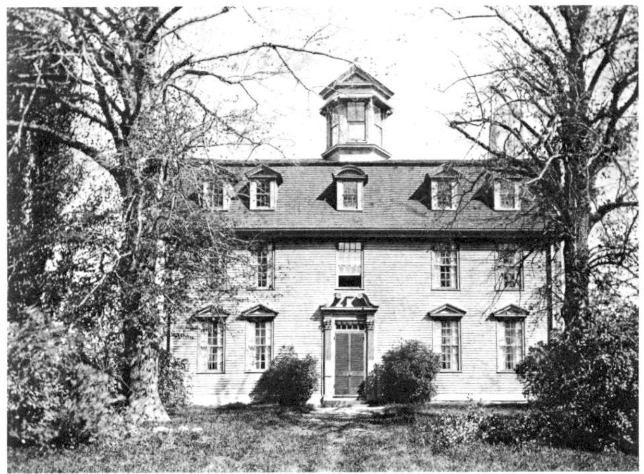

Fig. 2.3 Sparhawk Hall, Kittery Point, Maine, 1742. Demolished 1967. Photograph, ca. 1882. Courtesy, Society for the Preservation of New England Antiquities.

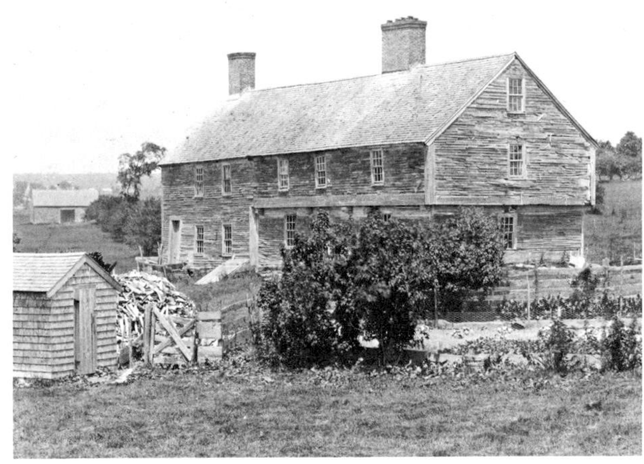

Fig. 2.4 McIntire Garrison, Scotland Parish, York, Maine, ca. 1711, with late eighteenth-century additions. Photograph, 1895–1915. Courtesy, Society for the Preservation of New England Antiquities.

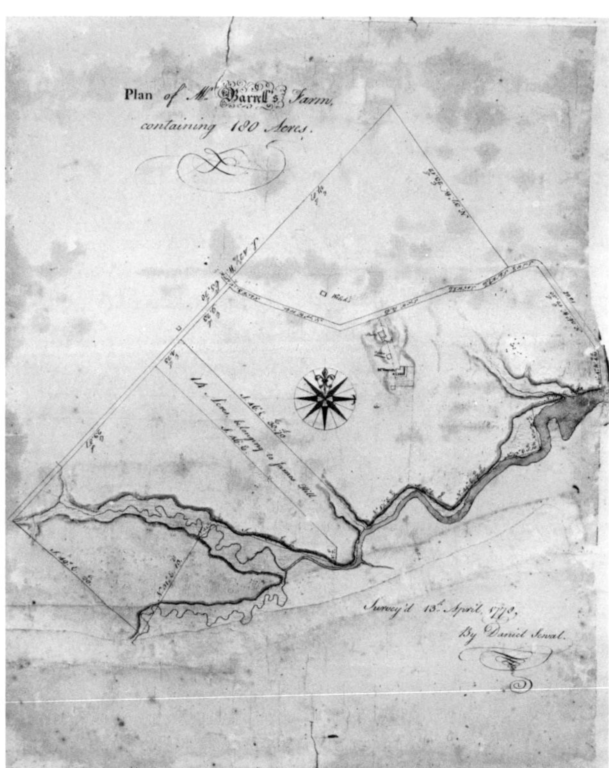

Fig. 2.5 *Plan of Mr. Barrell's Farm* , York, Maine, 1778. Pen and ink and watercolor on paper; H 17¾ (45.1), w 14½ (36.8). Private collection.

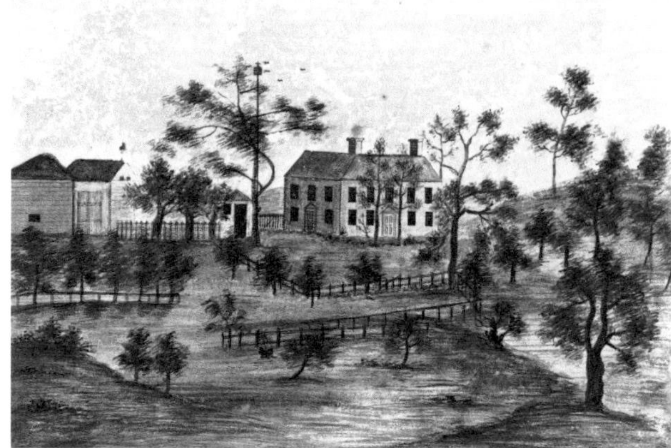

Fig. 2.6 Sophia Sewall Wood Monroe (1788–1878), *Barrell Homestead*, York, Maine, ca. 1800. Pen and ink and watercolor on paper; H 5¾ (14.6), w 8⅜ (21.3). Private collection.

Cleaves did. Across one end of this typical block he also built, possibly after 1804, a long room the entire depth of the house (fig. 2.8.3). The whole two-story extended house was covered by a hipped roof. The large single room had its own end chimney, which also warmed two chambers above, and its own front and rear doors as well as internal doors to the rest of the house. At the rear, a bulkhead led to apple bins in the cellar. Its hillside position permitted an unusual front portico, built over a staircase from street level, with a carriage house beneath.[20]

Architect-Builders of Southern Maine, 1795–1815

Some members of the local elite continued to own or build traditional houses with a central-chimney, five-room floor plan or with the Georgian plan of two rooms on either side of a central hall. However, new variations of the L-shaped plan appear at the end of the century. At the corner of Union and Main streets in Kennebunkport is a one-room-deep house built in 1805 by house-joiner Samuel Davis for Simon Nowell. Nowell was a taverner and by 1816 was among the upper 2 percent of the town's wealthiest men. His house had two chimneys, giving each room a fireplace without requiring the old central stack. One chimney was placed against an end wall and another was set behind the rear wall near the juncture of the ell. Floor plans employing multiple chimneys in various locations became common in new houses after about 1800. This generally relegated the kitchen to the rear ell, freed the stairway from the central chimney stack, and provided two formal ground-floor rooms.[21]

In 1816 Captain Joseph Perkins owned two houses, including one of this new type which is still located above the Kennebunkport wharves. One room deep, with a central hallway, it has two chimney stacks inside the back wall of the house; one originally heated both the front room and a

Other ways of modifying an older central-chimney house could also be seen during the last years of the eighteenth century. In 1816 Abigail Emerson, the widow of Edward Emerson, Jr., was the second highest taxpayer in York. The younger Emerson's home, in the heart of the village, was a mid-eighteenth-century central-chimney house of two-room plan that had formerly been used as a tavern. After Edward Emerson bought it in May 1794 for $2,250, he reoriented it toward the street by adding a broad central hallway across the back of the old house and two new rooms beyond (figs. 2.8.4 and 2.9). With its new southern facade and tall hipped roof, the old house was transformed into a two-story, double-pile, post-colonial Georgian mansion. Judge Sayward recorded in November 1795 that he enjoyed "agreeable entertainment with a number of gentlemen and their wives at Mr. Edward Emerson Jun'r at his remove into his elegant House."[19]

Daniel Cleaves's Biddeford home (fig. 2.10), located on a rise above his wharves and opposite Saco Village, represents yet another variation on the traditional New England central-chimney house. At its core was a five-room, central-chimney, and "leanto" plan, but with a range of three rooms across the rear at *both* stories. Five-room floor plans were common throughout the eighteenth century at only the first story (the "saltbox") or including the second story as kitchen in the rear ell. Both the main block and its ell are covered by straight gabled roofs without the typical hipped corner. If its 1790s date is correct, it may reflect a rapid impact on local vernacular building from such stylish houses as Coventry Hall in York (fig. 2.11) and the Frost house in Kennebunk which made their appearance in the same decade.

Coventry Hall was the home of the first federal justice in Maine, Judge David Sewall (fig. 4.2), who married for the second time in 1790. Located directly across the street from the Edward Emerson, Jr., house, Coventry Hall was York Village's only elaborate, completely new mansion of the federal era. Jonathan Sayward noted on July 31, 1794: "Judge Sewall his Grand new house was raised[;] it will when finished be one of the Grandest built in the County." On November 11, 1796, Susanna Emerson and her husband Edward Emerson, Jr., "went to Judge Sewall's new house to see them the first time since they have moved." The next day Sayward described the "agreeable company at Judge Sewalls at his New . . . very Elegant House."[22]

Set upon a broad terraced front lawn enclosed within a fence of urn-topped posts, the two-story mansion is L-shaped but the main block is more than one room deep (fig. 2.8.5). The main rooms are separated by a wide central stair hall; these stairs lead to a hallway that in turn leads to smaller rooms behind and connects large and small rooms along the length of the ell. A pair of chimneys heat three rooms on each floor. Another in the ell contains built-in kettles next to the kitchen fireplace and a smoke-room off the small end room on the second floor. These chimneys rise above a low hipped roof partly hidden by the balustrade of alternating solid panels, attic dormers, and open railings with turned balusters. Its width (including the rear ell) more than equals that of the main facade. The ell is connected to sheds and a stable set at an angle to the main block. In scale and proportion, as well as in decorative embellishment, Coventry Hall set a new standard for the region's domestic architecture.

In contrast to surrounding vernacular buildings, its facade was ornamented with neoclassical elements akin to designs recently built in Boston by Charles Bulfinch or those emerging along the upper Connecticut River in the work of Asher Benjamin. This treatment was very different than the earlier introduction of Adamesque detailing in Portsmouth. There it was mainly expressed in the interior finish of the ca. 1785 Woodbury Langdon brick house. Begun in 1794, Coventry Hall was with Montpelier, General Knox's Thomaston home built during the same years, one of the first high-style neoclassical seats in the District of Maine. Sewall's Coventry Hall facade is flush-boarded and divided by four two-story Ionic pilasters supporting entablature blocks under the cornice, refinements which echo the somewhat heavier features of the 1760 facade of the Lady Pepperrell house at Kittery Point. Sewall's central doorway is set off by a pair of engaged columns and pilasters supporting a broken entablature and an elliptical fanlight in the newest style. Inside, the parlor and chamber mantels are decorated with some of the same "composition" swags, urns, and floral chains as Bulfinch's 1795–1796 first Harrison Gray Otis house in Boston or the 1797 Captain James Means house in the Stroudwater section of Portland.

In its adoption of the "antique" Ionic order with "Greecian" molding profiles, the facade of the house was either entirely avant-garde for 1794–1797 New England or the product of a major remodeling based on published sources ten or more years later. There is no known evidence that Sewall remodeled his home in later years or any reason to expect him to have done so. It is, therefore, important to seek precedents for major features of this house among urban commissions of the early 1790s. Bulfinch, for example, used giant order Ionic pilasters on the Tontine Crescent (1793–1794) in Boston, including a combination of pilasters and attached columns like that of Sewall's doorway. The Tontine Crescent, probably derived from Robert Adam's 1768–1772 London project known as the Adelphi, was one of many major Bulfinch commissions by which the elements of Greek antiquity were introduced to Boston. The elliptical fanlight, uncommon in Maine until after 1800, first appears in Bulfinch's work in a drawing for the 1791–1792 Boston home of Joseph Coolidge, Sr. The upper stories of the Coolidge house were based on Robert Adam's 1772–1774 Royal Society of Arts in London. Its fanlight, like that at Coventry Hall, was used in combination with paired pilasters and/or columns beneath a broken entablature. In Salem, Samuel McIntire began using the elliptical fanlight as early as 1793, presumably on the basis of having seen Bulfinch's work. Bulfinch's 1795 plans for Joseph Coolidge,

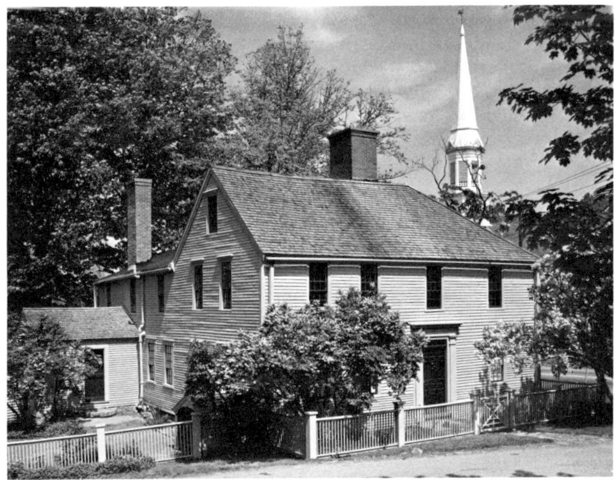

Fig. 2.7 Emerson-Wilcox house, York, Maine, ca. 1742, with 1760–1821 additions. Photograph, 1984. Old York Historical Society: Photo, Douglas Armsden.

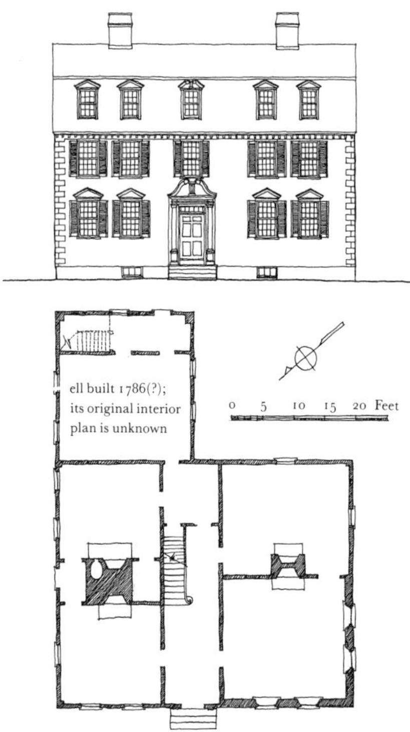

Fig. 2.8.1 Floor plan and elevation, Cutts house, Saco, Maine, 1782. Drawing, Scott Benson after Historic American Buildings Survey.

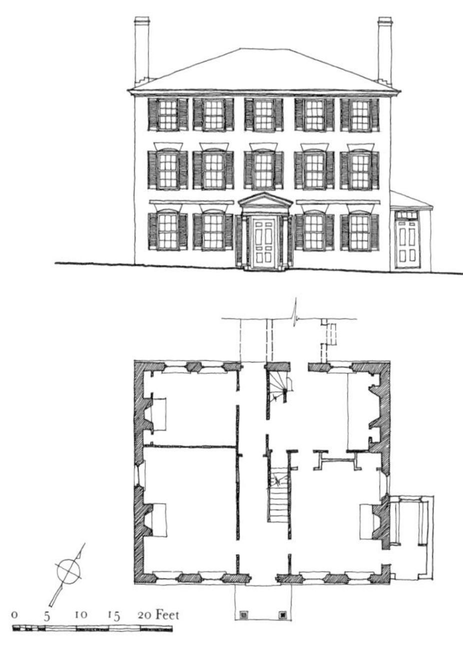

Fig. 2.8.2 Floor plan and elevation, Wadsworth-Longfellow house, Portland, Maine, 1785, with 1815 alterations. Drawing, Scott Benson after Historic American Buildings Survey.

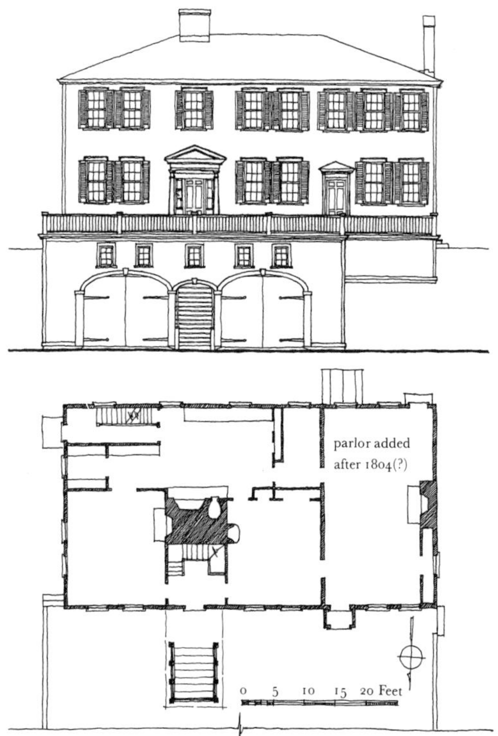

Fig. 2.8.3 Floor plan and elevation, Cleaves house, Biddeford, Maine, 1791(?), with additions by 1804. Drawing, Scott Benson after William E. Barry.

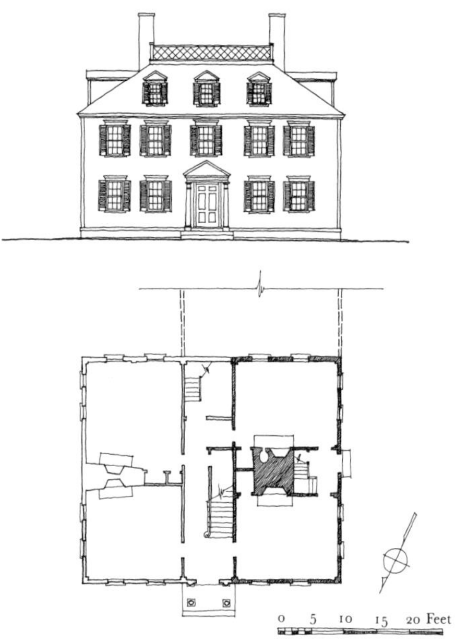

Fig. 2.8.4 Floor plan and elevation, Edward Emerson, Jr., house, York, Maine, 1740, with alterations ca. 1795. Drawing, Scott Benson and Thomas C. Hubka.

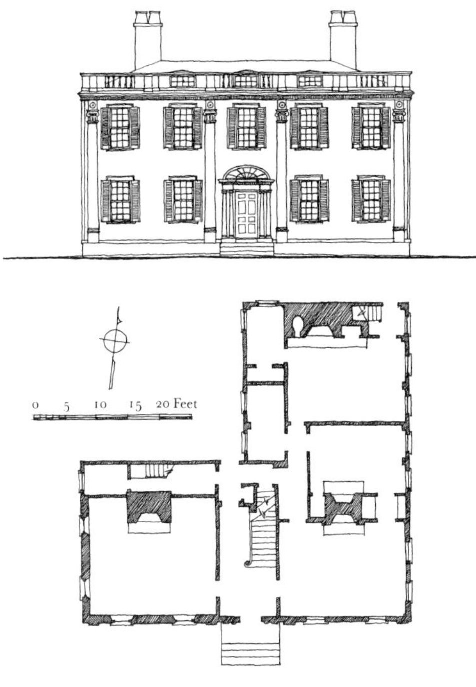

Fig. 2.8.5 Floor plan and elevation, Coventry Hall, York, Maine, 1794–1796. Drawing, Scott Benson after Frederick Porter.

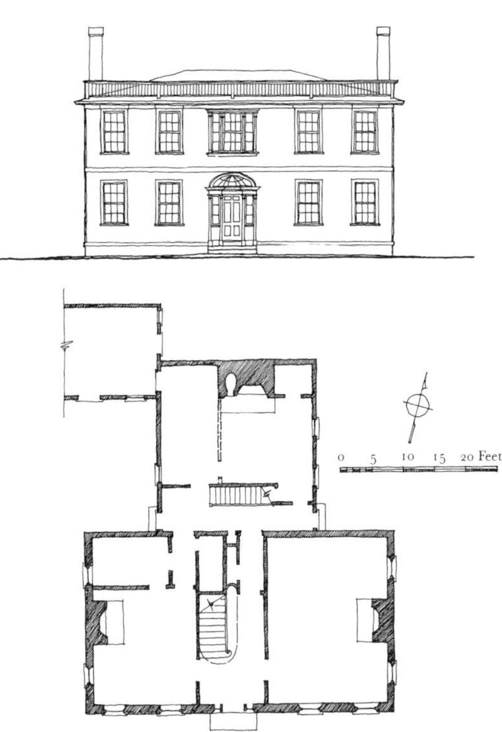

Fig. 2.8.6 Floor plan and elevation, Wallingford Hall, Kennebunk, Maine, ca. 1804. Drawing, Scott Benson after Orrin S. Ross, 1883.

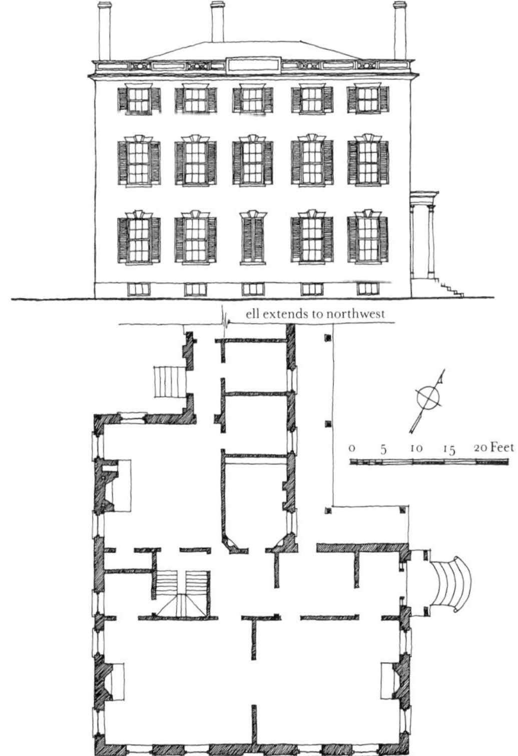

Fig. 2.8.7 Floor plan and elevation, Preble house, Portland, Maine, 1806–1807. Drawing, Scott Benson after Alexander Parris, 1805.

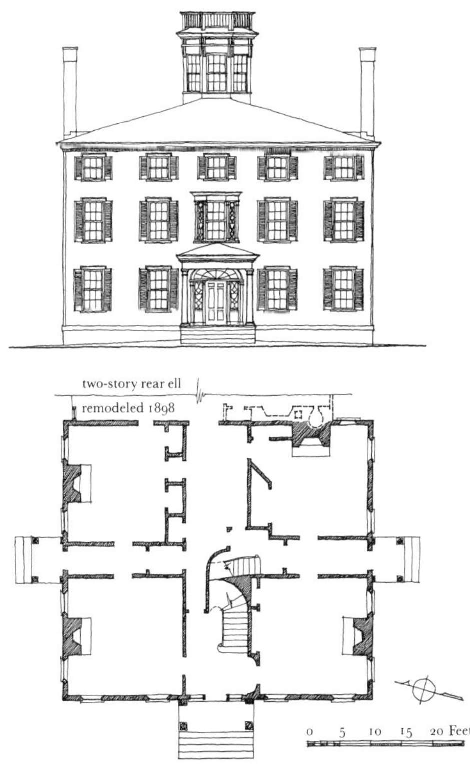

Fig. 2.8.8 Floor plan and elevation, Nathaniel Lord house, Kennebunkport, Maine, 1815. Drawing, Scott Benson after Joseph P. Clark.

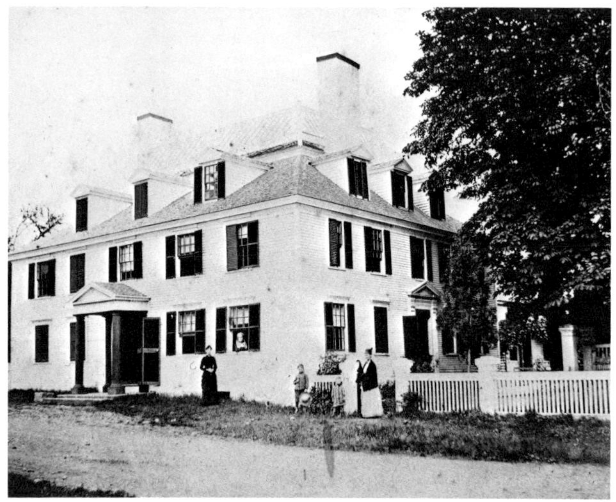

Fig. 2.9 Edward Emerson, Jr., house, York, Maine, ca. 1740, with alterations ca. 1795. Photograph, ca. 1890. Private collection.

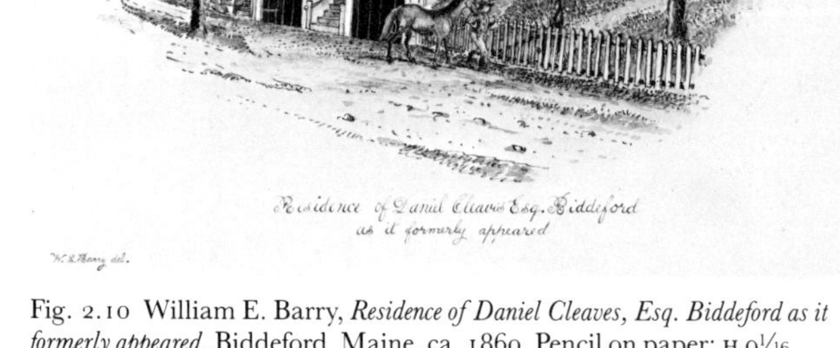

Fig. 2.10 William E. Barry, *Residence of Daniel Cleaves, Esq. Biddeford as it formerly appeared*, Biddeford, Maine, ca. 1860. Pencil on paper; H 9¹⁄₁₆ (23.0), W 12 (30.5). York Institute Museum.

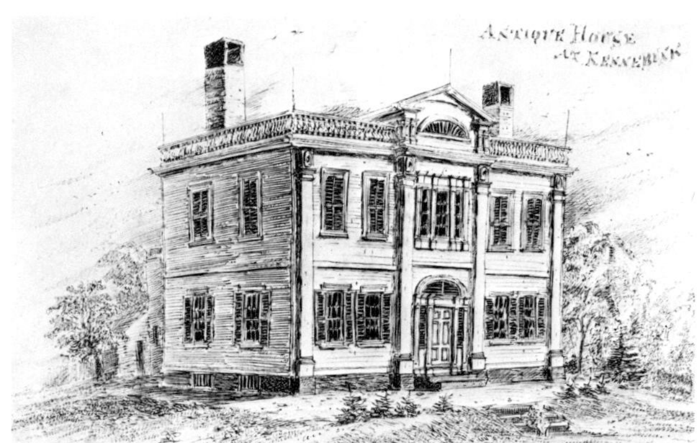

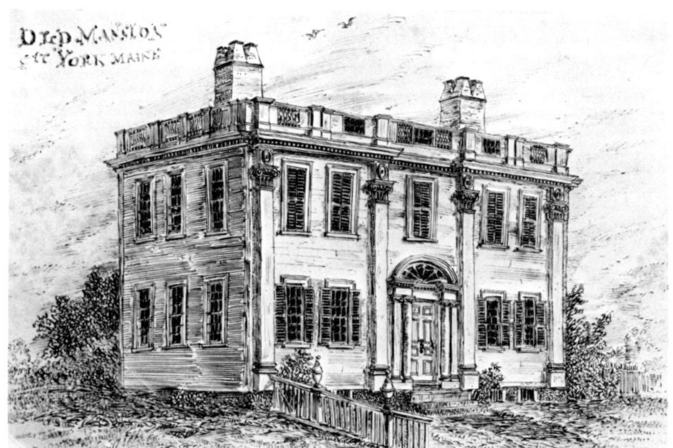

Fig. 2.11 William E. Barry, *Antique House at Kennebunk* (Jonas Clark house above). Pen and ink on paper; H 5⅝ (14.3), W 9¼ (23.5). *Old Mansion at York Maine* (Coventry Hall below). Pen and ink on paper; H 6¹⁄₁₆ (15.4), W 9¼ (23.5). For *Pen Sketches of Old Houses* (Boston, 1874). The Brick Store Museum.

Jr.'s, house and first Harrison Gray Otis house, both in Boston's expanding west end, employ rear ells that mask an intermediate room between the parlor and the kitchen similar to the plan of Coventry Hall.[23]

Although the tools to make advanced neoclassical embellishments were not commonly available to Maine carpenters until much later, Bulfinch's designs must have influenced many ambitious builders in Boston.[24] They impressed McIntire in Salem, to whom Coventry Hall has sometimes been attributed. He was soon duplicating the new style as did many urban craftsmen in Boston. To accept the early date of Coventry Hall's facade one does not have to attribute the design directly to either Bulfinch or McIntire. There were several Boston housewrights and joiners who could have been employed by Sewall to design and build a major commission such as this.

Although the designer or builder of Coventry Hall is not known, its great similarity to several Kennebunk homes, including that of another judge, suggests it may be the work of Thomas Eaton. The Judge Jonas Clark house (fig. 2.11) is one of a small group of Kennebunk buildings traditionally assigned to Eaton, a local housewright who married at Wells in 1793. Few of these are well documented except for the enlargement of the Kennebunk meetinghouse in 1803–1804, during which Eaton nearly fell from the roof.[25] The spire Eaton added to the meetinghouse, moreover, helps link many of the buildings attributed to his hand during the earliest years of his work. The three-stage tower (fig. 2.12.1) suggests that Eaton had access to Asher Benjamin's *The Country Builder's Assistant* (1797), the first American architectural builder's guide (fig. 2.12.2). The octagonal upper stages, above the open archways of the belfry, echo Benjamin's

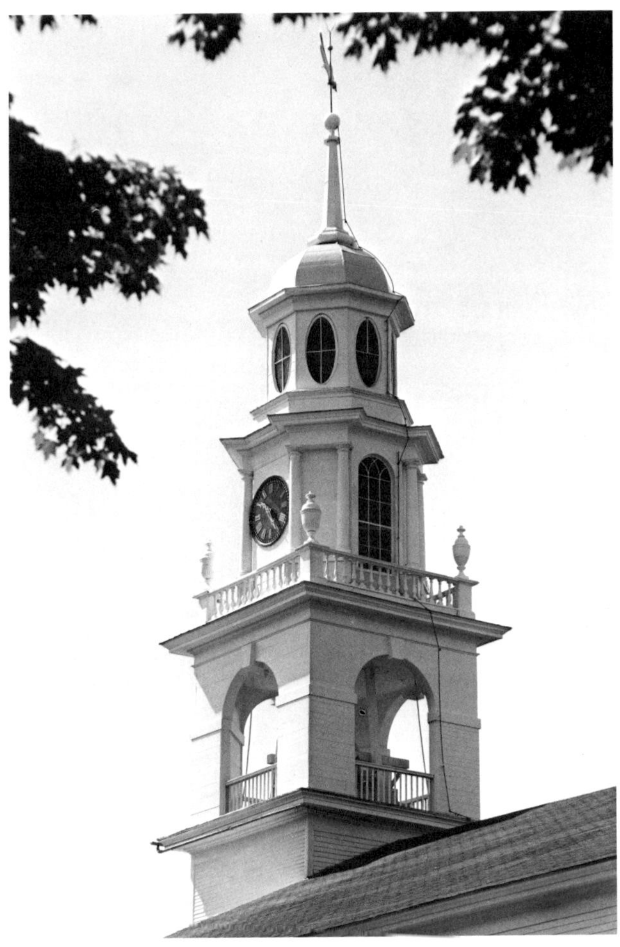

Fig. 2.12.1 Spire, First Parish Church, Kennebunk, Maine, 1803. Thomas Eaton, architect-builder. Historic American Buildings Survey.

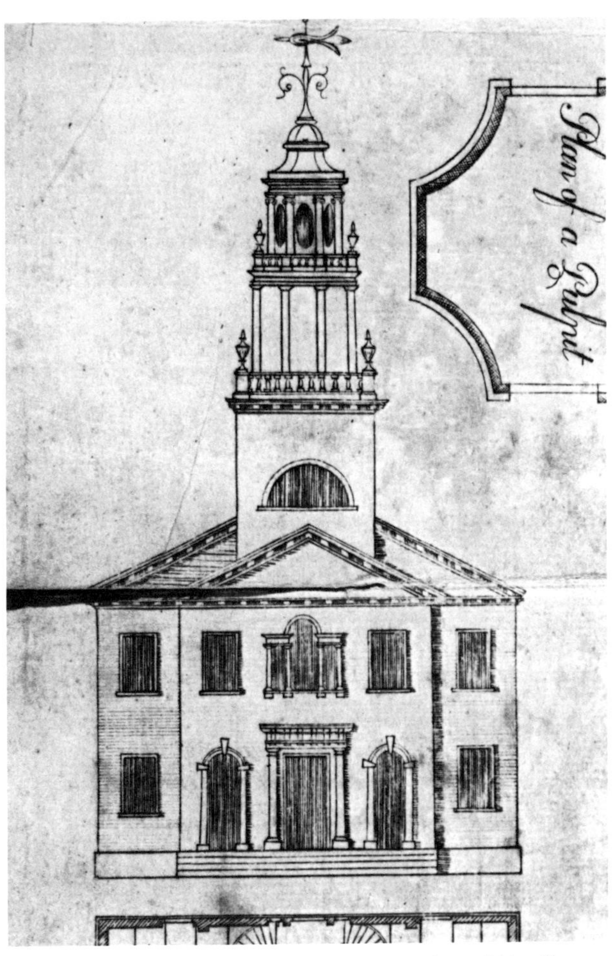

Fig. 2.12.2 Asher Benjamin, "Design for a Meetinghouse" (detail). From *The Country Builder's Assistant* (Boston, 1798), plate 33. Courtesy, American Antiquarian Society.

designs, especially the railing with corner urns and the oval openings of the cupola.[26]

Diagonally across the street is the 1799 Frost house, the earliest house in Kennebunk to be associated with Eaton. Like Coventry Hall, it is an L-shaped plan, although of smaller scale. It has a second-story Palladian window (a three-part opening with arched window in the center) over its front door and side lights similar to one found in Benjamin's first builder's guide. This suggests that Eaton owned an early copy of Benjamin's influential work, perhaps the Boston edition of 1798. The doorways and mantelpieces of the ca. 1803–1804 Taylor-Barry house on Summer Street also reflect Eaton's familiarity with this book.

According to local tradition, the addition to an older house Judge Clark bought in 1789 was made by Eaton sometime between 1800 and 1803. Its obvious source is not a published guidebook but Coventry Hall (fig. 2.11). Its plan uses end chimneys to heat large rooms on either side of its central hallway. Small unheated rooms are located behind

the major rooms, while the old house forms a central rear ell. Doric pilasters were substituted for the Ionic order employed in York and set off the projecting central bay; a beltcourse separates the two stories. The front door has both fan and side lights, a flat-top triple window lights the upper hall, and a lunette fills the raised pavilion gable. Some of these features suggest familiarity with other more recent houses near Boston, but similarities in the doorway and the facade indicate a close relationship to Coventry Hall. Interior evidence of an arched door beneath the stair landing appears both at Coventry Hall and acts as something of a signature in Eaton's Kennebunk houses during the next two decades. This suggests that Eaton was probably one of the craftsmen who worked on Coventry Hall during its more than two years in construction, perhaps as an apprentice or journeyman joiner under the direction of an unidentified Boston master.[27]

The George W. Wallingford house, Wallingford Hall, is also assigned to Eaton's hand and is customarily dated 1804 on the basis of a brick incised "Thurs. 16th of August 1804"

found in its rear chimney (see chapter 3 and fig. 3.9).
Although a smaller two-story house than Clark's, it shares
the flat-topped tripartite window over an elliptical fanlighted
doorway with sidelights. Its many doors and built-in
cupboards are painted in imitation of grained mahogany and
inlaid banding which prefigures similar work at other Eaton
houses. Its unusual plan (fig. 2.8.6) looks back to Judge
Jonas Clark's addition. Wallingford Hall is also T-shaped,
with a lower two-story rear ell containing the kitchen which
is separated from the front block by a cross-passage and rear
stairs. The house has a single chimney in each side wall and
a rear kitchen chimney with a second-story smoke oven. A
large parlor occupied the whole depth of the high-studded
main block to the right of the central stairhall. To the left of
the stairhall is a sitting room and a small anteroom at the
rear corner. Above are chambers over each main room; the
two left rooms have corner fireplaces from the single stack.
Curved walls between the rear hall and the right chambers
are also like those at the Clark house. Stretching south from
the ell is a run of connected outbuildings, the stable arcaded
with circular windows above. Whether these were built with
the house or evolved more slowly is not clear. Wallingford
owned this house and three outbuildings on twenty-three
acres for which he was taxed only $8.68 in 1816.[28]

Another important meetinghouse in Saco adds to our
knowledge of federal-style architecture in Maine during the
first decade of the nineteenth century. Its builder was
Bradbury Johnson, a joiner from Exeter, New Hampshire,
who moved with his family to Pepperrellborough in August
1802. James Garvin has demonstrated that, in the years after
Johnson helped the older architect-builder Ebenezer Clifford

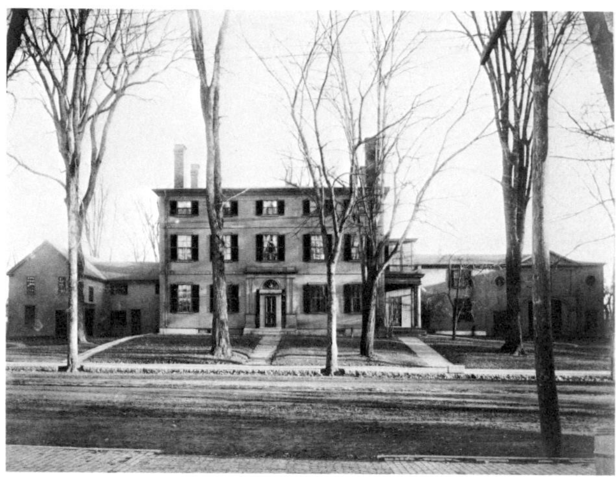

Fig. 2.14 Joseph Leland house, Saco, Maine, ca. 1803. Photograph, ca.
1910. Courtesy, Society for the Preservation of New England Antiquities.

design and erect the meetinghouse in Exeter between 1798
and 1800, he had a major influence on the stylistic development of the Piscataqua region. His presence in Saco by
November 1802, when the town approved construction of a
new meetinghouse, helped win him the commission.
Construction began in 1803 and the exterior was apparently
finished the next year; interior work continued during the
next two years. When Timothy Dwight returned to Saco in
1807, he described the new church as "a structure superior to
any other" in Maine and "inferior to very few in New
England." Another visitor added that the "new church is
built and painted in the gayest style."[29]

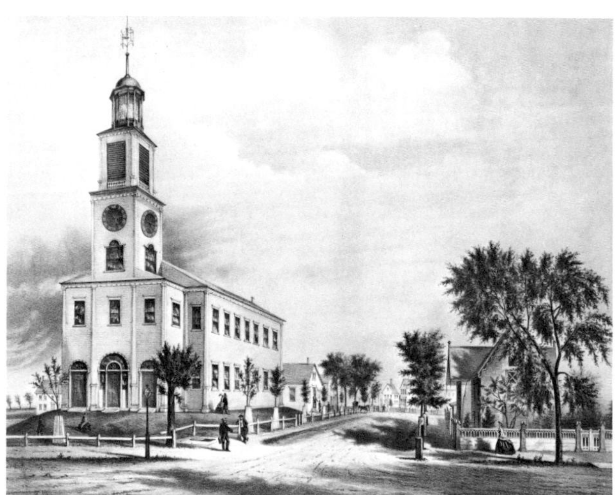

Fig. 2.13 Charles H. Granger, *The Old Congregational Church, Saco*, Saco,
Maine, 1803–1806. Bradbury Johnson, architect-builder. Lithograph,
Boston, ca. 1860. H 17½ (44.5), W 20⅞ (53.0). York Institute Museum.

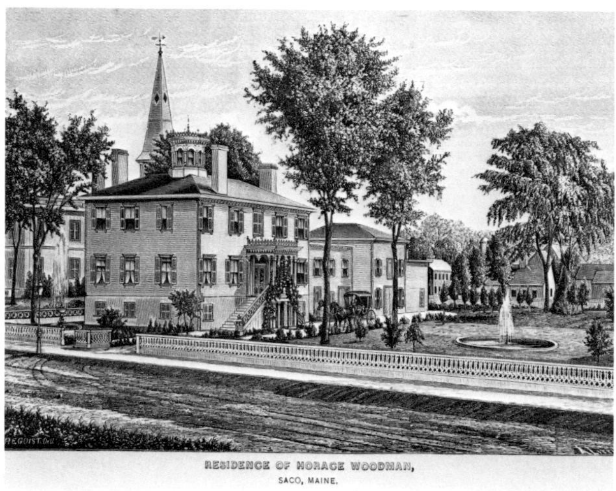

Fig. 2.15 Cyrus King house, Saco, Maine, 1807. From *History of York
County, Maine, with Illustrations and Biographical Sketches of its Prominent Men
and Pioneers* (Philadelphia, 1880). The Brick Store Museum.

The Saco meetinghouse (fig. 2.13) adopted the new convention of a pavilion projecting from the gable end, supporting the multistoried spire and serving as an entry. It had its genesis in Bulfinch's Pittsfield, Massachusetts, meetinghouse of 1790–1793 and the form was popularized by Benjamin's 1797 publication. Johnson also may have been directly familiar with the 1800 meetinghouse for the First Society of Newburyport. Like that church, Johnson's had a deep entry pavilion accommodating the stairs. Its exterior detail, more delicate and attenuated than contemporary Boston work, echoed some of the most recent high-style architectural decoration in Portsmouth. Narrow pilasters, some on pedestals, divided the entrance facade and marked the building's corners. Three semicircular fanlights over the entry doors bore similarities to those Johnson used in 1804 for the New Hampshire Fire and Marine Insurance Company office in Portsmouth. The Palladian windows in the lowest stage of the tower were familiar details in his earlier work.[30]

While Bradbury Johnson is said to have constructed "many of the best structures" in Saco during his brief residence there, only two long-destroyed houses have been previously identified. Others owned by the highest taxpayers in 1816 might also be attributed to him on the basis of both style and date. The strongest possibility among this group is Joseph Leland's ca. 1803 house (fig. 2.14). It may have been the first four-square, central-hall, three-story federal mansion with four chimneys marking its major rooms ever built in Saco. It was certainly among the earliest of this type erected in any town between Portsmouth and Portland. Surviving decoration above its front door includes a waffle-like design

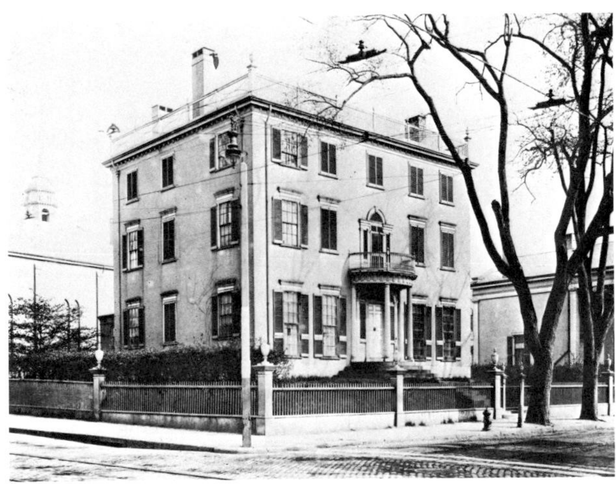

Fig. 2.16 Hugh McLellan house, Portland, Maine, 1800. Photograph, ca. 1900. Maine Historical Society.

found in earlier Portsmouth work; archways over doors separating the front and rear stairhalls employ alternating flutes and rosettes similar to those used in the same location in that city's Pierce mansion (1799) and the same motif Johnson employed on the 1798 Exeter meetinghouse. Johnson could also have built the large home of Foxwell Cutts (cat. 35), who died debt-ridden in 1816. It was later occupied by Thomas G. Thornton (cat. 36), Thomas Cutts's son-in-law, before being transformed into a Greek revival-style hostlery in the 1830s and later destroyed.[31]

Bradbury Johnson's sons and apprentices, John and William S. Johnson, stayed in Saco after their father returned

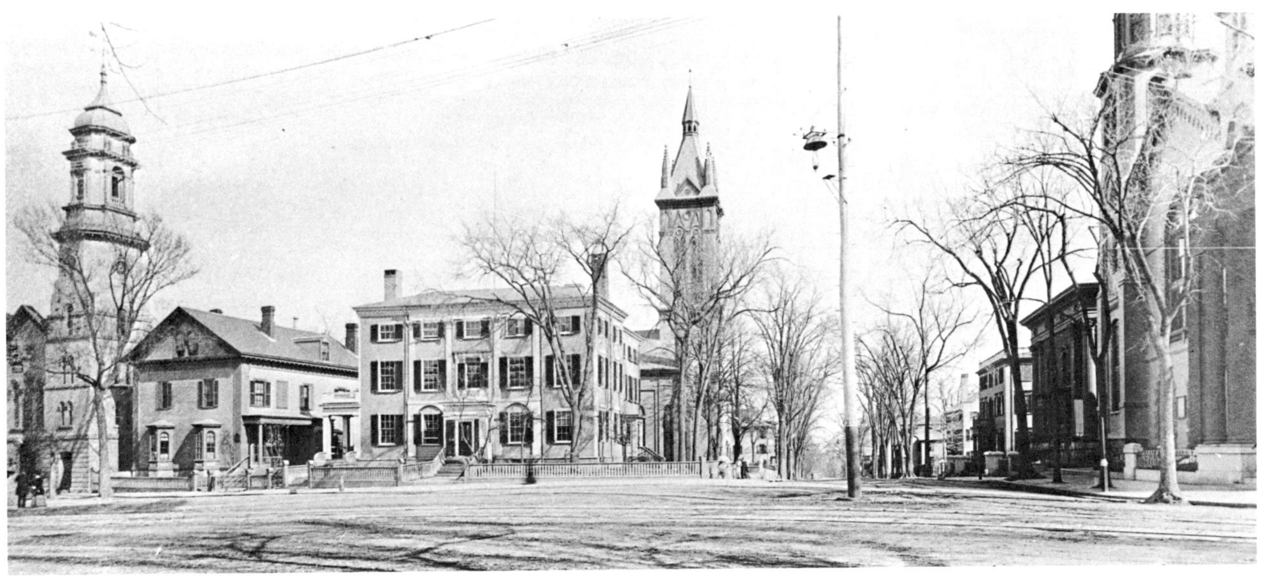

Fig. 2.17 Matthew Cobb house, Portland, Maine, 1801. Alexander Parris, architect. Photograph, ca. 1885. Maine Historical Society.

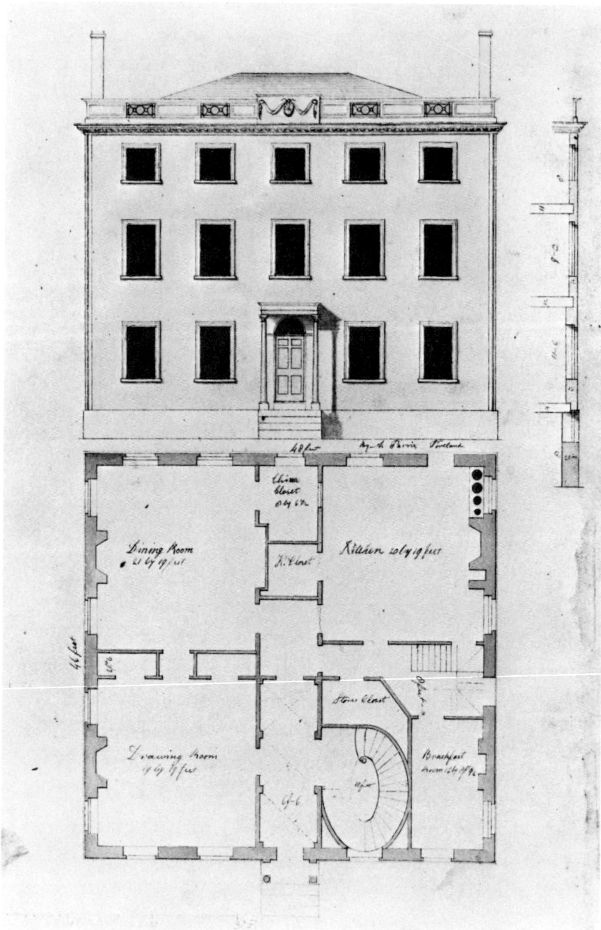

Fig. 2.18 Alexander Parris, *Elevation and plan*, Hunnewell house, Portland, Maine, 1805. Ink, ink wash, watercolor on paper; H 11⅛ (28.3), W 8½ (21.6). Boston Athenaeum.

to New Hampshire. Both were recorded as joiners in 1808, but William left after 1813 and was in New York City when his father died there in 1819. John married in 1814 and built his own Saco house in 1827. He is remembered for having "erected many of the finest and most substantial residences and public buildings in Saco and Biddeford" during a long life which ended in 1875.[32]

In addition to the Johnsons, Saco's rapid growth attracted other carpenters and house joiners such as Sherburne Tilton, who built the Reverend Jonathan Coggswell house on Main Street in 1818, and Valentine Clark, whose 1810–1813 house on High Street also survives.[33] These are more typical of Saco's vernacular building during this era—two-story homes facing the street, often with ells and stables forming a courtyard to one side.

The 1807 home built for Cyrus King, however, was an unusual variant of these common plans (fig. 2.15). Not only was it raised over a high foundation, but it was also sited so

that its long facade faced into a large side garden instead of the street. A two-story ell to the stables was connected to the far end of the basement and first story. Opposing chimneys on front and back walls heated double parlors across the street side; a third chimney was located in the rear. A cupola above the hipped roof suggests the possibility of an original elliptical stairway lit from above that preceded the present Victorian one. While little remains of its trim, the exterior cornice employs a design recommended in Benjamin's *Country Builder's Assistant* and used by joiners throughout the region. Its situation facing into the garden does not suggest a European model, as claimed by local tradition, but a familiarity with the newest domestic planning in Portland.[34]

Portland boasted some twenty known housewrights during this post-Revolutionary building boom, the most outstanding of whom were John Kimball, Sr., his son John, Jr., and the young Alexander Parris. The senior Kimball is credited with designing and building houses for two brothers, Stephen and Hugh McLellan in 1800. These brick, three-story, four-square mansions, with lower third stories beneath hipped roofs, set a new standard for domestic architecture among the town's elite (fig. 2.16). Each has a handsomely decorated central doorway, wide window surrounds topped with flat entablatures on the first two stories, and a Palladian window above the front portico. Hugh McLellan's house also has another Palladian window lighting the stair landing on the rear wall.[35]

Alexander Parris, who arrived in Portland from Massachusetts while the McLellan houses were under construction, was apparently impressed with their design. He was soon executing a series of mansions of his own design for the city's mercantile elite. In 1801 he designed new houses for Joseph H. Ingraham and Matthew Cobb. The former was a silversmith and land speculator who went bankrupt during the 1807 Embargo; his house was still held by the Maine Bank in 1816. Cobb was one of those who not only survived the economic crisis but also flourished in postwar Portland. Both wooden houses employed flush-board facades with pilasters segmenting the upper two stories and a flat-topped window over the portico (fig. 2.17). Although the Cobb house is gone, the Ingraham house survives with some of its interior intact. The parlor mantel is decorated with the same central composition ornament—probably imported from Boston—found in the Sewall and Means houses built just a few years earlier.[36]

In 1804 Matthew Cobb's business partner, Captain Asa Clapp (fig. 1.8), also employed Parris to remodel his house. Originally built in 1794 for Daniel Davis, the house stood at the corner of Congress and Elm streets. Parris added a third story, enlarged the hallway, and built a circular staircase lit by a new octagonal cupola. He was also probably responsible for a new door with fan and sidelights, as well as the portico with an unusual semicircular projecting roof. Edward

Zimmer, Parris's recent biographer, has identified this same feature in the work of Charles Bulfinch, the architect who inspired many aspects of the younger Parris's own work.[37]

For example, Parris's 1805 brick house for Cumberland County Sheriff Richard Hunnewell was strongly influenced by Bulfinch's unexecuted plan for the Elias Hasket Derby mansion in Salem, Massachusetts. Parris knew this design through the intermediate plans of another housewright, his friend Thomas W. Sumner. Hunnewell's house (fig. 2.18), which Matthew Cobb acquired by 1816, had an elliptical staircase to the right side of the entrance, groin vaulting in the entry, and a rear staircase on the side wall between the kitchen and front room such as Bulfinch proposed for Derby in 1795. Parris's plan (after that of Sumner) also marks the introduction of the Rumford oven to Portland kitchens and a sideboard niche in the dining room. Another 1805 house attributed to Parris, the four-square, three-story, brick mansion of merchant Robert Boyd, also has groin vaulting in the entry ceiling. This plaster decoration is located between the front doorway, with its semicircular fan and sidelights, and a matching inner screen with identical decorative glazing.[38]

"In 1806," Parris later wrote, "I was employed by the late Commodore Preble to build him an extensive dwelling."[39] Edward Preble (cats. 1–3), whose 1804 victory over the Barbary pirates off Tripoli won him fame and honor, was an active client. Parris drew upon a full battery of sources, published designs as well as those of his colleague Sumner, to provide Preble with multiple variations in plan and elevation. In the process he created what Zimmer calls "the most innovative of the young builder's Portland houses."[40]

Preble's three-story brick house as built in 1806–1807 had two major facades (fig. 2.19). Significantly, the entrance does not face Congress Street but is oriented toward a side garden and private drive. In breaking away from the street-side front entrance, the architect provided a pair of matching drawing rooms across the front of the main block with a chimney in either side wall. The entry was placed behind the front rooms with a hall and circular staircase separating a small library from the kitchen in the rear of the main block. Extending beyond was a lower central ell of service rooms with windows within arches on one side. A one-story porch connecting the house and its ell faced the garden. The house was not yet complete when Preble died in 1807. His widow, Mary, continued to occupy the house as is shown in the tax records of 1815 (chart 4).

Another side entrance house, sometimes credited to Parris because of its similarity to the Preble plan and its date of 1807, was the State Street home of Prentiss Mellen (cat. 30). This Saco lawyer, who moved to Portland about that time, was among the highest taxpayers in 1815. A nineteenth-century newspaper memoir, however, states that the builder was Thomas Eaton of Kennebunk. He, too, relocated in Portland about this date and must have been watching Parris's construction of the Preble house carefully.[41] The similarity of the unusual side entrance, if not its scale or plan, makes one wonder if Eaton also designed the Cyrus King house in Saco that same year.

Parris's architectural legacy in Portland also included two major monuments to the city's commercial life: the Maine Fire and Marine Insurance Company office of 1803 (fig. 2.20) and the Portland Bank of 1806. Both employed

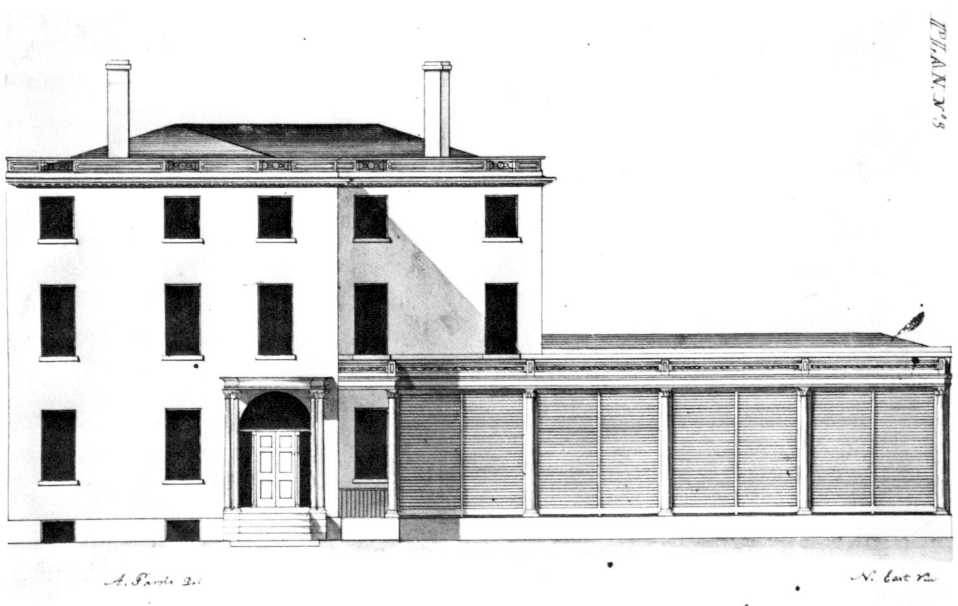

Fig. 2.19 Alexander Parris, *Plan No. 3*, Edward Preble house, Portland, Maine, 1805. Ink, ink wash, watercolor on paper; H 9¹³⁄₁₆ (24.9), w 7¹¹⁄₁₆ (19.5). Courtesy, American Antiquarian Society.

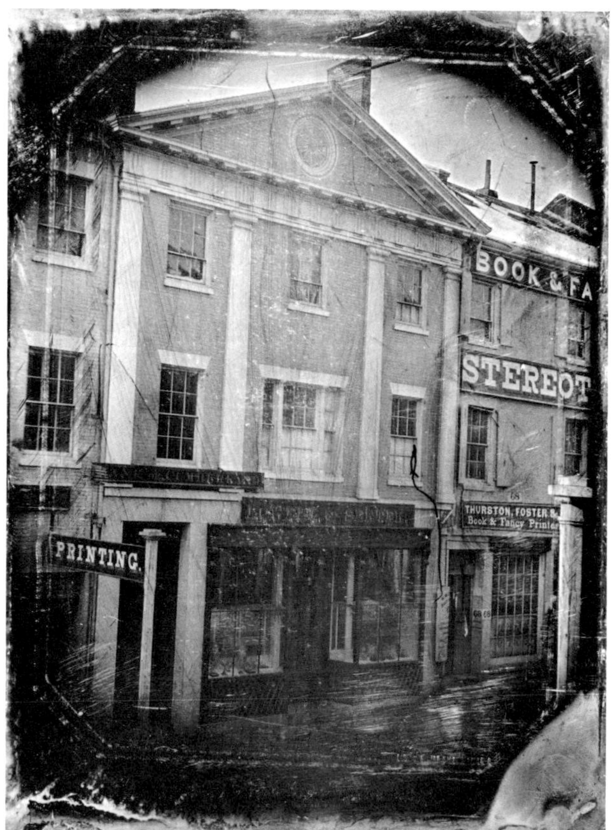

Fig. 2.20 Maine Fire and Marine Insurance Company, Portland, Maine, 1803. Alexander Parris, architect. Daguerreotype, ca. 1848. Maine Historical Society.

three vertical divisions of the upper stories with applied pilasters or engaged columns. The bank's arcade of semicircular windows and door fanlight reinforced this vertical segmentation. Its flat roof, skylit circular stairs, groin vaulting in the central hall, and large curved rooms at the rear (fig. 2.21) made this bank the most complex example of federal commercial architecture in the city.[42]

With the imposition of the Embargo and the subsequent failure of many of the city's merchants, Parris may have used his connection with Commodore Preble to secure a position superintending the construction of Fort Preble and Fort Scammell in Portland's harbor (cat. 12). Remaining in Portland two more years for this work, Parris then removed to Richmond, Virginia, and Boston where he continued his successful architectural career.[43]

Likewise, Thomas Eaton, who appeared in Portland in 1807 when he built the Mellen house, left the city by 1811. He returned to Kennebunk, where he built a group of much more elaborate houses undoubtedly influenced by his Portland sojourn. The key to Eaton's later work is found in the probate records of Nathaniel Lord of Kennebunkport. Lord began a new house in April 1814, moved in the following October, and died in February 1815. His estate papers include, among the administrator's expenses, several payments to Eaton and local cabinetmaker Edward White, who provided a fence. The earliest recorded payment is to Thomas Eaton in January 1816 for his bill on "contract for stairs & blinds [$]30." In November White was paid for painting and "making stair railing in the large house,

Fig. 2.21 Alexander Parris, *Section of Portland Bank, April 25, 1806*, Portland, Maine. Ink, ink wash, watercolor on paper; H 9⅜ (24.4), w 7¼ (18.4). Courtesy, American Antiquarian Society.

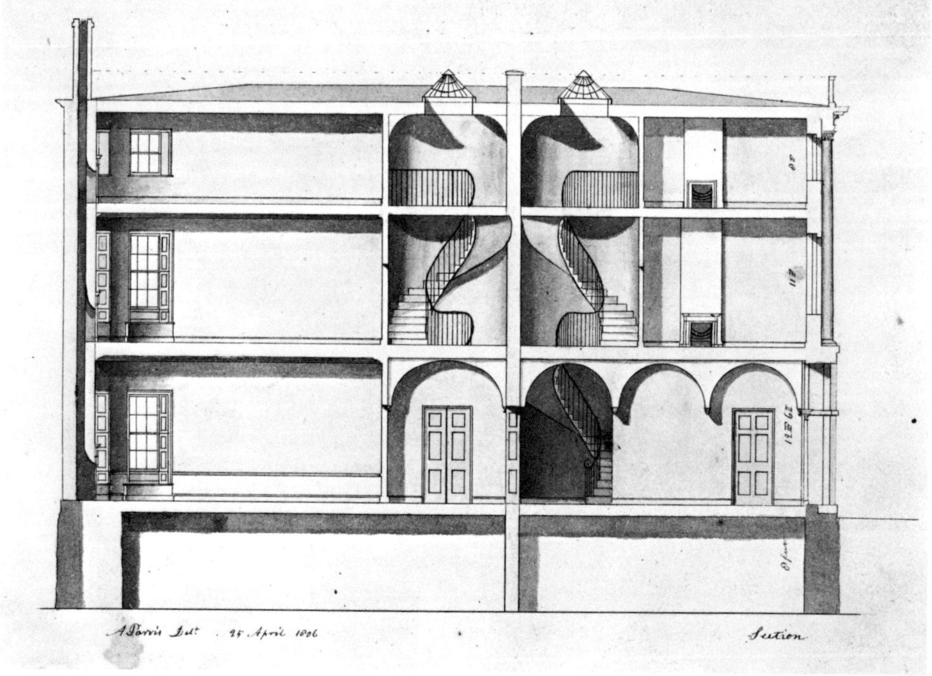

contracted for with T. Eaton. [$]42." Payments continued in 1817 to Edward Goodwin for ironwork and to Oliver Hodsdon, who made "blinds for the large house."[44]

Nathaniel Lord's house, the larger of two dwellings built at the same time, is the most important three-story federal mansion in Kennebunkport (fig. 2.22). Among its features are a central cupola, front and rear curved staircases, side-wall chimneys in its major rooms, curving interior walls, a flat-topped tripartite second-story central window, and handsome fanlighted doorways on three sides of the house. A two-story rear kitchen ell was added later. It thus matches Anne Royall's description of Portland's impressive four-square federal mansions (see Chapter 3 and fig. 3.11). When assessed for Lord's inventory, the "three story dwelling house with the outbuildings and half an acre of land" were valued at $6,200, compared to the "two story dwelling house adjoining the same" on an equal lot worth $2,800.[45]

On the basis of Eaton's hand in the design and construction of the Lord mansion, another Kennebunk house may now be more strongly attributed to him. The John Usher Parsons mansion (fig. 2.23) is set back from Kennebunk's main street much like the nearby Storer house. It suffers from a slight uncertainty of date, usually said to be 1812 or 1814. The advocate of the latter date claims that Mrs. Parsons died (July 3, 1815) "six months after" the house was built and that the house was sold the next year. Actually John U. Parsons signed the deed (as did his wife Susanna) selling the house "where I dwell" to Daniel Sewall on June 29, 1815.[46]

The Parsons-Bourne house, as it is known, shares with the Lord mansion several features of interior ornament that suggest it could have been built by Thomas Eaton only after his return from Portland. Despite the legend that the house was copied from one in Newburyport to please Mrs. Parsons, who came from that city, the house is as much a fine Portland-style mansion. It has doors on three of its four sides, side chimneys for the major rooms, a rear-wall stack for the kitchen, a Palladian window over the fanlit front door, and a single arched window lighting the curved staircase on the rear wall. Connected by a rear shed were two barns or stables, set off at right angles at the rear, with round windows over their archways.

Thomas Eaton, Bradbury Johnson, and Alexander Parris were mobile and talented builder-architects who helped transform these coastal communities in the first two decades of the nineteenth century. Each learned much by moving from one area to another. Parris saw Bulfinch's work firsthand, Eaton had to have known Coventry Hall and saw Parris's work in Portland, and Johnson brought the newest ideas from Newburyport, Exeter, and Portsmouth to the rapidly growing town of Saco. Through their craft training, their familiarity with published sources and their knowledge of recent building, new ideas were transferred from town to town and made solid.

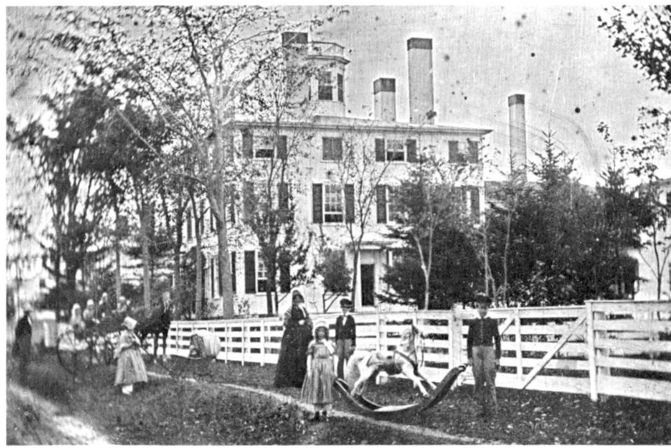

Fig. 2.22 Nathaniel Lord house, Kennebunkport, Maine, 1815. Thomas Eaton, architect-builder. Photograph from a daguerreotype, ca. 1850. Courtesy, Society for the Preservation of New England Antiquities.

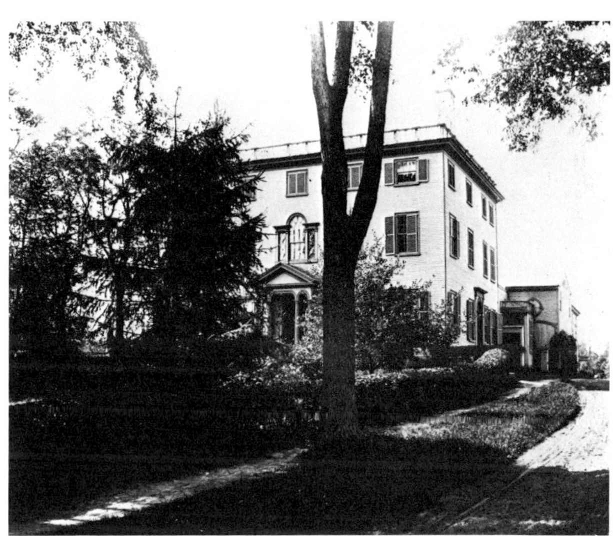

Fig. 2.23 Parsons-Bourne house, Kennebunk, Maine, ca. 1814. Photograph, ca. 1890. The Brick Store Museum.

This clearly differentiated them from other local builders who constructed the many smaller vernacular structures that made up these coastal towns. Many carpenters could extend or remodel an older home, build new ones much like their neighbors, and finish the interior with decent joiners' work. Eaton, Johnson, the Kimballs, and Parris created the architectural landmarks that define a town. It was their meetinghouses and mansions that travelers recalled when describing their memories of a journey through the District of Maine. Architect-builders such as these created the "appearance of enterprise and improvement" which best symbolized the worldly success of the coastal elite of southern Maine.[47]

1 La Rochefoucault-Liancourt, *Travels*, 1:462.

2 I have explored the various factors affecting the creation and growth of Maine communities in "From Revolution to Statehood: Maine Towns, Maine People, 1784–1820," in Clark and Leamon, *Maine in the Early Republic.*

3 Sewall, "Topographical Description of York," 8; Dwight, *Travels*, 2:205.

4 Subscription for an addition to the courthouse, July 25, 1799, typescript, William Frost Papers, OYHS.

5 York Parish Minutes, November 25, 1811, William Frost Papers, OYHS; Edward C. Moody, *Handbook of the Town of York* (Augusta, Me.: Kennebec Journal Co., 1914), 97. The building was remodeled after the courts moved to Alfred in 1832, again in 1873, and enlarged in 1893 as the present York Town Hall.

6 Dwight, *Travels*, 2:208. Hülswitt, *Journals*, 14, as translated by Fritz Richter. Joyce Butler located this source and kindly shared the translation. Royall, *Black Book*, 2:333.

7 Dwight, *Travels*, 2:168–169, 208.

8 Willis, *Journals*, 408–417.

9 Royall, *Black Book*, 2:214.

10 Banks, *History*, 2:340; Kendall, *Travels*, 45; 8th District of Massachusetts (York County, Maine), List of taxes payable on lands, lots and dwelling houses under the Act of Congress of March 5, 1816, December 1816 (photocopy, YCRD).

11 Indenture, October 7, 1810, typescript, William Frost Papers, OYHS; YCRP, docket 18217 (Seth Storer); lease, February 27, 1809, Daniel Cleaves Papers, MEHS; for Cleaves's business dealings with other tenant farmers, see Daniel Cleaves, account books, 1813–1818, Dyer Library and YIS.

12 Royall, *Black Book*, 2:214.

13 For early views of the Cutts mansion and other notable houses in this area, see Barry, *Sketches*. See John Mead Howells, *The Architectural Heritage of the Merrimack* (New York: Architectural Book Publishing Co., 1941) and *The Architectural Heritage of the Piscataqua* (1937; reprint, New York: Architectural Book Publishing Co., 1965) for similar examples north of Salem; for the Connecticut Valley, see Kevin M. Sweeney, "Mansion People: Kinship, Class, and Architecture in Western Massachusetts in the Mid Eighteenth Century," *Winterthur Portfolio* 19, no. 4 (Winter 1984): 231–255.

14 The Sayward house was later remodeled on the interior in 1761 for his son Jonathan by the local joiner Samuel Sewall. Nylander, "Sayward House," 567–577.

15 Banks, *History*, 2:60–63; George Ernst, *New England Miniature: A History of York, Maine* (Freeport, Me.: Bond Wheelwright Co., 1961), 170–177.

16 The Emerson-Wilcox house, a museum of the OYHS, is listed on the National Register of Historic Places. Building histories for this and Barrell Grove were taken from the typescript National Register nominations, courtesy of Earle G. Shettleworth, Jr., director, Maine Historic Preservation Commission, Augusta. I wish to thank Ann Reiss Cole, architectural historian, OYHS, for furnishing information on many of these York houses. For the Alexander McIntire house, see George Alex Emery, *Ancient City of Georgeana and Modern Town of York*, 2d ed. (Boston: By the author, 1874), 54n; Frederic Hutchinson Porter, "A Survey of Existing Colonial Architecture in Maine: Town of York . . . Part VII," *Architectural Review* 11 (1920): 41–48 (plate 22).

17 "The McCulloch House," *Old Houses.*

18 Remich, *History*, 360; Historic American Buildings Survey, Kimball House, 1936 measured drawings (ME-14) and photographs (ME16-Ken-4), Library of Congress; Remich, *History*, 129, 537–538.

19 Ernst, *New England Miniature*, 191, 255; Jonathan Sayward, journals, American Antiquarian Society, Worcester, Mass., record the purchase May 1, 1794, as well as the housewarming for the completed remodeling on November 13, 1795. The addition is also documented in the 1803 inventory made for the estate of Edward Emerson, Jr. The house was then worth $2,100, barn $180, stable $140, wood and "shais" house $300, together with sixty acres worth $2,280 (or almost the $2,250 he paid for the original property in 1794). YCRP, docket 5174 (Edward Emerson, Jr.). Fragments of federal wallpaper still remain in the new front parlor, together with composition ornaments around the fireplace which may have been later restored when the house was moved.

20 Annotated sketch plans and elevations by the late nineteenth-century architect William Barry for the "Estate of Daniel Cleaves, Esq., Biddeford, Maine" are among the Barry Family Collection, BSM. Map accepted at Biddeford town meeting, May 21, 1804, Dyer Library, Saco, shows a perspective view of the Cleaves house with only a five-bay facade; if this was an accurate representation, the long parlor may date later.

21 Those listed in chart 3 with five-room plan, central-chimney houses include: Moses and Issac Lyman in York, Capt. Joseph Hatch (34 Summer Street, Kennebunk), Eliphalet Perkins's 1802 house above Kennebunkport's Dock Square, and Daniel Walker's "cup and saucer" house in the same town. Early federal-period versions of the central-hall double-pile include: Perkins's ca. 1813 house on Union Street and Daniel Walker's Pearl Street "mansion" there. I wish to thank Joyce Butler for assisting in locating these structures and for pointing me to her article, "Samuel Davis," in "Kennebunk and Kennebunkport Cameos," *The Tourist News* (August 20, 1980), 7, 28. For a brief discussion of vernacular house types in rural Maine, see Thomas A. Hubka, *Big House, Little House, Back House, Barn: The Connected Farm Buildings of New England* (Hanover, N.H.: University Press of New England, 1984), 37–38n.

22 Sayward, journal, July 31, 1794, and November 12, 1796, American Antiquarian Society. Susanna Hovey Emerson, journal, November 11, 1796, Maine State Library, Augusta (photocopy, OYHS). Mrs. Emerson also reported on November 17, 1796, "young Gentlemen and Ladies of the most respected Families in the Town met to Congratulate Judge Sewall and Lady at their new dwelling house." Sayward lists Elisha Perkins of Connecticut among the visitors, and notes "Mr. Little of Kennebunk though upwards of 70 was Life of the Company." For Sewall, see Clifford K. Shipton, *Biographical Sketches of Those Who Attended Harvard College in the Classes 1751–1775 with Bibliographical and Other Notes*, Sibley's Harvard Graduates, vol. 13 (Boston: Massachusetts Historical Society, 1965), 638–644; Ernst, *New England Miniature*, 178–182.

23 For Bulfinch's work, see Harold Kirker, *The Architecture of Charles Bulfinch* (Cambridge: Harvard University Press, 1969), 40–124; Carolyn S. Parsons, " 'Bordering on Magnificence': Domestic Urban Planning in the Maine Woods," in Clark and Leamon, *Maine in the Early Republic*; and Abbott Lowell Cummings, "Charles Bulfinch and Boston's Vanishing West End," *Old-Time New England* 52, no. 2 (Fall 1961): 31–49. For the Langdon house and other early federal designs in Portsmouth, see Garvin, "Academic Architecture," 293–304. For Coventry Hall, see Porter, "Survey," 83–186 (plates 13–21); and Myers, *Maine Catalog*, 32–35, 37. For McIntire's houses, see Fiske Kimball, *Mr. Samuel McIntire, Carver: The Architect of Salem* (Portland: Southworth-Anthoensen Press, 1940), 30–33 and figs. 6, 88.

24 I greatly appreciate the useful correspondence and conversation with James Garvin over the meaning of molding profiles at Coventry Hall. For discussion of the required molding planes, see James L. Garvin and Donna-Belle Garvin, *Instruments of Change* (Canaan, N.H.: Phoenix Publishing for New Hampshire Historical Society, 1985), 11–13.

25 Remich, *History*, 310, 352. Oral tradition for Eaton's Kennebunk Village houses is found in Andrew Walker, diary, February 26, 1880 (7: 398), Kennebunk Public Library. This includes only the Clark, Frost, Taylor-Barry, and Wallingford houses. Martha Gandy Fales kindly brought this reference to my attention.

26 For a detailed summary of the relation of Benjamin's design to the transformation of New England church design in the early federal period by many builders like Eaton, see Abbott L. Cummings, "Meeting and Dwelling Houses: Interrelationships in Early New England," in Peter Benes, ed., *New England Meeting House and Church: 1630–1850*, Proceedings of the 1979 Dublin Seminar for New England Folklife (Boston: Boston University, 1979), 4–17.

27 Myers, *Maine Catalog*, 35. Walker, Diary, February 20, 1880 (7:398), Kennebunk Public Library; for a more detailed investigation of

Eaton, see Arthur Gerrier, "Thomas Eaton," in *A Biographical Dictionary of Maine Architects*, ed. Earle G. Shettleworth, Jr. (Augusta: Maine Historic Preservation Commission, forthcoming). I thank both for their contributions to this essay. The Clark (later "Robert Lord") house is illustrated with Coventry Hall in C. Howard Walker, "Some Old Houses on the Southern Coast of Maine," *The White Pine Series of Architectural Monographs* 4, no. 2 (April 1918): 5–11. Also see Porter, "Survey . . . Part VIII," *Architectural Review* 12 (1921): 73–75.

28 "Wallingford Hall" (1804), *Old Houses*; Remich, *History*, 111, dates the house "about 1810." The dated brick and measured plans by Orris S. Ross for William Barry, March 1883, are in the Barry Family Collection, BSM. Massachusetts assessments, 1816 (photocopy, YCRD).

29 Garvin, "Academic Architecture," 377–379, 403–405; Dwight, *Travels*, 2:227; Kendall, *Travels*, 45.

30 Garvin, "Academic Architecture," 406–407.

31 Garvin, "Academic Architecture," 408, notes as Johnson's the Capt. Asa Stevens house (burned 1876) and attributed Joseph Bartlett's "Folly" (built 1804, destroyed 1872) on the documented basis of a "concrete" roof like that Johnson used in Portsmouth. See comparison with other building ornament, 303, 333–334. John Haley, "Historical Notes on Saco" (manuscript, YIS), 74, gives 1803 as the date of Leland's Main Street house. Other writers give 1801 and 1802. Born in 1756 in Grafton, Massachusetts, Leland was a Revolutionary hero and settled in Saco as a merchant after the war. He married Dorcas King, daughter of Richard King of Scarborough, in 1786 and sired ten children. Politically active, he served in the Massachusetts senate from 1805 to 1808. See Folsom, *History*, 287, 290. Only the Seth Spring house (1795 to 1808, sources differ) on Spring Island in Biddeford and the Dominicus Cutts house formerly on Cutts Island (visible in cat. 39) were potentially earlier three-story mansions. Spring's interior paneling points to the 1790s for its similarity to that of the Thomas Cutts house. See Historic American Buildings Survey drawings and photographs of "Lafayette House," ME-8 (1936), Library of Congress, and Myers, *Maine Catalog*, 36, 206. It is unclear if Spring's mansion is earlier or if it was always three stories. Its later use as a tavern suggests the third story may have been added. This was the case in the William Jefferds tavern (now destroyed) near the falls in Kennebunk; a third story was added to a new 1790–1792 tavern sometime before 1816. Bourne, *History*, 761; Remich, *History*, 115. William Barry's pencil drawing of the Jefferds' "Tavern Doors," at BSM, confirms the late eighteenth-century appearance of its lower story. Foxwell Cutts's house is said to have been built during his shipbuilding career "several years previous" to the War of 1812. Both men appear in chart 3. Folsom, *History*, 296, 305; YCRP, docket 3870 (Foxwell Cutts).

32 W. W. Clayton, *History of York County, Maine*, Part 1 (Philadelphia: Everts & Peck, 1875), facing 172; cited in Garvin, "Academic Architecture," 408. Obituary of Bradbury Johnson, *The New York Post* (December 14, 1819). William S. Johnson's Saco work is drawn entirely from York County deeds.

33 See 372 Main Street and 45 High Street, "Saco Architectural Survey" (typescript, Dyer Library, Saco).

34 271 Main Street, "Saco Architectural Survey." It was later owned by Horace Woodman and is illustrated in Clayton, *History of York County*, facing 152; see also fig. 2.15. It is today the Parish House of the Most Holy Trinity Church. Cyrus King settled in Saco about 1799 and became a leading Federalist, serving as U. S. representative from 1812–1816. He died April 25, 1817, at age forty-four. See Folsom, *History*, 302–303. The Cyrus King Papers, Columbia University Rare Book and Manuscript Library, New York City, contain no document identifying the architect for the house. However, an undated pen and ink sketch among documents dating 1806–1820 illustrates a four-square, central-chimney, two-story, hipped roof with facade dormer house (44′ across the facade and figured at various depths from 35′ to 38′) drawn in elevation showing the facade and end. A variation on the reverse shows the same plan in three stories, with shorter windows in the top story and a lower hipped roof.

35 William Goold, "Old Houses and their Builders," no. 8, September 28, 1892, William Goold, Scrapbook; Myers, *Maine Catalog*, 38–41; Zimmer, "Parris," 26–29. Both Hugh and Stephen McLellan failed after the Embargo of 1807 and their houses were apparently held by the banks until after 1816.

36 Zimmer, "Parris," 32–46.

37 Zimmer, "Parris," 56–67.

38 Zimmer, "Parris," 69–81; also see Christopher Monkhouse on T. W. Sumner in Philip C. F. Smith, *East India Hall: 1824–1974* (Salem, Mass.: East India Marine Society, 1974). Parris Collection, plan and elevation of the Hunnewell house (fig. 2.18), and T. W. Sumner, "Plan No. 3" (September 21, 1804), Boston Athenaeum. CCRD; 65:368, 76:146, show that Cobb acted as surety to Hunnewell's notes on the Maine Bank in 1812. Apparently he foreclosed prior to the execution of the second deed as Hunnewell was not taxed in 1815. Boyd was a successful merchant, weathering the Embargo and staying among the top taxpayers in 1815. He continued to occupy his house until his death in 1827.

39 Alexander Parris to Levi Lincoln, March 16, 1838, cited in Zimmer, "Parris," 18.

40 Zimmer, "Parris," 88; for discussion of the Preble house designs and their evolution, see 88–102, 119–120.

41 "W[illiam]. G[oold].," "The Judge Mellen House and Its Owners," *Portland Daily Press* (August 17, 1877). I wish to thank Earle G. Shettleworth, Jr., for bringing to my attention this early attribution to Mellen's "builder from Biddeford [Thomas] Eaton, the father of Stephen W. Eaton who died a few months ago." Arthur Gerrier has followed Eaton's appearance in the Portland tax records and will document his work there in his forthcoming biographical sketch cited above. Mellen purchased the State Street land in 1806 from Joseph Holt Ingraham, adding an additional six feet in September 1807 which may confirm the date. CCRD; 44:222, 52:505.

42 Zimmer, "Parris," 55–58, 103–112, points to Parris's use of William Pain, *Practical House Carpenter* (Boston, 1796), plate 110, a section for a house design, as the English source for the flat-roofed bank's two skylit circular stairs.

43 Zimmer, "Parris," 133–138.

44 See Chapter 1 and notes in this volume for the documentation of the date of Nathaniel Lord's mansion; D. W. Lord's journal, MEHS, notes that between August and October 1824 there was an addition to the mansion house which may be the two-story rear ell. YCRP; 26:567–570. I thank Laura Sprague for bringing this new discovery from her extensive reading of the federal-period inventories to my attention. Thomas Eaton reappears in the Kennebunk land records in 1810 and 1811 (YCRD; 81:190, 84:241). Edward White and Daniel Hodsdon were in partnership between 1810 and 1818 at The Landing for the manufacture of cabinetwork, including "bell-back and bamboo chairs." Remich, *History*, 234, 251.

45 YCRP, docket 12247 (Nathaniel Lord). The smaller house, long known as the Taylor house, survives across the street. It has heretofore been incorrectly dated 1804 or earlier, but apparently correct in its attribution to Eaton. "Taylor House," *Old Houses*.

46 "The Bourne Mansion," *Old Houses*, and William Barry, *Chronicles of Kennebunk* (Kennebunk: By the author, 1923), give 1812; Remich, *History*, 345, claims 1814. The latter would place it in conflict with construction of the Lord mansion, but his misdating of the sale makes him somewhat suspect. YRCD; 93:65: J. U. Parsons to Daniel Sewall, 3 acres house and lot, $7,000. Sewall was clerk of courts and recorder of probate for York County in 1815 when he moved from York to Kennebunk; see Remich, *History*, 187, and cats. 91, 102. In 1816 he was taxed for property in both towns; Parsons removed from Kennebunk to Parsonsfield, retaining a number of business properties in Kennebunk reflected in his tax (see chart 3).

47 Morris, "Tower," 46.

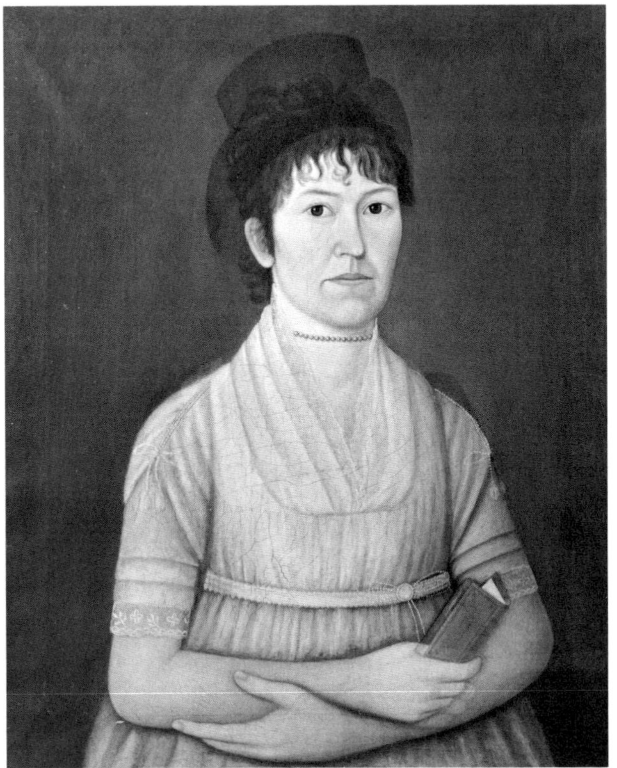

Cat. 28

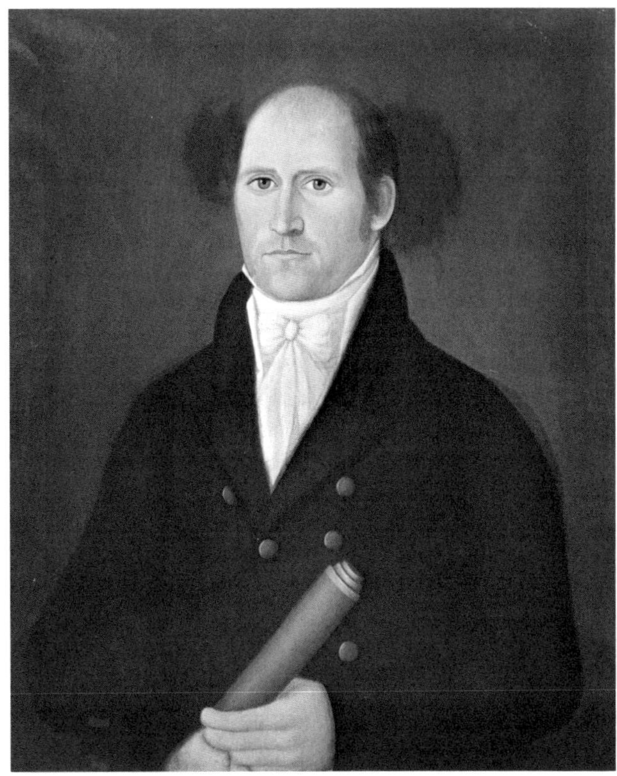

Cat. 28

28

John Brewster, Jr. (1766–1854)
Thomas Perkins (1769–1816)
Susannah Perkins Perkins (1766–1854)
Kennebunkport, Maine, 1797
Oil on canvas
Inscribed (on back of *Thomas Perkins*) "August 21,th
1797 / age 28 / John Brewster Junr. / Limner"
Inscribed (on lower stretcher of *Thomas Perkins*) "pint / pinxt"
Inscribed (on lower stretcher of *Susannah Perkins*)
"Brewster John"
H each 30½ (76.5); W each 25¾ (65.4)
The Brick Store Museum
Gift of Clifford Perkins Gould, 1980

Thomas Perkins was the great-grandson of Ensign Thomas Perkins who removed to Arundel in 1719 from Topsfield, Massachusetts. In 1790 Thomas married Susannah Perkins; she was the daughter of Thomas, Jr., and Susannah Hovey Perkins, and the granddaughter of Captain Thomas Perkins of Greenland, New Hampshire, founder of the second Perkins family to settle on the Kennebunk River in the early eighteenth century.[1]

John Brewster, Jr., was actively painting in Maine in 1796 and 1797; this signed and dated portrait of Thomas Perkins documents his earliest work here. Although not dated, the portrait of Susannah was painted at the same time.[2] They share several characteristics, notably the use of a solid brown background and gray underpaint that is visible through the translucent flesh tones. The pentimento about the heads indicates that the artist changed his mind at least once as to the shape of Thomas's head and Susannah's hair before the portraits were completed. The pencil inscription on the bottom stretcher of *Thomas Perkins* — "Mr. Moses Lester [Jr. or of ?] Preston [n?] County [?] [New?] Londo[n?]" — may reveal that Brewster prepared the Perkins canvas on a stretcher he had not used during a Connecticut visit.

A ship captain and merchant, Thomas is dressed in traditional attire with a black coat with high rolled collar, white waistcoat with standing collar and a white shirt with white cravat tied in a large bow. His spyglass is mute testimony to his career and its tragic ending; he was lost at sea in 1816. Susannah's sister, Sarah, died that same year. In 1819 Susannah married Sarah's widower, James Perkins, Jr. (1769–1845), the brother of her late husband.[3] The portraits descended to the donor, a great-grandson of James Perkins, Jr.

In addition to these, Brewster painted at least fifteen other portraits of Kennebunkport and Kennebunk residents between 1797 and 1809, most of them members of the Perkins or Lord families.[4] Four portraits of women—Susannah Perkins, her sister Abiel Perkins McCulloch, and their neighbors Elizabeth Pickering Stone and Phebe Walker Lord—bear striking resemblances in dress, hairstyle, and pose of bent and crossed arms. Susannah, Elizabeth, and Phebe all wear light-blue dresses; Abiel's is pale rose. The dresses had fashionable high waistlines and were decorated with cording and lace trim. A white scarf is tucked into the bodice and all the women wear a short string of gold beads. With hair piled into a chignon held with a black band and fringed bangs, their hairstyles, too, are similar. Phebe Walker married Nathaniel Lord in 1797 and her portrait could date to that time. While Elizabeth's portrait could also date to 1797, it seems more likely that it was painted at the time of her marriage to Jonathan Stone of Kennebunkport in 1798. It may also have been at this time that Brewster painted the portrait of Susannah's sister, Elizabeth, and her husband John Bourne, who were married in 1795 (cat. 139).[5]

Brewster returned to Kennebunkport in 1805 when he produced a full-length portrait of Francis Osborne Watts, the two-year-old son of Mehitable Lord Watts and Francis Watts, and a portrait of Tobias Lord III, Mehitable's brother. In December 1808 Elizabeth Wallingford sat for Brewster (cat. 41). The next year Brewster painted the portraits of Eliphalet Perkins and his wife Elizabeth Stone Perkins with their son, Charles.[6] In 1821, after a long hiatus, Brewster was again painting the portraits of Kennebunkport residents. Daniel Walker Lord, the son of Nathaniel and Phebe Walker Lord, recorded in his journal: "July had my portrait taken by Mr. Brewster."[7]   LFS & CSP

1 Bradbury, *History*, 267–270.
2 Little, "John Brewster, Jr.," 99, 113. The portrait of Susannah was published as unsigned.
3 Harold C. Durrell, comp., *Arundel Records* (n.p., n.d.), 49, BSM.
4 Little, "John Brewster, Jr.," 108–109, 112–113. In addition to those listed here are the portraits of James Perkins, the brother of Thomas Perkins, and his wife Sarah Perkins, the sister of Susannah Perkins, who were married in 1791; and the portraits of Elizabeth Pickering Stone, Nathaniel Lord, and Capt. John Low and his wife. See Brewster-related materials in John Brewster, Jr., Collection, BSM, and notes 5 and 7 below.
5 The Stone portrait is in the collection of the New Hampshire Historical Society. The name of Kennebunk merchant and ship-builder, Nathaniel C. Little, was inscribed on the left stretcher; he removed to Bangor in 1804. Donna-Belle Garvin kindly brought this portrait to our attention. Elizabeth Stone was related by marriage to the Perkins family. See Harold C. Durrell, "Marriage of Kennebunkport Families" (typescript, MEHS); and Robert Henry Eddy, *Genealogical Data respecting John Pickering of Portsmouth, New Hampshire* (Boston, 1884), 16–17. The Bourne portraits retain their unusual original stamped brass frames, as do these portraits of the Perkinses; see Little, "John Brewster, Jr.," 109.
6 Little, "John Brewster, Jr.," 108–109, 112.
7 Daniel Walker Lord, journal, MEHS.

29

Attributed to John Brewster, Jr. (1766–1854)
Samuel Deane (1727–1814)
Eunice Pearson Deane (1727–1812)
Portland, Maine, 1796–1800
Oil on canvas
H each 32½ (82.5); W each 29⁷⁄₁₆ (74.7)
Maine Historical Society
Gift of Alfred W. Lord, 1893

Surviving portraits of clergymen, merchants, ship captains, lawyers, and statesmen by John Brewster, Jr., indicate that Brewster satisfied the demands of many of Maine's most prominent citizens. This pair of portraits of the Reverend Samuel Deane and his wife, Eunice Pearson, attributed to Brewster, were painted shortly after the artist's arrival in Maine.

On November 22, 1795, Brewster's brother Royal married Dorcas Coffin, the daughter of Paul Coffin (1738–1821), pastor of Buxton's Congregational Church, and himself the subject of a Brewster portrait.[1] It is possible that Brewster was commissioned to paint the portraits of the Deanes at the suggestion of the Coffins. Clergymen in Maine were often in close communication. The Reverend Caleb Bradley of Westbrook noted in his journal a funeral in Windham where he, Dr. Deane, Mr. Kellogg, Mr. Jewett, and Mr. Marrett served as pall holders; all were clergymen. The portrait of Daniel Marrett of Standish was painted by Brewster in 1831.[2]

Brewster was in the Portland area from May 1796 to September 1797.[3] The portraits of the Deanes could have been painted at this time, or perhaps closer to the turn of the century, as the choice of background color is markedly similar to that of the portraits of Thomas and Elizabeth Scamman Cutts (cat. 33).

Samuel Deane graduated from Harvard College in 1760 and that year contributed to a volume of congratulatory addresses presented to George III on his accession to the throne. In 1764 he moved to Portland where he joined the Reverend Thomas Smith at the First Parish Church. He preached with Smith until Smith's death in 1795 and continued at the parish until his own death in 1814. In 1790 Brown University honored Deane with a doctorate in divinity, the source for his parishioners' name for him, "good Doctor Deane."[4] The minister is portrayed here in ecclesiastical attire holding a psalm book or Bible. In his seventies, Deane would have been used to the wig as an adornment.

The diaries kept by both Smith and Deane span nearly a century and are one of the most important sources in the study of eighteenth-century Portland history. After the sale of his property in 1814, Deane's diary found its way to

William Willis who published extracts of it jointly with the diary of Thomas Smith.[5]

Between 1795 and the arrival of the Reverend Ichabod Nichols in 1809, Deane preached alone at "Old Jerusalem," as the church was affectionately called. In 1787 part of the congregation split to form the second parish church; in March 1807 there was more dissent with the subscription for a new meetinghouse. Ann Smith reported that she "was very much grieved to have our good Doctor Deane loos[e] some of his parish, because it will hurt his feelings and he deserves better things from them . . . it is cruel to dessirt him in his old age. I fear they will not get so good a man." The following September Deane noted "N[athaniel] Cross' Meeting house raising," the building for the third parish.[6] Nevertheless, Deane was greatly respected and faithfully served his community for half a century.

The Deanes' house was located just to the west of the church on a three-acre lot that extended behind the house to Back Cove. Built at the time of his marriage in 1766, the two-and-one-half-story house had a hip roof with "luthern" or dormer windows.[7]

Deane, a member of the American Academy of Arts and Sciences, was devoted to agricultural improvements and published the results of his experiments in his 1790 *Newengland farmer, or Georgical Dictionary*. In 1803 as a member of the American Board of Agriculture, Deane served with John Quincy Adams and Peleg Wadsworth on the Committee of Correspondence for Massachusetts.[8] He frequently recorded the activities in his extensive garden in his diary. Staple wheat, rye, and barley were sown along with beets, potatoes, corn, turnips, and carrots. The Deanes, however, also dined on peas, strawberries, asparagus, and fruits from the orchard. Trees ranged from common pear, apple, and plum to the more experimental varieties of "blue pearmains," "sweet greenings," "sweet russets," "catharine pear," and "hotspur pear." Willis reported that Deane was the best gardener "among us" and exchanged his surplus with his parishioners. As a child Willis was lured to the orchard and nursery and was not deterred by the high garden fence. By 1849, however, Willis reported that the trees were gone and other parts of the garden had been destroyed.[9]

In addition to the labors on earth, Dr. Deane was also fascinated by the heavens. In 1780, 1792, and 1806 he recorded the eclipses of the sun, in the latter year noting the movement of the moon in great detail.[10] Just as the young Willis was attracted to the garden, so were other children delighted by Deane's knowledge of the planets and stars. Abigail May and the Wadsworth girls happily forfeited another frolic to Broad's Tavern for the opportunity to visit the parsonage. They

spent a much more agreeable evening viewing the moon Jupiter Mar's and other of the heavenly bodies thr'o an excellent telescope which the good doctr appear'd to take great pleasure in directing and accomodating to our convenience — and answer'd our questions with great good humour. we did not get home till past ten — late hour's for the Reverd & Lady.[11]

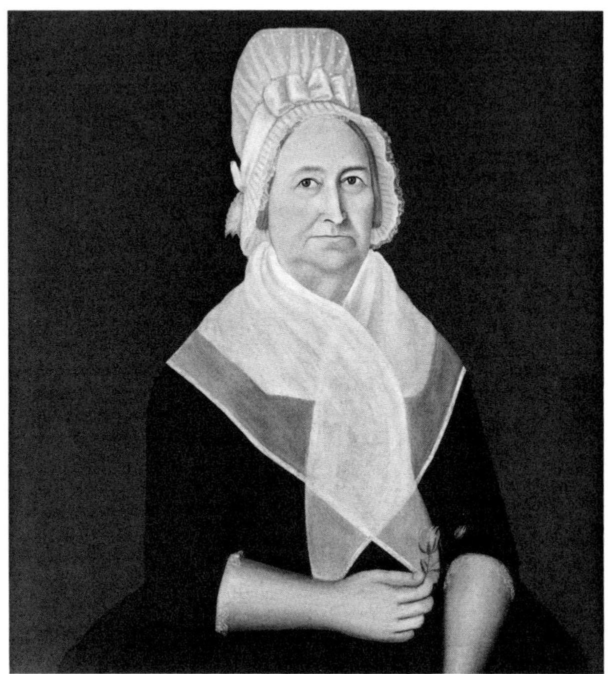

Cat. 29

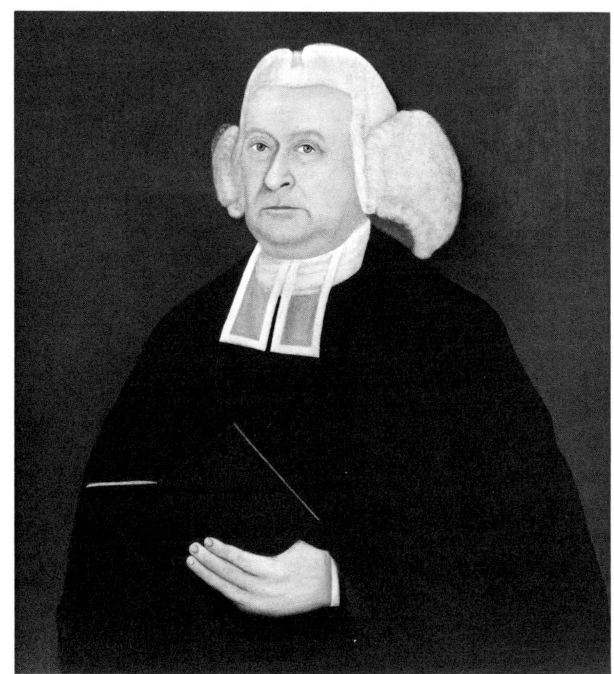

Cat. 29

Unfortunately, less is known of Mrs. Deane. One event, however, where she figured prominently was the "spinning day" held at the Deanes' on May 1, 1788. On this occasion, more than one hundred married and single women assembled, "most of whom were skilled in the important act of spinning." The newspaper account continued: "An emulous industry was never more apparent than in this beautiful assembly. The majority of fair hands gave motion to not less than sixty wheels." Others attended to the preparation of the materials and entertainment. "Near the close of the day, Mrs. Deane was presented by the company with TWO HUNDRED AND THIRTY SIX seven knotted skeins of excellent cotton and linnen yarns." Through the newspaper, Mrs. Deane took the "opportunity of returning her thanks to each, which the hurry of the day rendered impracticable at the time."[12] She is portrayed here in a conservative style befitting an older woman; her gown with fichu, and bonnet are very similar to those worn by Elizabeth Scamman Cutts (cat. 33). Although older than Elizabeth Cutts, Eunice appears in better health and more contented. Eunice and Samuel Deane had no children.   LFS & CSP

1 Little, "John Brewster, Jr.," 111–112.
2 Excerpts of Bradley's diary dating to 1799 are cited in William Goold, Scrapbook, 102. The portrait of Marrett is at Marrett house in Standish, SPNEA, and recorded in Little, "John Brewster, Jr.," 112–113.
3 Little, "John Brewster, Jr.," 99.
4 Willis, *Journals*, 289–292, 296.
5 Samuel Freeman published extracts of Smith's diary in 1821. See cat. 157.
6 Willis, *Journals*, 294, 391. Ann Smith, diary, March 13, 1807, MEHS.
7 Shettleworth and Barry, *Mr. Goodhue*, no. 19; for more on the house, see William Goold, Scrapbook, 113.
8 Willis, *Journals*, 296, 381. Another edition was published in the 1830s by Samuel Fessenden in Boston.
9 For examples of his entries, see Willis, *Journals*, 356, 359–360, 368, 381.
10 Willis, *Journals*, 348, 367, 387.
11 Abigail May, diary, MEHS.
12 Willis, *Journals*, 362, and *Cumberland Gazette* (May 8, 1788).

30

Attributed to John Brewster, Jr. (1766–1854)
Prentiss Mellen (1764–1840)
Saco or Portland, Maine, 1800–1810
Watercolor on ivory
H 2¹¹⁄₁₆ (6.8); w 2¹⁄₁₆ (5.2)
Maine Historical Society
Bequest of M. Persis Mellen Bailey, 1931
Color plate on page 43

John Brewster, Jr., customarily advertised himself as both a portrait and miniature painter. However, unlike his oil-on-canvas portraits, no documented Brewster miniatures were

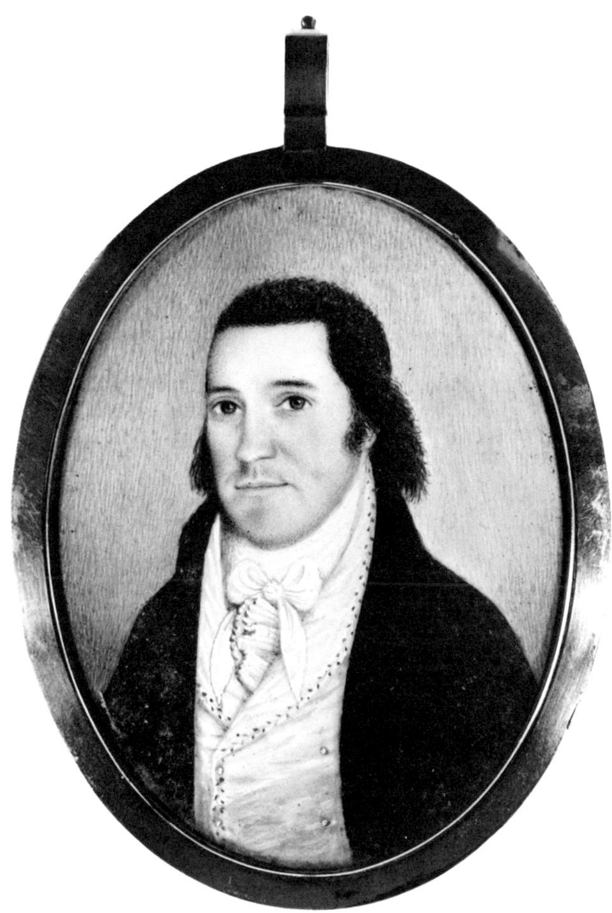

Cat. 30

known until the 1809 portrait of Benjamin Apthorp Gould of Newburyport was published in 1983.[1]

This miniature of Prentiss Mellen is attributed to Brewster on the basis of its similarity to his large-scale portraits and the Gould miniature. The angle of Mellen's body and his straightforward gaze are indicative of the artist's work; specific elements of Brewster's style are seen in the handling of Mellen's dress. The shirt ruffle and stock, although miniaturized, are painted in nearly identical style to those of the oil-on-canvas portraits of Thomas and Foxwell Cutts (cats. 34–35). With the aid of reducing and magnifying glasses, Brewster could employ his standard formula on a much smaller scale.

Brewster took Mellen's likeness during the first decade of the nineteenth century when the young attorney was rising to prominence. A miniature of Daniel Cleaves of Biddeford, attributed to Brewster, also dates between 1800 and 1810. Brewster was in Portland in January 1806 when he painted the miniature of Eliphalet Smith, a dry-goods merchant, and the Mellen work could date to this time. Eliphalet's wife recorded in her diary that she purchased "of [silversmith]

Joseph Lovis a gold Setting to My good mans Miniature for which he charges 18 dollars." The gold frame of Mellen's miniature is original.[2]

A native of Sterling, Massachusetts, Prentiss Mellen graduated from Harvard College in 1784. After several years of unsuccessful attempts to settle in a prosperous location, Mellen moved to Biddeford in 1792 at the suggestion of Judge George Thacher. Mellen described the humble years of his early Biddeford practice:

I opened my office in one of old Squire Hooper's front chambers, in which were then arranged three beds and half a table and one chair. My clients had the privilege of sitting on some of the beds. In this room I slept, as did also sundry travelers frequently, the house being a tavern.[3]

Nonetheless, Mellen is believed to have had access to George Thacher's extensive library, one that received favorable comment by the visiting Duke de la Rochefoucault. Mellen succeeded in Biddeford and as demand grew, he expanded his business. In 1804 he began to ride the circuit, eventually practicing in every county in Maine. By 1806 Mellen had purchased property in Portland, the county seat and largest town in the District. That year he built an elegant dwelling house on State Street (see Chapter 2).[4]

Beginning in 1818, Mellen served the District of Maine as United States senator. It was a short-lived position, however, for he left Washington in 1820 to assume his post as chief justice of the new state. It was at this time that Mellen began to publish poems and articles in the local newspapers. His writings elicited the comment that he was "well known in this State as an ultra temperance man and moralist." As chief justice, Mellen traded a lucrative private practice for public duty. Perhaps a sign of financial need was his return to the bar after he retired from the bench at the age of seventy. Mellen, himself, reported that this was "for the purpose of deriving a competency for my family." Shortly after his retirement in 1834 he sold the family's house and purchased a lot across the street where he built a small house. Mellen eventually left this house and lived out his days as a widower in a boarding house at the corner of Congress and Ann streets.[5]

As a lawyer and public servant, Mellen received favorable reports from his contemporaries. Simon Greenleaf reflected that Mellen "administered the hospitalities of social life with all the graceful liberality and good taste which were exhibited by gentlemen of what we now with melancholy truth, denominate '*the OLD school.*'" Greenleaf further described him as "elegant," "courtly," and always dressed in the "best style." A founding member of the Maine Historical Society, Mellen served as president for six years. Happily married for forty-three years to Sarah Hudson of Hartford, Mellen reminisced that he "married for love; and that, in those days, was an enduring cement." On occasion, Mellen took the opportunity in his writings to defend women and the value of

their education. His children pursued artistic and literary careers.[6]   LFS & CSP

1   Little, "John Brewster, Jr.," 100–102. Joyce Hill, "Miniatures by John Brewster, Jr.," *The Clarion* 49 (Spring / Summer 1983): figs. 1, 1a. Hill kindly brought the attribution of the Brewster miniatures to our attention.
2   The Cleaves miniature was bequeathed to The Brick Store Museum by Edith Cleaves Barry and Julia Barry Bodman in 1969 but was never received by the museum; its whereabouts are unknown. Jean Lipman and Tom Armstrong, eds., *American Folk Painters of Three Centuries* (New York: Hudson Hills Press, in association with the Whitney Museum of Art, 1980), 25. Ann Smith, diary, March 1, 1806, MEHS. Lovis was in the jewelry business at the Sign of the Golden Watch on Portland's Fish Street; see Henry N. Flynt and Martha Gandy Fales, *The Heritage Foundation Collection of Silver, with Biographical Sketches of New England Silversmiths, 1625–1825* (Old Deerfield, Mass.: Heritage Foundation, 1968), 270.
3   William Willis, *A History of the Law, the Courts, and the Lawyers of Maine* (Portland: Bailey & Noyes, 1863), 165.
4   La Rochefoucault-Liancourt, *Travels*, 1:462. Willis, *History of the Law*, 166.
5   Ellyn C. Ballou, "Prentiss Mellen, Maine's First Chief Justice, A Legal Biography," *Maine Law Review* 28, no. 2 (1977): 371, 375. The boarding house was constructed in 1784 as part of the Robison, Edgar, and Reed development of Ann Street. Enlarged and operated as a boarding house, it became known as the Jones-Mussey Tavern.
6   Ballou, "Prentiss Mellen," 368–369. Some of the Mellen Family Papers are at MEHS.

31

Unidentified artist
John Quinby (1758–1806)
Possibly Portland, Maine, ca. 1800
Watercolor on ivory
H 2¹⁄₁₆ (5.2); W 1⁹⁄₁₆ (4.0)
Maine Historical Society
Gift of Arthur Sewall II, 1940

Following the British naval bombardment of Falmouth in 1775, John Quinby moved with his family to Saccarappa (Westbrook). In October 1782, he was married to Eunice Freeman (1762–1790) by the Reverend Samuel Deane (cat. 29). Within the next eight years, John and Eunice had six children, the eldest of whom was Eunice (see cat. 154), before Eunice died in childbirth and John was left a widower. In 1783, with capital inherited from his father, Quinby purchased a large lot in Stroudwater, land that had been confiscated from Francis Waldo, a Tory. The property commanded a view of the Fore River and was bounded at the rear by the Stroudwater River, a source of power for mills and fresh water.[1]

In 1785 housewright John Kimball billed John Quinby £50 for "fraiming & bording Shingling & Clabbording your house." Of two-and-one-half stories, it featured a central chimney and "luthrum" or dormer windows. Quinby and his partner Archelaus Lewis constructed a two-story shop on the south side of the Great Bridge across the Fore River and from there carried on their trade.[2]

An active shipbuilder, Quinby was full or partial owner of seven brigs, a barque, and six smaller vessels which traded at Lisbon; Liverpool; Cronstadt, Russia; the West Indies; and ports along the Atlantic seaboard. While Quinby certainly profited from shipbuilding during the Neutral Profits Era, he took a great loss when two ships and their cargoes were captured by the French. In 1797 the ship *Eunice*, en route from Liverpool to Philadelphia, was captured, and the schooner *Mary* was also taken. Quinby filed suit against the French government; under the authority of the French Spoilation Claims, reparation was finally made to the family for the *Eunice* in 1896.[3]

Miniatures were extremely popular personal items and Quinby's likeness was carefully executed in watercolor on an ivory ground. The surface of the ivory had to be lightly roughed to hold the pigments which had been mixed with gum arabic, glycerine, or other materials to achieve the desired consistency. The pigments were applied to the ivory in thin washes with a damp brush. After the basic shapes were blocked out, hatching, stippling, or a combination of both techniques were used to define the likeness. Facial highlights were achieved by leaving areas of the naturally translucent ivory bare while opaque white pigment was often used as a heavier accent for clothing. The miniaturist's work was accomplished with the aid of reducing and magnifying glasses mounted on stands to free the artist's hands. The subject would be studied through the reducing glass, enabling the artist to obtain the correct proportions while the magnifying glass would assist with the fine detail in the portrait itself.[4]

While John Quinby's portrait was executed in miniature, his sons Moses (1786–1857) and Levi (1787–1828) chose the oil-on-canvas format when their portraits were taken by John Brewster, Jr.[5] Although the artist of this miniature has not been identified, Quinby chose from a number of options when he decided to have it painted (see Chapter 4).   CSP

1 Lovejoy, *This was Stroudwater*, 129–130, 132–133.
2 Account, John Kimball to John Quinby, 1785, Andrew Hawes Collection, MEHS. Many of Quinby's papers were collected and preserved by his great-grandson Andrew Hawes. Lovejoy, *This was Stroudwater*, 133.
3 Lovejoy, *This was Stroudwater*, 136–138, 144.
4 Mona Leithiser Dearborn, *Anson Dickinson the Celebrated Miniature Painter, 1779–1852* (Hartford, Conn.: Connecticut Historical Society, 1983), xxiii, 8.
5 The portrait of Moses's wife Anne Titcomb Quinby was also painted by Brewster. For the three Brewster portraits, see Henry Cole Quinby, *Genealogical History of the Quinby (Quimby) Family* (New York, 1915). The portrait of Moses Quinby is in the collection of the Bowdoin College Museum of Art.

32

Attributed to John Coles, Jr. (1776 or 1780–1854)
Nathaniel Barrell (1732–1831)
Boston, Massachusetts, or York, Maine, 1816
Oil on panel
H 26⅜ (67.0); W 22⁷⁄₁₆ (56.9)
Old York Historical Society
Gift of Eunice Wheeler, 1963

The staid and stodgy countenance of Nathaniel Barrell in this portrait suggests a restrained pillar of the community. By the age of eighty-four, Barrell had indeed become a respected citizen, but in his youth he was one of York's more eccentric and outspoken characters.

Born in Boston in 1732, Nathaniel was the son of John and Ruth Greene Barrell. Like his father and brothers, he was a merchant and had trade interests in Portsmouth, New Hampshire, in the 1750s.[1] In 1758 he married Sally Sayward, the daughter of York's wealthiest merchant, Jonathan Sayward (see cat. 131 and Chapter 3). From 1760 to 1763 Nathaniel's business took him to England; upon his return to Portsmouth he was joined in his enterprises by his brother Colburn.

In 1764 Nathaniel became a convert of Robert Sandeman, a radical Englishman who preached in Portsmouth, Boston, and Connecticut. The Sandemanians were fiercely

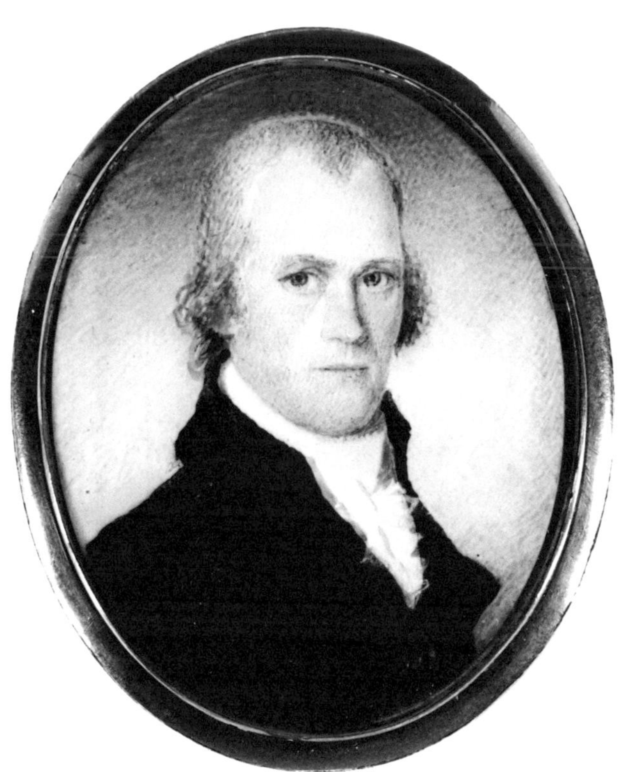

Cat. 31

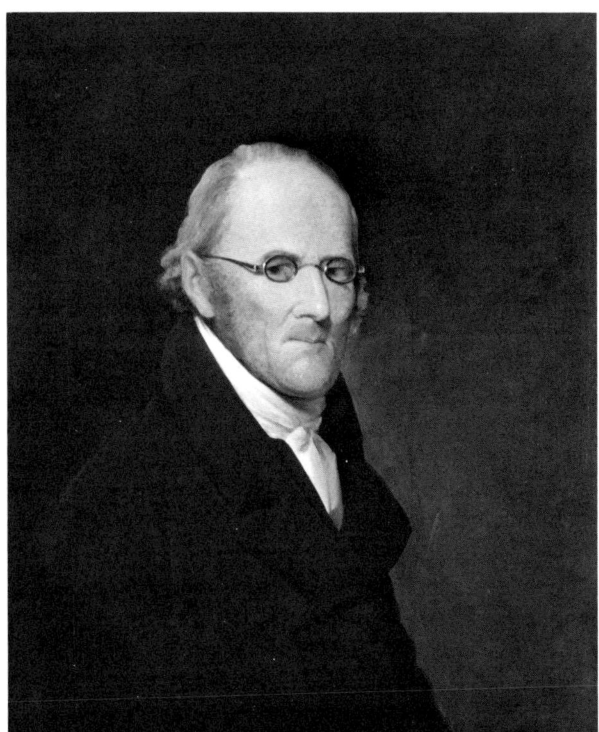

Cat. 32

inscription: "This Picture of Nathaniel Barrell / taken of him when he was eighty / four years old, was painted by the celebrated artist Cole in the / summer of eighteen hundred / and sixteen." The "celebrated Cole" may refer to John Coles, Jr., a Boston painter who studied under Gilbert Stuart and was painting portraits in Boston from 1807 to 1820. Coles's portraits are generally on panels and are characterized by lead color backgrounds.[5] The inscription may also relate to Moses Dupré Cole (b. 1783), a Newburyport portraitist who was working in Maine in 1817. In that year Cole advertised his services with a cut of a portrait in Portland's *Eastern Argus*.[6]   KAO

1 See cat. 101 for further discussion of the Barrell family.
2 George Ernst, *New England Miniature: A History of York, Maine* (Freeport, Me.: Bond Wheelwright Co., 1961), 170–177.
3 Joseph Barrell to Nathaniel Barrell, reprinted in Marston, "A Lady of Maine."
4 This is one of three similar portraits executed of Barrell. A second is at the Sayward-Wheeler house, SPNEA; the third is in a private collection.
5 Mantle Fielding, *Dictionary of American Painters, Sculptors and Engravers* (1926; revised ed., Green Farms, Conn.: Modern Books and Crafts, 1977), 72.
6 *Eastern Argus* (December 2, 1817). Martha Gandy Fales kindly brought this reference to my attention.

loyal to George III, which earned them political enemies, and Nathaniel lost many allies when he openly criticized the tenets of the established Congregational church. A hostile philosophical climate and heavy contributions to the Sandemanian church nearly bankrupted him in the late 1760s. Nathaniel retired to Barrell Grove, the estate in York built for him by Sayward, where he waited out the Revolution as a passive Loyalist (figs. 2.5 and 2.6). There he put his energies into experimental farming, planted orchards, and exotic crops, and tested new methods of germination and harvesting.[2]

Nathaniel was back in the public eye in 1787 when the anti-Federalist citizenry of York elected him and Esaias Preble as delegates to the Massachusetts constitutional convention. After considerable debate and impassioned letters from his Federalist brother, Joseph, Nathaniel reconsidered his opposition to the constitution.[3] In the end he was one of the slim majority of nineteen delegates who voted for ratification of the document, in spite of the opposing views of his constituents in Maine. Thereafter Barrell lived a quiet family life in York, making frequent trips to Boston. He died at the age of ninety-nine in 1831.

This oil on panel depicts a bust-length image of Barrell, gray-haired and bespectacled, in a brown frock coat and white shirt and cravat. A plain gray-black ground surrounds the sitter.[4] Penciled on the reverse of the panel is a later

33

Attributed to John Brewster, Jr. (1766–1854)
Colonel Thomas Cutts (1736–1821)
Elizabeth Scamman Cutts (1744/45–1803)
Saco, Maine, 1800–1801
Oil on canvas
H each 74⅝ (189.5); w each 30⅛ (76.5)
York Institute Museum;
Gift of George Addison Emery, 1867
Color plates on page 44

By practising the most rigid economy, even to the preparation of his own food, thereby avoiding the expense of board, and with the aid of an uncommon aptitude for business, Mr. Cutts within a short period enlarged his capital, and became engaged in lucrative and extensive transactions.

So reported George Folsom in his *History of Saco and Biddeford*, published nine years after the death of York County's wealthiest citizen.[1]

These full-length portraits of Colonel Thomas Cutts and his wife, Elizabeth Scamman Cutts, are significant in that they are the only examples known of adults in a standing pose attributed to John Brewster, Jr., the most prolific painter of Maine personalities during the federal period. A deaf-mute from birth, Brewster was the son of a respected and cultured Hampton, Connecticut, doctor and was encouraged to learn to read and write. By the early 1790s, his talent for painting had been developed under the direction of the Reverend Joseph Steward (1753–1822), a portraitist, and Brewster's early work reflected the styles of artists such as Steward and Ralph Earl (1751–1801). Following the convention of late eighteenth-century portraiture, the subjects of Brewster's earliest portraits were seated in chairs and placed in interiors with brightly patterned carpets or floorcloths.[2]

In the Cutts portraits, the artist depicted a patterned floor covering, but one with black figures on a drab brown-green ground rather than the bright colors of his earlier paintings. Brewster's knowledge of composition is apparent in his use of a walking stick placed on the diagonal to balance the mass of furniture in the lower right corner of Cutts's portrait, while his professional training taught him to extend Mrs. Cutts's dress beyond the edge of the canvas, creating an impression of stability in a portrait that would otherwise be too tall for its width.

Thomas Cutts's preference for conservatism was apparent in many aspects of his life, including his house (Chapter 3) and his wardrobe (cat. 158). In assessing the value of his estate, the appraiser described his clothing by the type of fabric or by the adjective "black."[3] Brewster painted Cutts dressed primarily in black, relieved only by a white stock and dark blue coat. Others of Cutts's generation and of lesser social status were wearing embroidered or striped silk waistcoats (cat. 157).

Like her husband, Elizabeth Cutts is portrayed in conservative attire. Her dress, fichu, and bonnet are the same articles of clothing worn by her contemporary, Eunice Pearson Deane (cat. 29). The small round box she holds is likely a container for snuff, a habit indulged in by both women and men.

With his gift of these portraits, great-grandson George Addison Emery commenced the "art gallery" at the York Institute Museum where they "are now and always have been a prominent attraction to all visitors to the museum."[4]

CSP

---

1 Folsom, *History*, 260.
2 Beatrix T. Rumford, ed., *American Folk Portraits* (Boston: New York Graphic Society, 1981), 65.
3 YCRP; 29:260.
4 *Biddeford Daily Journal* (December 16, 1890).

34

Attributed to John Brewster, Jr. (1766–1854)
Thomas Cutts, Jr. (1769–1839)
Saco, Maine, 1800–1801
Oil on canvas
H 26¹¹⁄₁₆ (77.7); W 25⁵⁄₁₆ (64.?)
York Institute Museum
Gift of the estate of George Addison Emery, 1934

John Brewster, Jr., painted waist-length portraits of two of the sons of Thomas and Elizabeth Cutts (cat. 33), his most common adult format. In contrast to the portraits of their parents, and befitting their age, the younger Cutts family members are portrayed in fashionable attire. Thomas, Jr., is dressed in a blue coat with bright buttons and a cravat tied with a large bow over a white shirt, the front ruffle clearly visible. His colorful striped vest is of a type popular in the early nineteenth century: a fancy front with an economical linen back. Cutts's spyglass is a symbol of his occupation as a ship captain, builder, and merchant. Thomas sports a typical turn-of-the-century hairstyle. The Reverend Caleb Bradley of Westbrook wrote in his journal on November 11, 1799: "had my hair cut off." For him the switch to a shorter, unfettered hairstyle was an event worth noting.[1]

Captain Thomas Cutts followed his father as shipbuilder and shipowner. His headquarters at Biddeford Pool consisted of his dwelling house, large store, and a shipyard. Shipping records maintained by him during the 1790s reveal his

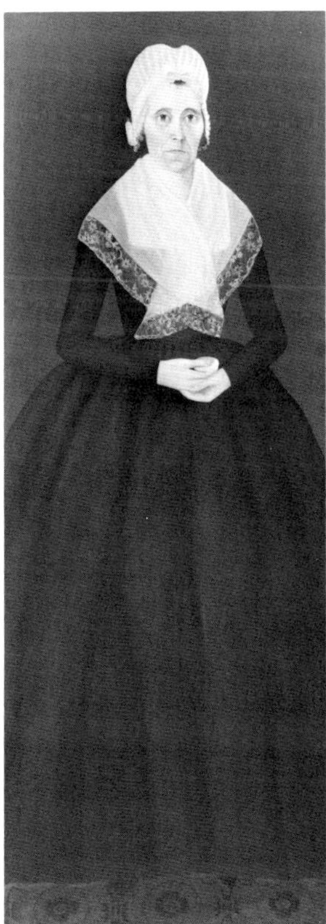

Cat. 33

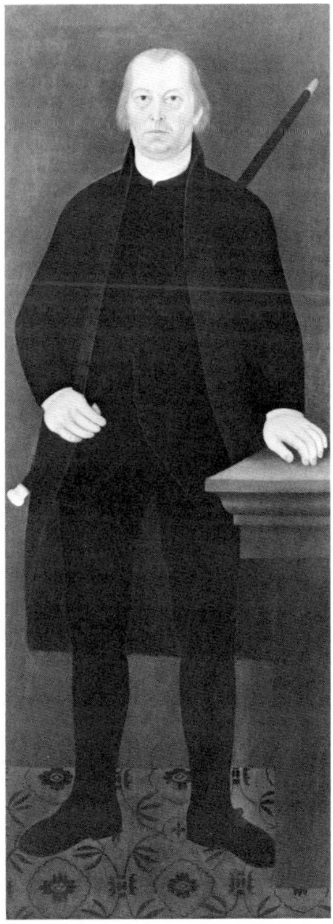

Cat. 33

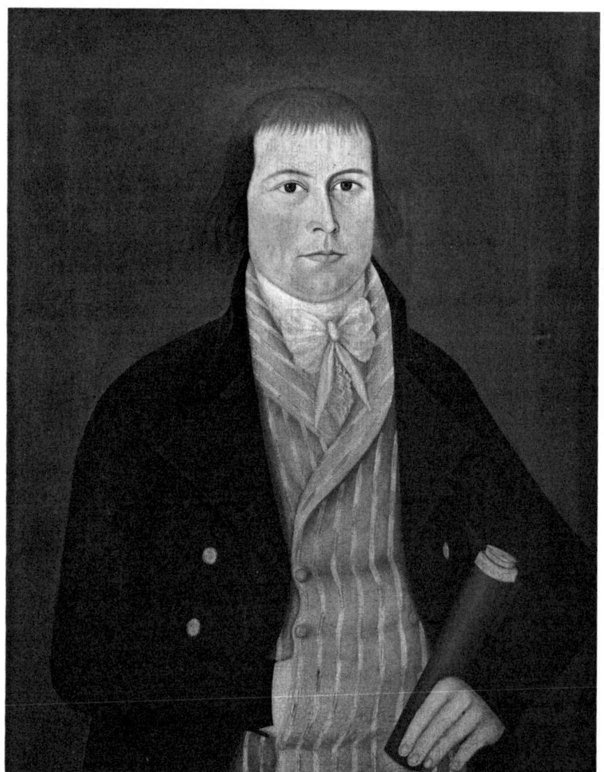

Cat. 34

extensive trade. Many of the cargoes he transported in his father's vessels were loaded in Liverpool and bound for Boston, Philadelphia, and ports in North Carolina. While commanding the ship *Minerva* between September 1793 and December 1795, he called at Bordeaux; Amsterdam; Hamburg; Brest; and Norfolk, Virginia; before returning to Bordeaux. On a voyage of the *Minerva* in 1794, the ship was taken by a French frigate and detained for a month in Brest.[2]

Constant access to foreign ports provided the opportunity for men like Thomas to acquire goods for their own and their family's personal use. Along with a cargo of textiles and earthenware onboard the *Betsey* from Liverpool in August 1790, Thomas Cutts had a crate marked "T.C. 8" containing "2 Kidderminster Bordered Carpets 4 by 3½ yards," "32 yards wide Kidderminster carpeting" and 22 yards of half width, "36 brass stair rods, 26 [inches] long," and "72 eyes" to hold them.[3] This amount would cover two rooms, probably two sets of stairs, and the first- and second-floor halls. Although the carpeting may have been for the Cutts mansion (see Chapter 3), it could also have been for the dwelling house of Foxwell, who had recently married Sarah Scamman (cat. 35).

In 1802 Thomas married Elizabeth Hight of Berwick. After her death, he married Mary Augusta Cook of Wiscasset. In contrast to his parent's silver, the hollowware given to

Thomas and Elizabeth was in fashionable neoclassical style—an urn-shaped sugar bowl and helmet-shaped creamer.[4]

During the War of 1812 Thomas Cutts continued to build ships in Biddeford Pool despite pressure from his family. "Your Father is anxious for you to have your Vessels moved out of danger of the Enemy," wrote Dominicus to his brother Thomas in April 1814; "I have always since the War advised you not to risque any property at the Pool that could be moved away." Cutts paid dearly for not heeding the warnings of his family. On June 16, 1814, the *Bulwark*, an English frigate of ninety guns, anchored nearby and landed. The whole detachment made its way to the Pool, where it destroyed two of Cutts's ships and took merchandise from his store. The damage was valued at $23,000 and included a ship carried off, later ransomed by Cutts for $6,000. According to local history, the appearance of the *Bulwark* was a response to an affront by Cutts to an English captain who put in at the Pool before the war. The captain became one of the officers of the *Bulwark*, and is credited for prompting the attack. Cutts's property might have been saved had there been a gun boat stationed in Winter Harbor as promised by the Navy Secretary to Richard Cutts; the boat never arrived and the harbor was left unprotected (see cat. 12).[5]

Thomas Cutts died in 1839 in possession of extraordinary wealth. Listed in the inventory of one of his houses is a portrait of "T Cutts" worth thirty cents and "1 Portrait" valued at $4. It is difficult to determine which entry, if either, related to this portrait of Thomas Cutts, Jr. Extremely low values were often placed on portraits of relatives determined to be of little or no interest outside the context of the family.[6] CSP & LFS

1 William Goold, Scrapbook, 102.
2 Thomas Cutts, Jr., book of invoices of goods shipped on the ship *Minerva*, 1792–1796, Cutts-Thornton Papers, MEHS. This is one of several shipping record books in this collection. Owen, *Old Times in Saco*, 82.
3 Invoice, August 4, 1790, book of invoices, 1790–1793, Cutts-Thornton Papers, MEHS.
4 This hollowware, along with a pair of sugar tongs and cat. 46, was photographed in a Biddeford studio in the late nineteenth century; Maine History Room, Dyer Library, Saco. The covered bowl and creamer are now in the Currier Gallery of Art, Manchester, N.H.
5 Owen, *Old Times in Saco*, 109–111.
6 YCRP; 50: 375–376.

35

Attributed to John Brewster, Jr. (1766–1854)
Foxwell Cutts (1765–1816)
Sarah Scamman Cutts (1768–1806)
Saco, Maine, 1800–1801
Oil on canvas
H each 30¹¹⁄₁₆ (78.0); w each 25⁵⁄₁₆ (64.2)
York Institute Museum
Gift of the estate of George Addison Emery, 1934

It is rather misleading to classify John Brewster, Jr., as an itinerant limner, for although he traveled in his work, he operated from an established base for most of his career. From his arrival in the District of Maine about 1796, Brewster lived with his brother Royal. On March 18, 1833, "John Brewster of Buxton, portrait painter" purchased from his brother Royal Brewster, Esq., eighty acres of land "which constitute the farm on which I now live" for the sum of $3,500.[1] His ability to purchase property is an indicator of his success as an artist. This success, reflected by the ownership of property and other assets, contradicts the myth that traveling artists worked solely for food and shelter and suggests widespread acceptance of the professional artist in rural Maine.

Brewster made painting trips to Maine, Massachusetts, New Hampshire, Vermont, and as far west as New York state.[2] However, a great deal of his work was executed close to home in York and Cumberland counties. These likenesses of Foxwell and his wife Sarah Cutts are two in a remarkable series of Cutts family portraits painted by Brewster during a period of twenty years and are typical of Brewster's Maine work. Although his later portraits show a degree of relaxation in the subjects' poses, the early single works, like these, tend to be rather stiff, with nose, chin, and hands aligned along the central axis of the painting. A man's hand is often slipped into the front opening of a waistcoat in Napoleonic fashion while the other is either not visible, as in this case, or is holding a symbol of the sitter's profession (cat. 34). Women's hands are usually flat and poorly defined. Brewster directed his creative energy instead toward the execution of the face and costume.

Foxwell, Colonel Cutts's oldest son, excelled in shipbuilding and shipowning until the Embargo and War of 1812. He was a member of the building committee of the First Parish Church in Saco, built by Bradbury Johnson (see Chapter 2 and fig. 2.13).[3] He died nearly insolvent in 1816 "by the misfortunes incident to merchants and the depressed state of commerce," and the contents of his estate were sold at auction. The broadside published for the sale revealed that

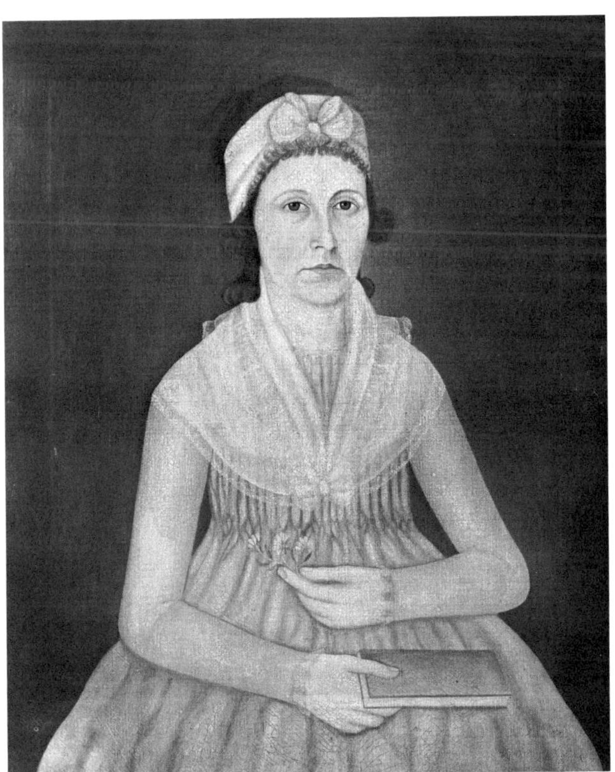

Cat. 35

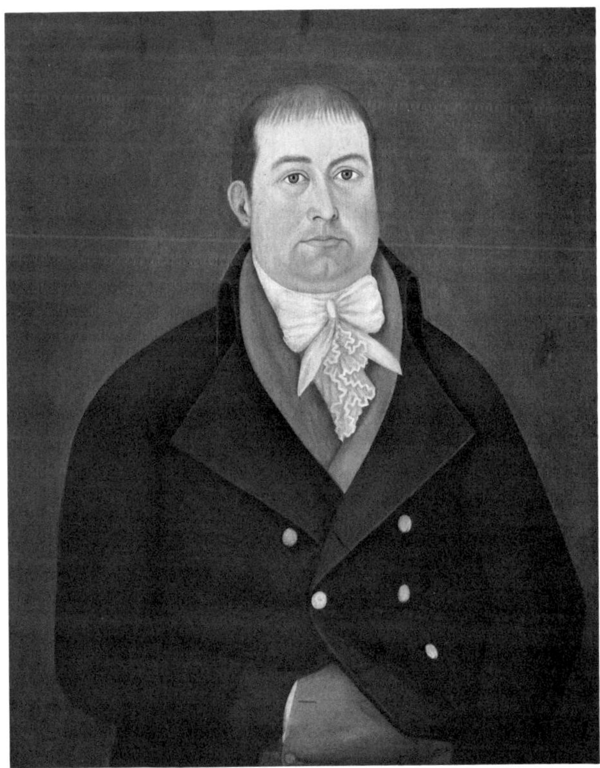

Cat. 35

$46,000 had to be raised. Allowances were made for his widow, Hannah, but she was not able to remain in her home.[4] Foxwell's sister Sarah and her husband Thomas Thornton gained occupancy of the Foxwell Cutts house on Main Street.

Sarah, Foxwell's first wife who died in 1806, is fashionably attired in a pink dress with a fitted bodice. The long sleeves are decorated with lace. Like many of her contemporaries, she has a short hair style, possibly a wig, ornamented with a wide band with bow. Brewster included a conventional spray of flowers and book, perhaps in reference to Sarah's education. CSP & LFS

1 Little, "John Brewster, Jr.," 103.
2 Little, "John Brewster, Jr.," 100–102. Joyce Hill, "Miniatures by John Brewster, Jr.," *The Clarion* 49 (Spring/Summer 1983): 49, 50.
3 Folsom, *History*, 296, 305.
4 Necessities to widow, January 1817, YCRP; docket 3870.

36

Attributed to John Brewster, Jr. (1766–1854)
Thomas Gilbert Thornton (1768–1824)
Sarah Cutts Thornton (1774–1845)
Saco, Maine, ca. 1820
Oil on canvas
H each 30¹⁵⁄₁₆ (78.6); w each 25⅝ (65.0)
York Institute Museum
Gift of the estate of George Addison Emery, 1934

Boston-born Thomas Gilbert Thornton settled in Saco in 1791. Two years later he married Sarah Cutts, the third daughter of Colonel Thomas Cutts. They had twelve children, eight of whom lived beyond infancy.

A practicing physician, Thornton left medicine for a more lucrative mercantile career, and in 1803 President Thomas Jefferson appointed him marshal for the District, a post he held until his death in 1824. The office of United States marshal was profitable for Thornton, especially during the years 1812–1815 when captured vessels, war prizes, and smuggled goods passed through his hands in great numbers.[1] After the capture of HM brig *Boxer*, it was Thornton's duty to settle the claims and divide the prizes (see cats. 12–15). His thousand dollar donation to Saco Academy, incorporated in 1811, was acknowledged by the change in name to Thornton Academy.

Thornton's duties required him to spend much of his time in Portland, although his family continued to live in Saco. During the frequent journeys between the two towns, Thornton characteristically wore a scarlet cloak (see cat. 161), a long buff vest, a shirt with a ruffled neck opening, and a sword. Thomas Thornton and Richard Hunnewell, Sheriff

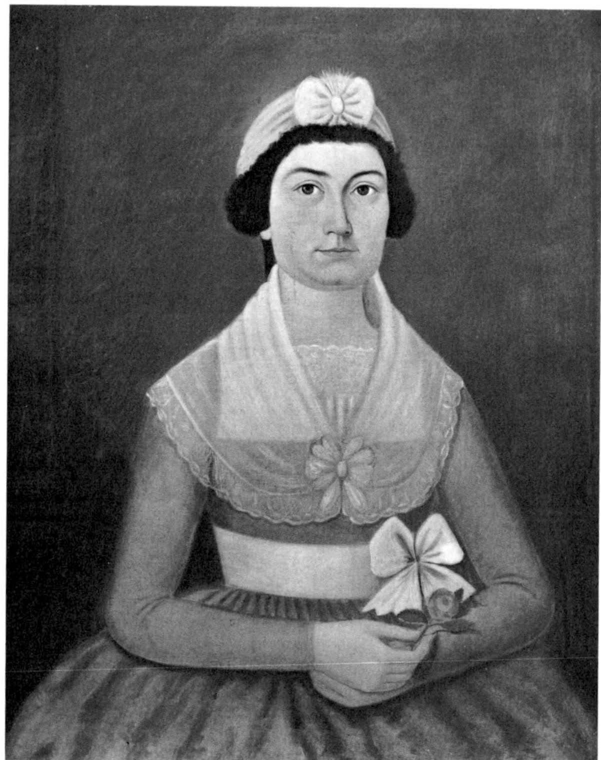

Cat. 36

of Cumberland County, were the last practitioners of this style of official dress, one that also included a cocked hat.[2]

Thomas Thornton was recorded as a genial although eccentric man, prominent among a group of Saco and Biddeford men "of intelligence and refinement" who periodically entertained at evening parties in their homes.[3] Although Thornton was celebrated for the elegant suppers that he gave at his large three-story house on Main Street, his wife was equally renowned as a hostess. It was Sarah who gave the Peace Ball in 1815 and, after the death of her husband, entertained General Lafayette.

These portraits of Thomas and Sarah Thornton were most likely painted in 1820, at the same time as those of their children, James, Elizabeth, and Sarah (cat. 37). By the 1820s Brewster had altered his technique to allow gray priming to show through thin layers of paint; complexions were ruddier and less delicate than the skin tones of his earlier work. Costumes, however, received the same attention to detail. Thornton was portrayed wearing a plain stock around his neck and a "spotted" double-breasted waistcoat, fashionable for the period. Waistlines for women's gowns had dropped from just below the bosom to a more natural location; the waistline of Sarah's light blue dress was emphasized by a large bow.

The portrait of Sarah Cutts Thornton was familiar to her

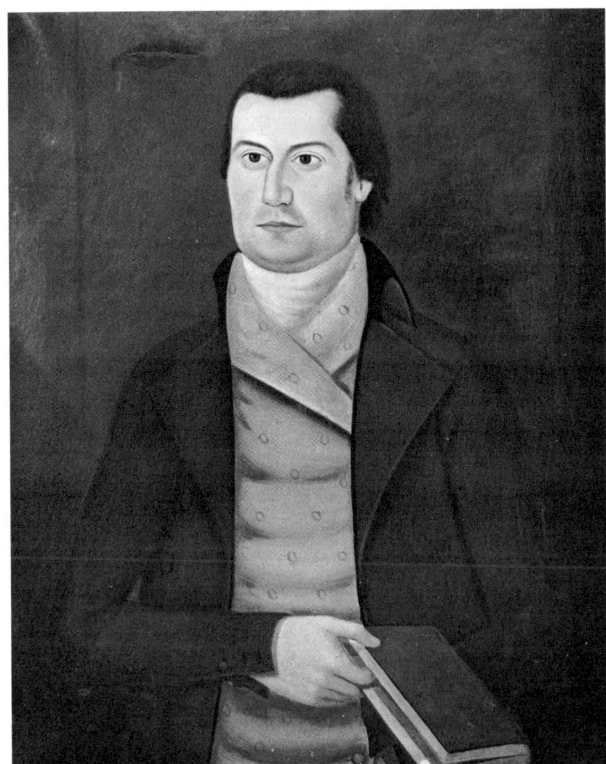

Cat. 36

John Brewster, Jr. (1766–1854)
Probably *James Brown Thornton* (1794–1873)
Saco, Maine, 1820
Oil on canvas
Inscribed (stretcher) "John Brewster Jr. pinxt
February 28, 1820"
H 30⅜ (77.2); W 24½ (62.2)
York Institute Museum; Gift of Sarah Bradbury Elden, 1896

37B

John Brewster, Jr. (1766–1854)
Elizabeth Cutts Thornton (1799–1841)
Saco, Maine, 1820
Oil on canvas
Inscribed (stretcher) "John Brewster Jr pinxt.
March [1]st 1820"
H 26⁷⁄₁₆ (67.2); W 25⅛ (63.8)
York Institute Museum; Gift of Sarah Bradbury Elden, 1896

37C

John Brewster, Jr. (1766–1854)
Sarah Cutts Thornton (1801–1892)
Saco, Maine, 1820
Oil on canvas
Inscribed (stretcher) "[pi]next Feb.y 1820
[possibly John Brewster]"
H 30¾ (78.1); W 25⅜ (64.5)
York Institute Museum; Gift of Sarah Bradbury Elden, 1896

This portrait of a young man (cat. 37A) is presumed to be
the likeness of James Brown Thornton, the eldest of the
Thornton offspring. It is the earliest dated portrait of a group
of five known of the Thornton family, including the parents
(cat. 36) and two sisters, Elizabeth and Sarah, discussed
here. This portrait is not of William Albert Cutts (1833–
1877) as previously thought, as it predates his birth.[1]
Another possible sitter is William Temple Cutts, the eldest
son of Thomas Cutts, Jr. (cat. 34). Confirmation of the
sitter's identity, however, awaits further research.

James Thornton was a successful merchant at Saco. He
not only inherited money but also "achieved a fortune" in his
own right. He married Eliza Gookin of North Hampton,
New Hampshire, on January 20, 1817. Their son John
Wingate Thornton was an early antiquarian who studied
Maine and New Hampshire history. In 1849 James's
portrait was taken again, this time in Boston by John
Greenough who worked his profile in cameo.[2]

daughter Anne Payne Thornton and her husband John
Fairfield, later governor of Maine. While serving as a senator
in Washington, D. C., John wrote to his wife in 1836
describing the dress of a woman "said to be the fashion latest
from Paris," the sleeve of which was snug in fit and reached a
little more than halfway to the elbow. Fairfield compared the
new style to the full sleeves that were previously popular: "I
never thought they were graceful or added in any way to the
beauty of the form. If I recollect rightly, your Mother's dress
in her portrait will be all the go, though I don't feel very
positive about the dress in the portrait." The donor, George
Addison Emery, was a grandson of Thomas and Sarah
Thornton. These portraits were recorded among the
"pictures of prominent local personages" on exhibit in the
Institute in 1890.[4]   CSP & LFS

1 Extensive Thornton Papers recording Thomas's activities as marshal
   as well as family matters survive in MEHS and the New England
   Historic Genealogical Society, Boston.
2 Portland Scrapbook, 24 vols., 2:50, MEHS.
3 Portland Scrapbook, 2:50, MEHS.
4 Cited in Arthur G. Staples, ed., *The Letters of John Fairfield* (Lewiston,
   Me., 1922), 115–116. *Biddeford Daily Journal* (December 16, 1890).

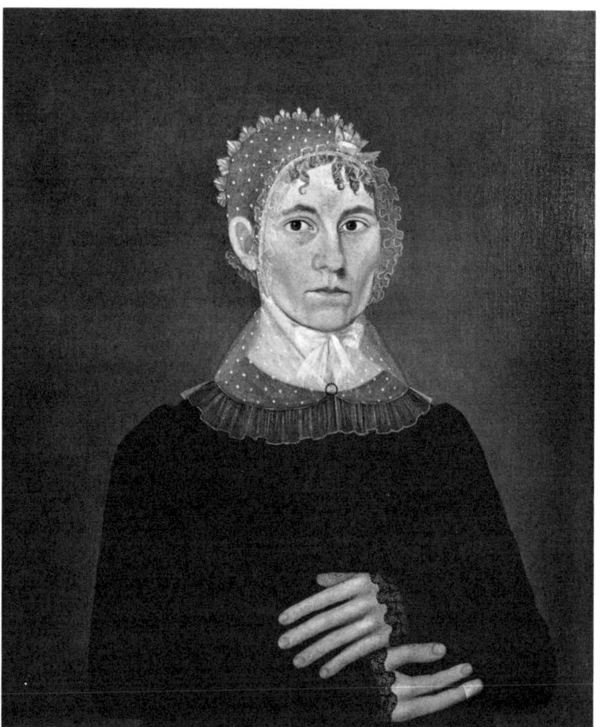

Cat. 37B

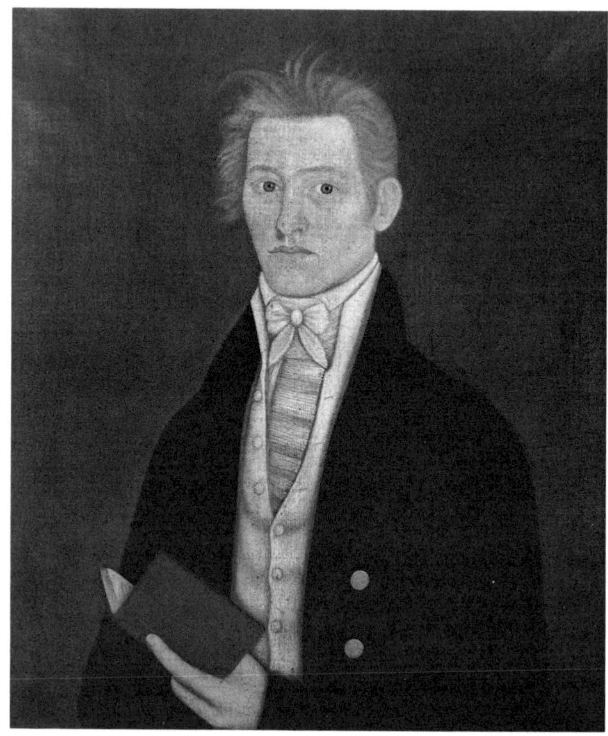

Cat. 37A

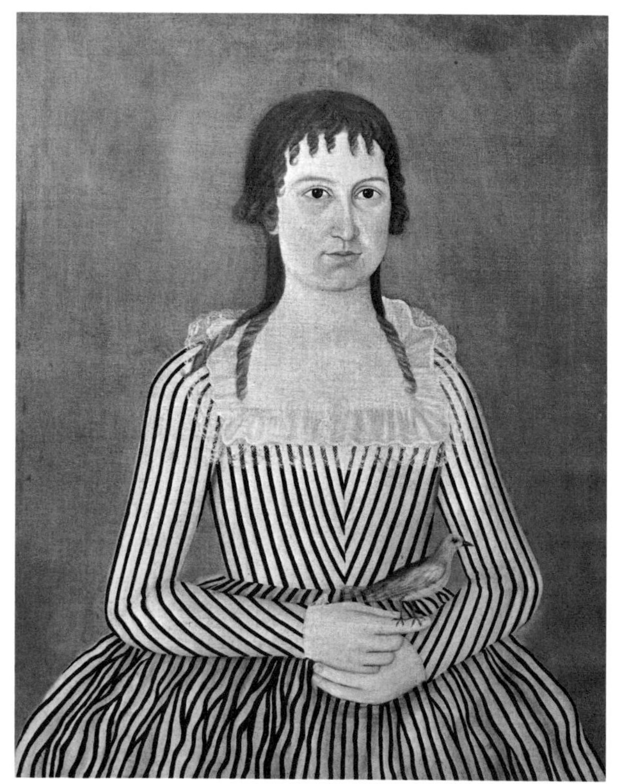

Cat. 37C

This portrait of Elizabeth (cat. 37B) was painted the year of her marriage to her cousin William Cutts (1786–1867) of Berwick. Her matronly status is represented by the cap covering her head. The thimble worn on her finger is atypical; sewing tools and other objects used exclusively by women were not often depicted in Brewster's work. Her plain black dress is softened only by a ruffled fichu which matches her cap. Her hollow cheeks, tight mouth, thin fingers, and the overall severity of the portrait indicate a denial of promise and good health that is evident in her pleasingly plump younger sister. Although she did marry and had three children, Betsy predeceased her mother (cat. 36) by four years, and siblings James and Sarah by fifty years.[3]

Of the three portraits of the Thornton children, the likeness of Sarah (cat. 37C) is most striking. She is dressed in the height of fashion with hair to match. Like the dress of her mother, hers of vivid pink and black stripes reflects the trend back to a natural waistline. Brewster effectively used the stripes to accentuate the difference between the tight sleeves and bodice and the full skirt. The severity of the bodice is softened by a white ruffle edged in lace. A small bird perched on Sarah's index finger is a convention used by Brewster in his portraits of women and young children. Like the portraits of the parents, Brewster's priming shows through the thinly applied paint and gives a gray cast to this and the other canvases.[4]

In 1823 Sarah married Moses Emery. Their youngest
child, George Addison Emery, presented the portraits of
Colonel Thomas and Elizabeth Cutts (cat. 33) to the York
Institute at the time of its founding in 1867 and gave other
family possessions in the early twentieth century.   CSP & LFS

1 It was published as the "son of William Cutts" in Little, "John
   Brewster, Jr.," 109.
2 Portland Scrapbook, 24 vols., 2:50, MEHS. Eliza Gookin was a
   descendant of the Reverend Nathaniel Gookin of Hampton; her son,
   James Brown, filled the Hampton pulpit in 1864. Joseph Dow, *History
   of the Town of Hampton* (1893; reprint, Somersworth, N.H.: New
   Hampshire Publishing Co., 1970), 458. For a partial bibliography of
   John Wingate Thornton's Maine writing, see Joseph Williamson, *A
   Bibliography of the State of Maine*, 2 vols. (Portland: Thurston Print,
   1896), 2: 517–518. Many of the manuscripts he collected are in the
   New England Historic Genealogical Society, Boston. The cameo is at
   MEHS.
3 Cecil Hampden Cutts Howard, comp., *Genealogy of the Cutts Family in
   America* (Albany, N.Y.: Joel Munsell's Sons, 1892), 82, 159.
   Elizabeth's miniature was painted on ivory when she was a young girl
   (1807–1810) and is at YIS. Sarah Elden gave the portrait of her
   husband, William Cutts, to YIS at the same time.
4 The portrait was previously published as Sarah Cutts (1774–1845)
   but, because of the date and other evidence, it represents instead her
   daughter; Little, "John Brewster, Jr.," 105. Although Sarah's
   youngest sister, Anna Payne, attended the Saunders and Beach
   Academy in 1822, the schools Elizabeth and Sarah attended have not
   been identified. See bill, Mrs. Saunders and Miss Beach to T. G.
   Thornton, August 20, 1822, Thornton Collection, New England
   Historic Genealogical Society.

38

Unidentified artist
Plan of Ann Street, Portland
Portland, Maine, ca. 1802
Pen and ink and watercolor on paper
L 38¹³⁄₁₆ (98.5); W 11¹¹⁄₁₆ (29.7)
Maine Historical Society
Gift of Charles Thornton Libby, 1909

Upon his arrival in Portland from Ontario in 1783, Thomas
Robison (1747–1806) launched an extensive building
program (see Chapter 2). He opened Ann Street (now Park)
from Congress Street to the water. The lower end of Ann
Street was the hub of his activity: his dwelling house, wharf,
warehouse, distill house, and cooper's shop were located
there. This plan of Robison's estate is a rare document that
reveals the scope of a prosperous Maine merchant's estate
and the conveniences it afforded. It was drawn at the time of
its pending sale, and Robison's subsequent departure from
Portland.

   The "explanation" accompanying the plan details the
property. The first four references are to his business enterprises:

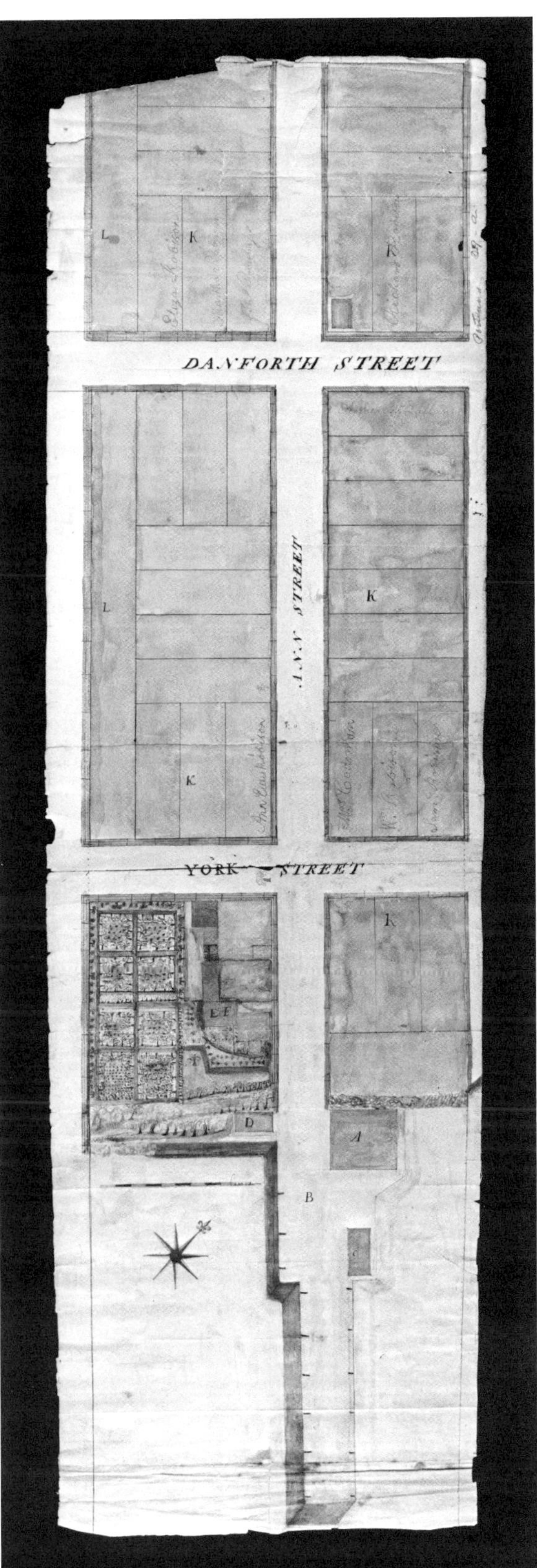

Cat. 38

*A. A Distill house with every thing proper to distill spirits. it is Built
with bricks & Stone and is the first in America of its size
B. A Wharf agreeable to the scale built with large Logs of Wood and
covered with Stone and Earth. Vessels of 11 feet water may load along
side of it. if it were run out 180 feet more it would extend to the Channel
where there is five fathoms at low water
C. A Store house on the wharf 50 feet long 25 feet broad and 3 stories
high
D. A Coopers Shop 40 by 20 feet*

To find men who could design and operate his distill
house, Robison enlisted the assistance of his Boston agent,
Robert Jenkins. Getting the business underway took
patience. In February 1784, Jenkins wrote: "the Gentleman,
whome I purpose[d] to get to draw you a plan of a *Distill-
house*, is a member of our General Assembly, which is now
setting and when his hurry is a little over, he will do it—I
don't hear of a person yet for [operating] your distillery—."[1]
Robison, familiar with the distilling business, ordered
literature on the subject, but Jenkins could not "find the two
Books you mention'd on distillation & Architecture." During
March 1784, the "Gentleman's time is so much taken up
with Genl. Assembly that he can't drawn the plan for your
Stillhouse as yet." By April, however, Daniel Ilsley assured
Robison that he would "superintend making Rum." Another
delay was that bricks in Boston were "very scarce. They may
be had here, but have risen to 8 Dollrs pr M [thousand] for

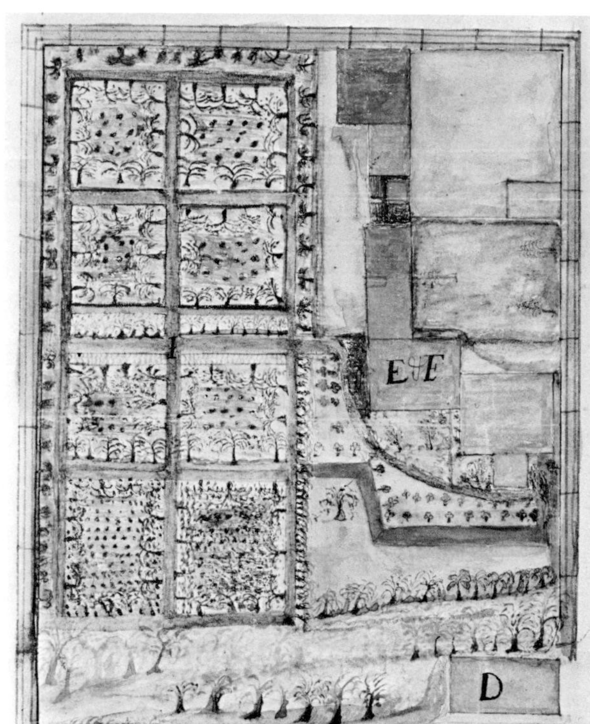

Cat. 38 detail

what they have on hand—no more can be made until next
June."[2] Nevertheless, Robison perservered and his distill
house was in operation by January.

Robison's domestic estate and gardens are outlined by
three parts of his "explanation":

*E & F A house and Out houses with a fine Cellar under the whole[.]
the house has two parlors 8 bed Rooms, a large Kitchen and many other
conveniences, the Stable will hold 8 tons of hay two horses & two
Cows, a good place for 2 Chaises a Place that will hold a quantity of
Wood—a place for keeping poultry & c. a Place for drying and
bleaching linnen[.] the whole commands a fine prospect of the town of
Portland and all the neighbouring Islands.*

Housewrights Smith Cobb and Isaac Little were two
joiners who worked on these buildings. In their accounts are
many references to architectural details that document the
decorative interior and exterior ornamentation of "Capt.
Thomas Robinsons House." For the front hall were "27 yds.
wainscot with frees [frieze] Pannell," "9 yds ditto up ye
Stairway," and "two Ramp and twisted rails . . . Banisters &
Caping Posts." Smith Cobb made "the Arch over the Stair
Case with the Moulding & Lamp[?] Panells." Outside, the
lobby, or projecting porch, may have been listed as "the
Platform, Steps, with Posts & Rails Capt & Chinees Railing." Many accounts with cabinetmakers and other
craftsmen describe the work done for and in these buildings,
including cutting pigeonholes in the wood house and
mending the drawers in the dining room.[3]

Around Robison's house was:

*I. A Garden of almost an Acre of Ground with fine fruit Trees from
Princes Garden. there are fine Currents & Gooseberries planted all
around[.]*

Abigail May, a friend of Robison's daughter Martha whom
she called Matty, made frequent trips to the Robison house,
"New Scotland." She described one of her afternoon visits to
"the mansion of hospitality":

*Matty and I took our work and seated ourselves under the willows at the
bottom of the garden where the air from the water was quite rifreshing
. . . all nature was gay and laughing the birds chanted their wild carrols
on every tree a delightful piece of water murmur'd at our feet and the
prospect beyond was more enchanting than fancy can conceive or
language describe[4]*

In 1867 a historian noted that "the tide then flowed up to
[Robison's] garden wall, on the bank he planted willows,
which have been recently taken down after having stood
sentry upon the bank for seventy years."[5]

Robison owned the property along Ann Street including,

*K Lots of Land for building on; each lot is 150 by 50 feet the whole of
the land is on a fine declivity which will make everything appear more
agreeable than if it was on a dead flat.*

John Seymour, the English cabinetmaker whom Robison patronized, lived in a house owned by Robison, designated here as the block on the corner of Ann and Danforth streets, now the site of the Morse-Libby mansion (see Chapter 4).[6] Although Robison had plans for the full development of these lots, particularly for the rope walks, this did not come to fruition under his supervision or during his lifetime.

When Thomas Robison and his wife left this house around 1802 to return to Ontario, it remained in the family. His son Thomas, Jr., carried on a very successful distillery trade, but by 1867 no family members remained in town. It was in this year that historian William Willis lamented the demise of "the seat of an elegant hospitality," further describing it as a "house which retained all its original features . . . which has had to yield to the advancing progress of the time."[7] Robison's development of Ann Street has since the late nineteenth century gone unnoticed, overshadowed by the building of the rowhouses on Park Street around 1830 just north of "New Scotland."

This plan is the finest known for federal Maine.[8] The house and outbuildings are picked out in red; the lots, in green; and the garden, in green and brown. When Robison purchased this property in partnership with William Edgar of New York, the parcel extended to Congress Street. This plan includes only that part which Robison retained at the dissolution of the partnership in 1788. The names of Robison's children are inscribed in pencil on the lots on Ann Street and probably indicate the property division. Accompanied by Robison's extensive contemporary accounts, this plan documents, as no other source can, one entrepreneur's domestic and commercial environment.   LFS

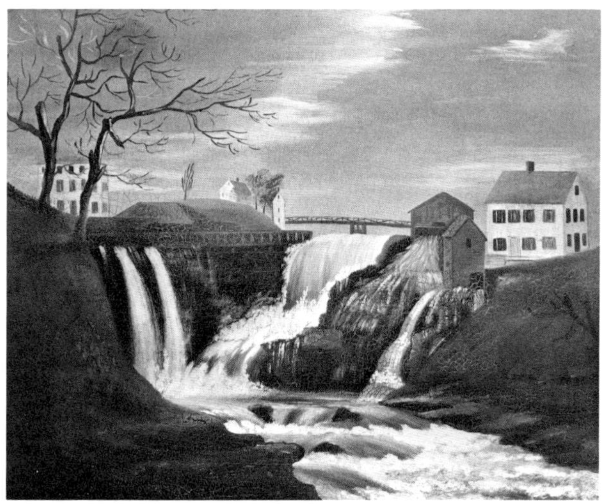

Cat. 39

39

William Stoodley Gookin (1799—after 1872)
View of Saco Falls
Saco, Maine, 1829
Oil on canvas
Inscribed (stretcher) "View of Saco Falls/ William S. Gookin/1829"
H 24⅞6 (62.0); W 30⅛ (76.5)
York Institute Museum

The Saco River was central to the development of northern York County. Timothy Dwight recognized the importance of the waterfall in Saco to the area's economic development and commented on it in 1807:

At a small distance above this island, a ridge of rocks crosses the Saco, and presents to the eye of a traveler a noble cataract, descending fourty feet in a great variety of wild and magnificient torrents. On this fall is a collection of sawmills, said to have cut four million feet of boards annually before the late American war, and to furnish still a very great quantity. The Saco is navigable for vessels of one hundred tons to the foot of this fall. Logs are floated down to these mills from the distance of sixty miles. As the lands on both sides are not likely soon to be cultivated, they may, if prudently managed, continue for a long time to yield a large supply of timber.[1]

The growth of industry along the Saco River during the first quarter of the nineteenth century changed the face of the landscape and shaped the progress of the future. This image of the powerful falls evokes that development. At the head of the falls on both banks are two clusters of mills; two sawmills and two gristmills on each side of the river. These represent the earliest types built. By the mid-nineteenth

1 Robert Jenkins to Thomas Robison, Boston, February 18, 1784, Robison Papers, MEHS.
2 See distillery record book, 1776–1784, Robert Jenkins to Thomas Robison, March 11, 1784; and Thomas Robison to Enoch Ilsley, April 24, 1784, Robison Papers, MEHS.
3 Account, Smith Cobb to Thomas Robison, 1784; and account, Isaac Little to Thomas Robison, August 1784. For two examples of the work of other craftsmen, see account, John Seymour to Mr. Robison, December 24, 1784, and account, John Seymour to Mr. Robison, March 16, 1787, Robison Papers, MEHS.
4 Abigail May, diary, MEHS.
5 William Willis, "Another Relic Gone," *Portland Daily Press* (May 9, 1867), Scrapbook, 1865–1869, 3 vols., 3:17, MEHS.
6 For a discussion of Seymour and his work for Robison, see Sprague, "John Seymour in Portland, Maine."
7 William Willis, Scrapbook, 3:17, MEHS.
8 The plan of James Rundlet's Portsmouth estate is illustrated in Robert D. Mussey, Jr., "Rundlet-May House, Portsmouth, New Hampshire," *Antiques* 129, no. 3 (March 1986): 644.

century, they were replaced by fortress-like brick industrial structures on Cutts Island. The changes in the name of this prominent and important property, seen at the left, once Indian Island and later Factory Island, reflect the growth of Biddeford and Saco.

On the right, in Saco, is a white two-story gable-roofed house, typical of late eighteenth-century construction. The large house on Cutts Island was built by Richard Cutts (1771–1845), the third son of Colonel Thomas, around the time of his 1804 marriage to Anne Payne, Dolley Madison's sister. It reflects the style of domestic architecture preferred by the coastal elite; the four-square block of three stories with a low hipped roof was painted yellow. Between 1801 and 1813 Cutts served in the United States Congress and traveled between Saco and Washington. After 1813, when he became superintendent of military supplies and resided in Washington, his house was occupied by Dominicus (1778–1844), his younger brother. Situated on the edge of the high island, the land between the house and the river was terraced.[2]

The bridge spanned the Saco River east of Cutts Island. The first bridge constructed in this location in 1760 was financed by a lottery authorized by the General Court; the first drawing was held in May 1759. A freshet in 1785 destroyed the Lottery Bridge and in 1786 the inhabitants of Pepperrellborough voted to provide lumber to build a new bridge; Colonel Thomas Cutts, whose own bridge connected Cutts Island and the Biddeford shore to the west, was awarded the contract.[3] Dwight elaborated on these vital structures:

Colonel Cutts . . . is also the proprietor of the bridge, which is said to yield him a handsome profit from the toll. A Mr. Spring, who lives on another island a little farther up, was building a second bridge, intending to turn the traveling by his own house, which he expected to accomplish by making the passage free.[4]

Maine landscapes from this period are rare, although they are known to have been painted; occasionally they decorated overmantel panels and fireboards (fig. 4. 3). Although this example is the only oil painting of a local landscape scene that dates before 1830 in the collections discussed here, it represents the shift from portraiture that paralleled the increasing awareness of Americans in their new land (see Chapter 4). Such an interest was expressed by Ann Smith after a ride in the countryside around Portland: "On our route we had one of the finest views I ever saw. The prospect so fine that [I] regretted my not being a landskip painter. I am not capable of describing its beauties."[5]

Twenty years after Dwight's visit, when Anne Royall reported on the scene, the beauty of the landscape and importance of industry were interwoven:

The buildings of the factory stand on an Island; this and the falls . . . the bustle of the workmen, the noise of the numerous mills, &c., the view and roaring of the falls, renders Saco a lively, delightful, and picturesque town. The scenery is by far the most handsome and variegated of any town in Maine. The land on the opposite shore being hilly and wooded — the falls in the center of the town. It has a most wild and fanciful appearance. There are three bridges over the Saco river at this place, connecting it with Biddeford, and the shipping in the harbor, all adds to its beauty.[6]

Later in the century, artists painted landscapes of Biddeford and Saco with a greater frequency. The enthusiasm of artists such as Gibeon Bradbury of Salmon Falls matched Gookin's early efforts.[7]

Born in 1799, the sixth child of Nathaniel and Elizabeth Gookin, William S. Gookin was responsible for the view of the Saco Falls taken in April 1829, and reproduced as the frontispiece to George Folsom's *History of Biddeford and Saco* (1830). This painting—taken from a slightly different view—was probably painted at the same time. A small pastel landscape at the York Institute is attributed to Gookin.

By 1837 William Gookin lived in Dover, New Hampshire, where he worked in several different genres. Although portraiture was his mainstay, he continued to paint landscapes that were generalized views of pastoral scenes. He also painted "fancy pictures," shaped to fit fireplace openings. One such work was a landscape Gookin painted for George Wadleigh of Dover. By copying daguerreotypes, Gookin found a new specialty. He took "Miniatures of Deceased persons, that no one can do and [gave] satisfaction to the friends of the deceased persons."[8] KDM & LFS

1 Dwight, *Travels*, 2:154.
2 Henry S. Burrage, "Richard Cutts," *Collections of the Maine Historical Society*, 2d ser., 8 (1897): 7, 24; and Henry S. Burrage, "Some Letters of Richard Cutts," *Collections of the Maine Historical Society Collections*, 2d ser., 9 (1898): 16.
3 Owen, *Old Times in Saco*, 55–56, 79.
4 Dwight, *Travels*, 2:154. Cutts charged only "strangers"; see Folsom, *History*, 275.
5 Ann Smith, diary, August 28, 1806, MEHS.
6 Royall, *Black Book*, 2:333.
7 Many of Bradbury's paintings are at YIS; see Kerry A. O'Brien, *Gibeon Elden Bradbury (1833–1904), Painter of the Saco Valley* (Saco, Me.: York Institute Museum, 1986). His sketchbooks are owned by MEHS.
8 Cited in Frank O. Spinney, "William S. Gookin, Portrait Painter of Dover, New Hampshire," *Old-Time New England* 34, no. 4 (April 1944): 61–66.

40

Unidentified artist
Tavern sign
New England, probably Maine, 1790–1820
Eastern white pine
H 12⅜ (31.4); W 37¹³/₁₆ (96.0)
Old York Historical Society

This tavern sign may have been observed by Edward
Kendall on his travels through York County. He commented
on the dwellings "on the road, in the intervals between the
villages . . . not a few of them have boards hung out, on
which are uncouth inscriptions offering *spirituous liquors for*
sale."[1] In this case the painter misspelled the word fruit; the
second *u* had to be corrected and left a gap in the word.

In addition to illustrating Kendall's observation, this
board is of interest because of the glass decanter which has
been included as part of the decoration. Its plain, sugar-loaf
shape is a standard of the federal period.

On his death in 1790, Samuel Jefferds, a tavernkeeper in
Wells, owned "1 sign for a tavern" valued at 1*s.* 6*d.*[2]   LFS

1 Kendall, *Travels*, 45. Other tavern signs have been recorded in local
  histories; see one recorded in Banks, *History*, 2:326 inscribed, "Rum,
  Wine, Brandy Sold here."
2 YCRP; 16:268.

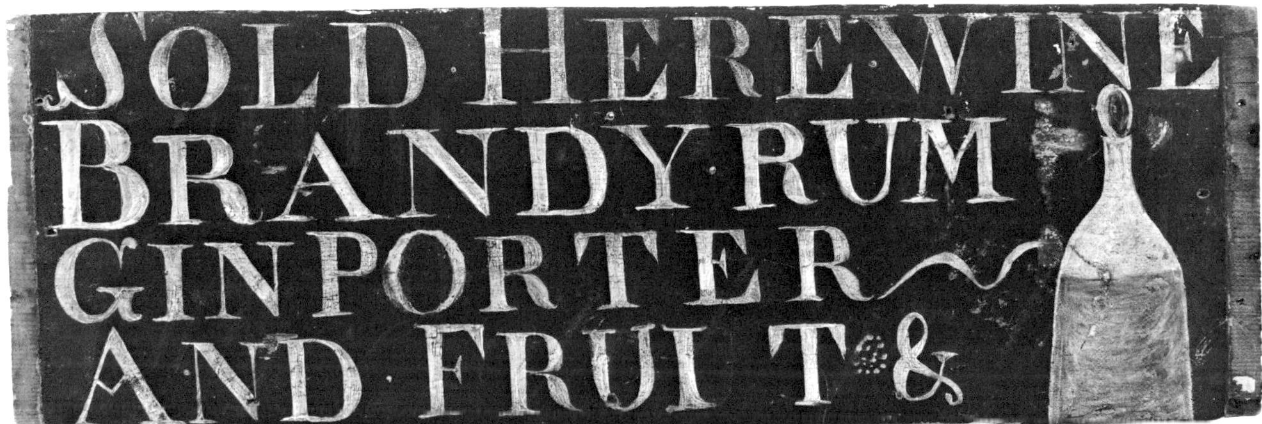

Cat. 40

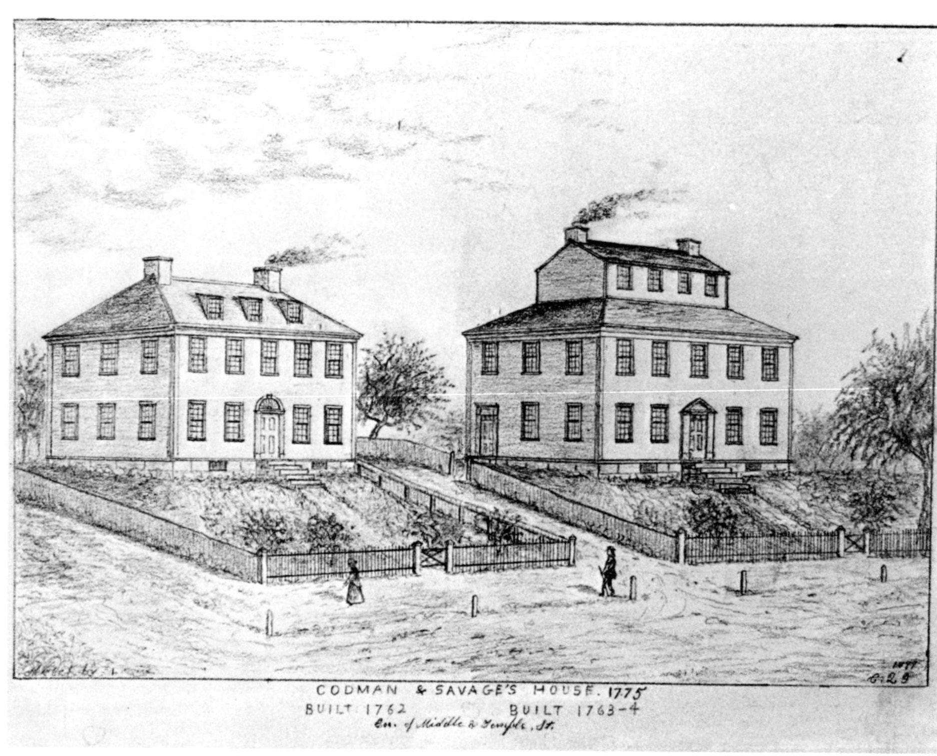

Fig. 3.1 Charles Q. Goodhue, *Codman & Savage's House. 1775*, Portland, Maine, 1899. Pencil on paper; H 9 (22.9), W 12 (30.5). Codman house (left) built 1762. Maine Historical Society.

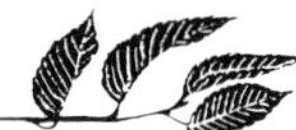

Chapter 3

"Fit for a Noble Man":
Domestic Interiors and the Style
of Living in Coastal Maine

Laura Fecych Sprague

On July 9, 1774, while on the Superior Court circuit in Maine, John Adams dined with Richard Codman, a Bostonian who had moved to Falmouth in the 1760s. In a letter to his wife Abigail, Adams wrote of his "very genteel Dinner" and described Codman's house. It was "A large spacious, elegant House, Yard, and Garden &c. I thought I had got into the Palace of a Nobleman" (fig. 3.1).[1] Codman's commercial success as a merchant was reflected by his dwelling house in the heart of eighteenth-century Falmouth. In 1785 Jonathan Sayward of York visited Theodore Lyman at "his seat," a newly built mansion house in Kennebunk (fig. 3.2). Sayward recorded in his diary that "it is fit for a noble man & I have seen nothing like it in this County and Scar[ce]ly any where."[2] To what degree did the enthusiastic reviews of Adams, Sayward, and other visitors in Maine from the 1770s to the 1820s correspond to the sophistication of the interiors and styles of living they actually encountered?

From the start of the eighteenth century, fashionable two-story Georgian-style houses with spacious central halls first appeared in, but were not limited to, urban centers such as Boston.[3] This preferred architectural style was transplanted as merchant families expanded their business enterprises to the northeast. Prosperous members of the merchant class had built large, elegant houses of this type in Maine throughout the colonial period. Of particular note are the houses in southern York County built by the Pepperrell family. Colonel William Pepperrell's house on Kittery Point was built in 1683 with changes in the early eighteenth century to increase formal first-floor spaces. Sparhawk Hall (1742), built for Sir William Pepperrell's daughter and son-in-law (fig. 2.3), and the Lady Pepperrell house, built in 1760 for his widow, featured large formal parlors on the first floor.[4]

The influence of this family and the northerly spread of the central-hall plan is documented by the house built in the Stroudwater district of Falmouth in 1738 by Charles Frost, Colonel Pepperrell's grandson. A cupola was recorded in 1756 on this two-and-one-half-story gambrel-roofed house.[5] Although few houses of pre-Revolutionary Falmouth survive, primary and secondary sources reveal a surprising number of two- or two-and-one-half-story houses with central halls. Another extant example in Stroudwater was built in 1760 by Francis Waldo, son of Samuel Waldo of Boston.[6]

Some members of the merchant class chose to build Georgian-style houses with the central-chimney plan. Thatcher Goddard's two-story house (ca. 1787) on the Kennebunk River is an example (fig. 3.3). Despite small rooms, Goddard created large spaces. The three rear chambers on the second floor were divided by two movable walls. Installed on hinges, the walls could be raised and secured by hooks to the ceiling, thus creating a large room for public gatherings or family entertainments.[7]

The most prevalent type of dwelling house in Maine from the mid-eighteenth to the mid-nineteenth century was of one or one-and-one-half stories. One or two rooms deep, the living spaces were built around a central chimney; this arrangement restricted the size of the rooms. To move from one room to another, passage through other rooms was required, thus limiting privacy. This style was frequently found in the countryside.[8]

Following the Revolution, a desire for richness in interior

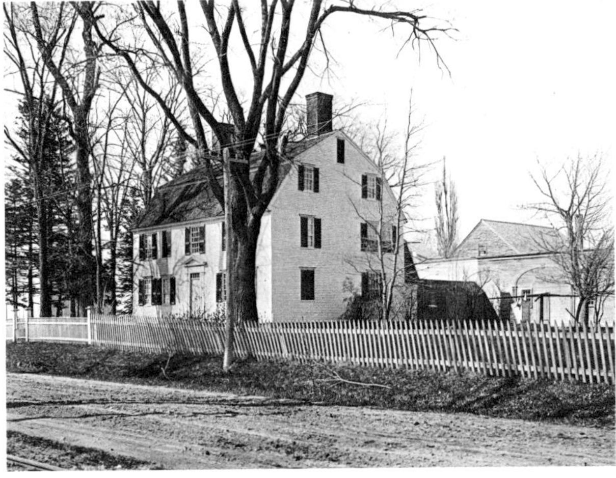

Fig. 3.2 Lyman house, Kennebunk, Maine, 1784–1785. Photograph, ca. 1890. The Brick Store Museum.

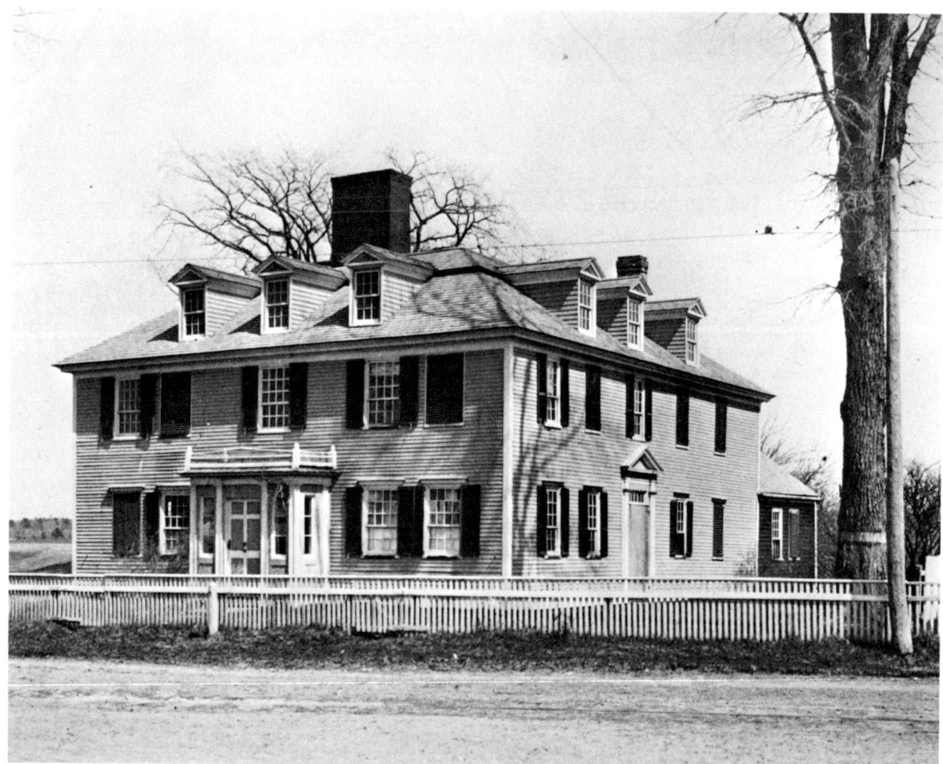

Fig. 3.3 Goddard-McCulloch house, Kennebunk, Maine, ca. 1787. Photograph, ca. 1900. The Brick Store Museum.

decoration flourished among the leading members of Maine society. In 1832 William D. Williamson acknowledged it in the conclusion to his *History of Maine*:

Man is a creature of expense; and in this particular, the dwellinghouses, furniture, dress and habits of the people, within a century past, have undergone essential changes. When pecuniary circumstances favor or permit, men consult convenience, taste, and even elegance. . . . [The colonial period] was succeeded by the overflowing influx of foreign fabrics; and when a passion for finery pervaded the community, families aspired to destinction by means of luxury and extravagance.[9]

Interior decoration and the style of living in Maine were comparable to that found in sophisticated urban centers, as Josiah Pierce noted in 1824 on attending the splendid *"wedding levee"* of Colonel Charles Q. Clapp:

Mr. Clap's furniture is richer than any I ever saw — candlesticks, lamps, tumblers, waiters, & all &c. all of massive silver. the most superb Turkey carpets & chairs, tables, & sofas, the best that could be found in Philadelphia.[10]

Many families that flourished during the federal period not only invested their wealth in new houses in "the best modern style of architecture," but also furnished them fashionably. The greatest changes came in scale, proportion, and ornament. The houses were larger; some were not just two stories with a dormer floor, but were three full floors, a size rarely found in New England's greatest colonial houses. Well-proportioned, with delicate ornament of classical inspiration, these houses suited the tastes of the affluent. Because of its association with the Roman republic, the neoclassical style was considered appropriate for Americans in their new democracy. It was chosen by increasing numbers of well-to-do families and can be found in great quantity in coastal communities from Rhode Island to Maine.[11]

During the federal period, families preferred the central-hall plan over the central-chimney plan because it allowed them greater control over their domestic activities. Although their house styles changed, the plans did not radically break from tradition. Public spaces were set apart from private ones; the increased number of rooms provided separate spaces for family members. In some houses, folding or sliding doors divided two rooms but could be opened to create a large double parlor. This was a particularly useful feature when a family valued large entertainments.[12] The innumerable references in period correspondence and diaries to visits, teas, and parties suggest they were constant. In their size and interior arrangement, these houses reflected the social concerns of their occupants.

Rooms that had figured prominently in colonial-period houses developed into spaces with new names and new purposes. For example, through most of the colonial period, the term "hall" described a room that served as a main living and sleeping area. By the federal period, the "hall" came to mean the general reception area. The "front room" or parlor was located directly off the hall upon entering the house through the front door. It was the setting for formal entertainments or special family events. The furnishings there were among the most highly valued in the household, indicating the wealth and status of the inhabitants. Across the hall, opposite the parlor and nearer the kitchen, the dining room was a second formal room devoted to entertainment. Rooms intended for a particular use, such as the dining room, provided spaces for specialized furniture. Of considerable importance among these was the sideboard, a form introduced in this period and owned by a number of Maine families.

Although some rooms had a specific purpose, they were not always given distinct names in inventories and other sources that reflected their use. General living spaces of families were frequently described as "parlor," "best room," or "sitting room." More often the rooms were referred to by the compass point or position within the house, such as "N[orth]. W[est]. front room" and "S[outh]. W[est]. front room."[13] The furnishings found in these first-floor rooms reflect a flexibility in use. Regardless of the name, these spaces were used as informal living spaces as well as for formal entertaining.

Primary sources contain numerous references to the multipurpose nature of first-floor living spaces. A guest of the Gardiner family in 1829 noted that after rising at six o'clock "the bell is rung again for prayers. All assemble in the library, which is large and is used most constantly for the sitting-room." In 1796 the parlor of the Frothinghams' Portland home was the setting for a "supper party," and one night at the Hannafords' "the carpet was taken up in the dining room and a negro servant who plays the violin very well: struck up a sprightly tune[.] the drawing room was soon left vacant." A group of schoolgirls in Hallowell who had formed an "art club" met regularly to draw and paint; one of the participants "had the use of her mother's parlor for the occasion." Two hours during the afternoon would be spent "drawing and painting landscapes and flowers, and all sorts of things, chatting together, admiring each other's work, and asking each other's advice."[14]

Bedchambers—in unusual instances recorded as "bed rooms"—were generally located on the second floor, where they were sufficiently removed from public areas of the house. Some houses were designed with second-floor bedrooms that could be opened up to form large ballrooms, as in the Goddard-McCulloch house in Kennebunk. This arrangement or double parlors on the first floor provided ample spaces for large formal entertainments. A guest at a "splendid ball" at the Warrens' in Hallowell in 1823 described the extent to which domestic spaces were used for formal entertainments:

there were two parlors which opened into one by means of Folding doors, when I went in there were about 50 young ladies and gentlemen, after we had been 1–2 hour the folding doors were thrown open & we were desired to walk into the other parlour, where the carpet had been previously taken up, the other carpet was speedily removed & commenced dancing to the sound of a violen and clarionet, we danced until 1–2 past nine, when we were marched up stairs into a room where there was a very splendid supper set out[.] after supper coffee was handed round, we then went down stairs & again commenced dancing, I got home at 1–2 past 11.[15]

Late one afternoon in the summer of 1796, a musical entertainment began after tea at "New Scotland," Thomas Robison's house; it evolved into a dance that lasted past sunset (cat. 38). Instead of moving to the second floor, the guests

sprang into the garden; . . . the Moon shone as bright as day . . . the water servd as reflector to the moon, and presented a broad blaze of light, beyond which appeard the shore and houses of Pappuduck—and the islands on the other side the bay—the prospect was almost unbounded; we strolld round the garden admiring and exclaiming—when the flute and clarinet playd 'rise Cynthia rise'—all was hush! not a word spoken—presently the tune changd to a sprightly reel and 2 or 3 sets stood up they danced till they were weary and a set for country dances formd—the 'little fifer and others [went to] the grass plot before the lobby—those who stood upon the stepts said it lookd like fairy ground.[16]

Kitchens were situated to the rear of the main block of the house or in the attached ell. Some of the large houses had two kitchens with the "outer" kitchen located in the ell. The ells served as additional space for domestic operations. In homes where servants were employed, the kitchen was not a room family members would necessarily frequent. Ann King of Saco may have preferred to avoid the kitchen one December evening, but the circumstances gave her no choice:

I am setting at the kitchen table away from the fire[.] my fingers stiff with the cold—the servants chatting and laughing in the comfortable chimney corner . . . no fire in the parlour—Aunt and Mr. Porter working upstairs by a candle on the mantle peice[.] no table at hand for poor me.[17]

In contrast, Mary Kent of Portland was in the kitchen regularly, where

her excellence appears in domestic affairs, she superintends every thing up early and late; and what makes this trait a great virtue there is no necessity for her doing it—four domestics and quite a small family—but she chuses to make all the pastry cakes' preserves &cc and gives orders in all branches of business—few people that see the beautiful and elegant Mary Kent in a large company superbly dress'd—and informd . . . would expect these useful acquirments.[18]

Others seemed to enjoy the informality of the space just as

we do in the twentieth century. On attending a party in Portland, Josiah Pierce reported: "I went, to *see* more than for any thing else, & after all I should quite as lief be at home in the kitchen."[19]

The aspirations of the merchant and upper-middle class are documented in coastal Maine through the written record and surviving objects. An examination of this evidence reveals the sophistication of the domestic environment. Furniture and wall, window, and floor treatments were the major components of the overall interior design and provided as much, if not more, "destinction by means of luxury and extravagance" than many elements of the exterior.[20]

The front entry or hall was the first space encountered on entering the house. Wallpapers, or paper hangings as they were called, often covered the walls here, and sometimes featured large-scale architectural designs. Double- or triple-hung prints were a standard decorative technique in this space. Many probate inventories record carpeting in the hall and on the stairs. "The lower entry" of Jonathan Hamilton's Berwick home had a "canvass carpet to remain in the house," a painted canvas floor cloth, as well as two large "matts of grass." References to "brass carpet rods & gear" describe a means of securing a carpet to the stairs. Carpets were also nailed to the stairs, a standard means used as well to secure wall-to-wall floor coverings.[21] Tables and chairs lined the walls in close proximity to main rooms, so they were readily accessible when needed.

The concern for social display is revealed by the number and value of objects found in the first-floor rooms. Parlors and sitting rooms were filled—sometimes to the point of overflowing—with furniture of the newest taste, including sideboards (cat. 48), card tables (cat. 94), lolling chairs (cat. 56), sofas (cat. 55), and increasing numbers of windsor and painted fancy chairs (cats. 59, 105–108). The extreme cost of furnishings such as pianofortes was not prohibitive for certain families. In some instances, pianofortes had a higher value than high-post bedsteads which, with all the appurtenances, were traditionally the single most expensive item in an estate (cats. 50–51). Looking glasses, often specified as having gilt frames, appear regularly, although mahogany-framed glasses were standard furnishings (cats. 109–111). Silver-plated, brass, or glass candlesticks and lamps lit interior spaces. In sunlight or by artificial light, "rubbed" or polished furniture would "shine like Mirrors," even in more modest homes. Parlors were decorated with fresh flowers.[22]

While some floors were decorated with only paint, Scotch ingrain, Kidderminster, Brussels, or Turkey carpets covered the floors of the affluent. Scotch ingrain or Kidderminster carpets were of a flat reversible weave and were the carpets most frequently found in New England homes. Because of the reversible weave, some patterns had large repeat designs. Kidderminster carpets were of fine quality and newspaper advertisements document their importation.

Brussels carpets were made by drawing yarn up into close, uncut loops to form the pattern. "Turkey" carpets had a velvety texture and were highly prized. Not necessarily the products of Persia or the Far East, they could be of European or English manufacture, expertly knotted in the Oriental manner. Although Maine references are rare, Daniel Cleaves owned "1 Turkey carpet." Valued at $50 in 1818, it was among the most costly of his furnishings and equal in value to his "mahogany case clock" (cat. 88). Josiah Pierce noted the Turkey carpets in Charles Q. Clapp's house in plural.[23]

To protect these expensive coverings, "crumb cloths" of lightweight baize could be spread on the carpet, and small carpets, often described as "hearth rugs," were placed by the fireplace along with brass fire sets or fenders. Wall-to-wall carpets, like the ingrain or Kidderminster carpet, might have been used in second-floor chambers, but generally small carpets and "rag rugs" furnished these rooms.

Second-floor chambers provided additional living spaces for family members. Chairs, tables, desks, and looking glasses, as well as beds, filled these rooms. High-post bedsteads with curtains furnished the best chambers, but bedsteads of other styles were made for secondary sleeping spaces. For the most part, the furnishings reflect the more private nature of these rooms. Federal-period inventories reveal increased numbers and types of specialized forms such as "toilet tables" (cat. 65), wash stands with basins and pitchers, and "night tables" that were used for personal care.[24]

Window curtains are not recorded in contemporary documents as often as bed hangings, carpeting, or upholstered furniture. Their infrequent use in federal Maine is not unexpected; research on window curtains in early America has shown that they were used less often than previously thought. When listed in Maine's probate inventories, window curtains are found in the finest homes, generally in second-floor chambers, but are not often described in detail. Rare and intriguing references, however, do survive. By 1803 Jonathan Hamilton of Berwick had furnished his stair entry with "2 Entry window Curtains & Cornices," valued at the high sum of $36. Cornices at the top of the windows concealed the lines and pulleys used to draw curtains up into festoons or the poles for "French rod curtains" which worked on the same principle as modern transverse rods. In Hamilton's southwest chamber, four window curtains and cornices were included in the listing of bed curtains and chair coverings, suggesting they were all of matching fabric, perhaps a copperplate-printed cotton (see cat. 51). This coordination of fabrics is documented to bed chambers. Stored in a trunk at Hamilton's house was "1 pr coarse Calico Window Curtains" valued at sixty-six cents. The 1818 inventory of Daniel Cleaves included "12 windo. curtains," but it is not known where the curtains were hung. Appraised at $24, they were nearly equal in value to his sofa.[25]

The following case studies reveal how these patterns of

interior furnishings were adapted by five different families in York, Saco, Portland, and the Kennebunks. Extant houses or documentation, household inventories, objects in historical collections, and other sources illustrate not only the houses of the wealthiest families, but also those of the upper-middle class. In the post-Revolutionary years, houses of the Georgian style continued to be built. However, by the opening years of the nineteenth century, a more refined neoclassicism in architecture and domestic interiors had become firmly established in the communities.

Although styles were changing, most families did not abandon their earlier homes and family possessions. Furnishings made of "our indigenous cherry, black-birch, and curl maple, which received so fair a polish in the service of our grandmothers" may have been "shoved from the parlour and setting-room, to admit articles of foreign mahogany, and perhaps of foreign workmanship," but they were not necessarily thrown out.[26] On his death in 1793, William Leighton of Kittery willed twelve chairs to his sons. One son received "six leather back & leather bottomed chairs." These were probably early eighteenth-century chairs like those made in Boston. John Leighton received the chairs further described as "six cain back chairs which are lately new bottomed." The father valued these chairs sufficiently to have them repaired in order to provide furnishings for his children.[27]

The Sayward-Wheeler House

Similarly, interior spaces were adapted for different needs or preferences by the succeeding generations. The Sayward-Wheeler house on the York River provides a valuable example of this kind of adaptation. Built around 1720, on the central-chimney plan, it was owned and occupied for much of the eighteenth century by Jonathan Sayward, a prosperous colonial merchant (fig. 3.4). It was decorated in the most fashionable taste of the 1760s. On his death in 1795, Sayward left his "homestead, with the buildings of every kind thereon and appurtenances therewith belonging," to his grandson, Jonathan Sayward Barrell.[28]

During Barrell's lifetime, funds were not available to undertake major renovations. Without capital to purchase land on which he would erect a new building, Jonathan Sayward Barrell remained in his grandparents' home with his inherited furnishings. However, he did make changes in order to update certain parts of the colonial interior with new and stylish furnishings. Barrell left the parlor as it had been furnished by Sayward in the 1760s, but added new wallpaper. He focused more particular attention on the sitting room, the largest room of the house (fig. 3.5). Jonathan Sayward had used the sitting room for many purposes. He kept his tall clock and desk and bookcase in this room, and during the cold winter months he moved his

bed into it from a small adjoining bed chamber. Within ten or fifteen years after Sayward's death, Barrell altered the use of this room. Not content with the "bofat," a corner cupboard, in the parlor where his grandparents had displayed their best Chinese porcelain and glass tablewares, Barrell purchased a mahogany sideboard. Living in an older house that did not have a large specialized space for a dining room, Barrell transformed the "sitting room" into a room for dining simply by adding this sideboard. Of generous proportions, it sat, slightly cramped, along one wall. Barrell decorated the room with a layer of stylish wallpaper and English prints of Shakespearian scenes. Otherwise, the first floor of the house remained much the way it was when he inherited it.[29] This house serves as the traditional style against which the new architectural preferences of the federal-period elite can be contrasted.

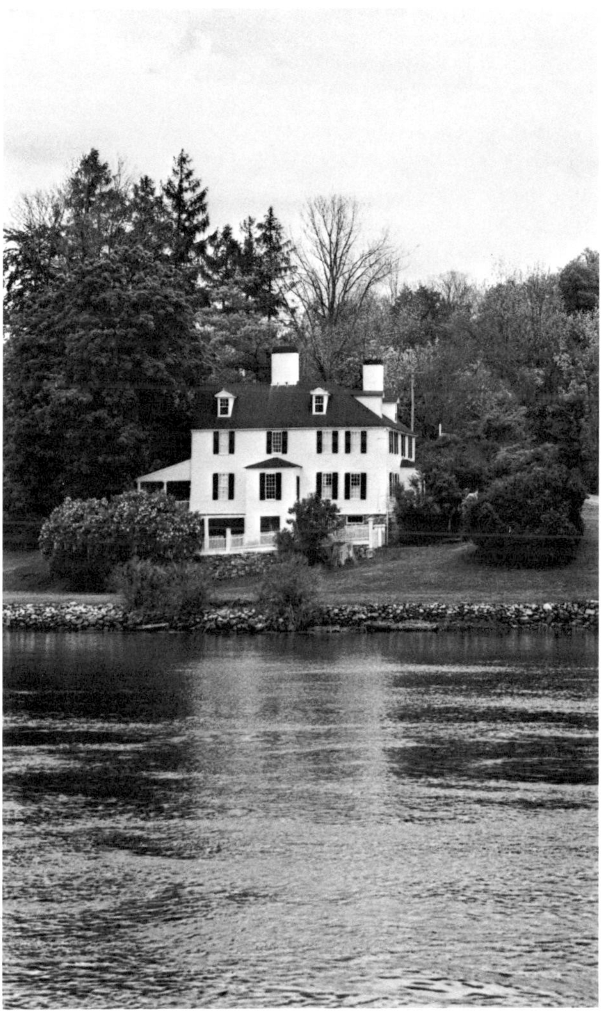

Fig. 3.4 Sayward-Wheeler house, York, Maine, ca. 1720, with alterations ca. 1767. Photograph, 1982. Courtesy, Society for the Preservation of New England Antiquities.

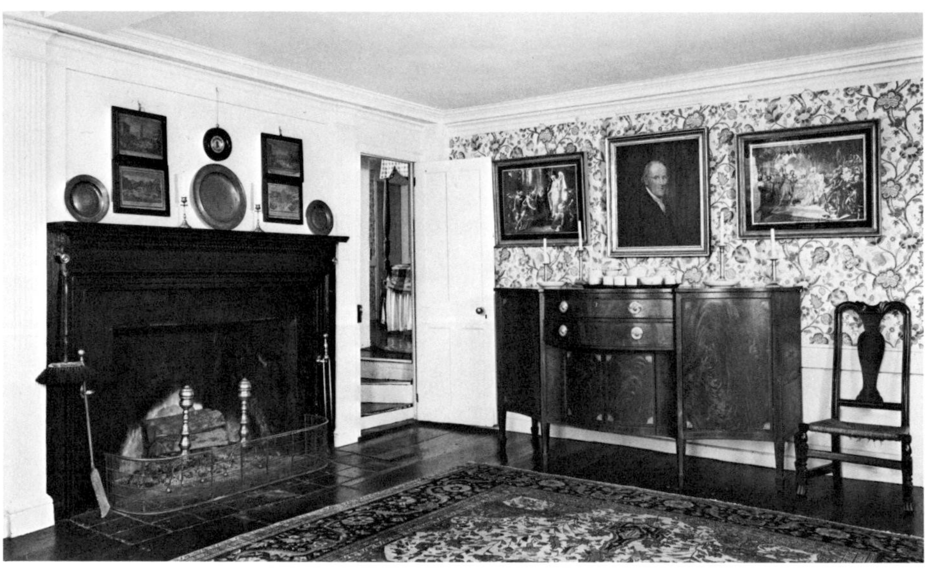

The Colonel Thomas Cutts Mansion

Built in the early federal period, the Thomas Cutts mansion in Saco was Georgian in style, a design the middle-aged Cutts was familiar with when he erected this house in 1782 (fig. 3.6). The two-and-one-half-story house was designed on the central-hall plan but appeared even larger because of the gambrel roof and dormers. At the gable end, not only a third, but also a fourth floor was articulated. Its sheer size set it apart from colonial counterparts while its site increased its monumentality. Located on the crown of Indian Island in the middle of the Saco River, the Cutts mansion, orchard, and garden was "the best in its situation." The "large house upon the top of [the island] which is very high," commanded the river basin.[30]

The family's wealth was expressed through the scale of the rooms, their decoration, and their furnishings. Cutts's conservative nature is evident in the old-fashioned paneled walls; their extensive use in first, second, and third-floor rooms reveals his ability to afford such ornamentation. However, his probate inventory, extant family possessions, and other primary sources document the sophisticated interior of his home with its costly new furnishings in the neoclassical taste. Wallpapers from this house do not survive, but documented examples from other York County houses provide images of a likely interior appearance. The two-story hall was probably decorated with an architectural paper, or another large-scale design, such as the paper Jonathan Hamilton selected for his home in South Berwick around 1785.[31]

The "long Entry" provided a spacious formal hallway and regulated access between the formal rooms at the front of the house and the kitchen and ell at the rear. A door at the back of the hall, just beyond the staircase, allowed persons to pass through the kitchen and one of the rear first-floor rooms without disturbing the more formal activities in the front part of the house. Fireplaces dominated the rooms which were arranged four-over-four. A two-story gambrel-roofed ell at the rear of the house has the appearance of three stories because of the dormers in the roof and window in the gable end. With a third chimney here, the ell provided a second or "outer" kitchen on the first floor. Eight rooms on the second and third floors in the main house and rooms in the ell provided separate sleeping chambers for Cutts, his wife and eight children, quarters for servants, and storage (fig. 2.8.1).

Expensive furniture was found in the formal "north lower room or parlour," the smaller of the two front rooms. Its size and exposure to the northwest reflected its more limited use, reserved for entertaining. The fireplace wall was fully paneled; molded pilasters flanked the fireplace and closets were built to either side. Seats were built-in under the three windows. One of Cutts's sideboards was placed in this room, along with a large looking glass and "6 red & 2 arm chairs," which were probably fancy chairs. Glass and ceramic tablewares in the form of wine coolers, decanters, wine-glasses, and tumblers were displayed "on the sideboard." The silver was stored or displayed in this room. It ranged from flatware to a tankard, four canns of pint and half-pint capacity, old and new porringers (cat. 46), a cream pitcher, "sugar pot & tongs," two "pepper cast[or]s," and "butter boats."[32] When compared with other merchant-class families who owned spoons and a few forms of hollowware, this assortment was impressive. A closet held an additional 123 pieces of "chinaware." Although not specified, some of these must have been English or Oriental porcelains.

Across the hall from the "north lower room or parlour"

was the larger "lower west room." Facing southwest, its desirable setting was enhanced by its furnishings which were equally costly, including a second sideboard, two card tables, two large looking glasses, eight leather-bottomed chairs, a mahogany desk, and a floor carpet. The three "worked pictures" (needlework) decorating the walls were highly valued at $4 each (cat. 142). A "glass chandelier" in this room was a luxury rarely found in domestic settings of this period.[33] Cutts divided his "crockery and glassware," "china and glassware," and "china" into closets identified as "North," "East," and "West."

Family portraits were hung in these front rooms (cats. 33–34). Although no portraits are included in Thomas Cutts's 1821 estate records, at least one was recorded as part of the estate of his son, Thomas, Jr., in 1839 (see cat. 34). A "Turkey Carpet, (old)" in the son's house may have been owned by Thomas, Sr., although the earlier inventory does not fully describe it.[34] The house also was furnished for a time with a pianoforte, although it does not appear in the father's inventory. A letter from Sarah Cleaves to her father in Biddeford, who was within sight of Cutts Island, documents the Cutts pianoforte and may explain why it disappeared from the house: "I was thinking Papa that I wished you could hire a Piano for us to play on while we are at home [on vacation from school.] Capt. Cutts at the Pool owns one it is at his Father's, I believe they do not use it." At the death of Daniel Cleaves within a year of the letter, his estate

contained a "pianoforte and stool" valued at the high sum of $150.[35]

Thomas Cutts used the room behind the parlor as his "bed room." Accessible from the front hall, this first-floor room was located at the rear of the house near the kitchen. It had a favorable southeastern exposure and a view down the river. As an elderly widower, Cutts may have found this location more convenient than a chamber. The room was crowded with furniture and personal effects. Six maple chairs, six "bow back" chairs, and a roundabout chair were kept here along with an easy chair, sofa, and armchair. His bedstead with its bedding and curtains, appraised for $25, had the highest value in the room. Cutts's tall clock and desk were found here along with his library. Other personal and household possessions included his large assortment of wearing apparel (cat. 158), liquor cases, "Shaving apparatus," walking canes, and glass bottles, "crockery ware," and trunks in the closet.

On the second floor, three of the five chambers were furnished with high-post bedsteads dressed with bed curtains. The best bedstead was in the "lower west chamber," the second-floor room with the most extensive paneling. With its curtains and bedding, this bedstead had the single highest value among Cutts's household furniture. Card tables, an easy chair, and a desk and bookcase that also furnished these rooms reveal that these chambers were not used solely for sleeping.

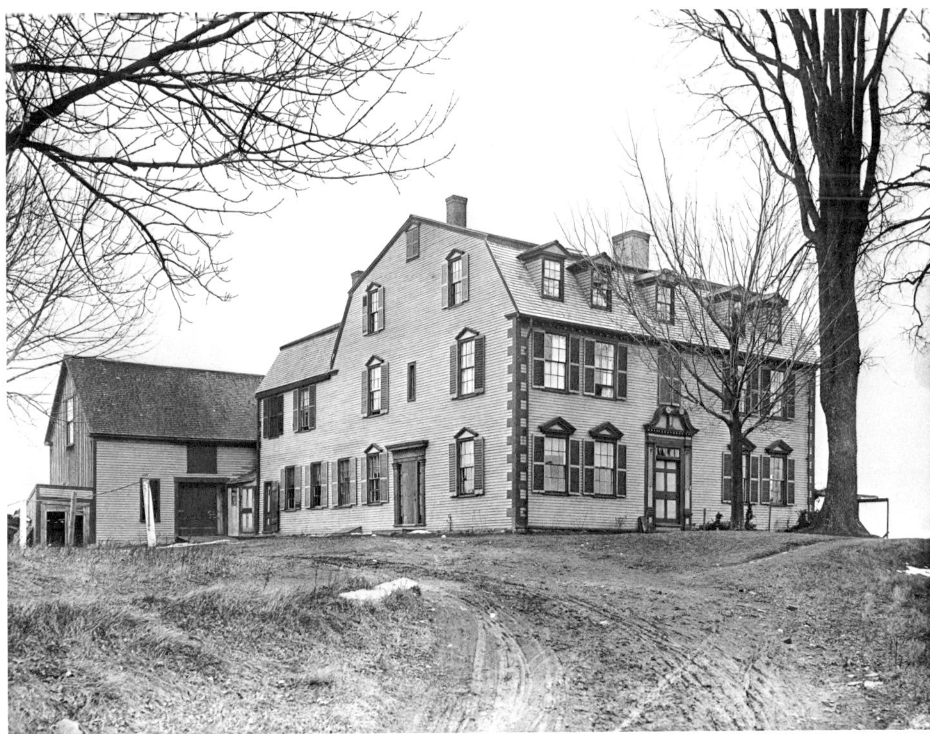

Fig. 3.6 Cutts house, Cutts Island, Saco, Maine, 1782. Four Moody brothers, builders. Removed from site and radically altered, 1937. Photograph, ca. 1900. Courtesy, Society for the Preservation of New England Antiquities.

One of the "upper" or third-floor chambers contained two bedsteads and bedding; another held bedding and a table. In the "uper West Chamber" were many more types of furnishings, and from the descriptions—such as " 1 kitchen table"—it appears that objects no longer desired or needed on the first or second floor were sent there for storage. Six "high back arm chairs," and ten "old chairs" were probably left over from a previous generation. By 1821 the Cutts children had all married and moved into homes of their own. Therefore, it is not surprising to find the rooms used simply for storage.

The Wadsworth-Longfellow House

Another prominent Maine citizen, General Peleg Wadsworth, began construction in 1785 of a two-story dwelling house. He chose a location in the "New Town," beyond the war-torn colonial center of Portland.[36] Although construction began while the Cutts house was being completed, Wadsworth rejected a colonial-inspired design and turned instead to the newest taste (fig. 3.7). Wadsworth made an additional effort to symbolize his position in the community by constructing his residence of brick, which he imported from Philadelphia. A large central hall, running the depth of the house to a back door, was flanked by two rooms on each side. Wadsworth went to the further expense of building four chimneys on the exterior walls, providing fireplaces in all eight rooms, four-over-four.[37]

On the east side of the house, the dining room was in front with the kitchen directly behind. On the west side of the house, the parlor opened off the hall at the front (fig. 2.8.2). Behind this large formal room was a small "back" room. The central hall was decorated with a stylish Boston wallpaper and border (cat. 67). The stairs rose in three runs to the second floor where four rooms corresponded to those on the first floor. These served as sleeping chambers for the family members. A back staircase provided access from the kitchen to the back second-floor hall.

Directly to the east of the house, Peleg constructed a two-story wooden building that served as his store. There is evidence that a narrow wooden passageway was built between the store and eastern parlor to provide direct access. Wadsworth kept his desk, a merchant's most important article of furniture, in the store. His work area was tied to the living space, yet was separate.[38]

This house served the Wadsworth family from 1786 until 1807. With a family of ten children, the residence was crowded. Objects that furnish the house today are mainly Longfellow family additions; only a few of the Wadsworth family furnishings are known. However, from letters written by daughter Zilpah Wadsworth (cat. 126) and other primary sources, it is possible to determine how the various rooms

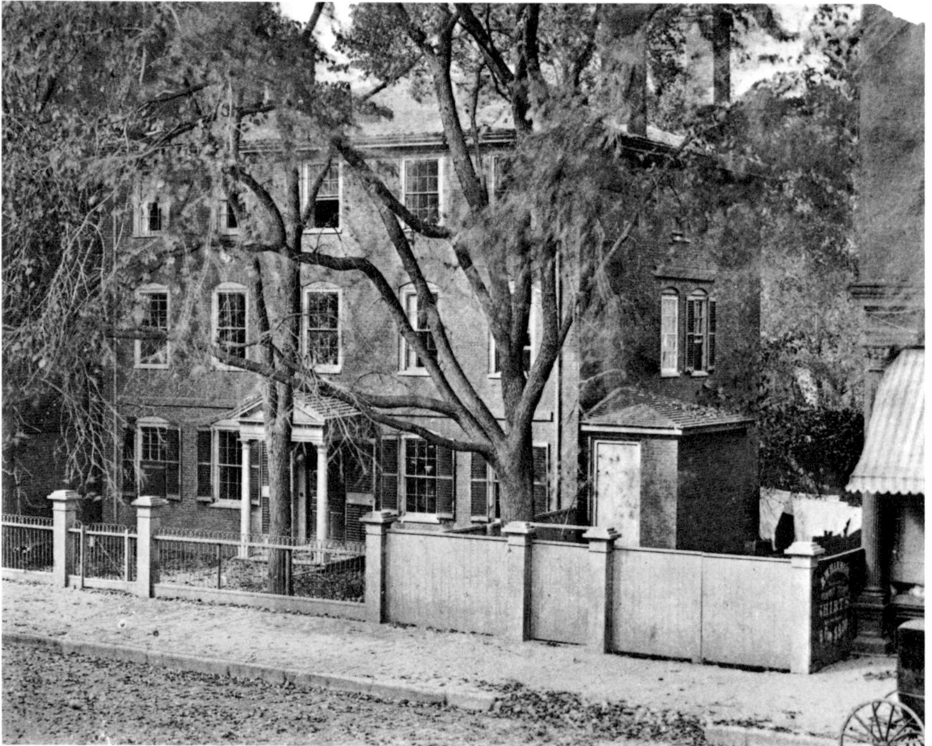

Fig. 3.7 Wadsworth-Longfellow house, Portland, Maine, 1785, enlarged 1815. John Nichols, mason. Handcolored photograph, ca. 1880. Maine Historical Society.

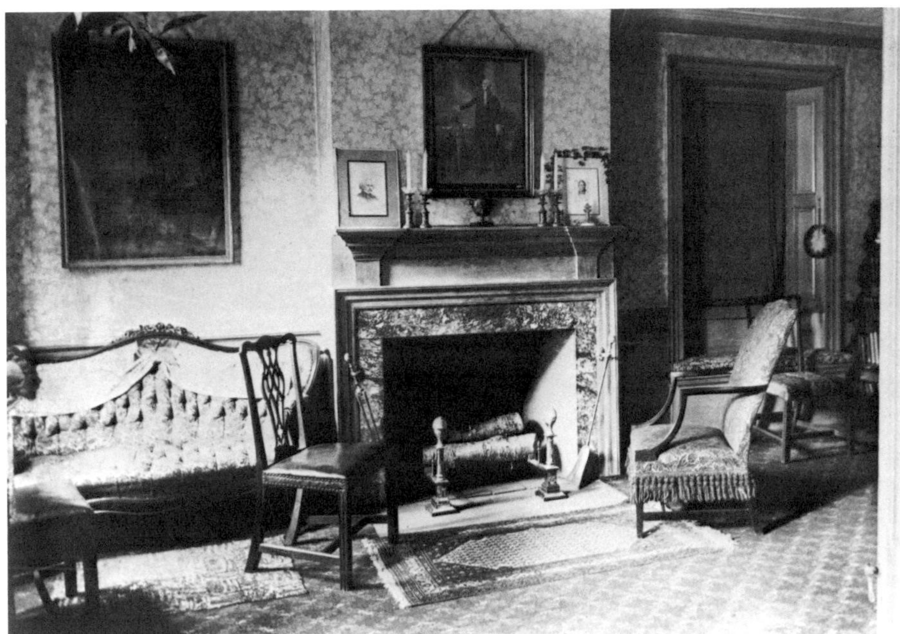

Fig. 3.8 Parlor, Wadsworth-Longfellow house, Portland, Maine. Photograph, ca. 1880. Maine Historic Preservation Commission.

were used. The names used to identify the rooms sometimes changed, but their purposes generally remained the same.

The parlor to the left of the front door, measuring nearly 20′ by 15′, was the largest room in the house (fig. 3. 8). Special entertainments or other important events took place here. It traditionally contained the spinet which was a focal point for family gatherings. Its blue wallpaper with white swags must have given an elegant appearance to the space (cat. 69). The role of this room in the Wadsworth family life was vividly described by Zilpah in the winter of 1799:

There sits Mama in her lolling chair by the fire. Betsy is playing on the piano 'Ye Tribes of Adam Join.' John and Lucia are singing at the back of her chair. George, Alexander, and Sam are singing in different parts of the room. Little Peleg is stepping about the floor surveying one and another. Charles is sitting at the table with me. . . . Harry is reading beside me . . . I have been singing as I wrote. . . . Ten children! What a circle! I should like to know what are Mama's thoughts as she looks around on us.[39]

Zilpah cited the "largest parlor" as the room where her sister Eliza died in 1802 (cat. 42). Family tradition maintains that Zilpah and Stephen Longfellow were married in this large formal space in 1804, as was their daughter, Anne, in 1832. In 1834 Zilpah named the "drawing room" as the one where Stephen met with Portland Academy trustees. Zilpah seems to be referring to the same room as the "largest parlor" of thirty years earlier, but it now had a new name.[40]

The slightly smaller room to the right of the hall, 19′2″ by 14′ 15½″, was frequently used for dining; it was called both a "dining room" and a "parlor." When the family entertained, large groups would gather here. On one occasion, guests of General and Mrs. Wadsworth "assembled to the number of thirty." Abigail May noted that at one point in the evening she "was in the dining room listening to the music & singing."[41] This room would come to serve a very different purpose in the early years of the nineteenth century.

The room behind the larger parlor had various uses. According to family tradition, it served as a bedchamber for Peleg and his wife Elizabeth. In 1799 Zilpah referred to it as the "little back room." Here she and her family passed the day reading, writing, and talking. "This is the room in which we used to read, to digress, to return, but to digress again."[42] Between 1816 and 1826 it was used as the family's dining room.

By 1807, when Peleg Wadsworth retired to his estate in Hiram, he allowed his daughters Lucia and Zilpah, and Zilpah's husband, to live in the Portland house. Upon his death in 1829, Wadsworth bequeathed the house to Zilpah and Lucia. Stephen Longfellow paid for furnishings, but he never owned the house. It was Peleg who spent considerable sums on its renovation.[43]

What Peleg Wadsworth considered fashionable in 1785 was outdated by early nineteenth-century standards and Zilpah and Stephen began to update the house. The changes they made provide evidence about the adaptation of rooms for use by a second generation during the federal period. Not only did the interior accommodate the Longfellows, but it also expressed the new generation's preferences for the neoclassical style. The house and its adaptation also are useful as a case study because the house belonged to a member of the upper-middle class. The Longfellows did not have "an independent fortune" and were not among the elite.[44]

As a leading Portland attorney, state representative, and United States congressman, Stephen Longfellow was aware of the latest styles. He could not have missed the activities surrounding the construction of large and fashionable three-story mansion houses along the streets of his town, particularly the one Commodore Edward Preble was building next door (see Chapter 2). Alexander Parris's designs for this and other Portland houses included such fashionable amenities as recessed alcoves to hold sideboards (fig. 2.18), and "windowed china closets." George Hepplewhite's London pattern book mentions that sideboards were "often made to fit into a recess," and thus encouraged their production by noting that "the conveniences it affords render a dining room incomplete without [it]."[45]

The Longfellows purchased a sideboard, and evidence of early nineteenth-century interior moldings confirms that an alcove was created to hold it (cat. 49). Hooks in the wall above the sideboard support the theory that a large looking glass or picture hung over it. At the same time Stephen also constructed a large china closet next to the alcove. Within the closet, a large working space was created with a drawer below and shelves above. A sliding door provided a pass-through from the closet to the kitchen. Like the alcove in Parris's designs, this small storage and work space may have been inspired by the small "china closets" in Parris's dining rooms. The dining room thus offered many conveniences in addition to having a stylish appearance.

In 1807 the Longfellows effectively updated the appearance of the parlor by replacing the paper hangings that had been hung twenty years earlier (cat. 70). The fireplaces in the dining room and parlor were altered. In simple architectural style, the mantels were never decorated with costly composition ornament seen in the best houses. The family's updating was limited to blue marble facings and sandstone jambs. Building jambs at an angle threw the heat into the room with greater efficiency (fig. 3.8).

After a fire in 1814 damaged the roof, the Wadsworths and Longfellows made major alterations to the house; Peleg contributed $500 to the construction. The addition of a third floor rather than an ell made the exterior more in keeping with the current style and reflected the ambitions of the occupants. With its third floor and low hipped roof, this four-square house now resembled those of the town's elite. This additional floor provided increased living space for the Longfellows' expanding family and was heated through the use of stoves. There were seven rooms including two small windowed spaces traditionally thought to be large closets,

but which Stephen included in his description of the "seven convenient chambers." Servants may have used the smaller chambers. The other rooms were used by the children, who by 1819 numbered eight, and their Aunt Lucia. Lucia occupied the large chamber on the southeast side of the house, and also had use of a small adjoining room. These rooms were comfortable and provided Lucia a wonderful view of the harbor.[46]

The second-floor rooms were bedchambers for the parents and visitors. Correspondence of Zilpah and Stephen reveals that their home was always filled with guests. It is not thought that any of the second-floor rooms provided space for public functions. The front rooms, however, did have a stylish appearance with high-post bedsteads dressed with fabric, and decorative window treatments. New furniture was acquired for these rooms, but the plan and use of the second floor changed little from the time of the Wadsworth occupancy.[47]

With the desire to impress townspeople with new building, it might also be expected that the public rooms on the first floor would, again, have received attention. They did. The parlor wallpaper of 1807 was outdated and it was replaced in 1815 (cat. 71). A second door from the hall to the parlor was added, giving this important public room the symmetry found in other fashionably decorated parlors. It also provided more convenient access to the rear hall and kitchen. In 1815 the hall was rehung with bamboo and drapery wallpaper in pastel colors (cat. 68), and between 1815 and 1835 the parlor received two additional changes of stylish rainbow wallpapers (cat. 72). After 1824, Stephen's portrait by Charles Bird King was hung in the parlor (cat. 43).[48]

In January 1815 the building Stephen was using as a law office burned. He turned to his dwelling house and adapted the dining room for new office space.[49] The sideboard remained in the alcove and, in order to accommodate Stephen's library, a bookcase with glass doors was designed to sit on top of it (cat. 49). A grain-painted bookcase also may have been constructed for this room. It would have provided ample and convenient storage for small books, pamphlets, receipts, and legal documents in its five covered shelves and pigeonholes (cat. 52). The writing-arm windsor chair Longfellow owned was a standard furnishing for offices (cat. 61). The transformed sideboard, painted chair, and bookcase provided both unusual and typical furnishings for Longfellow's office. With this large room converted to an office, the family used the small "back chamber" across from the kitchen as a dining room.

Expansion continued; a small ell on the eastern side of the house was built as a waiting room for clients. Incorporating the existing doorway, this brick ell replaced the wooden passageway Wadsworth had constructed. In 1807, when Longfellow moved to the house, his law office was elsewhere

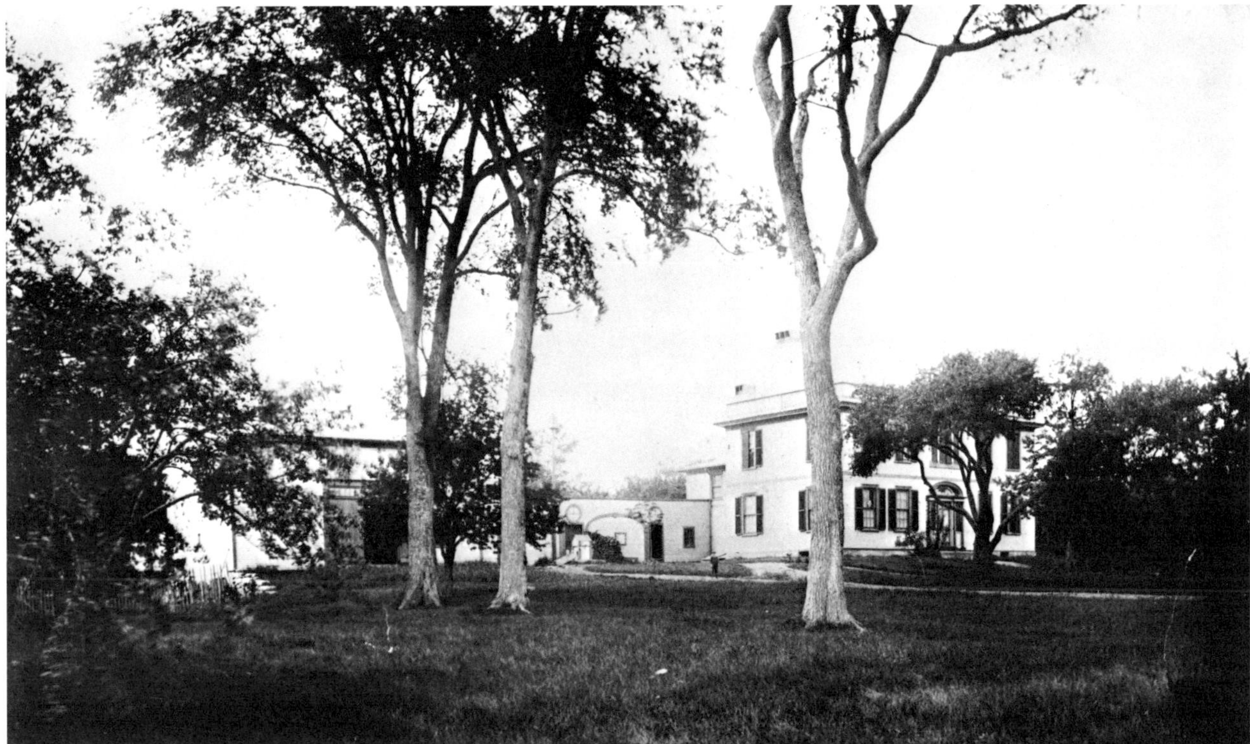

Fig. 3.9 Wallingford Hall, Kennebunk, Maine, ca. 1804. Thomas Eaton, architect-builder. Photograph, ca. 1880. The Brick Store Museum.

in town. The family did not need the adjoining store and rented the space; the store was moved off the site during the 1815 renovations. The new side entrance gave a more professional access to the office by diverting business-related visitors from the main door of the house and the family's central hall.

Between 1816 and 1826, Stephen paid Peleg $200 a year rent for the use of the space as his office. On occasion, Stephen's son Henry used the ell as a place to read and study as a child. In 1827 Stephen established a separate office on Exchange Street. A letter written by Henry in 1829 documents the conversion of the ell from an office entrance to a storage area, and the main first-floor room's return to its original use as a dining room. Henry regretted that the ell he remembered fondly had been transformed into a china closet: "no soft poetic ray has irradiated my heart—since the Goths and Vandals swept over the Rubicon of the 'front entry' and turned the Sanctum Sanctorum of the 'Little Room' into a China Closet."[50]

The Longfellows' constant renewal of their interior documents their social consciousness. Although some aspects of the family's style of living confirm their interest in the local "nabobs," others, such as the dining room office, indicate the limitations of the middle class.

Wallingford Hall

Like Longfellow, George Washington Wallingford was an attorney and member of the upper-middle class. When he built a new house in Kennebunk in 1804, he selected a style of architecture chosen by other affluent families in Maine: a two-story, hipped-roof house designed with a central-hall plan and an attached ell (fig. 3.9).[51] His choice indicates that, by this time, high-style building types had spread beyond the upper echelons of society. Wallingford created a stylish and visually impressive facade on York Street, just south of the Mousam River. The main part of the house was basically one room deep with three rooms and a large hall on the first floor (fig. 2.8.6).

From the front door one entered the hall, a grand two-story space. Even though it was not divided by a central chimney, this central hall did not run the full length of the house. It was divided by a door into the ell below the landing of the stairs. The staircase and walls were handsomely decorated with reeded woodwork. Wainscot paneling was grain-painted in imitation of mahogany. The walls could have been papered, but a less expensive alternative was a painted ground with stenciled border. A black design bordering a strong salmon-pink ground at Kennebunk's

Taylor-Barry house, also built in 1804, is a particularly fine example of this decorative technique that imitated plain papers and borders, one that would have been available to Wallingford.[52]

The parlor to the right ran the full depth of the block; at 26' by 19' it was not only the largest room in the house, but it was also more spacious than the parlors in some of Kennebunk's largest mansions. It traditionally served as an "assembly room" for formal entertaining.[53] Guests would enter this room from the hall near the front door of the house.

The left side of the house was divided by a wall just at the rear of the fireplace, creating a narrow anteroom behind the main room. The front room may be what appears in the 1824 probate inventory as the "setting room," used for dining and general living space. A second doorway was built next to the anteroom door; this entered the rear hall. When this door was closed, it would have cut the room off from the activities in the service spaces in the back of the house. With the anteroom door open, living space offered by the "setting room" was increased.

Not only does this room arrangement reveal the close proximity between the spaces used for living and entertaining and those for cooking and service, but also that there was ample space for both. A door at the rear of the parlor opened into the ell, giving convenient access to three closets under the stairs and to the kitchen in the ell. The china closets provided generous storage space for the family's large assortment of blue-printed earthenwares and glassware.

On the second floor, the largest bedchamber was over the parlor, though it did not run the full length of the house. A door at the rear of the room led to a back hall, and off that, behind the parlor chamber, to a small chamber. The left side was divided as on the first floor. Wallingford's two-story ell supplied sufficient sleeping chambers for his six children. Back stairs provided passage from the rear of the main block into the lower-posted ell.

Although Wallingford's inventory indicates that the three main rooms on the first floor were sparsely furnished, they did contain a mahogany sideboard and costly portrait. The portrait of Wallingford's eldest daughter, Abigail, was painted by John Brewster, Jr. (cat. 41), although, as is often the case, the painting was not listed in the household inventory. Much of the furniture was probably purchased at the time of his marriages in 1806 and 1811. An "old mahoghany Secretary," an "old Desk," and an "old 4 foot Mahogany table," may have been inherited family furnishings.[54]

Windsor chairs were listed in abundance throughout the house: "1 dozen black windsor chairs," "½ dz. yellow windsor Chairs," and "3 Black yellow striped windsor chairs" (see cat. 59). They outnumbered the flag-bottom chairs in the parlor chamber and "3 old stuffed bottomed chairs," probably in one of the second-floor chambers. Appraised at fifty cents each, the "stuffed bottom chairs"

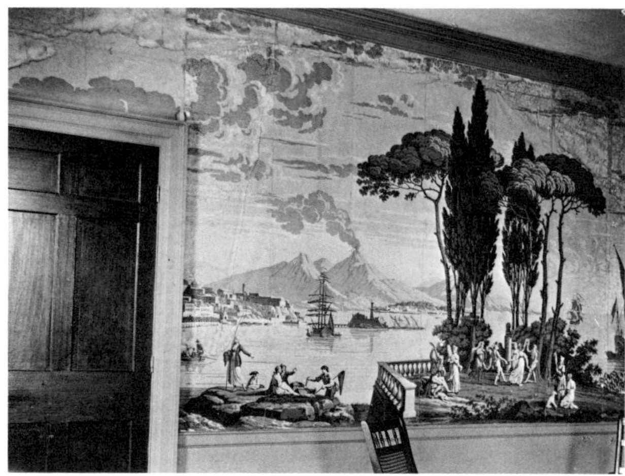

Fig. 3.10 Parlor chamber, Wallingford Hall, Kennebunk, Maine. Photograph, ca. 1880. The Brick Store Museum.

were equal in value to many of the windsor chairs.

Valued at $60, the most expensive article of furniture in Wallingford's house was the "1 mahogany high post bedstead" with bedding, counterpane, and "net curtains." This undoubtedly furnished the "best chamber" over the parlor. The carpet for this chamber was specified and valued at $13.50. Probably after Wallingford's death in 1824, this chamber received a layer of fashionable wallpaper. French in origin, the paper's monochromatic scenes depict *Les vues d'Italie*, first made by Dufour et Leroy in 1822–1823 (fig. 3.10). Often referred to as "The Bay of Naples" because the scene includes Mount Vesuvius, the design was imitated by other paper manufactories and was widely available in federal America.[55] Other furnishings in this room appear to have been a mahogany bureau, a mahogany dressing table, a half-dozen flag-bottom chairs, and a pine toilet table.

The remaining sleeping chambers were filled with a variety of furnishings. The eight beds listed in addition to the one in the best chamber were described as two "short post bedsteads," three "field bedsteads" (two of maple), a "cross-legged bedstead," "a narrow maple bedstead," and a "small crib bedstead," although their location is not specified. Their values ranged from $28 for the maple field bedstead, the next in value after the mahogany high post bedstead, to $2 for the narrow maple bedstead. Wallingford had seven children, the youngest born in 1822. Like the Longfellow family, perhaps the Wallingfords set some of these rooms aside for guests, other family members, or domestics residing with them.

In 1820 Wallingford purchased a store and lot closer to the town center and, according to local historians, occupied this space as his office. Wallingford's law library at his office and "articles of furniture for the use of the same" are listed separately from his "household furniture." Wallingford

reserved his best furnishings for his family's use; the ten
articles of furniture in the office were described as "pine,"
"small," or "old," three adjectives associated with inexpensive wares. The "pine writing desk and bookcase" valued at
$2 had the highest value. With a "small pine writing desk" at
seventy-five cents, two old pine tables, and "5 old Chairs" at
$1.25, these furnishings served their purposes at low expense.
On the completion of the house, perhaps Wallingford used
the anteroom behind the sitting room in the same way
Longfellow converted his family's dining room as an office.
Entry to the office could have been through exterior doors in
the ell, thus removing clients from family spaces.[56]

The Nathaniel Lord Mansion

Five miles away in Kennebunkport, Nathaniel Lord constructed his new three-story mansion house in 1814 (fig. 2.22).
Fourth in wealth in the county to Cutts, Cleaves, and Storer,
he chose the most up-to-date architectural style (see Chapter
2, chart 3). His home documents the evolution of a preferred
house type among the elite between the Georgian style
of the 1782 Cutts mansion and this high federal-style thirty
years later. The Lord mansion resembled the houses Lord's
builder-architect Thomas Eaton had seen and built in
Portland (see Chapter 2). Despite the dispersal of the family
furnishings, the original appearance of the interior can be
documented by a general 1815 inventory, the house itself,
and other surviving evidence.[57] In size, room arrangement,
and interior decoration, the Lord house represents a sophisticated scheme.

From the entrance hall, a door led through an arch to a
larger rear hall and stairs rose elliptically to the second floor.
The best parlor, on the northwestern side of the house, was
indicated by the extra ornamentation of the fireplace
surrounds and wallpaper printed *en grisaille* with "landscape
figures" (fig. 3.11).[58]

Across the hall, the door to the eastern parlor was inset
into a curved niche. This unexpected configuration is
explained by an alcove built to the left of the door on the
staircase wall. The alcove is not recessed and reserved *for* a
sideboard, it *is* a sideboard, with built-in drawers and
shelves. The drawers are grain-painted in imitation of
mahogany. The walls were hung with a wallpaper featuring
another large-scale repeating pattern, appropriate for best
rooms.[59]

Through a door at the rear of the room, one passed
through the axial hall leading to the cupola staircase into a
room of equal proportion (fig. 2.8.8). This space was
traditionally used for dining; it, too, had a "sideboard" built
into the wall. Although these rooms on the eastern side of the
house were divided by the hall, they provided an alternative
to a double parlor. The rear room was in close proximity to
the kitchen. An ell for the kitchen was added after the house
was built. Originally the kitchen may have been located in
the cellar with a dumbwaiter providing the necessary access
for food service.

The limited number of objects listed in the probate
inventory cannot represent a completely furnished house.
Perhaps the sketchiness can be explained by Lord's prema-
ture death in February 1815. Among the forms listed were
two secretaries, six card tables, a sofa, a clock, and four
looking glasses. Nathaniel and his wife, Phebe Walker Lord,

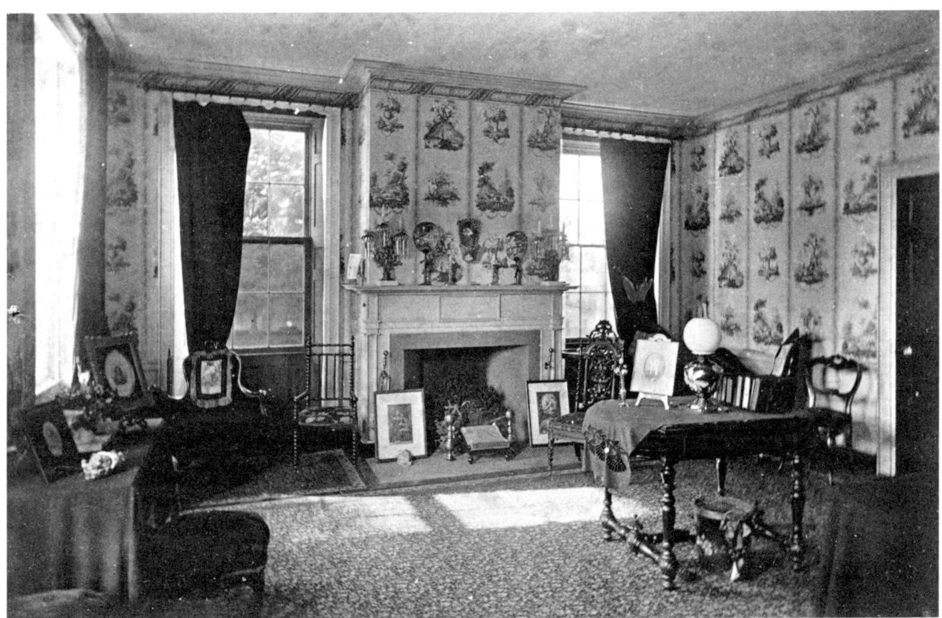

Fig. 3.11 Northwest parlor,
Nathaniel Lord house,
Kennebunkport, Maine, 1815.
Thomas Eaton, architect-builder.
Photograph, ca. 1890. Courtesy,
Society for the Preservation of
New England Antiquities.

had their likenesses taken by John Brewster, Jr.; these portraits (or at least the one of Phebe) hung in the best parlor of the house.[60]

As with other families, changes were made in the Lord mansion to update interior styles. Although the 1815 wallpapers in the front parlors remained undisturbed, a fancy rainbow paper was added in the 1820s in one of the rear first-floor rooms or better second-floor chambers.[61]

Conclusion

Whether building a new house of two or three stories, or altering an existing structure into a fashionable dwelling, a family's choice of architecture was one public statement of its aspirations and wealth. Symbols of prosperity were also expressed through interior room arrangement, decorative treatments, and stylish furnishings. Improvements in conveniences and ease of living were also represented in many of these homes.

Hyperbole is often used to express delight and to compliment. John Adams and Jonathan Sayward may have been overstating what they actually saw on their travels in Portland and Kennebunk, but it was only because they were pleased by what they found. They drew parallels with the places they knew in Boston and other sophisticated Massachusetts towns; Maine compared favorably. Evidence firmly proves that fashionable life was possible in Maine. The amazement with which visitors acknowledged this fact throughout the federal period continues to the present day. Cosmopolitan Maine residents were linked to the same values and styles of living as their Massachusetts counterparts. It, therefore, should come as no surprise that these northern New Englanders were equal partners in the Massachusetts commonwealth and "not a whit behind any . . . in the Union."[62]

1 L. H. Butterfield, ed., *Adams Family Correspondence*, 2 vols. (New York: Atheneum, 1965), 1:134.
2 Jonathan Sayward, journals, July 28, 1785, American Antiquarian Society, Worcester, Mass. For Lyman house wallpapers dating to this time, see Nylander, Redmond, and Sander, *Wallpaper*, 54–55, plate 3. Fragments of these papers also survive at BSM.
3 Abbott Lowell Cummings, "The Beginnings of Provincial Renaissance Architecture in Boston, 1690–1720," *Journal of the Society of Architectural Historians* 42, no. 1 (March 1983): 45, 50; for a discussion of Georgian-style architecture in New England, see Kevin M. Sweeney, "Mansion People: Kinship, Class, and Architecture in Western Massachusetts in the Mid Eighteenth Century," *Winterthur Portfolio* 19, no. 4 (Winter 1984): 231–255.
4 John Mead Howells, *The Architectural Heritage of the Piscataqua* (1937; reprint, New York: Architectural Book Publishing Co., 1965), plates 166, 169, 42, 43, 6, 10–12, 14. Garvin, "Academic Architecture," 94–95, 103, 213.
5 Lovejoy, *This was Stroudwater*, 63, 68; the 1756 map illustrating the Frost house is reproduced in Barry, *Tate House*, facing 97. For a house in the Piscataqua region with an early eighteenth-century cupola, see the MacPhaedris-Warner house, Portsmouth, in Garvin, "Academic Architecture," 52.
6 Lovejoy, *This was Stroudwater*, 111.
7 Thompson, *Maine Forms*, 64. Wallpaper made by a Boston paper stainer which depicts July 4, 1776, is recorded here. For a discussion and illustration of this paper, see Nylander, Redmond, and Sander, *Wallpaper*, 61–62. William E. Barry published a drawing of the movable walls in his *Sketches*.
8 Thomas Hubka, *Big House, Little House, Back House, Barn* (Hanover, N.H.: University Press of New England, 1984), 32–37.
9 Williamson, *History of Maine*, 2:703.
10 Josiah Pierce to Harriot Pierce, January 24, 1824, private collection.
11 Williamson, *History of Maine*, 2:703. William H. Pierson, Jr., *American Buildings and Their Architects* (1970; reprint, New York: Anchor Books, 1976), 228–230.
12 The double parlor in Hallowell's Warren house is described below; see n15. The Colonel John Black mansion in Ellsworth was also built with a double parlor; see Myers, *Maine Catalog*, 209.
13 This example is cited from Edward Emerson, Jr.'s probate inventory, YCRP; 19:429.
14 For the Gardiner house description, see Morris, "Tower," 48; the Frothingham and Hannaford references are in Abigail May, diary, MEHS; and for Hallowell, Emma Huntington Nason, *Old Hallowell on the Kennebec* (Augusta, Me.: Burleigh & Flynt, 1909), 220–221.
15 Nason, *Old Hallowell on the Kennebec*, 274.
16 Abigail May, diary, MEHS.
17 Ann King to [Caroline King ?], December 15, 1820, Erving-King Family Papers, New-York Historical Society, New York City.
18 Abigail May, diary, MEHS.
19 Josiah Pierce to Harriot Pierce, January 24, 1824, private collection.
20 Williamson, *History of Maine*, 2:703.
21 For Hamilton carpets, see YCRP; 19: 220–222; for stair rods, see YCRP; 26:174; and for nailed carpets, see account, Thomas Robison to John Seymour, December 24, 1784, Robison Papers, MEHS.
22 Butterfield, *Adams Correspondence*, 1:123. Ann Bryant Smith decorated her parlor with flowers; see her diary, MEHS.
23 For an example of a large repeat pattern, see the portraits of Thomas and Elizabeth Cutts (cat. 33); the floor coverings depicted could be a Brussels carpet, although canvas floor cloths were painted in imitation of more costly textiles. Nina Fletcher Little, *Floor Coverings in Early New England Before 1850* (Sturbridge, Mass.: Old Sturbridge Village, 1967), 8, 10–12; for an example of Brussels stair and floor carpets, see YCRP; 26:173; Kidderminster carpeting in the "newest patterns" was advertised in *Eastern Argus* (July 5, 1815); Cleaves's Turkey carpet is recorded in YCRP; 26:544.
24 Edward S. Cooke, Jr., "Domestic Space in Federal Period Inventories of Salem Merchants," *Essex Institute Historical Collections* 116, no. 4 (October 1980): 253–254.
25 For a discussion of window curtains and their use in early America, see Florence M. Montgomery, *Textiles in America, 1650–1870* (New York: W. W. Norton, 1984), 49–69. YCRP; 19:221–222 (Hamilton), and 26:543 (Cleaves).
26 Williamson, *History of Maine*, 2:703.
27 YCRP; 16:281; Jobe and Kaye, *New England Furniture*, 336–342; the cane-back chair illustrated on 337 descended in the Cutts family of Saco.
28 YCRP; 17:347.
29 Nylander, "Sayward House," 567–577.
30 Sweeney, "Mansion People," 241–242; although the house was moved in this century and so altered to be unrecognizable, the plan of the interior was recorded by photographs and drawings in 1936 as part of the Historic American Buildings Survey. A series of photographs and drawings is in SPNEA Archives. Bentley, *Diary*, 1:65–66. Bentley further commented that "by studying convenience within [the house, Cutts] has deranged all his windows, & destroyed the style of the building."
31 Thomas Cutts's inventory is recorded in YCRP; 29:254–272; for Hamilton house wallpapers, see Nylander, Redmond, and Sander, *Wallpaper*, 59–61; another stylish wallpaper treatment for a hall was Henry Knox's plain bright yellow papers with borders; see Nylander, Redmond, and Sander, *Wallpaper*, 72–74.
32 Thomas Cutts's tankard and "butter boats" are illustrated in *The*

Cornelius C. Moore Collection of Early American Silver, Sale 5430 (New York: Sotheby's, 1986), lots 108, 127; for a porringer made by Stephen Emery, see lot 129 and cat. 46. The tankard was lent to MEHS by Charles Thornton Libby and returned to him in 1939; accession records, MEHS.

33 Jane C. Giffen, "Chandeliers in Federal New England," *Antiques* 101, no. 3 (March 1972): 528–534; the chandelier purchased in 1826 for the First Parish Church in Portland is illustrated in fig. 5.

34 Thomas Cutts, Jr., owned his own dwelling house at Winter Harbor (Biddeford Pool) and "the house at Saco"; his extensive inventory is recorded in YCRP; 50: 358–383; the carpet reference is on 375.

35 Sarah Cleaves to Daniel Cleaves, March 16, 1816; typescript in Edith Cleaves Barry, comp., "The Fairfield, Cleaves, and Lord Families of Maine" (scrapbook, BSM); YCRP; 26:543. At some point, a piano was moved to the Cutts house in Saco, for one valued at $35 was listed there in Thomas, Jr.'s, inventory, YCRP; 50:376.

36 La Rochefoucault-Liancourt, *Travels*, 1:459.

37 Nathan Goold, *The Wadsworth-Longfellow House* (1901; reprint, Portland: Anthoensen Press, 1973), 10; for details of the Wadsworth house construction, see William Goold, "Old Houses and their Builders No. 5," [April] 1892, William Goold, Scrapbook, 114. For a discussion of federal-period dwelling houses in Maine, see Myers, *Maine Catalog*, 45–85.

38 Zilpah Wadsworth to Nancy Doane, letter journal, November 29–December 19, 1799, Wadsworth-Longfellow Papers, LNHS. This and all following references from the Wadsworth-Longfellow Papers at LNHS were kindly supplied to me for this discussion by Joyce Butler. For documentation on the desk in the store, see Zilpah Wadsworth to Nancy Doane, November 27, 1796, letter journal, Wadsworth-Longfellow Papers, LNHS. The passageway between the store and the southeast parlor is referred to in Peleg Wadsworth to George Wadsworth, February 25, 1804; see copies of letters from Peleg Wadsworth to his sons George and John, 2 vols., Wadsworth Papers, MEHS. He gave instructions how to barricade the passageway at "the shop door (into the Parlor) with Bricks, or a succession of Planks" in case of fire. Arthur Gerrier kindly brought this latter reference to my attention.

39 Zilpah Wadsworth to Nancy Doane, letter journal, November 29–December 19, 1799, Wadsworth-Longfellow Papers, LNHS.

40 Zilpah Wadsworth to Nancy Doane, September 1, 1802; Zilpah Wadsworth Longfellow, diary, February 16, 1830, Wadsworth Longfellow Papers, LNHS.

41 Abigail May, diary, MEHS.

42 Zilpah Wadsworth to Nancy Doane, letter journal, November 22, 1801, Wadsworth-Longfellow Papers, LNHS. Report of the Committee for the New Library, 1901, MEHS.

43 Will, Peleg Wadsworth, 1829, Wadsworth Papers, MEHS.

44 What Lucia may have had to say of the changes is not known. Zilpah W. Longfellow to Alexander Longfellow, May 16, 1836, Wadsworth-Longfellow Papers, LNHS; Richard Candee's research of the tax list of 1816 reveals that Longfellow was among the top 20 percent, not the top 2 percent.

45 Hepplewhite, *Cabinet-Maker's Guide*, 6.

46 I am indebted to Earle G. Shettleworth, Jr., and Arthur Gerrier for their assistance in determining the changes the Longfellows made. Joyce Butler shared her discovery that Peleg Wadsworth provided the funds for the third-floor addition; see Peleg Wadsworth to George Wadsworth, September 4, 1814, Wadsworth Papers, MEHS. Stephen's description of the chambers is in Stephen Longfellow to Zilpah Longfellow, August 15, 1815, Wadsworth-Longfellow Papers, LNHS. See also Goold, *The Wadsworth-Longfellow House*, 42–43.

47 There are numerous references in the Wadsworth and Longfellow Papers at both MEHS and LNHS to servants, but they do not reveal if they boarded. The papers are also full of the names of visiting friends and relatives who stayed with the family. For an example see Zilpah Longfellow to Stephen Longfellow, February 18, 1824, Wadsworth-Longfellow Papers, LNHS, about the expenses involved with company. Curved wooden cornices are attached at the top of the window frames and were probably covered with fabric.

48 Other houses with symmetrical doorways, including those with false doors, built in the opening years of the nineteenth century, include the Hugh McLellan house in Portland. Arthur Gerrier kindly provided this information.

49 The 1815 fire of Stephen's office is recorded in the records of the Portland Benevolent Society, 1814–1878, 1, MEHS. Joyce Butler kindly brought this event to my attention.

50 Receipts, 1816–1826, Longfellow Papers, MEHS. Joyce Butler brought the office rent to my attention. *The Portland Directory* (Portland, Me.: A.W. Thayer, 1823), 43; *The Portland Directory and Register* (Portland, Me.: James Adams, Jr., 1827), 46; Hilen, *Letters*, 1:305.

51 A brick from the Wallingford house kitchen chimney dated August 16, 1804, is among the Barry collection at BSM. Wallingford bought parcels of property in 1803 and 1806 that may have been the site for his house, see YCRD; 69:143 and 76:108, respectively.

52 The Taylor-Barry house is owned by BSM.

53 William E. Barry lived in the Wallingford house and described the largest parlor as the "great-room" or "assembly room" in his Biography Scrapbook, 1846–1932, BSM.

54 YCRP; 33: 296–306. My thanks to Mrs. Benjamin Flayderman, Norman Flayderman, and Barbara Storer of Stukas Realty of Wells for making the house accessible for study.

55 Lynn, *Wallpaper*, 200–203. Barry published the scene of Virgil's tomb in his *Sketches*.

56 YCRD; 104:80; Remich, *History*, 113.

57 YCRP; 25:587–588.

58 For more on landscape figures, see Nylander, Redmond, and Sander, *Wallpaper*, 118–119.

59 For a discussion of these parlor papers as well as other papers used in the Lord mansion, see Nylander, Redmond, and Sander, *Wallpaper*, 129–132. Lynn, *Wallpaper*, 277.

60 The portrait of Phebe Lord was photographed in the parlor ca. 1900. Private collection, courtesy Captain Nathaniel Lord Inn, Kennebunkport.

61 Nylander, Redmond, and Sander, *Wallpaper*, 142, plate 17.

62 Royall, *Black Book*, 2:216.

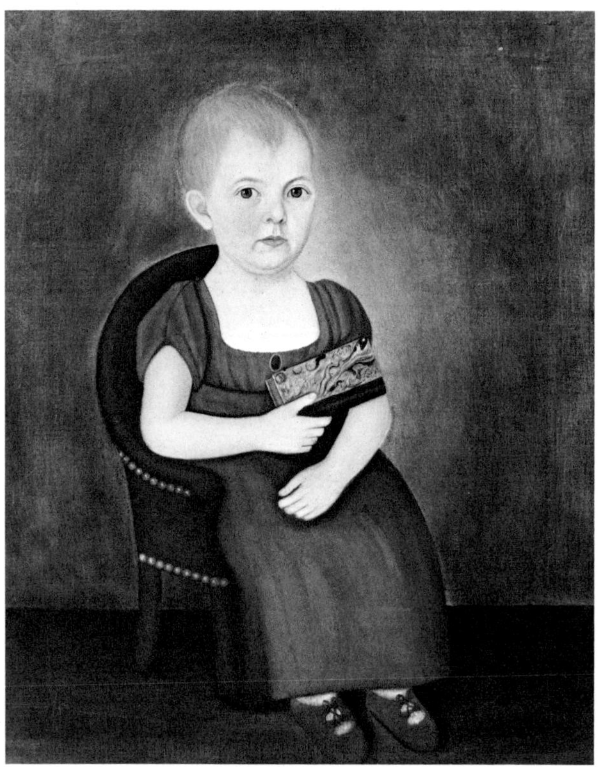

Cat. 41

Elizabeth's red dress and shoes are frequently found in early nineteenth-century portraits of children. The red stone brooch bears her mother's initials "AW." The armchair, upholstered in green fabric secured with shiny brass nails, documents the occurrence of such chairs, scaled down in size for children but treated in the same way as adult models. However, few, if any, upholstered children's chairs survive from this period.

The book with its marbleized paper cover symbolizes the importance of learning for this child. In 1819, when Elizabeth was sent away to a school for young ladies, her father wrote:

This is the first time it has ever devolved on me as a duty to address, by letter, an absent child and it is accompanied with sensations, mingled with pleasure and anxiety—pleasure in the thought that you are happy and that you are now improving in those necessary, useful and important accomplishments which enlarge the understanding and improve [the] mind— Which dignify and adorn our nature—Anxiety that your conduct will be such as will secure the love and esteem of your instructors, and those with whom you are associated—That you may have a proper sense of your own duty, of the importance of paying a due attention to the studies and pursuits assigned you, and also that you take the necessary care of your health.[1]

Her father's encouragement to "Write us often—it will familarize you to communicating your thoughts with ease," was tied, in part, to her inability to come home during the summer for vacation as "the distance is too great."[2]

Elizabeth Abigail Wallingford married Dr. Samuel Dow on October 8, 1829. Preserved in her or her family's cookbook is the recipe for "Elizabeth A. Wallingford's Wedding Cake." Made with six pounds of flour, two pounds of sugar, four pounds of butter, and four dozen eggs, this great cake, cylindrical in shape, would have been a prominent feature of Elizabeth's wedding reception. Six pounds of currants, mace, nutmeg, citron, and wine with "a few cloves" flavored this pound cake recipe. Slices of such large cakes were often sent to friends.[3] The joy brought by this occasion came to an abrupt end—Abigail died the following May at twenty-three, the same age as her mother at her death.   CSP & LFS

41

John Brewster, Jr. (1766–1854)
Elizabeth Abigail Wallingford (1806–1830)
Kennebunk, Maine, 1808
Oil on canvas
Inscribed (stretcher) "John Brewster Jr.
pinxit Decr 12th, 1808"
H 30³⁄₁₆ (76.6); W 25¹⁄₁₆ (63.6)
The Brick Store Museum; William E. Barry estate
through Edith Cleaves Barry, 1936
Color plate on page 253

This portrait of Elizabeth Abigail Wallingford, daughter of George and Abigail Chadbourne Wallingford of Kennebunk, is an unusual example of a child's portrait by John Brewster, Jr., for she is shown full-length, seated in a small armchair. When painting full-length likenesses of children, Brewster characteristically posed them in a standing position. Elizabeth's mother died in January 1808; before the year was out her father had arranged to have the portrait of his first child painted. She was the only offspring of Wallingford's first marriage; she had just turned two.

1 George Wallingford to Elizabeth Wallingford, Kennebunk, June 6, 1819, Wallingford Family Papers, BSM.
2 George Wallingford to "Dear Daughter" [Elizabeth Wallingford], Kennebunk, July 15, 1822, Wallingford Family Papers, BSM.
3 Wallingford family genealogy, and Elizabeth A. Wallingford, cookbook, BSM. Louise Conway Belden, *The Festive Tradition: Table Decoration and Desserts in America, 1650–1900* (New York: W. W. Norton, 1983), 183, 189.

42A

Unidentified artist
Probably *Stephen Longfellow* (1776–1849)
Probably Portland, Maine, ca. 1801
Watercolor on ivory
H 2½ (6.4); w 2 (5.0)
Maine Historical Society; Wadsworth-Longfellow House

42B

Attributed to John Roberts (1769–1803)
Elizabeth Wadsworth (1779–1802)
Portland, Maine, ca. 1801
Watercolor on ivory
H 2½ (6.4); w 2 (5.0)
Maine Historical Society; Wadsworth-Longfellow House

In 1798 Stephen Longfellow graduated from Harvard College and returned to Portland to practice law. He studied with Salmon Chase and in 1801 was admitted to the Maine bar. In 1799 both Zilpah and Eliza, Peleg Wadsworth's daughters, enjoyed the company of their "favorite Longfellow."[1] Despite a close friendship with Zilpah, it was to Eliza that Stephen was betrothed.

There is some confusion over the identity of the male sitter in this miniature (cat. 42A). An old society label records him as Stephen's younger brother, Samuel (1789–1816), who lived at the family homestead in Gorham, but there is nothing further to support that attribution. However, Stephen is known to have had a miniature painted as a young man. When Zilpah wrote to Stephen in 1825, "I wish you were here at this moment to hear your good friends commenting on your youthful miniature," Stephen replied, "it would give me great pleasure to join in your family circle and enjoy your sport and amusement, even at the expense of my poor miniature."[2]

This miniature of Stephen may have been painted about the time of his engagement to Eliza in 1801. Although the artist has not been identified, it may be the work of an itinerant who had added Portland to his list of stops. The likeness resembles that of the same man taken twenty-four years later (cat. 43) and supports the description of Stephen as "plain, straight-forward, and effective."[3]

It was Elizabeth Wadsworth, called both Eliza and Betsy

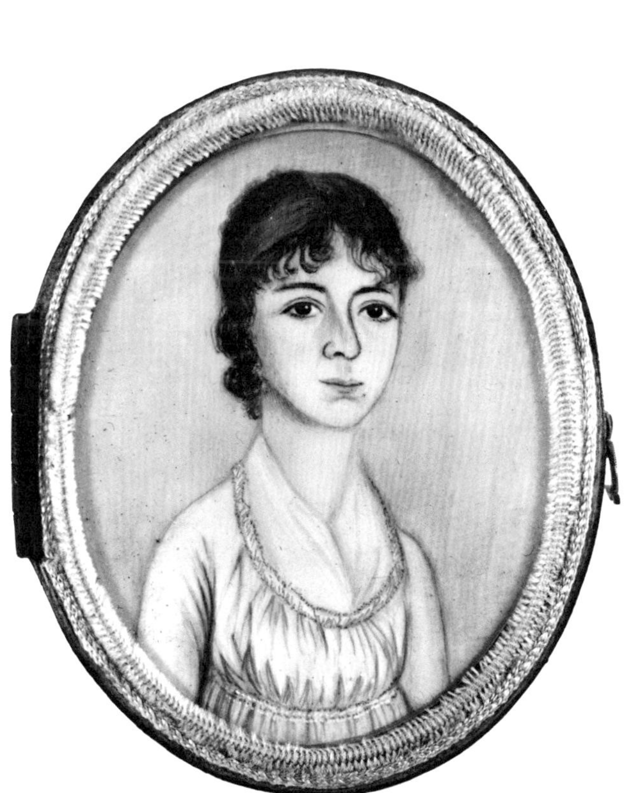

Cat. 42B

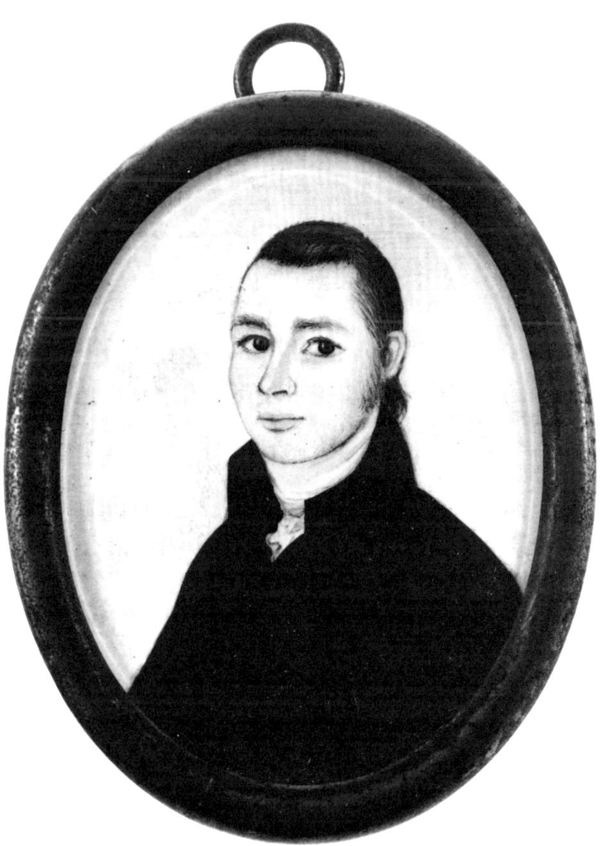

Cat. 42A

by her family, who, on the death of George Washington in 1799, wrote to her father in Washington, D. C., requesting a sample of Washington's handwriting or a lock of his hair (see cat. 75). Her white high-waisted dress is typical of styles that were popular at the turn-of-the-century and is like the white cotton assembly dress worn by her sister Lucia during the same time (cat. 165). Her hair is short and held with a ribbon in a style similar to that worn by her contemporary, Sarah Scamman Cutts (cat. 35).

This portrait (cat. 42B) may be the work of John Roberts. On October 18, 1801, Zilpah wrote to her cousin in Boston:

Should you like to see Betsy's miniature? I hope to have it in my power to show you a very good likeness though I cannot say as yet how good it will be, for it is not finished. It is taken by Roberts. I am unacquainted with his celebrity as a painter. . . . This miniature of my sister was taken at the request of a particular friend.[4]

A native of Scotland, Roberts came to America in 1793 where he was an active portrait and miniature painter, engraver, and inventor until his death in 1803. William Dunlap described him as talented, but noted that his eccentricities prevented him from taking advantage of many good opportunities.[5] In traveling the circuit, Roberts visited Portland at least three times. During August 1801, he advertised in the *Portland Gazette* as a "miniature and portrait painter. . . . Those who may please to favor him with their commands, may depend on having the most striking resemblance."[6] It must have been Roberts who was pleased by the response to his advertisement, for in October he was back in Portland and painted Eliza's miniature. The following spring, Roberts was again in Portland where he "beg[ged] leave to return his thanks to the Ladies and Gentlemen of Portland, for the liberal encouragement he has met with in the line of his profession." If three or more persons applied at one time during his short stay, he offered to paint their miniatures at the reduced rate of $10. He noted that he was intending to depart next for the West Indies. On March 14, 1803, he advertised as a miniature painter and drawing master, and announced plans to open a school.[7]

Zilpah may have been referring to Stephen as the "particular friend" who requested the work, since the miniature dates to the time of the marriage intentions between him and Eliza. With its flat, harsh lines, the likeness is not graceful, but it is probably accurate. By this time, Eliza was in the early stages of consumption. The texture of the ivory is visible through the blue wash of the background. The miniature is mounted in its original red leather-covered case.

The larger dimensions and light-colored pale blue backgrounds of both miniatures are representative of those painted at the beginning of the nineteenth century; these replaced the locket-size, eighteenth-century likenesses with their darker opaque grounds. A characteristic of American miniatures of this period was "honesty" to the subject; the popularity of the medium was rooted in the artist's attempt to capture an actual likeness of the sitter and to stimulate the memory "of a particular friend."

Before the wedding of Stephen Longfellow and Eliza Wadsworth took place, Eliza died. Responding to her cousin's letter and invitation to visit Boston, Zilpah reflected on the death of her sister: "in this house only, in this room where she died . . . I can recollect her most perfectly . . . I presume you know of which room I speak, it is the largest parlor, unfrequented by the family excepting such as retire for meditation." Between the lines "hours and hours I have watched here, frequently with Stephen" one might read her interest in her sister's intended.[8] Indeed, on January 1, 1804, within two years of Eliza's death, Zilpah married Stephen Longfellow.   LFS & CSP

1 William Willis, *A History of the Law, the Courts, and the Lawyers of Maine* (Portland: Bailey and Noyes, 1863), 362. Zilpah Wadsworth, diary, April 25, 1799, Wadsworth-Longfellow Papers, LNHS. Joyce Butler kindly brought this and the following LNHS references to our attention.
2 Zilpah Longfellow to Stephen Longfellow, January 17, 1825; and Stephen Longfellow to Zilpah Longfellow, February 27, 1825, Wadsworth-Longfellow Papers, LNHS. Hugh D. McLellan, *History of Gorham* (1903; reprint, Somersworth, N.H.: New England History Press, 1980), 641.
3 Willis, *History of the Law*, 364.
4 Zilpah Wadsworth to Nancy Doane, letter journal, October 18, 1801, Wadsworth-Longfellow Papers, LNHS.
5 George C. Groce and David H. Wallace, *The New-York Historical Society's Dictionary of Artists in America, 1564–1860* (New Haven, Conn.: Yale University Press, 1957), 539; and William Dunlap, *A History of the Rise and Progress of the Arts of Design in the United States*, 3 vols. (1834; reprint, Boston: C. E. Goodspeed & Co., 1918), 2:115, 134. William D. Barry kindly brought Dunlap's comments to our attention along with the newspaper references cited below.
6 *Portland Gazette* (August 3, 1801).
7 *Portland Gazette* (March 29, 1802; March 15, 1803).
8 Zilpah Wadsworth to Nancy Doane, September 1, 1802, Wadsworth-Longfellow Papers, LNHS.

43

Charles Bird King (1785–1862)
Stephen Longfellow (1776–1849)
Washington, D. C., 1824
Oil on canvas
H 29¹¹⁄₁₆ (75.4); W 24¾ (62.9)
Maine Historical Society; Wadsworth-Longfellow House

During the winter of 1824, Congressman Stephen Longfellow wrote from Washington, D. C., to his wife Zilpah broaching the subject of commissioning a portrait of himself. Through this and subsequent letters we are able to track the painting of this portrait of Longfellow by Charles Bird King. On February 19, 1824, Longfellow wrote to Zilpah:

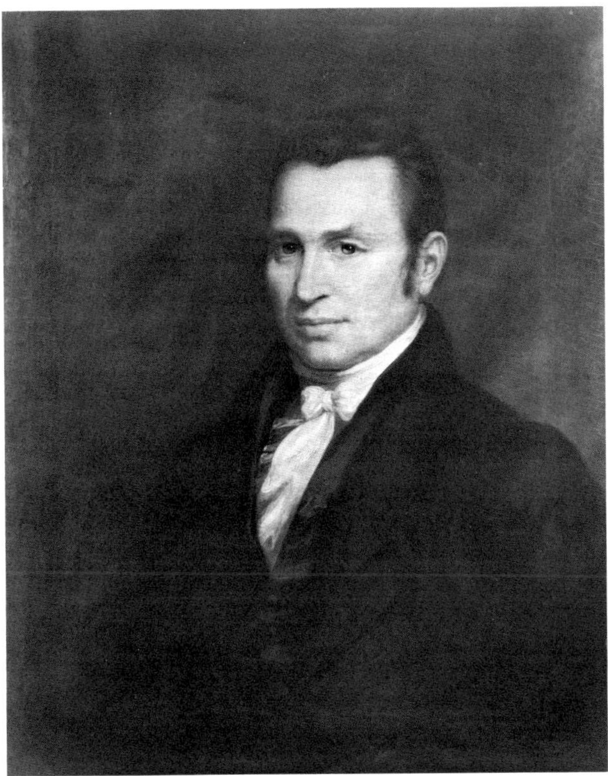

Cat. 43

There is a fine portrait painter here by the name of King. He has a public room about 30 feet wide & 40 long, lighted from the top, which is filled with portraits & other paintings of his own execution, many of which are very excellent. As I take great pleasure in viewing good paintings I frequently go in, & rest me in my walks. If you were here I would certainly have our portraits painted. Regretting as I do that we have no portraits of our parents, & sensible that that regret will be much [greater], if we should survive them & feeling also a hope that if I should be taken away my wife & children would not view with indifference the portrait of one so dear to them as a husband & parent, I have been almost tempted to have mine painted. What think you of it? It will cost $40 exclusive of the frame. . . . I was about to ask which you would prefer as a present, a gold watch or a portrait of your husband but perceiving the indelicacy and impropriety of the question I forbear.[1]

On March 7, Zilpah answered: "We shall all vote for the portrait, my dear husband, and I am rejoiced that you have an opportunity to have one taken by a good painter." Longfellow, however, began to have second thoughts about the portrait commission. On March 21 he reported to Zilpah that he had "done nothing respecting the portrait & the more I think of it, the more doubtful I feel as to the expediency of obtaining it." On April 4 he wrote that he "had given up the idea of obtaining the portrait but as you appear desirous of having it, I believe I must see the man." Zilpah

continued to persuade her husband, and by April 11 Stephen "could not resist the appeal, and it was commenced yesterday. Mr. King says he should be able to get an excellent likeness, but I don't see much resemblance to anything yet." On April 18 Zilpah wrote to thank Stephen for his "compliance with my request to sit for your portrait. I hope Mr. K. will do his best, and be successful in the likeness."

King was quick to complete the portrait as Stephen indicated on April 22 that "The portrait is nearly finished. I satt the last time today. I think he has got a pretty good likeness, & hope you will think so." On May 14, 1824, Stephen

sent to Alexandria, to be shipped to Portland, two boxes, one containing books, documents, etc., etc. & the other containing a portrait which I hope you will recognize as the likeness of one who tenderly loves you. . . . As no frames could be obtain[ed] here without sending to Baltimore for them I thought it best to obtain one at Portland.

Fastened to the stretcher is a fragment of King's receipt indicating that he was paid for the work in 1824. In the bust-length view of the forty-eight-year-old man, Longfellow wears a black coat and waistcoat and a white stock. The high regard in which he was held by both Maine citizens and visitors was related by Anne Royall on her visit to Portland in 1828:

Hon. Stephen Longfellow, (he ought to be called good fellow,) is also an able Counsellor, and one of the first lawyers. Mr. L. is a stout man, middle aged, dark complexion, staid countenance, with a large full intelligent black eye; his manners are of the first order, and if I were to judge, I would say he was among the most benevolent men of the age.[2]

The portrait descended to Stephen's son Alexander and was hanging in the dining room of his house when it was photographed in the late nineteenth century.[3]

Charles Bird King, a Newport, Rhode Island, native, first studied informally with Samuel King (1748/9–1819). His apprenticeship with Edward Savage (1761–1817) in New York City between 1800 and 1805 and further instruction during the years 1806–1812 in London with Benjamin West (1738–1820) allowed King to develop his skills and broaden his artistic tastes. During the summer of 1824 Charles Willson Peale (1741–1827) noted that King had in his studio not only portraits but also still lifes, landscapes, and emblematic pieces; during the period, artists did not commonly work in a variety of genres. After seven years as an itinerant painter moving from Boston to Norfolk, King settled in Washington during the winter of 1819–1820, responding to the security that a steady stream of portrait commissions provided. Following the examples of Peale and Savage, he opened a studio-gallery-museum at the corner of 12th and F streets that for four decades served as the focus of the art life in Washington. Not only was King's "Gallery of Paintings" a haven for visiting artists in Washington, but it was also a link in the chain of galleries from Portland to Charleston where artists could show the large exhibition pieces that became especially popular from the 1820s on, and upon which their survival depended. King himself depended on profitable portrait commissions to subsidize his penchant for painting subject pictures and to support his elaborate establishment through which, in turn, he was able to assist many other artists.[4]

John Quincy Adams appointed King to the first governmental art commission charged with judging entries for the pediment sculpture on the east facade of the Capitol. Adams believed the artist was also "an ingenious thinking man, with a faculty of conversing upon almost any topic."[5] William Dunlap visited Washington in 1824 and

found Mr. King full of business and a great favorite, assiduously employed in his painting room through the day, and in the evening attending the soirees, parties, and balls of the ambassadors, secretaries of the cabinet, president or other representatives and servants of the people, and justly esteemed every where.[6]

Congressman Longfellow and numerous other visitors to Washington found both visual pleasure and intellectual stimulation in frequenting the gallery of Charles Bird King, and they brought their expectations and their paintings back home to Portland and other communities.[7] Thus, this artist brightened not only the cultural scene in the immediate Washington area, but also played a part in the development of American artists and an appreciation of their skills on a national level. CSP

1 Letters, Stephen and Zilpah Longfellow, February 29 through May 16, 1824, Wadsworth-Longfellow Papers, LNHS. Joyce Butler generously provided these references.
2 Royall, *Black Book*, 2:219.
3 Alexander W. Longfellow house, photograph of interior, SPNEA Archives.
4 Andrew J. Cosentino and Henry H. Glassie, *The Capital Image: Painters in Washington 1800–1915* (Washington, D. C.: Smithsonian Institution Press, 1983), 39–40, 50, 264. Many King portraits were of Indian representatives in Washington, painted for the "Indian Gallery" established as early as 1817 by the Bureau of Indian Affairs. Some of these images were incorporated into the work of other artists. See also Andrew J. Cosentino, *The Paintings of Charles Bird King (1785–1862)* (Washington, D. C.: Smithsonian Institution Press, 1977). The portrait of Stephen Longfellow is not included in this catalogue.
5 Andrew Oliver, *Portraits of John Quincy Adams and His Wife* (Cambridge, 1970), 92; cited in Cosentino and Glassie, *The Capital Image*, 39.
6 William Dunlap, *A History of the Rise and Progress of the Arts of Design in the United States*, 3 vols. (1834; reprint, Boston: C. E. Goodspeed & Co., 1918), 3:29.
7 General Joshua Wingate (1773–1846) and his wife, Julia Cascaline Dearborn Wingate (1780–1867), of Portland, and Cyrus King (1772–1817) of Saco, also had their portraits painted by King; see Cosentino, *Charles Bird King*, 141, 163. The portrait of Mrs. Wingate is at MEHS.

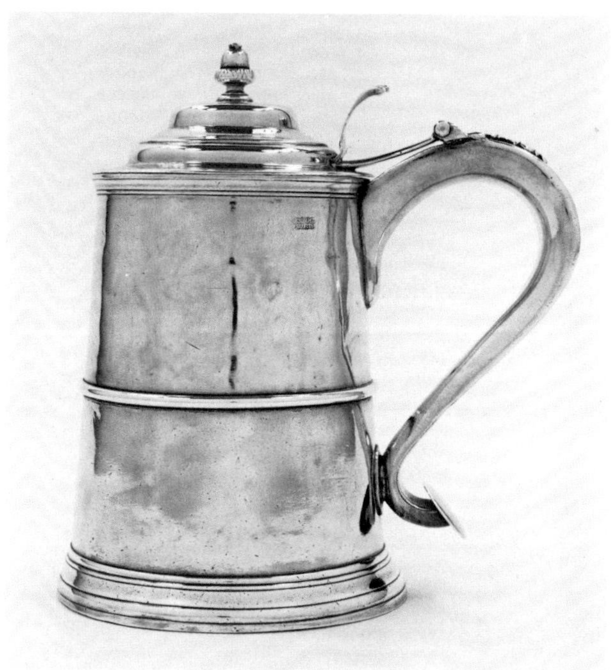

Cat. 44

44

Benjamin Burt (1729–1805)
Tankard
Boston, Massachusetts, 1750–1773
Silver
Marked (on body left of handle) "Benjamin / Burt"
H 7¹¹⁄₁₆ (19.5); w 4⅞ (12.4)
Old York Historical Society; Museum purchase, 1958

This tankard was made for Jonathan Sayward and his wife Sarah of York, who were married in 1736. Its handle is engraved with their initials "s / i * s." A large and important object, it served the succeeding generations as well. Sayward recorded in his diary in March 1773, "I let my son barrel have a silver tankard markd iss makers nam burt — to use in his family and took a Rec[ei]pt for the same to be returnd when demand[.] at the same time I gave him 2 Dol. as to pay for sedoring [soldering] on a Rim that was wanted on the Same."[1] It remained in the family until its purchase by the museum in 1958.

The practice of drinking communally from tankards on special occasions lasted longer in America than in Europe. This custom, along with the persistence of the tankard form, distinguished New England from European customs. Gerald

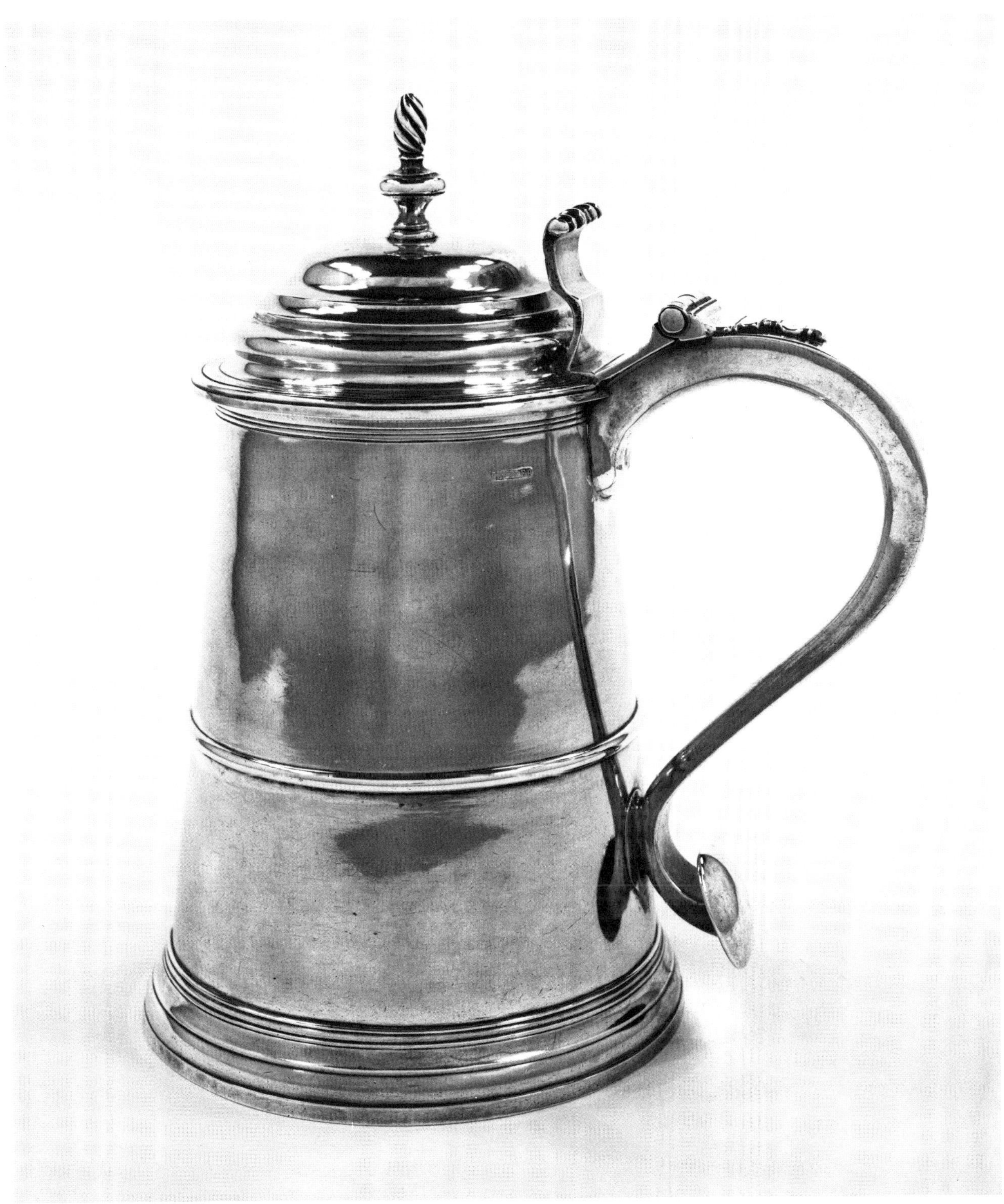

Cat. 45

W. R. Ward has suggested that the retention of traditional forms, such as tankards, may have provided a degree of stability and compensated for rapidly changing social conditions.[2] AAE

1 Jonathan Sayward, journals, March 15, 1773, American Antiquarian Society. SPNEA owns an unmarked silver tankard that is the companion to this one. Of slightly different proportions, it is also engraved s/1*s on the handle. See Penny J. Sander, ed., *Elegant Embellishments, Furnishings from New England Homes, 1660–1860* (Boston: Society for the Preservation of New England Antiquities, 1982), 35.
2 Gerald W. R. Ward, "Silver and Society in Salem, Massachusetts, 1630–1820: A Case Study of the Consumer and the Craft" (Ph.D. diss., Boston University, 1984), 137.

45

John Butler (1734–1827)
Tankard
Probably Portland, Maine, 1764–1785
Silver
Marked (on body left of handle)
"I. BUTLER" in rectangle
H 8⅞ (22.5); W 6¾ (17.2); Diam. bottom 5⁵⁄₁₆ (13.5)
Maine Historical Society; Gift of Richard H. Dana, Richard de Rham, and Mrs. Arthur L. Shipman, Jr., 1980

Traditional family history maintains that when blacksmith Stephen Longfellow died in 1764, he left his Harvard-educated son, Stephen, a small legacy. In gratitude, the son sent the silver coins to Boston to have made into useful silver objects. However, the Boston-bound vessel was lost. Stephen Longfellow gathered the necessary amount again and received, in return, two porringers, a cann, and a tankard.[1] The original Latin inscription engraved on the bottom of the tankard, "s.L /*Ex Dono Patris*," confirms that it was made "out of the gift of the father."

This tankard could well be the earliest known example of Maine-made silver hollowware. Marked "I. BUTLER," it is the work of John Butler, who moved to Portland in 1761 and worked there until 1785. Butler was known as "a handsome, gay, and accomplished man, but his misfortunes by losses of property and children, unthroned reason from her seat." Known thereafter as "Crazy Butler," his goldsmith tools were sold in 1785. In 1812 when Butler dined with the Reverend and Mrs. Deane, Deane reported that Butler was "tolerably sober and conversable."[2]

This tankard was donated to the Maine Historical Society by direct descendants of the original owner. It appears to be the tankard photographed in the home of Alexander W. Longfellow (d. 1901), and in 1913 it was at Craigie house in Cambridge, the home of Alexander's brother, Henry.[3] AAE

1 "Henry Wadsworth Longfellow," *Proceedings of the Maine Historical Society* (Portland: Hoyt, Fogg and Donham, 1882), 31.
2 Fales, "Early Maine Silver," 340. Willis, *History*, 792; Willis, *Journals*, 191, 401.
3 Alexander W. Longfellow house, photographs of interior, SPNEA Archives. Henry Wadsworth Longfellow Dana, *The Longfellow House, History and Guide* (Cambridge, Mass.: H. W. L. Dana, n.d.), 13.

46

William Simpkins (1704–1780)
Porringer
Boston, Massachusetts, 1762–1780
Silver
Marked (on handle) "Simpkins" in rectangle
H 2⅛ (5.4); W 7⅞ (19.9); Diam. 5³⁄₁₆ (13.2)
York Institute Museum

Many porringers survive that are engraved with the initials of a husband and wife and may have been wedding presents. This porringer was originally owned by Thomas and Elizabeth Scamman Cutts of Saco. Dating between 1762, when Thomas and Elizabeth married, and 1780, when Simpkins died, the porringer has engraved block letters "C /

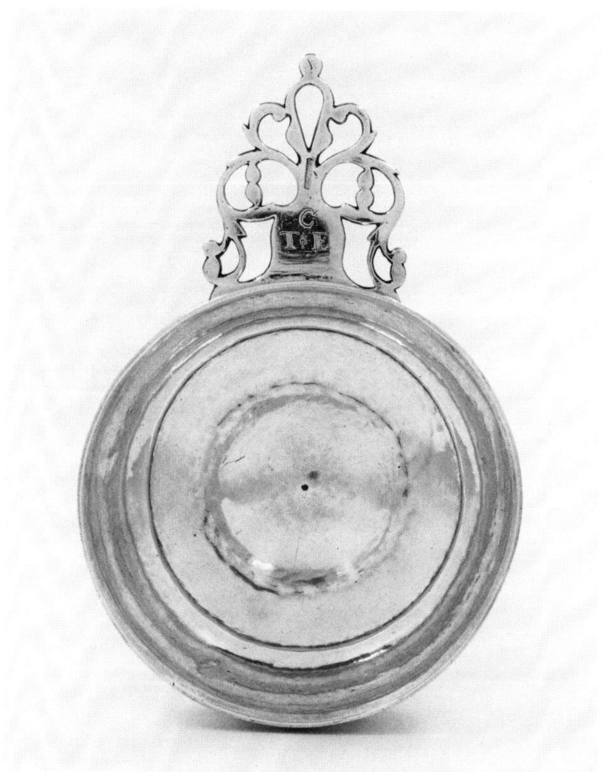

Cat. 46

T * E" on the handle. Thomas and Elizabeth Cutts owned
two similar porringers made by Boston silversmith Stephen
Emery.[1]

This porringer appears in Cutts's 1821 inventory as
either one of "2 old silver poringers 16 oz @ $1 − = $16.−"
or "2 new silver poringers 20 oz @ 1.21 = 24.17," valued
more highly (see Chapter 3).[2]

Although porringers were made extensively in the
colonial period, their production and use continued long
after the Revolution (see cat. 112). Between 1792 and 1796,
Elizabeth Cutts requested that Thomas Cutts, Jr., purchase
"2 silver Porringers with Cutts and Scammon Coats of arms
on rim" while on a voyage to England and Europe.[3] Although
Thomas, Jr.'s, mother was a Scamman and may have placed
the order which contained her maiden and married names, it
seems more likely that the porringers were meant as gifts to
her son, Foxwell Cutts. He had married Sarah Scamman in
1789 (cat. 35).

Local silversmiths sold porringers at least as late as 1804.
In that year, Portland's Enoch Moulton advertised silver porringers "just received from London."[4] Although Americans
continued to use porringers longer than did the English,
these references suggest that the production of porringers
continued abroad, perhaps primarily for export.   AAE

1 Philip H. Hammerslough, *American Silver* (Hartford, Conn.: Privately
  printed, 1965), 41; *The Cornelius C. Moore Collection of Early American
  Silver*, sale 5430 (New York: Sotheby's, January 31, 1986), lot 129.
2 YCRP; 295: 262.
3 Thomas Cutts, Jr., book of invoices of goods shipped on the *Minerva*,
  1792–1796, Cutts-Thornton Papers, MEHS.
4 *Eastern Argus* (November 30, 1804).

47A

Robert Brookhouse (1779–1866)
Spoon
Salem, Massachusetts, 1806–1819
Silver
Marked (on back of handle) "RB" in script in oval
L 4¹¹⁄₁₆ (11.9)
The Brick Store Museum; William E. Barry estate
through Edith Cleaves Barry

47B

Spoon
Maine or Massachusetts, 1806–1811
Silver
Unmarked
L 4⅜ (11.0)
The Brick Store Museum; William E. Barry estate
through Edith Cleaves Barry

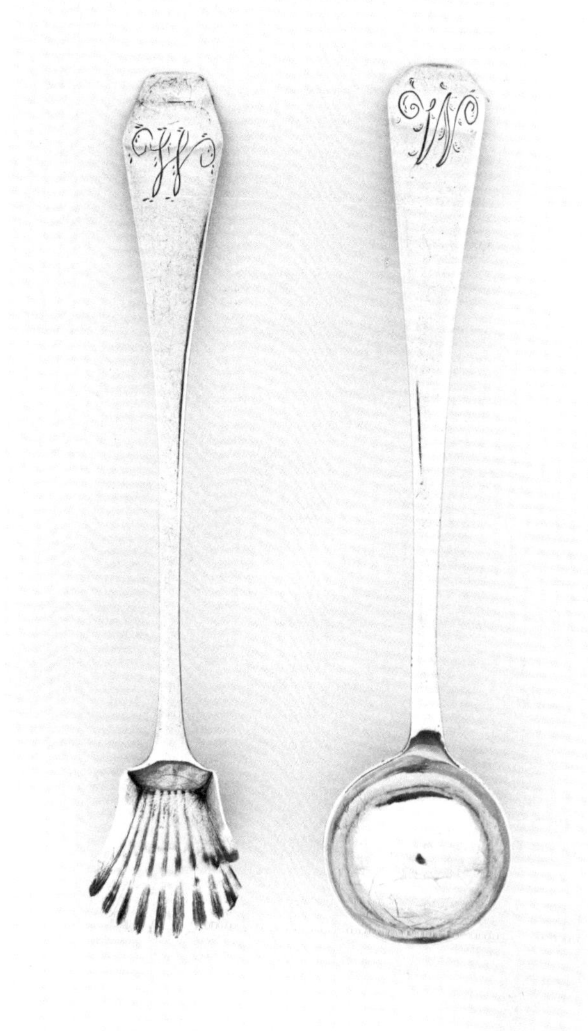

Cat. 47A and Cat. 47B

These flatware forms illustrate the specialization of serving
implements and the growing availability of these wares
during the early nineteenth century. Implements were
designed for a particular use and are associated with salt,
mustard, and other dried seasonings. They have short bowls
and long handles.

These spoons probably belonged to George Washington
Wallingford of Kennebunk; both handles are engraved with
a "W" in script. The spoon made by Robert Brookhouse of
Salem has a slender coffin-shaped handle and terminates in
a ribbed shovel-shaped bowl. It dates between the time of
Wallingford's marriage in 1806 to Abigail Chadbourne, or
his second marriage in 1811 to Mary Fisher, and the end of
Brookhouse's silversmithing career in 1819. The unmarked

spoon has a coffin-shaped handle and a deep rounded bowl.
Both were inherited by William Barry from his wife Florence
Hooper Wallingford, who was the granddaughter of George
and Mary Fisher Wallingford.[1]

Charles Farley was apprenticed to Robert Brookhouse in
Salem before he started his career in Portland in 1813. This
relationship is further indication of the ties between Boston-
area craftsmen and clients in southern Maine.[2]   AAE

1 William E. Barry lived in Wallingford Hall in the late nineteenth
   century. His collection formed the basis of The Brick Store Museum,
   founded by niece Edith Barry in 1936. See Wallingford family
   genealogy, BSM.
2 Churchill, "Crafts in Transition," 302; see also Maine silversmith
   files, Maine State Museum, and Gerald W. R. Ward, "Silver and
   Society in Salem, Massachusetts, 1630–1820: A Case Study of the
   Consumer and the Craft" (Ph.D. diss., Boston University, 1984),
   278–283, 288–289.

48

Sideboard
Possibly Maine, 1800–1810
Mahogany, mahogany veneer, *eastern white pine*
Branded "ss" in block letters
H 40¹⁵⁄₁₆ (106.5); W 71¼ (181.0); D 22⁷⁄₁₆ (66.9)
York Institute Museum; Gift of George Addison Emery

At his death in 1821, Thomas Cutts owned not one, but two
sideboards. One valued at $30 was found in "the lower west
room" along with his card tables and glass chandelier. He
furnished "the North lower room or parlour" with a second
sideboard valued at $20.[1] This is one of Cutts's sideboards,
known to have descended from him to his great-great-grandson, George Addison Emery. Large rooms in some federal-

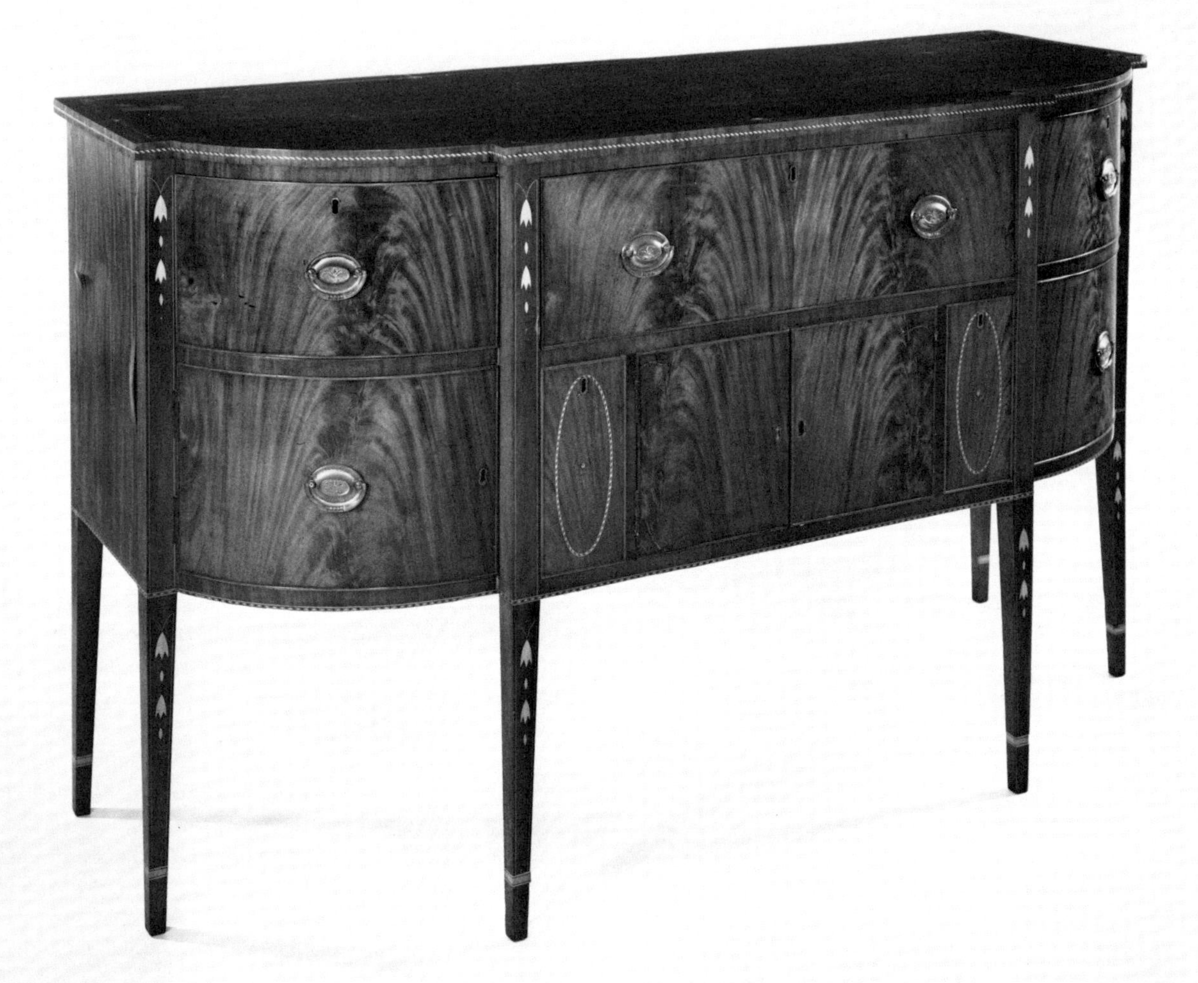

Cat. 48

style houses provided space for specialized pieces of furniture.
Of considerable importance among these rooms was the
dining room, which on occasion contained an alcove or niche
designed for a sideboard. Although Cutts's dining room had
no alcoves, this did not prevent him from purchasing two
sideboards (see Chapter 3).

Bills or other forms of documentation remain to be found
to establish the maker of this sideboard. An important clue
to its place of manufacture lies in the initials "ss" branded in
block letters on both rear legs just below the top. However,
further research is needed to determine who these initials
identify.

This sideboard is similar in form and arrangement to
another with a Maine history.[2] In both sideboards, the front
of the large top drawer folds down to form a writing desk, a
useful feature that many sideboards do not have. Unlike
other sideboards that have a top of expensive mahogany or
marble, the top of this example is covered in oilcloth painted
dark green. The construction suggests that it was originally
intended to be this way in order to provide a practical serving
space on an otherwise decorative and costly furnishing. The
surface pattern of this sideboard is created by mahogany
veneer with inlaid bellflowers and oval drops. Stringing
decorates the edge of the top, skirt, cuffs, and the bottle
drawers.

Of ample proportion, sideboards offered convenient
storage space. The merchant class in Maine evidently
believed in fashionable utility, because early nineteenth-
century probate inventories contain many references to this
form.   L F S

1 YCRP; 29:261–262.
2 Owned by Captain William Carr (1792–1827) of Bowdoin, Maine,
  the sideboard is at SPNEA. I would like to thank Brock Jobe for
  bringing it to my attention, and Jane Tucker for the provenance.

49

Attributed to Benjamin Radford (1775–1862)
and his brothers, William Radford (1779–1858)
and Daniel Radford (b. 1786)
Sideboard and bookcase
Portland, Maine, ca. 1807 (sideboard)
and ca. 1815 (bookcase)
Mahogany, mahogany veneer, *birch, holly,*
eastern white pine
H 95¹⁵⁄₁₆ (243.7); H sideboard 37⅝ (95.6);
W 67⅛ (170.5); D 26¹³⁄₁₆ (68.1)
Maine Historical Society; Wadsworth-Longfellow House

For many years the bills of the Radford brothers for furniture
sold to Stephen Longfellow have served as important

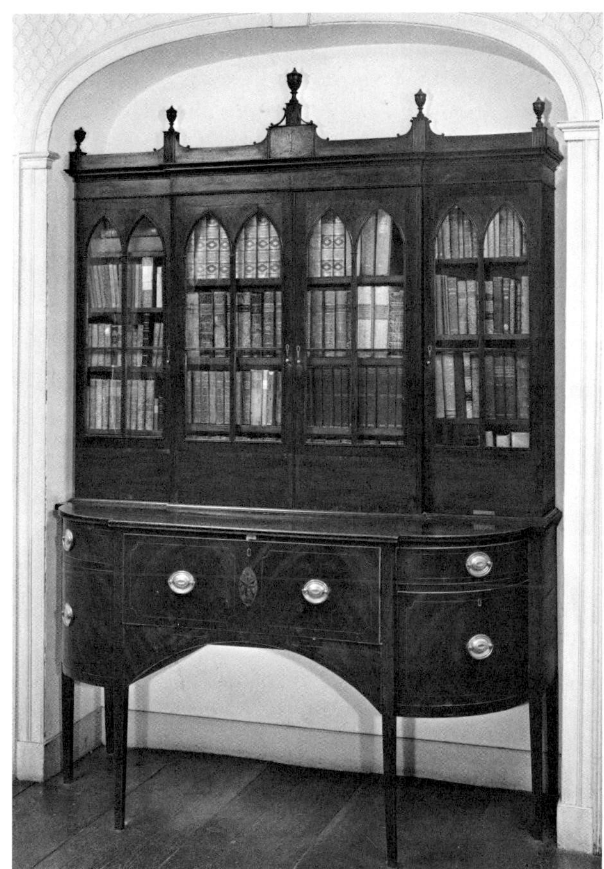

Cat. 49

references in the discussion of furniture made in federal-
period Maine. Although this sideboard is not included in the
bills, it has been attributed to the Radfords on the basis of its
close similarity to the documented furniture.[1]

Longfellow probably purchased the sideboard in 1807
when he moved into the house on Congress Street after the
Wadsworth family had removed to Hiram. Around 1815
renovations began at this house; the family's dining room
was adapted into a law office (see Chapter 3). At this time,
Longfellow is believed to have patronized a local cabinetmaker, possibly the Radford brothers again, to build a
bookcase for his law library.

The case was constructed to sit on top of the sideboard in
the alcove. The doors are veneered with mahogany panels
and crossbanding. Bordering the windows with their Gothic
arches is a double-bead molding, gathered near the top to
resemble reeds. Capping the case is a cornice with urn finials
supported by reeded plinths. The stringing on the doors,
drawers, and arch of the sideboard is made of holly. The
light color of the wood provides a decorative and striking
contrast against the dark mahogany.

In the center of the sideboard, a drawer folds down to

form a writing space like a desk, a feature also seen in
another sideboard attributed to a Maine craftsman (cat. 50).
With a drawer that functions as a work space, this sideboard
may have served Longfellow in place of a more typical desk
and bookcase, especially during the years he occupied the
room as an office. The bookcase remained with the sideboard
even after the room was returned to its use as a dining room,
and provides an excellent example of the innovative inter-
changeability of furnishings within Maine homes.[2]   LFS

1   Three bills, Benjamin Radford to Stephen Longfellow, January 1805;
    September 5, 1805; and July 16, 1808; Longfellow Papers, MEHS;
    and Shettleworth, "Portland Cabinetmakers," 285–289.
2   It is visible in a late nineteenth-century photograph of the room,
    Wadsworth-Longfellow house, MEHS.

50

Attributed to Benjamin Radford (1775–1862)
and his brothers, William Radford (1779–1870)
and Daniel Radford (b. 1786)
High-post bedstead
Portland, Maine, 1808
Mahogany, *soft maple, eastern white pine*
H 86⅝ (220.0); W 56½ (143.5); D 77¹⁵⁄₁₆ (198.0)
Maine Historical Society; Wadsworth-Longfellow House

On July 16, 1808, Benjamin Radford of Portland billed
Stephen Longfellow $20 for a "high post bedsted, & bottom
& cornishes." Charges were added for "painting cornishes"
and for "one line." This high-post bedstead is thought to be
the bed listed on the bill. The bed retains its "cornishes," a
pine cornice with a beaded upper border installed at the top
to connect the posts. The painted decoration on the cornice
is original, though the bright yellow color has faded. Raised
panels featuring painted oak leaves and acorns further
decorate the centers of the cornice on its three visible sides.[1]

The "bottom" listed on the bill refers to a sacking
bottom, a canvas support for the feather beds and hair
mattresses. "One line" refers to the rope used to attach the
bottom to the rails by lacing it through holes. Although the
sacking bottom does not survive on the bed, holes in the rails
confirm its original presence.

The mahogany footposts are turned and reeded. The
blocks are decorated with stringing seen in other furniture
made by Maine cabinetmakers.[2] This turned and inlaid
decoration would have been visible, but required more labor
and increased the cost of the bed. By contrast, the hexagonal
headposts, which would not have been seen, were made of
locally available maple. Shaped inexpensively with a plane
or drawknife, they would have been covered with bed curtains.
Three or four inches have been cut off the lower part of the legs.

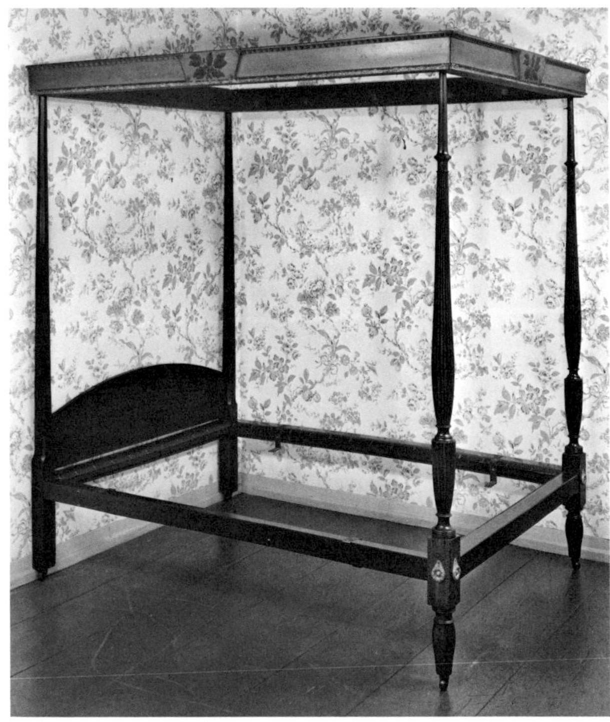

Cat. 50

Some of the original hardware survives on the posts.
Cloak pins at the headposts just above the rails may have
been used to draw up curtains in festoon draperies. The
L-shaped brackets just below the cornice would have held the
iron or wooden curtain rods.[3]

Bed hangings, feather beds, pillows and bolsters, and
mattresses, along with other required bedding such as
sheets, blankets, and quilts, added significantly to the overall
cost of the bed. Ann Bryant Smith purchased a "new bed
tick" from Edward Howe, the Portland upholsterer, in
December 1806. Containing forty-eight pounds of down, it
alone cost $64.24.[4]

This was not the only bed Radford made for the Longfellows. A second bill, dated January 1805, includes two beds, a
"mahogany field bedstead" for which he charged $15, and
a "burch" field bedstead for $5 less. Radford's entry on this
bill for $13 "cash paid for sackin bottoms" reveals the high
cost of this necessary feature. Radford's payment in cash
indicates that someone else, probably an upholsterer,
provided the canvas bottoms.[5]

Field bedsteads made of birch, a light-colored wood
available locally, were often painted in plain colors or stained
to look like the more expensive imported mahogany. Three
bedsteads of lesser quality wood made in Portland for
Thomas Robison received coats of red and green paint.[6]
Field bedsteads were fitted with "sweeps," arched tops of
different shapes. A number of cabinetmakers in Portland

made field bedsteads which are frequently referred to in probate inventories.   LFS

1 Bill, Benjamin Radford to Stephen Longfellow, July 16, 1808, MEHS. For a detail of the cornice, see Shettleworth, "Portland Cabinetmakers," 285; and a color plate in Churchill, *Simple Forms and Vivid Colors*, 10.
2 See the desk and bookcase made in Brunswick by Dinsmore and Batchelder, Decorative Arts Photographic Collection, Winterthur Museum; for a detail of the stringing on the footposts, see Shettleworth, "Portland Cabinetmakers," 285.
3 Richard Nylander kindly identified the use of the hardware. Beds rarely survive without adaptations. In addition to the shortened legs, metal braces have been installed on this frame to support modern box springs.
4 Ann Smith, diary, December 15, 1806, MEHS.
5 Bill, Benjamin Radford to Stephen Longfellow, January 1805, MEHS; a high-post bedstead photographed in the home of Longfellow's son, Alexander, has footposts and cornice of the same shape; as similar as it is, however, it is not this bed because the original decoration has been covered with paint; Alexander W. Longfellow house, photographs of interior, SPNEA Archives. A sacking bottom could also be nailed to the rails. This technique survives intact on the bed made by Benjamin Frothingham for Henry Knox, now at Montpelier in Thomaston, and the 1827 bed at the Colonel Black house in Ellsworth.
6 Account, John Seymour to Thomas Robison, April 19, 1786, Robison Papers, MEHS.

51

Bed curtain, one of two (detail)
England, 1775–1785
Cotton
H 80½ (204.5); w 50⅛ (127.3); w fabric 25 (63.5)
York Institute Museum
Bequest of Almira Locke McArthur, 1950

With copper plate-printed cottons like this example, the English textile industry found an enormous market in the United States. For the printing process, a copperplate was engraved with a design. After being inked, the surface of the plate was wiped cleaned, leaving dye in the incised lines. Under pressure of the press, the color was drawn from the grooves and the design transferred to the fabric. Although the plate was costly to produce, once made it provided a economical means of producing vast amounts of decorated yard goods. This type of fabric is commonly referred to in period documents as "copperplate." Probate inventory references reveal the widespread use of such printed goods in the decoration of bedchambers.

This curtain is one of two from a set of bed hangings used in the household of Daniel Cleaves. Measuring more than six feet in height, it would have dressed a high-post bedstead. Its sepia-printed designs of sheep shearing and dipping and of harvesting activities must have appealed to Cleaves, who prospered as the owner of numerous tenant farms in York County. This design was produced a decade prior to the

1795 marriage of Daniel and Sarah Fairfield Cleaves. It is not surprising, however, that it continued in popularity.[1]

Bed curtains included a head cloth, a tester at the top of the canopy, valances, a counterpane, and a flounce. In order to have the chamber decorated en suite, sufficient fabric needed to be ordered for window curtains and for slipcovers on furniture if desired.

Dressing a bedstead was an expensive undertaking and the best bedstead with all its appurtenances was often the single most expensive furnishing in a house (see cat. 50). An invoice of goods that Thomas Robison imported from Boston in 1784 reveals that while his "Maple long post field Bedsted Complete" cost £3.18.0, twenty-nine yards of "copper plate Furniture" at £5.11.2 were nearly twice as much. When Robison added feathers for a mattress, a "fine Bed Tick," blankets, "pillowbeers," and sheeting at a cost of £20.5.0, he increased the cost of bedding and hangings alone to £25.16.2.[2]

Textiles were printed in a great variety of patterns. Red- and other sepia-printed cottons are known with Maine histories. Hugh McLellan of Portland favored a red-printed scene depicting the "Apotheosis of Benjamin Franklin and George Washington." The Wadsworths dressed a high-post bedstead at their home with a cotton featuring a satirical British military encampment scene.[3]   LFS

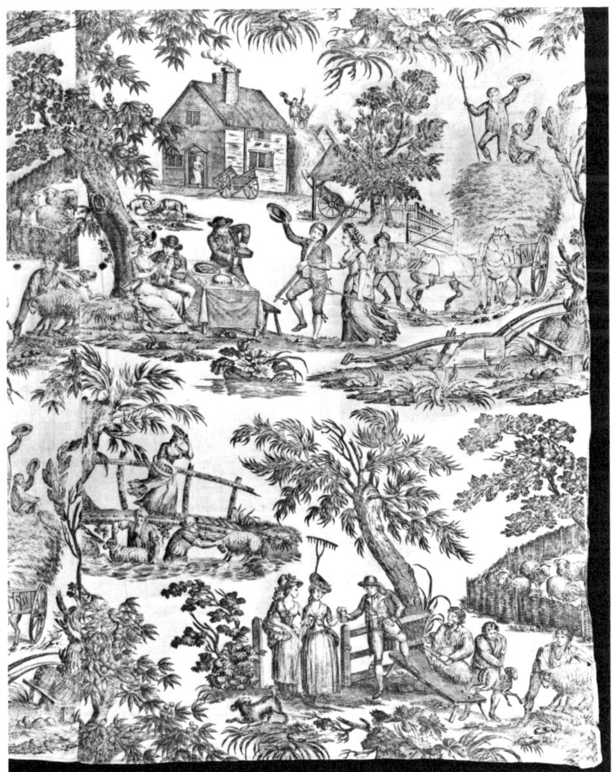

Cat. 51

1 Florence M. Montgomery, *Printed Textiles: English and American Cottons and Linens 1700–1850* (New York: Viking Press, 1970), 212, 261.
2 Invoice, January 22, 1784, Robison Papers, MEHS.
3 The McLellan fragment is in the Portland Museum of Art; a fragment of the militia-printed cotton was used to line the slipcover for cat. 57. In 1901 two valances of the Wadsworth curtains were exhibited at the Wadsworth-Longfellow house; see photographs of interior, MEHS. The print is illustrated in Montgomery, *Printed Textiles*, 262. Another fragment of a cotton bed curtain at the Portland Museum of Art has a McLellan history and is printed with "The Dance" and "The Departure" in blue; see Montgomery, *Printed Textiles*, 278.

52

Bookcase
Portland, Maine, 1805–1815
Eastern white pine, red pine
H 79 9/16 (201.1); W 61 7/8 (157.2); D 13 1/4 (33.7)
Maine Historical Society, Wadsworth-Longfellow House;
Gift of the family of Alexander W. Longfellow

This unusual object is thought to have been among the furnishings of Stephen Longfellow's law office. Although it is not known if Stephen had it made on commencing his practice in Portland or around 1815 when his office was

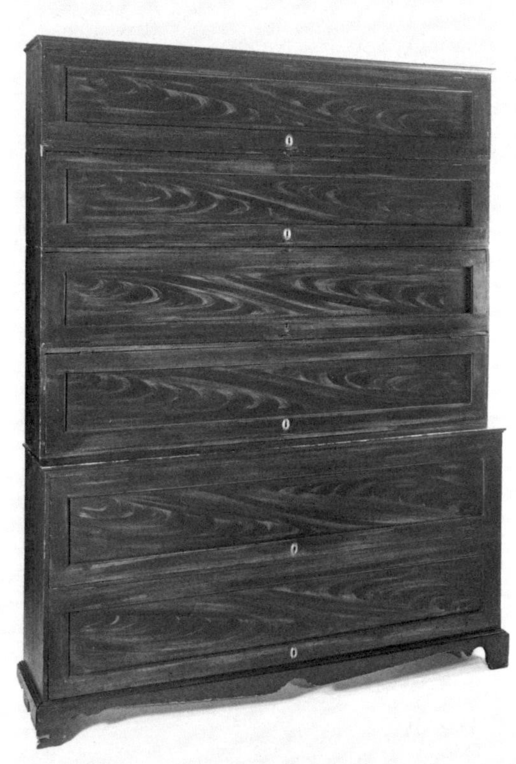

Cat. 52

moved to the converted family dining room, it does fit on the staircase wall opposite the fireplace and to the left of the sideboard and bookcase in the alcove (see Chapter 3 and cat. 49). It is typical of office furniture owned by other Maine lawyers. The desks and tables in George Wallingford's Kennebunk office were described in his probate inventory as made of pine.[1] Woods of lesser quality were painted, as vividly illustrated by the red graining which decorates the front of this case in a handsome diagonal pattern.

The case is constructed in five sections. The upper four cases are narrow, measuring 11 3/8 inches high and 9 1/4 inches deep. Each part rests on top of the case below, secured only by wooden pegs that project from the top of the lower case into the bottom of the upper case. The doors are hinged at the top. One would open the case only long enough to extract the needed pamphlet, book, or papers, thus avoiding the need to construct supports for doors hinged on the bottom edge.

The two lower cases are larger and built as one. The interiors of these cases were divided by partitions and provide a convenient means to sort or store receipts, promissory notes, and other folded or rolled papers.   LFS

1 YCRP; 33:305. Merchant Thomas Robison's desk and bookcase in his store was made of pine; the one furnishing his home was of mahogany and imported from London (see Chapter 4).

53

Attributed to Benjamin Radford (1775–1862)
and his brothers, William Radford (1779–1870)
and Daniel Radford (b. 1786)
Chest of drawers
Portland, Maine, ca. 1805
Mahogany, mahogany veneer, *eastern white pine*
H 38 13/16 (98.6); W 42 1/2 (108.0); D 23 1/8 (58.7)
Maine Historical Society; Wadsworth-Longfellow House

In January 1805 Benjamin Radford billed Stephen Longfellow for "1 Mahogney Beurow" that cost $20. This bow-front chest of drawers in the Wadsworth-Longfellow house is one of two that fit the general description and may be the object referred to on the bill.[1] The second chest is extensively decorated with contrasting panel veneers and stringing on the drawer fronts. Furniture associated with the Radfords displays only a limited use of veneer and stringing; therefore it is unlikely that this second chest is from their shop. The chest of drawers under consideration here is more stylish and more expensive than the birch chest (cat. 54) the Longfellows also may have bought from the Radfords.

Decorated with crotch veneer that creates a scrolled or swag pattern across the front of the piece, the drawer fronts

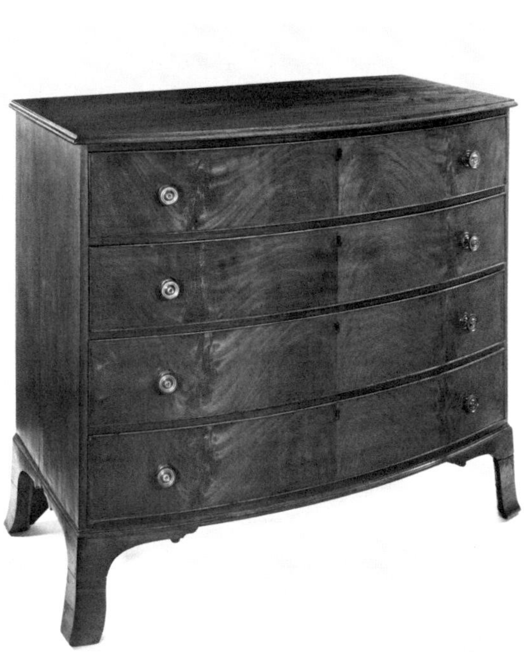

Cat. 53

was not the only form Maine craftsmen were capable of making; it simply illustrates a less expensive option. Locally available birch was stained to imitate imported mahogany. The edges of the drawer fronts are incised to simulate an applied, beaded edge. A modest example, it is enhanced by a decorative skirt. This chest retains its original brass hardware. A large script initial L was inscribed in chalk on the backboards, perhaps to mark it as a Longfellow purchase.

While chests of drawers like this one provided storage space and were rarely moved, others served more unusual purposes, sometimes going far afield. Writing from St. Croix in the Virgin Islands in 1811, R. R. Clark advised his cousin John Fox to forward his "half press and Bureau" via a Portland vessel. "They are based up but as [the captain] promised to put the Bureau in the cabin I think it would be best to mat it or cover it with wrapping. Has many things put up in the Drawers and those articles sells very high in this part of the world."[1] LFS

1 R. R. Clark to John Fox, April 19, 1811, John Fox Papers, MEHS.

are surrounded by an applied bead. The top is finished with a molded edge. Supported by French feet, the chest is further ornamented with a delicately shaped skirt. The stamped brass pulls are original.

This chest appears in a photograph of the parlor chamber taken shortly after the house was given to the society.[2] Traditionally this room was used by Zilpah and Stephen Longfellow. The chest bears no later Longfellow family labels to indicate that it had ever been removed from, and subsequently returned to, the house. LFS

1 Bill, Benjamin Radford to Stephen Longfellow, January 1805, Longfellow Papers, MEHS.
2 Wadsworth-Longfellow house, photographs of interior, MEHS.

54

Probably by Benjamin Radford (1775–1862)
and his brothers, William Radford (1779–1870)
and Daniel Radford (b. 1786)
Chest of drawers
Portland, Maine, 1805–1815
Birch, eastern white pine
H 38½ (97.8); W 41⁹⁄₁₆ (105.5); D 20 (50.8)
Maine Historical Society; Wadsworth-Longfellow House

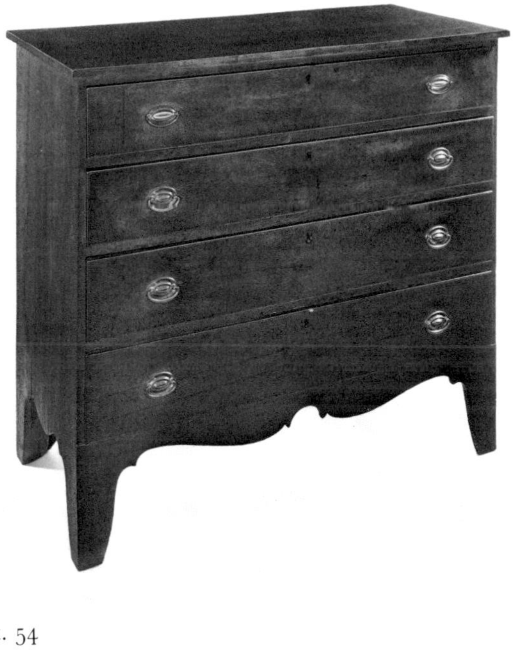

Cat. 54

For many years, a four-drawer chest of this type was the form most readily attributed to Maine cabinetmakers. This chest

55

Sofa
Probably Boston, possibly Maine, 1800–1810
Mahogany, *birch*, *basswood*
H 36⅝ (93.0); W 32¹¹/₁₆ (83.0); D 22⁷/₁₆ (57.0)
York Institute Museum
Bequest of Almira Locke McArthur, 1950

Like a set of Boston side chairs (cat. 103), this sofa descended in the family of Almira Cleaves Dummer of Hallowell and Saco, Maine. It is similar to a pair with a history of ownership in the family of William Bond, a silversmith who settled in Portland around 1785 and later moved to Boston. The top of the back and ends of both sofas are upholstered, a feature that differs from the crest rails of veneered wood and wooden arms with stringing found on many northeastern Massachusetts or coastal New Hampshire examples.[1]

The original linen under-upholstery, webbing, stuffed straw or grass, and horsehair have survived on this example and reveal the crisp outlines of the sofa's cake, or foundation. Fragments of green wool have survived under and along the internal horizontal back support and may have originally covered the sofa. Of a plain weave, it was a standard upholstery fabric.[2] One strip of canvas webbing is printed with the mark "BRUSGIN" and the number 16 stitched in blue thread. A second strip also bears the number 16 which must refer to the size of the webbing. Brusgin may have been an English or northern European maker or exporter.

While Maine cabinetmakers may have been making this form of furniture in their shops, no references have been identified to document that possibility. However, there are entries recording sofas being brought to Maine in the coastwise trade. In October 1800, Enoch Preble of Portland purchased a sofa in Boston at the high cost of £10.[3]

Nathaniel Deering appears to have purchased his sofa outside of Portland; he paid £1.4.0 for its "Freight Truckage & Wharf." The "soffa Frame" cost £3. "Stuffing [the] soffa" cost £5.8.0, nearly twice as much. A "soffa case" was made for 12s. Thirteen-and-one-half yards of "binding" were used during the upholstery, but it was the six yards of decorative fringe at £9 that increased the cost of the final product to £18.5.7.[4]

Whatever the source for the frames, local upholsterers advertised that they were able to "stuff sofas" and make coverings for them. Edward Howe also advertised that he sold "Sofas with and without Hair Cloth." He probably purchased the frames from a cabinet shop and then covered them with black horsehair, a standard upholstery fabric seen on other furniture (cats. 102, 104).[5] "Sofas without Hair

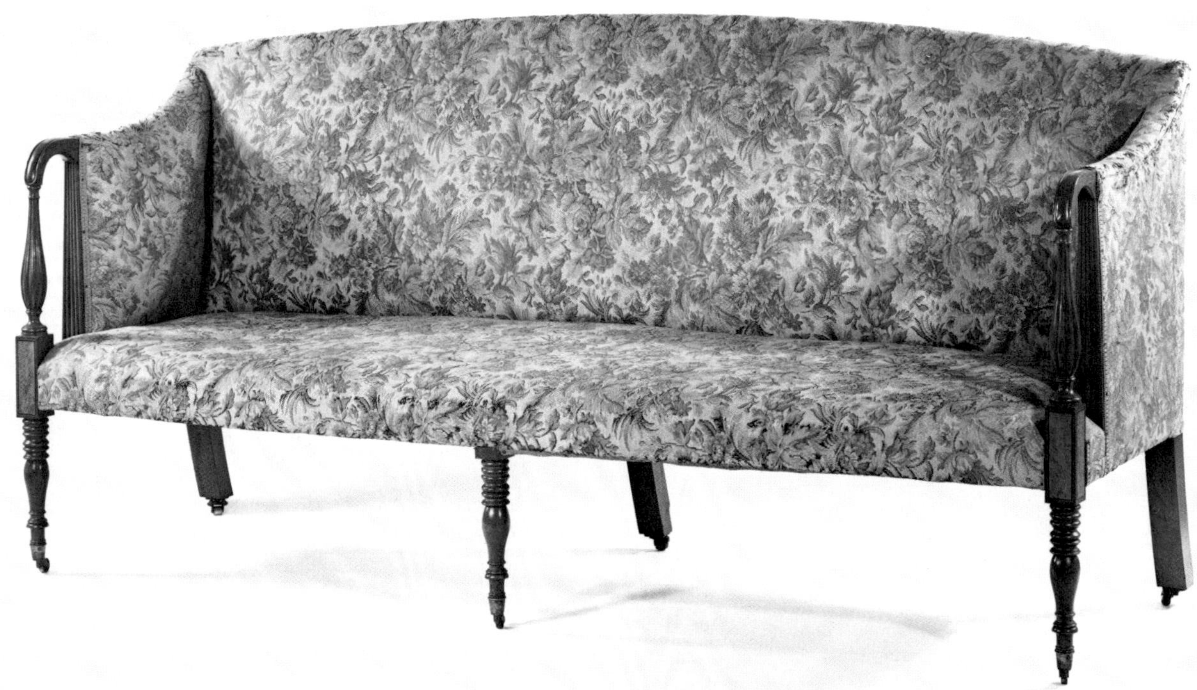

Cat. 55

Cloth" could have been covered with the fabric chosen by the customer.

Loose pillows were often added to the deep seat of the sofa to improve comfort. Both sofas in Jonathan Hamilton's formal first-floor rooms were recorded with their "Covering & 2 Pillows."[6] The "covering" could refer to slipcovers used to protect the expensive upholstery fabric.

Couches and daybeds, two forms of seating furniture referred to in pre-Revolutionary household inventories, were owned by the wealthiest of Maine citizens.[7] Sofas, still an expensive form of furniture, appear more frequently in households of the federal period than in their colonial counterparts.   LFS

1 Montgomery, *American Furniture*, 307–308. A sofa from the Waite family of Portland at the Portland Museum of Art is said to have been made in Portland. Although slightly smaller than this sofa, its curved back and arms are upholstered. The wooden arms and legs have similar turnings.
2 Elizabeth Lahikainen kindly identified the wool.
3 Enoch Preble, expense book, MEHS.
4 Nathaniel Deering, account book, 1793–1795, MEHS.
5 *Eastern Argus* (November 8, 1805); *Eastern Argus* (December 3, 1807).
6 Wendy A. Cooper, *In Praise of America: American Decorative Arts, 1650–1830* (New York: Alfred A. Knopf, 1980), 56–57; YCRP; 19:220.
7 Jobe and Kaye, *New England Furniture*, 315–318.

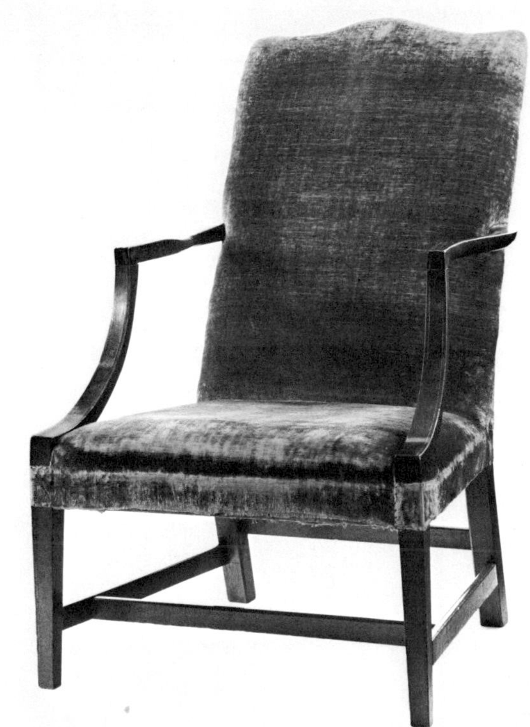

Cat. 56

56

Attributed to Benjamin Radford (1775–1862)
and his brothers, William Radford (1779–1870)
and Daniel Radford (b. 1786)
Lolling chair (one of a pair)
Portland, Maine, ca. 1805
Mahogany, *soft maple, birch*
H 41 (104.1); H seat 15 (38.1);
W seat 25 15/16 (65.9); D seat 21 (53.3)
Maine Historical Society, Wadsworth-Longfellow House;
Gift of Alice Longfellow, 1921

Lolling chairs were a new form of the neoclassical period. An expensive form of furniture with their upholstered backs and seats, lolling chairs were among the formal furnishings in rooms used for entertaining.[1]

Once the frame of the chair was constructed, an upholsterer provided the foundation and covering. Edward Howe advertised in Portland newspapers that he was "stuffing . . . lolling chairs . . . and making covering for d[itt]o." Fragments of fabric tacked to the rear seat rail reveal that a striped green and beige silk was originally used to cover this chair.[2]

The combination of the woods used to construct these chairs and the light-colored stringing which arches at the top of the front legs is found on other furniture at the house attributed to the Radford brothers. The serpentine crest rail, s-curved arms, and stretchers—all features found on other chairs with Portland histories—also relate to others with coastal Massachusetts histories. Considering that the Radford brothers, as well as other cabinetmakers, emigrated from Essex County to Portland, it is not surprising to find chairs of this type being made in Maine (see Chapter 4). Without the documentation and wood analysis, it would be difficult, if not impossible, to distinguish these chairs from those made in northeastern Massachusetts.[3]

This pair of chairs was divided after Stephen Longfellow's death in 1849. One remained in the house and appears in a late nineteenth-century photograph of the parlor (fig. 3.8); it was covered with a later brocade and decorated with fringe attached to the seat rails. This chair descended to Henry Wadsworth Longfellow and was among his furnishings in Cambridge. When it was returned to his parents' home by his daughter Alice in 1921, she wrote that it had belonged to Stephen. It was "in the old house during his lifetime. I think it stood in the drawing room on the left."[4]
LFS

1 Montgomery, *American Furniture*, 155–156.
2 *Eastern Argus* (November 8, 1805). R. Bruce Hoadley identified the fabric as silk.
3 Shettleworth, "Portland Cabinetmakers," 285–289; and Montgomery,

American Furniture, 158–159, 162; similar examples can be found at the Portland Museum of Art and in the Decorative Arts Photographic Collection, Winterthur Museum.

4 A photograph at the Wadsworth-Longfellow house shows Mary Longfellow Greenleaf seated in one of these chairs; Alice Longfellow to [MEHS], December 13, 1921, Longfellow Papers, MEHS. Joyce Butler brought this letter to my attention.

57

Side chair (one of two)
Boston, Massachusetts, 1765–1780
Mahogany, *soft maple*
H 38⅛ (96.8); H seat 18 (45.7);
w seat 21½ (54.6); D seat 17½ (44.5)
Maine Historical Society; Wadsworth-Longfellow House

With its pierced splat, serpentine crest rail, and straight, molded legs, this chair is representative of a type made in Boston between 1765 and 1780. Other chairs of similar

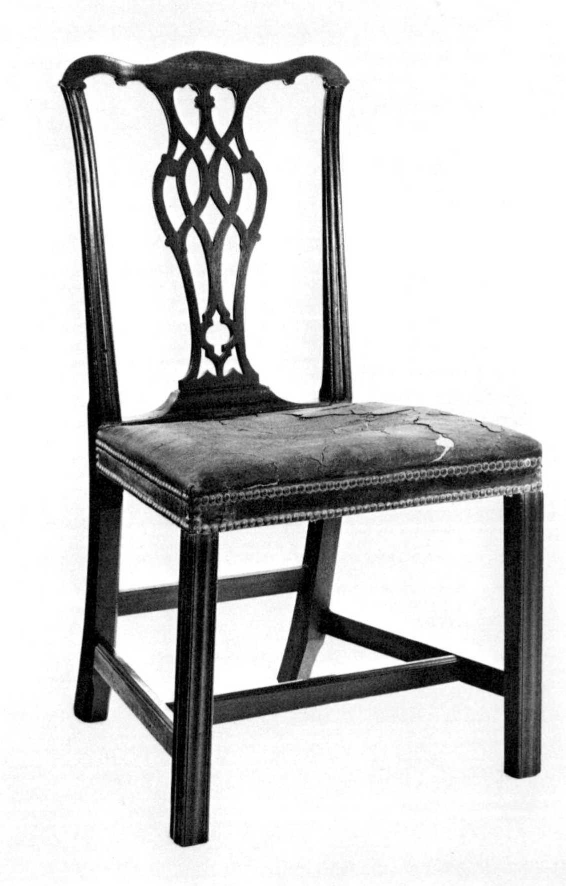

Cat. 57

design are known with Massachusetts histories.[1] The leather upholstery is original, an exceptional and rare document. Further ornamentation is found in the double row of gilt brass nails along the upper and lower edges of the seat rail and front corners. This type of chair appears to have appealed to Maine families because there are numerous references in late eighteenth-century probate inventories to "leather bottom'd chairs mahogany."[2]

This chair is one of a pair at the Wadsworth-Longfellow house that is part of a larger set. Three chairs from the set are visible in a late nineteenth-century photograph of the parlor (fig. 3.8); they retain their leather upholstery in good condition. The second chair at the house has been stripped of its original upholstery and covered with a modern fabric.

The upholstery of this chair has deteriorated badly. It must have been heavily used because by the 1830s a chintz slipcover had been made for the chair. It appears that because the roller-printed cotton of the slipcover was not thick enough to cushion the rough leather, a second fabric was used to line it. The fabric selected was the sepia-printed copperplate cotton that the Wadsworths had used in one of their bedchambers around 1786. The copperplate is very worn with several repairs. It seems likely that when a lining was needed, an old worn-out fabric was used. The chintz slipcover was well made, with carefully stitched corners and tape sewn along the edges. Its survival is rare.[3] When the next cover was added in the late nineteenth century, it was simply tacked over the chintz slipcover, thus preserving rather than replacing it. Another layer was added in 1901 when the house was opened to the public. The survival of these layers documents the use of slipcovers early in the nineteenth century and the subsequent updating throughout the century.

The set of chairs was divided upon the deaths of Stephen and Zilpah Longfellow. Anne Longfellow Pierce cherished her family's chairs sufficiently to display one of the set prominently in her photograph.[4]   L F S

1 I am grateful for the assistance of Brock Jobe in the identification of this chair; others of this type are in the Groton Historical Society and the Metropolitan Museum of Art. For another mahogany leather-bottomed chair with a Maine history, see Jobe and Kaye, *New England Furniture*, 389–391.
2 YCRP; 19:429.
3 Robert Mussey and Brock Jobe kindly removed the later fabrics and identified the slipcover.
4 It is displayed in the Wadsworth-Longfellow house.

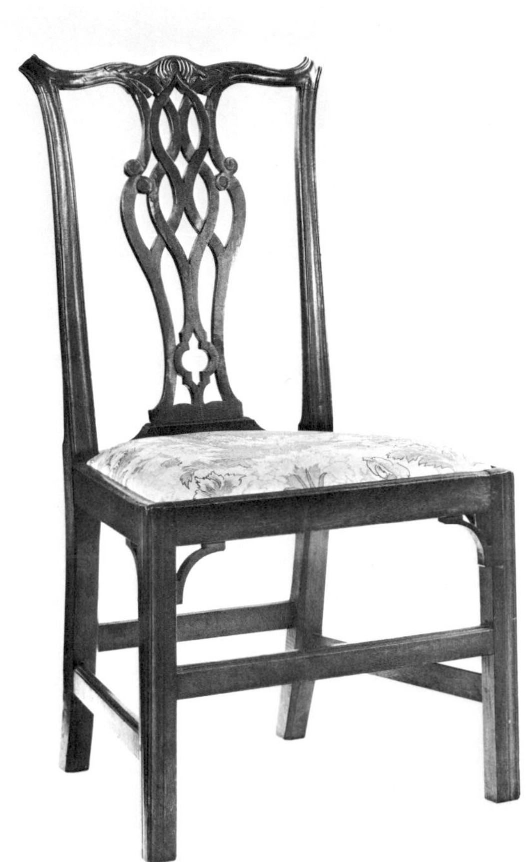

Cat. 58

58

Side chair
Possibly Portland, Maine, 1775–1790
Birch, soft maple
H 38⅛ (96.8); H seat 16½ (41.9);
W seat 20⅜ (51.8); D seat 16¹/₁₆ (40.8)
Maine Historical Society; Wadsworth-Longfellow House

This chair, marked VI, is from a set acquired by the
Wadsworth or Longfellow family late in the eighteenth
century. Photographs of the Portland home of Stephen
Longfellow's son, Alexander, reveal that by the late
nineteenth century two chairs from this set had been divided
among family members.[1]

The style, construction, and ornamentation of this chair
suggest that it may have been the product of a Portland
cabinetmaker. The chair's low proportions and the stretcher
between the front legs are indications of a craftsman working
outside an urban area. The outside edges of the front legs are

molded in a manner that is not seen on other coastal Massachusetts chairs, and may be unique to the maker.[2]

The frame of the chair was made of birch, a wood that
gave way to mahogany in more expensive furniture. This
chair has been mahoganized, in imitation of the more
desirable wood. Birch was also used to fashion less costly
chairs, those not embellished with carving or fitted with
upholstered slip seats.[3] This slip seat retains its original
stuffing and webbing, and reveals the flatness of the seat.

Portland has never been recognized as an important
eighteenth-century town for cabinetmaking. Craftsmen,
however, were active here in the colonial period. Between
1768 and 1772 they were proficient enough to send their
products coastwise. British customs records reveal that
chairs were the chief form of furniture made for this trade
during that five-year period. [4]   LFS

1   The slip seat, also marked VI, belongs to this chair; Alexander W.
    Longfellow house, photographs of interior, SPNEA. Two other chairs
    from this set were given to Henry Wadsworth Longfellow's Cambridge
    home between 1882 and 1912. They reportedly came from the
    Wadsworth house in Duxbury.

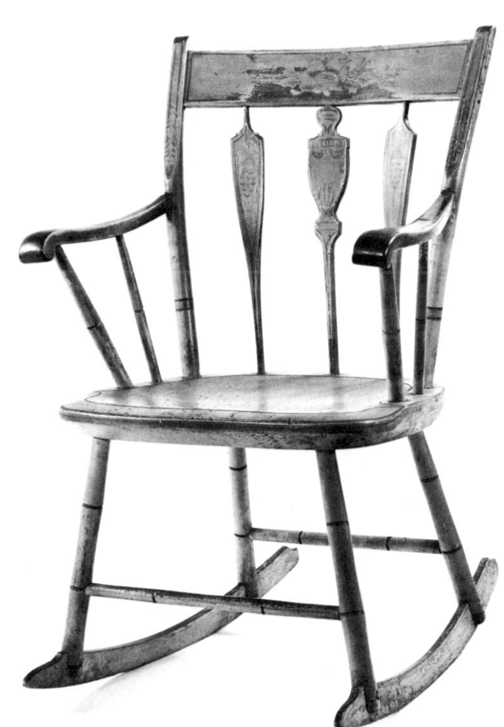

Cat. 59

2 These features may reveal the work of a Portland craftsman, as suggested by Brock Jobe, August 1, 1985.
3 For one example, see Jobe and Kaye, *New England Furniture*, 427–428.
4 "Imports and Exports (America), 1768–1775," *Public Documents: Great Britain Customs Office*, Customs 16 / Vol. 1 (microfilm at Joseph Downs Manuscript and Microfilm Collection, Winterthur Museum Library).

59

Armchair (one of a set)
Portland, Maine, area, ca. 1820
Mahogany arms, *beech, birch, eastern white pine*
H 32 5/16 (82.0); H seat 17 3/4 (45.1); W seat 16 1/8 (41.0);
D seat 15 (38.1)
Maine Historical Society; Wadsworth-Longfellow House

This chair, one of a set of three side chairs and two rocking armchairs, probably originated in the Portland area in the 1820s. Although the seat, legs, and back are painted yellow, the chairmaker constructed the arms of mahogany, a costly imported wood. The combination of mahogany arms on painted chairs is found on the most stylish windsor chairs. The urn motif of the central splat, commonly associated with high-style mahogany chairs, is here executed in paint rather than the slower and more costly process of carving. Chairs like these satisfied a demand for fashionable furniture at a modest price.[1]

By the 1780s windsor chairs had become part of Maine household furnishings. A 1799 inventory listed "5 old windsor chairs," and in 1817 when Cyrus King died, he owned "8 yellow bowback chairs" and "6 dark bowback chairs." James Littlefield of Wells owned half a dozen each of blue and green windsor chairs. These references and the presence of "7 roundabout windsor chairs" in Simon Fernald's 1806 York inventory reveal the variety of types and colors.[2] AAE

1 Nancy Goyne Evans, Winterthur Museum, letter to author, April 19, 1985. The paint on the side chairs and second armchair is badly worn. The "12 oval back'd white color'd Arm chairs with mahogony Arms" that Henry Knox of Thomaston purchased from William Cox of Philadelphia in 1794 are an excellent example of this treatment in one of Maine's most fashionable homes; bill, May 29, 1794, Knox Papers, MEHS. See Carolyn S. Parsons, "'Bordering on Magnificence': Urban Domestic Planning in the Maine Woods," in Clark and Leamon, *Maine in the Early Republic*. Michael Ettema, "Technological Innovation and Design Economics in Furniture Manufacture," *Winterthur Portfolio* 16, nos. 2/3 (Summer/Autumn 1981): 197–223.
2 The inventory of Stephen Palmer of Fryeburg listed "5 boo [bow?] back chairs" in 1781; YCRP; 14:42. Solomon Coit's 1788 Pepperrellborough inventory included "6 windsor chairs," YCRP; 15:291. See also YCRP; 18:89 (Chadbourne); 27:316 (King); 18:476 (Littlefield); and 20:546 (Fernald). An 1809 listing of Stephen Longfellow, Jr.'s, Gorham furniture included "12 yellow windsor chairs"; see Samuel Stephenson Papers, MEHS.

60

High chair
Northeastern New England, possibly Maine, 1790–1810
Pine, maple, ash
H 36 3/16 (91.0); H seat 21 11/16 (57.0); W seat 11 13/16 (30.0);
D seat 11 7/16 (29.0)
Maine Historical Society, Wadsworth-Longfellow House;
Gift of Warren W. Mansfield
and Lewis Pierce Mansfield, 1972

Although this rod-back windsor high chair has been associated with Henry Wadsworth Longfellow, it is more likely that Stephen and Zilpah Longfellow purchased it for their oldest child, Stephen, born in 1805. It was given to the Wadsworth-Longfellow house by two great-great-nephews of Anne Longfellow Pierce, sister of Stephen and Henry.

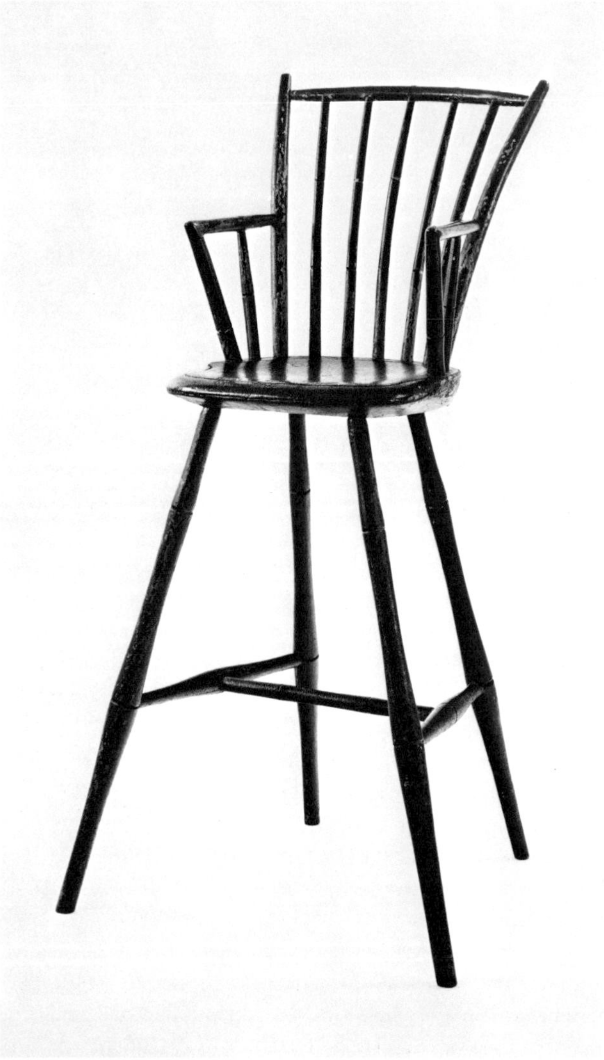

Cat. 60

Chairs for children were made in the same manner as those for adults. The chairmaker scooped the softwood seat from a sawn plank and shaped it with an adze and a drawknife. The turned legs, made of a harder wood such as maple, were fitted into holes in the plank seat. Because the seats, spindles, and other parts were generally constructed of a variety of lesser quality woods, windsors were painted; colors referred to in probate inventories include green, blue, white, and yellow. This high chair has a coat of red paint, under which appear earlier applications of red and black.

Although their listing is infrequent, high chairs and other children's furniture do appear in late eighteenth and early nineteenth-century probate inventories; Aaron Libby owned "1 green high chair" in 1799.[1] More often, perhaps, they were passed on to the next generation or included among other chairs. In 1825 Chadbourn and Junkins of Kennebunk advertised children's chairs, but whether they were scaled-down adult chairs or high chairs is unclear.[2] Small chairs for children were both practical and useful for a child's amusement; they suggest increased attention to a child's comfort and play.   AAE

1 YCRP; 18:135.
2 *Kennebunk Gazette* (June 15, 1825). Abigail Wallingford sat in an upholstered armchair when her portrait was painted (cat. 41).

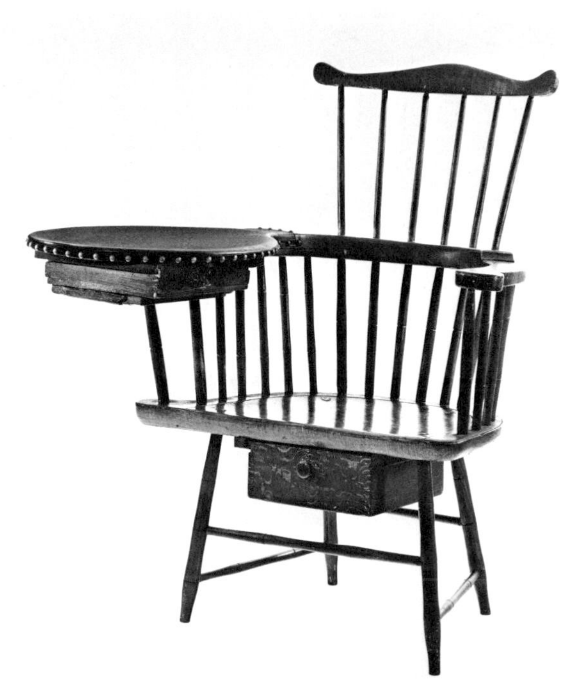

Cat. 61

61

Writing-arm windsor chair
Northeastern New England, 1790–1820
Birch, *eastern white pine, soft maple, aspen (populus species)*
H 44⅞ (114.0); H seat 17½ (44.4); W seat 21⅞ (55.5);
D seat 17¾ (45.1)
Maine Historical Society; Wadsworth-Longfellow House

According to family tradition, and an inscription on the bottom of the lower drawer, this chair was owned in 1775 by Stephen Longfellow (1750–1824), a school teacher in Portland. Although it is unlikely that he purchased it then, because of its later style, it is more certain that it belonged to his son, Stephen, the Portland attorney.

Men with professions that required routine writing and correspondence, such as lawyers or ministers, often owned chairs of this type. Biddeford lawyer and judge George Thacher owned at his death in 1824 "1 Armed Writing Chair & Inkstand" (Chapter 2).[1]

An original oilcloth cover for the writing arm has been replaced, but the chair's painted decoration, a distinct yellow grained pattern, survives in remarkable condition. In addition to the practical writing arm, this chair offered other convenient features. The small drawer, attached to the underside of the arm, is divided into three compartments, and slots in the drawer sides indicate that other compartments could have been made. A small glass inkwell with a cork stopper fits into the smallest space. When extended, a slide below the drawer bottom expands the working space. When pushed in, it fits around the arm support, locking the drawer into place. A second drawer is located under the seat.

Cushions were made for windsor chairs and are documented in Maine by written sources such as the "½ doz winsor chairs with cushions" in Ebenezer Libby's Scarborough household.[2] A cushion not only contributed to the chair's comfort, but it also protected the painted surface of the plank seat.   AAE

1 YCRP; 33:382.
2 Ebenezer Libby estate inventory, 1817, Libby Family Papers, MEHS.

62

Side table
Boston, Massachusetts, ca. 1800
Mahogany, mahogany and bird's-eye maple veneer,
birch, eastern white pine
H 30¼ (77.0); W 53⅜ (135.5); D 27¾ (69.0)
York Institute Museum
Bequest of Almira Locke McArthur, 1950

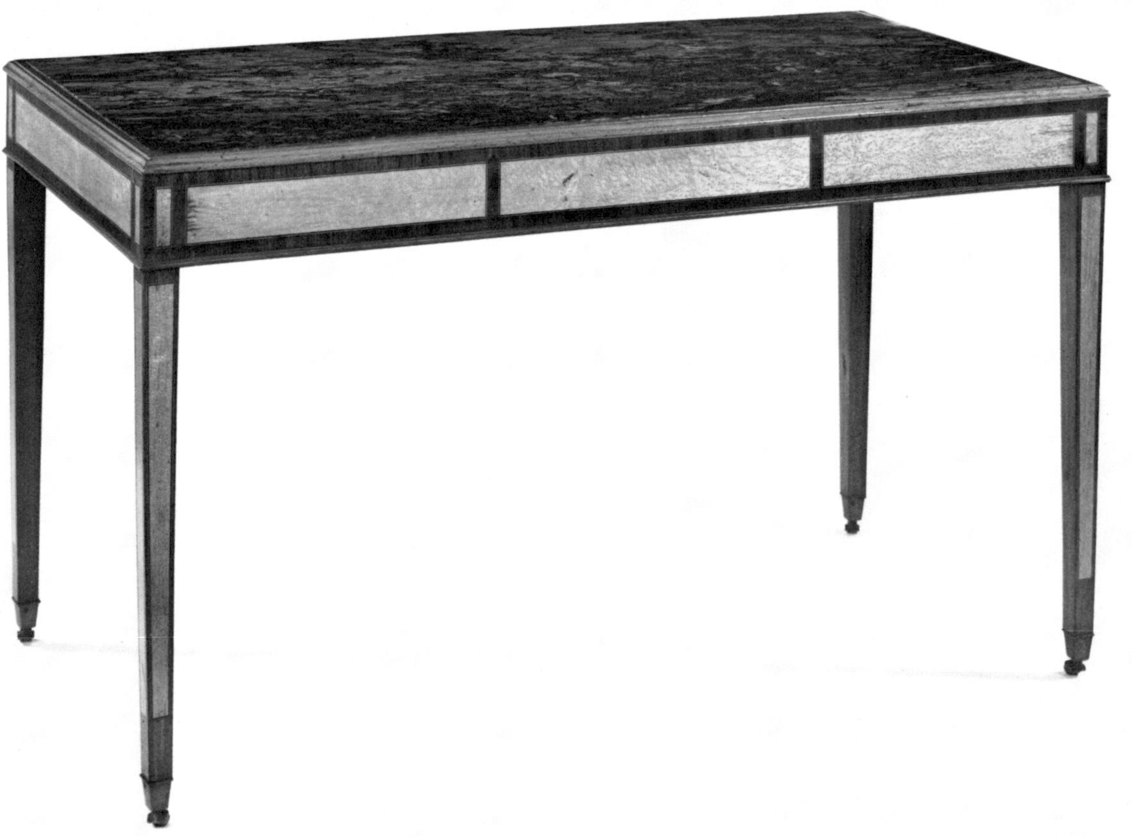

Cat. 62

This table is an elegant example of the fashionable objects that furnished Maine homes. Impervious to liquid, the gray-veined marble top provides a practical surface for the serving of food and drink. Although slightly larger than a similar table with a Boston provenance, it is not as highly embellished.[1] Its fine construction and ornamental detail are features of sophisticated Boston shops. It descended in the family of Daniel and Marcia Tucker Cleaves and may have originally belonged to her father, Jonathan Tucker of Saco. Around 1804 Tucker built a stylish house on Main Street next door to Cyrus King (see Chapter 2).

Several marble-topped tables are known with Maine histories, but this one is more unusual. Its form and large size make it less typical than other marble-topped tables with Maine histories or attributions. A pair of stone-topped tables associated with the Deering family feature inlay, and turned and reeded legs, and may have a Maine or North Shore origin. Another table with similar turned and reeded legs, but with less decorative inlay, is thought to have been owned by the Edward Preble family; it may have been made in Portland.[2] Marble tops were among the products sold by local artisans. Bartlett Adams, a "sculptor & stone cutter" in Portland, advertised in 1800 that he had "a few Italian MARBLE TABLE SLABS."[3] Given the number of cabinetmakers active in Portland, it would not have been difficult to secure a frame.   LFS

1 The table is at the Winterthur Museum; see Montgomery, *American Furniture*, 363.
2 *Antiques* 57, no. 1 (January 1950): 23. Earle G. Shettleworth, Jr., kindly brought this advertisement to my attention. The whereabouts of the pair is unknown. The Preble table is in a private collection.
3 *Portland Gazette* (September 15, 1800). Arthur Gerrier brought Adams's notices for table slabs to my attention.

63

Attributed to Benjamin Radford (1775–1862)
and his brothers, William Radford (1779–1870)
and Daniel Radford (b. 1786)

Drop-leaf table
Portland, Maine, 1805
Mahogany, *birch, eastern white pine*
H 29¹¹⁄₁₆ (75.4); w closed 18¾ (47.6); D 36⅛ (91.7)
Maine Historical Society; Wadsworth-Longfellow House

In 1805 Benjamin Radford billed Stephen Longfellow for "1 mahagney Pembroke table" costing $10. This is the table referred to on the bill. Although the form of this table had been illustrated by Thomas Chippendale in the mid eighteenth century, it had widespread use during the federal period.[1] The form is known from period sources as both a Pembroke and a breakfast table.

This table is simply decorated with a narrow veneered band on the edges of the skirt. The same figured wood is inlaid on the legs at the cuff. Light stringing further decorates the tapered legs. Recessed wooden brackets attached to the frame fold out on a hinge to support the drop-leaves. Tables were also made with slides under the top which were pulled out to support the leaves.[2]

For breakfast, tea, cards, writing, or any activity requiring a small table, Americans found the breakfast table to be a convenient size. In many inventories, descriptions of tables of this type are followed by entries to "oil cloth" or "green baize," which suggest these were used to protect the table surface.[3]   LFS

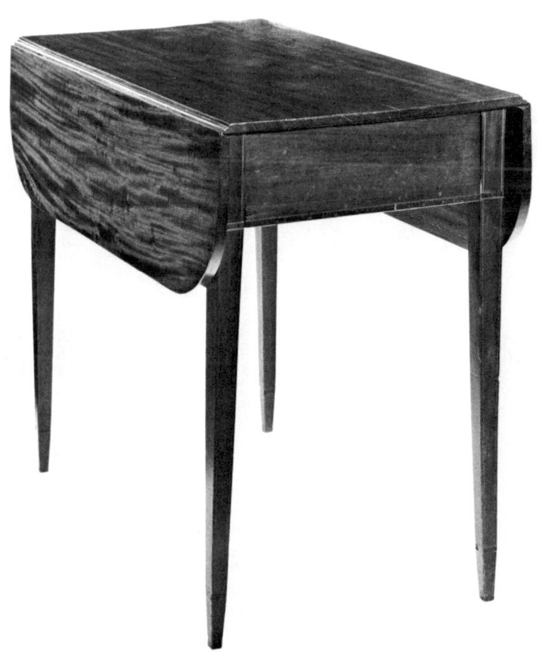

Cat. 63

1 Bill, Benjamin Radford to Stephen Longfellow, January 1805, Longfellow Papers, MEHS. Thomas Chippendale, *The Gentleman and Cabinet-Maker's Director* (1762; reprint, New York: Dover Publications, 1966), plate 53.
2 A Maine-owned and possibly Maine-made mahogany table with this construction is in the Portland Museum of Art.
3 For references to oilcloth and baize table covers, see YCRP; 50:363 and 36:289, respectively.

64

Possibly by Benjamin Radford (1775–1862)
and his brothers, William Radford (1779–1870)
and Daniel Radford (b. 1786)
Tilt-top stand
Portland, Maine, ca. 1805
Mahogany, *soft maple, birch*
H 28¼ (71.7); w top 23⁵⁄₁₆ (59.2); D top 16¹³⁄₁₆ (42.7)
Maine Historical Society, Wadsworth-Longfellow House;
Gift of Mary L. Greenleaf by request of Anne Pierce

This oval-topped stand was made of mahogany, maple, and birch. The light-colored stringing on the legs and crossbanding on the cuffs is similar to that found on other furniture in the Wadsworth-Longfellow house. These woods and simple decorative treatments are associated with the Radford shop (cats. 52, 58). Although "a stand" is not itemized, Benjamin Radford billed Stephen Longfellow for six tables in 1805, five of which are described as "Dining," "Pembroke," "Citchin," and "toilet" (cats. 63, 65). This stand could have been made at about the same time.[1]

Small, portable stands with folding tops were widely used in Maine households. The hinged tops could be turned up and the table moved against the wall, requiring little space. In 1789 John Seymour made a mahogany stand for Nathaniel Deering which cost ten shillings. "A lock and screws for D[itt]o" at one shilling confirm it as one with a top that folded and locked into place when in use. When another Portland cabinetmaker, Alexander Barr, charged Thomas Robison fifteen shillings for a "light stand," he identified one of its uses.[2]   LFS

1 Shettleworth, "Portland Cabinetmakers," 285–289; two bills, Benjamin Radford to Stephen Longfellow, January 1805 and September 5, 1805, Longfellow Papers, MEHS.
2 Account, John Seymour to Nathaniel Deering, March 1787, account book, 1787–1789, 30, MEHS. Tilt-top tables of larger size are found referred to as "snap tea tables" because of the sound made when locked into place; see Jobe and Kaye, *New England Furniture*, 304–305. Account, Alexander Barr to Thomas Robison, October 6, 1787, account book, 1787–1789, 36, Robison Papers, MEHS.

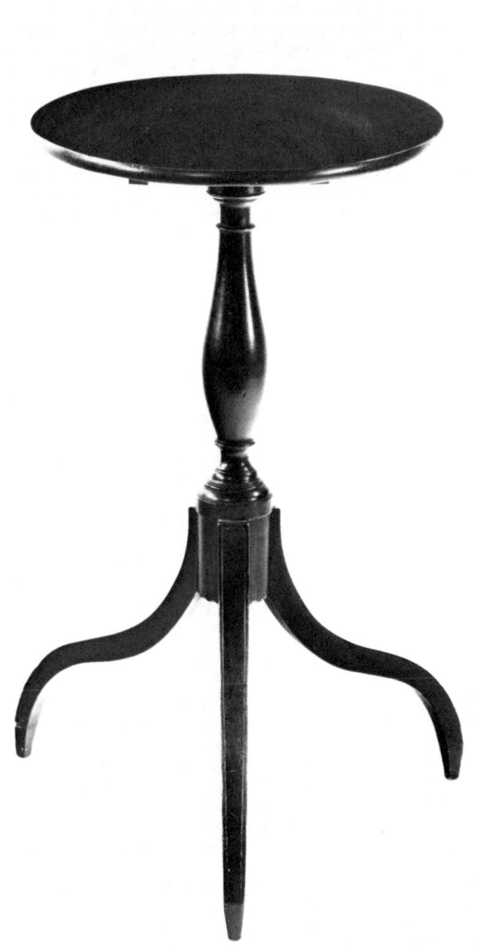

Cat. 64

65

Attributed to Benjamin Radford (1775–1862)
and his brothers, William Radford (1779–1870)
and Daniel Radford (b. 1786)
Toilet table
Portland, Maine, 1808
Eastern white pine
H 31⅛ (79.1); W 28¼ (71.8); D 17⅛ (43.5)
Maine Historical Society, Wadsworth-Longfellow House;
Gift of Mary L. Greenleaf

In January 1805 Benjamin Radford billed Stephen Longfellow for "2 toilet tables," each costing $1. This table is one of
them.[1] It is simply constructed; the two rear legs are joined
by a mortice-and-tenon joint to the third leg, which projects
toward the front of the table. Although there is no evidence
of paint, the wood has been stained.

Many toilets tables were meant to be covered with cloth,
thus hiding from view their construction of inexpensive pine
boards. Although the legs of this table are finished with
molded corners, regularly spaced tacks under its top, several
holding threads of cotton, document the use of a skirt.[2]
When draped with fabric, the serpentine top created a
decorative effect.

References in account books and inventories document
the use of toilet tables in Maine. As early as 1786, John
Seymour constructed a "toilet table" for Thomas Robison
for 6s. 8d. Sarah Cutts Thornton owned three, each appraised at fifty cents. They were inexpensive items in
bedchambers that were furnished with card tables and
lolling chairs, valued at three times as much, and "1 Extra
large Looking glass" valued at $10.[3]   LFS

1 Bill, Benjamin Radford to Stephen Longfellow, January 1805, MEHS.
2 R. Bruce Hoadley kindly identified the cotton fibers.
3 Account, John Seymour to Thomas Robison, April 19, 1786, Robison
  Papers, MEHS. YCRP; 58:71; for a painted toilet table with a
  Portsmouth history, see Jobe and Kaye, *New England Furniture*,
  294–295.

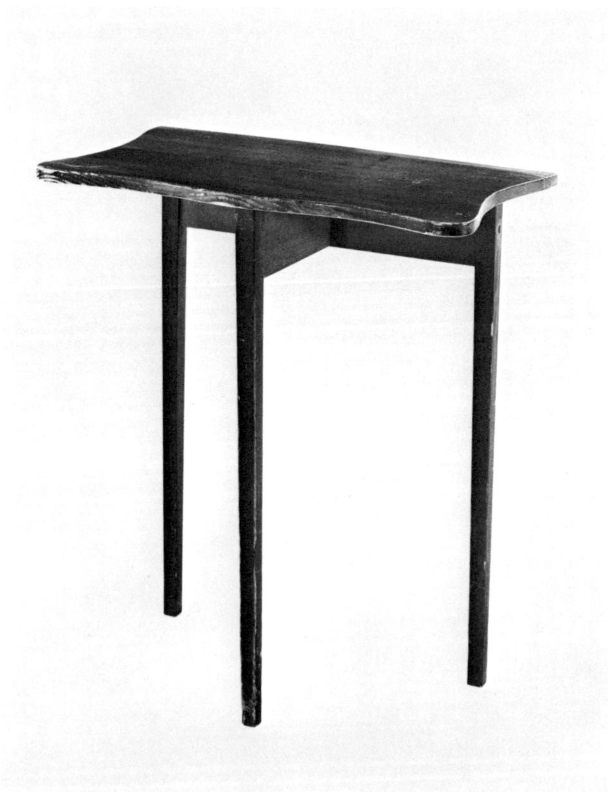

Cat. 65

66

Unidentified artist
Fireboard
Probably Maine, 1800–1820
Eastern white pine
H 25 (83.5); w 42⅞ (108.9)
York Institute Museum

Fireboards were frequently used in New England homes to close up fireplaces during the warm summer months or when otherwise not in use. Wooden fireboards are known with painted designs ranging from baskets of flowers to landscapes.[1] This one provides an unusual medium for the display of the heraldic arms, "By the Name of Nye." While heraldic iron firebacks are known that date from the seventeenth century, during the federal period coats of arms were most frequently painted in watercolors (cat. 74).

While some families located arms for their surname in design books, others had them adapted (see cat. 3). No coat of arms for the Nye family has been found in eighteenth-century source books, suggesting that elements including a bend, doves, and crescents were simply selected at random for this fireboard.

Colonel Thomas Cutts's youngest daughter Eunice married Samuel Nye in 1803. Samuel's 1826 probate inventory does not list fireboards along with the "Brass fire setts" and "fire dogs and shovels."[2] His sister-in-law, Sarah Cutts Thornton, however, owned five fireboards at the time of her death. They were found in the best first-floor rooms as well as in second-floor chambers. Two were valued at ten cents each, and one at six cents.[3]

This fireboard is constructed of two boards simply joined by a tongue-and-groove joint. Cabinetmakers in Maine made these inexpensive domestic items. On November 8, 1787, John Seymour in Portland made "2 Fire Boards" at 3*s.* each.[4]

This may have been among the "valuable relics of this family" including "unique specimens of furniture . . . and minor articles" in the York Institute as early as 1892.[5]   LFS

1 Nina Fletcher Little, *Little by Little: Six Decades of Collecting American Decorative Arts* (New York: E. P. Dutton, 1984), nos. 127–132, 134–136. Other examples with Maine histories include those painted with Portland landscape scenes by Charles Codman for the Deering family in the collection of the Portland Museum of Art and Fruitlands (fig. 4.3).
2 YCRP; 36:288–290.
3 YCRP; 58:67–72.
4 Account, John Seymour to Thomas Robison, March 16, 1787, Robison Papers, MEHS.
5 Cecil Hampden Cutts Howard, comp., *Geneology of the Cutts Family in America* (Albany, N.Y.: Joel Munsell's Sons, 1892), 88.

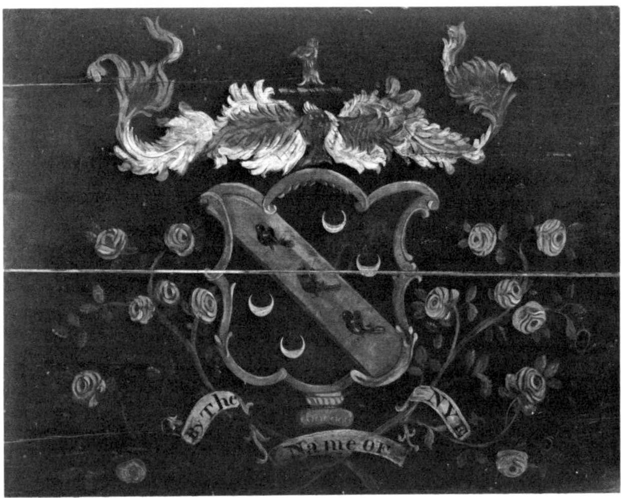

Cat. 66

67

Wallpaper with border
Probably Boston, Massachusetts, ca. 1786
Black and orange block-printed on light blue ground;
border: black, white, and two pinks block-printed
on a dark blue ground
H fragment 12⅛ (30.8); w fragment 22¹⁵⁄₁₆ (58.3);
H repeat 2¹⁵⁄₁₆ (7.5)
Maine Historical Society; Wadsworth-Longfellow House

After 1901, when the Wadsworth-Longfellow house was converted from a private residence to a public museum, the interior was "modernized," a colonial revival inspiration. Although much wallpaper from the eighteenth and early nineteenth century was removed, a remarkable series has survived that documents the choices of the two families (see Chapter 3).[1]

About 1786 the Wadsworths selected this overall star and ribbon pattern for their two-story hall. The black and orange printed on a light blue ground is a sharp and striking combination of colors.[2] It covered the walls from the ceiling to the wainscot paneling throughout the front hall.

Fragments of a festoon border attached to the paper document its use along the ceiling molding. The design may have been printed from the same blocks that were used to print another sample found in a Sutton, Massachusetts, house. The Sutton border, however, was used with a more elaborate, French inspired, arabesque design.[3]

A reproduction of this paper, without its border, was installed in the parlor chamber in the 1950s.   LFS

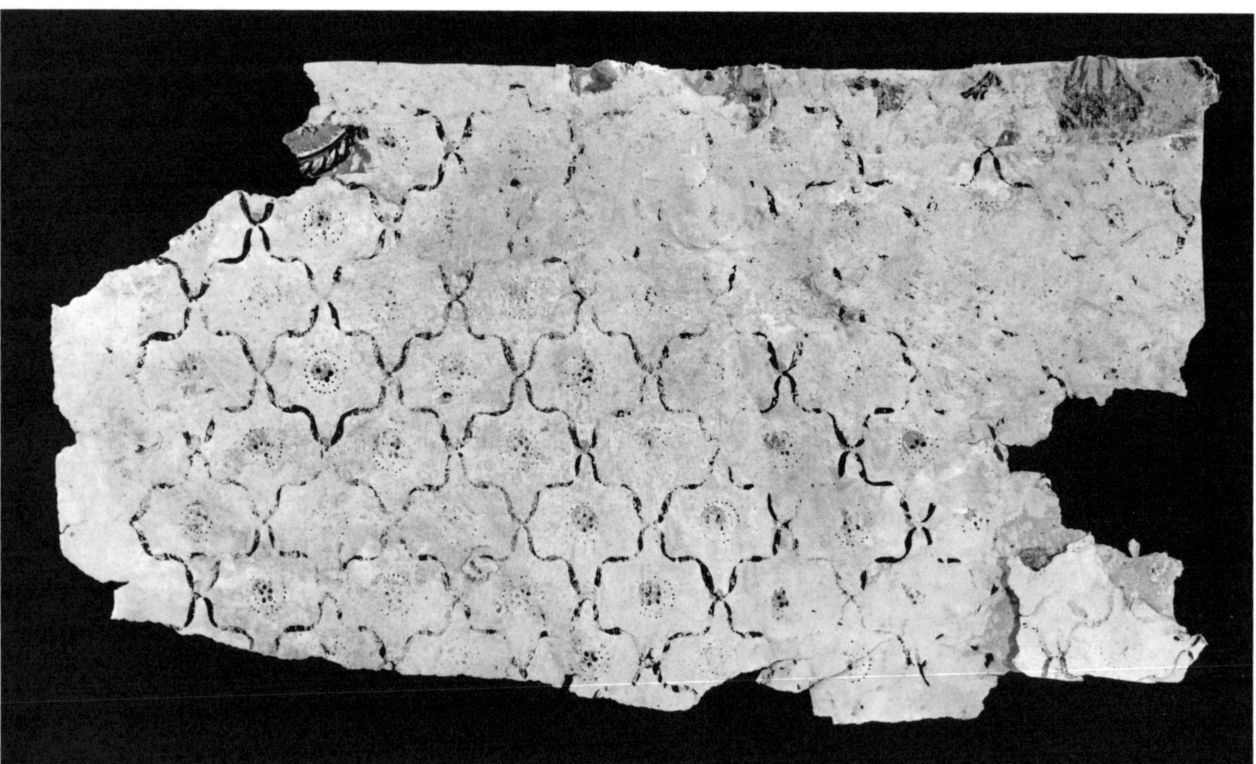

Cat. 67

1 I am indebted to Richard C. Nylander for identifying the wallpapers discussed here and for kindly bringing related examples to my attention.
2 Nylander, Redmond, and Sander, *Wallpaper*, 64–65, fig. 11.1.
3 Nylander, Redmond, and Sander, *Wallpaper*, 91, fig. 20a.

68

Moses Grant, Jr., and Co. (1811–1817)
Wallpaper and border
Boston, Massachusetts, 1811–1817
One roll: white, blue, gray, and dark gray
block-printed on blue gray ground;
second roll: two whites, two grays, and pink
block-printed on gray ground
w roll 22 (55.9); h repeat 21½ (54.6)
Maine Historical Society; Wadsworth-Longfellow House

This wallpaper, patterned with vertical bamboo columns alternating with drapery and tassels, was applied over the star and ribbon paper installed in the hall in the late 1780s (cat. 67). It is thought to date between 1811 and 1817, which coincides with the expansion of the house in 1815.[1]

Close scrutiny of this paper reveals that the Longfellows alternated two wallpapers of the same pattern, but printed in two different series of colors. One paper was printed with white, blue, gray, and dark gray on a blue-gray ground. The white and blue drapery was highlighted with white. This roll was alternated on the walls with a paper printed with two whites, two grays, and a pink on a similar blue-gray ground. The gray and white drapery was highlighted on the second paper with pink.

This is an unusual arrangement which may have been the result of not having an adequate supply of one or the other type of paper. In the alternating colors, however, the drapery must have created a shadowy illusion. Where the drapery met on the edges of the paper, half was highlighted by white, the other by pink.

Although not visible here, a fragment of an elegant French border survives under the wallpaper that was installed between 1845 and 1855. Nine separate blocks were used to print a Greek key, an olive branch swag, and rich foliage in blue-green, dark blue, light green, black, bright orange, blue, gray, white, and pink.

In December 1815, Edward Howe advertised that he had just received from Bordeaux "a large assortment of very *Rich French Paper-Hangings*, with suitable bordering to match." His stock also included American paper hangings.[2] The Longfellows mixed both. The domestic product decorated the walls; a more expensive French import used only as the border suited them and their pocketbook.

This paper remained on the walls until 1845–1855, the date range of the only other layer. A long span of years for the use of this paper is not unusual. Great expense accompanied papering a two-story hall; papers used in these spaces for many years are documented in other New England homes.   LFS

1 Nylander, Redmond, and Sander, *Wallpaper*, 112.
2 *Portland Gazette* (December 26, 1815).

69

Wallpaper
Probably Boston, Massachusetts, ca. 1786
White block-printed on bright blue ground
H fragment 14 (35.6); w fragment 16¹⁵⁄₁₆ (43.0);
H repeat 10³⁄₁₆ (25.9)
Maine Historical Society; Wadsworth-Longfellow House

On completion of their house in 1786, the Wadsworth family selected this paper for the largest and best room, the parlor. With its southeastern exposure, the room with these white festoons printed on a brilliant blue ground must have had a rich appearance. This paper was on the walls when Eliza Wadsworth died in the room in 1802, and when Zilpah married Stephen Longfellow two years later.

Boston supported a number of paper-staining establishments. In 1786 when the Massachusetts legislature prohibited the importation of wallpapers, it only encouraged the craft industry's success.[1] This paper is probably the product of a Boston wallpaper maker. Its design required only one block to be cut and used in the printing; it was a handsome as well as affordable choice.   LFS

1 Lynn, *Wallpaper*, 109.

70

Wallpaper
Boston, Massachusetts, ca. 1807
Two greens, black, and white on gray ground
H fragment 23½ (59.7); w fragment 21¾ (55.2);
H repeat 5 (12.7); w repeat 10½ (26.7)
Maine Historical Society; Wadsworth-Longfellow House

When the Longfellows redecorated in 1807, they changed the paper in the parlor. Replacing the elegant white swag was this "trellis" or lozenge pattern. The green, black, and white pattern was hung with the widest part of the diamond on the horizontal. The diamonds enclose foliate sprays.

The products of Boston wallpaper makers were available locally. David Pease kept paperhangings and borders from "the manufactories in Boston" in stock, and he could purchase patterns not in stock "as shall be ordered by any

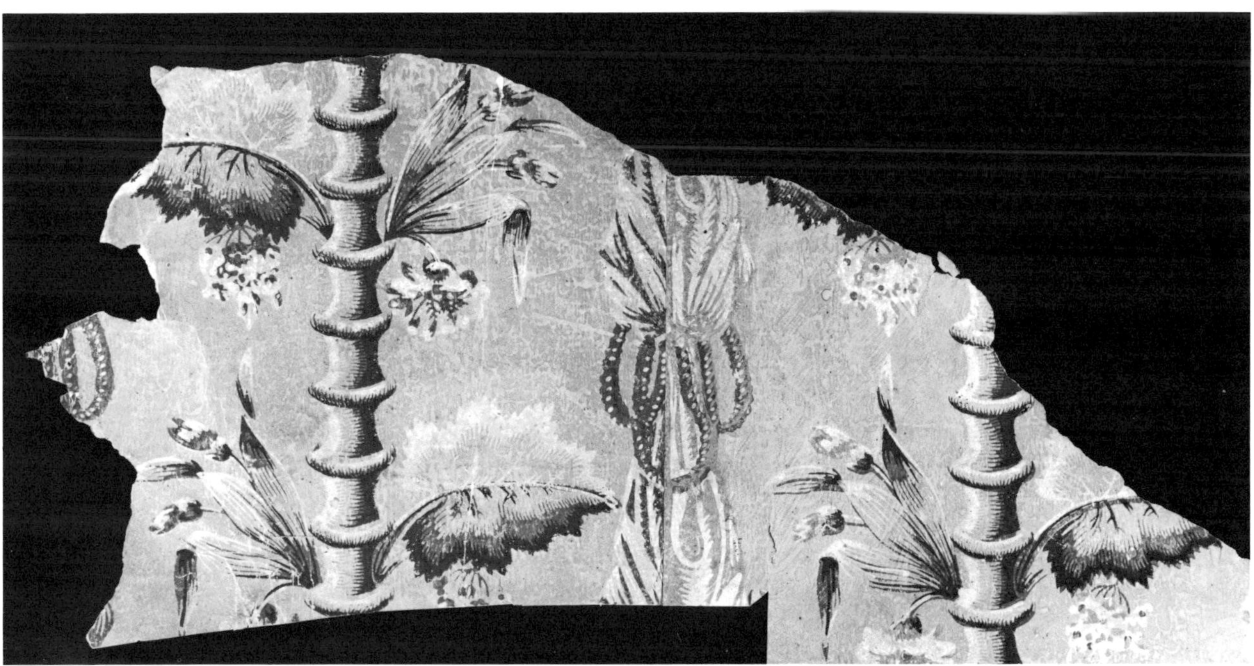

Cat. 68

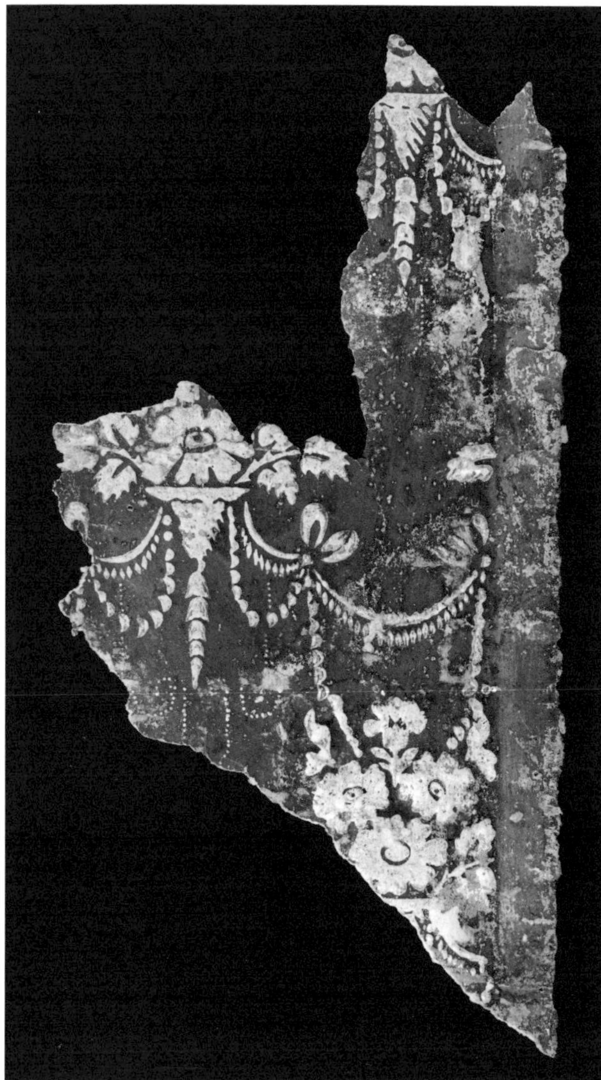

Cat. 69

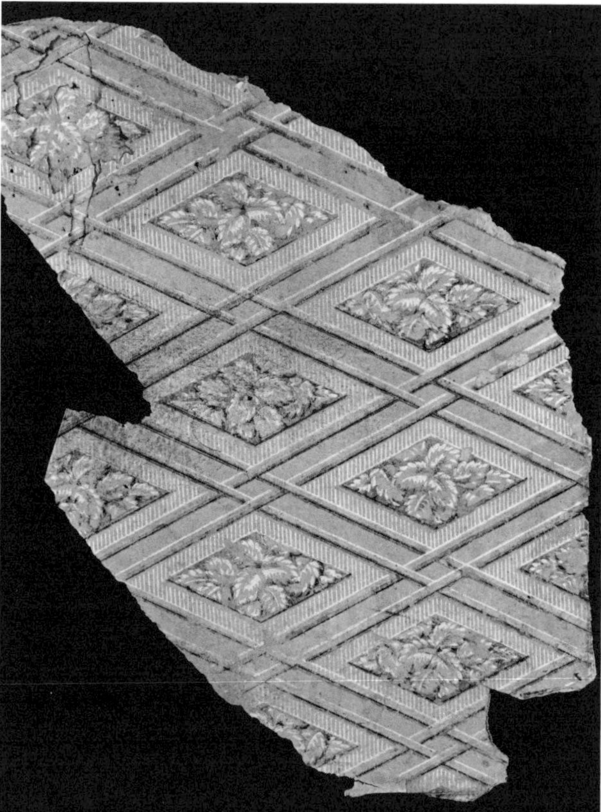

Cat. 70

gentleman." [1] Individuals could also obtain papers directly from Boston themselves. On April 30, 1811, Captain Samuel Nye of Saco bought of Moses Grant and Son "6 Rolls Paper" for $9 and "16 yds Border" for $5.34, sufficient for a room twelve feet square. [2]   LFS

1   *Eastern Argus* (May 16, 1806).
2   Bill, Moses Grant and Son to Samuel Nye, Boston, April 30, 1811, Nye Family Papers, Dyer Library, Saco.

71

Wallpaper
Boston, Massachusetts, ca. 1815

White and peach block-printed on a yellow ground
H fragment 19¾ (50.2); W fragment 7¼ (18.4);
H repeat 8¼ (21.0)
Society for the Preservation of New England Antiquities

In the parlor of the Wadsworth-Longfellow house, five wallpapers were hung between 1786 and 1835, one covering another, documenting the succession of their installation. This third paper is layered between the lozenge paper (cat. 70) and the rainbow paper (cat. 72). It is most likely a product of Moses Grant, Jr., and Co., the Boston paper stainers. [1]

This sample is one of the Wadsworth-Longfellow papers that made its way into the collections of the Society for the Preservation of New England Antiquities sometime before 1966. Unlike other papers from this house in the Society, however, the provenance of this paper was unclear. The group of papers discussed here confirms its location in Portland.

The Society's sample has been included here because the Portland sample remains layered between earlier and later papers and the pattern repeat cannot be seen. The white-printed ribbon cascades down the paper, creating reserves for leafy sprays.   LFS

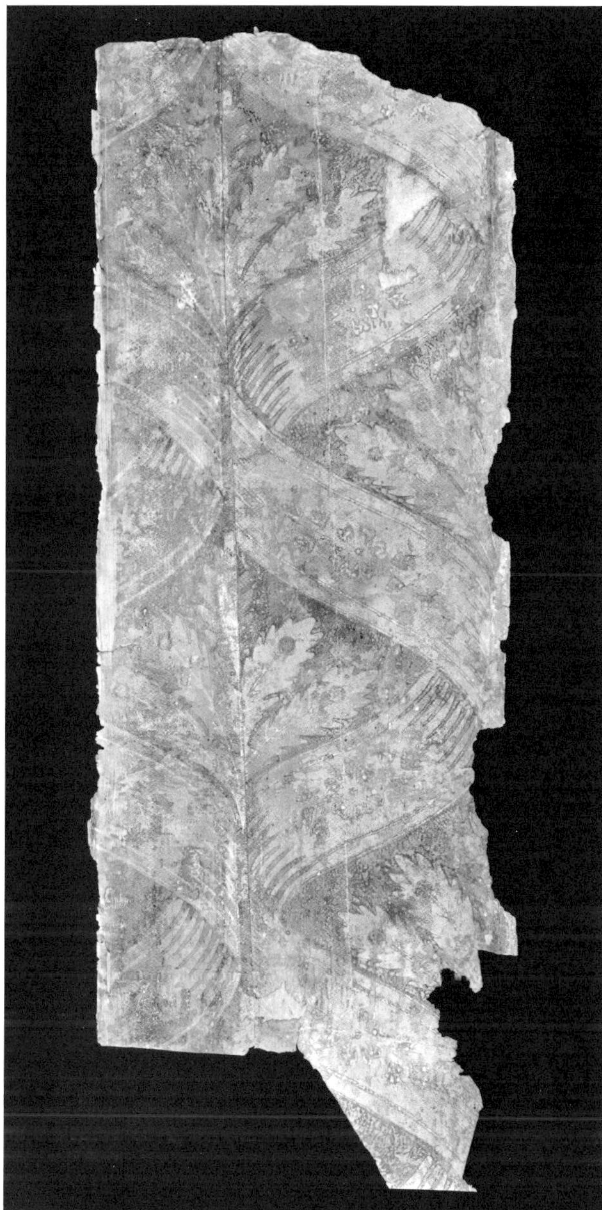

Cat. 71

1 For a discussion of the Grant manufactories, see Nylander, Redmond, and Sander, *Wallpaper*, 87–88, 129–132.

72

Wallpaper
France, 1825–1835
Gray and yellow block-printed on a blended bright green, gray, and orange ground

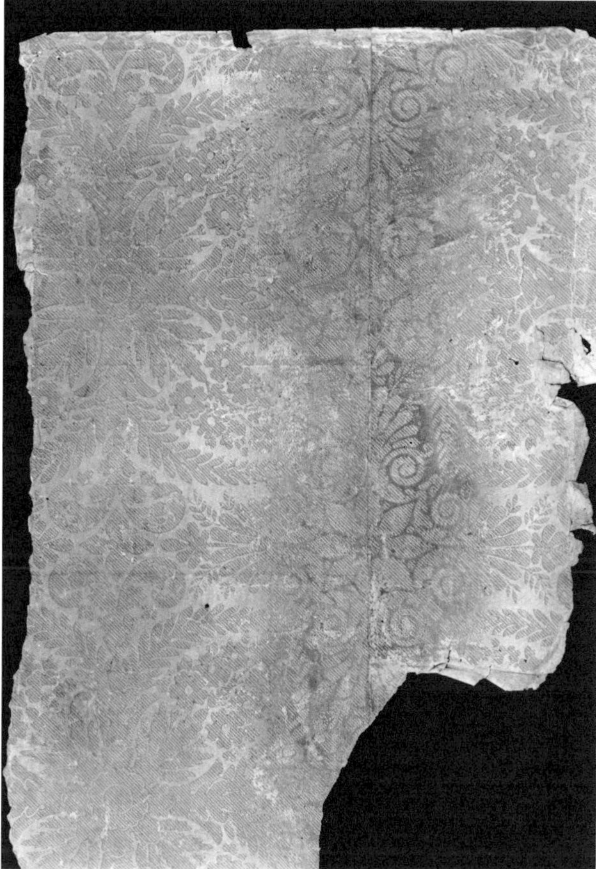

Cat. 72

w roll 19¾ (50.2); H repeat 19 (48.3); w repeat 19⅛ (48.6)
Maine Historical Society; Wadsworth-Longfellow House

The installation of this paper in the parlor may correspond with a renewal of the first-floor front rooms about 1827 when Stephen Longfellow moved his office from the house to Exchange Street (see Chapter 3). Another activity in the late 1820s that may have prompted new paperhangings was the engagement of Elizabeth Longfellow to William Pitt Fessenden. She died, unexpectedly, in 1829, before the marriage.

In this paper, many small stylized elements create a large and active pattern, contrasting bright green, orange, and gray. By 1835 this rainbow paper was replaced by another featuring a floral pattern on a blue ground. The installation of the second rainbow paper may coincide with the marriage of Anne Longfellow to George Washington Pierce in 1832. Rainbow papers were highly fashionable during the 1820s and 1830s. One was chosen to decorate the Nathaniel Lord mansion in Kennebunkport.[1]

This earlier rainbow paper appears elsewhere in the house. Outdated, it was enlisted for the decoration of a bandbox, now in a closet on the third floor. Although it is difficult to determine exactly when the paper was applied to the box, it overlapped an 1845 newspaper lining.[2] It covered wallpaper with a blue, black, and white floral sprig pattern printed on a pink ground that may be another paper used earlier by the Wadsworth or Longfellow family.   LFS

1 Cynthia J. Murphy, comp., "Wadsworth and Longfellow Genealogy" (typescript, MEHS). The second rainbow paper is among the wallpaper samples at MEHS. For the Lord rainbow paper, see Nylander, Redmond, and Sander, *Wallpaper*, 142, and plate 17.
2 Lynn, *Wallpaper*, 294.

73

Attributed to Samuel Gore (1750/1–1831)
Coat of arms
Probably Newburyport, Massachusetts, ca. 1795
Oil on panel
H 14⅞ (37.8); W 11⅟₁₆ (29.0)
The Brick Store Museum; William E. Barry estate
through Edith Cleaves Barry

In its composition and style, this coat of arms of the Fairfield family is similar to the arms of the Cleaves family at the York

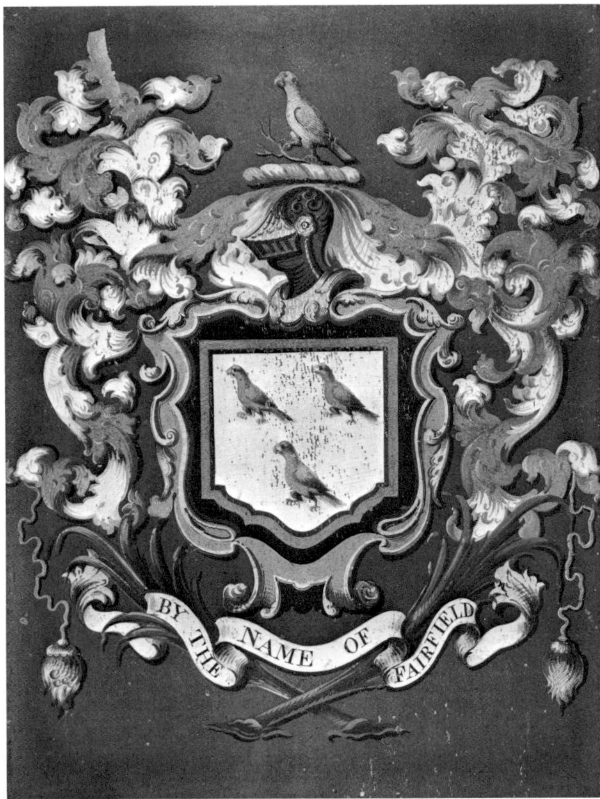

Cat. 73

Institute Museum. Both are painted on a panel with a dark green ground and exhibit nearly identical cartouches, highlighted in red and gilt. They may have been commissioned together when Sarah Fairfield and Daniel Cleaves married in 1795. Their division and descent in the Barry and Locke families is documented by many other Cleaves family furnishings included in this catalogue.

The composition of the Fairfield and Cleaves arms is similar to those painted by George Searle (ca. 1751–1796) of Newburyport. However, it is more likely that they were painted by Samuel Gore, Searle's cousin who moved to Newburyport after 1789 and continued as a heraldic painter there after Searle's death in 1795.[1] Contact between Maine patrons and Samuel Gore is documented in more than one instance between 1783 and 1799 (see cats. 142, 154). The arms of Fairfield and the arms of Cleaves were probably derived from designs in John Guillim's *Display of Heraldry*, published in six editions between 1611 and 1724. Although a copy of this book has not been documented to Samuel Gore's possession, his father owned the 1724 edition; his cousin Searle is thought to have also owned this edition.[2]

Samuel Gore was the son of John Gore (1718–1796), a decorative painter in Boston, and the brother of Christopher Gore, a governor of Massachusetts. The tradition of painting in the Gore family was carried on by Samuel's sons George and Christopher; the latter was in partnership with his father by 1807.[3]   KDM

1 Harold Bowditch, "Early Water-Color Paintings of New England Coats of Arms," *Publications of the Colonial Society of Massachusetts* 35 (1944): 203. This Fairfield arms appears to be the one Bowditch published from a negative at the Essex Institute. Although Bowditch never saw the original and did not know its whereabouts, the negative may have found its way to the Essex Institute through John Corning, a Kennebunk resident and the son of Howard Corning, a director of the Essex Institute. John Corning and the panel's owner, Edith Cleaves Barry, were friends.
2 Bowditch, "New England Coats of Arms," 174.
3 Bowditch, "New England Coats of Arms," 181–182.

74

John Coles, Sr. (1749–1809)
Coat of arms
Boston, Massachusetts, 1798
Pen and ink and watercolor on paper
Signed and dated on reverse
H 13¹³⁄₁₆ (35.0); W 9¾ (24.7)
The Brick Store Museum
Gift of Mr. and Mrs. Theodore O. Kingsbury, 1978

When asked who might bear a coat of arms in America, William Sumner Appleton, founder of the Society for the Preservation of New England Antiquities, replied, "Everyone . . . who is not restrained by a sense of the absurdity of so

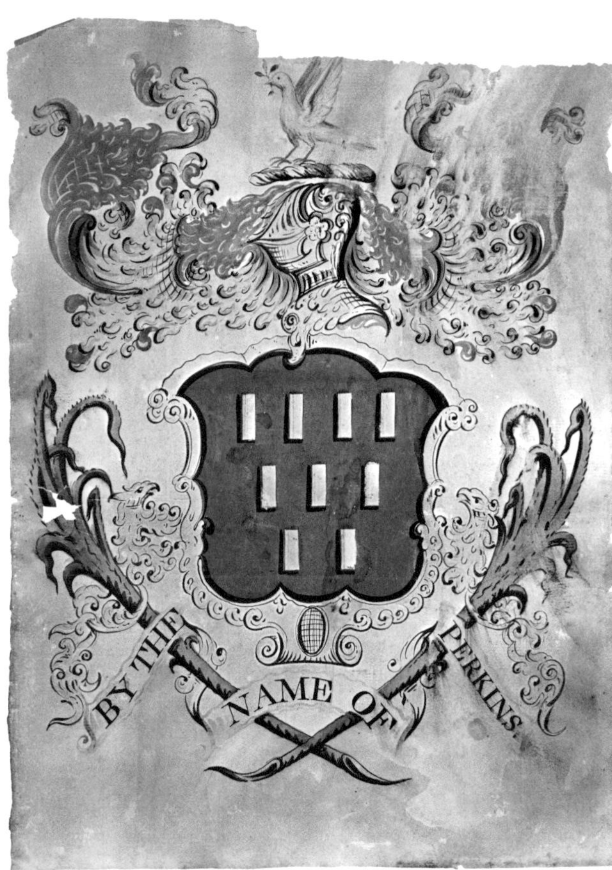

Cat. 74

Heraldic decorations, however, were good business and painters like John Coles encouraged their production. Coles owned two source books on heraldry—the 1724 edition of John Guillim's *Display of Heraldry* and a version of Guillim's work by Samuel Kent, *The Banner Display'd*.[4] One need not despair if his surname was not listed in the major source books: Perkins is listed in neither Guillim nor Kent. Coles adapted a coat of arms for the Perkins family from one of the hundreds listed, further attesting on the label he attached to the back that the arms were "copied directly from the arms of the Perkins family of the County of Kent, England."

The style of the coats of arms painted by Coles is distinctive. The mantle does not fall below the shield and breaks the composition into two sections. The mantle consists of short feathery brush strokes with cross-hatching to indicate shading.[5] John Coles was first listed in the *Boston Directory* in 1782 as a publisher and painter; in that year he published a portrait of George and Martha Washington, designed by Benjamin Blyth of Salem and engraved by John Norman. In 1788 Coles was listed as a painter, and in 1796, as a heraldry painter. He was followed in the business by his son, John Coles, Jr. (1776 or 1780–1854), who painted portraits and miniatures in addition to heraldic decorations (cat. 32).[6]   KDM & LFS

doing."[1] Indeed, the use of heraldry in America seems opposed to the nation's democratic foundations. By displaying coats of arms, Americans emulated the European gentry in an attempt to establish themselves as members of a new elite, and perhaps in an effort to establish their American roots.

Thomas Perkins (1700–1752) settled in Arundel (Kennebunkport) in 1719. By commissioning this coat of arms, perhaps his son, Thomas, Jr., was expressing his family's connection to the area. Thomas, Jr., was a representative to the General Court and town clerk. After his death in 1794, his widow, Suzanne, married Edward Emerson of York (see Chapter 2). This watercolor drawing descended in the family of Perkins's daughter, Elizabeth Perkins Wildes Bourne (see cat. 139), to the donors.[2]

In the New World, it was not entirely clear which families had noble lineage, and therefore, a proper arms. The liberal use of heraldic designs led to a controversy later in the nineteenth century. In 1891 Appleton published "Positive Pedigrees and Authorized Arms of New England" and corroborated the claim to a coat of arms for only a handful of families.[3]

1 William Sumner Appleton, "Heraldry in America," *Proceedings of the Massachusetts Historical Society*, 2d ser., 15 (1901–1902): 164.

2 Bradbury, *History*, 267–268. A nearly identical Perkins coat of arms signed on the reverse by John Coles, Sr., and dated 1802 was reproduced with a facsimile of the inscription as the frontispiece to Annie Peabody Brooks, *Ropes' Ends: Traditions, Legends and Sketches of Old Kennebunkport and Vicinity* (Kennebunkport, Me.: By the author, 1901).

3 William Sumner Appleton, "Positive Pedigrees and Authorized Arms," *New England Historic Genealogical Register* 45, no. 3 (July 1891): 187–190.

4 Harold Bowditch, "Early Water-Color Paintings of New England Coats of Arms," *Publications of the Colonial Society of Massachusetts* 35 (1944): 174.

5 Bowditch, "New England Coats of Arms," 190–193. Many other examples painted for Maine families by Coles are known; see cat. 142.1, the Tucker and Cunningham arms dated 1794 at Castle Tucker in Wiscasset, and the McLellan family arms dated 1802 at the Gorham Historical Society.

6 George C. Groce and David H. Wallace, *The New-York Historical Society's Dictionary of Artists in America 1564–1870* (New Haven: Yale University Press, 1957), 139. A memorial to George Washington engraved by E. G. Gridley after a painting by John Coles, Jr., and probably published in 1800, descended in Kennebunk's Lord-Barry family and is now at BSM; it is from the same engraved plate as one in a private collection published as the frontispiece in *Antiques* 69, no. 2 (February 1956): 134–135.

75

Edward Savage (1761–1817)
George Washington
Philadelphia, Pennsylvania, 1801
Engraving
Inscribed "E. Savage Executd 1801 / George Washington"
H 31⅛ (79.0); W 24⁷⁄₁₆ (62.0)
Maine Historical Society; Wadsworth-Longfellow House

The Wadsworth family owned several objects which illustrated their admiration for President Washington. In
addition to this engraving after the Landsdowne oil portrait,
they had an image of the apotheosis of Washington, and the
"Washington in Glory" pitcher (cat. 88). In 1800 Eliza
Wadsworth earnestly wrote to her father Peleg, a Congressman in Washington, requesting a copy of the death
march composed for Washington's funeral, and "a scrap of
General Washington's hand writing, perhaps his name." She
continued, "Papa had he hair? A lock of that I should value
more highly still; but this I suppose impracticable, the first I
hope for." Eliza received her wish when Tobias Lear, Mrs.
Washington's secretary, forwarded the requested lock of hair
as "a memorial of veneration for his Character."[1]

More than twenty years later, when Peleg's son-in-law

Stephen Longfellow was in Washington, he traveled to
Mount Vernon where he acquired a piece of the cypress from
Washington's tomb. He sent it to his son, Henry Wadsworth
Longfellow, then a student at Bowdoin College. Henry
replied that he would keep it "as a sacred relick."[2]

Engravings frequently decorated the best rooms of a
house. George Lovis, a Portland goldsmith and jeweler,
offered for sale "A great variety of elegant PRINTS, with gilt
frames, suitable for parlour ornaments" and, more specifically, "Likenesses of Washington and Hamilton, elegantly
framed and glazed."[3] This engraving can be seen hanging
over the parlor mantelpiece in a late nineteenth-century
photograph of the Wadsworth-Longfellow house, where it
remains (fig. 3.8). The original frame bears the reverse-
painted inscription "G. Washington" at the bottom. Fragments of an 1802 newspaper are glued to the back.   AAE

1 A John James Barralet engraving of the apotheosis of Washington,
  1800–1802, survives at the Wadsworth-Longfellow house. Eliza
  Wadsworth to Peleg Wadsworth, January 19, 1800, and Tobias Lear
  to Peleg Wadsworth, April 5, 1800, Longfellow Papers, MEHS. A
  gold locket Henry Wadsworth Longfellow had made for the hair
  survives at MEHS and is inscribed: "Washington's Hair, / Given by
  Mrs. Washington / to / Miss Eliza Wadsworth / April 5th 1800./
  Henry W. Longfellow / 1850."
2 Hilen, *Letters*, 1:89.
3 *Eastern Argus* (January 31, 1806; July 19, 1805).

Cat. 75

76

Published by Bowles and Carver
*Robinson Crusoe carrying away on his Raft the most
useful remains of the Wreck*
London, 1795
Engraving
H 8½ (21.5); W 11⅜ (28.9)
Old York Historical Society
Gift of Mrs. H. Kingsbury, 1900

Daniel Defoe's novel, *Life and Strange Surprising Adventures of
Robinson Crusoe*, was first published in 1719, but has remained
popular to this day. Portland booksellers advertised the work
during the first decade of the nineteenth century.[1] The story
lent itself to pictorial representation. In 1795 the English
firm of Bowles and Carver printed a series of engravings
illustrating the adventures of Robinson Crusoe.

This is number three of a set of twelve prints, six of
which survive with a history of ownership in York. The set
depicts Robinson Crusoe from the time his ship sank to his
settlement on the island and discovery of human footprints
on the sandy beach.

Series of prints like this and the Prodigal Son (cat. 77)
were frequently grouped together on the walls of front rooms.

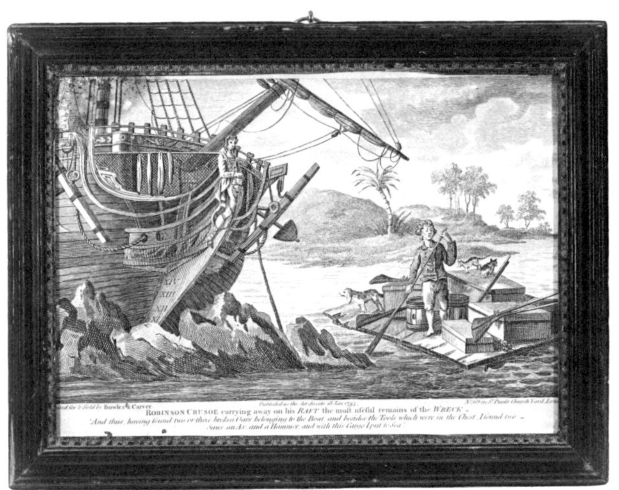

Cat. 76

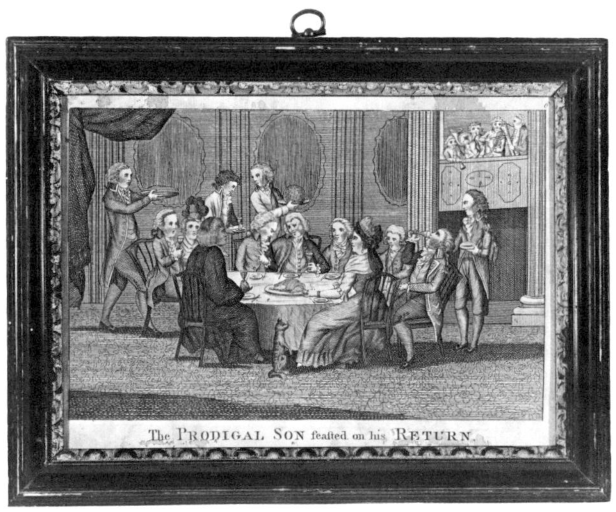

Cat. 77

In Edward Emerson, Jr.'s, northwest front room in York was "Washington's family large picture elegantly gilted [with] 4 small pictures by its Side, gilted." Emerson's southwest front room had "4 pictures of the seasons."[2] At the nearby Jonathan Sayward house, portraits, views of European cities, and scenes from Shakespeare ornamented the walls of the front rooms (fig. 3.5).

An invoice for engravings purchased in London by Thomas Robison of Portland listed both single and pairs of engravings. The order included individual prints of landscapes, battle scenes, and mythical subjects ("Nymphs Sporting") as well as pairs such as "Evening and Morning," and "2 Diana & her Nymphs." Many were framed in "pear tree Frame[s] carved in & out & Glass."[3]

Because frames and glazing were additional expenses, some prints were not protected this way. The 1804 probate inventory of Kittery resident Daniel Pierce indicated that of the nineteen "pictures," only five were "with frames and glass." Four were listed with wood frames, and three with brass. Two large pictures were "without glass" and two others were "without frames."[4]   AAE

1 *Eastern Argus* (December 14, 1806); *Freeman's Friend* (Portland) (September 19, 1807).
2 YCRP; 19:429–430. According to Edith Barry, a series of the seasons published in London by John Fairburn in 1796 and now at BSM decorated Wallingford Hall (see Chapter 3).
3 Invoice, Robert Wilkinson to Phyn and Ellice, April 24, 1784, Robison Papers, MEHS.
4 YCRP; 19:403.

77

Published by C. Sheppard
The Prodigal Son feasted on his Return
London, 1792
Engraving
H 6 (15.2); W 8 (20.3)
Old York Historical Society; Gift of G.W.S. Putnam

The biblical story of the Prodigal Son (Luke xv:12) was often depicted in engravings. According to the story, the son acquired his share of the inheritance, left home, and squandered it. Repenting his actions, he returned home where his family welcomed him joyfully.

Both American and English engravers illustrated the popular moralistic tale. Many versions share similarities in the placement of the figures and in the settings. Engravers used contemporary homes, furnishings, and clothing in their renderings of the parable. This and another set at the Old York Historical Society were engraved in London in 1792.[1]

Samuel Hadlock, Jr., of Cranberry Isles, Maine, traveled in Germany in the 1820s and commented on the "ladies of Pleshier" and the customs regarding prostitution. The men "return back like Progale [prodigal] son" after their encounters, he wrote, "and are hartley [heartily] received by thair companions."[2]   AAE

1 Joan D. Dolmetsch, ed., *Eighteenth-Century Prints in Colonial America: To Educate and Decorate* (Williamsburg, Va.: Colonial Williamsburg Foundation, 1979), 151. This set lacks "The Prodigal Son in Excess." The other set of engravings is complete, but framed together in a later frame. Castle Tucker in Wiscasset, Maine, owns three prints of a Prodigal Son series published in London by Robert Sayer & Co. in 1791.
2 Rachel Field, *God's Pocket: The Story of Captain Samuel Hadlock, Junior, of Cranberry Isles, Maine* (New York: Macmillan, 1934), 62.

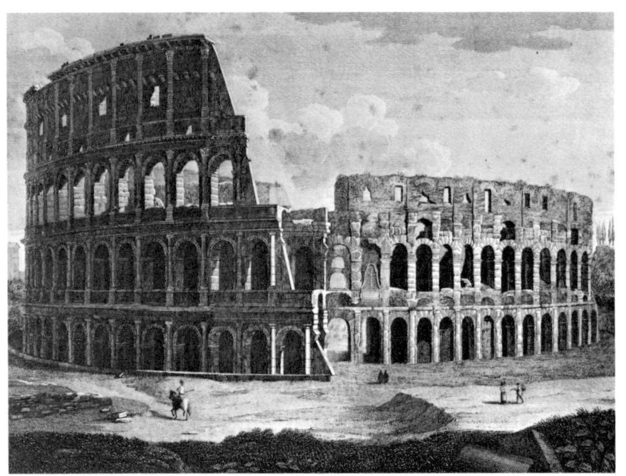

Cat. 78A

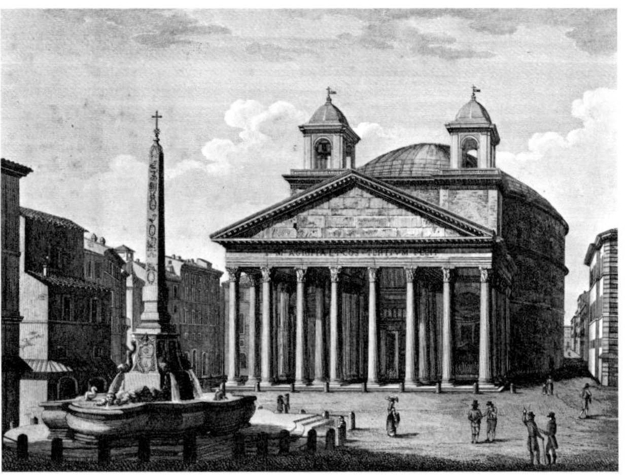

Cat. 78B

78A

Achille Parboni (w. 1820s–1830s)
Veduta dell' Anfiteatro Flavio detto il Colosseo,
cretto dall" Impre. Flavio / Vespasiano nei Giardini
di Nerone l'Anno 72. dell' Era volgare.
Vue de l'Amphitheatre Flavien apelle le Colossee,
erige par l'Empur. / Flavien Vespasien dans les Jardins
de Neron l'an 72 de l'Aire vulgre.
Italy, 1824
Engraving
Inscribed "Achil. Parboni . . . inc. 1824"
H 10⅜ (26.4); W 13⅝ (34.6)
Maine Historical Society; Wadsworth-Longfellow House

78B

Achille Parboni (w. 1820s–1830s)
Veduta del Panteon d'Agrippa in oggi Chiesa di S. Maria
ad Martyres, comunemente detta la Rotonda.
Vue du Pantheon d'Agrippa aujord'hui l'Eglise de
S.M.e ad Martyres, communement apellee la Rotonde.
Italy, 1825
Engraving
Inscribed "Achille Parboni inc 1825"
H 10⅜ (26.4); W 13⅝ (34.6)
Maine Historical Society; Wadsworth-Longfellow House

Engravings of European cities decorated many Maine
homes. Jonathan Sayward owned views of England, France,
and Italy (fig. 3.5), and Thomas Robison ordered engravings
from London, including "A View near Naples," "2 Views of
London," and "2 Views of Windsor."[1] Many years after
Thomas Robison ordered his prints, these engravings of

"Roman ruins" were purchased by Henry Wadsworth
Longfellow while on the Grand Tour. In 1828 Henry wrote:

*You can imagine nothing equal to the ruins of Rome. The Foro Romano
and the Colos[s]eum are beyond all I had ever fancied them: — and the
ruined temples — the mausoleums — and the old mouldering acqueducts
which are scattered in every direction over the immense plain which
surrounds the city — give you an idea of the ancient grandeur of the
Romans, and produce in your mind ideas, which cannot be easily
defined, nor communicated.*[2]

Achille Parboni was working in Rome during the 1820s,
but little about his work is known. In 1830 he and Pietro,
probably his brother, engraved *Nuova Raccolta di principali
Vedute de Roma*, a new collection of the principal views of
Rome. They also copied the works of Poussin.[3]

These engravings were photographed in the eastern front
room of the Wadsworth-Longfellow house in the late
nineteenth century, where they remain.[4]   AAE

1 Invoice, Robert Wilkinson to Phyn and Ellice, London, April 24,
  1784, Robison Papers, MEHS.
2 Hilen, *Letters*, 1:271.
3 Armando Pelliccioni, *Dizionario Degli Artisti Incisori Italiani* (Modena,
  Italia: Gualdi Germano & Figli, 1949), 127. Edith Schmidt of the
  Museum of Fine Arts, Boston, kindly assisted in the identification of
  Parboni.
4 Wadsworth-Longfellow house, photograph of interior, MEHS.

79

Henshall and Company (w. ca. 1790–1828)
Dinner set (selections)
Longport, Staffordshire, England, 1804–1815
Pearlware with transfer-printed decoration in blue
Marked (on bottom) "HENSHALL & CO."
· H tureen, cover, and stand 9¼ (23.5); L ladle 9¼ (23.5);

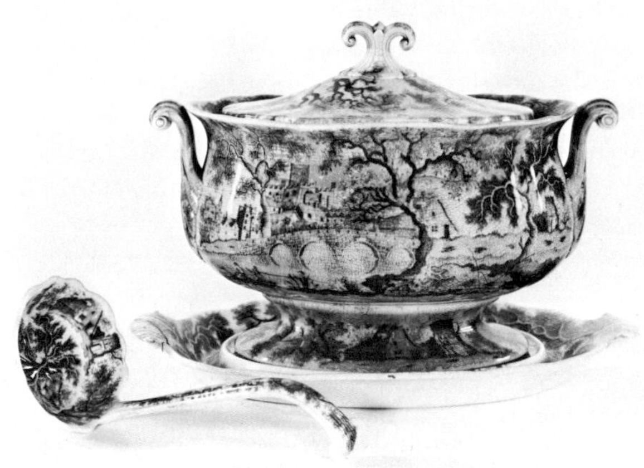

Cat. 79

H footed stand 4¾ (12.0); H footed bowl 4¼ (10.8);
Diam. plate 8 (20.3)
Maine Historical Society; Wadsworth-Longfellow House

"Elegant blue printed dining setts" were advertised for sale
in federal-period Portland. Part of a large, and by most
standards elegant, dinner service with blue-printed decoration survives at the Wadsworth-Longfellow house. It is of
particular interest because unlike the majority of tablewares
exported to America from unidentified factories, more than
half of the one hundred pieces in this service are marked by
the manufacturer. Henshall and Company operated under
various partnerships between 1790 and 1828. Family
tradition maintains this service was purchased as a wedding

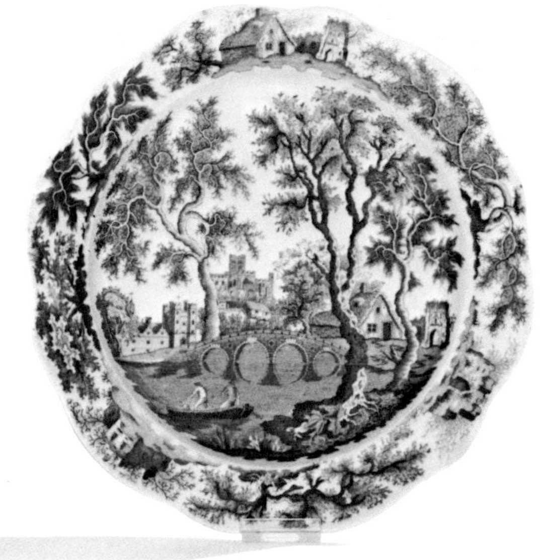

Cat. 79

present to Zilpah Wadsworth on her marriage in 1804 to
Stephen Longfellow. The castle and bridge pattern depicted
here is dated by ceramic scholars between 1810 and 1815,
but it may have been in production a few years earlier.
Products of this factory are known for their consistently high
quality.[1]

The majority of these wares are plates of varying sizes.
Illustrated here are some of the most unusual forms: a footed

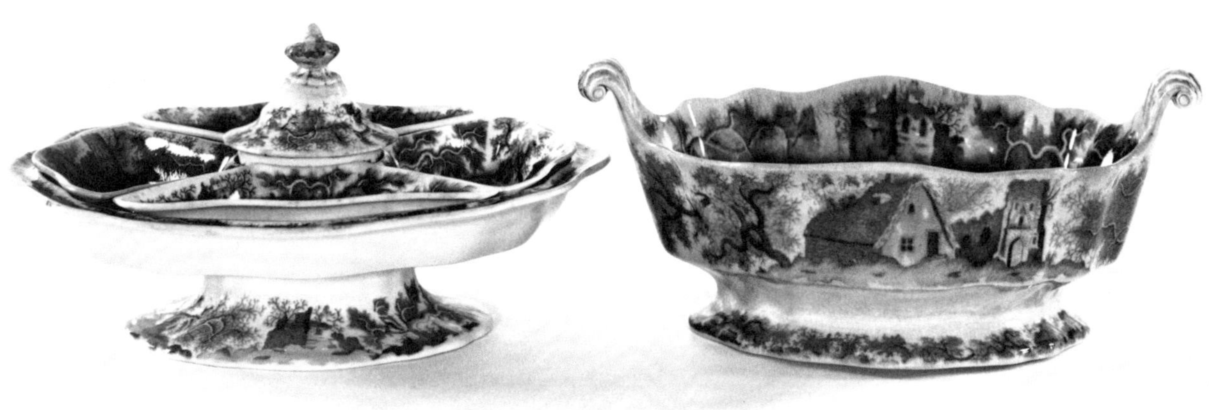

Cat. 79

stand with four removable dishes, probably used for serving relishes; a boat-shaped bowl with scrolled handles; and a large soup tureen with scrolled handles, and ladle. The tureen is surmounted by an uncommon fleur-de-lis finial.

Zilpah Longfellow highly valued these tablewares. In 1814 when in Boston, Stephen wrote to her asking if there was anything she needed. Her reply documents that this service was the best they owned.

"In response to 'What shall I bring you?' a pair of silver ladels for gravey tureens. I have just found out that two china ones are broken, belonging [to] my blue dining set."[2]

The ladle illustrated here is the only one to survive. Its size corresponds to the larger tureens. Two smaller "gravey tureens" survive in poor condition.

Although no bills have been found to document the purchase of this set, family tradition relates that it was particularly large, possibly two full services. Its division among family members, probably after the death of Zilpah in 1851, is confirmed by a photograph of the dining room at the Alexander Longfellow house in Portland, in which platters and plates from this service are visible in the alcove over the fireplace.[3] Another portion of the set went to daughter Mary. In 1901 when Anne Longfellow Pierce bequeathed the house to the Society, part of the service was stored in the "china closet," the small one-story ell off the family's dining room (see Chapter 3).

In his poem "Kéramos," published in 1877, Henry Longfellow noted his family's table service with the "willow pattern." He distinguished it from Italian maiolica and other ceramic masterpieces, describing it as "coarser household ware." In its role as utilitarian ware, however, Zilpah considered it her finest table service.[4]   LFS

1 *Portland Gazette* (August 2, 1813). A. W. Coysh and R. K. Henrywood, *The Dictionary of Blue and White Printed Pottery 1780–1880* (Woodbridge, Suffolk: Antique Collectors' Club, 1982), 173.
2 Zilpah Longfellow to Stephen Longfellow, February 11, 1814, Wadsworth-Longfellow Papers, LNHS.
3 Alexander W. Longfellow house, photograph of interior, SPNEA Archives.
4 Longfellow's verse reads, in part: "Nor less the coarser household wares, / The willow pattern, that we knew / In childhood, with its bridge of blue/ Leading to unknown thoroughfares; / The solitary man who stares / At the white river flowing through / Its arches, the fantastic trees / And wild perspective of the view." Joyce Butler kindly brought the poem to my attention.

80

Enoch Wood and Sons (w. 1818–1846)
Plate
Burslem, Staffordshire, England, ca. 1820
Earthenware with blue transfer-printing

Marked (in transfer-printed ribbon on bottom)
"Enoch Wood & Sons / Burslem"
Diam. 9⅞ (25.1)
Maine Historical Society; Wadsworth-Longfellow House

On December 22, 1820, the "Sons of the Pilgrims" celebrated the two hundredth anniversary of the founding of the Plymouth Colony. Plates depicting the arrival of the *Mayflower* are believed to have been commissioned and imported for the banquet held at Plymouth. Guests invited to this celebration are believed to have taken these plates home as souvenirs, though they were also available afterwards from Plymouth merchants.[1] The "Landing of the Fathers at Plymouth" plates may be the earliest known examples of ceramic objects commemorating the colonial past, a subject which Pilgrim descendant Henry W. Longfellow popularized through his poetry later in the nineteenth century.

Zilpah Longfellow's father, Peleg Wadsworth, was descended from Christopher Wadsworth and Henry Sampson, a passenger on board the *Mayflower*. Her mother, Elizabeth Bartlett, was born in Plymouth, the sixth generation of Puritan descent. This plate has survived at the Wadsworth-Longfellow house, although it is not known whether Portland family members traveled to Plymouth for the celebration.[2] The dark blue printing of this plate was very fashionable during the period and was produced in vast quantities for the American market by Enoch Wood's Burslem factory.

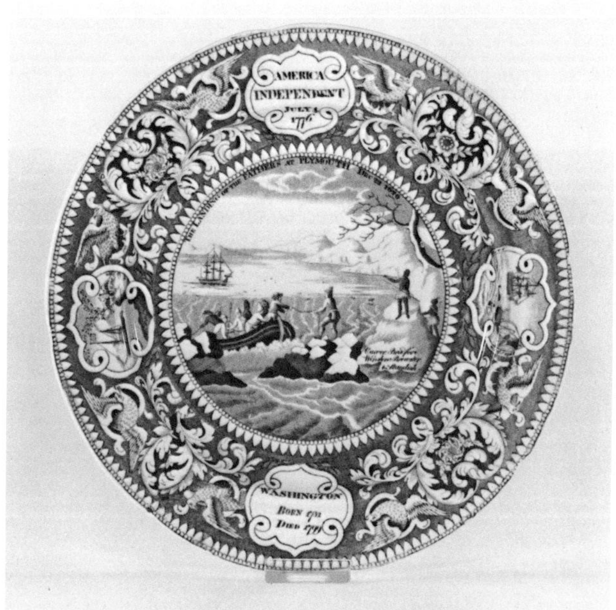

Cat. 80

A scene depicting the landing of the fathers at Plymouth was first engraved in 1800 and decorated admission cards to the anniversary dinner held that year. This engraving undoubtedly served as the source for the transfer-printed design, since in that portable form it would have been accessible to the engravers at the English potteries. Michele Felice Cornè was also inspired by the subject matter. His large oil painting *Landing of the Forefathers* was available for local inspection in 1825, when a museum in Portland exhibited it along with other paintings by Cornè.[3] LFS

1 Carl L. Crossman and Charles R. Strickland, "Early Depictions of the Landing of the Pilgrims," *Antiques* 98, no. 5 (November 1970): 777–781; see also Ellouise Baker Larsen, *American Historical Views on Staffordshire China* (1950; reprint, New York: Dover Publications, 1975), 8–9.
2 John Osborne Austin, *American Authors' Ancestry* (Providence, R.I.: E. L. Freeman Co., 1915), 60. The Portland Wadsworths were not listed on the official guest list which Lawrence Pizer of Pilgrim Hall kindly checked for me.
3 *Eastern Argus* (May 5, 1825).

81

Enoch Wood and Sons (w. 1818–1846)
Plate
Burslem, Staffordshire, England, ca. 1824
Earthenware with transfer-printing in blue
Impressed (on bottom) "Enoch Wood and Sons" around an American eagle and "Burslem"
Diam. 9 (22.9)
Old York Historical Society

Lafayette's visit to the United States was commemorated on ceramic tablewares made for the American market. Among the designs produced by the English potteries are the series depicting views of Lafayette's feudal chateau near Paris. This plate is one of the series showing "La Grange, The Residence of The Marquis Lafayette." It is transfer-printed in dark blue, a color fashionable during the 1820s. The firm of Enoch Wood and Sons is noted for its tremendous export of wares designed especially for Americans.[1]

Other potteries also produced earthenwares featuring designs celebrating Lafayette's visit. A scene entitled "Landing of General Lafayette at Castle Garden, New York, 16 August 1824," also transfer-printed in dark blue, decorates a plate made by James and Ralph Clews of Staffordshire. It represents the wares of another factory involved in the American export trade.[2]

When Henry Wadsworth Longfellow was studying in France in 1826, he sent his letter of introduction to Lafayette. The General replied that he hoped he "may Have at Lagrange our Share of your European tour." A few months later Henry wrote to his father that he had

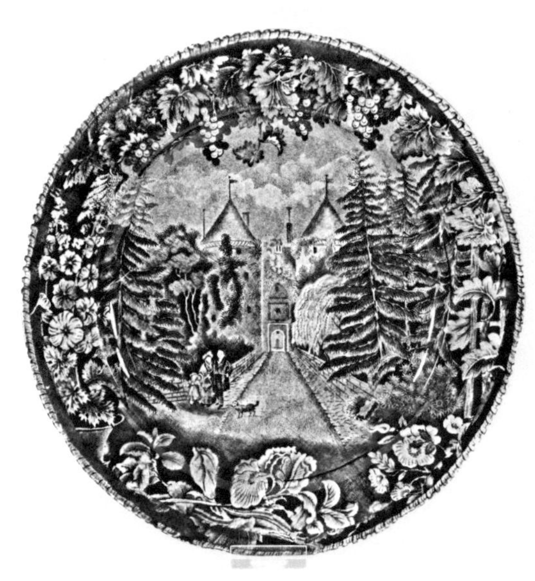

Cat. 81

met General Lafayette in the street not long ago: — he was alone — on foot — and nobody seemed to notice him particularly! What a difference from what it was in America! He gives a great dinner to all the Americans in Paris on the Anniversary of his return to France. I have not yet been at Lagrange. It is said that there are never less than thirty or forty at his table daily. So many visitors must be a great burden to him — this restrains me from going at present. He sends his regards to you.[3] LFS

1 Ellouise Baker Larsen, *American Historical Views on Staffordshire China* (1950; reprint, New York: Dover Publications, 1975), 254–255.
2 These plates are at OYHS.
3 Samuel Longfellow, ed., *Life of Henry Wadsworth Longfellow* (London: Kegan, Paul, Trench and Co., 1886), 1:89; and Hilen, *Letters*, 1:184.

82

Compotier
England or Ireland, 1780–1800
Colorless lead glass, blown and cut
H 7⅛ (18.2); W 10¼ (26.0); D 8 (20.3)
York Institute Museum
Bequest of Almira Locke McArthur, 1950

The compotier played an important role in federal-period dessert customs. While pyramids, created by stacking footed glass salvers, were used in Maine into the nineteenth century, serving preserved fruits or other sweetmeats in a footed compotier was also very fashionable. This oval form

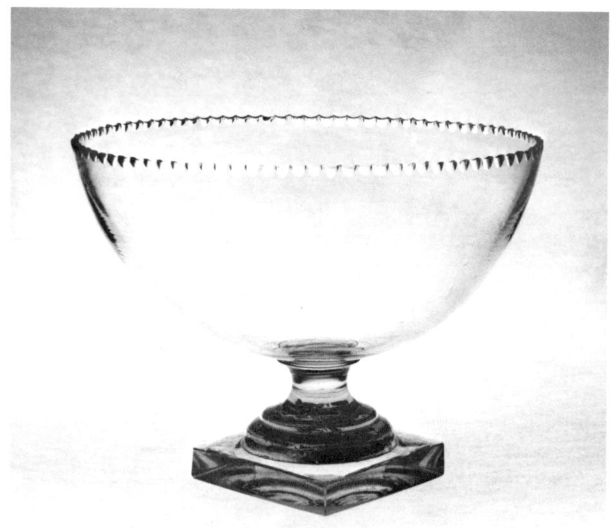

Cat. 82

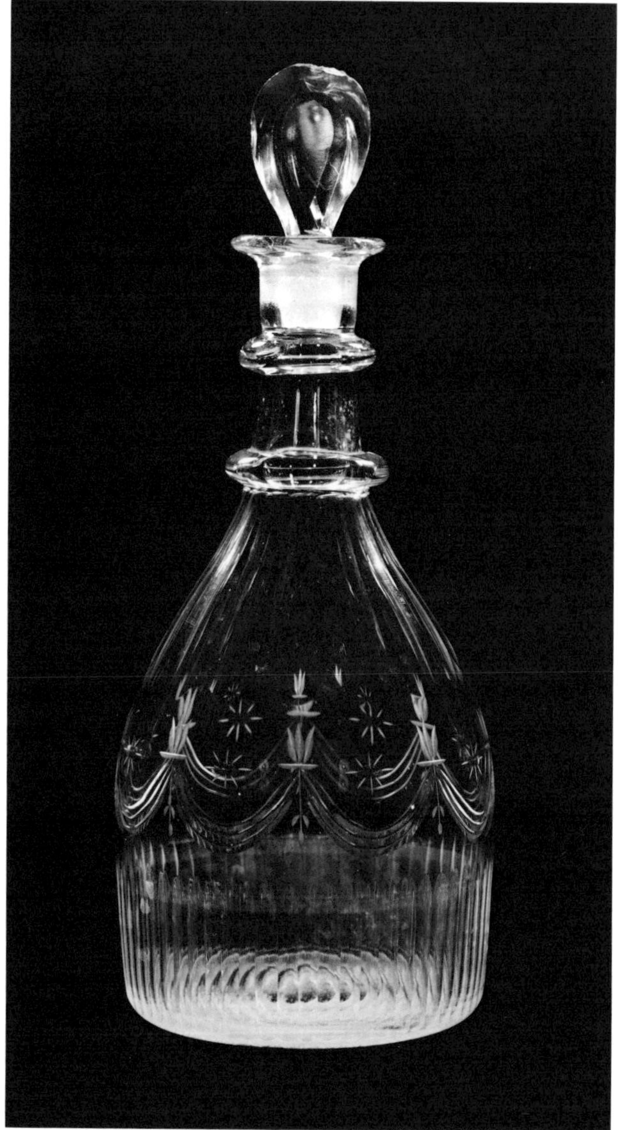

Cat. 83

with its cut scalloped rim and cut foot is typical of the period.[1] It would have received favorable attention as the centerpiece of a dessert arrangement.

Even more fashionable than pyramids or compotiers for serving desserts were epergnes with cut glass dishes set into silver frames. Cut dishes for two such epergnes survive in Ellsworth, owned in the early nineteenth century by John and Mary Cobb Black. In 1802 William King received "a glass epergne for [his] dining table" from his business associates in Liverpool. This is a rare reference to an extravagant gift sent as a "small acknowledgment of the friendship you have shewn us."[2]   LFS

1 Louise Conway Belden, *The Festive Tradition: Table Decoration and Desserts in America, 1650–1900* (New York: W.W. Norton, 1983), 59–60.
2 Hannay and Logan to William King, May 28, 1802, William King Papers, MEHS.

83

Decanter
England or Ireland, 1780–1800
Colorless lead glass, blown, cut, and engraved
H 11½ (29.2); Diam. bottom 4⅛ (10.5)
The Brick Store Museum; William E. Barry estate through Edith Cleaves Barry, 1936

Decanters were one of the most commonly used forms of tablewares. Eight of twenty-four casks of glassware that William King imported to Maine from Belfast, Ireland, were identified as decanters in quart, pint, and half-pint sizes. The remaining glass included "drams" or tumblers, cruets, mustard bottles, and salts. A box of glassware marked "K" was sent to William King from Liverpool. Probably for his personal use instead of resale, the glass included "4 cut quart Decanters."[1]

Thomas Robison's invoice for glassware included ten decanters in quart, pint, and half-pint capacity, "neat flower[e]d . . . with cutt stop[per]s."[2] One large two-quart decanter was also purchased. The quart decanter illustrated here fits the general description of the engraved decoration on Robison's glass. The shape of this decanter is sometimes noted in the period as "tapered" because of its sloping shoulders, but it was also referred to as a sugar-loaf shape, after the molded shapes of imported sugar.

This decanter appears in a watercolor drawing of the
Lord dining room rendered by William Barry in the 1880s; it
was probably among the tablewares used by the Lord or
Cleaves families. LFS

1 Invoice, Belfast, November 2, 1799, William King Papers, MEHS.
   Invoice, Thomas Holt to Logan, Lenox & Co., July 4, 1809, William
   King Papers, MEHS.
2 Invoice, Thomas Wilkinson to Phyn & Ellice, London, April 22,
   1784, Robison Papers, MEHS.

84

Keene (Marlboro Street) Glass Works (1815–1841)
Flask
Keene, New Hampshire, 1815–1841
Green glass, blown-molded
H 7⅛ (18.1); W 2¹³⁄₁₆ (7.1)
The Brick Store Museum; William E. Barry estate
through Edith Cleaves Barry

Small and portable, flasks or pocket bottles were used
extensively in eighteenth- and nineteenth-century Maine.
Pocket bottles were among the few glasswares offered for sale
by Falmouth merchant Jabez Fox in 1744. They would have
been "suitable to carry the *comfort of life* into the field," as one
New England merchant commented.[1]

New Englanders consumed tremendous quantities of
alcoholic beverages. Casks of a wide assortment of wines and
rum were among the household stores. Alcoholic drinks were
supplied for ceremonies as well as ordinary business transactions. The administrator of Daniel Moulton's York estate
recorded that he "p[ai]d Mr. Emerson for 2 quarts of wine
for the funeral." The estate of Jeremiah Littlefield, Jr., of
Wells was debited for "liquor found for the vendue."[2]

This flask bears a blown-molded decoration of a cor-
nucopia on one side and an eagle on the reverse.[3] Designs
related to prosperity and patriotism are frequently seen in
common and inexpensive items. This is a product of the
earliest New Hampshire bottle glassworks at Keene, established in 1815. That same year, Bradbury C. Atwood
advertised bottles and "an extensive assortment of flint
Glassware" for sale in his Portland shop from another New
England factory, the Boston Glass Manufactory.[4] While the
New England factories were able to capture a portion of the
market, bottles and flasks from England and Europe
remained an important trade item. LFS

1 Jabez Fox, account book, 1743–1745, MEHS. *Connecticut Courant*
   (June 21, 1790) as reprinted in Kenneth M. Wilson, *New England
   Glass and Glassmaking* (New York: Thomas Y. Crowell Co., 1972), 28.
2 YCRP; 16:148, 296.
3 A second example is in OYHS along with a flask attributed to this

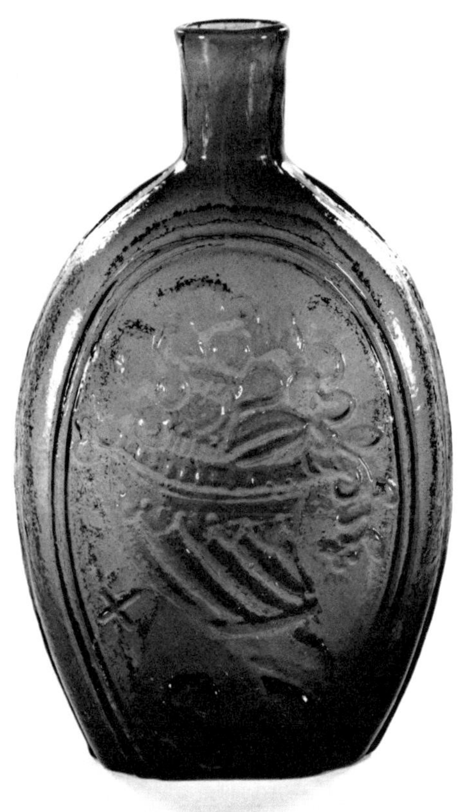

Cat. 84

factory, dated 1815–1817, with a molded sunburst decoration; see
   Wilson, *New England Glass*, 162.
4 *Eastern Argus* (November 8, 1815; August 9, 1815). In the *Portland
   Gazette* (September 21, 1819), Atwood advertised Keene factory
   window glass.

85

Case of bottles
England or Holland, 1740–1780
Fir, spruce, scotch or *red pine*; green glass, blown
H case 11¾ (29.8); W case 20 (50.8); D case 14⅞ (37.8)
Old York Historical Society

A 1793 inventory reference to "a case containing 12 bottles"
accurately describes this common domestic appurtenance.
Found in countless Maine households from the seventeenth
century, large square bottles were used to hold liquids.[1] They
were generally stored or transported in straw hampers or
baskets, or in wooden cases with partitions. The cases were
divided into nine, twelve, or sixteen units. Although apprais-

ers frequently listed the number of bottles found within a case, it is not always clear if the case was full. The overall size of the case would vary depending on the size of the bottles. Sometimes the size of the bottles was recorded, such as "2 quart case bottles." The average size of the bottles seen here is one quart.[2]

Case bottles held a variety of liquids ranging from alcohol to olive oil. In 1797 a cask of olive oil was shipped in bottles and in "4 boxes / 12 bottles in a box." Unlike other parts of the country, appraisers in Maine frequently called wooden boxes with bottles "gin cases." On his death in 1800, Mr. Hooper owned "3 empty gin cases without any bottles."[3] Although in the twentieth century the type of bottle shown here is often associated with gin, the history of its use reveals far greater versatility.

Cases and bottles were manufactured in England and northern Europe. Sometimes the latter was indicated by descriptions such as "a Dutch 12 bottle case."[4] This case retains its original hardware and an early coat of yellow paint. A shipping or consignment number, and initials, possibly those to whom it was consigned, have been carved into the upper right side of the box.

Fancy cases of bottles were also made. Colorless glass bottles, often with engraved decoration, fit into mahogany or mahogany-veneered cases, many of which were lined with wallpaper. An important Maine example is a green-painted case dated 1818 and inscribed with the name of the owner,

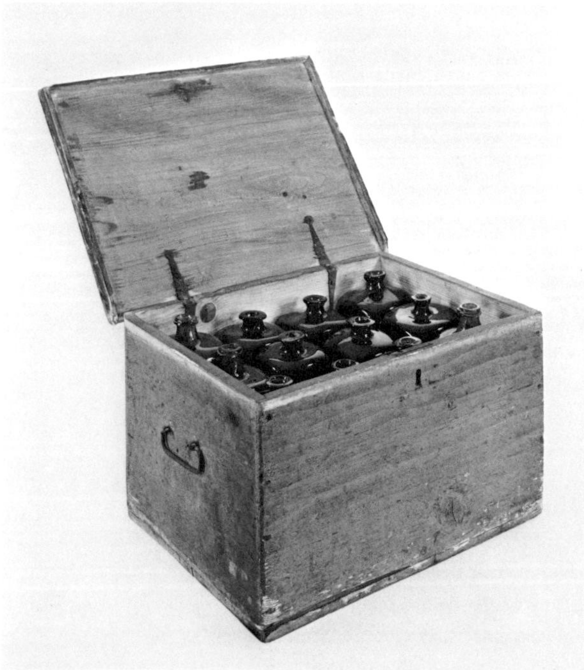

Cat. 85

Elbridge Drinkwater. It contains colorless bottles with engraved decoration. The interior retains fragments of wallpaper.[5]   L F S

1 YCRP; 16:414.
2 YCRP; 19:152.
3 Invoice, February 25, 1797, Robert Southgate Papers, New England Historic Genealogical Society, Boston. YCRP; 18:356. See 18:187 for "1 gin case with bottles."
4 YCRP; 14:204.
5 The Drinkwater case is at the Museum of Yarmouth History, Yarmouth, Maine.

86

Shaker community
Box (part of a nest)
Alfred, Gorham, or New Gloucester, Maine, 1820–1830
Maple, pine
H 3¹¹⁄₁₆ (9.4); W 10½ (26.7); D 7½ (19.1)
Maine Historical Society, Wadsworth-Longfellow House;
Gift of Mary L. Greenleaf

This is one of three oval boxes that survives in the kitchen of the Wadsworth-Longfellow house. A product of one of the Shaker communities in York or Cumberland county, its tapered maple laps are fastened with cut nails. By the 1820s virtually all the Shaker communities made oval boxes which they sold to the "world's people" or those outside their community. On April 22, 1826, Barnabas Palmer advertised in the *Kennebunk Gazette* that he had "Shaker's Wooden Ware of various kinds constantly for sale." "Boxes" were itemized along with woolen and linen wheels, dry measures, and tubs. While some boxes were painted, these examples were varnished to seal the wood.[1]

Shaker boxes are documented in probate inventories of Maine residents. "[One] Nest Shaker Boxes" in Thomas Thornton's estate was valued at sixty-five cents in 1824. At his wife's death, two Shaker boxes valued at twelve cents were in the kitchen and "4 Small Shaker boxes" were stored in a closet with baskets, pewter, and tinware.[2]

The Shaker communities in Alfred and New Gloucester, Maine, were founded during the 1790s. The Shakers at the short-lived Gorham community, founded in 1808, abutted the property of Stephen Longfellow (1776–1849). Upon their departure to both Alfred and New Gloucester in 1819, he purchased thirty acres of land from them.[3]   A A E

1 Eugene Merrick Dodd, "Functionalism in Shaker Crafts," *Antiques* 98, no. 4 (October 1970): 591. Edward Deming Andrews and Faith Andrews, *Shaker Furniture* (New York: Dover Publications, 1964), 96.
2 YCRP; 33: 274, and 58: 68, 72.
3 Deed, January 26, 1819, Longfellow Papers, MEHS.

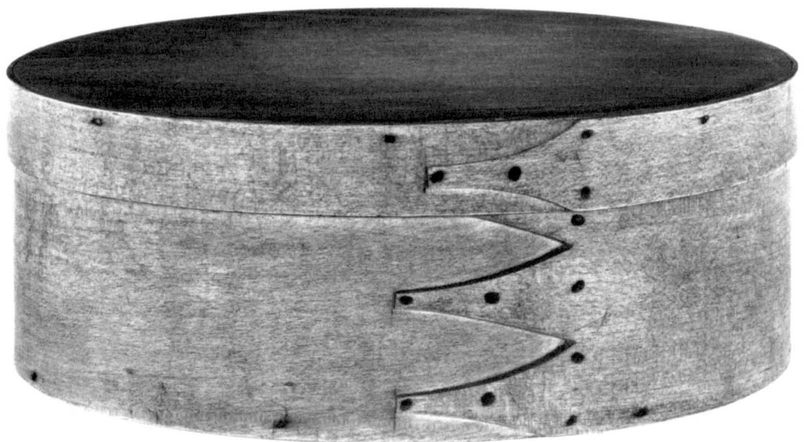

Cat. 86

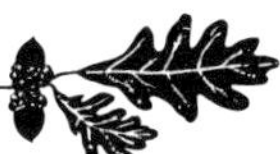

Chapter 4

Patterns of Patronage
in York and Cumberland Counties,
1784–1830

Laura Fecych Sprague

In December 1793 Thomas Robison of Portland, Charles Vaughan of Hallowell, and Samuel Sewall of York helped to found the Massachusetts Society for the Information and Advice of Foreigners Settling in our Country. These Maine residents joined others in Massachusetts, including architect Charles Bulfinch and silversmith Paul Revere, for the purpose of advising and informing "Foreigners who may come to settle among us." The membership of these prominent Maine residents in a Boston-based organization supported by leading Boston merchants and tastemakers documents not only Maine's ties to "Boston and its vicinity," but also its links to federal New England.[1]

Society members hoped to direct immigrants "in the way to be useful to themselves, and to the country which protects and befriends them."[2] The proper placement of these newcomers would improve the new nation's artistic standards and increase productivity. Members took an active role as sponsors of artisans, mechanics, and farmers coming to the new republic. The representation of Maine residents in the society provides a point of departure for the discussion of merchants, craftsmen, and artists who sought patrons in the Maine marketplace. Some of the well-to-do or well-connected Mainers were not isolated in a wasteland north of the Piscataqua River but were part of a large and flexible service economy. As energetic members of a maturing American society, they were keenly aware of the material and fashionable comforts of federal America. They were not limited in their choices when deciding on new acquisitions and were able to tap into a sophisticated northern New England network.

An examination of primary materials sheds light on how local availability and the expectations and preferences of the buyer affected patterns of patronage in Maine. Account books, invoices, newspaper advertisements, letters, and diaries reveal what objects were purchased, where they were purchased, and the extent of the interaction between availability, fashion, and cost. These sources further reveal how attitudes and decisions changed between 1784 and 1830. In the years just following the close of the Revolution, the local economy was limited and many goods could not be purchased in the coastal towns. Instead, residents sought necessary furnishings, both domestic and foreign, in urban centers. Distance to Boston or other ports was not restrictive; networks of business or social connections ensured that appropriate purchases were made. As the economy in the coastal towns grew and prospered in the early national period, inhabitants of southeastern Maine not only purchased more domestic objects to fill their larger houses but also purchased more goods from the increasing ranks of local merchants, craftsmen, and artists than ever before.

The economic prosperity that provided the means for new buildings and purchases in Cumberland and York counties attracted the attention of entrepreneurial merchants and artisans. For these businessmen, the northern district was an ideal market for the growing commercial and manufacturing interest of the old, more densely settled towns of New England.

William Shepherd, a Boston trader, explicitly referred to such a mercantilistic view in a letter to Thomas Robison in 1784:

Presuming from the variety of settlers daily removing to your part of the Country that one of my Packages of Plates & Glasses for the Table may easily find a Purchaser at Falmouth[,] I have taken the Liberty to send you a Tierce . . . hoping that some one of your Friends may be accommodated by buying it. . . . When you have found a Purchaser for that Parcel if you give me Encouragement I can send you one or two more.[3]

In this instance, Shepherd is presumed to be selling at wholesale prices English wares he had imported to Boston.

When Boston merchants acted as agents for Maine associates, they often patronized Boston craftsmen, but this was not always the case. Although in January 1784 Robert Jenkins had ordered "12 hollow back flag Bottom Chairs" from a Boston artisan, Jenkins felt no loyalty to the local craft economy nineteen months later when Thomas Robison requested windsor chairs and purchased instead those of Philadelphia manufacture. "The winsor Chairs made among us, are not worth much," he wrote, "they come exceeding Good from Philadelphia, we expect Vessels from there daily, perhaps they may bring some, as they frequently do."[4]

Just as merchants used agents to peddle their wares, craftsmen often took their own initiative to arrange a representative in the commercial sector to sell their goods, thus expanding their network to the Maine marketplace. Newspaper advertisements, merchants' accounts, and correspondence document this system, which apparently flourished for years.

In the *Eastern Argus* for November 8, 1805, upholsterer Edward Howe announced his arrival in Portland. His business included more than the sale of custom "stuffing" and "coverings"; he also retailed ready-to-purchase seating furniture (cat. 56), wallpaper, clocks, and carpets. The clocks were described as made in Boston by Simon Willard. In this way, Howe represented Willard who previously, in 1797, had come to Portland for a week to personally peddle his eight-day clocks.[5]

Howe represented other Boston craftsmen. An April 1807 entry in one of John Doggett's account books included an "Invoice of Looking glasses Left with Mr. Edward Howe at Portland to sell on Commission." Doggett, a large looking-glass manufacturer in Roxbury, sent both gilt-framed and mahogany-framed glasses. Doggett also supplied those items Howe specifically requested such as "1 Portrait frame" and "1 Embroidery frame." The frame came with "glass for d[itt]o with enameling." Satisfaction was guaranteed and the arrangement continued for nearly fifteen years. In 1820 Howe advertised that looking glasses from John Doggett's manufactory were being "sold at very reduced prices, to close the sale of the consignment."[6]

This advertisement signaled the end of Howe's role as agent for Doggett's looking glasses. Doggett entrusted his looking glasses to James Todd, a trained looking-glass maker who arrived in Portland in 1820. After the arrival of Todd, Howe then turned to other aspects of the furnishings trade. In 1827 Doggett wrote to Howe, "If you are in want of Carpeting and should favor us with an order we will put it up according to our best judgment, and when received, any pattern you may reject we will take back again." Doggett dealt with Howe in carpeting and wallpaper and channeled his looking-glass business through James Todd. Letters to Todd reveal the extent of Doggett's system. Todd placed orders for looking glasses ready made. If he ordered specific parts, such as glass plates or sizing, Doggett enclosed specific instructions for their use, indicating Doggett's concern for quality control.[7]

Other examples of this agent network are revealed through the sale of silver and furniture. Boston and Essex County silversmiths, and Boston and Philadelphia furniture makers also saw Maine as a growing market. The number and types of extant objects suggest that Massachusetts flatware and hollowware were exported to Maine in tremendous quantity. The majority of table, tea, dessert, mustard, and salt spoons, sugar tongs, and hollowware with York and Cumberland county histories was marked by Boston and Essex County silversmiths. The Boston silversmiths represented in Maine homes include Edward Watson (cat. 119), Stephen Emery (1725–1801), Paul Revere II (1735–1818), Ebenezer Moulton (cats. 113–114, 116–117), William Homes, Jr. (cat. 116), David Tyler (1760?–1804), and the partnership of Dyer and Eddy (working 1806). Salem is represented by Jabez Baldwin (1778–1819) and Robert Brookhouse (cat. 47); and Newburyport by Theophilus Bradbury (1763–1803).[8]

Salem cabinetmakers also found this trade lucrative and sent their goods northward. Cargo manifests for Salem between 1790 and 1820 reveal shipments of furniture to Kennebunk, Pepperrellborough, and Portland. Although it is not clear whether these were sent on consignment or to fill a particular family's order, the craftsmen in either case had identified the market and acted to profit by it. News of success traveled south. Boston furniture warehouses also supplied Maine's coastal towns. Adams and Libbey advertised in Saco's *Maine Palladium* "200 low priced Dining Chairs," and "400 prime Chairs" they had just received from Boston. Philadelphia chairmakers also found ready demand in the Maine market. In the late eighteenth century, they used Boston agents, such as Robert Jenkins, as middlemen to handle their transactions. By the 1820s, however, the Philadelphia craftsmen dealt directly with Portland retailers. Simon and Bavis consigned two shipments of chairs, totaling forty-two bundles, to Portland's George Clark, himself a cabinetmaker who kept "constantly on hand, a good assortment." The Philadelphia partnerships of Bailey and Willis, Rawlston and Lyman, and Stove and Todd used the same method to sell their furniture in Maine.[9]

An alternative to employing an agent was to open a branch shop. In February 1804 the peripatetic looking-glass makers Paul Cermenati and John Bernarda placed a notice in the *Portland Commercial Gazette* listing "all kinds of looking glass and picture frames, neatly made and gilt; [and] a large assortment of looking glasses of all sizes." Rather than rely on consignment or commission sales, they opened their own store on Free Street in Portland where they offered the same items as they did in Boston. Boston engraver Abel Bowen opened a shop on Middle Street in Portland, where he "solicit[ed] the Engraving of Bank Notes, Maps, Charts, Diplomas, Portraits, Bills of Exchange, Heads of Bills [and] Business and Address Cards."[10]

The growth of the economy and the lure of increasing consumer demand are documented by the number of artisans of all trades who migrated to Maine. This influx is indicated by the rise in advertising by craftsmen in the local newspapers. For example, while only Ebenezer Davis had advertised with any degree of regularity in the *Falmouth Gazette and Weekly Advertiser* during the 1780s, the number of cabinetmakers and chairmakers who advertised in Portland increased tenfold by 1810. At least fifty cabinetmakers are known to have worked in Portland between 1784 and 1823, and seventeen have been recorded in Kennebunk and Kennebunkport between 1790 and 1830. Others, previously unrecorded, continue to be identified in Saco, York, and other towns. They were ready and able to respond to concerns such as Sarah Sheppard's, who, on renting a "new dwelling" in Portland in 1812, wrote "the rooms are large & require more furniture."[11]

Significant among these immigrants were the cabinetmakers who moved from Boston and the North Shore to Maine. Benjamin Radford and his brother William learned the cabinet trade in Salem, emigrating to Portland in 1797, and Benjamin Ilsley came to Portland in 1796 from Newbury. Their training may have put them in contact with the latest furniture designs, but their abilities to produce fashionable styles had to be adapted to the demands of the local economy. It is critical to recognize that cabinetmakers trained in urban Boston or Essex County shops were capable of producing furniture in the District in the same way they had been taught in other parts of Massachusetts. The products of local craftsmen may not have always been chosen, but it was not because they were crude or poorly constructed.[12]

Manuscripts and other primary sources document the fact that the local cabinetmakers were able to compete in a brisk trade. Bills and invoices substantiate the claims of the cabinetmakers that their furniture was available in the "newest fashion" and "sold as cheap as can be bought in Boston." The prices Enoch Preble paid for some of the furniture he purchased in Boston were comparable to those charged by Portland cabinetmakers for similar forms. A mahogany bureau that John Seymour made for Nathaniel Deering in 1787 cost only 18s. less than the one Preble bought in Boston for £6.6.0. Preble's Boston bedstead at £5.16.0 cost only 12s. 5d. more than the one Deering bought from a Portland cabinetmaker.[13] With local purchases came the advantage of not having to pay for or worry about shipping.

Foremost among Maine cabinetmakers and one of the earliest to settle in Portland following the Revolution was John Seymour, who emigrated from Axminster, England, in 1784. Seymour first worked for Thomas Robison and his partners in December 1784 and his accounts reveal the extent of his joinery work. Although Seymour's income was supplied primarily by cabinetwork, it was supplemented by general construction, repair in and around local properties, and finishing work on board ships. Furniture accounted for 75 percent of his output. He was able to concentrate on furniture, in part, because his sons John and Thomas were contributing to the family income by painting walls, laying floors, and finishing ships' interiors. The refined craftsmanship and new types of furniture documented as the work of John Seymour attest to the emergence of the local market.[14]

That Thomas Robison acted as Seymour's patron during his Portland residency is shown by Robison's land transactions. In the deed dividing the property at the dissolution of one of Robison's business partnerships in January 1788, Robison retained his house at the foot of Ann Street, the distillery, and "the house now occupied by John Seymour," also identified as "lot No. 47" valued at £190 sterling (cat. 38). This property was valued at twice that recorded for other Portland cabinetmakers in 1798; the relationship with Robison directly affected Seymour's ability to succeed.[15]

Robison's patronage of Seymour and many other cabinetmakers, housewrights, and shipwrights in Portland gave him insights into the opportunities available and conditions affecting the woodworking trades. He must have been well informed when he attended a Portland meeting of the "Society of gaining information" in October 1792. This gathering is thought to have been a meeting of the Massachusetts Society for the Information and Advice of Foreigners settling in our Country. Robison's involvement with the Society may have led him to the conclusion that the talented Seymour needed a more advantageous location in which to excel. For whatever reason, Seymour moved to

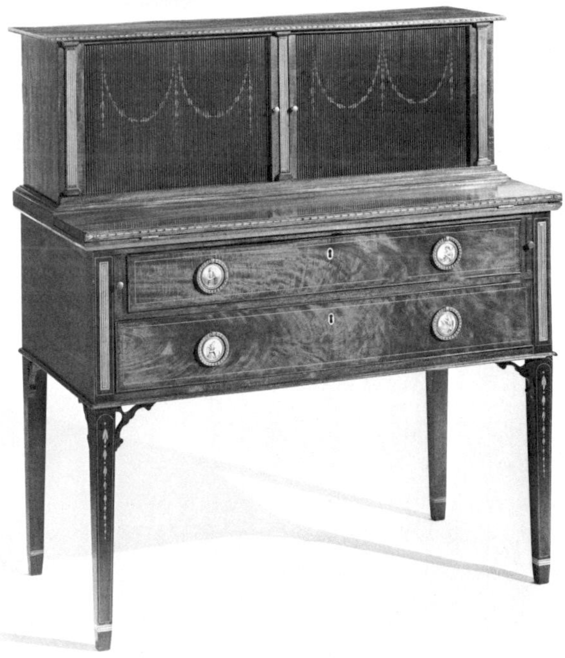

Fig. 4.1 John Seymour and Son, lady's writing desk, Boston, Massachusetts, 1796–1804. Mahogany, white pine, white elm, mahogany veneer; H 41⅜ (105.8). Courtesy, The Henry Francis du Pont Winterthur Museum.

Boston by 1796 and formed a partnership with his son Thomas. The metropolis of Boston would provide greater opportunities for the skilled cabinetmaker. Yet Seymour never completely severed his Maine connections. One of his best-known pieces of furniture was a finely built tambour desk for the Cutts-Thornton family of Saco (fig. 4.1).[16]

The career of Nathaniel Knowlton provides additional proof of the influence of the local clientele and economy upon a craftsman trained for a more sophisticated market. Knowlton, born in Eliot, Maine, came from a family with cabinetmakers among its members. Two of Knowlton's account books survive that record work he did between 1812 and 1859. Of particular note are the references to furniture Knowlton made for Benjamin Lamson, a cabinetmaker in Boston. Knowlton had moved to Boston where he worked for Lamson for two years either as an apprentice or journeyman. Between August 1812 and November 1814 Nathaniel Knowlton recorded more than 135 pieces of furniture he made for Lamson. These included 31 birch dining tables, 34 mahogany or birch Pembroke tables, 20 field bedsteads, 19 "elliptic" and 9 "straight" bureaus, as well as a "secretary and bookcase." On November 15, 1814, Knowlton "settled all accounts with Benjn. Lamson to this date" and must have returned to Eliot. When his entries began again in April 1815, his work had changed. Now for his customers in Eliot and surrounding towns, he not only made furniture but also coffins, wagons, and sleighs. He painted and repaired furniture and repaired tools. Although he may have brought an awareness of urban styles to southern Maine, the economy within his community did not support cabinetwork alone. By 1860 Knowlton referred to himself as a house carpenter and carriage maker.[17]

The local market grew steadily and with it came an influx of cabinetmakers seeking opportunity. However, these craftsmen did not always reap the benefits of patronage. Joseph Sylvester made costly mahogany furniture in Portland, but he ultimately was taken to court for debt. Others sought greener pastures elsewhere. Joseph Adams was working in Portland in 1786, but by 1789 had set up shop in Boston, the same move Seymour would make a few years later.[18] Robert Plummer was listed in the 1823 Portland city directory as a cabinetmaker. Within two years, he had a partner, John Dennett, and had left Portland. A letter written by Dennett on July 13, 1825, to his family in Kittery, Maine, reveals what became of them:

I have commenced busyness in compeny with Mr. Plumer a yong man from Portland[.] wee have taken two shops[.] he caryes on the cabinet busyness and I the turning busyness[.] wee have three journamen and two apprentaces. wee have a plenty of work and find vary good incouragement.[19]

By Maine standards, Plummer and Dennett had a good-sized furniture shop. Their business was not in any Maine town, however, but in Buenos Aires, Argentina. Large British investments there in the early years of the nineteenth century attracted the attention of merchants and craftsmen, the latter comprising the largest group of immigrants in that city in 1831. Plummer and Dennett must have been attracted by this activity just as earlier cabinetmakers had seen prospects for prosperity in the District of Maine.[20]

The ranks of silversmiths, like cabinetmakers, expanded in Maine during these years. Unlike cabinetmakers, however, they faced different challenges. Although their numbers and businesses increased, they focused on the production of such forms as spoons and buckles. There were advantages to this: it was easy to standardize production, there was constant demand, and little overhead was tied up in materials. The local silversmiths concentrated on making and retailing easily salable goods, and at the same time, had to compete with the wares of Boston and North Shore shops that flooded the market.[21] The dearth of Maine-made silver hollowware is due only in part to the competition Maine silversmiths faced. More importantly, the scarcity reflects the changing trends affecting silver manufacturing nationwide, just at the time when silversmiths began to practice in earnest in Maine.

The shift from full-service manufacturing to specialized merchandising in the silver trade occurred more in Salem and Boston, but it is illustrated in Maine by the career of Boston-born silversmith, Eleazer Wyer (cat. 117). On his 1806 arrival in Portland, Wyer described himself as a "goldsmith and jeweler," and sold tea, salt and mustard spoons, sugar tongs, jewelry, and small personal objects like thimbles and buttons. In 1814 he formed a partnership with Charles Farley, a Salem-trained silversmith (cats. 118–119). By combining forces, Wyer and Farley were able to increase their stock and capital. Together they advertised an extensive selection of goods "on hand" as well as objects they manufactured. This included a significantly larger number of forms than Wyer had advertised on his own. The partnership, however, was short-lived. After its dissolution in 1818, Wyer was forced to look to new fields. On June 5, 1821, he formed a partnership with Joseph Noble, an established Portland coppersmith and brass founder. Together, they turned their attention to the cast-iron stove industry. By 1823 Wyer no longer advertised his line of silver and fancy goods, committing instead his capital to stoves and other base-metal products. Wyer's divestiture reveals how he was forced by his economic circumstances to shift from being a craftsman carrying on a small trade to being an entrepreneur.[22]

The careers of late eighteenth and early nineteenth-century artists in Maine reveal a similar pattern of establishment. During the colonial period, some Maine residents went to Boston in search of an artist. One of the few colonial portraits to have survived the naval bombardment of Falmouth in 1775 is that of Elizabeth Ross by John Singleton Copley. In the federal period, Maine residents continued to have their portraits taken by artists in Boston and New York. Judge David Sewall of York sat for John Johnston in Boston in 1790 (fig. 4.2); other Mainers had their miniatures taken by Edward Malbone. Asa Clapp and his wife Eliza Wendell Quincy hired the highly regarded New York artist, John Wesley Jarvis, to paint their full-length portraits about 1808 while they were visiting the city (fig. 1.8). Charles Bird King painted a portrait of Stephen Longfellow while Longfellow served in the Congress in 1824 (cat. 43). Some ship captains even had the opportunity to have their portraits painted by English or foreign port painters.[23]

The demand for the work of local artists was not as great as for the products of merchants and craftsmen that filled houses. However, by the early nineteenth century, it had increased and local artists were patronized by "people who are not to be satisfied with the skill and taste of their doer of tavern-signs, Jersey-wagons, chairs and cradles," according to Portland-born John Neal, the first American art critic.[24] His observations that American artists, good and bad, were supported by increasing numbers of patrons—"critics in the furtherest off and most unheard of country villages"—continued:

Pictures of worth are beginning to be relished . . . they will soon become not merely an article for the rich, a luxury for the few, but things for everybody, familiar household furniture. Already they are quite necessary as the chief part of what goes to the embellishment of a house, and far more beautiful than most of the other furniture. If you cannot believe this, you have but to look at the multitude of portraits, wretched as they generally are, that may be found in every village of our country. You can hardly open the door of a best-room any where, without surprizing, or being surprized by, the picture of somebody, plastered to the wall and staring at you with both eyes and a bunch of flowers. And the fashion once set, even for bad pictures, there is a certain market for good ones in embryo.[25]

Itinerant painters were the first to take advantage of the market. The earliest to advertise in Portland was Josiah Flagg, who in August 1789 rented a room in the store owned by Peleg Wadsworth. A "Surgeon Dentist" by profession, he advertised "Miniature painting" in addition to his dental services. John Brewster, Jr., from Buxton, Maine, traveled to Portland, Kennebunk, and Saco to paint portraits and miniatures of local residents (cats. 28–30, 33–37, 41). He began in Portland in 1796, and later returned, hoping "that from his skill and experience in the various branches of painting, and the reasonableness of his prices, that those who favor him with their custom will find him worthy of the patronage of the public." While in Portland in 1806, he was commissioned to paint the portrait of Eliphalet Smith, a dry-goods merchant. Smith's wife recorded this activity in her diary as well as Brewster's social visits: "Judge Frothingham & Mr. Brewster passed the Evening with us. Mr. B. has this day finished a Miniature likeness of my good husband. I

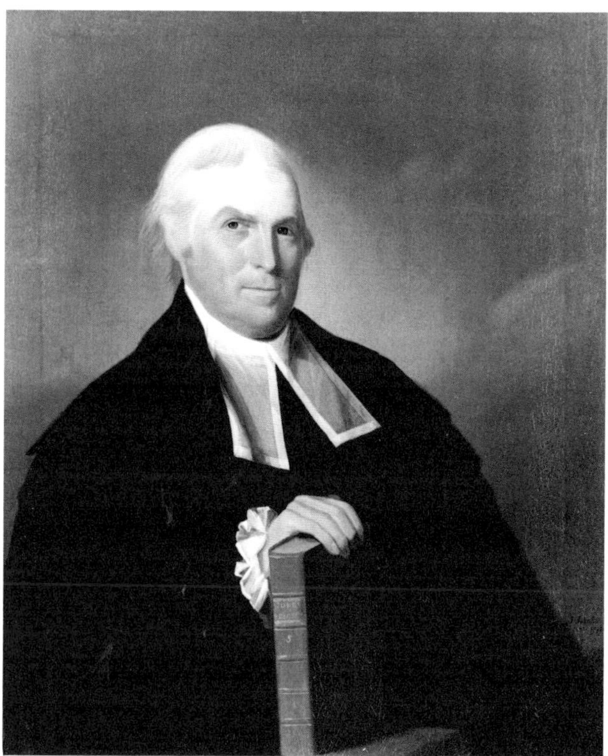

Fig. 4.2 John Johnston, *Judge David Sewall*, Boston, Massachusetts, ca. 1790. Oil on canvas; H 35⅜ (89.9), W 28⅞ (73.3). Bowdoin College Museum of Art.

could never prevail on him to sit for it before." Almost two weeks later, John Brewster dined with the family again. A number of other miniaturists followed these artists, including Nathaniel Hancock, John Roberts (cat. 42), and Anthony Meucci.[26]

Heraldic and decorative painters in Boston and Newburyport received the attention of Maine patrons. These artists worked in many media; they painted signs, militia company banners (cat. 154), and coats of arms (cats. 73–74). Members of the Gore family of Boston, especially John Gore (1718–1796) and his son Samuel (1750/51– 1831), were leading decorative painters in New England. In 1783 while attending school in Boston, Elizabeth Cutts sought Samuel Gore's advice when planning to embroider a coat of arms for her parents (cat. 142). In 1799, when young ladies of Portland commissioned a banner for the Portland Federal Volunteers, they specified Samuel Gore or an artist of better skill (cat. 154 and Chapter 5).

On June 10, 1811, the *Portland Gazette and Maine Advertiser* reported on the standard presented by the "Ladies of Portland" to the Portland Rifle Company. The account credited John Ritto Penniman (1782–1841) of Boston as the artist who "in paintings of this particular kind, stands unrivaled." In its design and execution, "this stand of

Colours is pronounced by adequate judges, to be superior to any thing of the kind ever exhibited in this state." A celebrated decorative painter, Penniman was versatile in many media. Although his ambition may have been to become an easel painter, he relied on a steady and wide range of ornamental commissions for his income. Penniman continued to cast an eye to the Maine market when, in 1822, he advertised in Portland's *Eastern Argus*.[27]

Penniman's business in Maine must have captured the attention of Charles Codman (1800–1842), who worked for Penniman. Within a year of establishing a portrait and decorative painting business with his brother William P. Codman in Boston, Charles quit that city and settled in Portland. In October 1822 he advertised in the *Eastern Argus* the modest tasks of lettering, painting, and enameling on glass for timepieces, looking glasses, and ladies' needlework. Like Penniman, Codman also decorated signs, banners, fireboards, window shades, and other objects, filling the local need for a competent painter.[28]

His enterprises, however, were not confined to the decorative painting business. He placed a notice in the *Portland Advertiser* that he executed landscapes in oils and watercolors, and views of gentlemen's seats. Following the tradition of many great artists, Codman proposed opening a school "for the instruction of young ladies and gentlemen in the art of drawing, painting and landscapes &c on wood,

glass or canvas."[29] John Neal credited him as "one of our earliest and finest land-scape painters," landscape being a subject that American artists were just beginning to address (cat. 39). Neal recollected some of Codman's other painting and the circumstances surrounding his first meeting with Codman:

While at table [at Portland's Elm Tavern], my attention was directed to what seemed the strangest paper-hangings I had ever seen, — a forest of large trees, reaching from the floor to the ceiling, and crowded with a luxuriant undergrowth. Upon further examination, I found these paper-hangings to be painted in oil; and learned, upon inquiry, that they were the work of a sign-painter. They were masterly, and I lost no time in hunting the artist up. I found him in the midst of his workshop, half buried in signs, banners, fire-buckets, and all sorts of trumpery.[30]

Neal ordered "a picture, which [Codman] spoiled by overdoing," and placed orders on behalf of other Portlanders. As Codman's style improved, Neal remarked to Codman that "I thought he must have begun life with some painter of tea-trays, or pottery, or clock-faces. He [Codman] laughed, and acknowledged that he had been apprenticed to Willard, the clock-maker of Roxbury, where he did paint nothing but clock-faces; and that after this, he worked for Penniman, the sign-painter of Boston."[31] Once discovered by Neal, who encouraged local patrons, Codman carried on a highly successful career. Many works signed by or otherwise

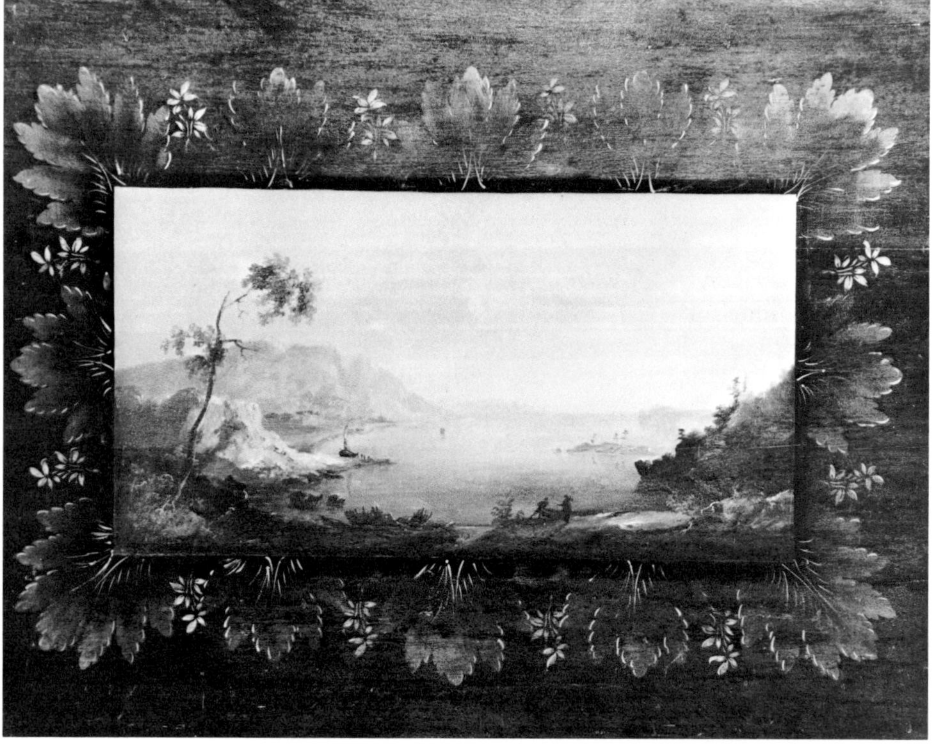

Fig. 4.3 Attributed to Charles Codman, fireboard with scene of East Cove, Portland, Maine, 1825–1830. Oil on panel; H 34½ (87.6), W 44 (111.8). Courtesy, Fruitlands Museum, Harvard, Mass.

attributed to him include landscapes painted in oils on canvas, panels for overmantels and fireboards (fig. 4.3), and decorative wall murals.[32]

Like artists, engravers also benefited from Maine patrons. The market for decorative engravings was filled by imports from other American cities and from abroad; this was not the market that Portland engravers sought (cats. 75–78). They looked instead to the job printing of bank notes, maps, charts, bookplates, bill heads, and merchants' and manufacturers' cards that would have been specifically ordered. Although it is not known if James Akin ever came to Maine, this Newburyport engraver found customers at a distance in Portland between 1800 and 1807 (cat. 9). Danforth Newcomb was the first engraver known to have settled in Portland. He arrived in 1820, the year Portland became the capital of the new state of Maine. A Quincy, Massachusetts, native, Newcomb died prematurely a little over a year after his arrival. His stock and tools were then purchased by Abel Bowen, a successful Boston engraver.[33] The activities of Abel Bowen in Portland parallel those of other Boston craftsmen. He advertised in the papers, but actually used his brother Sidney Bowen to oversee day-to-day operations.

Abel must have viewed the opportunity to take over Danforth Newcomb's shop as a way — with his brother's assistance — to increase his business. Shortly after Bowen's arrival, an interested party welcomed him to Portland and reported in the *Eastern Argus*: "I understand he contemplates publishing an Engraving, giving a view of this town, taken by a Camera Obscura, which, if well executed, would make a very handsome print; and as a friend to the arts, I sincerely wish he may receive sufficient encouragement to warrant the undertaking." It is not known if this print was ever executed, but Bowen did engrave *A New and Correct Plan of Portland Maine* in 1823 for a city directory. Success, however, was short-lived; Bowen's last advertisement was published in February 1823. The void his departure created was filled by Orramel Hinckley Throop, yet another Boston engraver who saw the Maine market as a good opportunity. He advertised many of the same services that Bowen had offered (cat. 128).[34]

Still, the paucity of known works of Portland engravers perhaps reflects more the nature of their work than the competition in the trade. While maps, charts, certificates, and diplomas may have been signed by the engraver, many of the commodities the engravers advertised, such as bank notes and business cards, were of simple design and did not warrant a signature. Given the skill and background of the engravers, the quality of the Portland-engraved works would be indistinguishable from those made in Boston. Well-established Mainers with factors in urban ports could just as easily purchase the printed materials they required outside of the District or state.

The following case studies of the acquisitions made by Maine residents discuss in detail the circumstances affecting their choices and decisions. Americans who made their homes in York and Cumberland counties, in a District of Massachusetts and later the state of Maine, were not mired in a backwater. Certain people made purchases far afield, based on their business and social contacts. For others, the local supply became an important source as the range and quality of goods increased.

The correspondence and business papers of Thomas Robison (1742–1806) provide valuable documentation of the acquisitions made by one merchant for a newly built mansion house on the banks of the Fore River. Robison often relied on his business and social network in London and Boston. His economic circumstances and those of his community played a major role in the decisions he made when purchasing objects for his house.

In 1783, when Robison emigrated from Ontario, Canada, Portland was just beginning to recover from the destruction of the 1775 British naval bombardment that destroyed the eighteenth-century town. The damage and eight-year hiatus in trade caused by the war restricted the local supply of household goods and forced him, initially, to look elsewhere. Robison took advantage of his friendships and long-standing credit with London merchants, and ordered an assortment of English furniture, silver, engravings, and glass and ceramic tablewares.[35]

By 1784 his associations with Boston merchants provided additional sources of supply. In January Robison sent to Boston for furniture, textiles, and a wide range of household furnishings. Correspondence between Robison and Robert Jenkins, his Boston agent, shows that this method was not always convenient or satisfactory. Chairs ordered in January took three months to make because "the weather has been so uncommon severe, that the person could not work on them, the weather has moderated, and he has near finish'd them, but am afraid will not be in time to go this Trip, unless the winds should keep the vessel here." A high-post bedstead which arrived on board a coastal schooner was "verymuch dirtied!" despite being wrapped for shipment.[36]

Soon, however, Robison found desirable goods in the local Portland shops. By the end of 1784 Robison had begun to purchase furniture from the first of several cabinetmakers who had moved to Portland after the close of the war in 1783. Seven cabinetmakers are known to have made furniture for Robison between 1784 and 1796: John Seymour and his two sons, John, Jr., and Thomas; Alexander Barr; Ebenezer Davis; Joseph Adams; and Joseph Sylvester. Robison's needs ranged from a desk and bookcase by Seymour to a wooden safe constructed by Davis. Both Adams and Sylvester were engaged to provide sets of mahogany chairs. These cabinetmakers also fashioned small domestic and personal items ranging from fireboards and clothes horses to fishing rods and rolling pins.[37]

The purchasing patterns of Portland lawyer Stephen Longfellow demonstrate a preference for Portland goods in the early nineteenth century. He found it convenient to patronize local cabinetmakers such as Benjamin Radford and his brothers. Shortly after Stephen married Zilpah Wadsworth in 1804, the couple acquired many furnishings even though they did not have their own permanent residence until October 1807, when they moved to her family's home on Congress Street. In 1805 Radford billed Longfellow for thirteen articles of furniture, including a mahogany bureau at $20 (cat. 53), a mahogany field bedstead at $15, and a cradle valued at $4. These are comparable to prices charged in Boston for similar forms.[38]

The Longfellows, however, were not restricted solely to local products. When Stephen was attending the Legislature in Boston in 1814, his wife asked that he bring home a new pair of silver ladles for her gravy tureens (see cat. 79). On a trip to Albany in 1822, Zilpah had a dress made in New York (cat. 170). While serving as a member of Congress in 1824, Stephen had opportunities to make purchases in Washington. In addition to convincing Stephen to have his portrait taken by Charles Bird King, Zilpah and her daughters also requested "a new parlor carpet and a new hearth rug" that could be sent from New York.[39]

Other prominent Maine families made little use of the local shops. Enoch Preble commanded ships along the coastal and transatlantic trade routes, and often found it convenient to purchase his furnishings while waiting in ports for cargo. While in Liverpool in 1801 and London in 1804, Preble had his portrait taken, and acquired silver hollowware and small household and personal possessions. These objects, typical of the purchases made by other travelers to England, are the type of goods and services which local artisans in Portland may not have been able to offer when Enoch wanted to buy them. For major pieces of furniture, however, Preble turned to American sources and filled his new house with furniture acquired in Boston during October 1800. He purchased costly mahogany furniture including a bedstead (£5.16.0), a secretary (£6.12.0), a bureau (£6.6.0), and a sideboard (£18). Four chairs were purchased for £4.16.0 "at auction," another popular means of purchase (see Chapter 1).[40]

In 1803 Richard Southgate of Scarborough began the construction of a new house near Dunstan Corner. His daughter Eliza had recently married Walter Bowne and was residing in New York City. Despite her distance, Eliza took an interest in her family's new house. On July 8 her comments implied her role in its furnishing: "How comes on the new house? . . . If you choose to send so far, I will purchase any kind of furnishing you wish, perhaps cheaper and better than you can get elsewhere."[41] Two years later Eliza's younger sister Octavia, in preparation for her marriage to William Browne, sent Eliza a detailed list of furniture, silver,

and linens she would like. Eliza replied, "Tis very lucky there is so direct an opportunity to Scarborough; we shall endeavor to send as many things as possible." Although sick in bed, Eliza sent her husband to the shops, assuring her sister, "my husband has both a great deal of taste and judgment in those things, and makes better bargains than I do." Octavia purchased both ready-made goods and custom-made silver, for Eliza reported that many of the items could be "procured before the vessel sails, but 'twill be impossible to get any *plate made* to send for several weeks."[42]

Eliza's comments concerning this silver order also demonstrate how a distant customer was able to initiate and control the design process. Printed references were the key. Eliza reported: "We made a sketch of the articles you wished . . . which cannot be very incorrect, as I took them all from our own furniture book," probably a pattern book. Octavia meant to have the silver engraved, but she "mentioned nothing of the Cypher on the Plate: O[ctavia]. S[outhgate]. or B[rowne].—or your crest, or William's crest, if you can find them out,—I suppose we could here,—or what?" Four days later, Eliza wrote: "Yesterday the Silversmith came for instructions respecting the plate, and bro't patterns for me to look at. . . . The man is to send me some patterns to look at which he thinks are similar to your description." In the meantime, Eliza purchased one "plated Castor best kind" for $12, and a "plated Cake Basket silver rims" for $18, although she does not identify the source. She wrote: "The Cake Basket is very cheap, $2 cheaper than mine, and rather handsomer I think." A bill in the Southgate papers documents the purchase of "1 Silver Sugar Dish & Milk Pot—Engraved with Ornaments & Cyphers" for £23.10.0 and "1 Silver Soup Ladle" for £5.0.6. John and Peter Targee of New York billed Walter Bowne "for the Order of S[outhgate]" in April 1806. Octavia asked for a barrel-shaped tea urn, but the Bownes had difficulty, even in New York, procuring one.[43]

A letter written in 1824 by Zadoc Long of Buckfield reveals an attitude toward acquisition quite different from that held by the Longfellows or Southgates. Writing to his fiancée Julia Davis, Long explained his personal preferences for local rather than imported wares:

Shall go to Boston in June, and will make such purchases as you shall direct. I have no right to control you as to the quantity or quality of furniture to be provided for housekeeping as it will be at your expense. I would however suggest that, as we don't own a house, it would be well to expend less for furniture now than at some future time if we live and prosper. You mentioned that you would like to have the Cabinet work made at Portland or Boston. Pardon me for offering an opinion that it would be better to get it done here by Mr. Jewett for a variety of reasons. His work is as elegant as I think you will wish to see in the house we shall occupy, and perhaps as elegant as you expect to get elsewhere. Considerable expense can be saved by the easy manner in which we can pay him; but the principal reason is that I would avoid any cause of exciting envy in our neighbors. I would not have them perceive, so far as it can be well avoided, that we are distinguished above them in our style of living.[44]

While some Maine citizens consciously worked at being distinguished and living "snug handsomely," others, like Long, preferred modesty.[45] The cabinetwork of James Jewett may have been "as elegant as you expect to get elsewhere," but Long revealed the inextricable nature of established buying patterns, or the strong will of his wife, when, four months later, he wrote to Julia:

I suppose you expected to receive the things which I bought for you in Boston before now. . . . I hope you will be satisfied with them. If you dislike any object return it to me and I can sell it at a profit here.[46]

He enclosed a transcript of the bill for $142.34 worth of personal and domestic possessions he had purchased. They included: "1 Doz Silver Tea Spoons" costing $8.50, "½ Doz. Silver Tea Spoons" at $2.25, and "⅓ Doz Silver Table Spoons" at $10. He also bought twenty-five yards of English carpeting for $31.25, "1 Hearth Rug" for $3.25, and "2 Plated Candle Sticks" for $2. On occasion, one's preferences could not entirely overcome the deep-rooted economic and social links to Boston that pervaded Maine's society.

Despite depressed years, the federal era was marked by stable government and a flourishing economy, an environment which nurtured the craft industry. Prosperity was accompanied by a general strengthening of these "various Branches" and there was a shift in the very method by which craftsmen did business. Early in the federal period, many craftsmen benefited by the patronage of powerful merchants and other leaders of society. As the nineteenth century progressed, more and more craftsmen sought success by aiming their products at a wide marketplace as demand required. The 1815 founding of the Maine Charitable Mechanic Association, a tradesmen's organization, was a sign of the increasingly businesslike approach of craftsmen. Among the chief purposes of the group was to relieve "the distresses of unfortunate mechanics and their families," and "to promote inventions and improvements in the Mechanic Arts." By 1827 its role and powers had been extended to support and enlarge a library for apprentices, another attempt to promote their work (cat. 124).[47]

Maine cabinetmakers, silversmiths, and other artisans were no longer satisfied to leave their social and economic welfare in the hands of wealthy merchants like those who organized Boston's Immigrants Society in 1793. Instead, they moved to control their own livelihoods — "to merit a share of patronage from a generous Public."[48] Despite continual competition from goods imported from domestic and foreign ports, Maine artists and craftsmen successfully promoted their wares, attracted customers, and conducted business in an increasingly entrepreneurial fashion.

I am indebted to Edward S. Cooke, Jr., for his helpful insights and generous assistance in the preparation of this essay.

1 "Society for the Information and Advice of Immigrants," Massachusetts Society for the Information and Advice of Foreigners Settling in our Country, broadside, Boston, December 30, 1793, Codman Family Manuscript Collection, SPNEA (hereafter cited as "Massachusetts Society for Information"); "Information for Immigrants to the New England States," Immigrants Society, broadside, Boston, October 27, 1795, Massachusetts Historical Society, Boston.

2 Immigrants Society, broadside, October 27, 1795, Massachusetts Historical Society.

3 William Shepherd to Thomas Robison, August 18, 1784, Robison Papers, MEHS.

4 Robert Jenkins to Thomas Robison, January 26, 1784; and Robert Jenkins to Robison, Edgar, and Read, September 5, 1785, Robison Papers, MEHS.

5 *Eastern Argus* (November 8, 1805); *Eastern Herald* (Portland) (October 21, 1797). Martha Gandy Fales kindly brought the Willard reference to my attention.

6 John Doggett, account book, April 17, 1807, and August 25, 1808 (photocopy), Joseph Downs Manuscript and Microfilm Collection, Winterthur Museum Library. I am indebted to Martha Gandy Fales for bringing this source to my attention. *Eastern Argus* (June 30, 1820).

7 John Doggett and Co. to Edward Howe, letter book, December 17, 1827; for a reference to his careful instructions, see John Doggett and Co. to James Todd, letter book, November 22, 1828, Downs Collection, Winterthur Museum Library.

8 This conclusion is based on the silver in the collections discussed in this catalogue. Spoons by Emery are at YIS; Paul Revere at MEHS; and Dyer and Eddy, Tyler, Baldwin, and Bradbury at BSM.

9 The Salem manifests are cited in Margaret Burke Clunie, "Salem Federal Furniture" (M.A. thesis, University of Delaware, 1976), 303; *Maine Palladium* (Saco) (June 6, 1827), Maine craftsmen files, Maine State Museum, Augusta, courtesy Edwin C. Churchill; consignments for Philadelphia furniture are cited in Kathleen Catalano, "Cabinetmaking in Philadelphia," *American Furniture and Its Makers: Winterthur Portfolio 13*, ed. Ian M. G. Quimby (Chicago: University of Chicago Press for the Henry Francis du Pont Winterthur Museum, 1979), 83. Catalano kindly identified which craftsmen sent these shipments to Portland.

10 *Portland Commercial Gazette* (February 15, 1804); for the Bowen notice, see *Eastern Argus* (September 17, 1822), as cited in Shettleworth, "Engravers," 60–61.

11 For Ebenezer Davis's advertisement, see Shettleworth, "Check List." The cabinetmakers and chairmakers have been identified through two 1823 Portland city directories; Shettleworth, "Check List"; Robison Papers, MEHS; and craftsmen files, BSM. Sarah Sheppard to John Sheppard, September 21, 1812, Sheppard Family Papers, New England Historic Genealogical Society, Boston (hereafter NEHGS). Laurel Ulrich kindly brought the Sheppard letter to my attention.

12 Shettleworth, "Portland Cabinetmakers," 285–289; Martha Gandy Fales, "Benjamin Ilsley, Cabinetmaker in Federal Portland," *Antiques* 105, no. 5 (May 1974): 1066–1067.

13 For these references and others, see Shettleworth, "Check List"; Enoch Preble, expense book, 1800–1804, MEHS; and Deering, account book, 1787–1793, 30, MEHS.

14 For Seymour's Portland work, see Sprague, "John Seymour."

15 CCRD; 17:12–14; "Massachusetts and Maine Direct Tax Census of 1798" (microfilm, NEHGS).

16 Montgomery, *American Furniture*, 229. Many bills of and accounts with cabinetmakers, housewrights, and shipwrights can be found in the Robison Papers, MEHS; Willis, *Journals*, 367; "Massachusetts Society for Information," broadside; Mabel M. Swan, "John Seymour and Son, Cabinetmakers," *Antiques* 32, no. 4 (October 1937): 176–180.

17 Charles Henry Wright, *The History and Genealogy of the Knowltons of*

England and America (New York: Knickerbocker Press, 1897), 70, 282–283; Bentley, *Diary*, 1:121, 157, 245; John E. Frost kindly confirmed the identification of the Knowlton family members in Eliot; Nathaniel Knowlton, account books, 1812–1859, 2 vols., MEHS. For more on Benjamin Lamson, see E. Page Talbott, "The Furniture Industry in Boston, 1810–1835" (M.A. thesis, University of Delaware, 1974), 66, 193; YCRD; 269:19.

18 Sylvester's mahogany chairs are recorded in account book, 1791–1801, May 23, 1793, Robison Papers, MEHS; and his debt in Records of the Cumberland County Court of Common Pleas, 5: 109, 118, 167, and 270, Maine State Archives; other cabinetmakers jailed for debt are recorded in Naomi Payton-Glixman, comp., "Incarcerated Craftsmen, extracted from the Cumberland County Sheriff's Calendar of Prisoners 1795–1825" (typescript, MEHS). Joseph Adams worked for Thomas Robison; see below and Ann Smith Lainhart, ed., "John Haven Dexter and the 1789 Boston City Directory," *New England Historical and Genealogical Register* 140 (January 1986): 30, where Adams was listed as a "cabinet and Windsor chair-maker."

19 John Dennett to William Dennett, July 13, 1825, Dennett Family Papers, Manuscripts and Archives Division, New York Public Library.

20 Henry Stanley Ferns, *Britain and Argentina in the Nineteenth Century* (Oxford: Clarendon Press, 1960), 76.

21 For the climate for Maine silversmiths during this period, see Churchill, "Crafts in Transition"; cited on 316–317 is an 1833 report submitted to the U. S. House of Representatives documenting the importance of the Maine market for Boston silversmiths.

22 For discussions of the shift within the silver craft and related fields, see the case study by Philip Zea, "Clockmaking and Society at the River and the Bay: Jedidiah and Jabez Baldwin, 1790–1820," in Peter Benes, ed., *The Bay and the River: 1600–1900* (Boston, Mass.: Boston University, 1982), 43–59; and Gerald W. R. Ward, "Silver and Society in Salem, Massachusetts, 1630–1820" (Ph.D. diss., Boston University, 1984). Churchill, "Crafts in Transition," 301.

23 William D. Barry, Earle G. Shettleworth, Jr., and Philip Grime have all been involved in the research of Maine artists. The Ross portrait is illustrated in Mellon and Wilder, *Maine and Its Role in American Art*, 26; Marvin S. Sadik, *Colonial and Federal Portraits at Bowdoin College* (Brunswick, Me.: Bowdoin College, 1966), 110–112. "Mr. and Mrs. Preble" sat for Malbone in Boston. Although a Malbone miniature of Edward Preble has not been identified, those of his wife Mary Deering Preble and brother Eben Preble painted by Malbone survive. He also painted the miniatures of Eliza Southgate Bowne and her husband (1803), and Mr. and Mrs. Robert Hallowell Gardiner (1805); see Ruel Pardee Tolman, *The Life and Works of Edward Green Malbone 1777–1807* (New York: New-York Historical Society, 1958), 145–146, 172–173, 233–234. The miniature of Mary Deering Preble is in the collection of the United States Naval Academy Museum, Annapolis. For portraits of Maine sea captains taken in foreign ports, see those of James Fairfield, BSM; Joseph McLellan, Portland Museum of Art; and Francis Rittal, Maine Maritime Museum.

24 Dickson, "Observations," 42.

25 Dickson, "Observations," 42.

26 *Cumberland Gazette* (August 28, 1789); *Portland Gazette* (August 23, 1805); Ann Smith, diary, January 1, 12, 1806, MEHS; William D. Barry provided the reference to Nathaniel Hancock; see *Portland Gazette* (August 11, 1800). For other artists in Portland, see Jordan Newspaper Index, Portland Public Library.

27 *Eastern Argus* (July 9, 1822); Carol Damon Andrews, "John Ritto Penniman (1782–1841), an Ingenious New England Artist," *Antiques* 120, no. 1 (July 1981): 147–170. I am indebted to William D. Barry who kindly shared his research on Penniman in Portland.

28 Dickson, "Observations," 91; *Eastern Argus* (October 22, 1822), as cited in Cooney, "Ornamental Painting in Boston," 27–28.

29 *Portland Advertiser* (November 25, 1823) and *Eastern Argus* (December 10, 1822), as cited in Cooney, "Ornamental Painting in Boston," 50.

30 Dickson, "Observations," 90–91.

31 Dickson, "Observations," 91.

32 Other examples of Codman's work are in the collection of Portland Museum of Art; Fruitlands Museum, Harvard, Mass.; Museum of Art, Rhode Island School of Design, Providence; and the Brooklyn Museum. His landscape murals are recorded in the Frost house by Lovejoy, *This was Stroudwater*, 68.

33 Shettleworth, "Engravers," 59–60.

34 The engraved plan appears in Nathaniel G. Jewett, *The Portland City Directory and Register* (Portland, Me.: Todd & Smith, 1823); see Shettleworth, "Engravers," 60–62.

35 Silver invoice, John Sterling to Thomas Robison, London, March 26, 1781; furniture invoice, Nicholas Phene to Mr. Pollard on account Thomas Robison, London, April 10, 1783; engravings invoice, Robert Wilkinson to Phyn and Ellice on account Robison and Edgar, London, April 24, 1784; and tablewares invoice, Thomas Wilkinson to Phyn and Ellice on account of Robison and Edgar, London, April 22, 1784; Robison Papers, MEHS.

36 Invoice, Boston, January 22, 1784; Robert Jenkins to Thomas Robison, March 11, 1784; and Thomas Robison to Robert Jenkins, [February] 1784; Robison Papers, MEHS.

37 In the Robison Papers there are numerous references to work by each of the cabinetmakers named. For examples see bill, John Seymour to Thomas Robison, December 24, 1784; Alexander Barr account, account book, 1787–1789, 36. His work ranged from 40′ by 20′ house frames for the West Indies trade for £ 12 to eight mahogany chairs of equal value. Bill, Ebenezer Davis to Thomas Robison, 1790; bill, Joseph Adams to Thomas Robison, June 18, 1789; Joseph Sylvester account, account book, 1791–1801, May 23, 1793, MEHS.

38 Bill, Benjamin Radford to Stephen Longfellow, January 1805, Longfellow Papers, MEHS. For comparison prices, see Enoch Preble, expense book, 1801–1804, MEHS.

39 Zilpah Longfellow to Stephen Longfellow, May 15, 1824, Wadsworth-Longfellow Papers, LNHS.

40 Enoch Preble, expense book, 1801–1804, MEHS. Daniel Walker Lord's journal at MEHS contains references to furniture purchased in Boston in 1829 when he went with his wife and sisters Betsey and Susan "for the purpose of purchasing Betsey's furniture" prior to her marriage.

41 Bowne, *A Girl's Life*, 165.

42 Bowne, *A Girl's Life*, 203.

43 Bowne, *A Girl's Life*, 203–206; bill, John and Peter Targee to Walter Bowne, April 5, 1806, Southgate Papers, NEHGS.

44 Pierce Long, ed., *From the Journal of Zadoc Long, 1800–1873* (Caldwell, Idaho: Caxton Printers, Ltd., 1943), 71.

45 Stephen Decatur, Jr., to Edward Preble, May 6, 1806, Edward Preble Papers, Manuscript Division, Library of Congress.

46 Long, *Zadoc Long*, 72–73.

47 *Constitution of the Maine Charitable Mechanic Association* (Portland, Me.: Bryant Press, 1965), 3–4.

48 Samuel Richard advertisement, *Eastern Argus* (November 10, 1803), as cited in Shettleworth, "Check List."

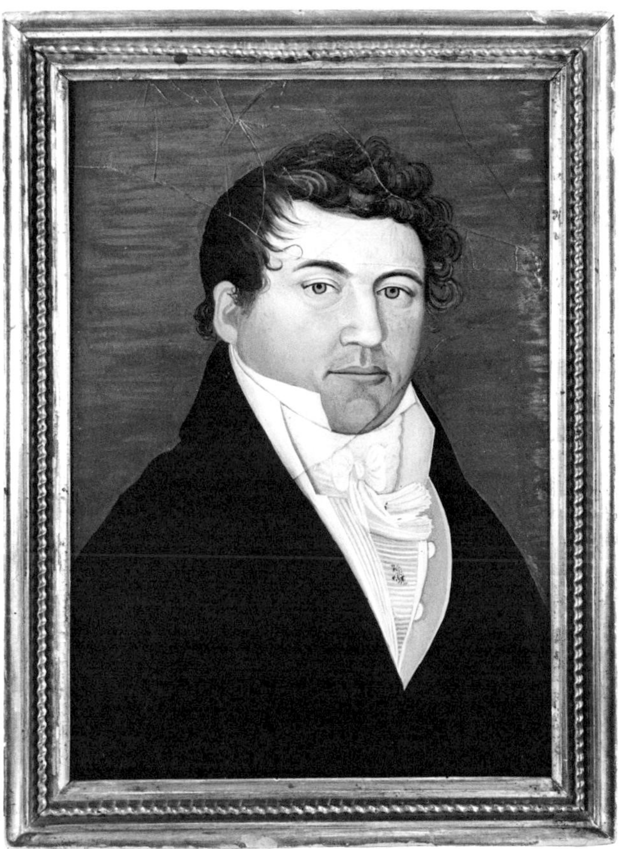

Cat. 87

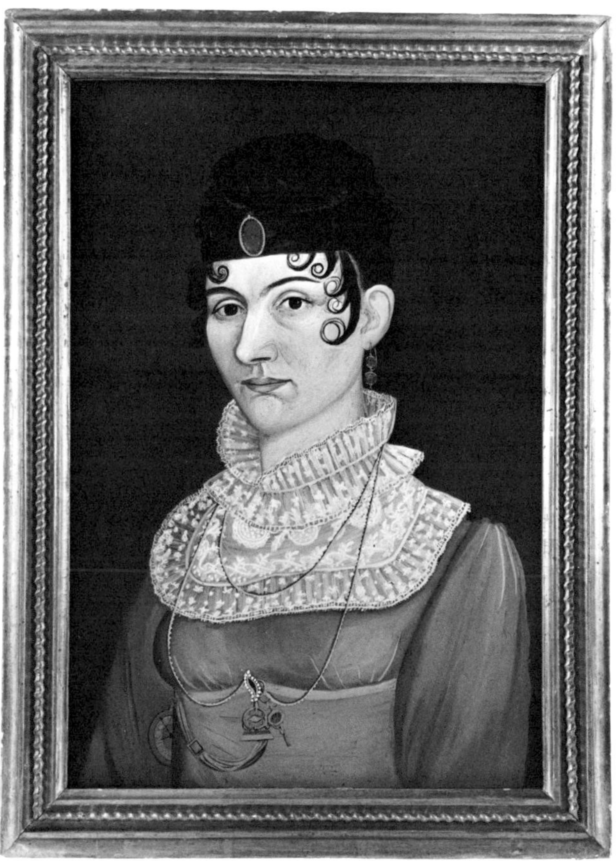

Cat. 87

87

Benjamin Greenleaf (1769–1821)
Parker McCobb (1785–1847)
Rebecca Hill McCobb (1790–1851)
Phippsburg, Maine, 1818
Reverse oil painting on glass
H each 16⅞6 (41.8); w each 11⅜ (28.9) sight
Maine Historical Society
Gift of the Alexander M. Burgess family, 1979

These portraits of Parker McCobb, his wife, Rebecca Hill McCobb, and a third portrait of their son, Henry Bromfield McCobb, represent the latest extant work of Benjamin Greenleaf, an itinerant artist whose characteristic medium was reverse oil painting on glass. They were executed in Phippsburg in 1818. A pencil inscription on the backboard now on Parker McCobb's portrait reads: "Henry Bromfeld [*sic*] McCobb / AE 7 years & 6 months / Painted by Benjamin Greenleaf / at Phipsburg May the 15. 1818." The backboard to Parker's portrait is now on Henry's frame. They were reversed at an unknown time.[1] Greenleaf painted the portrait of Mark Langdon Hill, possibly Rebecca's great-uncle, in

Phippsburg in April of that year.[2] These portraits are part of a group of a dozen three-quarter, bust-length views that have been identified as Greenleaf's work. His other portraits were profiles.[3]

The first known works of Benjamin Greenleaf, a Hull, Massachusetts, native, are the portraits of Jacob Gould and Dr. Cotton Tufts of nearby Weymouth. From the beginning of Greenleaf's career in 1803, the artist was linked by marriage or friendship to sitters from the South Shore area of Massachusetts. The ties of these family members accounted for many of Greenleaf's later clients in northern New England and underscore the importance of such relationships to an artist's career. Like other itinerants, notably Ruth Henshaw Bascomb, Greenleaf traveled a specific course from sitter to sitter, his commissions resulting from word-of-mouth recommendations between friends and relatives.

Greenleaf's trip to Phippsburg in the spring of 1818 was not his first to coastal Maine. In late 1816 he painted the portraits of Bath residents Dr. Samuel Adams, the Reverend John Wallace Ellingwood and his wife, Nancy Duke Ellingwood, and in December 1817, Dummer Sewall. The portrait of Dolly Smith Ripley was painted in Bath around 1817–1818. These sitters were all friends and were connected by birth or marriage to Hingham, Massachusetts, and nearby towns.[4]

Rebecca was the daughter of Jeremiah Hill of Biddeford. In 1810 she married Thomas McCobb of Phippsburg, a prosperous shipowner, and moved into his elegant neoclassical-style dwelling called the Spite house. Thomas was in partnership with his brother-in-law, Mark Langdon Hill. After Thomas's death in 1815, Rebecca married his nephew, Parker. He, too, was a shipbuilder and owner, and before Thomas's death commanded vessels for the partnership.[5] When Greenleaf visited Phippsburg in 1818, he painted the portrait of Henry Bromfield McCobb, Rebecca's son from her first marriage. Her second son was James Thomas McCobb; there were no children from her second marriage. Both Henry and James graduated in the Class of 1829 at Bowdoin College; James began his career as a lawyer, studying in Portland in 1834. By 1837 his mother and step-father had moved to that city. They are buried in Portland's Western Cemetery.

Rebecca McCobb's gray-blue attire is reminiscent of a dress of the period (cat. 168) with its high waist and fitted bodice. Greenleaf has detailed her ruffled white lace tucker and jewelry. Her red and gold drop earrings, gold chains, watch, fob, watch key, and gold pin with pearls were probably similar to those "Elegant Pearl, Amethyst, Topaz, Chrystal, Jett and Paste EAR-RINGS; . . . Gold Neck Chains; . . . Gold, Silver and Gilt Watch Chains, Keys and Seals" sold by Eleazer Wyer at his Portland shop.[6] The black band in her hair features an oval red-stoned brooch, possibly carnelian or coral.

Parker's attire is typical of a wealthy citizen. He wears a black coat and white cravat tied in a bow, ornamented by a gold and pearl pin. His likeness is set against an olive green ground; hers against a blue-green background. Both portraits survive in their original gilt frames.   LFS & CSP

1 Conservation report, MEHS files; Arthur B. and Sybil Kern, "Who was Benjamin Greenleaf?" *Antiques World* 13, no. 9 (September 1981): 47. The portrait of Henry Bromfield McCobb is illustrated in Mellon and Wilder, *Maine and its Role in American Art*, 38.

2 The backboard of the now-destroyed portrait of Mark Hill was inscribed: "The portrait of Mark Langdon Hill, Esq. Ae 46 Painted By Benjamin Greenleaf at Phippsburg, April 1818." It is illustrated in *Phippsburg—Fair to the Wind* (Lewiston, Me.: Phippsburg Historical Society, 1964), facing 5. Hill, the son of Jeremiah and Mary Langdon Storer Hill, was the nephew of Governor John Langdon of Portsmouth; Rebecca is not Mark Langdon Hill's sister as recorded in Kern and Kern, "Who was Benjamin Greenleaf?" They are separated by at least one generation, but further genealogical research is needed to confirm her relationship to Jeremiah Hill, husband of Mary Langdon Storer Hill. See Samuel A. Hill, "Hill Family of York County" (typescript, MEHS) and Mrs. Harold J. Staples, comp., "Biddeford, Maine, Town Records: Births, Deaths, and Marriages, 1768–1814" (typescript, MEHS), 198.

3 Since 1947 the artist of this body of work was thought to be Benjamin Greenleaf, the noted mathematician and educator from Bradford, Massachusetts. The mistaken identity persisted until the Kerns proposed this new identity and an additional thirty portraits were

added to the list of ten known works; Kern and Kern, "Who was Benjamin Greenleaf?" 38–47.

4 Kern and Kern, "Who was Benjamin Greenleaf?" 44, 46–47.

5 Staples, *Biddeford, Maine, Town Records*, 198. Mary Pelham Hill, ed., *Vital Records of Phippsburg, Maine* (Portland: Maine Historical Society, 1935), 259. Arthur Gerrier brought Rebecca's connection to the Spite house to our attention. Her sister-in-law Jenny McCobb married William Nickels, builder of the celebrated Nickels-Sortwell house in Wiscasset. Parker McCobb Reed, *History of Bath and Environs* (Portland, Me: Lakeside Press, 1894), 79–83.

6 *Eastern Argus* (January 9, 1821).

88

Movement by Ephraim Willard (b. 1755)
Tall clock
Boston, Massachusetts, 1800–1805
Mahogany, mahogany veneer, *birch, eastern white pine*
Inscribed "Warranted for Mr. Daniel Cleaves. / E. Willard. / BOSTON."
H 89 3/16 (226.5); W 20 1/16 (51.0); D 10 1/16 (25.5)
York Institute Museum
Bequest of Almira Locke McArthur, 1950

The importance of this clock lies not only in its maker but also in the clockmaker's inscription to the customer on the dial. The clock was "Warranted for Mr. Daniel Cleaves" by "E. Willard. / BOSTON." It was a costly possession; it had nearly the same value as a yoke of oxen in Cleaves's 1818 household inventory.[1]

Born in 1755, Ephraim Willard began his career in partnership with William Gowen, a Medford, Massachusetts, goldsmith. In 1801 Willard purchased a building on Sheafs Lane (now West Street) in Boston and was known as a "merchant" as well as a "clock-maker," probably because he both made and imported parts for the works. Willard is believed to have left Boston in 1805 for New York City with his wife, Hepzibah, and their son, who may have followed in his father's trade. Only a small number of clocks made by Ephraim Willard are known to survive.[2]

The case follows the Roxbury type defined by such craftsmen as the Willards and William Fisk. The form is characterized by a rounded hood surmounted by fretwork and three cup- or urn-shaped finials. Cleaves's clock has brass ball finials. The extensive use of inlay and stringing added value to the case: stringing had to be glued into prepared channels and pictorial inlay made or, more likely, purchased from a specialized maker. Stringing decorates the bonnet, door, and base. A vase of flowers within an oval is inlaid on the door and quarter-round foliate motifs decorate the lower corners of the base. On the inside of the door, blue and white furniture check was used to cover the joints in three places. The movements of the clocks were also expensive, since they were cast in brass locally or were imported.

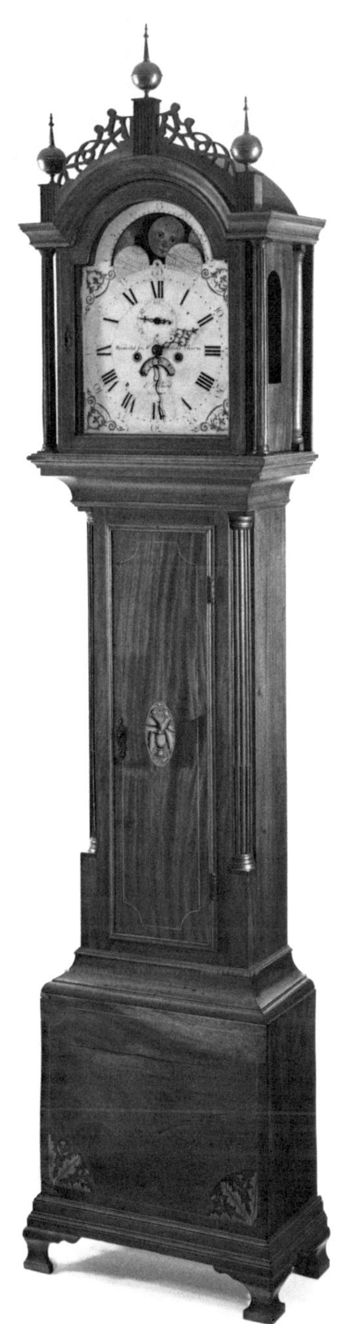

Cat. 88

The eight-day movement, found in this clock, was developed by Ephraim's brother, Simon, the well-known Roxbury clockmaker. It was preferred because it ran longer than the more common thirty-hour variety.[3]   KDM

1 YCRP; 33:544.
2 John Ware Willard, *A History of Simon Willard, Inventor and Clockmaker* (1911; reprint, Mamaroneck, N.Y.: Paul Appel, 1962), 101–104.
3 Montgomery, *American Furniture*, 191–192.

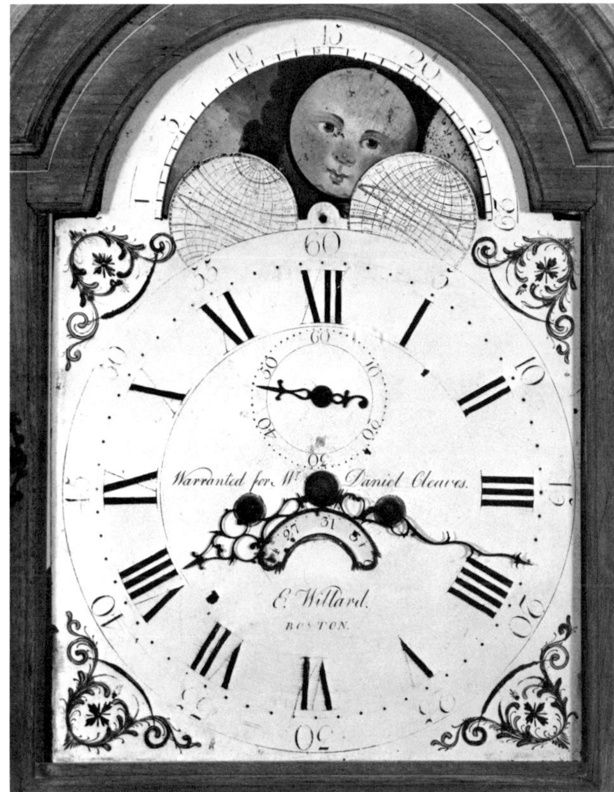

Cat. 88 detail

89

Movement by Edward S. Moulton (1778–1855);
case attributed to Abraham Forsskol (1790–1864)
Tall clock
Saco, Maine, 1810–1820
Mahogany, mahogany veneer, *basswood, birch, eastern white pine*
Inscribed "E. S. Moulton"
H 49¹¹⁄₁₆ (126.3); W 20¼ (51.5); D 10½ (26.7)
York Institute Museum; Gift of Katharine Deering

Edward S. Moulton began his metalworking career in Rochester, New Hampshire, and later moved to Saco, where he had a house and shop on Main Street. An inventory of Moulton's estate taken in 1855 records his tools for making both clock works and spoons. "Eight Day Time Piece[s]," as well as silver spoons, thimbles, and spectacles were among the stock in his shop. By expanding his business into the production and sale of less expensive household items, Moulton increased his market by reaching a larger segment of his community.[1]

The movement Edward S. Moulton produced is the same eight-day type as those made by Simon Willard. Although worn, the dial of the clock is signed "E. S. Moulton."

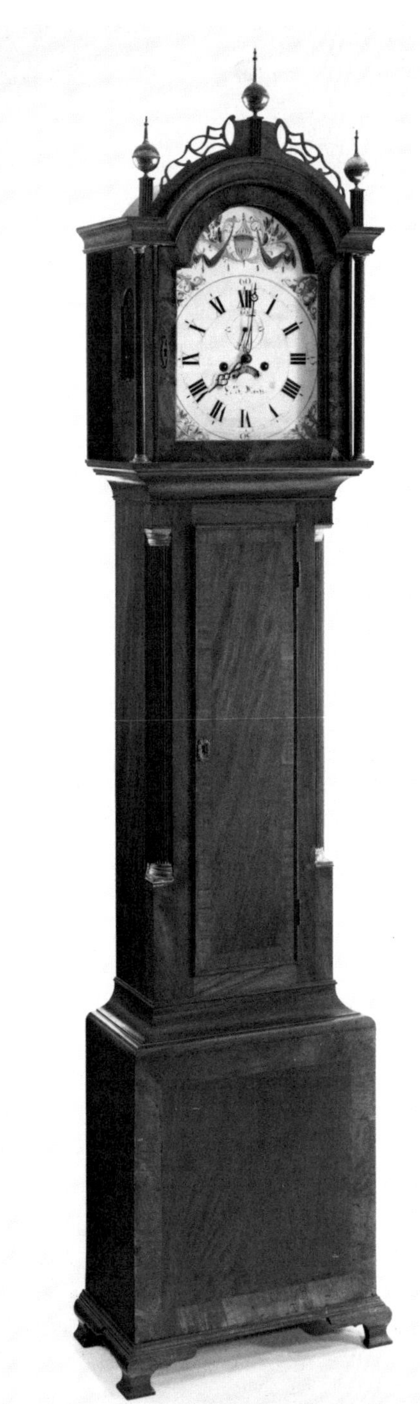

mounted by fretwork and three ball-shaped finials supported by fluted plinths. Other elements are found in the body of the case, such as the quarter-round fluted columns with brass capitals and bases that flank the door. These are seen on a second case (cat. 90) attributed to Forsskol.[2]

Abraham Forsskol was working independently in Saco as a cabinetmaker when this case was made. By 1824 he had formed a partnership with David Buckminster, another Saco craftsman. An inventory of their shop, made at the time of Buckminster's death in 1849, indicated that these joiners produced a variety of goods for local sale.[3]

Nine "high stools" and forty-four "low stools" were in the shop, as well as a "Lot of chair stuff," "turned" and "rift" or sawn. Two turning lathes and tools for turning were included in the inventory. A "Screw Sett for chairs" was also on hand, and was used to hold the turned pieces together while they were being glued. Buckminster and Forsskol also owned planes used to smooth boards and shape moldings for tables and case furniture. Judging by their stock of lumber, some furniture was made of mahogany, other of birch. Less expensive woods were painted; paints in stock included "French yellow," "Chrome [yellow]," "Prussian Blue," and "Rose Pink." The presence of a lolling chair frame along with a "Stuffing knife" and saddler's hammer indicated that Buckminster and Forsskol served as upholsterers. The partners were also undertakers, an allied trade for cabinetmakers; they made coffins in great number and owned a share in a hearse and harness. On March 13, 1824, they billed the estate of Thomas G. Thornton of Saco for $51.63. This included $22.92 for "one Lead Coffin," $6 for a pine coffin, and $2 for the "attendance by Buckminster & Forsskol at Funeral."[4]

The donor of this clock also owned papers of Moses Emery and George Addison Emery, members of the Thornton family. The clock undoubtedly has a Saco family history, but a provenance in the Thornton or Emery families awaits documentation. The bracket feet of this case replaced turned originals.[5]   KDM

Cat. 89

Its enamel decoration depicts an urn and swags in red, green, brown, and gilt.

Attributed by family history to Saco cabinetmaker Abraham Forsskol, the case of this clock demonstrates the pervasive influence of the urban Massachusetts cabinetmakers. Roxbury clock cases feature a bonnet which is sur-

1 A signed example of Moulton's Rochester, New Hampshire, work is in the collection of Old Sturbridge Village; Charles S. Parsons, *New Hampshire Clocks and Clockmakers* (Exeter, N.H.: Adams Brown Co., 1976), 55, 120–121. YCRP; docket 13674.
2 These features appear as far north as Augusta on clock cases made by Frederick Wingate. See Edwin A. Battison and Patricia E. Kane, *The American Clock, 1725–1865: The Mabel Brady Garvan and Other Collections at Yale University* (Greenwich, Conn.: New York Graphic Society, 1973), 50.
3 Account, estate of Thomas G. Thornton to Buckminster and Forsskol, March 13, 1824, Cutts-Thornton Papers, MEHS; YCRP; 64: 72–76.
4 Account, estate of Thomas G. Thornton to Buckminster and Forsskol, March 13, 1824, Cutts-Thornton Papers, MEHS.
5 Fairfield, *Sands*, 435. Museum records, YIM.

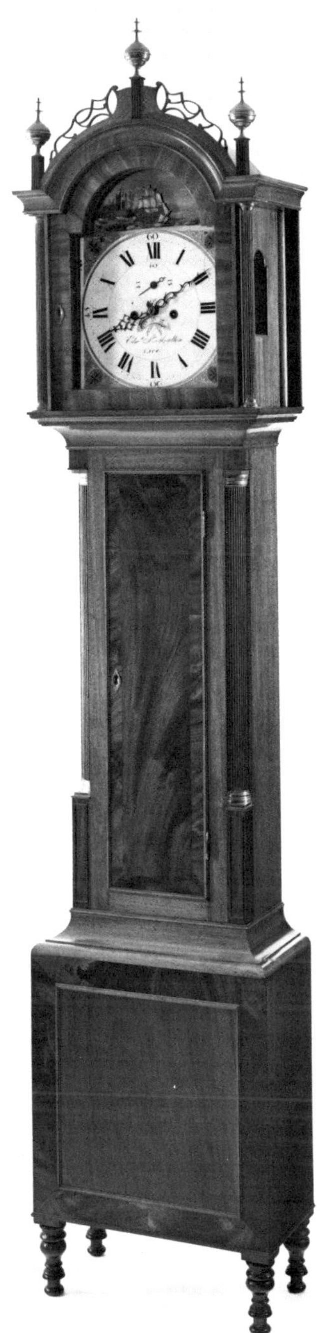

Cat. 90

90

Movement by Edward S. Moulton (1778–1855);
case attributed to Abraham Forsskol (1790–1864)
Tall clock
Saco, Maine, 1810–1820

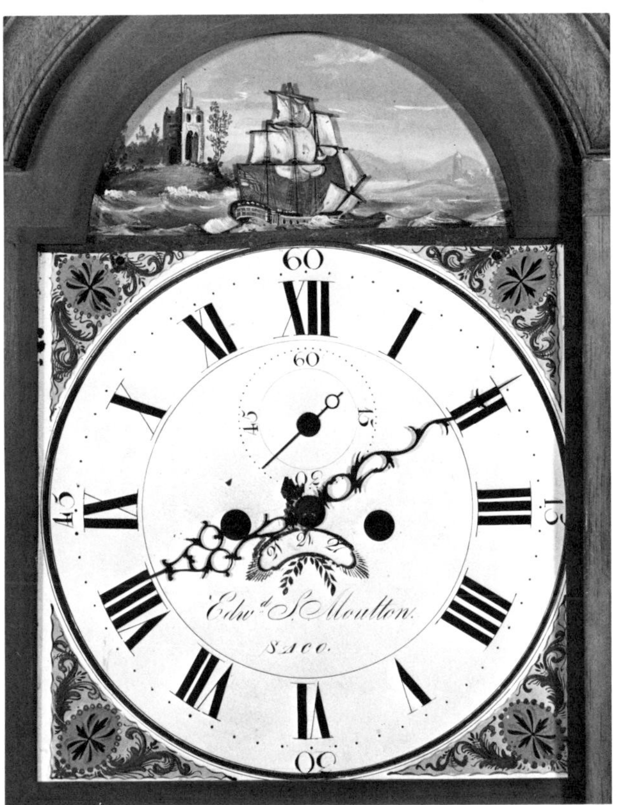

Cat. 90 detail

Mahogany, mahogany veneer, *basswood*, *birch*,
eastern white pine
Inscribed "Edwd S. Moulton. / SACO."
H 93 (236.0); W 19⁵⁄₁₆ (49.0); D 9½ (24.1)
York Institute Museum; Gift of George Addison Emery

In its construction and decoration, this clock case is very
similar to another (cat. 89) also attributed to Abraham
Forsskol. The bonnet is surmounted by fretwork cut from the
same pattern, the ball-shaped finials are supported by
similar thin fluted plinths, and arched glazed panels are set
into the sides of the bonnet. Other important similarities are
the secondary woods the craftsman used in the construction
of the bonnet. Basswood and birch are found in the same
parts of the bonnet; lightweight basswood for the arch, and
birch, a stronger wood, for the lower bonnet frame.

Plain colonnettes with brass capitals and bases flank the
doors. Both clock cases have reeded quarter-columns on the
waist, also decorated with brass bases and capitals. This
clock, however, was presumably more expensive. Not only
did the case have turned feet and triple beaded molding on
the lower part of the case, but the movement is also more
elaborate. More metal work was required to complete it,
since the rocking ship on the dial was an extra feature. This

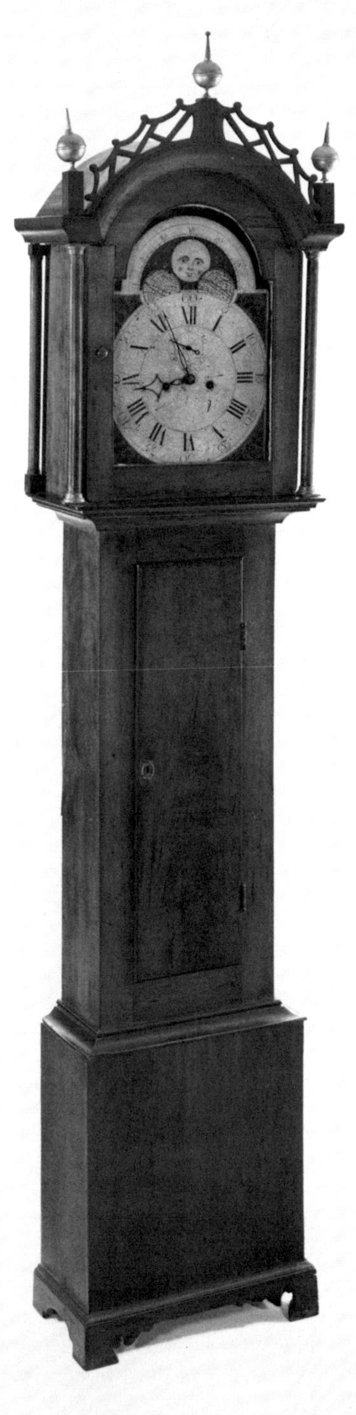

Cat. 91

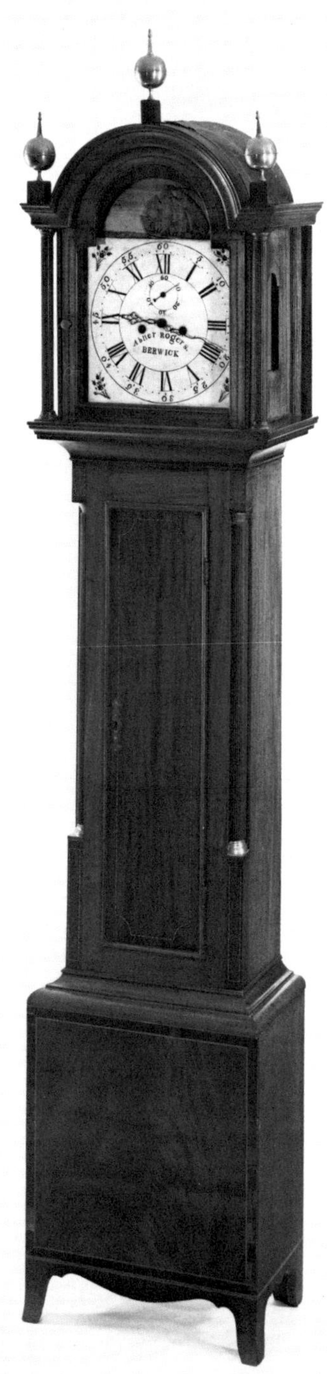

Cat. 92

clock is substantially taller than the other Moulton and
Forsskol example.

   Although the original owner of this clock has not been
identified, it is presumed to have belonged to a member of

the Cutts-Thornton family, since it was inherited by the
same descendant who gave the Cutts portraits (cats. 33–36)
and other important Cutts family possessions (cat. 142).
KDM

91

Movement attributed to Paul Rogers (d. 1818)
Tall clock
Berwick, Maine, 1800–1810
Black cherry, basswood, birch, eastern white pine
H 85⁷⁄₁₆ (217.0); W 20½ (52.0); D 9¹⁵⁄₁₆ (25.1)
The Brick Store Museum
Bequest of the estate of Edward E. Bourne III, 1982

This arched bonnet with its fretwork and ball-shaped finials
is a country version of examples made in urban shops about
1800. The use of smooth cherry columns on the waist as
opposed to those of fluted mahogany; the incised lines on the
bonnet door in place of stringing; and the finials supported
by blocks rather than by fluted plinths are all modifications
of the Roxbury form. Such changes to the formula made this
clock affordable to those who were not affluent enough to
purchase a clock from one of the urban shops, or a more
expensive local product.

The movement of this clock has been attributed to Paul
Rogers of Berwick on the basis of its similarity to examples
signed by him. Rogers is known to have made both shelf
clocks and tall clocks. They were probably less expensive
than those made near Boston, since the movements were
made principally of iron. Brass wheels have been recorded in
only one Rogers clock.[1]

Local cabinetmakers must have supplied the cases for the
clocks made by Paul and his son Abner (cat. 92). One
craftsman who may have been working with Paul Rogers was
Humphrey Chadbourne, Jr., of Berwick. Although listed as
a "yeoman" at his death in 1792, Chadbourne's estate
included "5 chair frames" and a note held against Paul
Rogers for £7.15.9.[2]

Paul Rogers's household inventory of 1818 indicates that
he was a moderately successful craftsman who also depended
upon farming for support. Rogers owned an anvil,
"blacksmith's vise," bellows, tongs, and "part of set of clock
maker's tools." He may have used his metalworking skills in
other practical ways.[3] Abner Rogers probably worked in his
father's shop.

This clock is one of two listed in a 1910 record of the
furnishings in the Parsons-Bourne house in Kennebunk.
Daniel Sewall, a brother of David Sewall (Chapter 2 and fig.
4.2), moved to Kennebunk from York in 1815. He purchased
the large three-story house built in 1812 by John Usher
Parsons (Chapter 2 and fig. 2.23). Sewall held the post of
register of probate for York County for thirty-seven years and
also served at various times as clerk of common pleas, and
clerk of the Supreme Court. Sewall's house and its contents
descended to his son, William Bartlett, and subsequently to
William's widow, Maria Moody Sewall. She left the house to
her nephew, Edward E. Bourne, Jr.

In his 1910 record of Bourne family furnishings, Edward
Bourne's grandson Harold noted a "Grandfather's" clock
that was inherited from Daniel Sewall, and a "small
mahogany" clock that was "from W. B. Sewall." The
"Grandfather's" clock is known to be a tall clock made by
John Roulston of Boston. Its finely constructed and carved
case makes it an important example. According to Harold
Bourne, "it was placed on the stairs in 1815." If Bourne's
date is accurate, the removal of the tall clock to the stairway
may be the earliest documentation known for the replacement of tall clocks by efficient shelf clocks introduced in 1814
by Eli Terry. Tall clocks on stair landings are most often
documented to the mid nineteenth century and the colonial
revival movement. William E. Barry sketched the Roulston
clock in its niche in the late nineteenth century. Both clocks
remained in the house and descended to another of Edward
E. Bourne, Jr.'s, grandsons, Edward E. Bourne III.[4]

This Rogers clock is believed to be the one identified as
the "small mahogany" clock. Its black cherry case, stained to
resemble mahogany, could easily have been misinterpreted
by Harold Bourne.   KDM & LFS

1 The clock, probably made by Rogers, is in a private collection; see H.
   G. Harris, *Nineteenth Century American Clocks* (Buchanan, N.Y.:
   Lakeside Books, 1981), 48. A tall clock that descended in the Adams
   family of Newburyport is in the Cheney Wells collection at Old
   Sturbridge Village; see Lura W. Watkins, "Highfields and its
   Heritage," *Antiques* 90, no. 2 (August 1966): 204–207.
2 YCRP; 16:193.
3 YCRP; 28: 276–278.
4 Remich, *History*, 530–532, 345. H. H. Bourne, "The Bourne Family of
   Kennebunk, Maine, Record of Old Furniture, 1910" (manuscript,
   BSM). Christopher P. Monkhouse and Thomas S. Michie, *American
   Furniture in Pendleton House* (Providence, R.I.: Museum of Art, Rhode
   Island School of Design, 1986), 13. The Barry drawing is at BSM.
   The Roulston clock remained in its niche until 1964. It is illustrated in
   Antiques 86, no. 4 (October 1964): 411. Dean and Martha Gandy
   Fales kindly brought the references to the Roulston clock to our
   attention.

92

Movement by Abner Rogers (1777–1808/9)
Tall clock
Berwick, Maine, 1804–1808
Mahogany, mahogany veneer, *basswood, eastern white pine*
Inscribed "Abner Rogers. / BERWICK."
H 93⅛ (236.5); W 19¾ (50.2); D 10⅛ (25.7)
The Brick Store Museum; Gift of the estate
of Jane Lord Thompson Burbank, 1943

The case of this clock, made by an unidentified Maine
craftsman, follows the form of other examples made in the
Roxbury style. Evidence of the urban Massachusetts
influence is seen in the arched bonnet surmounted by three
ball-shaped finials resting on reeded plinths. The use of

mahogany veneer with extensive stringing corresponds to clocks made in the Boston area at the same time.

The cases for this and other clocks made by Rogers must have been supplied by local cabinetmakers such as Abraham Forsskol of Saco or the nearby Eliot joiner, Nathaniel Knowlton. Boston-trained Knowlton is known to have made clock cases. In October 1817, he charged James Shapleigh $15 for one and for "finding the trimmings" (the brass hardware).[1] Basswood appears as a secondary wood in the Forsskol-related cases (cats. 89–90).

Abner Rogers was the son of Berwick clockmaker Paul Rogers. The absence of any clock-making tools or real estate in Abner's 1809 inventory suggests that he did not have his own shop but simply worked in his father's shop. In the spandrels of the dial are blue flowers. The lunette above is decorated with a sailing ship scene. The dial bears the inscription "Abner Rogers. / BERWICK." Although Rogers had prosperous customers, including Clement and Sarah Durrell Lord who traditionally owned this clock, the appraisal of his estate reveals that Abner achieved only a moderate degree of material prosperity.[2]

This clock descended in the Lord-Thompson family from the original owners to the donor. Two inscriptions on the bonnet reveal that Charles H. Thompson, the uncle of the donor, owned the clock later in the nineteenth century.[3]

KDM

1 Nathaniel Knowlton, account books, 1812–1859, 2 vols., MEHS.
2 YCRP; 21:550–551. The dial appears to have been repainted.
3 The inscription on the bonnet, "C H Thompson / Kennebunk / Maine / May [20# 176?]" is incised in the paper; in the wood on the right side appears "Chas H. Thompson/ May 18[6?]1." See Lord family scrapbook, BSM.

93

Attributed to William Hackett (1780–1864)
Sideboard
Kennebunk, Maine, 1800–1806
Mahogany, mahogany, curled and bird's-eye maple veneer, *basswood, eastern white pine*
H 41⅜ (105.0); W 53¹¹⁄₁₆ (136.4); D 22⁷⁄₁₆ (57.0)
The Brick Store Museum; Gift of Edith Cleaves Barry in memory of Jane Lord Burbank, 1948

This sideboard originally belonged to Clement and Sarah Durrell Lord of Kennebunk; family history also maintains it was made by Kennebunk cabinetmaker William Hackett. Born in Newburyport, Hackett was "[a]mong the immigrants and energetic young men" who came to Kennebunk around 1800. He took over the cabinetmaking shop William Hooper had established some twenty years earlier. In January 1802 William Hackett, "cabinet maker," purchased a house lot in "that part of Wells called Kennebunk." By

November 1803 Hackett was active in his shop, and advertised that he carried on the "Cabinet Making Business" and had on hand a handsome assortment of mahogany furniture. He specified sideboards in the list. Other forms included secretaries; bureaus; dining, card, and Pembroke tables; bedsteads; sofas; and easy chairs. Some of these forms were part of his line of maple furniture, which he distinguished from the mahogany.[1]

In an 1803 advertisement, Hackett requested the services of a "smart active LAD, about 16 or 17 years of age as an Apprentice to said business." A journeyman whom Hackett employed was responsible for a fire that destroyed the shop. Although the exact date is unknown, the fire appears to have occurred about 1806. Reportedly discouraged by the loss of his tools and stock, Hackett abandoned cabinetmaking and went into business selling English and West India goods and dealing in lumber. With Nathaniel Frost, a former chairmaker, Hackett operated a store on Main Street in Kennebunk, but by 1809 the partnership had been dissolved. In September 1814, Timothy Frost and William Hackett, "both of Wells, traders," purchased a store and store lot. By 1820 Hackett described himself as a "merchant." In 1823 Hackett moved inland to Limerick, Maine, with his wife Lydia Dutch (1793–1848) and their three children, and sold farm products and lumber. Hackett remained interested in coastal activities; he owned shares in ships and in 1846 signed a petition to dredge and straighten the Mousam River to improve its navigability.[2]

One distinctive feature of this sideboard is its wide arched opening with tambour doors. The same arrangement was used on an enclosed pier table made by Mark Pitman of Salem between 1800 and 1810. An Essex County native who was undoubtedly trained there, Hackett must have been familiar with this form. The deep cavity behind the doors provided ample storage space for linens or tablewares. Bottle drawers flank the doors. The front of the case is highly patterned. Panels of curled and bird's-eye maple veneer on the drawer fronts and stiles are contrasted by the dark mahogany veneer. Dark and light checkered stringing is used extensively along the edges of the top, the arch, the skirt, and the cuffs of the legs (see cat. 99). In its size, use of bottle drawers flanking a lower compartment, and contrasting veneers, Hackett's sideboard also relates to a Newburyport sideboard table by Abner Toppan.[4]

Basswood, found in the interior framing, is the same secondary wood used in other furniture attributed to York County cabinetmakers. It appears in the bonnets of the clock cases attributed to Abraham Forsskol of Saco (cats. 89–90) and in those made for the Rogerses of Berwick (cats. 91–92).

This sideboard has the same provenance as the Abner Rogers tall clock (cat. 92) and, like it, appears in an interior photograph of the Burbank house in Saco. Both objects were bequeathed to the donor, Edith C. Barry, by Jane Lord

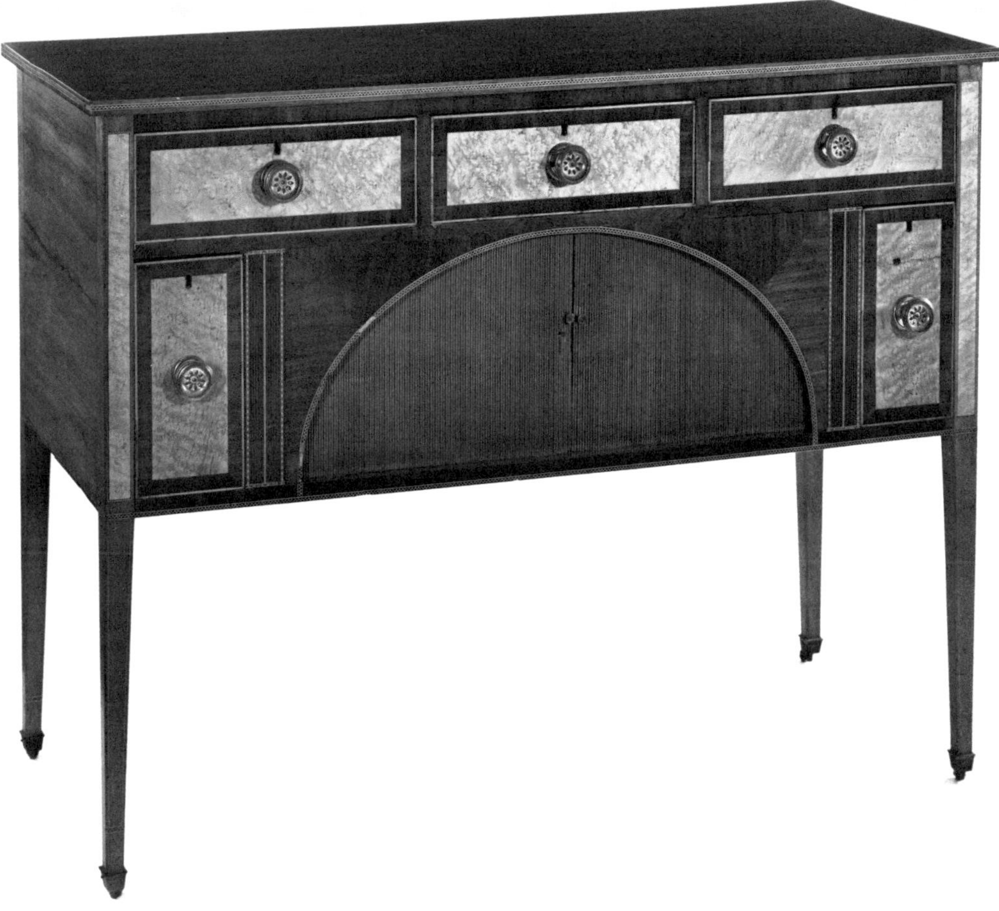

Cat. 93

Burbank (1887–1941), the granddaughter of Kennebunk's Captain Nathaniel Lord Thompson (1811–1889) and his first wife, Jane Stone Lord (1816–1851). Miss Barry was related to Jane Burbank through Nathaniel L. Thompson, whose second wife was Edith's maternal grandmother. Nathaniel L. Thompson's third wife was Nancie F. Hackett (1825–1883), daughter of William Hackett. A sideboard, chest of drawers, and two card tables attributed to Hackett descended in the family of their daughter Mary Hackett Thompson (b. 1865). On the death of Nathaniel L. Thompson, his furnishings descended to the children of all three marriages.[5]   KDM

1   Bourne, *History*, 581. *Annals of the Times* (December 1, 1803). William Hackett file, BSM.
2   *Annals of the Times* (December 1, 1803). Remich, *History*, 135, 232, 339, 377–378. YCRD; 69:101; 90:200; 104:105.
3   Montgomery, *American Furniture*, 372.
4   See Montgomery, *American Furniture*, 371.
5   Burbank family scrapbook, BSM. Natalie Green kindly provided the historical information on the Hackett-Thompson family.

94

Attributed to Ichabod Fairfield (1763–1824)
Card table (one of a pair)
Saco, Maine, or Salem, Massachusetts, 1795–1805
Mahogany, *birch, eastern white pine, hickory* (hinge pin), curled maple and rosewood(?) veneer
Inscribed (in chalk under top) "Fairfield"
H 4 11/16 (72.5); W 36⅛ (91.5); D closed 16 13/16 (42.7)
York Institute Museum
Bequest of Almira Locke McArthur, 1950

Card tables in the neoclassical style were a prevalent form of furniture in Maine homes as they were throughout New England. Small and lightweight, they were moved about the house as needed. Many styles were available. Hardwood examples with tapered legs such as these were one choice; tables with turned legs were another. A customer could also have one made to his own specifications.[1]

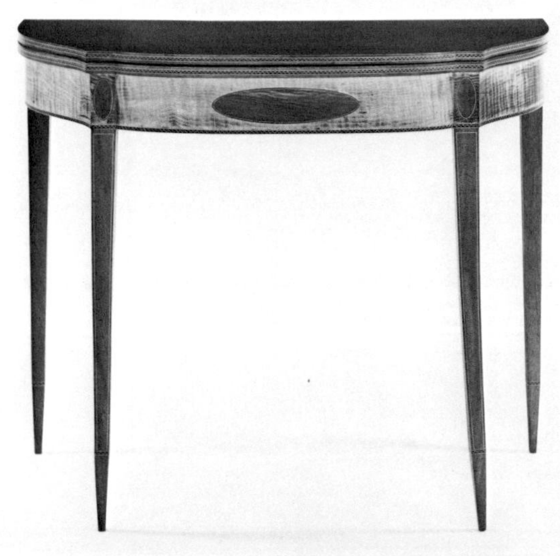

Cat. 94

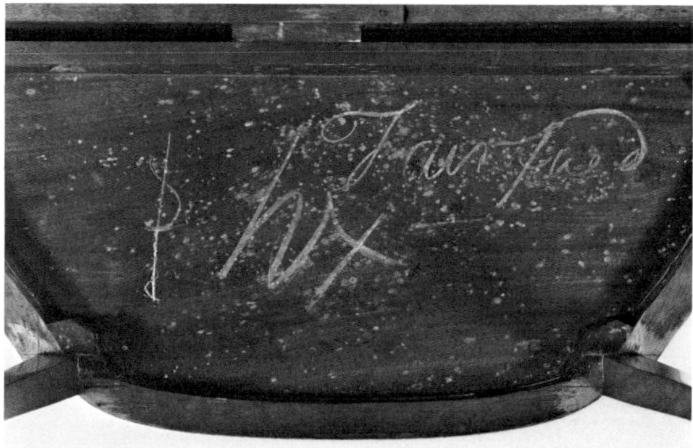

Cat. 94 detail

According to recent research, the shape and construction features of this table point to a Boston-area origin. The table is square with an elliptical front and serpentine ends. The decorative features of Boston-area tables are also found on this example. The skirt is decorated with light figured veneer, which sets off the contrasting inlaid oval. However, many Boston-trained cabinetmakers migrated northward, resulting in the spread of similar conventions to northern Massachusetts, New Hampshire, and Maine.[2]

Family tradition maintains that these tables, like a desk and bookcase (cat. 95), were made by Ichabod Fairfield for his sister, Sarah, at the time of her marriage to Daniel Cleaves in 1795. When Almira McArthur left these tables to the York Institute Museum, she noted that they were inherited from the Tucker family. Almira's grandmother, Marcia Tucker Cleaves, could have inherited them from

Daniel Cleaves, her father-in-law, or Jonathan Tucker, her father. If the chalk inscription "Fairfield," written in chalk under the top, does refer to Fairfield as the maker, these tables offer valuable evidence of the pervasive Boston influence in Maine cabinetwork.

This table may be one of the "4 mah[ogan]y card tables" listed in Daniel Cleaves's estate inventory of 1818. When his widow died in 1838, there were still four card tables in the house: two in the parlor, one in the sitting room, and one in the chamber over the sitting room.[3] Although not specified in these documents, card tables were often made as pairs.

Card playing, a popular entertainment in homes, occupied increasing amounts of leisure time during the federal period. Games besides cards were played on these tables. Inventories and diaries often mention backgammon boards and checkerboards. Maine residents, however, also played games in public assembly halls and taverns, where fashionable tables like these were not to be found; almost any table surface would have served the purpose. In the spring of 1801, Eliza Southgate and her friends spent an evening at Broad's Tavern. "We played cards, talked and wrote crambo [a rhyming word game]; after we had scribbled the backs of two packs of cards, cut half of them up and eat our supper, we set out for home, about one o'clock."[4]   LFS

1 See Montgomery, *American Furniture*, 327–328; and Benjamin A. Hewitt, Patricia E. Kane, and Gerald W.R. Ward, *The Work of Many Hands: Card Tables in Federal America, 1790–1820* (New Haven, Conn.: Yale University Art Gallery, 1982) for examples of these various choices.
2 Benjamin A. Hewitt, "Regional Characteristics of American Federal-Period Card Tables" in Hewitt, Kane, and Ward, *The Work of Many Hands*, 55–106, 137–139. Other features of construction based on this research are plane fly-leg construction, hinged rail design one, no leaf-edge tenon, no medial brace, two horizontal laminations in the front and end curved rails. Oval inlays further decorate the stiles. The edges of the top and skirt and the cuffs are inlaid with patterned stringing. Light-colored stringing decorates the legs.
3 YCRP; 26:544 and 48:454–455.
4 See Gerald W. R. Ward, "'Avarice and Conviviality': Card Playing in Federal America," in Hewitt, Kane, and Ward, *The Work of Many Hands*, 17. Bowne, *A Girl's Life*, 45.

95

Attributed to Ichabod Fairfield (1763–1824)
Secretary
Possibly Saco, Maine, ca. 1795
Mahogany, mahogany and satinwood (?) veneer,
birch, eastern white pine
H 85¹³⁄₁₆ (218.0); W 48¹³⁄₁₆ (124.0); D 19¹¹⁄₁₆ (50.0)
York Institute Museum
Bequest of Almira Locke McArthur, 1950

When Almira McArthur, the great-granddaughter of Daniel and Sarah Fairfield Cleaves, left her desk and bookcase to the

York Institute, she wrote that it was made by Sarah's brother, Ichabod, "for a wedding present at the time of her marriage to Daniel Cleaves in 1795." The "1 maghogy. secretary" listed at $30 in Daniel's 1818 inventory, and again in 1838 as part of Sarah's estate as the "secretary and bookcase" at $12, undoubtedly records this object.[1]

Family history further relates that Ichabod trained as a cabinetmaker in Portsmouth or Salem. Unfortunately, other documentation of his work as a craftsman, journeyman, or apprentice in those towns has not come to light. This attribution, however, is supported by the pair of card tables with the same family tradition, one of which is signed "Fairfield" (cat. 94). When Fairfield acquired property in Saco in 1800, he referred to himself as a gentleman, not a cabinetmaker.[2] This association, however, does not preclude his occupation as a cabinetmaker. It reflects his mercantile activities and perhaps shows the change in his activities during his adult life, a shift in trade that occurred with other Maine cabinetmakers (see Chapter 4).

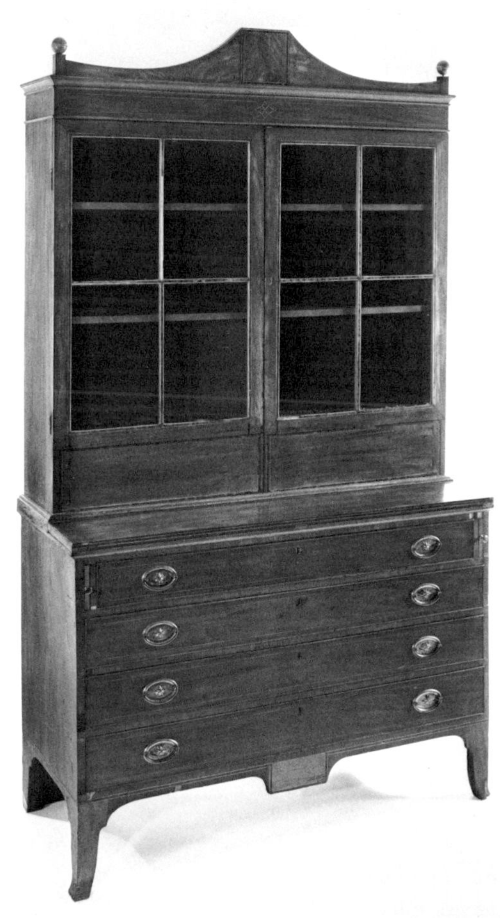

Cat. 95

The form and decorative style of this secretary is in the Salem and Portsmouth traditions. Among the typical elements in the lower case are a dropped veneered panel in the skirt and French feet. The drawers with their beaded edges also feature light stringing. The oval brasses with embossed star design are original.

Two large doors open to reveal shelves over drawers and pigeonholes. The inside of the bookcase is stained dark green, a surface that may be original. The large panes of glass are set into birch doors covered by mahogany veneer and stringing. In the cornice, light stringing intersects a diamond of similar stringing, a motif often associated with Salem. The cornice with its veneered central crest is decorated with dark stringing; on the ends, reeded plinths support brass finials. A central finial is missing.

The desk and bookcase form was well within the range of Maine cabinetmakers. John Seymour produced a pine desk and bookcase for the Portland firm of Robison, Edgar, and Reed in 1785. It cost £2.16.0. Brunswick partners Dinsmore and Batchelder produced one with handsome inlay and stringing, and tambour doors.[3] Although they were available locally, when Andrew Titcomb needed a desk and bookcase, he sent his brother bargain hunting in Boston. His brother replied: "I have put on board Capt McLellan['s vessel] a Desk and Book Case for you. Inclosed is the Bill. I could not get one under that price at any of the Cabinet Makers in Town, It appears to be a good piece of Work & I hope it will answer your expectations."[4]

The desk and bookcase is a symbol of the merchant class. For Samuel Abbott, a "trader" in Saco, his desk was the single most valuable furnishing in his estate.[5] Merchants and shopkeepers found it a convenient form. Writing space was created when the desk top folded out. In this example, the surface was probably originally covered with baize. Drawers in the desk provided storage space; the bookcase held ledgers and other account books.

The upper section was often made to lock. This provided security for one's papers, but made it inconvenient if one lost the key. During his family's move from Essex County to Maine, Edward Little wrote to his sisters in Newburyport: "When I was at your house a week or 10 days since I left my desk key, pray find it & send it to me as I have never been able to find one to unlock it."[6]   LFS

1 Accession records, YIS. YCRP; 33:544, and 48:454.
2 YCRD; 66:151.
3 Account, John Seymour to Robison, Edgar, and Reed, February 16, 1785, Robison Papers, MEHS. For the Dinsmore and Batchelder desk and bookcase, see the Decorative Arts Photographic Collection, Winterthur Museum.
4 Moses Titcomb to Andrew Titcomb, Boston, September 6, 1800, Andrew Hawes Collection, MEHS. The bill is missing.
5 YCRP; 17:138.
6 Edward Little to Sarah and Mary Little, January 28, 1814, Little Family Papers, MEHS.

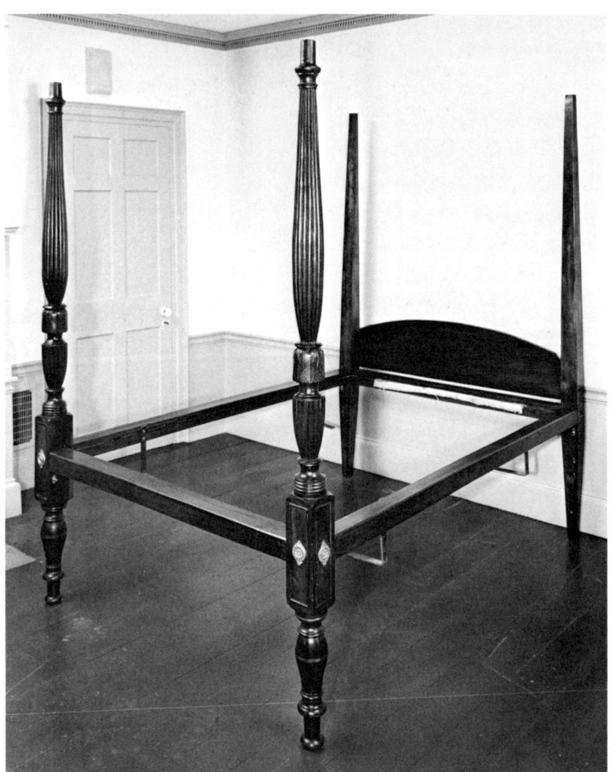

Cat. 96

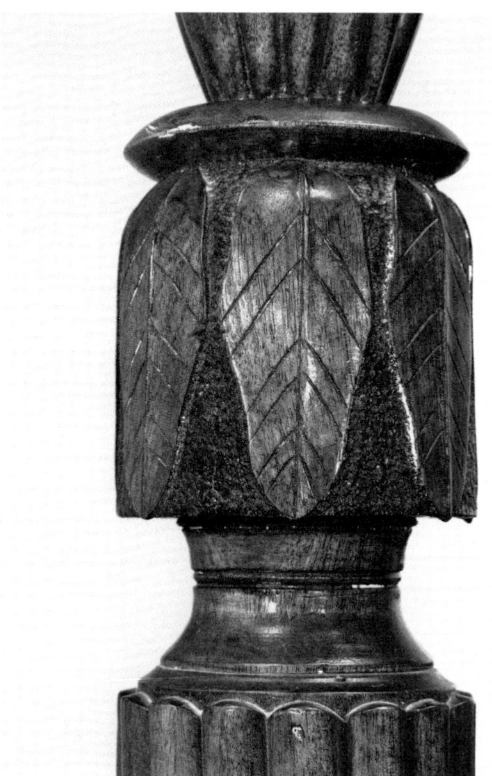

Cat. 96 detail

96

High-post bedstead
Possibly York County, Maine, ca. 1816
Mahogany, *birch*
H 80 (202.2); W 56¼ (143.5); D 61⅞ (157.0)
The Brick Store Museum
Gift of Mrs. John B. Corning, 1974

By the early nineteenth century, the use of high-post
bedsteads made of imported mahogany became widespread
among the merchant class. The extent of the turned and
carved decoration of this example suggests that it was an
expensive purchase. The carved motif on the posts, a
waterleaf against a punched background, is similar to that
on a stand owned by the Cleaves family (cat. 100). Water-
leaves and punched work appear frequently on furniture
made in the Salem, Massachusetts, area after 1800. Here,
those motives are not as crisp and appear to have been
interpreted by a rural maker, suggesting a York County
origin. Traces of the original sacking bottom remain tacked
to the head rail.

Daniel Wise (1761–1825), a successful merchant, is
believed to have had this bed made for his daughter Mary
(1793–1825). Mary married Moses Morrill in 1816. Family

history maintains that the cotton coverlet that still accompanies the bed was made for Mary Wise (cat. 139). Daniel
Wise was in Kennebunk by 1790 and in 1824 formed a
partnership with John W. Bodwell to sell "general merchandise" in the Phoenix Building, later known as the "Old
Brick."[1]   KDM

1 Remich, *History*, 415.

97

Commode
Possibly York or Hancock counties, Maine, ca. 1800
Mahogany, mahogany veneer, *eastern white pine*
H 36³⁄₁₆ (91.9); W 47½ (120.7); D 23¼ (59.1)
York Institute Museum
Bequest of Almira Locke McArthur, 1950

In 1787 when George Hepplewhite published a design for
this form in his pattern book, he recommended that it be
"adapted for a drawing room" as it "require[d] considerable
elegance." It had its practical features as well; interior spaces
"answer[ed] the use of a closet or cupboard."[1]

This stylish form required more labor and materials in its manufacture than a standard chest of four drawers. In addition to four large drawers, eight small drawers were constructed. These side drawers were hinged and open to reveal triangular-shaped compartments. All the drawers were graduated and their curved facades were veneered. These features all increased the cost of construction. This chest retains its original hardware, including the brass acorn-shaped keyhole covers.

More elegant examples of this form are known which incorporate elaborate veneer and stringing into the decoration.[2] The maker of this chest eliminated the inlay, thus adapting a highly fashionable design into a less costly product. In his changes, however, the craftsman still adhered to Hepplewhite's stipulation that the commode provide ample storage space. Drawers in the center of the case replace the doors and interior shelves of the pattern book design.

Two interior boards bear the pencil inscriptions "Thos Eayres" and "Thomas Eayres / Newmon." The inscriptions could refer to the maker, since their location on a drawer divider would have been an awkward and difficult place for an owner to inscribe his name. Newmon may designate a town, or simply be another name whose association is now unknown. There was no such town in Maine. A few Eayres families are recorded in Massachusetts and New Hampshire towns in the 1800, 1810, and 1820 census. However, the 1800 Maine census listed ten households of Eayres in York and Hancock counties. John and Joseph Eyrs were recorded in Portland in 1810, and York County deeds reveal families of Eayres in Saco and other towns. This commode is another

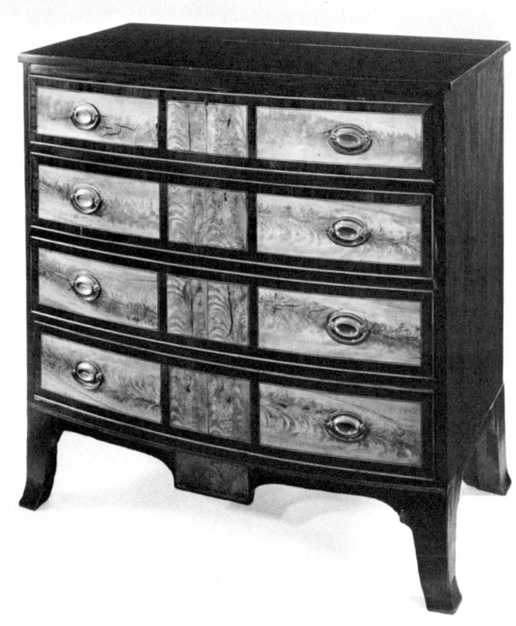

Cat. 98

of the many objects that descended to Almira McArthur, and it most likely furnished a Saco home shortly after it was made.   LFS

1 Hepplewhite, *Cabinet-Maker's Guide*, 14, plate 78.
2 Philip Zea, "New England Furniture," *Antiques* 127, no. 3 (March 1985):661.

98

Chest of drawers
Portsmouth, New Hampshire,
or York County, Maine, 1800–1815
Birch, flame birch or satinwood, and mahogany veneer,
eastern white pine, basswood
H 38⅝ (98.1); W 38½ (97.8); D 20⅞ (53.0)
Old York Historical Society; Museum purchase, 1971

The abundance of surviving Portsmouth furniture with histories of ownership in southern York County illustrates the level of trading activity between the two towns throughout the eighteenth and nineteenth centuries. As York's harbor was too small to accommodate ships bound for England or the Continent, commodities from these distant ports could be secured in Portsmouth, which was easily accessible by sail or the King's Highway. Several York merchants, including Edward Emerson, Sr., and Nathaniel

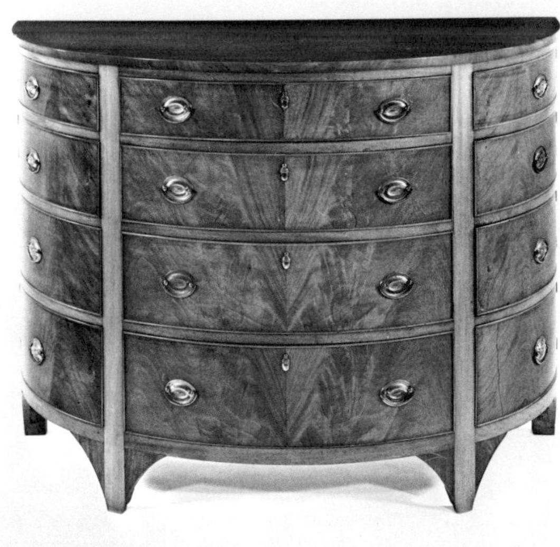

Cat. 97

Barrell (cats. 34, 101), advertised in Portsmouth newspapers and had retail shops in the town. While there were cabinet shops in York, notably those of Caleb Preble and Cotton Bradbury, wealthy families often looked to Portsmouth, Salem, or Boston when purchasing furniture.[1]

This bow-front chest of drawers supported by French feet is typical of the regional furniture available in early nineteenth-century York and may have been made in a Portsmouth or York shop.[2] The pine drawer fronts are veneered with contrasting birch and mahogany in a three-part pattern. The skirt features a drop panel, typical of Portsmouth area furniture, which is painted in careful imitation of the panels above. Basswood was used as a secondary wood by other York County cabinetmakers (cats. 89–90, 93). The brasses and backboard are not original. Nathaniel Knowlton of nearby Eliot, Maine, made veneered chests in this style (see Chapter 4).

Based on family records and correspondence, Captain Samuel Sewall (1748–1826), a York mariner, purchased this chest for his wife Hannah Moulton Sewall (1756–1805).[3] After her death the Sewall daughters continued to run the household for their father until 1822, when daughter Susan and her husband, Captain John Thompson, bought the house next door. They took the chest with them and it remained in the Thompson family until its purchase by the Old York Historical Society in 1971.[4] KAO

1 For an important cabinetmaker working in York during the colonial period, see Myrna Kaye, "The Furniture of Samuel Sewall," *Antiques* 128, no. 2 (August 1985): 276–284.
2 See Helen Comstock, *American Furniture* (New York: Viking Press, 1962), fig. 466.
3 See cat. 172 for the wedding dress of the Sewall's daughter, Ruth Sewall Putnam.
4 The provenance was traced in 1971 by Katharine D. Thompson, a descendant of the original owners and last owner.

99

Chest of drawers
Possibly Kennebunk, Maine, 1800–1810
Mahogany, mahogany and maple veneer,
eastern white pine
H 38 (96.5); W 43 (109.2); D 21¾ (55.2)
The Brick Store Museum; Gift of Julia Barry Bodman

This chest of drawers descended in the Lord and Barry families of Kennebunk. Through shipping enterprises, the Lord family had ample opportunity to purchase furniture in Boston and other urban ports. However, chests of this type also were made locally. Kennebunk cabinetmaker William Hackett (cat. 93) advertised in 1803 that among the furniture he had on hand were "Swelled Bureaus," a contemporary name for a bow-front chest. The crossbanded inlay along the

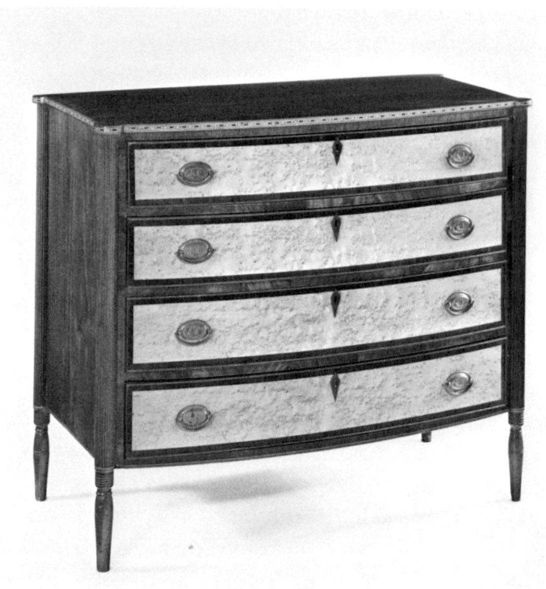

Cat. 99

edge of the top of this chest, panels of figured maple veneer and beading on the drawer fronts, inlaid mahogany escutcheons, and engaged reeded columns have been executed by a skilled craftsman. These features all added to the original cost of this object.

A straight-front chest of drawers based on family tradition to be the work of Hackett has engaged reeded columns similar to these. The sideboard attributed to him features the same checkered stringing found here.[1] The brasses are old but not original to the chest. KDM

1 William Hackett file, BSM.

100

Work table
Possibly York County, Maine, 1805–1820
Mahogany, mahogany veneer, *eastern white pine*
H 29⁷⁄₁₆ (74.8); W 20 (50.8); D 18¼ (46.3)
The Brick Store Museum; William E. Barry estate through Edith Cleaves Barry, 1969

Small in size, this form provided storage for tools and supplies associated with domestic work (see cat. 151). The top of the two drawers is partitioned to hold small items such as needle books and thread. The lower galleried shelf offered additional storage space and is a feature associated with New Hampshire and Maine.

The carving of the flat waterleaf against a star-punched
background is similar to the carving on the footposts of a
bedstead owned by the Wise family of Kennebunk (cat. 96).
These decorative motifs appear frequently on federal
furniture made in Salem.[1] However, the carving on this work
table, because of its simplification, appears to be an interpretation of a high style by a carver once removed from the
design source. The construction and design features also
suggest that the table was made in York County.

Family history maintains that this table was owned by
Daniel and Sarah Cleaves. The 1818 household inventory of
Daniel included a listing of "1 mahogy. workstand," valued
at $7, that may refer to this object.[2] It descended in the
Cleaves and Lord families to the donor.   KDM

1 Margaret Burke Clunie, "Salem Federal Furniture" (M.A. thesis,
  University of Delaware, 1976), 89.
2 YCRP; 26:544.

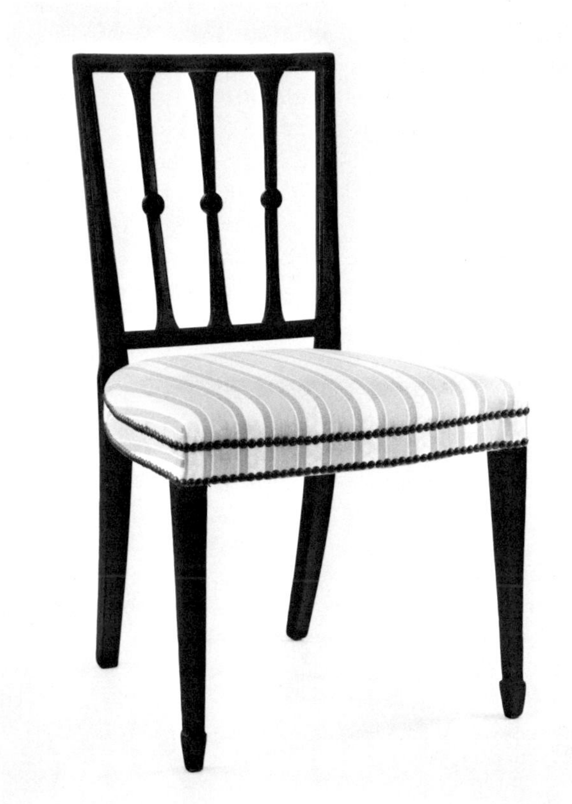

Cat. 101

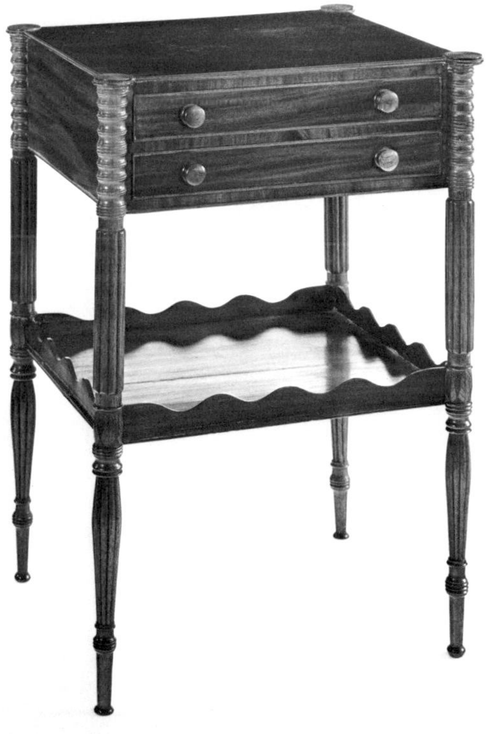

Cat. 100

101

Side chair (one of a pair)
Probably Portsmouth, New Hampshire, 1790–1815
Mahogany, *beech*
Branded (on rear seat rail) "THEODORE / BARRELL."
H 34⅝ (88.0); H seat 18⅜ (46.6);
W seat 20⅝ (52.4); D seat 17½ (44.5)
Old York Historical Society; Museum purchase
in memory of Mrs. Elizabeth Sewall Winton, 1978

The simple and delicate design of these mahogany chairs is
typical of furniture produced in Portsmouth in the early
nineteenth century. Their brands—"THEODORE / BARRELL."
on the center of the rear seat rails—also suggest a Portsmouth
provenance. While the branding of furniture by owners was
not a common practice in New England, a substantial
number of chairs, tables, and case furniture with Portsmouth
histories and marked in this way have been discovered. The
owner of these chairs may have branded them in accordance
with local customs, or for storage or moving.[1]

The ownership of the pair has been traditionally linked
to Theodore Barrell (1741–1796), the son of John and Ruth
Green Barrell of Boston, and brother of Portsmouth retailers

Colburn and Nathaniel Barrell (cat. 32). Theodore's mercantile activities included interests in the West Indies, and business connections with his brothers undoubtedly brought him to Portsmouth during his career. The chairs would have been of the latest fashion in the mid 1790s and, if they were indeed owned by Barrell, must have been purchased toward the end of his life. He died in Boston in 1796.[2]

The chairs may have been made in the first decade of the nineteenth century and owned by a younger Barrell. A Theodore Barrell, the son of John "of Barbados" and Maria Blackner, had his portrait painted in miniature around 1810.[3] While this younger Theodore, who would have been assembling a household around the time his portrait was executed, may be a more likely owner of the chairs, his Portsmouth connections are unknown.

The square back and double-beaded legs, stiles, and splats of the chairs suggest the work of Langley Boardman (1774–1833). Born in Ipswich, Massachusetts, Boardman probably apprenticed in Salem. He was working in Portsmouth by 1798 and five years later established what would become a large and lucrative workshop on Congress Street.[4]   KAO

1 Myrna Kaye, "Marked Portsmouth Furniture," *Antiques* 113, no. 5 (May 1978): 1098–1104.
2 The activities of the Barrell family are chronicled in Marston, "A Lady of Maine."
3 Miniatures of Theodore and his parents are in the collection of Cincinnati Art Museum which includes miniatures of prominent Portsmouth men and women, as well as an image of the elder Theodore Barrell (1741–1796).
4 See Montgomery, *American Furniture*, 85, for a similar side chair which descended in the Boardman family, and *Plain and Elegant, Rich and Common: Documented New Hampshire Furniture, 1750–1850* (Concord, N.H.: New Hampshire Historical Society, 1978), 22–29, 141–142.

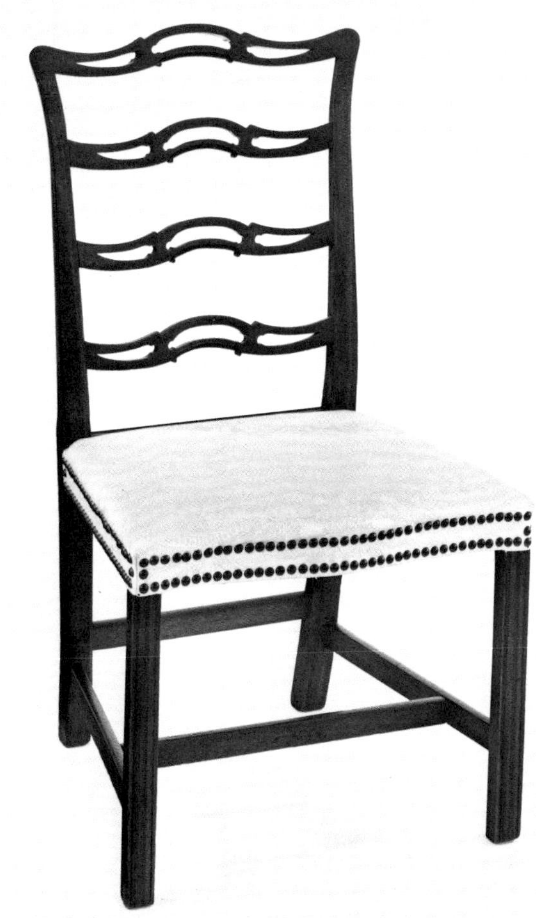

Cat. 102

102

Side chair
Maine or Massachusetts, 1775–1805
Mahogany, *maple*
H 36¾ (93.3); H seat 17 (43.2); W seat 21 (53.3); D seat 18 (45.7)
The Brick Store Museum
Gift of Mr. and Mrs. Dean A. Fales, Jr., 1977

The three decorative slats of this chair back repeat the design of the crest rail. This style was found on chairs starting around 1770; it was popular in Massachusetts for the remainder of the century. Elaborately carved examples with New England histories are known, as well as more modest designs. This chair back is one of many representing the middle range.[1] With its history in Kennebunk, this example documents that the style was also chosen by consumers in the District.

The pierced crest rail and slats are composed of three sections; the lower edge of the center section is carved. The stiles are simply planed to create molded edges and the straight molded or Marlboro legs are invariably seen with this type of chair back.[2] The seat is upholstered over the rails and further decorated with a serpentine front rail. Although the upholstery seen here is a replacement, a small scrap of black horsehair under a tack documents the fabric originally used. Because brass nails along the seat rails are known to have decorated chairs of this type, those seen here may have replaced the originals. Sets of side chairs with horsehair upholstery appear in household inventories as "6 Hair. bottomd chairs."[3]

This chair descended to Edward E. Bourne, Jr., from William B. Sewall, the son of Daniel Sewall. It was probably originally owned by Daniel Sewall and furnished his three-story house in Kennebunk (fig. 2.23). The chair appears to have been listed in 1910 in the "Record of Old

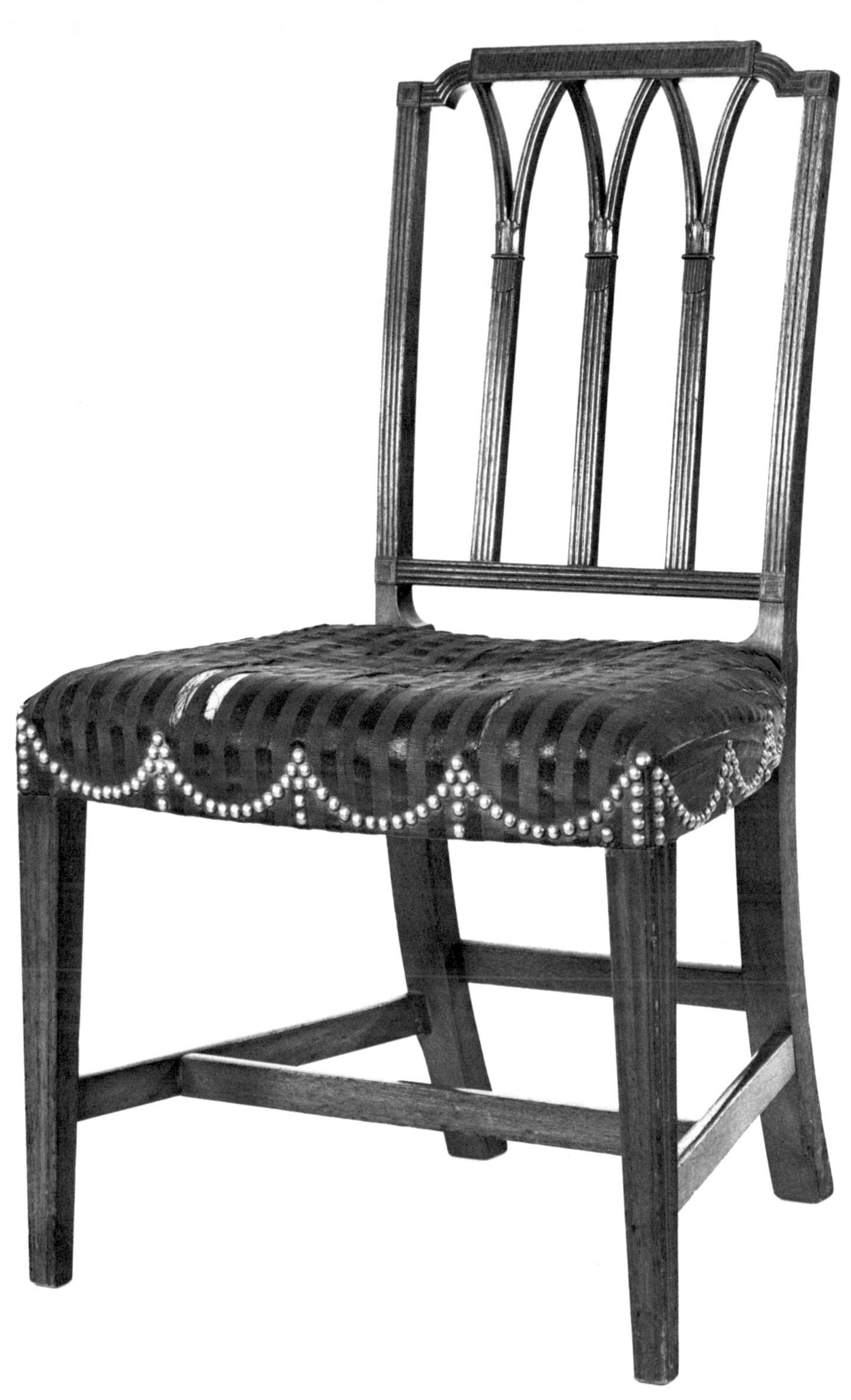

Cat. 103

Furniture" compiled by Harold H. Bourne, a grandson of
Edward E. Bourne, Jr.[4] The Sewall furnishings remained
together in the house for five generations until their sale in
1964. Purchased at that time, this side chair was later given
to the museum where it complements other Bourne family
possessions in the collection (see cats. 91, 108).   LFS

1 Jobe and Kaye, *New England Furniture*, 423–431.
2 Jobe and Kaye, *New England Furniture*, 423.
3 YCRP; 36:288.
4 Harold H. Bourne, "The Bourne Family of Kennebunk, Maine, .
   Record of Old Furniture, 1910" (manuscript, BSM). The chair was
   listed as "No. 34."

103

Side chair (one of three)
Boston, Massachusetts, 1785–1810
Mahogany, *birch*, *cherry*
H 36¹³⁄₁₆ (93.6); H seat 18½ (47.0);
D seat 17⅜ (44.0); W seat 15⅜ (39.0)
York Institute Museum
Bequest of Almira Locke McArthur, 1950

Inspired by the "gothick" taste, this chair descended in the
family of Almira Cleaves Dummer, a daughter of Daniel
Cleaves. It is exceptional for its original striped horsehair
covering which is further ornamented by the swags of brass
nails along the front and side seat rails. Such a survival is
rare and is of importance as documentation for the appearance and contour of upholstery in the federal period.[1]

The shape of the back of this chair is described in an
1802 English price book as "square back chair with elliptic
cornered top containing a tablet."[2] The inlaid tablet along
the crest rail appears to be of figured birch; the corners are
decorated with inlaid stringing. The reeded arches in the
back of the chair are decorated with carved sheaves of wheat
at the intersections. Other chairs of Boston manufacture
with similar backs are known. Cabinetmakers in that city
offered several options. Crest rails could be inlaid with other
woods such as mahogany; legs could be reeded or molded,
with tapered or spade feet.[3]   LFS

1 The other two chairs do not retain their original covering, although
   the hair stuffing and webbing of the under-upholstery survives.
2 Montgomery, *American Furniture*, 83.
3 Richard H. Randall, Jr., *American Furniture in the Museum of Fine Arts*
   (Boston, Mass.: Museum of Fine Arts, 1965), 212–213.

104

Side chair (part of a set)
Probably Boston, Massachusetts, 1815–1825
Mahogany, *birch*
H 33⅜ (84.8); H seat 15⅞ (40.3);
W seat 18 (45.7); D seat 15¼ (38.7)
York Institute Museum
Bequest of Almira Locke McArthur, 1950

This sophisticated klismos-type chair is one of eight that
survive in the York Institute Museum and The Brick Store
Museum. The Roman numerals marking the rear seat rails
and slip seats indicate that there were at least twenty-one
chairs in the set. Twenty-four chairs would have comprised a
large set of chairs.[1]

Grecian in inspiration, the form reflects the neoclassical
aesthetic of the early nineteenth century. While klismos
chairs were imported from England at the end of the
eighteenth century, the first domestic examples were
probably produced by New York cabinetmaker Duncan
Phyfe by 1815. The lyres on these chairs, "strung" with brass
rods and enriched with flat foliate carving, relate to lyres
found on Boston tables. More expensive versions of this type

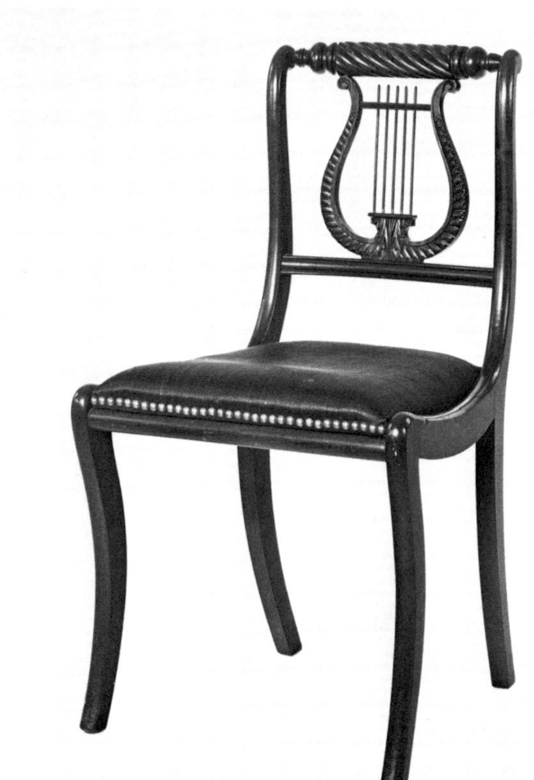

Cat. 104

of chair feature front legs carved in imitation of fur and terminating in brass lion's-paw feet.[2]

This chair, and the remaining armchair and three side chairs at the York Institute Museum, retain their original black horsehair upholstery. Although the three side chairs at The Brick Store Museum have lost their horsehair covering, they do retain the original under-upholstery. Brass nails ornament the edge of the front seat rails. The birch slip seats fit into the front and side rails and rest on the rear seat rail, further secured by iron pins which project from the front and rear seat rails into the slip seats.

The five York Institute Museum chairs and three Brick Store Museum chairs descended in the Almira Cleaves Dummer family of Hallowell and Saco, Maine, and the Sarah Cleaves Lord family of Kennebunk, respectively. They may have originally belonged to the parents of these women, Daniel and Sarah Cleaves. Daniel died in 1818, so it seems more likely that the set furnished the home of the younger Sarah, married in 1820, or of Almira, who married seven years later.[3]

These chairs are strikingly similar to two side chairs at the Portland Museum of Art. They are about the same size; the main difference of the Portland chairs is that the front seat rails have a double beaded molding. Like the chairs illustrated here, they retain their original black horsehair upholstery and brass nails along the front of the slip seat. The Portland chairs were in the McLellan-Sweat mansion when the house was given to the museum in 1908. Although the identity of the original owners is unclear, Margaret Jane Mussey Sweat belonged to the Mussey, Wingate, Clapp, and Dearborn families of Portland.[4]   KDM & LFS

1 The seat rails and corresponding slip seats of the Saco chairs are numbered IV, XIV, XVI, and XXI, and the Kennebunk chairs I, VII, and XIX. The armchair is not numbered.
2 Montgomery, *American Furniture*, 126–127; Patricia E. Kane, *Three Hundred Years of American Seating Furniture: Chairs and Beds from the Mabel Brady Garvan and other Collections at Yale University* (Boston: New York Graphic Society, 1976), 177–178; Page Talbott, letter to author, April 15, 1986. The lyres on four of the chairs have undergone repairs.
3 BSM chairs were from the estate of William E. Barry through Edith Cleaves Barry.
4 The Portland Museum chairs are numbered XI or IX on the rear seat rail (1908.13) and VI (1908.14).

105

William Seaver and James Frost (w. 1800–1803)
Armchair
Boston, Massachusetts, 1800–1803
Maple, pine
Branded (on bottom) "SEAVER & FROST"
H 38⅜ (97.5); H seat 18⁹⁄₁₆ (47.0); W seat 20¹⁄₁₆ (51.0);
D seat 17⅝ (44.7)
The Brick Store Museum
Gift of Mary McCulloch Marshall, 1942

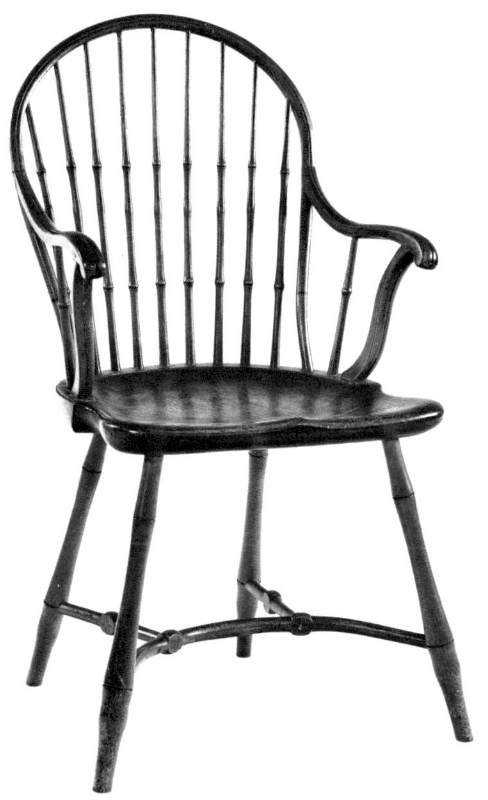

Cat. 105

This is one of two windsor armchairs with York County histories and the maker's brand of "SEAVER & FROST." One has a provenance in the Jeremiah McIntire family of York; this chair belonged to Kennebunk's Hugh McCulloch family and was used at their house at The Landing (fig. 3.3). William Seaver and James Frost were partners in Boston at the turn of the nineteenth century and advertised their sale of windsor chairs and settees.[1]

The influence of imported goods in America is evident in both the turnings and arrangement of the stretchers. Bamboo turnings on windsor chairs began to replace baluster turnings on legs and stretchers during the 1780s and reflected the influence of the China trade. Some chairs have turnings that imitate bamboo almost to exaggeration and may be the type referred to as "bamboo chairs" in the 1818 inventory of Cyrus King. Earlier English windsors with this same curved stretcher configuration probably served as a prototype for this chair.[2]

Painted surfaces withstood the moisture and sun that stained and faded costly upholstered furniture. Consequently, windsors were also used on porches, in gardens, and on board ships. This chair was painted mustard-yellow with dark striping on the spindles. With close attention to detail, the decorator painted flowers to ornament the stretchers. The paint survives in good condition because for many years it was "swaddled in old comforters. . . . On removing the disfiguring swaddling clothes it appeared as you see it; too lovely," its donor said, "to live outside a Museum."[3]   AAE

1   The OYHS owns the McIntire chair. Nancy Goyne Evans, Winterthur Museum, letter to OYHS, October 17, 1974.
2   Nancy Goyne, "American Windsor Chairs: A Style Survey," *Antiques* 95, no. 4 (April 1969): 539–540; Jonathan L. Fairbanks and Elizabeth Bidwell Bates, *American Furniture, 1620 to the Present* (New York: Richard Marek Publishers, 1981), 288. YCRP; 27: 315. John T. Kirk, *American Furniture and the British Tradition to 1830* (New York: Alfred A. Knopf, 1982), 297–298.
3   Disbursements for ship *Alexander*, 1803, William King Papers, Maine State Library. Four windsor chairs costing $5.67 were purchased in Liverpool for use on board the ship. Note attached to chair by donor; see object file, BSM.

106

Side chair
Northeastern United States, 1800–1825
Birch, eastern white pine, ash
Incised (on bottom) "EB"
H 35¾ (90.8); H seat 17½ (44.5);
w seat 15½ (39.4); D seat 15⅞ (40.3)
Maine Historical Society; Wadsworth-Longfellow House

Windsor chairs displaying decorated crest rails and back slats became popular at the turn of the nineteenth century. Referred to in the early nineteenth century as "bent-back" or "square back" chairs, windsors like this one were decorated with the same floral and abstract motifs and striping that also appeared on fancy chairs.[1]

Graining, gilding, striping, and other options offered a multitude of possibilities for a chair's decoration. Skilled decorators painted freehand designs at first, but as mass production increased, stencilling replaced, or at least reduced, the amount of freehand decoration and brought semi-skilled workers into the decorating process. Green leaves and ovals of yellow-orange appear in a stylized, repetitive pattern on the crest rail of this chair, and gold-painted foliate designs spill down the chamfered rear stiles and also ornament the middle of the front legs.

Chairmakers and merchants who advertised windsors often sold fancy chairs as well. By the beginning of the nineteenth century, fancy chairs began to replace windsors as elegant, though affordable, seating furniture for parlors, halls, and other rooms.[2] The identity of the craftsman who incised the back-to-back initials "EB" on this chair is unknown.   AAE

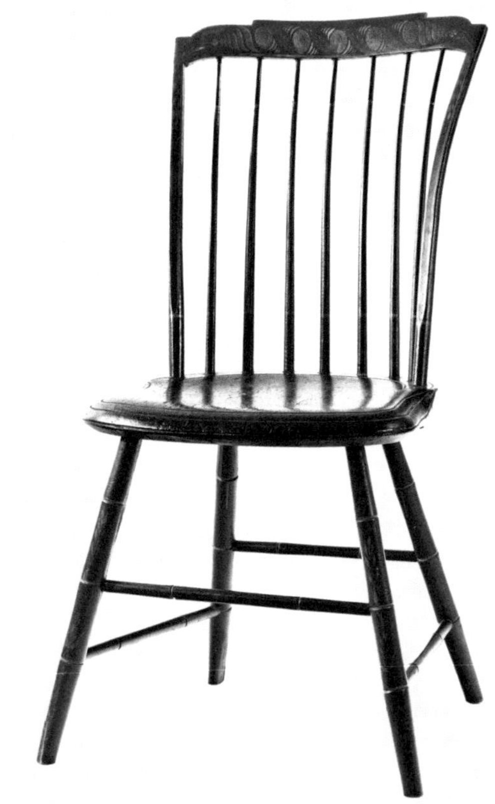

Cat. 106

1   Nancy Goyne Evans, Winterthur Museum, letter to author, October 2, 1985. No period documentation has provided an obvious description of what is currently referred to as a "step-down" windsor.
2   This chair is illustrated in Zilla Ryder Lea, *The Ornamented Chair: Its Development in America 1700–1890* (Rutland, Vt.: Charles E. Tuttle Co., 1960), 68.

107

Side chair (one of four)
York or Cumberland County, Maine,
or Boston, Massachusetts, 1820–1835
Birch, beech, maple, basswood
H 32¹¹⁄₁₆ (83.0); H seat 18⅛ (46.0);
w seat 18½ (46.9); D seat 16⅜ (41.5)
The Brick Store Museum; William E. Barry estate through Edith Cleaves Barry

This chair, one of a set of four, has red and black graining simulating rosewood, and could be the type of chair described as "fancy Red flag bottom" in Thomas Thornton's 1824 inventory. His twelve side and four arm chairs were in a room furnished with a fashionable mahogany sideboard and

sofa.[1] The curly abstract design on the rectangular crest rail
is painted a mustard-gold, and imitates ormolu mounts and
applied brass ornaments found on high-style pier tables,
sideboards, chairs, and other objects.

Chairs like this could have been sold by Saco merchant
Lauriston Ward, who advertised in a Kennebunk newspaper
in 1832. His notice bears a woodcut illustration similar to
these chairs and lists "FANCY FLAG BOTTOM CHAIRS,"
"Double back Yellow and Rose Wood do," and other items.
Other local merchants advertised that they sold "Boston
Furniture." Daniel Wise of Kennebunk advertised "Brown,
Yellow and Green Chairs with gilt backs" and the Ken-
nebunk firm of Chadbourn and Junkins likewise advertised
"BOSTON FURNITURE . . . consisting of Yellow, Red, Green
and Brown CHAIRS, Flag Bottom do."[2]   AAE

1 YCRP; 33: 273.
2 *Kennebunk Gazette* (February 18, 1832; August 13, 1825; June 25,
  1825). Two fancy chairs at BSM with a Lord-Barry family provenance
  have a similar back and stretcher configuration; they retain their
  original mustard-yellow paint.

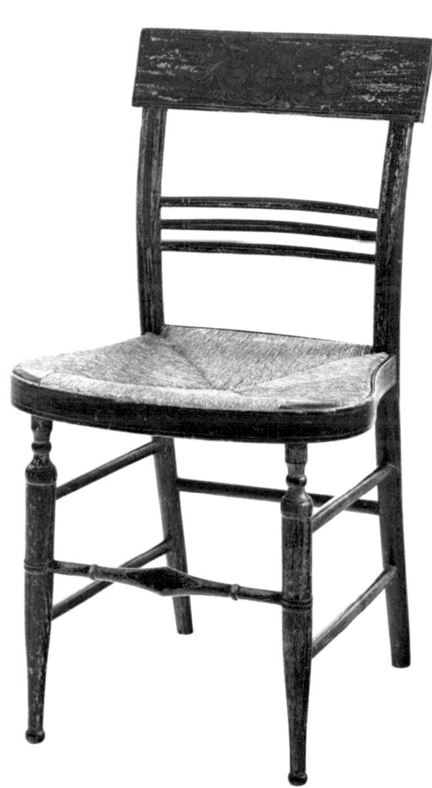

Cat. 107

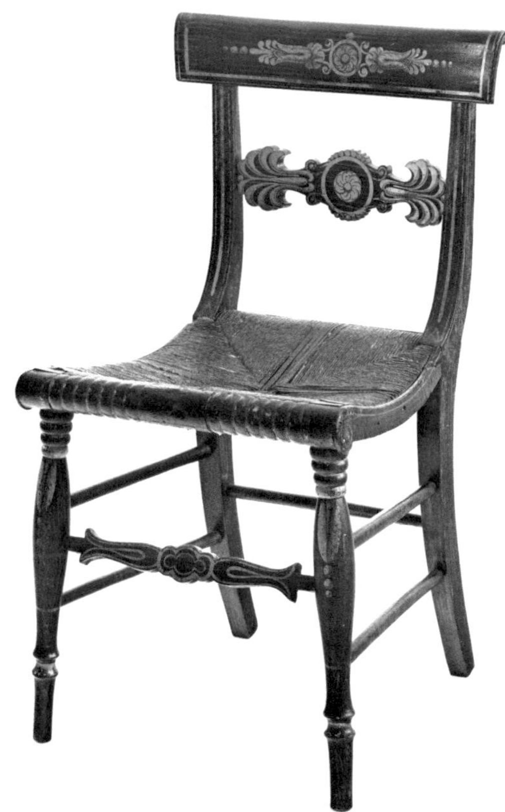

Cat. 108

108

Side chair
New York City or Philadelphia, Pennsylvania,
1810–1830
Yellow poplar, soft maple, hickory, red gum
H 32⅝ (82.8); H seat 17¹⁵⁄₁₆ (45.6);
W seat 14⁵⁄₁₆ (36.3); D seat 16⁹⁄₁₆ (42.0)
The Brick Store Museum
Gift of Mr. and Mrs. Dean A. Fales, Jr., 1977

This chair owned by Kennebunk's Bourne family is indicative of the wide range of goods that trade brought to coastal
towns. Grained and painted to simulate rosewood with
ormolu mounts, it imitates contemporary high-style chairs
based on classical furniture forms. Similarly fashionable, this
chair was available at a more moderate price.[1]

Elements adapted from antiquity and used in furniture
were more than just stylistic imitations. When Englishman
Thomas Hope published a collection of furniture designs in
1807 based on Greek and Egyptian forms, he wrote: "the

association of all the elegancies of antique forms and ornaments . . . might be capable of enobling" common furniture forms. His furniture designs could also refine "the intellectual and sensible enjoyments of the individual; and . . . produce farther advancement in virtue and patriotism."[2]

This chair was purchased in 1964 when the contents of the Bourne mansion were sold; it was later given to the museum (see cats. 91, 102). Harold Bourne, a descendant, noted that the chair had belonged to Benjamin Nason, who was from another branch of the family.[3]   AAE

1 Montgomery, *American Furniture*, 456. See also Dean A. Fales, Jr., *American Painted Furniture* (New York: E. P. Dutton, 1972), 192–193. Six similar chairs with grain-painting over a yellow ground and painted decoration in imitation of ormolu mounts are at the Macphaedris-Warner house in Portsmouth, New Hampshire. Family history maintains that the chairs were part of a larger set used in the house ca. 1815. One of the chairs appears in a 1928 photograph of Evelyn (Eva) Sherburne, the last member of the Warner-Sherburne family to inhabit the house.
2 Thomas Hope, *Household Furniture and Interior Decoration* (1807; reprint, New York: Dover Publications, 1971), 7.
3 H. H. Bourne, "The Bourne Family of Kennebunk, Maine, Record of Old Furniture, 1910" (manuscript, BSM). The Faleses kindly brought this reference to my attention.

109

Looking glass
Northern Europe or England, 1770–1800
Mahogany veneer, *spruce*, *scotch* or *red pine*,
white oak, composition, gilt
H 41½ (105.4); W 22½ (57.2)
Old York Historical Society

Often associated with the colonial period, new mahogany-framed looking glasses continued to be purchased at the end of the eighteenth century. Although this glass has no confirmed history in a Maine family, it illustrates a standard type that appears frequently in York County household inventories and other primary sources. In 1788, Samuel Abbott (d. 1792) married Mary Cutts, the oldest child of Colonel Thomas Cutts. In September Abbott traveled to Boston where he purchased "1 Large Mahogany frame Glass" for £5.8.0 from Oliver Brewster. Among the looking glasses that Thomas Cutts, Jr., imported in the ship *Minerva* was "1 sq. [looking glass,] feather top, 32 x 19."[1]

Mahogany frames with feather or scroll tops gave way to the gilt and composition frames that survive in quantity (see cats. 110–111). In October 1800 when Enoch Preble was in Boston, he purchased four looking glasses. The one identified as "mahogany framed" cost £4.10.0. The "Gilt Looking Glass" at £9 cost twice as much.[2] Because of the expense of gilded frames, those made of mahogany continued to satisfy the demand for more modestly priced looking glasses.

This looking glass could have been imported from Holland or England. A looking glass that may be a Dutch import survives at the Marrett house in Standish. "Dutch looking glasses" were advertised for sale in Portland in 1815.[3]

Heavy looking glasses had to be firmly secured to the walls. Thatcher Goddard sold his house in 1801 to Hugh McCulloch with the condition that he reserved the right "of taking down and carrying away . . . 1 looking glass which [is] screwed or nailed to the walls" (see fig. 3.3).[4]   KDM

1 Montgomery, *American Furniture*, 253. Bill, Oliver Brewster to Samuel Abbott, September 24, 1788, YIS. The yard of gauze he purchased at the same time may have been used to protect the glass. Thomas Cutts, Jr., shipping book, 1793–1797, MEHS.
2 Enoch Preble, expense book, MEHS.
3 The Marrett glass is discussed in Jobe and Kaye, *New England Furniture*, 458–459; *Portland Gazette* (December 26, 1815).
4 YCRD; 60:240. For an eighteenth-century glass *in situ*, see Nylander, "Sayward House," plate 5.

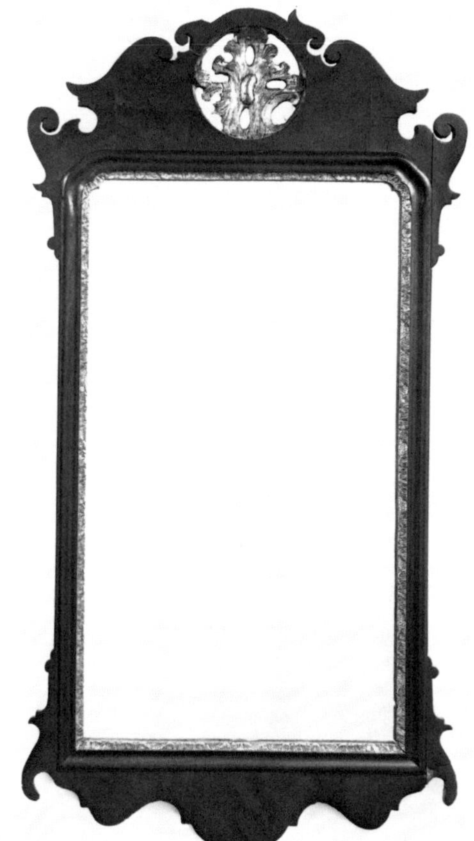

Cat. 109

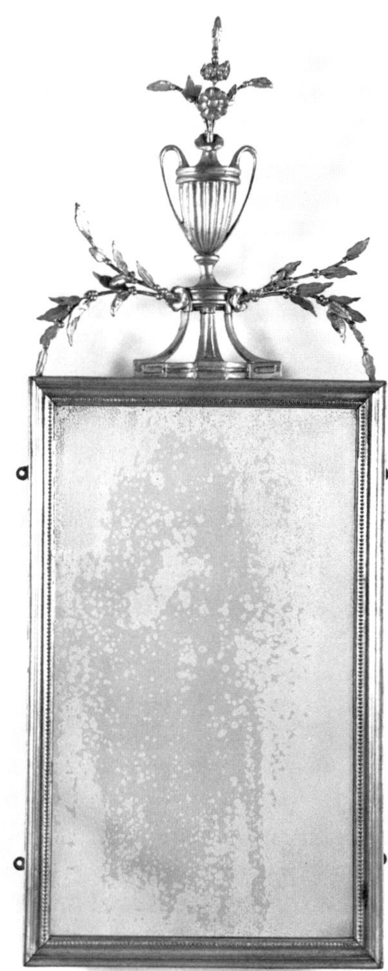

Cat. 110

110

Looking glass (one of a pair)
New England, possibly Boston, Massachusetts,
1790–1810
Pine, gesso, composition, gilt
H 42 (106.6); W 15¹⁵⁄₁₆ (40.5)
York Institute Museum
Bequest of Almira Locke McArthur, 1950

Family history maintains that this pair of looking glasses was purchased by Daniel and Sarah Cleaves at the time of their marriage in 1795. The 1818 inventory of Daniel Cleaves listed four looking glasses, valued collectively at $24.[1] The simple beaded frames are ornamented by handled urns sprouting gesso flowers and supported by pedestals.

Popularized by cabinetmakers' guides, looking glasses such as this were owned in number by wealthy families, like the Cleaveses, who decorated their houses in the neoclassical style. Looking glasses were imported throughout the eighteenth century; domestic production started about 1800. The domestic products were available in Maine through the coastwise trade, particularly with Boston. John Doggett of Roxbury, the largest looking glass manufacturer in New England, sent his glasses to Portland as did Stillman Lothrop, another Boston maker. Doggett also sold materials used in the manufacture of looking glasses to such firms as that of Paul Cermenati and John Bernarda, purveyors of looking glasses in Boston, Salem, Newburyport, and Portsmouth between 1803 and 1812. To capitalize on the growing market in southern Maine, Cermenati and Bernarda opened a shop on Free Street in Portland in February 1804. The firm advertised "a large assortment of looking glasses of all sizes, on the most *reasonable terms.*"[2]

A glass featuring the same large central urn and composition ornament was among the Lord family possessions in Kennebunk. It was drawn in the 1880s by the antiquarian William Barry.[3]   KDM

1 John S. Locke inscribed the information on the backboard when he "restored" the looking glass in 1888. YCRP; 33:544–545.
2 Montgomery, *American Furniture*, 253–257, 479. *Portland Commercial Gazette* (February 15, 1804).
3 The drawing is in BSM.

111

Looking glass (one of a pair)
Probably Boston, Massachusetts, 1795–1810
Red or *scots pine*, composition, gilt
H 43⅞ (111.4); W 22⅝ (57.5)
York Institute Museum
Bequest of Almira Locke McArthur, 1950

Owned by the Cleaveses, the same family that owned a pair of urn-topped glasses (cat. 110), these flat-topped looking glasses illustrate another type that received widespread attention during the federal period. Reverse-painted entablatures were a standard means of ornamentation, and the motifs are countless. They included American or patriotic symbols, and landscape views. Here, the scene consists of a swag of trumpet-shaped flowers, roses, and bows. The twisted columns along the sides of the glass were often described as "single pillar." Balls are standard ornaments on gilt frames.[1]

The glass plates in looking glasses were often broken and repaired. In many cases, the original wooden backing used to hold the glass within the frame has been replaced. These looking glasses are remarkable not only in the survival of their original glass plates, but also in the survival of the linen that was used to cover the back of the frame and protect the glass (cat. 111.1). The linen has been attached to the frame with small roseheaded tacks. Also visible is an iron nail driven through the back of the cornice that provided the hook for hanging. To the left and right of this center support are the pencil inscriptions "32 x 18" and "D. Cleaves," respectively. Once the pair had been selected by or for Cleaves, the measurements for the size of the glass plate to be set into the frames were noted as well.

Looking glasses were often covered with muslin or gauze to protect the glass and gilding from fly specks. In a letter published in the *Memoirs* of the American Academy of Arts and Sciences, Portsmouth minister Timothy Alden reported on the effects of lightning that struck a house near the Piscataqua River. It "threw down a large looking glass, which was broken, seemingly, into a thousand pieces; [and] burnt a considerable part of a muslin covering, which was drawn over the face of the glass."[2]   LFS

1 Montgomery, *American Furniture*, 257. Another glass with similar reverse-painted decoration descended in Kennebunk's Lord family and is in BSM.
2 See cat. 109, n1. American Academy of Arts and Sciences, *Memoirs* (Cambridge, Mass., 1809), 93–94.

112

Porringer
New England, 1743–1789
Silver
Unmarked
H 8³⁄₁₆ (20.8); Diam. 5⁵⁄₁₆ (13.5)
Maine Historical Society; Gift of Henry F. Homes

This porringer, with a keyhole handle similar to the Simpkins porringer (cat. 46), has a history of ownership in the Freeman family of Portland.[1] Samuel Freeman was born in 1743, and later served as judge of probate and clerk of courts

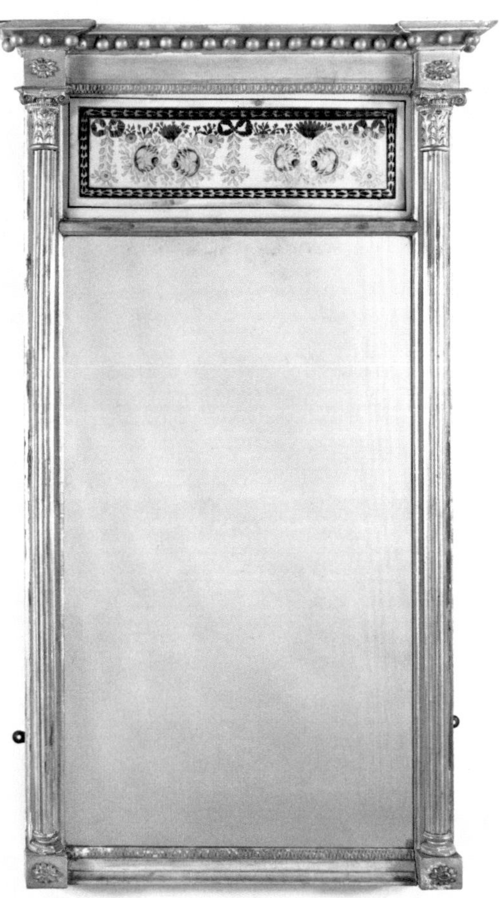

Cat. 111

Cat. 111.1

for Cumberland County (see cat. 158). The underside of the handle bears his initials "SF" in engraved block letters. The upper side of the handle bears a later script engraving, "DF," for his third daughter, Dorcas Freeman, born in 1789. It was presented to the Maine Historical Society by her grandson.

The expense of heavy hollowware objects was directly related to the amount of the precious metal required for their production. The intrinsic value of silver is evident in probate inventories, where silver possessions, including porringers, tankards, and canns, are sometimes recorded by total weight, rather than the worth of the individual objects.[2]

AAE

1 It differs from the Cutts porringer by the absence of two furls on the outer edge of the handle.
2 For one example, see YCRP; 14:56.

113

Ebenezer Moulton (1768–1824)
Creamer
Boston, Massachusetts, ca. 1795
Silver
Marked (on bottom) "MOULTON" in rectangle
H 5⁵⁄₁₆ (13.5); W 5⅛ (13.0)
The Brick Store Museum; William E. Barry estate
through Edith Cleaves Barry

Silver was an appropriate material for presentation gifts. This creamer is thought to have been given to Daniel Cleaves and Sarah Fairfield at the time of their marriage in 1795. It appears in the 1818 probate inventory of Daniel Cleaves as "1 silver creampot," valued at $7.

Cleaves, like other merchants, owned much silver flatware. Included in his estate were "11 silver table spoons" and "33 tea spoons" appraised at $27.50 and $22.50, respectively. This creamer is of interest because it is the only silver hollowware object recorded in the inventory, most of which was made of less-expensive plated silver, such as the tea and coffee set (cat. 117), a pair of salts, a pair of candlesticks, and a tray and snuffers.[1] This helmet-shaped pot, a shape introduced during the federal period, is decorated with well-executed bright-cut engraving. The oval medallion with a ribbon above encloses the cipher "DSC." A second medallion, without script initials, decorates the reverse.[2]

Technological changes affecting the craft are evident here. Until the late eighteenth century, silversmiths constructed most hollowware such as tankards and creamers by forging the forms from a silver disc. Other elements such as handles or cast decoration were then applied to the vessel. By the late eighteenth century, rolled sheet silver had become available and forms with flat surfaces became easier to make.

AAE

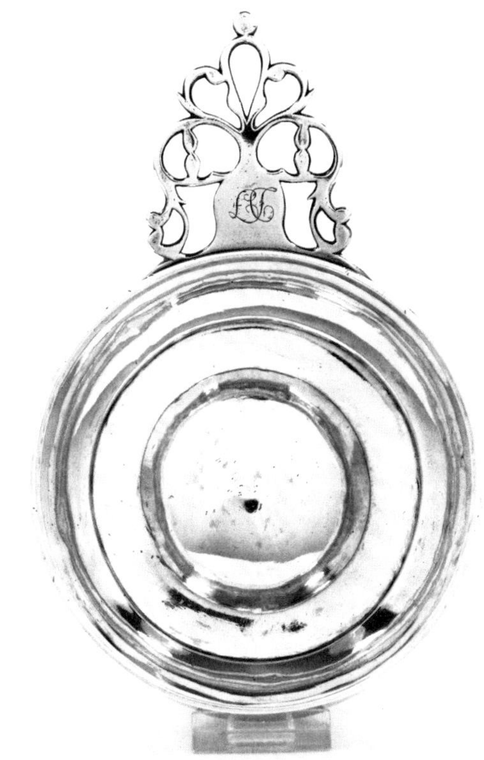

Cat. 112

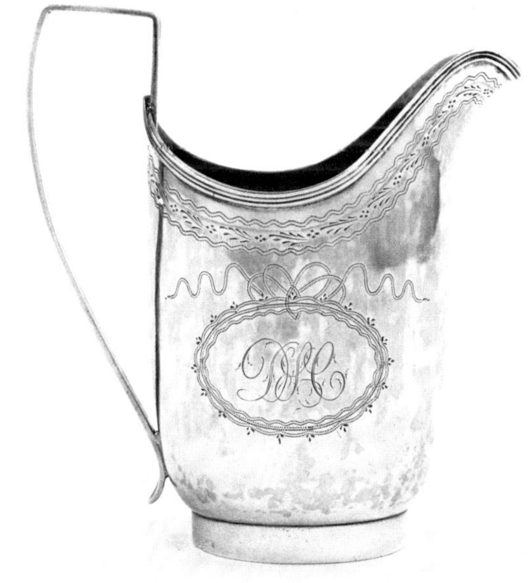

Cat. 113

1 YCRP; 26:544.
2 This creamer is similar in form and decoration to others attributed to
  Ebenezer Moulton. One, with a matching teapot and sugar bowl, was
  made for Judith Sprague on her marriage to Gershom Bradford
  Weston in 1820. See Kathryn C. Buhler, *American Silver from the
  Colonial Period to the Early Republic in the Worcester Art Museum* (Worcester,
  Mass.: Worcester Art Museum, 1979), 60–61. The Essex Institute
  owns a similar creamer engraved "AO."

114

Ebenezer Moulton (1768–1824)
Mug
Boston, Massachusetts, ca. 1808
Silver
Marked (on bottom) "MOULTON" in rectangle
H 3¹⁄₁₆ (7.8); Diam. bottom 2¼ (5.7)
York Institute Museum
Bequest of Almira Locke McArthur, 1950

With its horizontal banding applied at the rim and engraved
on the body, this small child's mug is typical of federal-period
hollowware forms and decoration. The molded handle
appears large for the size of the mug, but would have been
easy for a child to grasp. The initials "AMN" are engraved in
script opposite the handle.

    This mug was given to Ann Matilda Nye, probably at the

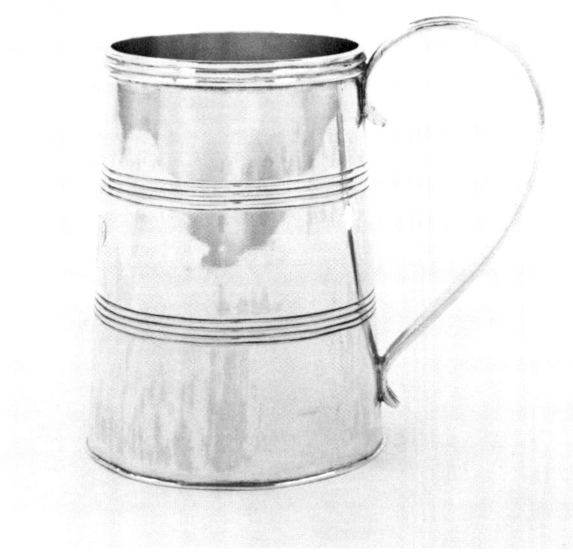

Cat. 114

time of her birth in 1808. Her parents Samuel and Eunice
Cutts Nye lived in Boston when Ann was born. The family
returned to Saco in 1812. Ann died unmarried in 1889.
Other Nye family objects were given to the York Institute by
1892.[1] AAE

1 Cecil Hampden Cutts Howard, comp., *Genealogy of the Cutts Family in
  America* (Albany, N.Y.: Joel Munsell's Sons, 1892), 88.

115

Coffee and tea set (selections)
England, 1795–1818
Fused plate, *boxwood*
Unmarked
H coffeepot 10¾ (27.4); H teapot 6½ (16.5);
H creamer 4½ (11.5); H sugar bowl 5 (12.7)
York Institute Museum
Bequest of Almira Locke McArthur, 1950

Fused-plated objects, made of a sheet of copper covered with
thin sheets of silver applied through heat and compression in
a rolling mill, were a popular alternative to sterling flatware
and hollowware. The fusion of the two metals was first
perfected in Sheffield, England, in the mid eighteenth
century; by 1780 it was readily available in the United
States. For many years fused-plated wares, generally known
now as Sheffield plate, were imported and sold by merchants
and jewelers as well as silversmiths.

    Inventories attest to the range of forms for which
Sheffield plate was made and used. Most frequently recorded
are cruet stands, candlesticks, "tray and snuffers," and items
associated with the service of coffee and tea. However,
Sheffield plate also appeared in other forms, such as Thomas
Thornton's pair of plated spurs and clasps (see cat. 125).

    This set, consisting of a coffeepot, teapot, creamer, and
sugar bowl, appeared in both the 1818 inventory of Daniel
Cleaves and the 1838 inventory of his widow, Sarah. An
illustration in an 1815 advertisement of Portland silversmiths
Eleazer Wyer and Charles Farley resembles the Cleaves set
in its gadrooning on the base and D-shaped handle. In 1820
Wyer and Farley advertised "Plated Tea Setts . . . Plated
Candlesticks—Snuffers and Trays," which they had purchased for resale.[1]

    Matched sets of silver became more widespread in the
federal period. Decorative boxwood handles, rectangular
ivory finials, and gadrooning added fashionable elements to
the design of this set. AAE

1 YCRP; 26:544; 48:454. *Portland Gazette* (1815), as reprinted in
  Churchill, "Crafts in Transition," 308. The cut was still in use five
  years later; see *Portland Gazette* (June 15, 1820). A pair of plated
  candlesticks at BSM have a history in Kennebunk's Lord family.

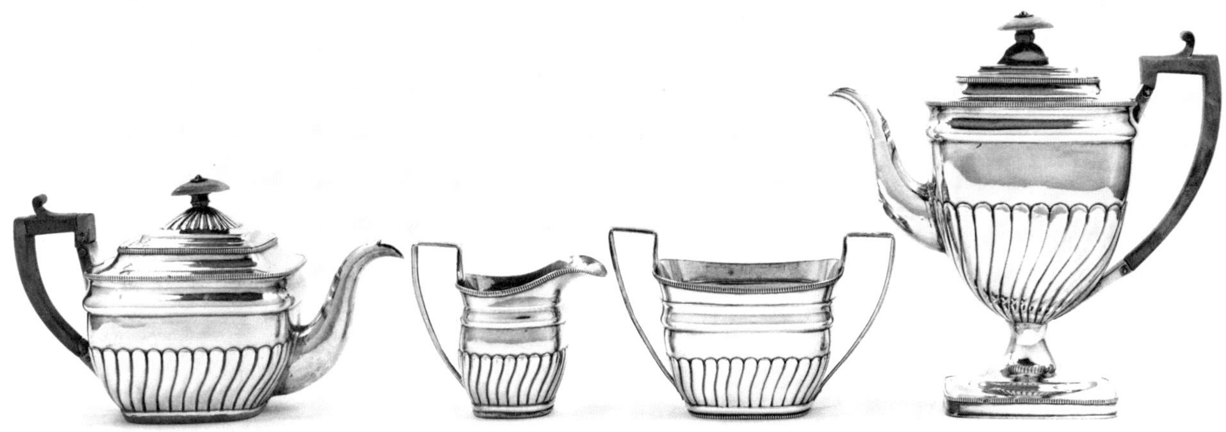

Cat. 115

116A

Ebenezer Moulton (1768–1824)
Tablespoon
Boston, Massachusetts, ca. 1795
Silver
Marked (on back of handle) "MOULTON" in rectangle
L 9¹⁄₁₆ (23.0)
The Brick Store Museum; William E. Barry estate
through Edith Cleaves Barry, 1936

116B

William Homes, Jr. (1742–1825)
Tablespoon
Boston, Massachusetts, ca. 1795
Silver
Marked (on back of handle) "WH" in rectangle
L 9¼ (23.5)
The Brick Store Museum; William E. Barry estate
through Edith Cleaves Barry, 1936

Flatware in the form of teaspoons, tablespoons, dessert, and
salt spoons comprised the largest number of silver objects
found in Maine households. Spoons surviving from the
federal period with Maine histories attest to the broad range
of styles available for purchase whether in or out of Maine.

Daniel and Sarah Cleaves owned Boston-made silver
including these tablespoons from the shops of both Ebenezer
Moulton and William Homes, Jr. The Moulton tablespoon
is engraved with their initials in a bright-cut oval and was

probably made about the time of their marriage in 1795.
This is one of two tablespoons and two teaspoons made by
Moulton for these customers.[1] Moulton also made a silver
creamer decorated with engraved initials (cat. 113).

William Homes, Jr., also crafted a tablespoon with
similar bright-cutting for the couple. These spoons along
with others were recorded in Daniel Cleaves's inventory as
"11 silver table spoons $27.50" and "33 teaspoons, silvr
$22.00."[2] Homes received the patronage of other Maine
residents. John Quinby (cat. 33) bought six silver table
spoons for $19 from Homes while on a trip to Boston.[3]   AAE

1 The other spoons are at YIS.
2 YCRP; 26:544. Teaspoons by Homes and Stephen Emery, also of
   Boston, with bright-cut engraving and the engraved initials "C/DS"
   within an oval, survive at YIS.
3 Account, W. Homes to John Quinby, n.d., Quinby Papers, MEHS.

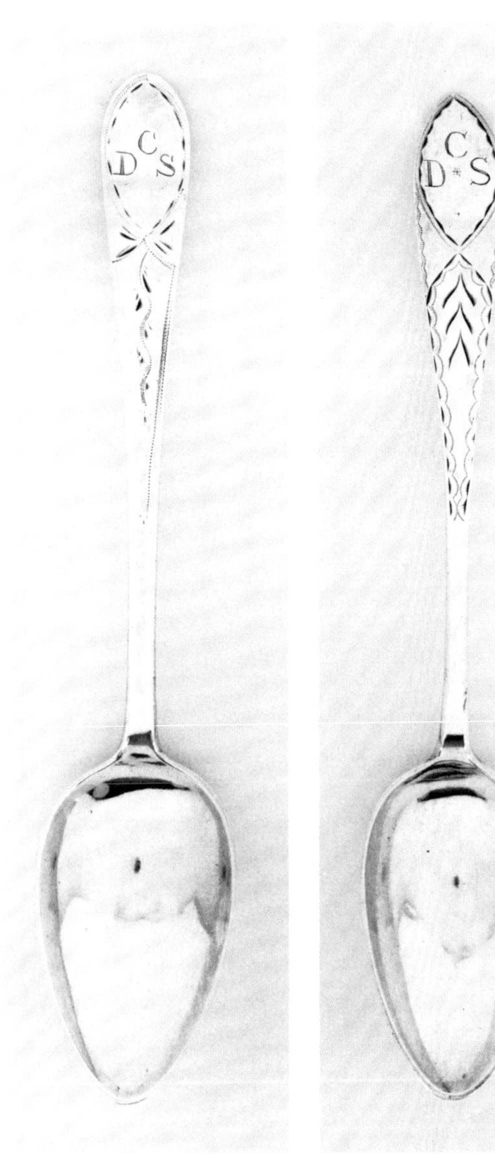

Cat. 116A

Cat. 116B

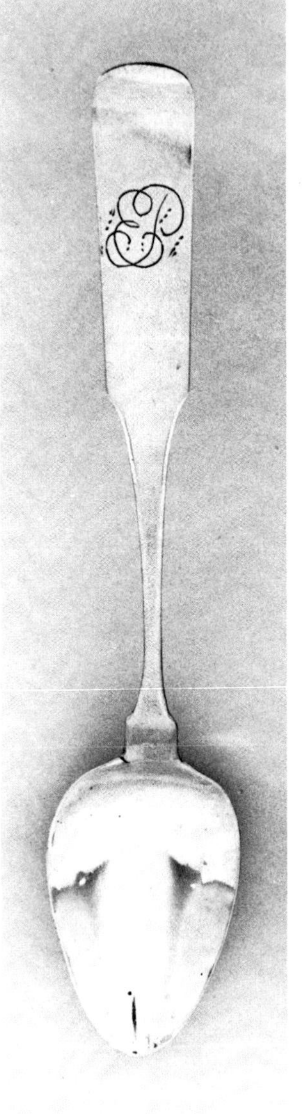

Cat. 117A

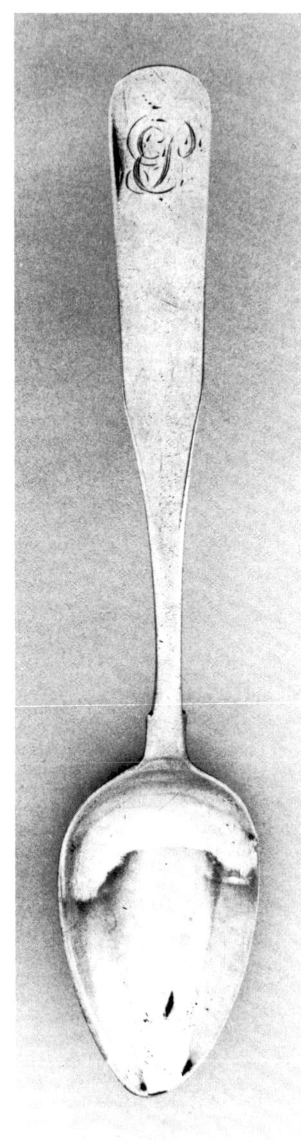

Cat. 117B

117A

Enoch Moulton (1780–1820?)
Teaspoon (one of four)
Portland, Maine, ca. 1810
Silver
Marked (on back of handle) "E. MOULTON" in rectangle
L 5⅜ (13.7)
Maine Historical Society
Gift of Mrs. William R. Smith, 1938

117B

Eleazer Wyer, Jr. (1786–1848)
Teaspoon (one of six)
Portland, Maine, ca. 1810
Silver
Marked (on back of handle) "E. WYER" in rectangle
L 5¼ (13.3)
Maine Historical Society
Gift of Mrs. William R. Smith, 1938

Simply engraved "EP," these teaspoons are two of ten that belonged to Experience Jordan, who married Samuel Parris in 1788. They represent the work of two Portland silversmiths. Four of the set were crafted by Enoch Moulton with fiddle handles and pointed bowls. The son of Joseph Moulton, a silversmith in Newburyport, Enoch was in Portland by 1803 when he advertised in the *Eastern Argus*.[1]

Experience also purchased flatware from Eleazer Wyer. A Boston native, he was in Portland by 1806 where he had a long career as a silversmith, retailer, and eventually, owner of a stove foundry business (see Chapter 4). Between 1814 and 1818 he was in partnership with Charles Farley (cat. 118). The spoons made by both silversmiths are similar; each has an oval pointed bowl, fiddle handle, straight shoulders, and is engraved "EP" in script.

According to the donor, this silver was part of the wedding silver of her great-grandmother, Experience Jordan Parris. However, the craftsmen who marked the spoons did not begin their careers until after her marriage. These spoons were probably acquired by her in later life as the need arose and finances allowed.

Experience and Samuel Parris have been difficult to identify. Experience may have married into the Parris family of Paris, Maine, and Pembroke, Massachusetts, which included Albion, a nineteenth-century governor of Maine, and Alexander, an architect (see Chapter 2).[2]   AAE

1 Henry N. Flynt and Martha Gandy Fales, *The Heritage Foundation Collection of Silver with Biographical Sketches of New England Silversmiths, 1625–1825* (Old Deerfield, Mass.: Heritage Foundation, 1968), 281.
2 William B. Lapham and Silas P. Maxim, *History of Paris, Maine* (Paris, Me.: printed for the authors, 1884), 687.

118

Eleazer Wyer, Jr. (1786–1848),
and Charles Farley (1791–1877)
Pair of spoons
Portland, Maine, 1816
Silver
Marked (on back of handles) "WYER & FARLEY" in rectangle
L 4¹³⁄₁₆ (12.2)
Maine Historical Society

These teaspoons made in the shop of Eleazer Wyer and Charles Farley are unusual in having engraved dates. The coffin handles, popular during the early nineteenth century, bear the engraved block letters "CR." Stipple engraving outlines the ends of the handles and forms diamond patterns down the handles of the spoons.

Wyer and Farley were young silversmiths and relative newcomers to Portland when they established a partnership in 1814, one that lasted only a short time. Wyer had been in town since 1806 and other examples of his flatware are known (cat. 117B). Farley had arrived in town in the fall of 1813, having completed his apprenticeship with Robert Brookhouse of Salem (cat. 47A). By spring he had joined forces with Wyer. As partners, they were able to offer a greater volume of goods than they could as single craftsmen. Their mark on these spoons lacks the flanking eagles that the partners are also known to have used.[1]

Because of its cost, silver in flat or hollow forms, could only be purchased by those with discretionary income. In modest households, silverwares often had a greater monetary value than any other portable possession. Obviously, this did not escape the attention of Brooks Tomes, for when he "eloped from this town [Portland] . . . [he] took from his wife's Bureau six large silver table spoons, made by Enoch Moulton of Portland."[2]   AAE

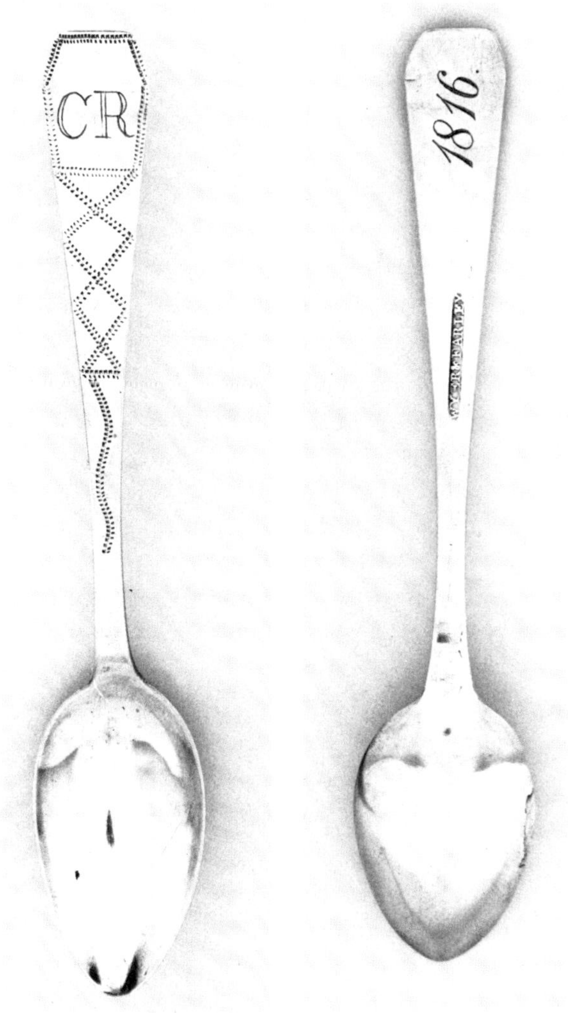

Cat. 118   Cat. 118

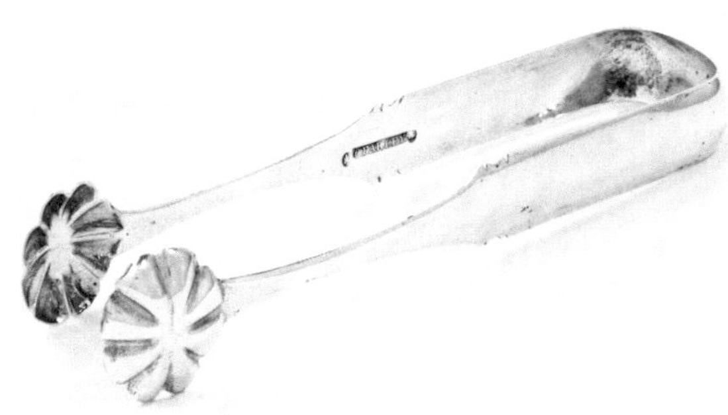

Cat. 119A

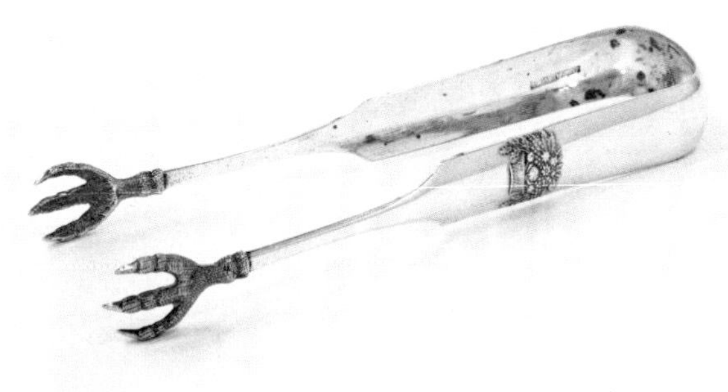

Cat. 119B

1 Churchill, "Crafts in Transition," 301–302; and Gerald W. R. Ward, "Silver and Society in Salem, Massachusetts, 1630–1820: A Case Study of the Consumer and the Craft" (Ph.D. diss., Boston University, 1984), 278–283, 288–289. Henry N. Flynt and Martha Gandy Fales, *The Heritage Foundation Collection of Silver with Biographical Sketches of New England Silversmiths, 1625–1825* (Old Deerfield, Mass.: Heritage Foundation, 1968), 363.
2 *Eastern Argus* (August 16, 1815).

119A

Charles Farley (1791–1877)
Sugar tongs
Portland, Maine, 1813–1825
Silver
Marked "c. farley" (twice on inside)
in rectangle flanked by eagles in ovals
L 5¹¹⁄₁₆ (14.5)
York Institute Museum
Bequest of Almira Locke McArthur, 1950

119B

Edward Watson (d. 1839)
Sugar tongs
Boston, Massachusetts, 1822–1838
Silver
Marked "E. Watson" in rectangle
L 6⅛ (15.5)
The Brick Store Museum; William E. Barry estate
through Edith Cleaves Barry, 1969

Bow-shaped sugar tongs were developed in the last third of the eighteenth century and were among the new forms of flatware that satisfied the needs of increasing numbers of families who served coffee and tea. The bow-shaped form, cut out of a flat sheet of silver, was easier and cheaper to produce than the cast scissor-shaped sugar tongs of the colonial period and became readily available during the federal period.

Charles Farley of Portland fashioned this pair of tongs in his Portland shop during the early nineteenth century. In 1814 he and his partner Eleazer Wyer advertised, "Sugar Tongs, Salt Spoons and Mustard Ladles, made to any pattern."[1] When Farley had his own business, he undoubtedly kept a few styles in stock to supplement sugar tongs he made to order. This pair of tongs has tapered arms and grips shaped into rosettes.

The other pair of tongs represents the work of Boston silversmith Edward Watson. More highly ornamented, the grips resemble the talons of a bird, and the handles are adorned with baskets of fruit and flowers. The basket appliqués were formed in a swage or die and then soldered to the tongs. Charles Farley also used the claw motif when he made tongs now in the Maine State Museum. The engraved "c" in script on the bow of these tongs may indicate a Cleaves family history.   AAE

1 *Portland Gazette* (June 6, 1814).

120

Nursing tube
Probably America, 1776–1793
Silver
Unmarked
H 2⁷⁄₁₆ (6.2); Diam. 1¼ (3.2)
The Brick Store Museum
Gift of Mrs. George Lord, 1946

Family history maintains that this silver nursing tube was used by Olive Jefferds (1793–1879), daughter of William and Olive Jefferds of Wells. It may date to the time of her

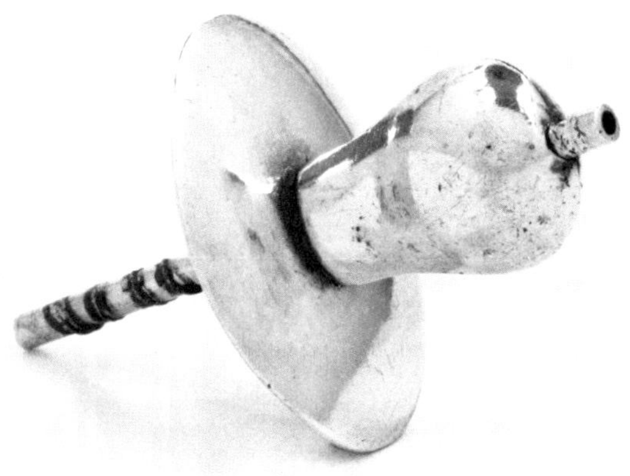

Cat. 120

birth in 1793, but it could have been purchased for one of her seven siblings, the oldest of whom was born in 1776. The hollow silver tube was threaded to fit another piece that served as a straw.[1]

"Tubes" were among the small domestic possessions Edward S. Moulton sold to and repaired for Thomas Thornton in 1818, along with "clasps" and "bosom pins."[2] Silver nursing tubes may not have been uncommon in the homes of wealthy families, but few have survived.　AAE

1　Kathryn C. Buhler, *American Silver 1655–1825 in the Museum of Fine Arts Boston*, 2 vols. (Boston: Museum of Fine Arts, Boston, 1972), 2:624.
2　Account, Edward S. Moulton to Thomas Thornton, 1817–1818, Thornton Family Papers, Dyer Library, Saco.

121A

Brooch
Probably eastern Canada or Maine, 1785–1820
Silver
Unmarked
Diam. 6¹¹⁄₁₆ (17.0)
Maine Historical Society
Bequest of Mary Purrington Putnam, 1938

121B

Brooch (one of a pair)
Probably eastern Canada or Maine, 1785–1820
Silver
Unmarked
Diam. 7½ (19.1)
Maine Historical Society
Bequest of Mary Purrington Putnam, 1938

The Abnakis, with whom these large brooches are associated, traded furs for silver, as did other Indians in the northeastern United States. These brooches serve as reminders of the relationships between native Americans and European colonists from the earliest days of settlement. Silver also played a role in the negotiations between the two groups and was often presented upon the conclusion of new treaty agreements.

In 1816 Maine historian William Williamson described a ceremony in Old Town. The Indians were "clad in coats of scarlet broadcloth and decorated with silver brooches, collars, armclasps, jewels, and other ornaments." Two years

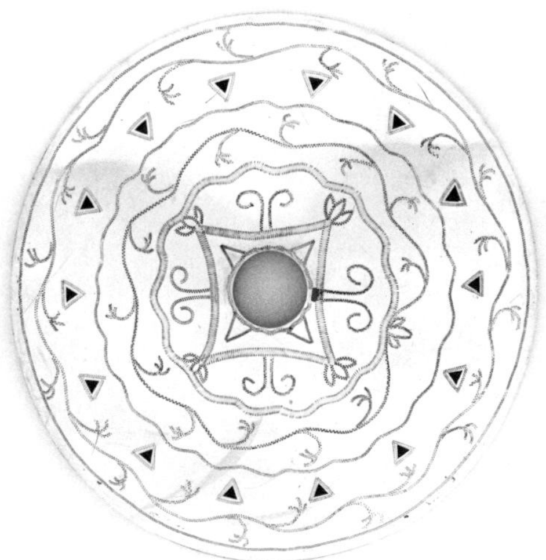

Cat. 121A

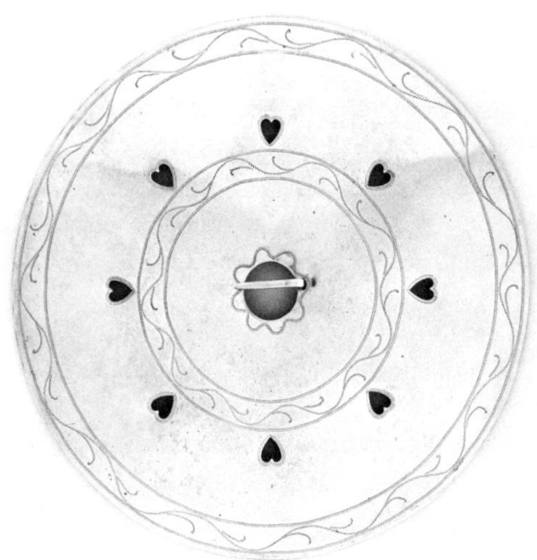

Cat. 121B

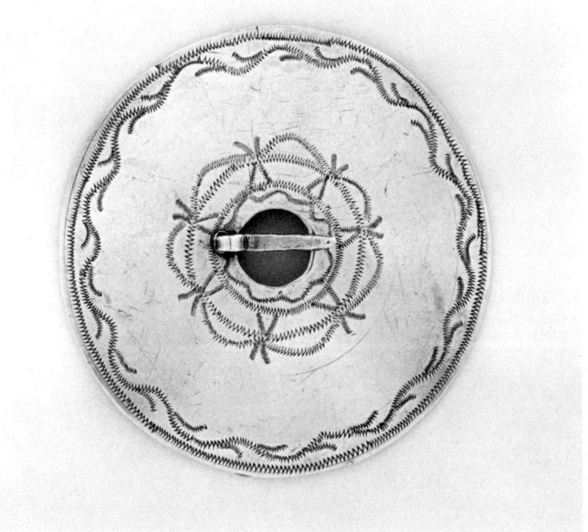

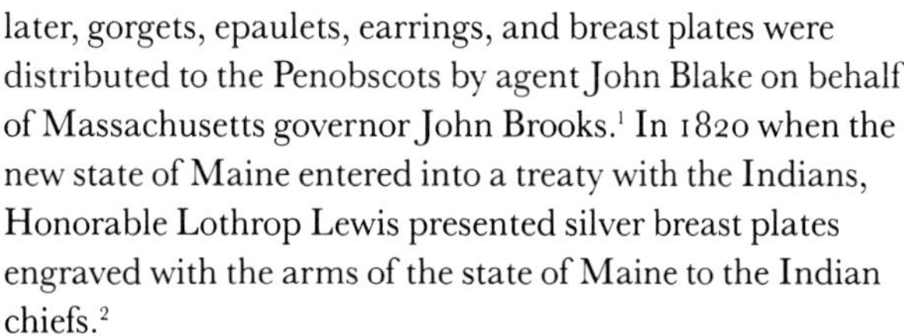

Cat. 122

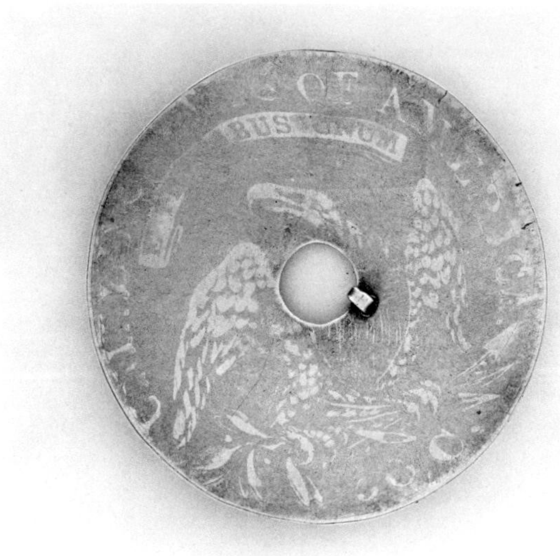

Cat. 122.1

later, gorgets, epaulets, earrings, and breast plates were distributed to the Penobscots by agent John Blake on behalf of Massachusetts governor John Brooks.[1] In 1820 when the new state of Maine entered into a treaty with the Indians, Honorable Lothrop Lewis presented silver breast plates engraved with the arms of the state of Maine to the Indian chiefs.[2]

Although these brooches bear no maker's mark, they could have originated in Quebec, a center for the production of Indian trade silver, or in Maine. A silver crown marked "J T" survives, perhaps the work of Montreal silversmith, Jonathan Tyler. Silversmiths in Bangor, a town not far from Old Town, are also known to have made Indian trade silver.[3]

Decorative silver brooches had native American prototypes because Indians adorned themselves with shells, stones, and other objects. Aware of the stylistic preferences of the Indians, silversmiths incorporated traditional Indian motifs into the silver made for their trade. The single brooch (cat. 121A) is engraved with the double curve motif, a design favored by the Penobscots, Abnakis, and Malecites in their beadwork and carving.[4] The pair (cat. 121B) is more simply decorated with bands of bright-cut engraving, with pierced hearts.

These large brooches were probably acquired by James Purrington while he acted as the Indian agent at Old Town between 1860 and 1864. They descended to his daughter, Mary Purrington Putnam.   AAE

1 *History of Penobscot County, Maine, with Illustrations and Biographical Sketches* (Cleveland, Ohio: Williams, Chase & Co., 1882), 42. Inventory for General Blake, 1818, John Blake Papers, Bangor Historical Society. For an illustration of an Indian wearing silver brooches and other ornaments, see the 1817 watercolor drawing of

Denny Soccabeson of Eastport, Maine, in Nina Fletcher Little, *Little by Little: Six Decades of Collecting American Decorative Arts* (New York: E. P. Dutton, 1984), 260, 262.

2 *Weekly Visiter* (September 9, 1820).

3 The crown is in the Bangor Historical Society. Bangor silversmith Zebulon Smith made a silver armband between 1810 and 1820. It is illustrated in Barbara McLean Ward and Gerald W. R. Ward, eds., *Silver in American Life: Selections from the Mabel Brady Garvan and other Collections at Yale University* (New York: The American Federation of Arts; Boston: David R. Godine, 1979), cat. 72.

4 Frank Speck, *Penobscot Man: The Life History of a Forest Tribe in Maine* (Philadelphia: University of Pennsylvania Press, 1940), 155. Bruce Bourque kindly brought related decorations to my attention.

122

Brooch
Probably northern New England, 1807–1815
Silver
Unmarked
Diam. 2⅜ (6.0)
The Brick Store Museum; Gift of Josephine Brazier, 1941

By the early nineteenth century, silver adornment had become a basic part of Indian dress. Possession of silver indicated rank, and the objects Maine Indians wore included arm bands, leg bands, and head bands, earrings, and brooches. Brooches used to ornament jackets, dresses, hats, and hair had the most widespread use, though other forms of jewelry survive. Brooches continued to decorate clothing in the early twentieth century, by which time Indian silversmiths began to produce their own silver items.[1]

While many brooches are known to have been made from Spanish coins, this example was hammered from an Amer-

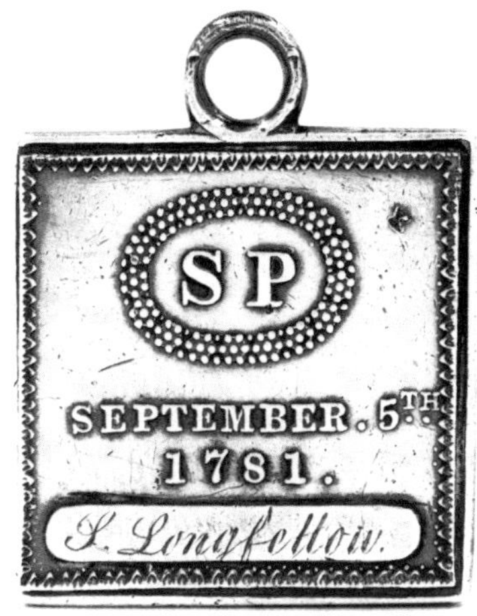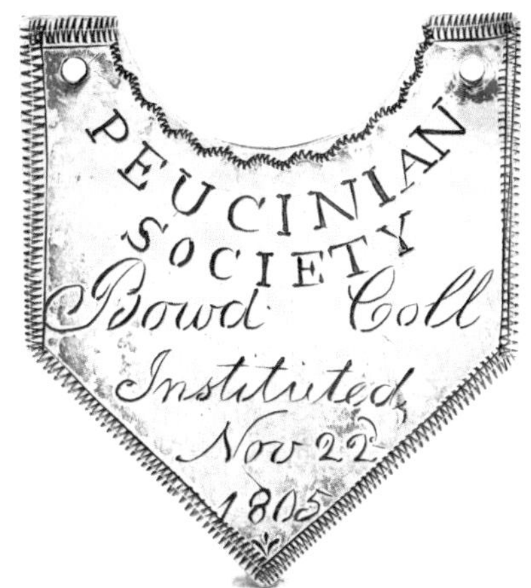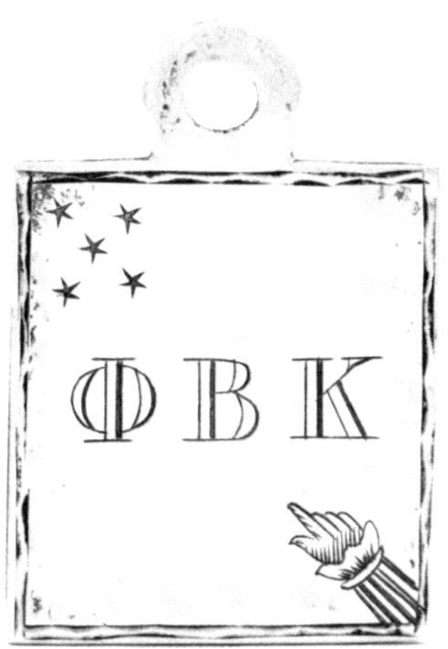

Cat. 123A, Cat. 123B and Cat. 123C

ican coin dating between 1807 and 1815.[2] On the reverse, traces of its minting are still visible (cat. 122.1). This small brooch is decorated with bright-cut engraving.   AAE

1 See cat. 121, n3. The Maine State Museum owns a pair of silver earrings and a small brooch with scalloped edges and pierced semi-circles and ellipses.
2 *The Covenant Chain: Indian Ceremonial and Trade Silver* (Ottawa: National Museums of Canada, 1980), 49.

123A

Phi Beta Kappa medal
Probably Boston, Massachusetts, ca. 1798
Silver
Unmarked
H 1 1/16 (2.7); W 1 1/16 (2.7)
Maine Historical Society; Wadsworth-Longfellow House

123B

Peucinian Society medal
Probably Portland, Maine, ca. 1823
Silver
Unmarked
H 1 3/8 (3.5); W 1 3/16 (3.1)
Maine Historical Society; Wadsworth-Longfellow House

123C

Phi Beta Kappa medal
Possibly Portland, Maine, ca. 1825
Silver
Unmarked
H 1 3/8 (3.5); W 15/16 (2.4)
Maine Historical Society; Wadsworth-Longfellow House

Silver medals were awarded for academic excellence, membership in organizations, or other achievements. Inscriptions of the schools or organizations, names of owners, dates, and ornamentation offer information about the people who awarded and received them. These Phi Beta Kappa and Peucinian Society medals have Longfellow family histories.

Stephen Longfellow, a member of the Harvard class of 1798, and his son, Henry Wadsworth Longfellow, who graduated from Bowdoin College in 1825, both were elected to the Phi Beta Kappa society in their respective colleges. The late eighteenth-century medal (cat. 123A) bears the inscription "September. 5th 1781.," the date of the society's establishment at Harvard, and below it in script, "S. Longfellow." Both obverse and reverse have a cast border.

Henry Wadsworth Longfellow and his older brother, Stephen, roomed together and both graduated in 1825 from Bowdoin. It was the studious Henry, rather than the more popular Stephen, who was a member of the Phi Beta Kappa Society.[1] His medal (cat. 123C) is thinner than his father's and has no engraved name. Both medals bear the Greek letters "Φ B K"; a hand with an extended finger points to stars in the opposite corner. The reverse of Stephen's bears six stars and the obverse of Henry's, five; the number of stars signified the chapter.[2]

Both medals also bear the initials "SP," which stand for "Societas Philosophiae," or Society of Philosophers. They are in block letters on the older medal. On Henry's, they are engraved on the reverse along with the inscriptions "Alpha of Maine" and "Feb.[ruar]y 22.d 1825."

As an underclassman, Henry Wadsworth Longfellow belonged to Bowdoin's Peucinian Society, organized in 1805 as the Philomanthian Society "to promote literature and friendship." Members debated current issues, wrote prose and poetry, and established a library. In June 1823 Henry wrote to his father in Portland: "I wish you to send me $3 to pay the initiation fee of the Peucinian Society." During an annual celebration of the society, members paraded down Maine Street in Brunswick wearing their society medals and blue ribbons; officers sported broad blue scarves.[3]

The engraved inscription on the obverse reveals the society's location and when it was founded (cat. 123B). On the reverse, two pine trees, symbols of the society, as well as of the college, flank the Latin motto *Pinos Locquertes Semper Habermus* ("We always have speaking pines") abbreviated to "*Pin Loq / Sem Hal*." The medal relates closely to others belonging to the class of 1825. The initials "FWS" are engraved on the reverse. Although these initials cannot be identified, it is believed that Henry may have acquired the medal from a former member.[4]   AAE

1 Nehemiah Cleaveland, *History of Bowdoin College with Biographical Sketches of its Graduates from 1806 to 1879*, ed. Alpheus Spring (Boston: James Ripley Osgood and Co., 1882), 29; and Bowdoin College Scrapbook, MEHS.
2 Reverend E. B. Parsons, comp., *Phi Beta Kappa Hand-Book and General Address Catalogue of the United Chapters* (North Adams, Mass.: Walden and Crawley, 1900), 256. See also William T. Hastings, *The Insignia of Phi Beta Kappa* (Washington, D.C.: United Chapters of Phi Beta Kappa, 1964).
3 Louis C. Hatch, *The History of Bowdoin College* (Portland: Loring, Short and Harmon, 1927), 304–306. Hilen, *Letters*, 1:47.
4 Hatch, *History of Bowdoin College*, 305. A search of the Society's records at Bowdoin College has not revealed the identity of the initials. Henry's classmate and future brother-in-law, George Washington Pierce, was also a member of the Peucinian Society. The medal may have come to the collection through his widow, Anne.

124

Charles Farley, silversmith (1791–1877);
David G. Johnson, engraver (w. in Portland ca. 1825–1845)
Maine Charitable Mechanic Association medal
Portland, Maine, 1826
Silver
Marked "FARLEY" in rectangle flanked by eagles in ovals and "D. G. Johnson, Sc"
H 3 (7.4); Diam. 2½ (6.3)
Maine Historical Society; Gift of S. A. Russell

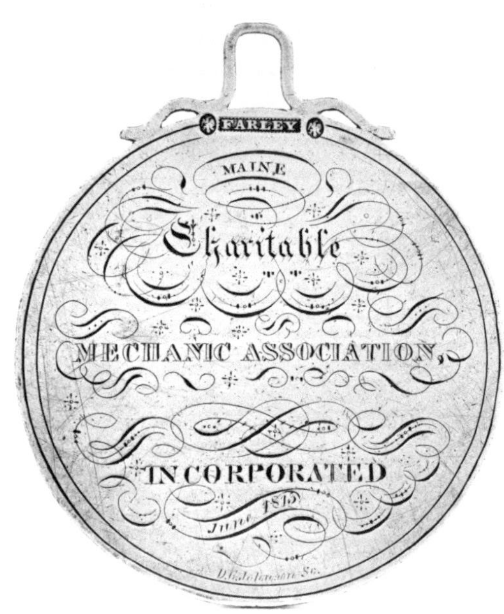

Cat. 124

Engraver David G. Johnson arrived in Portland late in 1824. In 1826 he collaborated with silversmith and retailer Charles Farley on this medal for the Maine Charitable Mechanic Association.[1] The inscription on the reverse reveals that it was presented to John W. Smith for his boot, judged to be second best at an apprentices' exhibition of manufactures held on July 4. Smith was apprenticed to Ephraim Wilber, who had a shoe manufactory and store in Portland "at the sign of the large Boot." By 1841 Smith had established himself as a cordwainer on Exchange Street.[2]

Nine other apprentices also received medals for their work, which included a lady's work table, a set of fancy chairs, a silver cup and ladle, and a chaise harness. Farley and Johnson collaborated on the silver medal presented to Daniel Woodman, Jr., for the best copper tea kettle and may have been responsible for the others.[3]

At the presentation in 1826, the president of the Association, Nathaniel Mitchell, addressed the apprentices. He stated that the medals represented "a perpetual memorial of your youthful skill." He hoped they would "constantly stimulate you to exertion, not only in the improvement of the arts, but in the improvement of your minds." But "should you . . . take to evil courses and neglect your business, then they will prove a source of mortification and only serve to remind us of what you once were, and what you might have been, but for your own folly."[4]

Star-shaped silver medals that may be the work of Farley are also known. One was awarded to Ann Quincy, a student at the Misses Dupees' school in Portland on May 2, 1818, for her achievement in geography. Another, awarded to Almira Deering, is engraved "Portland Academy March 1818," and bears the inscription "Almira Deering No 1 Latin." on the reverse.[5]   AAE

1 David G. Johnson lived in Portland until about 1830, after which he moved to New York City; Martha Gandy Fales, "An Unrecognized Portland Engraver," *Old-Time New England* 57, no. 3 (Winter 1967): 77.
2 *Eastern Argus* (February 10, 1824); *Eastern Argus* (July 11, 1826); Harlowe Harris, *The Portland Directory* (Portland, Me.: Arthur Shirley and Son, 1841).
3 Kathryn C. Buhler and Graham Hood, *American Silver, Garvan and Other Collections in the Yale University Art Gallery*, 2 vols. (New Haven: Yale University Press, 1970), 1:304.
4 *Eastern Argus* (July 11, 1826).
5 Martha Gandy Fales, "Early Maine Silver," 341–342. The Quincy medal is owned privately; the Deering medal is in the Maine State Museum.

125A

Clasp
Possibly Portland, Maine, 1785–1804
Silver
Unmarked
H 1⅛ (2.8); w fastened 1¹⁵⁄₁₆ (4.9)
Maine Historical Society
Gift of William Thrasher Nash, 1956

125B

Clasp
Probably England, 1785–1815
Fused plate
Unmarked
H 1³⁄₁₆ (3.0); w fastened 2³⁄₁₆ (5.5)
Maine Historical Society
Gift of William Thrasher Nash, 1956

Decorative silver clasps were used to close cloaks, belts, and other garments and were available through the shops of local silversmiths. In 1814 Thomas Thornton paid $1.24 to Saco clockmaker and silversmith, Edward S. Moulton, for "two pairs of silver clasps." Four years later, Moulton sold him another pair for fifty cents.[1]

These clasps, one pair of silver, the other of fused plate, belonged to Lucy Foxcroft Thrasher (1779–1815), the daughter of the Reverend Samuel Foxcroft of New Gloucester, Maine. The silver pair has coffin ends and wigglework ornamentation that resemble contemporary spoon handles. Fabric was fed through two silver posts on the back and secured by stitches. This pair is engraved "L.F." and dates before 1804, the year Lucy married Joseph Thrasher of New Gloucester.

Two heart-shaped pieces fasten together to create the second pair of clasps that are decorated with an engraved scalloped border. This pair had holes pierced in the edges and was sewn directly onto the fabric. Both pairs were presented to the Society by a great-grandson of Lucy Thrasher.   AAE

1 Bill, Edward S. Moulton to Thomas Thornton, December 16, 1814; and account, Edward S. Moulton to Thomas Thornton, 1817–1818, Dyer Library, Saco.

126

William King (w. 1804–1809)
Zilpah Wadsworth Longfellow (1778–1851)
Portland, Maine, ca. 1805
Negative cut on paper
Embossed (below shoulder) "W. King"
H 3¹⁵⁄₁₆ (10.1); w 3 (7.6)
Maine Historical Society
Gift of the Alexander W. Longfellow family

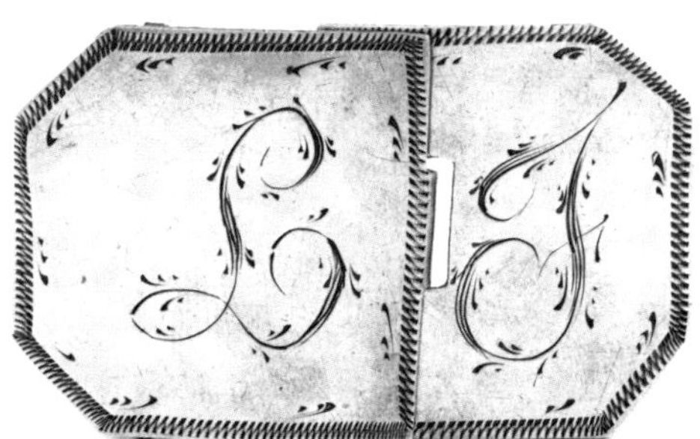

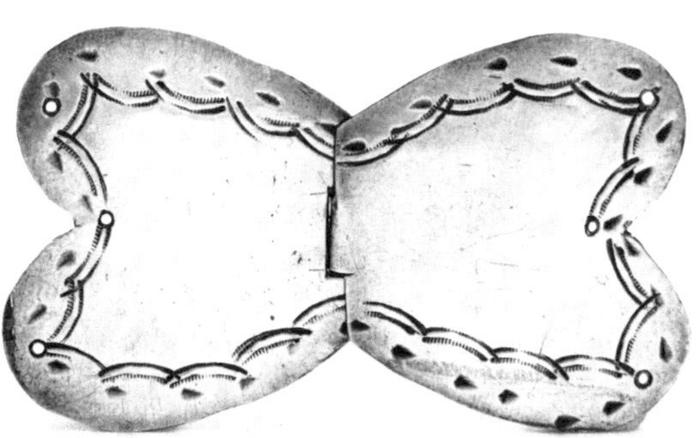

Cat. 125A and Cat. 125B

At least six profilists traveled to Portland and advertised their services in the city's newspapers between 1805 and 1828. They found a market for their trade in the growing port. Some profilists sold frames, though frames were also stocked by local jewelers and merchants.

William King, a Salem resident, visited Portland in 1805. Although he had carried on the crafts of cabinetmaking and ivory carving in Salem, he began taking profiles around 1804. He notified the people of Portland that he had "taken above 10,000 likenesses in Salem, Newburyport, Portsmouth, & their ajoining towns."[1] This negative cut silhouette of Zilpah Wadsworth Longfellow is one of two pairs King made of family members that survive at the Wadsworth-Longfellow house. Silhouettes were also cut of Zilpah's husband, Stephen, and her parents, Elizabeth and Peleg Wadsworth.[2] This bust-length view depicts a hair style preferred by young women with the hair in a bun at the back of the head and a small braid over the forehead.

Hollow-cut profiles, such as these, required that the image be cut from white paper and placed over a black background. Some silhouettists took a positive image, applying the black profile to a white ground. William King's advertisements indicate that he had a mechanical device for taking profiles. His notice mentioned his "patent delineating pencil" and that he charged twenty-five cents for two profiles

of the same person. Duplicate profiles would have made welcome gifts to friends or family.   AAE

1 Alice Van Leer Carrick, *Shades of Our Ancestors* (Boston: Little, Brown & Co., 1928), 48. William King took the profiles of Jonathan Sayward Barrell and his wife, Mary Plummer Barrell; see Nylander, "Sayward House," fig. 6 and plate X. *Eastern Argus* (April 26, 1805).
2 The cuts of Stephen Longfellow and Elizabeth Wadsworth bear King's mark.

127

William Bache (1771–1845)
Francis Douglas (1783–1820)
Portland, Maine, ca. 1811
Pen and ink wash on paper
Marked "Bache's / Patent"
H 4¾ (12.0); W 3¾ (9.5)
Maine Historical Society
Gift of Lucy D. Tuckerman, 1937

William Bache visited Portland in 1811 where he made this likeness of Francis Douglas, the editor of the *Eastern Argus*. Bache was born in England and emigrated to Philadelphia in 1793. On his arrival in Portland, he advertised years of experience as well as a technique which was his own invention:

W.B. having devoted the last 7 years to delineating the human countenance and having invented a machine upon principles less liable to error than those commonly used for drawing Profiles, he flatters himself able to give general satisfaction to those who may honor him with their attendance at his Profile Room.[1]

Bache's silhouette of Francis Douglas, highlighted with an ink wash, depicts in bust-length a man facing right, wearing a black coat, white shirt, stock, and jabot. Bache's stamp appears below the bust.

Bache married Anna Page of Philadelphia in 1811 and shortly after gave up his itinerant career as a profilist. Settling in western Pennsylvania, he became a merchant and postmaster general.[2]   AAE

1 *Eastern Argus* (February 2, 1811).
2 Alice Van Leer Carrick, *Shades of Our Ancestors* (Boston: Little, Brown & Co., 1928), 60.

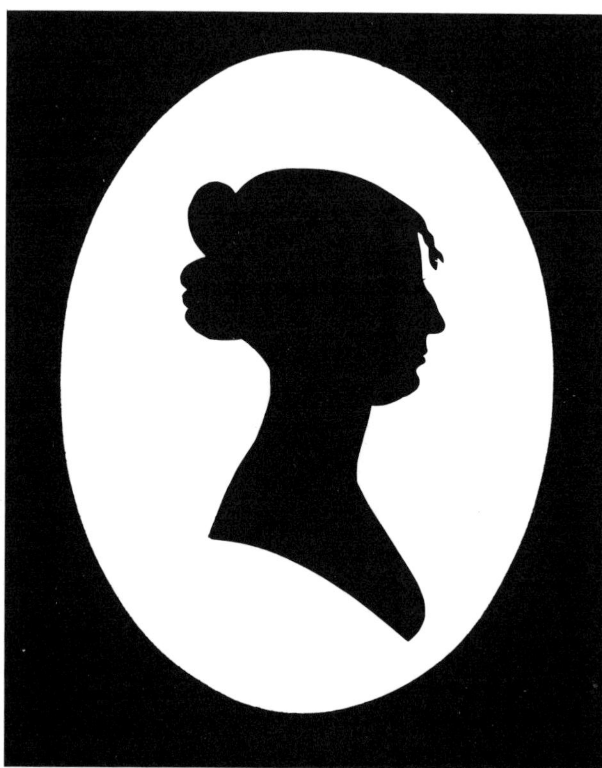

Cat. 126

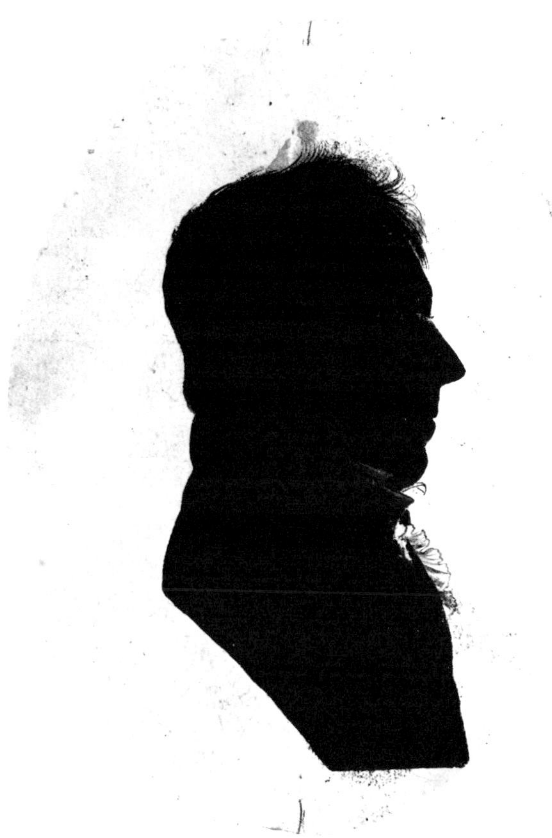

Cat. 127

Although Lafayette did not arrive until June of the following year, the Portland newspapers faithfully reported the speeches and toasts made during his American stops.

Lafayette's first Maine stop was Kennebunk. Amid the sounds of bells ringing and artillery firing, he entered the town accompanied by a cavalcade. People lined the streets and cheered; Dr. Samuel Emerson publicly welcomed him. At a public dinner, his chair decorated with flowers, over which a wreath of flowers formed an arch, Lafayette presented a toast: "I rise from this chair, so kindly, so beautifully ornamented, to propose to you—the Kennebunk Ladies." The guests responded with nine cheers. As the Marquis traveled up Main Street on his way to Biddeford and Saco, men working on William Lord's new store (now The Brick Store Museum) leaned out of the windows to cheer the passing hero.[1]

At Saco evergreens and flowers decorated the bridges, and triumphal arches spanned his route. At the Cleaves hotel and again at the home of Mrs. Thomas Thornton, citizens attended receptions in his honor. In Saco, the general lodged with his friend, Captain Seth Spring.

The following morning, the general arrived in Portland, then Maine's capital. A parade comprising a military escort of four companies in uniform, selectmen, a band, members

128A

Orramel Hinkley Throop (1798–after 1832)
Lafayette
Portland, Maine, ca. 1824
Engraving
Inscribed "Throop Sc"
H 3¹³⁄₁₆ (9.6); w 2⅝ (6.7)
Maine Historical Society; Wadsworth-Longfellow House

128B

David G. Johnson (w. 1825–1845)
Lafayette
Portland, Maine, 1825
Engraving on silk
Inscribed "D. G. Johnson Sc"
H 9¼ (23.5); w 1⅝ (4.1)
Maine Historical Society; Wadsworth-Longfellow House

The visit of the Marquis de Lafayette to Maine caused great excitement in the new state. In August 1824, the selectmen of Portland invited the "nation's guest" to visit their town.

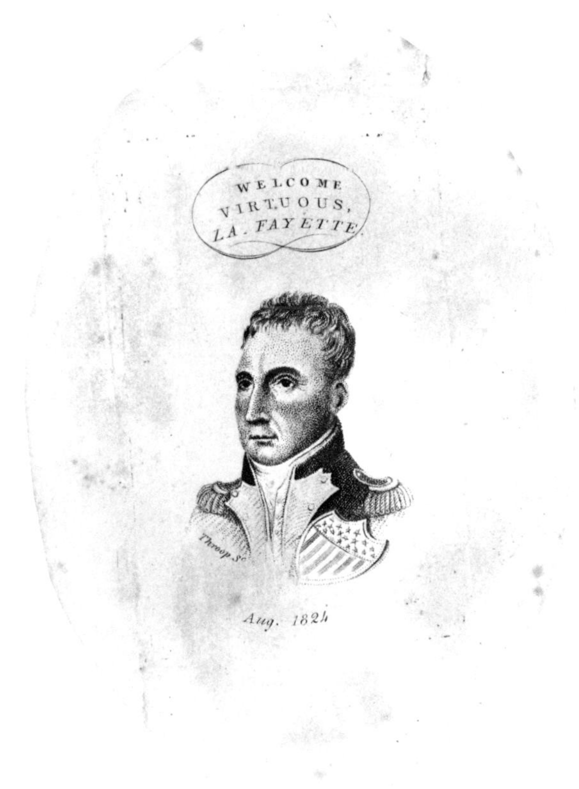

Cat. 128A

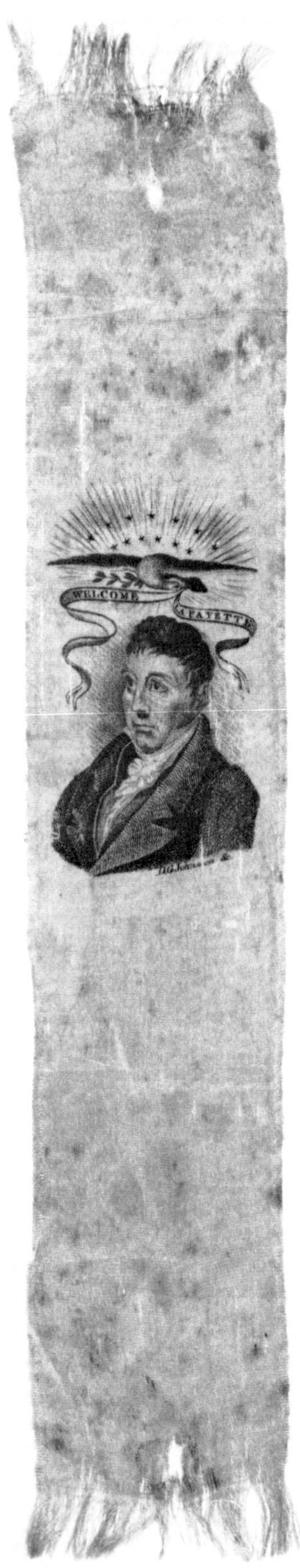

Cat. 128B

of the national and state legislature, and clergy accompanied Lafayette, who rode in an open carriage pulled by four white horses. As in Kennebunk, Saco, and other towns, bells in Portland rang, salutes were fired, and crowds cheered. Triumphal arches of evergreens and roses bore inscriptions welcoming the general and recalling his contribution to American independence. School children in uniform also took part; the little girls scattered flowers along the street. Other festivities included a dinner at Portland's Union Hall, a reception at the State House, and a ceremony in which Bowdoin College conferred on him an honorary degree.[2]

Despite thorough planning, the festivities were not without incident. A platform bearing notable Portlanders collapsed during the ceremony. Congressman Stephen Longfellow reportedly forgot part of his speech and had to consult the notes he had hidden in his hat. Pickpockets in Kennebunk and Portland roamed the streets and profited by the crowds.[3] One final, controversial episode occurred when Governor Albion K. Parris refused to escort the general out of town on the Sabbath, deeming it more proper to attend church.

The visit of Lafayette prompted the production of objects in his honor. Advertisements for badges and ribbons featuring his likeness appeared in Portland newspapers in August 1824, shortly after his arrival in the United States, and again in the early summer of 1825, just prior to his visit to Portland. Olive Currier, a milliner on Exchange Street, advertised "Lafayette belts and badges, similar to those worn by young misses and masters on the arrival of Lafayette in Boston and New York." Henry Quimby of Portland advertised "Lafayette Belts, Badges, and Watch Ribbons, Just received for Sale," which he had purchased for resale. A wide range of citizens bought these mementos. The *Eastern Argus* reported: "The little boys had each a printed label upon their hats, inscribed with 'Welcome Lafayette' above it."[4]

This ribbon, featuring Lafayette in civilian clothing with the banner inscribed "Welcome Lafayette," is probably similar to those worn by the schoolchildren. Family history relates that this ribbon, engraved by David G. Johnson in 1825, was the one Stephen Longfellow wore during the festivities.

The likeness of Lafayette in military dress was engraved by Orramel Hinkley Throop, who worked in Portland from late 1823 through August 1824.[5] A similar engraving executed the same year by John Peter Vanness Throop, the brother of Orramel, appears as the frontispiece of a book published in Portland in 1824. Facing the title page of John Foster's *A Sketch of the Tour of General Lafayette* is an engraving of Lafayette facing left, signed "J.V.N. Throop Sc." Its similarity to that by David Johnson suggests that both engravers based their renderings on the same source, or one copied the other.   AAE

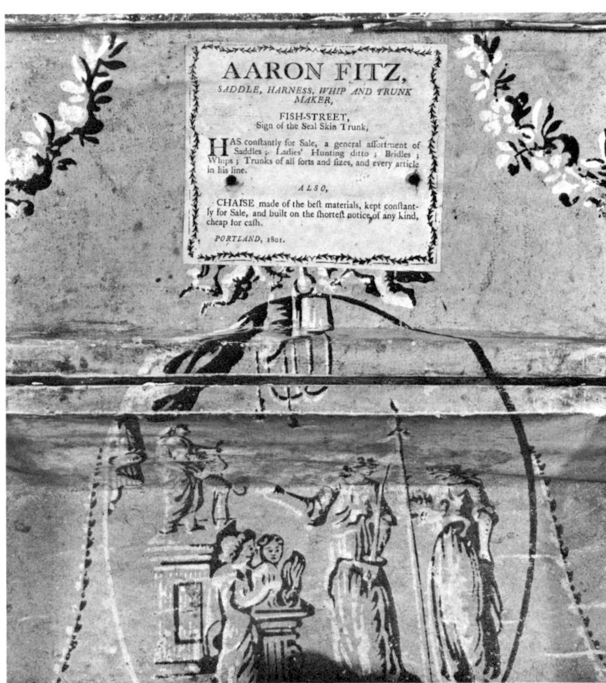

Cat. 129.1

1 *Eastern Argus* (June 27, 1825). Jane Bacon MacIntire, *Lafayette, The Guest of the Nation: The Tracing of the Route of Lafayette's Tour of the United States in 1824–25* (Newton, Mass.: Anthony J. Simone Press, 1967), 222.
2 *Eastern Argus* (June 27, 1825).
3 MacIntire, *Lafayette*, 222.
4 *Eastern Argus* (June 13, 1825; June 20, 1825).
5 Shettleworth, "Engravers," 62.

129

Aaron Fitz (1773–1813)
Box
Portland, Maine, 1801
Eastern white pine, leather
Paper label (pasted to inside of cover)
H 5¹¹⁄₁₆ (14.4); W 12 (30.5); D 6⅛ (15.6)
Maine Historical Society

This box is an example of the work of Portland saddler Aaron Fitz. A Newburyport native, Fitz had moved to Portland by the spring of 1801. In April of that year his

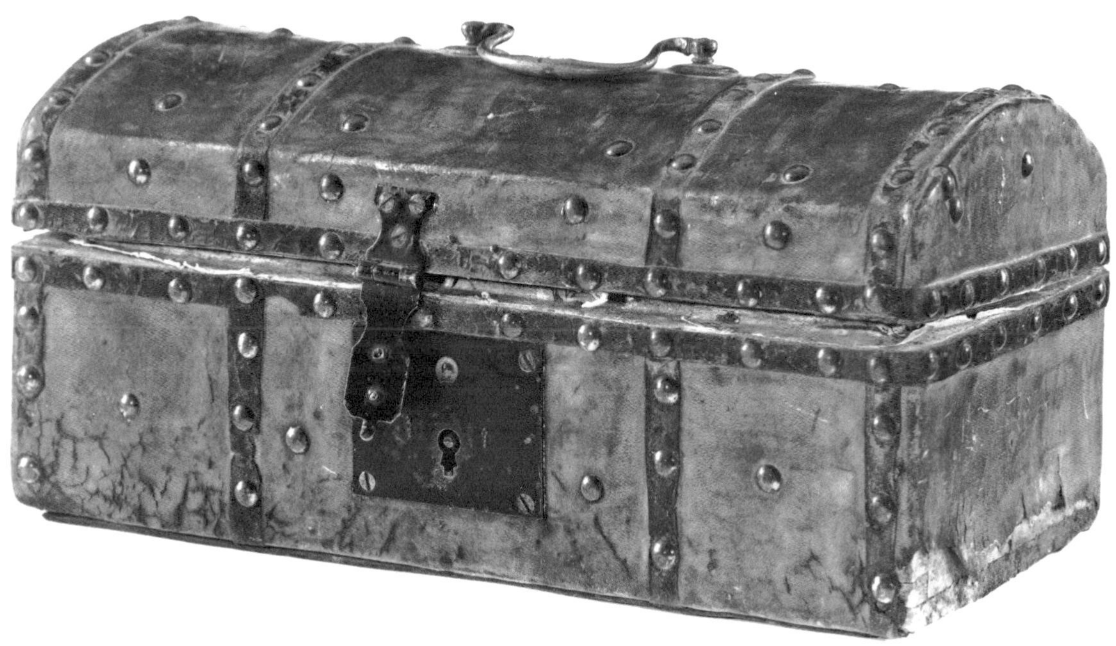

Cat. 129

notice in the *Portland Gazette* announced, "Aaron Fitz, Saddler and Chaise maker, Respectfully informs the public, that he has taken the shop in Fish Street . . . where he carries on the Saddle, Harness, & Trunk making business in their various branches."[1]

From that date until his death in 1813, Fitz worked in Portland making boxes and trunks of various styles and sizes, covered with sealskin, oilcloth, and different types of leather. In his shop "at the sign of the Trunk," he also made and sold chaises, saddles, post bags, bridles, whips, and firebuckets (cat. 130). By 1805 his business was flourishing, for he advertised the need to hire an apprentice and he purchased and sold partial rights to a house and lot of land on Middle Street.[2]

Many examples of Fitz's boxes and trunks are known; they were essential for storage and travel. Whether transported by land or sea for a brief or extended journey, trunks could hold clothing, jewelry, books, papers, and other articles. When her trunk disappeared from Barnard's tavern in 1804, Mary Augusta Cook (later Mrs. Thomas Cutts, Jr.) advertised for its safe return. Among the missing clothing was "1 long white satin Cloak, lined with white mode & trim'd with broad black lace," "1 white cambric Petticoat, with welts," "1 pair purple and white kid Shoes," "1 dimity morning Gown," and "Shirts and Cravats marked O.C." She also lost "1 Locket marked M.C.," "1 pair paste Bracelets, with blk velvet Ribbon," "1 Inkstand with knives and wafers [sealing paste]. . . and many other Articles that cannot be remembered."[3]

Constructed of wood, trunks could float in water, a feature that had its advantages. When his trunk was lost from the *Charles,* Seth Emery announced, "As it is probable said trunk and clothing will drift on shore on some of the beaches, any person who may pick it up and will return it to the subscriber or give him information so that it can be obtained, shall be generously rewarded."[4]

This leather-covered box bears Fitz's label dated 1801 on the inside of the cover (cat. 129.1). The grisaille wallpaper lining was probably the product of a Boston or Salem paper stainer. This design may have been called "Diana" during the period. Wallpaper remnants were often used to line boxes and trunks.[5] AAE

1 *Portland Gazette* supplement (April 16, 1801).
2 *Portland Gazette* (June 5, 1805); CCRD; 46:411; and 48:11–12.
3 A sealskin covered trunk (H 17 [43.2]; W 42¼ [107.3]) at Tate house in Portland bears this same label. Other examples are in the Portland Museum of Art. *Eastern Argus* (October 22, 1804).
4 *Weekly Visiter* (December 30, 1815).
5 A trunk at MEHS bears Fitz's label dated 1806. Signed "Akin, Sc," the label was engraved by James Akin (1773–1846) who was working in Newburyport at this time (see cat. 9). Nylander, Redmond and Sander, *Wallpaper,* 63, fig. 10a.

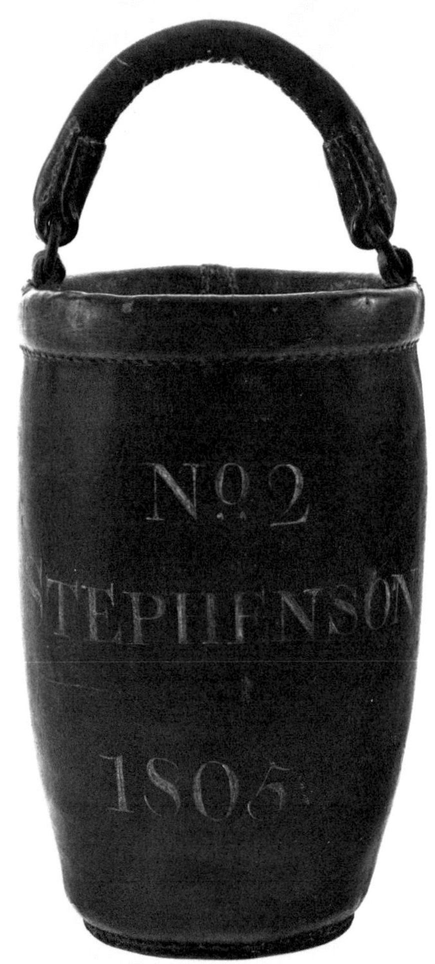

Cat. 130

130

Aaron Fitz (1773–1813)
Firebucket
Portland, Maine, 1805
Leather
Branded (on bottom) "A. FITZ"
H 18⁹⁄₁₆ (47.2); Diam. 8⅜ (21.3)
Maine Historical Society; Wadsworth-Longfellow House

An account of a fire in Portland in 1822 dramatized the ever-present danger of fire and the need for an efficient means of combating it:

The easterly side of the street was principally lined with wooden buildings, and in the vicinity were stables, barns, work-shops, bake-houses surrounded with faggots, soap-houses filled with tallow,

*and every thing was in perfect readiness, like a tinder-box, to burst into
a blaze from every falling spark. The winds were sporting with glowing
embers, scattering them in showers to the distance of half a mile, and
young fires starting up, like hydras, in every yard and on every building.*[1]

As early as 1783, prominent citizens established organizations and guidelines in an effort to protect their homes and
businesses. In that year, the Fire Society in Portland was
established. The town acquired a fire engine two years later.[2]

Portland's earliest documented fire engine was an
English-made, handtub-type "Cataract" that volunteers
pulled to many fires. Historian William Goold described it as
"painted vermillion, which gave it the appearance of an
immense lobster." Oil-burning torches attached to each of its
four corners helped to light the way as it was pulled through
the dark streets at night. Firebuckets dangled at its sides, and
people helping to fight the fire brought their own buckets
and firebags as well. The "Cataract" served Portlanders
from about 1801 until 1838.[3]

The Fire Society regulated fire-fighting equipment
owned by its members, the course of action to be taken in the
event of fire, and other activities. The rules in 1803 dictated
that each member have two leather firebuckets and two
firebags. Both were to be kept together "in good order in
some conspicuous part" of the house. Hung from large
wrought nails in the back stair hall, these buckets were easily
accessible. The firebags, used to salvage possessions at the
fire, were to be constructed of raven's duck, and "one yard
and one half long, and three quarters of a yard wide, with
strings at the mouths."[4] The owner's name was to be placed
on the firebuckets; omission of this resulted in a fine. By 1816
the Fire Society also required members to own a bed key.[5]

This is one of a pair of leather firebuckets belonging to
Portland Fire Society member Samuel Stephenson, Stephen
Longfellow's brother-in-law. On the bottom is the brand of
its maker, saddler Aaron Fitz, who also made trunks and
boxes (cat. 129). Painted black with red trim, the bucket
bears its requisite number and owner's name, as well as the
date.[6]

Although the dimensions of firebuckets were not regulated by the Fire Society, they were close in size and common
enough to be used as a unit of measure, in at least one
instance. On describing a sea monster sighted in Salem in
1820, an article reprinted in Portland noted that "his head,
which was black, resembling that of a common serpent . . .
was about the size of a common fire bucket."[7]   AAE

1 *Eastern Argus* (June 18, 1822).
2 Shettleworth and Barry, *Mr. Goodhue*, no. 25. Saco's fire society was
   founded in 1792 and Kennebunk organized one in the early
   nineteenth century.
3 Shettleworth and Barry, *Mr. Goodhue*, no. 25. Charles Quincy
   Goodhue's 1894 sketch of the "Cataract" is illustrated here.
4 *Rules and Orders to be Observed by the Fire Society, Instituted in Falmouth,
   February 24, 1783* (Portland: Thomas B. Wait, 1805), 3.

5 *Rules and Orders to be Observed by the Fire Society, Instituted in Falmouth, (now
   Portland,) February 24th, 1783* (Portland: Printed by A. & J. Shirley,
   1816), 4.
6 A pair of leather firebuckets belonging to Stephen Longfellow at the
   Wadsworth-Longfellow house are painted "S. Longfellow/1803," but
   are not signed. Other firebuckets dating to this period are in the City
   of Portland's Spring Street Fire Museum.
7 *Eastern Argus* (August 15, 1820).

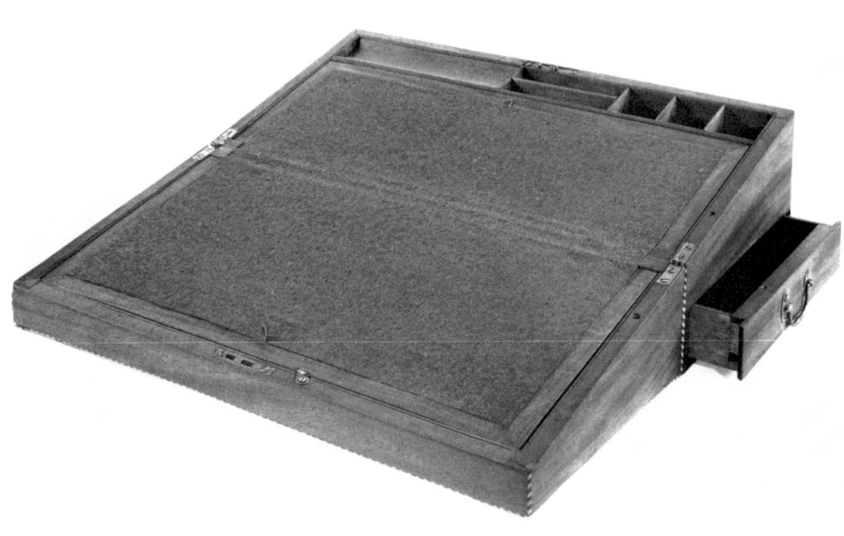

Fig. 5.1 Portable writing desk, probably Portsmouth, New Hampshire, 1800–1820. Cat. 131. Old York Historical Society.

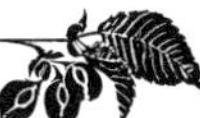

Chapter 5

"From the Fair to the Brave":
Spheres of Womanhood in Federal Maine

Laurel Thatcher Ulrich

Madame Wood's writing box unfolds like a Gothic novel, its raised lid unbending into a delicately compartmented desk fragrant with Spanish cedar and the scent of old fictions (fig. 5.1 and cat. 131). On this slanted surface, it is said, Sally Sayward Barrell Keating Wood (fig. 5.2) wrote the five books that secured her slim fame—*Julia and the Illuminated Baron* (1800); *Dorval; or the Speculator* (1801); *Amelia; or the Influence of Virtue* (1802); *Ferdinand and Elmira: A Russian Story* (1804); and *Tales of the Night* (1827). The titles promised dark adventures in remote places, the author all the while insisting "that not one social, or one domestic duty, have ever been sacrificed or postponed by her pen."[1]

Sally Wood was not the only Maine woman of her time to discover the pleasures of writing, although hers were the only published works. Between 1790 and 1820 a surprising number of women took to their pens. Surviving writings from coastal Maine include the fragmentary diaries of Eliza Wildes, Abby May, and Ann Smith; the brilliant letters of Eliza Southgate Bowne, more than two hundred pages in the printed edition; the self-consciously literary (and later oppressively pious) diaries of Sarah Connell Ayer; and the papers of Zilpah Wadsworth Longfellow, the mother of the poet; as well as scattered letters from families like the Sewalls of York and the Cleaveses of Biddeford. These women accepted—and exfoliated—woman's sphere. Their words give life to the patriotic and sentimental miscellany in Maine museums.

This essay will focus on four objects—the Sewall mourning embroidery at the Old York Historical Society, the Bourne coverlet at The Brick Store Museum in Kennebunk, the tiffany border at the York Institute in Saco, and the Stroudwater Light Infantry banner at the Maine Historical Society. Each object can be related to broad themes in the cultural history of the early republic: the mourning picture to the triumph of neoclassical images of death, the coverlet to the rising cult of domesticity and the concern for American manufacturing, the tiffany border to the effort to define a genteel yet appropriately republican education, and the militia flag to the problem of female citizenship in the new nation.

Despite a brief flurry of experimentation (some New Jersey women voted in the election of 1800), America settled for a traditional understanding of gender summarized in the ribboned motto of the Stroudwater banner—"From the Fair to the Brave." The Fair were to inspire rather than act, to complement rather than to share the duties of the Brave. Yet republican womanhood was never merely passive. Within their own realm women had adventures of a different kind, excursions of the heart, battles with indolence and luxury, and tournaments of will. Their lives are best comprehended through small dramas: Betsy Sewall, homesick in Boston, lettering her mother's death date on her silk embroidery;

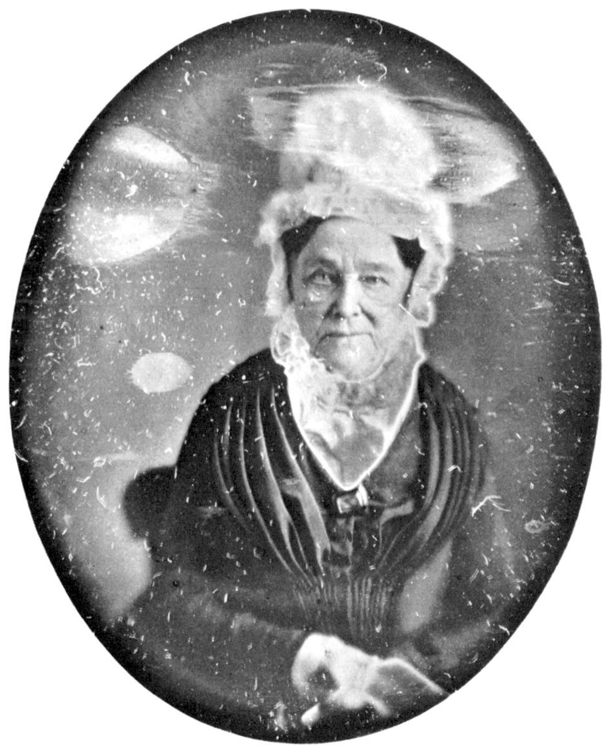

Fig. 5.2 *Sally Sayward Barrell Keating Wood* (1759–1855), probably Portland, Maine, ca. 1845. Daguerreotype; H 2¹³⁄₁₆ (7.1), W 2⅜ (6.0). Maine Women Writers Collection, Westbrook College, Portland.

Eliza Bourne in Kennebunk warping a coverlet as a hedge against the Embargo; Eliza Southgate on her way home from a Portland ball, tromping through snow drifts, laughing as she pulls off her wig with her bonnet; and Zilpah Wadsworth on the front step of her father's house giving a tremulous and reluctant speech.

Mourning: Elizabeth Sewall Embroidery

"I have been working a piece of embroidery in memory of my dear departed Mother," thirteen-year-old Betsy Sewall wrote to her father from Boston in July 1801. "I cannot express my feelings to you when I think what a loss I have met with. Mrs. Tucker called to see me. I dont know any body I should have been more glad to have seen except our family, she was quite affected when she first saw me I put her so much in mind of my Mother."[2]

It is easier for twentieth-century readers to identify with Betsy's sorrow than with the stylized embroidery (fig. 5.3 and cat. 132) that gave it expression. It has the expected elements—a bending tree (nature), a marble monument (art), and a dark-clad maiden curved toward the tomb, but nothing of Betsy or her mother. In historical context, however, Betsy's silken maiden seems almost rebellious. Traditional piety had seen expansive grief as evidence of faltering faith. To mourn too visibly for the loss of a loved one was a kind of idolatry, a substitution of earthly attachments for submission to God's will. There are echoes of such sentiments in Maine embroideries well into the nineteenth century. "Give up your comforts to the Lord," Joanna Poole's sampler of 1807 cautions. "He shall restore what you resign / Or grant you blessings more divine." As Mary Ann Twombly's 1817 sampler expressed it: "O Resignation heavenly power / Our warmest thoughts engage / Thou art the safest guide of youth / The sole supporter of age / Teach us the hand of law divine / In evils to discern / Tis the first lesson which we heed / The latest which we learn."[3]

In the picturesque serenity of Betsy Sewall's picture there is also a kind of resignation, yet it is a resignation achieved through an artistic ordering of grief that shifts the focus of consolation from divine will to human memory. "If I visited you in reality as often as I do in imagination and dreams, it would be often indeed," Betsy wrote her father from Concord, Massachusetts, seven years after her mother's death. "A few nights since I had a most pleasing interview in my sleep with our family, I was conversing very happily with my mother and awoke and found it to be a dream."[4] The figures of young women on memorial embroideries celebrated private sorrow and validated feminine sensibility.

For some girls, of course, mourning had no immediate reality. It was simply part of the curriculum in the fashionable new schools. When Eliza Southgate of Scarborough wrote to her sister Octavia, who was attending Susanna

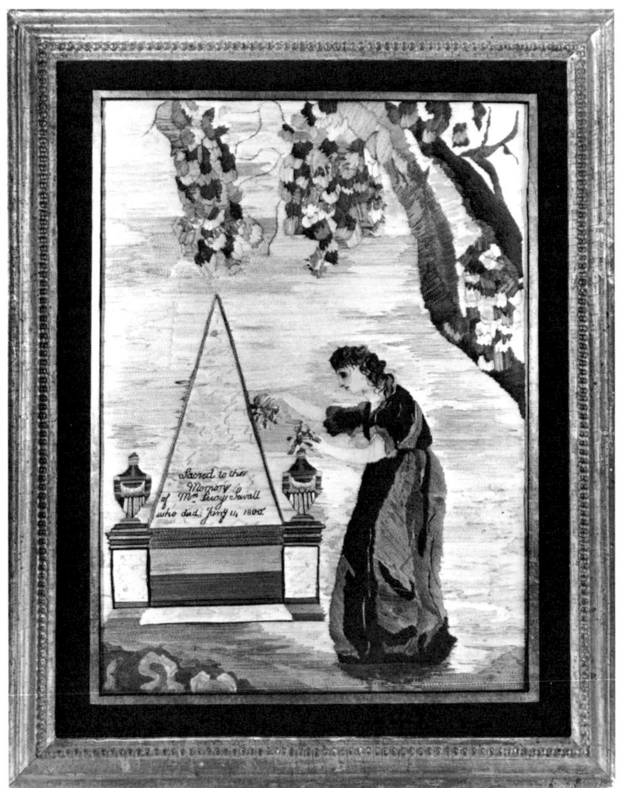

Fig. 5.3 Elizabeth Sewall, mourning picture, Boston, Massachusetts, ca. 1801. Cat. 132. Old York Historical Society.

Rowson's school in Boston, she enclosed instructions from "Mamma." Octavia was to work "a *mourning piece* with a figure in it, and two other pictures, *mates*." Her mother considered "figures of females . . . handsomer than Landscapes" although she assured her that "Mrs. Rawson knows what is best."[5] There had been as yet no death in the immediate family. For Octavia weeping would come later.

In life the new art of mourning joined rather than replaced the ancient religious rituals. When Sarah Connell spent the day with her Aunt Eustis, who was in the last stages of consumption, the dying woman begged her "to forsake the vanities of life" and "look to religion for that consolation which the World denies." Later, after losing four infants in as many years, Sarah would express the same feeling in much the same way.[6] Yet it is the new cult of mourning, not traditional piety, that colors her schoolgirl diary.

"In the forenoon I read the life of Petrarch which interested me much," she wrote on August 20, 1808. "In the afternoon we went up to burying hill. Here rose the marble mausoleum of the great, there the plain turf grave of the humble cottager. No stone tells whose ashes are deposited under yonder heap of earth, but the virtues of the good will remain in the memory of their friends, though no stone marks them to the passing traveller."[7] For the young Sarah it was human memory rather than divinity that sanctified death.

A few evenings later she and her friend John again walked to the burying ground. "The Moon cast a pale light on the surrounding tombs," Sarah wrote, "and I expected almost to see the spectre of some departed fellow Mortal. Immediately on our entrance soft music assailed our ears, which seemed to rise from the mansions of the dead, and was borne along the evening gale. John at length convinced me that it was a female voice, which rose from the Cottage below us." Despite the faint shiver of mystery, the diary entry is as tranquil as Betsy Sewall's picture—and as stylized. "We sought and found the grave of his departed Mother, and watered her grave with tears of love. Every discordant idea was hush'd into a calm, and all within was sweet serenity."[8] Significantly, John as well as Betsy watered the grave with tears, a detail omitted from the embroideries, almost all of which focus on the female form.

Sarah Connell's was a schooled response to an omnipresent reality. There was less of the weeping willow and more of the death's-head in the letter Nancy Sewall sent from York after the death of her own mother. There had been many people sick in the town that spring and a number of deaths. Aunt Lyman was gone. So were Mr. Lount and Deacon Sewall. "Capt Donnel that married Polly Darby died last week of a consumption," and "a maloncally event took place in our neighborhood a few weeks since. Mrs. Molly Harmon was found dead in a well and it is thought she threw herself in." The woman had been subject to melancholy but had been free of it until a few weeks before her death. "Her daughter had been dangerously sick but began to recover and her mother distressed herself for fear she would die for want of the necessaries of life. She would not be Comforted." Nancy had neither the sensibility nor the literary inclination to seek beauty in death. Her comforts were the traditional ones. "Time only heals our wounded hearts. No it does not heal, it only wears of[f] the sharp edge of affliction and now that is done I feel it selfish to wish my dear mother back to this transitory world, a world of trouble."[9]

Betsy Sewall's moonlit embroidery was created in that world of trouble, as were the fictions of Sally Wood, the journals of Sarah Connell, and the letters of Eliza Southgate. Sally Wood's first extant work is a consolation poem addressed to a neighbor. She was herself widowed twice, and she saw all three of her children die in young adulthood. Sarah Connell's diary grew more somber after she experienced four births and four deaths in as many years.[10] Betty Ring has noted that a significant number of the samplers and silk embroideries in museum collections were the work of unmarried women or short-lived girls.[11] The same may be true of manuscripts. The survival of Eliza Southgate's marvelous letters may well have something to do with her own death from consumption at the age of twenty-five. Betsy

Sewall, too, died young.[12] Ironically, the mourning embroidery she created for her mother became a lasting memorial to herself.

Domesticity: The Bourne Coverlet

Eliza Wildes of Kennebunk and Ann Smith of Portland were both hard-working women, better educated and more prosperous than most of their contemporaries, yet more practical and less leisured than Sally Wood, Eliza Southgate, or Sarah Connell. Eliza Wildes's husband was a mariner, Ann Smith's a retail shopkeeper. Both women kept their own kitchens and gardens, sewed, washed, and wove. Both kept diaries. The contrast between Eliza Wildes's terse entries of the 1790s, and Ann Smith's more sentimental diary of 1807, tells us less about changes in women's work than about changes in women's writing.

Where Eliza Wildes wrote, "I stayed at home all day and read the Pilgrim's Progress," Ann Smith composed a small vignette: "I seated at my writting table with a Large Bible on my left hand, and Perrys Dictionary on the Right—My sister Eliza sewing by the fire and the cat at rest in the corner."[13] Eliza Wildes noted what she did and with whom—"We washt a great many clothes. Mrs. Perkins washd with us"—but never how she did it or why. Nor did she comment on her own physical or emotional state. On June 6, 1790, she wrote, "Abigail Wildes was born," making absolutely nothing of the fact that she was Abigail's mother. Nor did she add anything to the entry for April 4, 1792: "I heard that shocking news of my poor husbands death."

In contrast, Ann Smith turned even the smallest occurrence into an event, as in this entry for June 8, 1807: "I was up this Morn before the (Lazy) sun, baked a Large loaf of bread in a Duch oven (our usual mode of baking in Summer) which I mixed & sit to rising last night) put on the tea kittle—while I was thus imployed our boy Ben harnessed the horse, & put him to the Chaise—My husband & self steped in, & had a charming ride and returned at Seven o'clock & took our breakfast." The casual aside to the reader ("our usual mode of baking in Summer") as well as the uncertain parentheses around "Lazy" (did she question the appropriateness of the adjective?) mark this as a composition, a self-conscious attempt to capture a moment and mood. Although she noted on one winter day that "My avocations differ so little, that the journal of one day, would serve for almost half a year," four days later she was composing a kind of memorial to herself simply by listing those avocations: "I at home all day—baked a good oven full of bread, got dinner (breakfast) & Supper, washed a bushell of dirty dishes, swept a basket full of Snow out of the entrys, tryed out a pot of tallow, & knitt part of a stocking. Smart!!!"[14]

Ann Smith's fragmentary diary was part of a larger celebration of domesticity in the early republic. By 1800 even the heroines of romantic stories knew how to cook. "I attended my little dairy, cooked my grandfather's provisions, took care that my house was always clean, and endeavoured to be cheerful to give him pleasure," declared the beautiful Julia of Sally Wood's first novel. When Julia's fiancé visited America he wrote back praising "Mrs. Murray" (Judith Sargent Murray, editor of *The Gleaner*) whom he had met in Boston. "I have dined with this lady, and was charmed with my entertainment, and pleased to find that her literary pursuits did not interfere with her domestic virtues; she is a most excellent wife, and one of the best of mothers, and the perfect order and arrangement of her house-hold declare her a complete house-wife."[15] Through devotion to household duty, women ensured domestic tranquillity in the nation as well as at home. As one of the graduates of Susanna Rowson's academy declared, "A woman who is skilled in every useful art, who practices every domestic virtue . . . may, by her precept and example, inspire her brothers, her husband, or her sons, with . . . just ideas of the true value of civil liberty."[16]

Such literature emphasized the moral rather than the economic consequences of domesticity. A different group of writers considered the more practical implications of women's work. In the introduction to his 1810 survey of American manufacturing, Tench Coxe lavished attention on what he called "our redundant southern cotton, which is every where for sale and pays no import duty or excise." The wide availability of such a material might "render every industrious female *an artizan*, whenever her household duties do not require her time," he wrote. Coxe was interested in household as well as factory production. Aged or childbearing slaves might spin and weave when they could not be employed in field work; northern housewives might profitably turn to cotton once their flax and wool was exhausted. "Fancy goods offer the greatest profits," he wrote, "and in many instances are easy of imitation."[17]

Eliza Wildes (now Eliza Bourne) could testify to that. Her white coverlet in The Brick Store Museum is direct evidence of Tench Coxe's contention (fig. 5.4 and cat. 139). The spinning and weaving recorded in her 1790 diary had by 1810 become a flourishing home industry. According to a Kennebunk newspaper of that year, no household manufacturer had exceeded her. She and her helpers had produced 228 yards of cloth and more than two dozen coverlets in a season, an output equal to "the constant labor of three women with the assistance of children."[18] Given the complexity of the Bourne household (Eliza was the mother and stepmother of fifteen children), it probably took a stream of helpers, daughters and neighbors, to secure the equivalent of the "constant labor of three women."

In the Bourne household, as elsewhere, factory spinning of cotton thread stimulated rather than retarded home weaving, housewives using factory spun thread alone or in combination with homespun wool and flax. Tench Coxe listed only three cotton factories in Maine in 1810, but Rhode Island thread was also available. Household production far exceeded factory production. In York County alone, according to the 1810 survey, 201,997 yards of cotton goods were produced in families.[19] If Eliza Bourne's two hundred yards represented unusually high production, as the newspaper account suggests, then cotton manufacturing was distributed over hundreds of households, factory-spun yarn having been integrated into old patterns of production that linked mothers, daughters, and neighbors in an intricate— and female managed—textile production system.[20]

The relation between the old production patterns and the new domestic ideals is difficult to determine, but in Eliza Bourne's household, for a time at least, the two came together. In 1810 her daughter Abigail (the child whose birth was recorded so unceremoniously in the 1790 diary) made a coverlet which she sent to Dolley Madison. Woven into the center were words that simultaneously celebrated married love and hinted at the dangers of public life: "Beneath this bed illustrious pair repose, / Secure from foreign and domestic foes. / May white plumed seraphs watch around this bed, / And heaven its kindlier influences shed." Even the president and his lady might retire to a domestic bower, and they might do so more happily knowing that women like Abigail Wildes were increasing American manufactures.

In a family memoir written in 1861, Edward Bourne described his mother's activities with affection. She was an old-fashioned woman, both pious and energetic, whose household sometimes included as many as twenty members. "The family were trained to activity; and I think no one can be named of the whole number, who had outgrown the training. True, I have heard my mother sometimes address the girls, as 'lazy drabs.' But such occasional interjections were only a part of the regimen, instituted for the purpose of fireing up the spirit, and rooting and grounding them in habits of industry." Through the combined efforts of herself and daughters, Eliza Bourne was able "to do much to meet the failure of income from other sources," to furnish the "fashionable apparel" and other commodities appropriate to "the social standing of the family."[21]

She was the perfect republican woman, able to combine industry with gentility, to simultaneously uphold her family's social position and inculcate habits of industry and self-reliance. No temptations to luxury and self-indulgence here. No, indeed! Her son Edward admitted that if his mother had one fault it was her indifference to the niceties and comforts of life. "Without doubt, she could have sat down with Dr. Franklin, and made a comfortable repast on his sawdust pudding." On one memorable morning, she almost made a meal out of lampblack. The boys had dropped it in the drawer of an old coffee mill, and when the

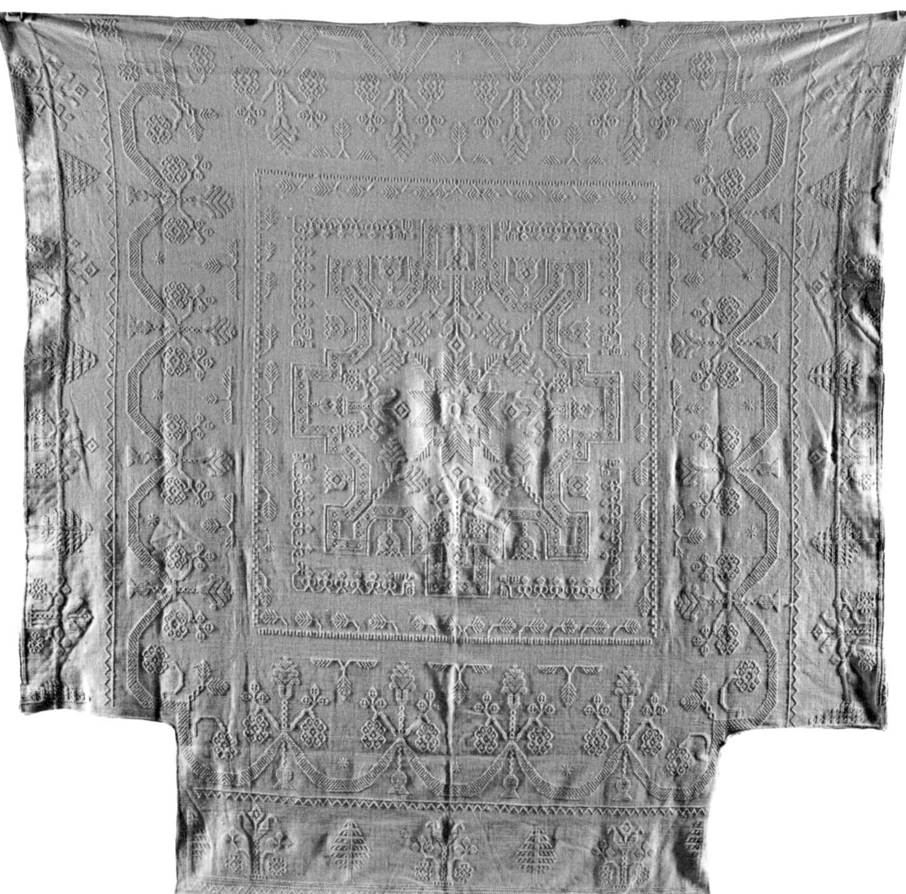

Fig. 5.4 Elizabeth Wildes Perkins Bourne, coverlet, Kennebunk, Maine, ca. 1810. Cat. 139. The Brick Store Museum.

maid came to make breakfast by candle light, she took it by mistake. "What is the matter with this coffee?" the children complained. "It is good enough," the mother replied, "only a little oily, strange you can't be satisfied." Not until the mistake was discovered was she willing to admit defeat. "But probably, had she been alone, she would have taken her usual portion in Christian resignation and trust."[22]

This humorous anecdote from a nineteenth-century memoir suggests real tensions in the early republic between the virtues of civilization and the dangers of luxury. As Richard Candee has shown (Chapter 2), the Maine gentry lived in an island of privilege in comparison with their true country neighbors. The scenes of pastoral happiness depicted in their needlework and poetry portray a mythical world sealed off not only from the deaths and financial reverses that were realities for these women or their acquaintances but from the tragedies of less-privileged people around them.

Idealizing the "simple life" was of course one way of assuaging anxiety over one's privileges. On September 10, 1808, Sarah Connell again took a romantic walk, this time in the company of female friends. Her diary entry might have

described an engraved or embroidered pastoral rather than a real day in an actual New England village: "We pursued our way through the woods till we arrived at the great Pear tree, where we all stopped and hung up our bonnets. We then passed through the little gate, and entered the little cottage, which is not visible till within a yard of the door, and it then discovers itself peeping through the foliage. The old Woman was ironing, but our abrupt visit did not seem to disturb her. Her daughter, Mrs. Fish, was nursing her little infant, while her little boy, apparently four years old, was expressing his delight at our visit. We were received with unfeigned hospitality. Pears and Cyder were set before us, with the recommendation of a hearty welcome. How much superior is the sweet cheerfulness of the honest rustics, and their friendly repast, to all the parade of ceremony, and the insincerity of the Great. Tenderness supplies the place of refinement. . . . They are happy, they are all the World to each other."[23]

Eliza Southgate was less sure about the "honest rustics." In a letter to her cousin Moses Porter, she complained, "Our novelists have worn the pleasures of rural life threadbare. . . . Yet let us judge for ourselves,—we all have seen what the pleasures of rural life are, and whatever Poets may have ascribed to it, we must know there is as much depravity and consequently as much discontent in the inhabitants of a country village as in the most populous city. They are generally ignorant, illiterate, without knowledge to discover the real blessings they enjoy by comparing them with others, continually looking to those above them with envy and discontent and imagine their share of happiness is proportioned to their rank and power."[24] (By this time, of course, "envy and discontent" in some parts of Maine had already resulted in armed protest against the wealthy landowners who were attempting to impose their own boundaries on disputed lands.)

Eliza was less idealistic than Sarah, but she too showed little ability to understand her neighbors on their own terms, nor did she see any irony in the decorations constructed in 1803 for a New York dinner in honor of her uncle, Rufus King. Down the center of each table, she wrote, was "an enclosure about 2 feet wide, filled with earth, and railed in with a little white fence and little gates every yard or two . . . some places flocks of sheep, some cows laying down, beautiful little arches and arbors covered with green."[25] In the world of fantasy at least one could enjoy the pleasures, without the labors, the inconveniences, or the tumults, of country life.

Education: Tiffany Border

"I found the mind of a female, if such a thing existed, was thought not worth cultivating," Eliza Southgate wrote in 1801, commenting on her own fashionable education. "I disliked the trouble of thinking for myself and therefore adopted the sentiments of others—fully convinced to adorn my person and acquire a few little accomplishments was sufficient to secure me the admiration of the society I frequented."[26]

A disdain for "little accomplishments" permeated the literature of the period. In novels as in reformist essays like those of Judith Sargent Murray or Benjamin Rush, sensible women skilled in domestic pursuits were elevated above mere ladies of fashion. Part of this impulse came from the old religious mistrust of worldliness. "A cold unpleasant day, but I have a good fire, and much better health than for months past, & many, very many of the good things of this World for my Ease, Gratification & Convenience. O My God may they not Endanger my Eternal Salvation," Ann Smith wrote in

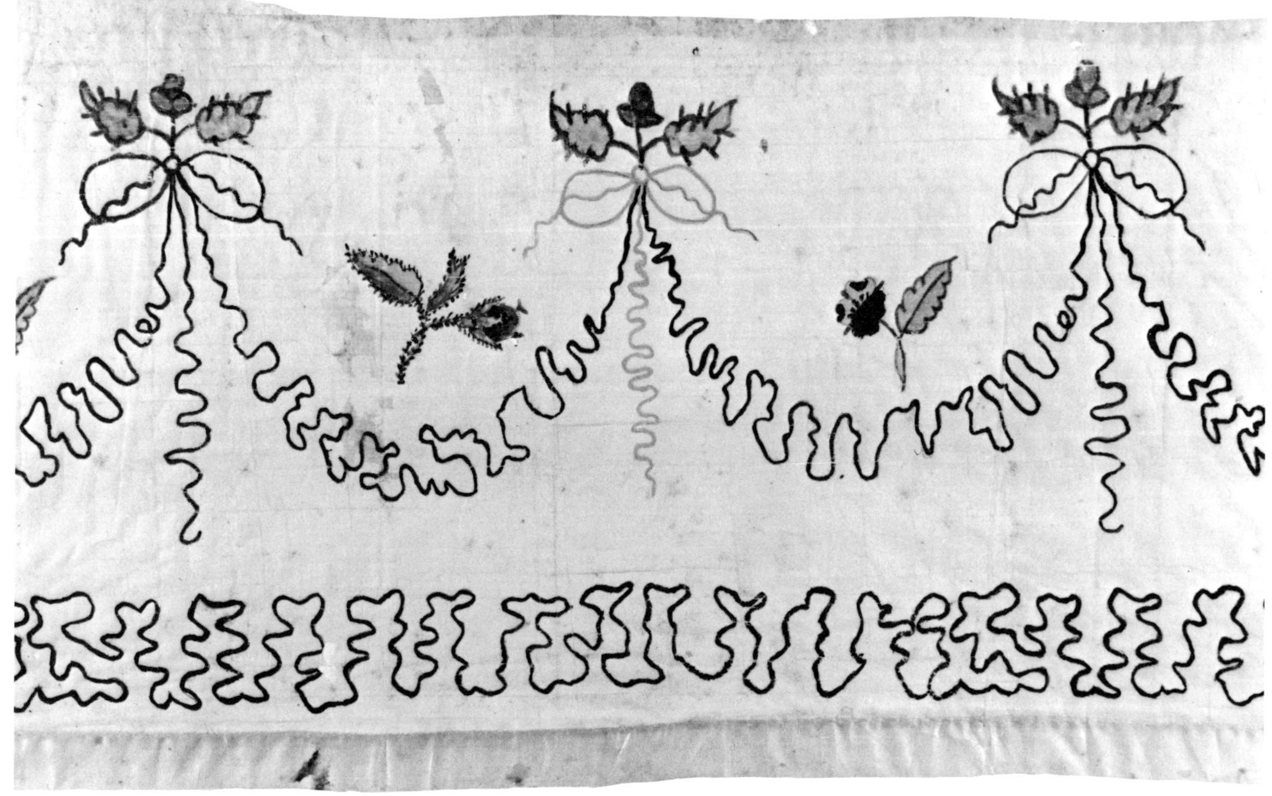

Fig. 5.5 Tiffany border or flounce, probably Saco, Maine, ca. 1797. Cat. 141. York Institute Museum.

February 1806. But for the reformers, the danger was not loss of salvation but loss of self. A republican woman *"should reverence herself,"* Judith Sargent Murray insisted, arguing not only for an enlarged respect for practical skills but for deliberate cultivation of the mind.[27]

The study of geography, Benjamin Rush had suggested, would qualify American women for "a general intercourse with the world," while the development of skill in bookkeeping would allow them to become "stewards and guardians of their husbands' property."[28] In most schools of the period such subjects were simply grafted on to the ornamental arts that had long been the province of ladies. "You wish to know my studies," Betsy Sewall wrote her father from Boston in September 1805, "I attend to the useful studies the same as the rest of the schollar[s], Grammar, Geography, writing, reading etc. I have worked they say a handsome work. I am now working a pair of sleves on linen cambric."[29]

In 1797–1798 Eliza Southgate had attended the best schools in Medford and Boston, including Susanna Rowson's famous academy where she studied arithmetic, writing, and geography, in addition to embroidery and music. "I left school with a head full of something, tumbled in without order or connection," she later complained.[30] By the second decade of the nineteenth century that same "tumble" of subjects was available in Maine. Ann Grant's "Academy," established in Kennebunk in 1813, offered "Reading, Writing, Grammar, Orthography, Geography, Drawing, Painting, Embroidery, Print-Work, fillegree, tambour, plain Sewing, Marking, Working Muslin, etc.," the proprietress promising to give "due attention to the improvement and morals of her scholars."[31]

Did such academies promote ornamental at the expense of useful knowledge? Did they substitute a flickering gentility for a vigorous and productive womanhood? Some contemporaries thought so. "I cared but little for the mind," Eliza Southgate admitted. "I learned to flutter about with a thoughtless gaiety—a mere feather which every breath had power to move."[32] Should that fragile strip of silk identified in the collections as a tiffany border or flounce be seen, then, as a commentary on the ephemeral quality of young ladies' learning in the period (fig. 5.5 and cat. 141)? A few little accomplishments and a desire for self-adornment—these Eliza Southgate saw as the sum total of her education.

Her strictures should not be taken at face value. What her own letters show, beyond doubt, is the liberating power of the genteel education she had received. Her first stilted letters, perhaps copied as penmanship exercises, gave her the rudimentary control of her pen that made her later writing possible. "My dear Parents: I hope I am in some measure sensible of the great obligation I am under to you for the inexpressible kindness and attention which I have received of you from the cradle to my present situation in school," she wrote in one letter from Medford, and in another, "Your

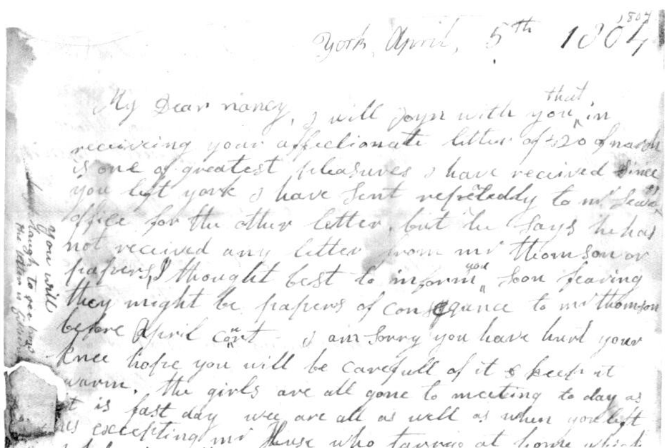

Fig. 5.6 Hannah and Joanna Sewall to Nancy Sewall (details), York, Maine, April 5, 1804. Old York Historical Society.

letter shall be my guide from home, and when I again behold our own peaceful mansion then will I again be guided by my Parents' happiness."[33] The distance from home required the letters, the instruction gave them form.

The significance of Eliza's stiff and formulaic little compositions can be glimpsed in Sarah Cleaves's comment in a letter to a daughter who was away at school: "I recived a letter from Mary and I wrote her one and hers was the first I have written this twenty years; now yours is the second. . . . My Dear I see the want of Lerning now more than ever I did; you must try and Lerne."[34] The distance between generations is apparent in the handwriting on a letter written jointly by Hannah Sewall and her daughter Joanna. Joanna's penmanship is confident, her mother's a mere scrawl (fig. 5.6). Without a comfortable mastery of pen and ink, women's words—and lives—were lost.

Regardless of the curriculum, the experience of living away from home was in itself educational, even more so as the girls learned to negotiate—in writing—the delicate territory between obedience and self direction. Betsy Sewall from Boston, September 8, 1805: "The exhibition is the 1st of October. I shall wish if convenient for you to send me some money to get some things that are necessary for that purpose. I know it will be pleasing to you to have me appear as well as the other schollars. I shant get any but what is necessary." Eliza Southgate from Medford, September 30, 1797: "You say that you shall regret so long an absence; not more certainly than I shall, but a strong desire to possess more useful knowledge than I at present do, I can dispense with the pleasure a little longer of beholding my friends and I hope I shall be better prepared to meet my good parents towards whom my heart overflows with gratitude."[35]

Eliza Southgate sought "useful knowledge," yet she later insisted that her fashionable schooling had left her fluttering about, with no sure direction. She proposed the correspondence with Moses Porter both "for pleasure and instruction," acknowledging the superiority of his education, begging him to become her instructor. Like other bright women of her age, she had tasted enough of books to realize how little she really knew. "I never was of opinion that the pursuits of the sexes ought to be the same," she told her cousin. "Yet to cultivate the qualities with which we are endowed can never be called infringing the prerogatives of man. . . . Do you suppose the mind of woman the only work of God that was 'made in vain.'" Unfortunately, Moses's letters have not survived, but the intensity of Eliza's arguments suggests he had responded with the traditional objections to learned women. "I am aware of the censure that will ever await the female that attempts the vindication of her sex," Eliza rejoined. "Yet I dare to brave that censure that I know to be undeserved. It does not follow . . . that every female who vindicates the capacity of the sex is a disciple of Mary Wolstoncraft. Though I allow her to have said many things which I cannot but approve."[36]

The ideas in Eliza Southgate's letters appear in more developed form in the published writings of her contemporaries, Judith Sargent Murray and Charles Brockden Brown. Even with only one side of the correspondence, however, her dialogue with Moses Porter has a vitality missing from their work or from New England novels of the period. For her the correspondence opened a kind of fictional space in which she could fully be herself. She urged Moses to speak to her with the same openness as with a male friend, to abandon the affectations and conventions of traditional gender relations so that they might "step aside from the world, [and] speak to each other in the plain language of sincerity."[37]

In her letters, Eliza tried to invent a new kind of exchange between the Fair and the Brave. Her writing is both candid and teasing, self-deprecating and saucy, satirical and serious. She composed lyrical descriptions, then mocked them, erected arguments only to dismiss them, dancing with words as she might have with Moses at a ball. Like Jane Austen she was tuned to the subtleties as well as the comic absurdities of a provincial social life.

"Thursday it snowed violently," she wrote, "indeed for two days before it had been storming so much that the snow drifts were very large; however, as it was the last Assembly I could not resist the temptation of going, as I knew all the world would be there. About 7 I went down-stairs and found young Charles Coffin, the minister, in the parlor. After the usual enquiries were over he stared awhile at my feathers and flowers, asked if I was going out,—I told him I was going to the Assembly. 'Think, Miss Southgate,' said he, after a long pause, 'think you would go out to *meeting* in such a storm as this?' Then assuming a tone of reproof, he entreated me to examine well my feelings on such an occasion. I heard in silence, unwilling to begin an argument that I was unable to support."[38]

Eliza went out into the snowstorm with her feathers and flowers and didn't get home until Monday. "Such a frolic! Such a chain of adventures I never before met with, nay, the page of romance never presented its equal." In the luxuriously detailed letter she sent Moses, she polished every comic character she had encountered, from the "sweet little, trembling, delicate, unprotected fellow" who planted himself in the midst of the ladies' carriage to the beau who gallantly offered to carry her through the snow to the house, then sank under "such a weight of sin and folly."[39]

In the apologetic (and anonymous) preface to *Julia and the Illuminated Baron*, Sally Wood echoed Eliza Southgate's dismissal of female education. Describing herself in the third person, she wrote, "Her abilities are too scanty, to allow her to understand either religious or philosophical subjects in others, much more inadequate to the attempting them herself; incapable of undertaking the labours of history, or of attaining the sublime heights of poetry; the only path which lay open, was that of Romance."[40] One wonders what might have happened had Eliza Southgate been free to take that course. In her hand ballrooms and carriages, tiffany and feathers, swags and frolics, became assertions of self.

Patriotism: The Stroudwater Light Infantry Banner

The silk standard of Washington's Life Guards depicts the Spirit of Liberty, a demure young woman in classical garb, presenting the commander's flag to an officer of the guard. The image is both allegorical and literal. Although female seamstresses and upholsterers sometimes *made* flags, as in the Betsy Ross tradition, elite women more commonly *presented* them, raising money for silk and painting, then offering the finished standard with an appropriate speech. Such a custom was well-established throughout America by the end of the Revolution. As early as 1748 the *Pennsylvania Gazette* reported the presentation of "Colours . . . by the good Ladies of this City, who raised Money by Subscription among themselves." Zilpah Wadsworth presented a flag to the Federal Volunteers of Portland in 1799, Eunice Quinby the Stroudwater Light

Infantry banner in 1805 (fig. 5.7 and cat. 154), and Sarah Grant the Kennebunk militia flag of 1813.[41]

Zilpah left a remarkable account of her experience. Because her father, Peleg Wadsworth, was a prominent military figure, her selection was a natural one, but she resisted it. "The week before it was given I went to Saco to pass a fortnight, secretly congratulating myself that all would be over before I should come home. But it was not so to be. I was sent for and coaxed to consent to present it. Every argument was used that would conduce me, & my reluctance, though not banished was overcome."

According to the official account the troops marched in platoons to the Wadsworth house where Zilpah presented the standard "in behalf of the Young Ladies of Portland," offering a "truly Elegant Address." Zilpah's account adds the music and the trembling: "Capt. Boyd drew up his company very near to the gate. The ladies all went out into the front yard before me, they were much nearer the company than I was and all around me. I only went to the large stone step & then the Ensign advanced to receive the standard. The music continued all the time so that it was no matter whether or not anything was said. I cannot describe it Nancy. I wish you had been here to see for yourself. I have not said a word of the spectators, they were innumerable, I never saw so large a collection in this town but I did not dare look at them till they began to disperse."

The experience was both better and worse than she expected. It wasn't the speech itself. In retrospect, that really wasn't so difficult. "When it was over and the Ensign waved the standard, had it never more been mentioned, my name I mean, I had been content to have made the sacrifice I did to gratify the Captain & the company. But then to have one's name handed about so publicly & in the newspapers it was too much. I was mortified & distressed." By her own account, Zilpah was both helpless and powerful, an inspirer of men and a hostage to public opinion. Too frightened to look at the crowd, she had nevertheless soaked in the admiration of the troops.

"The company were all young men," she wrote. "It was very gratifying to them & inspired them with enthusiasm to have it from the ladies in person. . . . And then it gave them an opportunity of making a ball, and gave us all a very agreeable evening. The volunteers appeared to be very happy, some of them I suppose never before spent such an evening. I dare say they will as long as they live love the ladies the better for it." What worried Zilpah was the publicity. Would other people, not knowing how reluctant she had been, think she had sought the honor? "There is nothing will sooner or more deeply tinge my cheeks than thinking of these things," she wrote, "and so I bid the ungrateful subject adieu."[42]

Insisting she had acted from the highest motives, Zilpah Wadsworth nevertheless feared a loss of reputation. One would suspect her of being coy if Eliza Southgate had not expended a long letter to Moses Porter trying to explain just such a problem. "Reputation undoubtedly is of great importance to all, but to a female 'tis every thing,—once lost 'tis *forever* lost. Whatever I may have said, my heart too sensibly tells me I have none of that boasted independence of mind which can stand collected in its own worth, and let the censure and malice of the world pass by. . . . I have ever thought that to be conscious of doing right was insufficient; but that it must appear so to the world."[43] The treacherous journeys, hidden dungeons, and mistaken identities in Sally Wood's novels had at least a psychological reality in Maine.

Flag presentations, parades, and balls drew women, however reluctantly, into the rituals of military culture. "We were awakened at four in the Morning by Martial music playing near our window," Sarah Connell wrote while visiting a friend in Newburyport, Massachusetts, in October 1809. "We both rose, opened the shutter, and seated ourselves on the window seat. The Moon was in her last quarter, and her silver light, illumined all around. The whole World seemed hushed to sleep, save the Musicians. Nought was heard save the warlike sounds of the drum and fife. They played the most Patriotic tunes, calculated to excite the patriotism of the soldier, and to arouse him from disgraceful slumbers to protect the honour and independence of

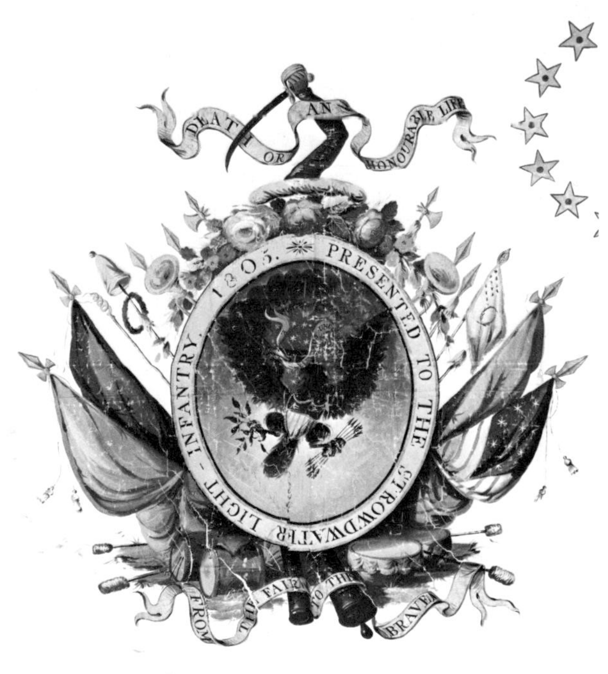

Fig. 5.7 Stroudwater Light Infantry Company banner (detail), Boston or Newburyport, Massachusetts, 1805. Cat. 154. Maine Historical Society.

America. America! Dear Native Land. Never may thy privileges, and rights be invaded by British tyranny and oppression."[44] Clearly the drum and fife had awakened Sarah as well as the soldiers. Although she pronounced the ball that evening "uninteresting," her diary entry confirms the evidence of Zilpah Wadsworth's papers: young women not only provided an audience, they helped to create the meaning of military events.

The presentation of banners symbolized women's relation to the state. The "fair" were to inspire and support the "brave," sometimes by contributing funds for flags and supplies, always by releasing them from private responsibilities (or pleasures) to pursue the public good. As Solomon Aiken of Newburyport put it, the soldiers of the revolution "were stimulated by the fire of *female patriotism*: which unlocked the arms of the fair, from the most tender embraces . . . saying 'go! go . . . and save our country.'"[45]

In peacetime, of course, the men went not to war but to the nearest tavern. The Stroudwater banner hung in Broad's Tavern, the scene on patriotic holidays of all-male drinking parties that were the federal counterpart of the revolutionary gatherings of the Sons of Liberty. Newspaper accounts of such events typically listed the fifteen or sixteen toasts proposed by the gentlemen. Usually the culminating toast, after The Constitution, The People, True Republicanism, and The Bright Star of Literature, was to The Fair. A militia gathering in 1800 hailed "the Ladies of Portland, whose Banners we bear," while a group at Mr. Motley's tavern on July 4, 1793, drank to "The fair daughters of Columbia; May their lips speak wisdom—their cheeks, health—and their eyes the language of love." At another dinner a gallant toasted "The fair sex throughout the world," adding "may the men hear of no chains, but those forged by their charms; nor feel any darts but the lightning of their eyes."[46] As Carl Bridenbaugh has pointed out, ritualized tributes to the ladies on such occasions did not preclude bawdy jokes and heavy drinking.[47] Describing one such occasion a Portland newspaper wrote (with no apparent irony), "The usual number of toasts were given, and the company retired after passing the day with the most uninterupted hilarity."[48]

As war with England loomed in 1812, Zilpah Longfellow laughed at the antics of five-year-old Henry, who was "ready to march," with "his tin gun prepared and his head powdered."[49] Some years later, as Henry and his brother reached military age, their patriotic masquerades seemed less charming. Noting the approach of training day, Zilpah wrote, "For my part I wish the day were well over, I always have a thousand fears for young people on such high days, they are then most apt to go astray."[50] Abigail Dutch of Augusta, Maine, put it more vividly. In a letter to her sister, she wrote, "Fourth of July as usual here was a tremendus day. People generally were very *high and* of course noisy, but your Brother's let tell it to their honour were both sober—

Charles worked all day on the farm, and William altho he dined with them returned home steady, while boys much younger [than] he were reeling about the streets, and while Mr. Bridge and other respectable men, let me speak it to their shame, were roaring at the streets. O abomanable. . . . Mr. Dutch & Mr. Nason started that day for Boston, and so got released to my great joy."[51]

When Sarah Grant, the proprietress of a young ladies academy, presented a flag to the Kennebunk militia in 1817, she urged the men to remember their standard had been "given by females who believe that humanity no less than valor, is an ornament to the soldier."[52] She said no more. Perhaps the men understood that learning to "love the ladies" meant adding self-restraint to valor.

Sometime after 1815 Sally Wood wrote an unpublished story, "War, The Parent of Domestic Calamity—A Tale of the Revolution." The opening chapter, ostensibly about the evacuation of Portsmouth, New Hampshire, after the burning of Falmouth in 1775, could just have well been based on her own experience in Wiscasset in the autumn of 1812 as British warships lay offshore. As she described those events in a letter to her father, "Castine, Belfast & Camden are now in the hands of the British, and an attack upon Portland or this Plain is daily expected. The Navy are hovering about our coast, every Precaution has been taken to repel the invaders, and there is at this time three or four thousand soldiers in town & two Regiments will be added this afternoon. . . . at this moment there are three companys landed in front of my house, ten more advancing, eight drums, & twice the number of fifes playing."[53]

Against the background of troop movements and civilian hardship, Madame Wood constructed a frothy romance, a love story involving a British officer and a young New Hampshire woman whose father was a Loyalist and whose brothers had enlisted in the American army. For forty-nine of the fifty-two pages of the tale nothing seemed capable of disrupting the course of true love. Romance overcame history as the gallant British lover saved the life of the heroine's rebel brother, an equally gallant American assisting him in pursuing his courtship behind enemy lines. In a world where there is no country but love, the soldier won the lady. The father and mother gave their consent. The wedding was about to take place when out of the night came the patriotic American brothers. Seeing but not recognizing their own father helping their sister into a sleigh, they concluded she was being abducted by a traitor in an enemy uniform.

In two breathless pages the story came to its macabre conclusion. The men's "blood boiled in their veins and they were so impelled by rage and shame, that to decide and act was the impulse of the same moment. . . . a pistol was discharged with too good aim to miss its object and it penetrated the backs of both father and daughter, who gave one convulsive start and sunk to the bottom of the sleigh."

The English lover and the assailant then fired at each other, the two of them falling dead beside "the murdered father and the sacrificed sister."[54] It is not difficult to imagine why the tale was never published. The brutal ending fractured the delicate treaty between the Fair and the Brave, cutting through the harmonious ceremonies of love to the Gothic horror of war.

Eliza Southgate. Sally Wood. Sarah Connell. Ann Smith. Zilpah Wadsworth. And others. Between 1790 and 1820 Maine women circumnavigated woman's sphere, sketching delicate pastorals, subtle interior maps, and lively genre pieces that give life to the souvenirs of womanhood they left behind.

1 *Julia and the Illuminated Baron* (Portsmouth, N.H., 1800), iv.
2 Elizabeth Sewall to Storer Sewall, July 28, 1801, Sewall Papers, OYHS; Charles L. Clark, Corrections to "York Necrology" (OYHS), 11; Sewall Genealogy (typescript, OYHS), 12.
3 These samplers are cats. 145 and 147.
4 Elizabeth Sewall to Storer Sewall, August 1807, OYHS. On the broader change, see Philippe Ariès, *Western Attitudes toward Death: From the Middle Ages to the Present* (Baltimore and London: Johns Hopkins University Press, 1974), Anita Schorsch, *Mourning Becomes America: Mourning Art in the New Nation* (Philadelphia: William Penn Memorial Museum, 1976), and Barton Levi St. Armand, *Emily Dickinson and Her Culture* (Cambridge: Cambridge University Press, 1984), chap. two.
5 Bowne, *A Girl's Life*, 25.
6 Ayer, *Diary*, 53.
7 Ayer, *Diary*, 57.
8 Ayer, *Diary*, 58–59.
9 Nancy Sewall to "My Worthy Friend and Cousin," n.d., OHYS.
10 Marston, "A Lady of Maine," 207; Ayer, *Diary*, 209.
11 Betty Ring, *Let Virtue Be a Guide to Thee: Needlework in the Education of Rhode Island Women, 1730–1830* (Providence: Rhode Island Historical Society, 1983), 263.
12 Bowne, *A Girl's Life*, vi, 238; Sewall Genealogy, 12.
13 Eliza Wildes, diary, December 26, 1790; Ann Smith, diary, March 21, 1807, MEHS.
14 Ann Smith diary, February 3, 7, 1807, MEHS.
15 *Julia and the Illuminated Baron*, 18, 82.
16 Quoted in Linda Kerber, *Women of the Republic: Intellect and Ideology in Revolutionary America* (Chapel Hill: University of North Carolina Press, 1980), 229.
17 Tench Coxe, *A Statement of the Arts and Manufactures of the United States of America for the year 1810* (Philadelphia, 1814), xxix.
18 Excerpt from *The Weekly Visiter* (1810) in Remich, *History*, 221. Sandra Armentrout kindly shared her sources for Bourne's home industry.
19 Coxe, *Arts and Manufactures*, 2. There were 811,912 yards produced in Maine households.
20 I have described that system as it existed in one Maine family in the late eighteenth century in "Martha Ballard and Her Girls: Women's Work in Eighteenth-Century Maine," in Stephen Innes, ed., *Essays in the New Labor History of Early America* (forthcoming).
21 Edward E. Bourne, "History of the Bourne Family of Kennebunk" (1861), par. 236–237, 246, BSM.
22 Bourne, "History of Bourne Family," par. 297, 300–301. The typescript of Bourne's history says "Camp black." I have assumed this is an error in transcription.
23 Ayer, *Diary*, 60.
24 Bowne, *A Girl's Life*, 100.
25 Bowne, *A Girl's Life*, 168.
26 Bowne, *A Girl's Life*, 57.
27 Quoted in Kerber, *Women of the Republic*, 206.
28 Quoted in Kerber, *Women of the Republic*, 210–211.
29 Elizabeth Sewall to Storer Sewall, September 8, 1805, OYHS.
30 Bowne, *A Girl's Life*, 3, 4, 6, 8, 11, 15.
31 Remich, *History*, 240; *Weekly Visiter* (May 1, 1813; March 12, 1814; April 25, May 30, 1818).
32 Bowne, *A Girl's Life*, 56.
33 Bowne, *A Girl's Life*, 5.
34 Sarah Fairfield Cleaves to Almira Cleaves, August 6, 1818, William Lord Papers, BSM.
35 Bowne, *A Girl's Life*, 11.
36 Bowne, *A Girl's Life*, 60–61.
37 Bowne, *A Girl's Life*, 66–67.
38 Bowne, *A Girl's Life*, 92.
39 Bowne, *A Girl's Life*, 93–97.
40 Wood, *Julia and the Illuminated Baron*, iv.
41 Edward W. Richardson, *Standards and Colors of the American Revolution* (Philadelphia: University of Pennsylvania Press, 1982), 90, 132, 265–274, 121, 321. *Pennsylvania Gazette* (January 12, 1748); *The Autobiography of Benjamin Franklin* (New York: Modern Library, 1981), 139.
42 Zilpah Wadsworth to Nancy Doane, letter journal, September 1799, (filed with 1797), Wadsworth-Longfellow Papers, LNHS. Zilpah's retelling of the story for her own children may have influenced a poem written in 1825 by Henry, "Hymn of the Moravian Nuns," which describes the presentation of a flag to Count Pulaski by the Moravian sisters of Bethlehem.
43 Bowne, *A Girl's Life*, 50–51.
44 Ayer, *Diary*, 131.
45 See Kerber, *Women of the Republic*, 99–105, for an example of Philadelphia and New Jersey women organizing to raise money for troops; Solomon Aiken, *An Oration Delivered Before the Republican Citizens of Newburyport, and Its Vicinity, July 4, 1810* (Newburyport, Mass.), 1810), 13.
46 *Portland Gazette* (July 7, 1800); *Eastern Herald* (July 6, 1793; July 5, 1794). Similar descriptions appear in *Eastern Herald* (October 1, 1792; February 24, 1794; July 8, 1797; February 23, 1797); *Portland Gazette* (July 9, 1798); *Eastern Argus* (July 10, 1816; July 17, 1816).
47 Carl Bridenbaugh, *A Gentleman's Progress: The Itinerarium of Dr. Alexander Hamilton, 1744* (Westport, Conn: Greenwood Press, 1973), xvii, 43.
48 *Portland Gazette* (July 6, 1801).
49 Laurance Roger Thompson, *Young Longfellow* (New York: Macmillan, 1938), 10–12.
50 Zilpah Longfellow to Stephen Longfellow, September 15, 1823, Wadsworth-Longfellow Papers, LNHS.
51 Abby Dutch to Susan Sewall, July 8, 1814, Manley Scrapbook, Maine State Library, Augusta.
52 Bourne, *History*, 695–696.
53 Sally Wood to Nathaniel Barrell, September 11, 1814, in Marston, "A Lady of Maine," 222.
54 Sarah Sayward Barrell Keating Wood, "War, the Parent of Domestic Calamity—A Tale of the Revolution," in *A Handful of Spice: Essays in Maine History and Literature*, University of Maine Studies, 88 (1968): 53–105.

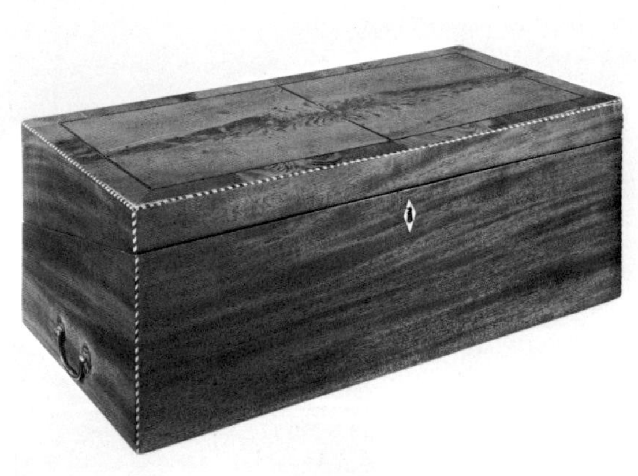

Cat. 131

131

Portable writing desk
Probably Portsmouth, New Hampshire, 1810–1820
Mahogany and birch veneer, *eastern white pine,*
Spanish cedar
H 8 (20.2); W 22 (56.0); D 11 (27.9)
Old York Historical Society; Museum purchase, 1976

Tradition traces the ownership of this portable writing desk
to the family of Sally Sayward Barrell (1737–1805) of York.[1]
Sally was the only child of Jonathan and Sarah Mitchell
Sayward. One of the town's leading citizens and a Loyalist
during the Revolution, her father served as a justice of the
court of common pleas, judge of probate, and justice of the
Province of Maine. From the family's mansion house
overlooking York Harbor, Sayward oversaw his ships,
wharves, and warehouses (fig. 3.4).

In 1758 Sally Sayward married Nathaniel Barrell
(1732–1831), a merchant in Boston and Portsmouth (cat.
32). Her father built them a large house inland on the York
River, where the Barrells settled in the late 1760s to farm and
raise eleven children (figs. 2.5–2.6). Their most famous
offspring was the eldest daughter, Sally Sayward Barrell
Keating Wood (fig. 5.2), who became Maine's first female
novelist, writing under the pseudonym "A Lady of Massachusetts" and, later, "A Lady of Maine." Sally Wood
surely received a literary and genteel upbringing under her
mother's tutelage, for Sally Sayward Barrell was an avid
reader and correspondent. In 1759 she wrote to friends in
Boston: "Books are my principal entertainment in the
country: as there are no Balls, no Assemblies, no Concerts of
Musick etc."[2] Indeed, the letters of both mother and
daughter frequently included pleas for books of all sorts.
Sally Wood is known to have written six novels and a hymnal

for children (see Chapter 5). She may also have operated a
female academy in Portland for a brief period.[3]

This refined writing desk would have been an appropriate
accessory for a member of this family. The figured birch
veneers and delicate stringing are typical of Portsmouth
furniture of the early nineteenth century. The box opens to a
baize-lined writing surface with a storage compartment and
a single drawer in one end, made fragrant by the use of
Spanish cedar (fig. 5.1).   KAO

1 When this was sold at auction with a number of other objects from a
   York family, it was consigned with the Sayward-Barrell family history.
2 Sally Sayward Barrell to Mr. Savage, cited in Marston, "A Lady of
   Maine," 13.
3 John T. Hill, ed., *Centennial Celebration of Portland 1786–1886* (Portland,
   Me., 1886), 200.

132

Elizabeth Sewall (1792–1812)
Mourning picture
Boston, Massachusetts, ca. 1801
Silk and watercolor on silk
H 18⁹/₁₆ (45.1); W 15¾ (40.0)
Old York Historical Society; Probably the gift
of the Reverend Frank E. Sewall, 1900

Nine-year-old Elizabeth Sewall of York stitched this memorial to her mother while attending school in Boston in 1801.
She wrote home to her father Storer Sewall in 1801, "I have
been working a piece of embroidery in memory of my dear
departed Mother, I canot express my feelings to you when I
think what a loss I have met with" (see Chapter 5 and fig. 5.3).[1]

Elizabeth employed long satin stitches for the white and
blue background, while the arms, face, and hair were
painted in watercolors. Shorter satin stitches in curved
configurations created a marbleized effect on the tomb, the
impression of folds on the dress, and a sense of vitality in the
leaves. The rich and vibrant greens, now faded to blue, in the
foreground, offer a sense of the original brightness. Stitched
on the tomb is the inscription "Sacred to the / Memory of /
Mrs. Lucy Sewall / who died Jany 14 1800."

Painters, jewelers, and looking-glass makers offered their
services to embellish or frame needlework. In Portland,
Henry Williams noted, "Painting upon Glass, Silk and
Sattin; and FACES on Embroidery," and Charles Codman
advertised "Drawings for Ladies' Needle Work, also figures
and skies colored for the same." Portland looking-glass
maker James Todd offered "Needlework . . . framed to any
pattern."[2] Elizabeth Sewall probably obtained the painted
arms, face, and hair for her needlework, as well as the frame,
from Boston sources.   AAE

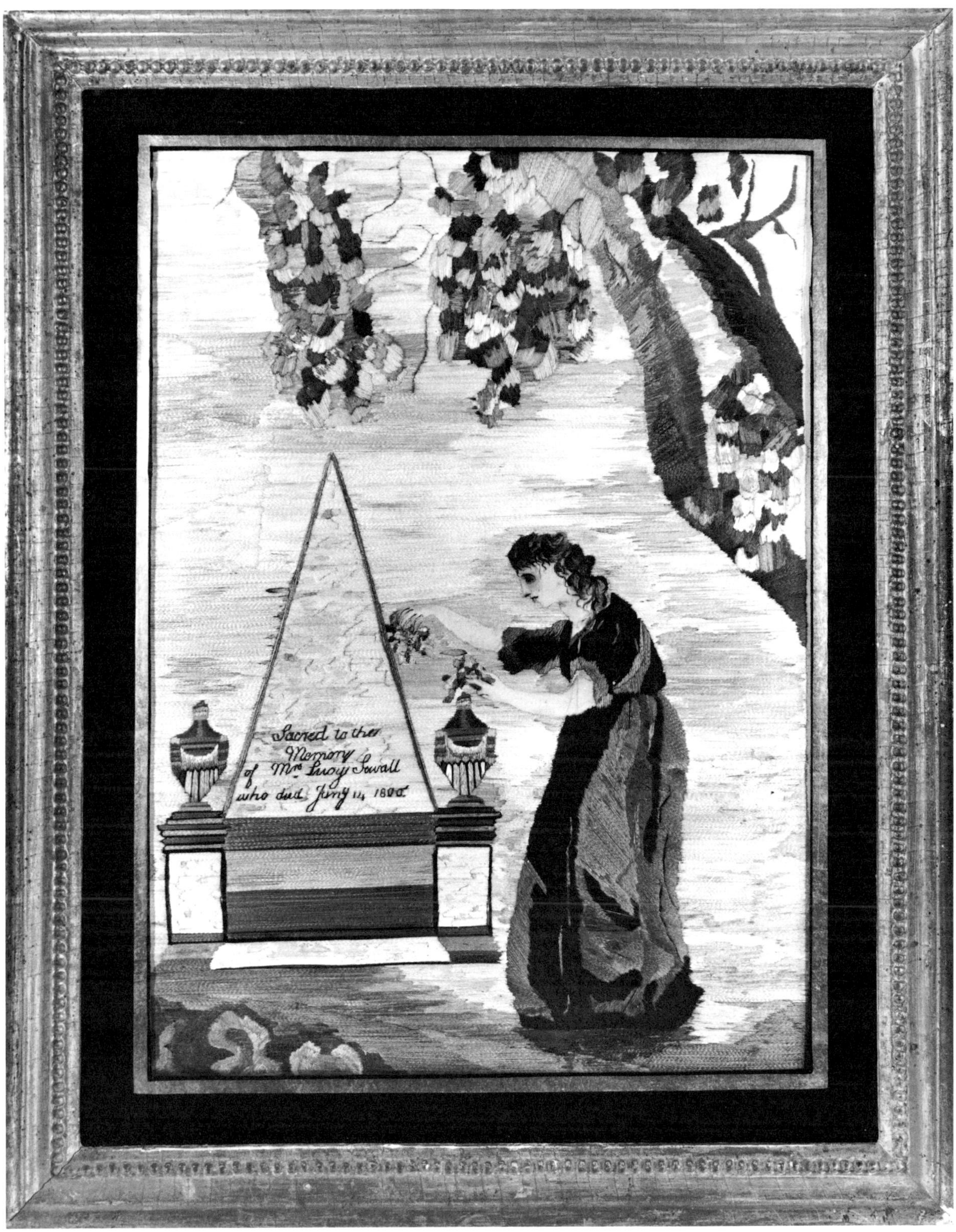

Cat. 132

1 Elizabeth Sewall to Storer Sewall, July 28, 1801, OYHS.
2 *Eastern Argus* (December 9, 1803); Nathaniel P. Jewett, *The Portland Directory and Register* (Portland: Todd and Smith, 1823), 79; *Eastern Argus* (June 10, 1823).

133

Mary Cleaves (1803–1871)
Mourning picture
Dorchester, Massachusetts, ca. 1818
Watercolor on velvet
H 22½ (57.2); W 18 (45.7)
The Brick Store Museum; Gift of Mrs. John B. Corning

Sarah Fairfield Cleaves believed strongly in the importance of education for her three daughters because she herself was inadequately trained. In August 1818, she wrote to her daughter Almira: "I have recived a letter from Mary and I wrote her one and hers was the first I have written this twenty years[;] now yours is the second[.] dont let it be seen[.] I have written this up hill the next I writte I will goe down hill. . . . My Dear I see the want of a Lerning now more than ever I did[;] you must try and Lerne."[1] Sarah's letter was written eight months after the death of her husband,

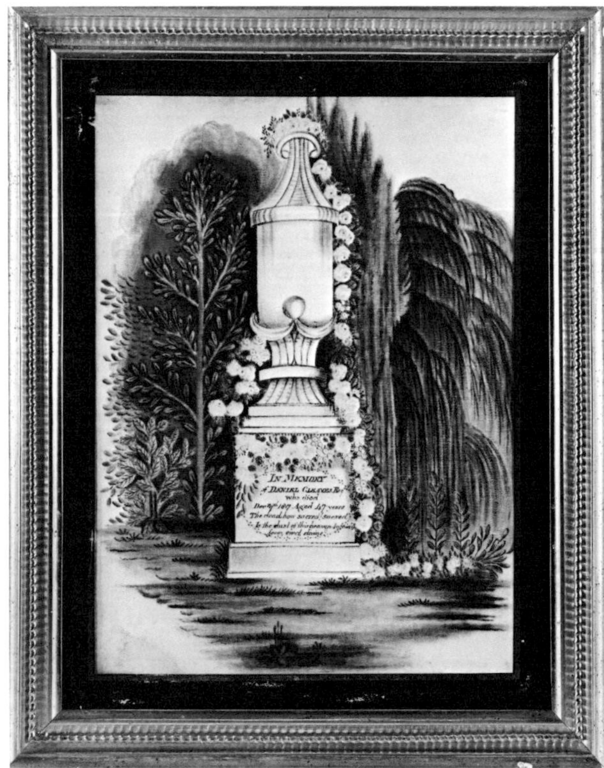

Cat. 133

Daniel Cleaves, who had evidently taken care of the family correspondence during his lifetime. His death, after twenty-two years of marriage, thrust new responsibilites on Sarah.

The three Cleaves girls studied at the Misses Martins' school in Portland between 1814 and 1815. By 1816 Mary and Sarah Cleaves were enrolled in the academy of Judith Foster Saunders and Clementina Beach on Meeting House Hill at Dorchester, Massachusetts. Evidently the Dorchester school offered superior instruction, because in July 1818, Mary reported: "I have taken five lessons in Musick, but make little progress in it. I have begun it all over again, for my Musick Master teaches in quite a different style from that in which I have been taught, and I think it rather difficult. He pays great attention to Time and the fingering; you know that was neglected very much by Miss Martin."[2]

The Saunders and Beach Academy attracted pupils from a number of wealthy Saco families, including Ann P. Thornton, daughter of Thomas G. Thornton; and Olive and Ann King, daughters of Cyrus King. Ann King reported in 1812, "Within a fortnight we had a ball and a concert, in each of which I was a performer: added to both was the attention and requisite to prepare the best specimens of our drawing and writing to ornament the hall."[3] In Dorchester the girls received instruction in ornamental needlework and painting, and created works that have been credited with an unusually high level of technical accomplishment.

A mourning picture, either painted or embroidered on silk, was often the culmination of a schoolgirl's artistic training. In July 1818 Mary Cleaves wrote to her sister Almira, "I have painted a little but hope soon I shall be able to paint so well as to do a Mourning-Piece for Mama. As she wished it, I shall do it with the greatest delight." Painting on velvet, more difficult than other techniques, was a major accomplishment, as is indicated in a letter from Olive King to her sister Mary: "I hope I shall begin to paint with colors soon[.] I have painted only with India ink landscapes[.] Ask Mama if I paint well enough & paint a mourning piece on velvet [if] I shall have it framed, if yes get me some line of poetry to put on it with the age of Papa when he died &c. (I am in no hurry for it)." Her father Cyrus had died in 1817.[4] This painting by Mary Cleaves—a memorial to her father who also died in 1817—was undoubtedly one of her finest works.

While many contemporary memorial paintings included figures dressed in the neoclassical taste, this one emphasized an angular gray monument with rose garlands set against a contrasting bright dark blue background and green willow trees. The inscription on the pedestal reads: "In Memory / of Daniel Cleaves, Esq. / who died on Dec. 7th, 1817 aged 47 years. / The dead how sacred! Sacred / Is the dust of this heaven-labour-ed / form, erect, divine!" The verse, as well as the composition, recalls other painted memorials made at the Saunders and Beach Academy.[5]   KDM

1 Sarah Fairfield Cleaves to Almira Cleaves, August 6, 1818, William
  Lord Papers, BSM.
2 Mary Cleaves to Almira Cleaves, July 17, 1818, facsimile, William
  Lord Papers, BSM.
3 Ann F. King to Hannah King, December 13, 1812, Cyrus King
  Papers, MEHS.
4 Mary Cleaves to Almira Cleaves, July 17, 1818, William Lord Papers,
  BSM. Olive Storer King to Mary C. King, August 18, 1819,
  Hale-King Papers, Special Collections, Bowdoin College Library.
5 The paintings on velvet by Almira Brown, in memory of Mrs. Susan
  Kendall (d. 1803), and Elizabeth Salter of Portsmouth, dedicated to
  Richard Salter (d. 1812), are similar to this painting by Mary
  Cleaves. See Betty Ring, "Mrs. Saunders' and Miss Beach's
  Academy, Dorchester," *Antiques* 110, no. 2 (August 1976): 312.

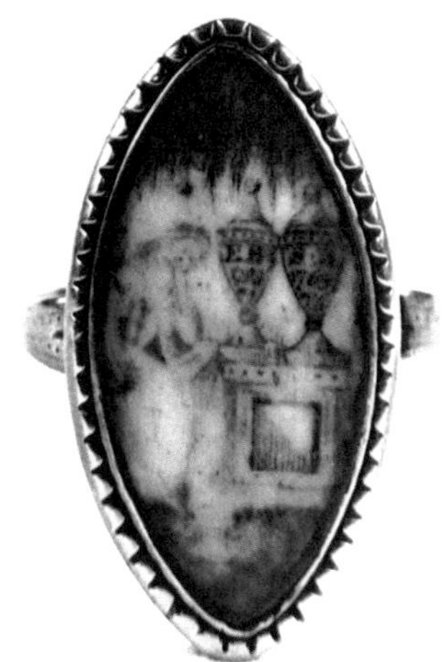

Cat. 134

134

Mourning ring
America, probably New England, ca. 1793
Watercolor on ivory and gold
Unmarked
H 1⅛ (2.8); W ⅝ (1.6)
Maine Historical Society, Wadsworth-Longfellow House
Gift of the Longfellow family, 1918

The custom of giving mementos of the deceased was such a
well-established and costly custom in New England by the
mid eighteenth century that in 1742 the Massachusetts
General Court passed an act limiting funeral gifts in order to
curtail funeral expenses.[1] In spite of this, the practice of
giving gifts at or after funerals continued beyond the early
nineteenth century. In federal Maine, rings or gloves were
often given as tokens of remembrance. Silversmiths advertised mourning jewelry and merchants, fancy goods dealers,
and milliners, such as Isabella Child, advertised "dark slate
colored gloves for mourning." [2]

The inventory of Daniel Pierce of Kittery in 1804 noted
his ownership of these types of personal possessions with its
references to a "death's head ring" and "a mourning ring."[3]
The "death's head ring," popular a century earlier, depicted
a skull in the center of the gold band.

The two urns in the painted memorial scene of this ring
are inscribed "s.b. / 1769" and "e.b. / 1793." Samuel and
Elizabeth Lothrop Bartlett, residents of Plymouth, Massachusetts, were the parents of Elizabeth Bartlett
Wadsworth. When Elizabeth Bartlett Wadsworth commissioned the ring after the death of her mother in 1793, she
honored her father as well, though he had died many years
earlier.

Attitudes toward death changed as the eighteenth
century progressed. This evolution is apparent in the gradual
shift from death's-heads on gravestones to willow trees and
urns. Like gravestones, rings also depicted classical and
sentimental mourning scenes.   AAE

1 Martha Gandy Fales, "The Early American Way of Death" *Essex
  Institute Historical Collections* 100, no. 2 (April 1964): 75.
2 *Portland Gazette* (November 11, 1788).
3 YCRP; 19: 403.

135A

Mourning ring
Maine or New Hampshire, ca. 1802
Gold, hair
Unmarked
Diam. 15/16 (2.4)
Old York Historical Society
Gift of Laura J. Williams, 1936

135B

Mourning ring
Maine or New Hampshire, ca. 1810
Gold, onyx or possibly jet, hair
Unmarked
Diam. 11/16 (1.8)
Old York Historical Society
Gift of Mrs. W. J. Neal, 1954

The mourning ring on the right (cat. 135A) was made for
Eunice Gerrish in memory of her husband, who was lost at
sea in 1802. Richard Gerrish (1769–1802) was born in

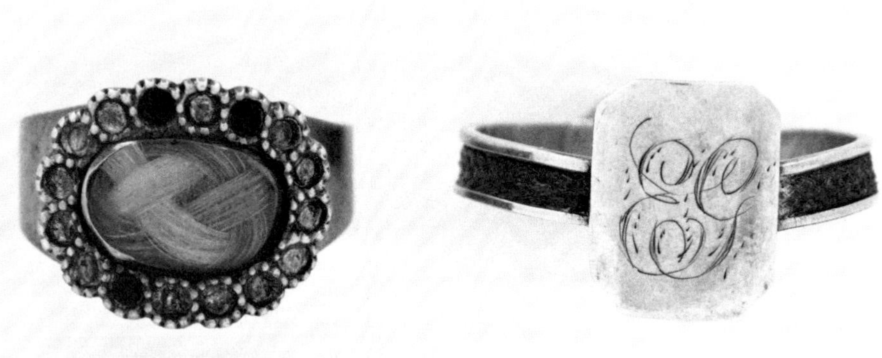

Cat. 135A and Cat. 135B

Kittery and later moved to York, where he married Eunice Donnell in 1793. Eunice may have saved a lock of her husband's hair which a jeweler or silversmith then fashioned into the ring. The band is set with an octagonal plaque engraved "EG." The inscription "Richd Gerrish, Ob AE 33 1802" is engraved on the inside of the band.

The other example with woven hair is the ring on the left (cat. 135B), made in memory of York's Isaac Lyman. The inside of the band is engraved "Rev. I. Lyman ob Mar 12, 1810 ae 85." Isaac Lyman was the pastor in York for more than sixty years. The father of nine children, some of whom predeceased him, Lyman was aware of his own age and mortality. He recorded in his diary in 1793, "Am this Day 68 years of Age. My Comrads have gone before me." A sermon preached at Lyman's funeral was published and, like this ring, served as a memento mori.[1]

The use of hair in jewelry became increasingly widespread as the nineteenth century progressed, but was not only associated with mourning. Eleazer Wyer of Portland advertised that he executed "All kinds of Fancy Hair Work," including hair hoops, bracelets, and necklaces. "Any person wishing to preserve a friend's hair, will do well to call." In 1802 Eliza Southgate Bowne received such a gift while visiting in Salem. She wrote that her friend Martha Coffin Derby had sent her "a beautiful bracelet for the arm made of her hair; she is too good — to love me as she says, more than ever."[2] AAE

1 Isaac Lyman, diary, 1785–1794, Massachusetts Historical Society, Boston. Reverend Moses Hemmenway, *A Sermon Preached at York, March 16, 1810, at the Interment of the Reverend Isaac Lyman, who deceased March 13, 1810, in the 86th Year of his age, and the 61st year of his ministry* (Boston: John Eliot, 1810).
2 *Portland Gazette* (October 23, 1809), as reprinted in Churchill, "Crafts in Transition," 306. Bowne, *A Girl's Life*, 143; Portland native Martha Derby was the wife of Richard, a son of Elias Hasket Derby.

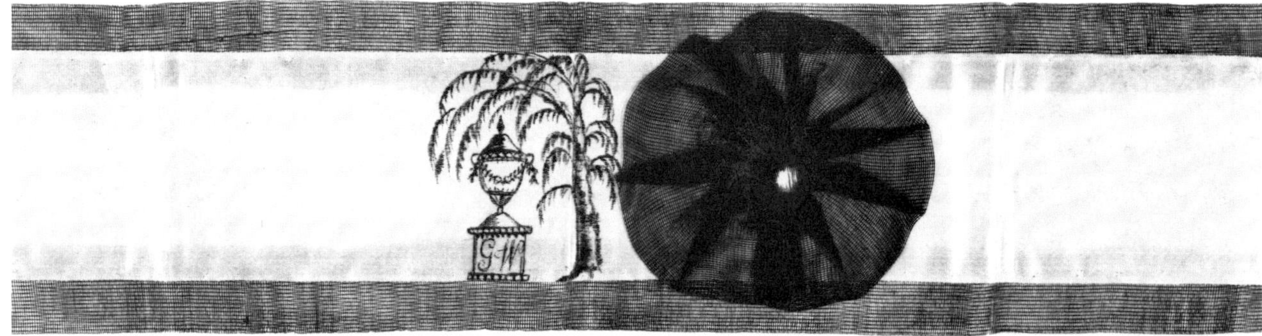

Cat. 136A

136A

Armband
New England, possibly Maine, ca. 1799
Silk
H 2 (5.0); W 13⅜ (34.0)
Maine Historical Society
Gift of Gilman Davis, 1885

136B

Badge
Probably New England, ca. 1826
Silk
H 6⅛ (15.6); W 2³⁄₁₆ (5.6)
York Institute Museum
Bequest of Almira Locke McArthur, 1950

Badges and armbands worn to mourn the death of national
leaders reflect the importance of a public display of bereave-
ment to express a sense of loss as well as patriotic sentiment.
After the deaths of both John Adams and Thomas Jefferson
on July 4, 1826, citizens purchased objects such as this
badge in their honor. Although printed examples like this
were available in stores, some people made their own
mourning emblems. The individual who fashioned this
armband stitched black binding to a white silk ribbon,
applied a rosette which resembles a cockade, and sketched in
ink a tomb with Washington's initials on it and a willow tree.
In February 1800 Eliza Southgate wrote from Boston, "For
mourning for Washington the ladies dress as if for a relation,
some entirely in black, but now many wear only a ribbon
with a line painted on it."[1]   A A E

1 Bowne, *A Girl's Life*, 22.

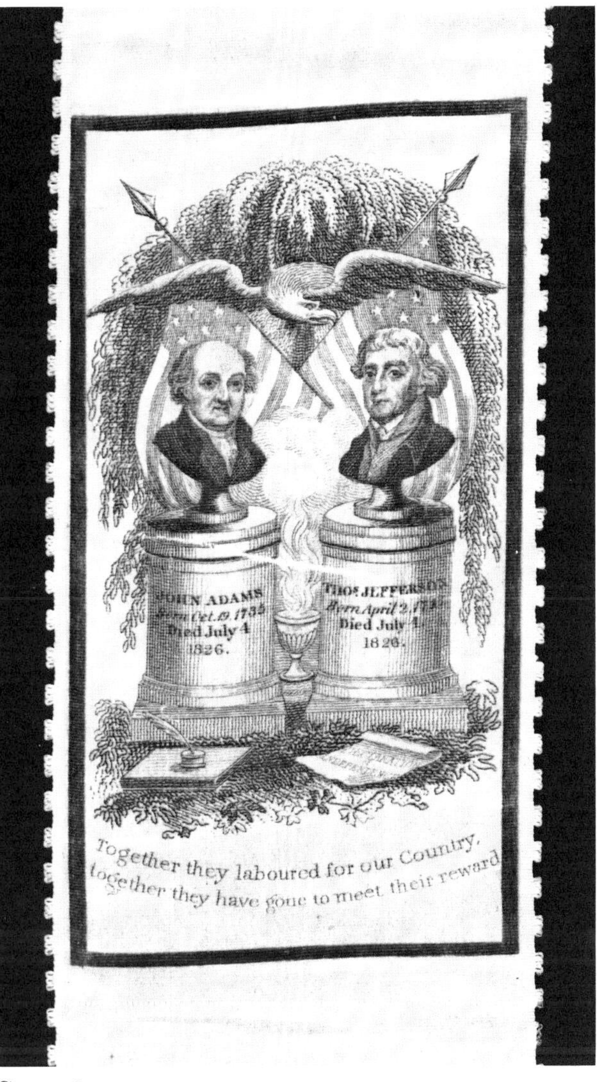

Cat. 136B

137

Thomas Clarke (w. 1796–1801)
Sacred to the Memory of the Illustrious G. Washington
Boston, Massachusetts, 1801
Engraving
Inscribed "T. Clarke Sculp: 1801 Boston"
H 8⅜ (21.2); W 8¹⁄₁₆ (20.5)
Old York Historical Society; Gift of Dorothy Hungerford

Both the number and the variety of surviving Washington
memorial prints indicate the popularity of the nation's first
president as a subject for engraving. Patriotic images such as
Charles Willson Peale's *George Washington at the Battle of
Princeton* and Gilbert Stuart's Vaughan-type and Athenaeum
portraits celebrated him during his lifetime. Following his
death, allegorical scenes and memorial prints identified him
as a symbol of the new nation.[1]

Americans honored Washington in ways other than
making or purchasing likenesses of him. Newspaper owner
Eleazer Jenks advertised for sale at his bookstore Washington's published will, and the eulogy, hymns, and dirges
composed for his funeral. The frequency with which John
Marshall's *Life of Washington* appears in probate inventories is
further evidence of Maine residents' interest in the president.
Ann Smith recorded in her diary in 1806, "Ben Hopkins
reading the History of Washington to us." A Mr. Packard
capitalized upon Washington's popularity at his Philosophical and Mechanical Museum. Besides a magician and
invisible lady, there was "a portrait of General Washington,

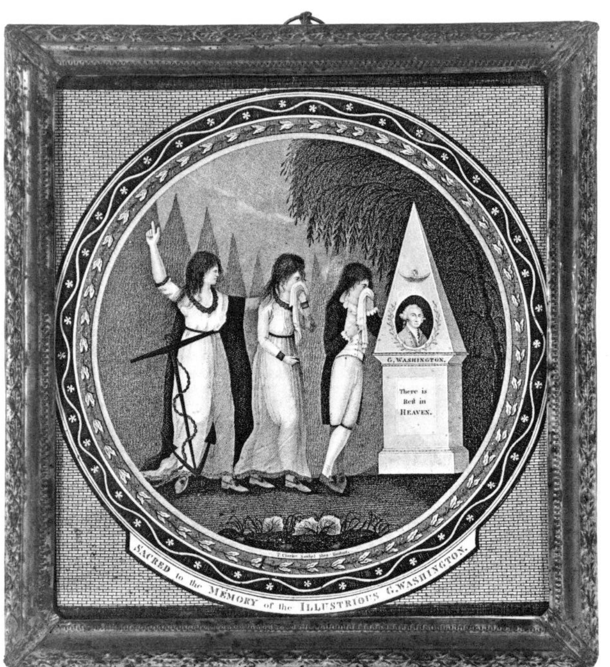

Cat. 137

A.F. & A.M. This "Herculaneum Pottery" mark in a straight line under an eagle may have been used for only a short time, replaced by the more common "Herculaneum Pottery Liverpool" mark which is printed in a curve under an eagle. A scene of peace, plenty, and independence decorates the reverse.[1]

A second example of an apotheosis design is at the Old York Historical Society and is impressed "HERCULANEUM" on the bottom. On the York pitcher angel heads surround the upper portion of the oval reserve and a ribbon under the scene bears the inscription "Apotheosis."[2] An apotheosis occurs when one is exalted to a divine rank. Considering America's admiration for Washington, it is not unexpected to find him so glorified.

This pitcher was among the ceramic tablewares photographed in the dining room of the Alexander W. Longfellow house in the late nineteenth century. It retains only traces of its original gilding.[3]   LFS

1 Nelson, "Transfer-printed Creamwares," 101–103. The Grand Lodge pitcher and its mark are illustrated in Sprague, "Liverpool-type Pitchers."
2 For this apotheosis print, see McCauley, *Liverpool Transfer Designs*, no. 64A, plate 25.
3 Alexander W. Longfellow house, photographs of interior, SPNEA Archives.

supported by two wax figures representing Liberty and Justice."[2]   AAE

1 Wendy Wick, *George Washington, An American Icon; The Eighteenth Century Graphic Portraits* (Washington, D.C.: Smithsonian Institution, 1982), 6.
2 *Eastern Argus* (January 27, 1800). Ann Smith, diary, January 15, 1806, MEHS. *Eastern Argus* (March 15, 1805).

138

Herculaneum Pottery (1796–1840)
Pitcher
Liverpool, England, 1802–1810
Creamware with transfer-printing in black, gilt
Marked (in transfer-printing under spout)
"Herculaneum Pottery"
H 9 (22.9)
Maine Historical Society, Wadsworth-Longfellow House
Gift of the Alexander W. Longfellow family

Earthenware pitchers transfer-printed with scenes in memory of George Washington were mass-produced by the English potteries. This scene of the apotheosis of Washington is recorded in many American collections, but only two pitchers are known bearing this mark (cat. 138.1) of the Herculaneum Pottery. The other pitcher known with this rare mark is also in Portland in the Grand Lodge of Maine

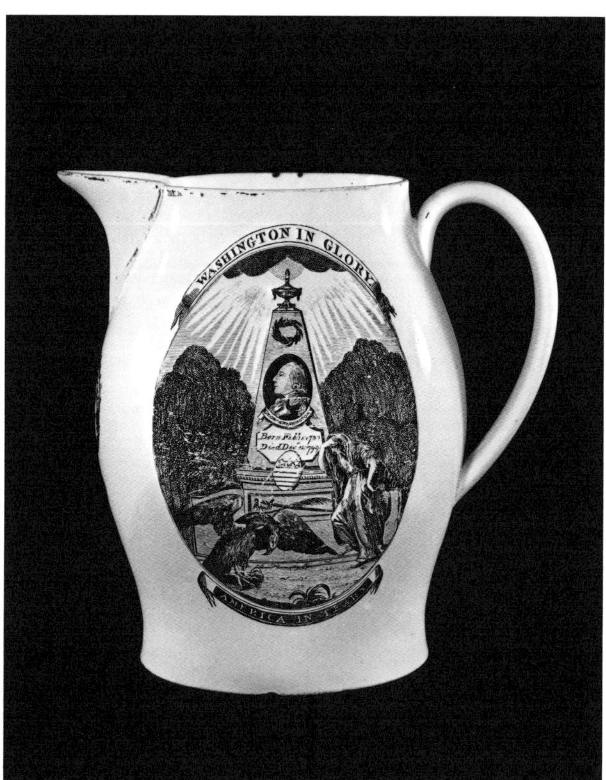

Cat. 138

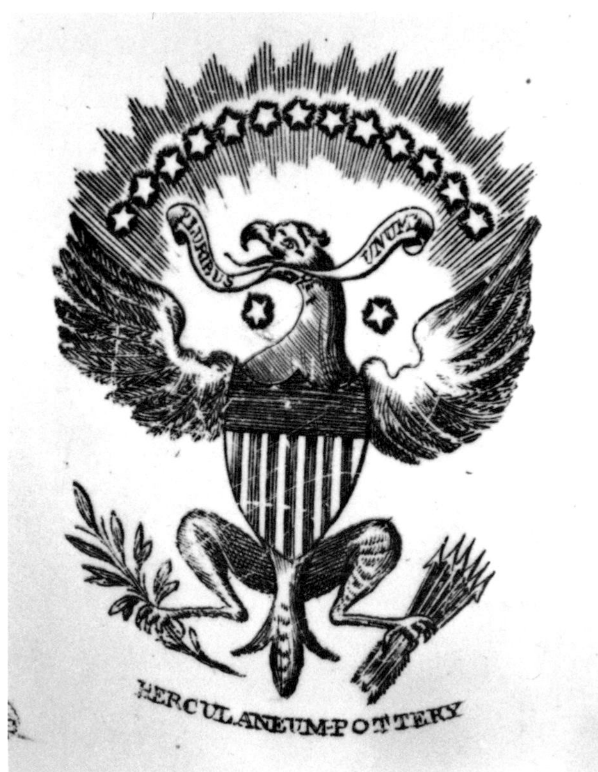

Cat. 138.1 detail

139A

Elizabeth Perkins Wildes Bourne (1765–1844)
and her daughters, Suzanne Wildes (1786–1829),
Elizabeth Wildes (1787–1875),
and Abigail Wildes (1790–1819)
Coverlet
Kennebunk, Maine, ca. 1810
Cotton
L 97½ (243.8); W 101 (256.5)
The Brick Store Museum; Gift of Mrs. William Henderson

139B

Attributed to Elizabeth Perkins Wildes Bourne
(1765–1844) and her daughters, Suzanne Wildes
(1786–1829), Elizabeth Wildes (1787–1875),
and Abigail Wildes (1790–1819)
Coverlet
Kennebunk, Maine, 1810
Cotton
Woven (in top edge) "Mary Wise 1810"
L 108¾ (276.4); W 107½ (273.3)
The Brick Store Museum; Gift of Mrs. John B. Corning

These woven cotton coverlets are evidence of a remarkable home industry that existed in Kennebunk during the first decades of the nineteenth century. One of the coverlets (cat. 139A) descended in the family of Elizabeth Perkins Wildes Bourne, whose work as a professional weaver can be well documented. The other coverlet (cat. 139B), made in 1810 for the trousseau of her neighbor, Mary Wise, is attributed to Elizabeth Bourne and her daughters.

Elizabeth (Eliza) Perkins, born in Arundel in 1765, married Captain Israel Wildes in 1785. During her married years, she kept a diary. In the portion that survives (1789–1793), she recorded daily activities of spinning, weaving, knitting, and a modest home industry of bonnet, gown, and cloak-making. Eliza mentioned spinning cotton, and in one entry she stated simply, "I made my white coverl'd."[1] The entries in Eliza's diary are significant for, although they do not provide a description of the 1789 coverlet, they prove that cotton was indeed being spun and woven in Kennebunk well before 1800.

Kennebunk sea captains who were involved in the West Indies trade, as was Eliza's husband, also called at southern ports and brought cotton in bales to Maine. Oliver Keating of Kennebunk Landing listed bales of cotton as cargo aboard the sloop *Elizabeth* in his account book between 1791 and 1795. In 1803 Samuel Hill advertised cotton thread and cloth as well as fifteen bales of cotton for sale. According to an 1809 Waterston and Pray advertisement in *The Weekly Visiter*, all groceries and dry goods will be "sold cheap for Cash, Butter, or Yard goods," especially "cotton cloth of good quality." The notice continues, "cotton warp and filling yarn at Factory prices kept constantly for sale at said stores on consignment from the justly celebrated Hope Cotton Manufacturing Company, Providence, R. I."[2]

Eliza was widowed in 1793 and left with three young daughters, Suzanne, Elizabeth, and Abigail. In 1795 she married John Bourne, a widower and father of six. Sometime

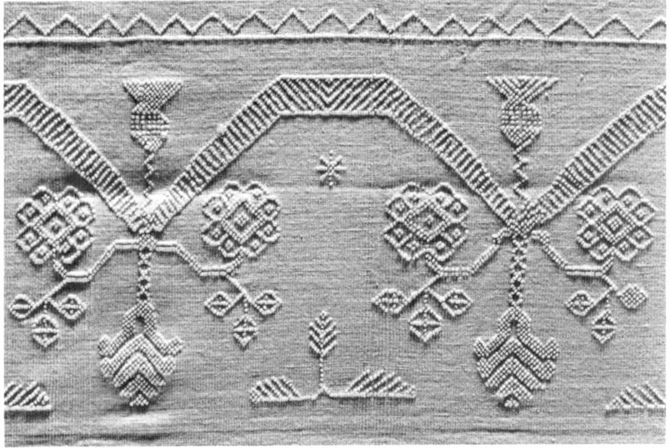

Cat. 139A detail

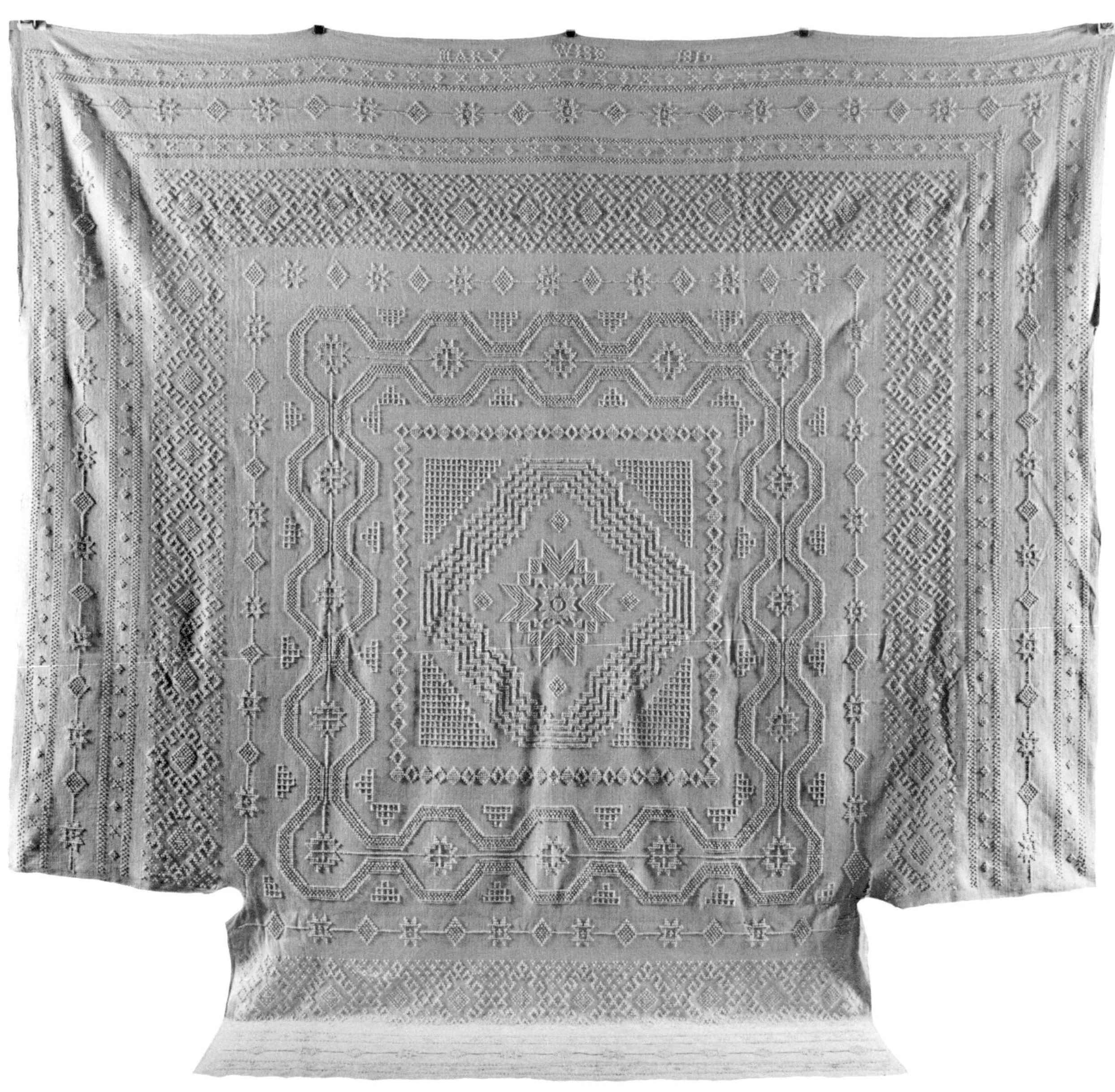

Cat. 139B

before 1806 the family moved into a large house at Kennebunk Landing where John Bourne had established a shipyard. By 1810 there were fifteen children in the household. To aid in the support of her large family during the period of economic hardship imposed by the Embargo, Eliza expanded her domestic industry to the home manufacture of cotton coverlets or counterpanes. In 1810 the Reverend Andrew Sherburne, a census-taker, was quoted in the *Weekly Visiter*:

Amongst the household manufactures in this division none have as yet been discovered who appear to have excelled a Mrs. Bourne, of Kennebunk. She occasionally employs three looms, one of which carries the fly-shuttle. Within eight months this family have woven two hundred and twenty-two yards of cloth of different kinds in this loom, which at the lowest value is worth one hundred and twenty-three dollars and ninety cents. The other two looms are constructed to weave cotton counterpanes the whole width. On one of these wide looms has been woven the season past, by one young woman, twenty one counterpanes,

*worth on an average seventeen dollars each, and in the other they have
woven ten counterpanes, worth ten dollars each, amounting in the whole
to four hundred and fifty-seven dollars, and the total manufactures to five
hundred and eight dollars and ninety cents. The labor expended is
thought not to exceed the constant labor of three women with the
assistance of children.*[3]

Further documentation of Eliza's home production is
provided by her son, Edward Emerson Bourne, who
published Kennebunk's first town history in 1871. It is in his
1861 unpublished family history, however, that Bourne
extolls his mother's virtues as a woman of industry:

*She was made of sterner material, and was not to be overcome by the
presence of any amount of active operations in the house. Far from it.
She was for enlarging, not contracting, the sphere of domestic labour
and enjoyment. . . . She added a new and important branch to her
business; that of the manufacture of white cotton counterpanes. This she
first attempted in the ordinary old fashioned loom. But woven thus in
pieces, they did not satisfy her tastes; and she had a loom made of
sufficient width to complete them in one piece. This new machine,
required two persons for its operation, and some considerable skill and
experience in sending the woof across the warp. But soon the mother and
daughters were able to carry on this new business to their entire
satisfaction.*[4]

White woven coverlets such as these made by Eliza and her
daughters are often referred to as "Bolton quilts or caddows"
after the type made in the home industry center of Bolton,

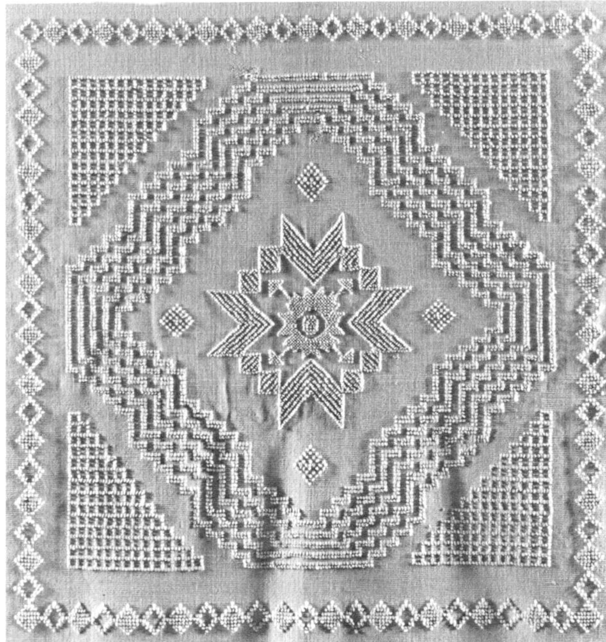

Cat. 139B detail

near Manchester, England.[5] Many similar coverlets appear
in American collections and are assumed to be of English
origin.

Before the discovery of the Bourne industry, the earliest
documented American coverlet of this type was made for
Colonel Henry Rutgers in Paterson, New Jersey, in 1822.
Woven in a single width measuring 107 by 99 inches, the
Rutgers coverlet was factory-made.[6] Apparently it has been
assumed that the wide-loom, fly-shuttle technology was not
utilized for home production. However, this improvement,
originally developed in England for the weaving of wide
woolens (cat. 15), was introduced in Rhode Island in 1789
and used extensively for the weaving of cotton goods. In
order to keep pace with the machine production of yarn
perfected in Rhode Island in 1790, and prior to the introduction of the power loom in 1817, many innovations were
developed to help facilitate home weaving. Some mills even
rented looms and other tools for home use.[7]

In 1984 The Brick Store Museum acquired out of the
barn on the former Bourne property a cloth beam measuring
127 inches. This evidence, combined with Sherburne's
account and E. E. Bourne's family history, substantiates
Eliza Bourne's highly sophisticated production system. It is
easy to imagine the older children in the family participating
in the production effort, and Eliza's three elder daughters
were surely genial apprentices. E. E. Bourne, in describing
the new wide loom fashioned for weaving coverlets in a single
width, credits his step-sister with special talent. "Abigail, the
youngest, was the most skilled cooperator on this new engine
of physical labor. The counterpanes had now acquired a
reputation almost throughout New England."[8]

In 1810 seventeen-year-old Abigail "conceived the
project of making a present of one, to the wife of the President
of the United States. . . . It was forwarded to Mrs. Madison."
Bourne recorded the inscription woven into the center of the
coverlet: "'Beneath this bed illustrious pair repose, / Secure
from foreign and domestic foes. / May white plumed seraphs
watch around this bed, / And heaven its kindlier influences
shed.'"[9]

Abigail's counterpane was one of the gifts that poured
into the White House during the Madison administration.
James and Dolley Madison did not always keep these official
gifts for themselves. They offered them for public sale or
reimbursed the donor in cash or in-kind for gifts they wanted
for their Virginia estate. That Dolley Madison kept the
counterpane is documented by her reply to Abigail: "I have
just now had the pleasure to receive the valuable and
beautiful counterpane from Miss Wildes which does much
credit to her ingenuity and industry." Enclosed were a "pair
of the richest gold earrings and a chain."[10]

Ironically, neither the "illustrious pair" nor their
possessions were safe from enemies. James and Dolley

Madison fled the White House in August 1814 after the British invaded Washington. The coverlet is believed to have been lost in the British burning of the White House along with "everything else belonging to the publick [and] our own valuable stores of every description."[11]

Donor history maintained that the coverlet attributed to the Bourne loom (cat. 139B) was made for Mary Wise, whose name is woven into the top edge with the date 1810. Mary Wise, who married Moses Morrill in 1816, lived at The Landing, near the Bourne residence; she and Abigail Wildes were contemporaries. Family history also maintained that the coverlet was used on the Morrill's bedstead (cat. 96).

The two Kennebunk coverlets are very close in size. Although the border designs differ, the central eight-pointed stars are identical. These coverlets have variations of the same stylized patterns and geometric motifs seen on other coverlets attributed to both English and American manufactories. Safford and Bishop refer to these as "candlewick spreads" and describe two types, "embroidered candlewick" and "woven candlewick," the curious nomenclature derived from the coarse white cording or "roving" made of soft twisted cotton which resembled the wicks used by candlemakers. Embroidered candlewick coverlets are usually made of linen or cotton twill with the design made by embroidering French knots or the cord "laid and couched" as in crewel work (see cat. 140B). In the woven process, a strong twisted cotton was used as warp and the soft roving (also called filling) used as weft. The weaver created the pattern by pulling up loops from the flat weave with a pick.[12] Coverlets of this type were made throughout the nineteenth century, and a modern machine-made version, the "George Washington Bedspread" made by the Bates Manufacturing Company in Lewiston, Maine, is still popular today.

Documentation of Eliza Bourne's early nineteenth-century home-textile production challenges earlier beliefs that all white woven coverlets of the Bolton type are of English origin. It not only expands the knowledge of this early Maine home industry but also highlights the importance of this activity in American textile history.   SSA

<hr>

1 Eliza Perkins Wildes, diary, 1789–1793, July 15, 1789, MEHS. For a discussion of the vernacular use of the terms "coverlid" and "coverlet," see Lisa H. Foote and Carol L. Haines, "Household Vernacular in Concord, Massachusetts, Probate Inventories: 1655–1800," in Peter Benes, ed., *American Speech: 1600 to the Present*, Annual Proceedings of the Dublin Seminar for New England Folklife 1983 (Boston: Boston University, 1984), 65–66.

2 Oliver Keating, account book, 1791–95, BSM; *Annals of the Times* (March 10, 1803); *The Weekly Visiter* (August 19, 1809).

3 Remich, *History*, 221.

4 Edward Emerson Bourne, "The Bourne Family of Kennebunk," paragraph 245 (manuscript, 1861, BSM).

5 Harold B. Burnham, "Bolton 'Quilts' or 'Caddows,' a Nineteenth Century Cottage Industry," *Bulletin de Liaison du Centre International D'Etude Des Textiles Anciens* (Lyon, France, 1971), 2: 22–23.

6 Esther I. Schwartz, "Notes from a New Jersey Collector, Early Commercial Weaving in Paterson," *Antiques* 74, no. 4 (October 1958): 330–331.

7 Paul E. Rivard, *The Home Manufacture of Cloth, 1790–1840* (Pawtucket, R.I.: Slater Mill Historic Site, 1974), 17–21.

8 Edward Emerson Bourne, "Bourne Family," paragraph 246.

9 Theodore O. Kingsbury, "Paper presented to the Kennebunk Fire Society" (typescript, 1951, BSM).

10 Conover Hunt, *Dolley and 'The Great Little Madison'* (Washington, D.C.: American Institute of Architects, 1977), 42–43. Dolley Madison to Abigail Bourne, January 20, 1810, Cutts Collection of Papers of James and Dolley Madison (microfilm), Library of Congress (facsimile, BSM). Bourne, "Bourne Family," paragraph 247.

11 Hunt, *Dolley*, 46.

12 Carlton L. Safford and Robert Bishop, *America's Quilts and Coverlets* (New York: Weathervane Books, 1974), 278–281.

140A

Possibly by Sarah Fairfield Cleaves (1769–1835)
Coverlet (detail)
Biddeford, Maine, ca. 1810
Cotton on linen
L 111½ (283.2); w 98½ (250.2)
The Brick Store Museum; William E. Barry estate through Edith Cleaves Barry, 1969

140B

Possibly by Martha Treadwell (1792–1827)
Coverlet
Kennebunk, Maine, 1818
Cotton
Embroidered (in top edge) "Martha Treadwell Kennebunk 1818"
L 89½ (227.6); w 83½ (212.3)
The Brick Store Museum; Gift of Mrs. William Curtis, 1957

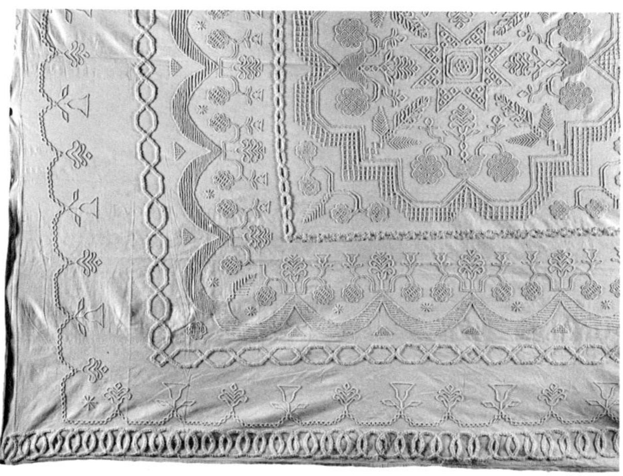

Cat. 140A detail

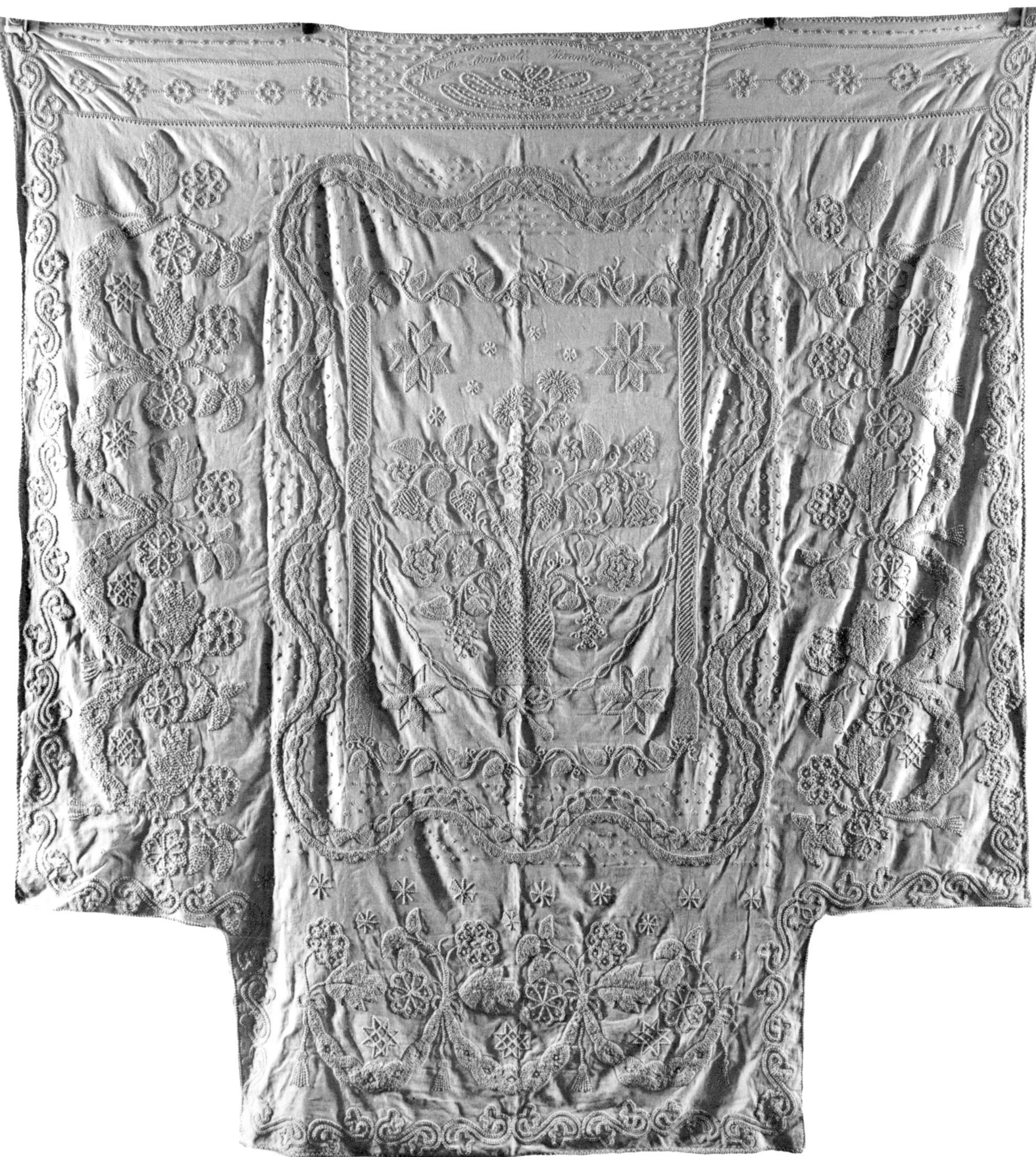

Cat. 140B

Interesting comparisons to the woven coverlets made by Eliza Bourne and her daughters (cats. 139A and 139B) are these embroidered "candlewick" coverlets. One (cat. 140A) descended in the Lord and Barry families of Kennebunk with a history of having been made by Sarah Fairfield Cleaves, wife of Daniel Cleaves. Their daughter, Mary, was an accomplished embroiderer and undoubtedly received sewing instruction from her mother, as well as at female academies in Portland and Dorchester (cat. 168). This coverlet, however, is the only evidence of Sarah Cleaves's skill as a needleworker. The other coverlet (cat. 140B) bears the inscription "Martha Treadwell Kennebunk 1818." Martha Treadwell lived in West Kennebunk; she died, unmarried, at the age of thirty-five.[1]

Embroidered candlewicking had its roots in English
needlework of the seventeenth and eighteenth centuries,
where typical patterns depicted flowers, fruits, and flowing
vines. This particular type of coverlet was worked in white
on homespun linen or cotton with a combination of French
knots, looped stitches and threads which were "laid and
couched."[2]

Candlewicking is acknowledged as an American deriva-
tion of English needlework. Many documented examples
substantiate a tradition of home manufacture before 1820.
The discovery of the Bourne coverlets establishes the
existence of weaving patterns and technology in America by
1810, which coincides with the earliest documented embroidered coverlets. A comparison of patterns and motifs used in
both embroidered and woven types reveals many similarities,
but identifying which is the source and which the imitation is
more difficult. A study of both the Cleaves and Treadwell
coverlets leads to a conclusion that these particular examples
were inspired by the overall effect and individual motifs of
the more complicated woven Bourne coverlets.

A skilled needleworker, Sarah Cleaves began with three
plain pieces of linen cloth, likely purchased, and sewn
together with two seams. Sarah's stitches follow perfectly
ruled geometric lines in exact imitation of the type of pattern
found in Eliza Bourne's woven coverlets. The patterns of the
woven coverlets were determined by raised loops counted
horizontally across the weft and built upon row after row.
Without the influence of a woven pattern, an embroiderer
would doubtless have followed a freer, more curvilinear
design, as Martha Treadwell did. Although Sarah's embroidered pattern is not the same as the Bourne coverlets, it is
remarkably similar to a woven one in the collection of the
Philadelphia Museum of Art.[3] Based on this evidence, one
can assume that patterns were somehow transmitted by

weavers to embroiderers with a written system of counted
threads and loops being adapted to a graph. Templates of
various repeated motifs could then be laid out and traced in
graphite directly onto the cloth. While Sarah's coverlet
appears almost identical to a woven coverlet, the design is
superimposed onto —rather than incorporated into— the
weave. The threads of Sarah's linen cloth are too fine and the
embroidery stitches too large to be considered a counted
thread pattern.

In the coverlet made by Martha Treadwell, patterns of
early nineteenth-century weavers and embroiderers are
mingled. Drawn from the traditional foliate motifs of English
crewelwork, the design Martha created was composed of
leaves, vines, and flowers embroidered in a curvilinear style.
The dramatic central motif is a large vase of flowers flanked
by twisted columns. Occasionally, however, Martha included
eight-pointed stars, triangles, and other geometric shapes
from the weaver's pattern vocabulary. The swag and tassel
border of the Treadwell coverlet is clearly derived from the
same inspiration as the border in the Bourne coverlet
(cat. 139A). However, the embroidered flowers and leaves
are more florid than the crisp geometric designs of the woven
work. The stitches, short on the underside with loops on top,
are consistent throughout the coverlet. The effect, especially
after wear and washing, is of tight rows of small tufts much
like the counted loop system of the weaver.   SSA

1 Little else is known of her. Bourne, *History*, 512; and Remich, *History*,
  153.
2 Carleton L. Safford and Robert Bishop, *America's Quilts and Coverlets*
  (New York: Weathervane Books, 1974), 279.
3 Safford and Bishop, *America's Quilts*, 280.

141

Tiffany border or flounce (detail)
Probably Saco, Maine, 1796–1805
Watercolor and pencil on silk
H 8⅝ (21.9); L 161⅛ (404.3)
York Institute Museum
Bequest of Almira Locke McArthur, 1950

This transparent silk border is painted in watercolors with
bowknots, floral sprigs, and vermiculated swags and border
motifs. Illustrated here is a full repeat of the pattern that
decorates more than thirteen feet of its length, now in two
pieces. A tape is sewn along the bottom edge; the selvage
runs along the top. This flounce is believed to have been used
as a decorative border along the hem of a formal dress. That
such flounces were made and decorated by young ladies in
Maine is documented by two sources.

While visiting Portland in September 1796, Abigail May
recorded in her diary, "I carried home a flounce I have been

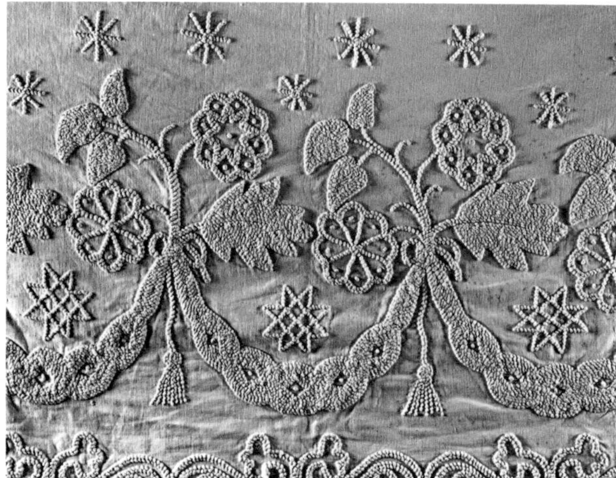

Cat. 140B detail

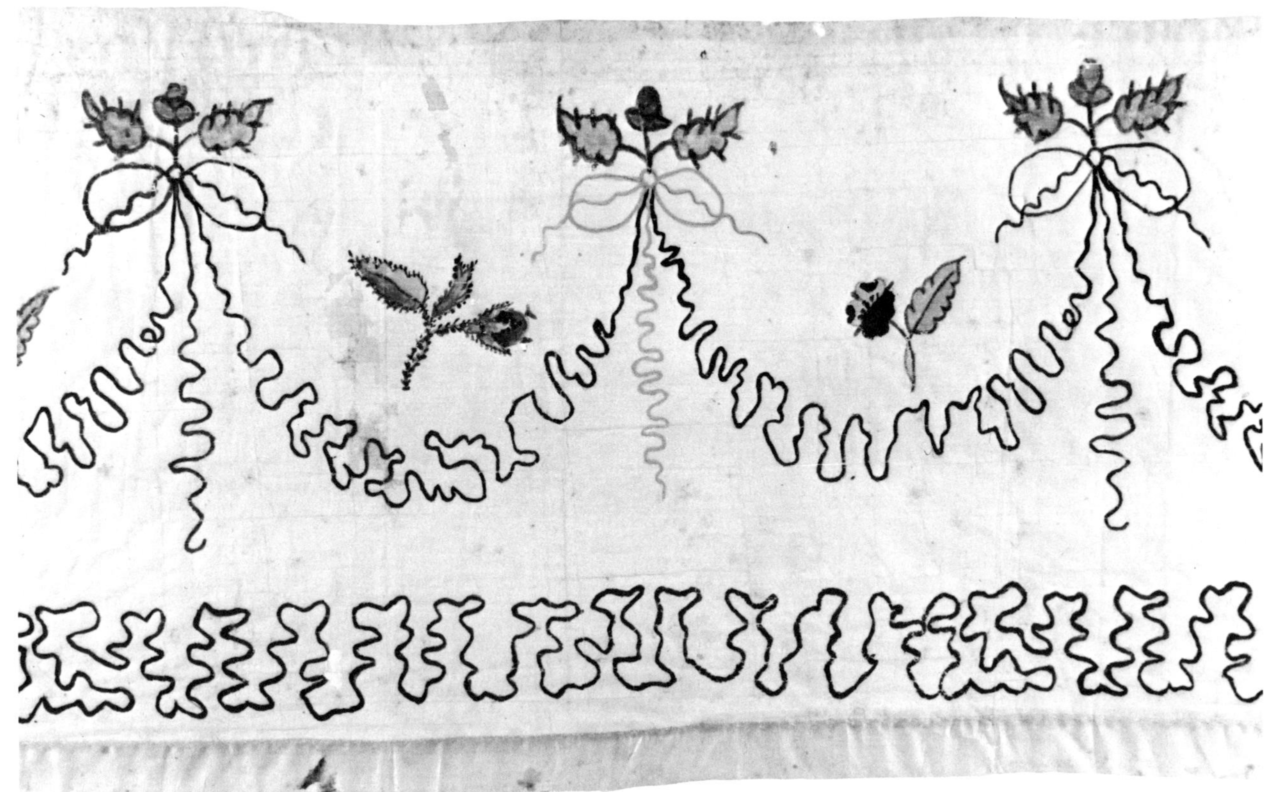

Cat. 141

painting for Matty [Robison,] the same pattern as that which Miss Elliot sent me from Washington. She appears much pleased with it and says it shall grace the first ball we have."[1] The following year, Zilpah Wadsworth described a white assembly dress "with painted tiffany borders, our own handy work. The pattern was the one we took from Mrs. Ducs skirt."[2]

Both these references provide important details in the identification of this flounce. Zilpah described the borders as tiffany, which was a type of thin transparent silk or transparent gauze muslin. Abigail and Zilpah both describe the borders as painted, which accurately describes this example. The design was first sketched in pencil and then filled in with watercolors. The skill of the painter varied, as one young lady noted. "They are not as well done as I could wish, but they are as well done as I who never learnt to draw could do them."[3] Both girls acquired the patterns from visitors or friends outside Maine. Tiffany could also be used in other ways. In the same letter, Zilpah further described an "all white musslin skirt and train . . . spangled tiffany Head dress with a plume."

Zilpah and Abigail were using their tiffany to make highly fashionable ornamentation for their dresses. This use is confirmed by an account of tiffany worn at a ball to honor George Washington in Charleston, South Carolina, in 1791.

The ladies and dresses were really superb — painted tiffany and silver twice was quite common . . . the most elegant . . . was a tiffany gown and coat — with a border a quarter deep of the most superb painted tiffany . . . in festoons the flowers very small and very distinct. They seemed to be made of foil spangles and painting so that it was extremely brilliant.[4]

The extent of the fashion for decorative borders on dresses is vividly illustrated by a flounce embroidered by Lady Emma Hamilton in England. Metallic threads were used in a pattern of ovals and swags and the inscriptions "Bronte" and "Nelson." It celebrated Admiral Horatio Nelson's Dukedom of Bronte, a gift from the King and Queen of Naples after the Battle of the Nile in 1798.[5]

The association of the York Institute flounce with a special event must, in part, explain its survival in the bottom drawer of the desk and bookcase (cat. 95) from the Cleaves family, although no further written history has been located.
LFS

1 Abigail May, diary, MEHS.
2 Zilpah Wadsworth to Nancy Doane, letter journal, September 1797, Wadsworth-Longfellow Papers, LNHS; according to Jane C. Nylander, the design of this flounce is similar to embroidery patterns

for white work on leno or muslin for the 1790–1800 period; conversation, February 5, 1986.

3 Miss Smith of Philadelphia to Miss Yeates of Lancaster, September 14, 1800, as cited in Elisabeth McClellan, *Historic Dress in America 1800–70* (Philadelphia: George W. Jacobs and Co., 1910), 35.

4 Florence M. Montgomery, *Textiles in America, 1650–1870* (New York: W. W. Norton, 1985), 366.

5 Fragments of this flounce survive in the National Maritime Museum, London. See Norah Lofts, *Emma Hamilton* (New York: Coward, McCann and Geoghegan, Inc., 1978), 91, for a similar embroidery of "Nelson" and "Bronte" on muslin.

142

Elizabeth Cutts (1766–1810)
Coat of arms
Boston, Massachusetts, ca. 1783
Silk and metallic thread embroidery and spangles
on silk ground
H 35½ (90.2); W 35½ (90.2)
York Institute Museum; Gift of George Addison Emery

Hatchments, or lozenge-shaped panels displaying coats of arms, served as heraldic symbols of mourning and as decorative devices. Following European precedent, the earliest hatchments were often painted on a black background, carried in funeral processions, and hung in churches or placed on the exterior of the deceased's house. In eighteenth-century New England, hatchments were the work of professional embroiderers or produced by young women as part of their education. These fragile embroidered coats of

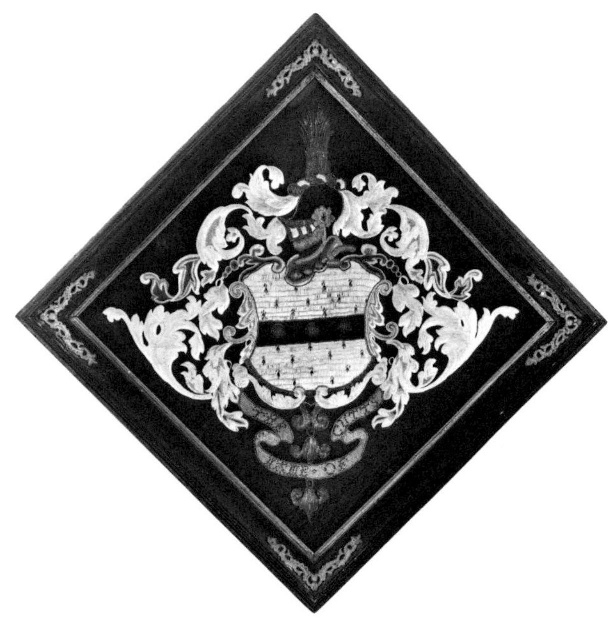

Cat. 142

arms were not likely to be hung outside or used in funeral processions.

This coat of arms was worked in silk by Elizabeth Cutts of Saco. It relates stylistically to a group of hatchments featuring flowing acanthus leaves encompassing a central arms-bearing shield, the lower edge of which is echoed in a three-part banner. The design covers all available space within the frame. A hatchment worked by Submit Boyd of Portsmouth, New Hampshire, ca. 1795, corresponds closely to the Cutts coat of arms. A limited number of coats of arms worked by young women from northern New England survive.[1]

Elizabeth Cutts was attending school in Boston when she began her hatchment in 1783. The design, however, did not originate with her teacher but rather was provided by a Boston color shop. Elizabeth Cutts wrote to her father Thomas:

I have been to get the Coat Arms prepared for working, and Mr. Gore shewed me two Arms by the name Cutts, the one belonging to a Family from London, and the other from Chelsey, both Arms different; and Papa as you chuse I should work your Arms, I should be fond of making no mistake & of working the right, if your business permitted your letting me know by name the right one, it would be sufficient, without further trouble, as my utmost abilities shall be exerted to please Mama & yourself sir in the working.[2]

John Gore (1718–1796) owned a color shop for the sale of pigments and oil at the "sign of the Painter's Arms in Queen Street." He supplied coats of arms that were popular with the rising American aristocracy and his work was known in Philadelphia as well as Boston. It was his son Samuel (1750/51–1831), however, who assisted Elizabeth, for the elder Gore, a Loyalist, was absent from the country between 1776 and 1785.[3] The Gores may have supplied girls attending various schools with the overall design for their coats of arms because there is a remarkable consistency of style and size in Boston-area hatchments of the second half of the eighteenth century.

John Guillim illustrated a coat of arms in *A Display of Heraldry* pertaining "to the ancient family of the Cutts of Arkesden in the County of Essex . . . the heart of which family is at present Richard Cutts of the said Place, as also of Childerley in Cambridgeshire, Esq." The arms were described as an "*Argent* on a Bend engrailed *Sable* three plates." According to Guillim, "Plates in Armory are Emblemes of Justice and equall dealing among men."[4] A coat of arms executed in watercolor on paper in this format and attributed to John Coles, Sr. (1749–1809), survives in the Cutts Family Papers at the Dyer Library in Saco (cat. 142.1). Elizabeth Cutts worked instead a similiar coat of arms, that of the Bramston family, illustrated on the same page in the 1624 edition of Guillim's book, and inscribed it "The Name of Cutts." It would have been more difficult to

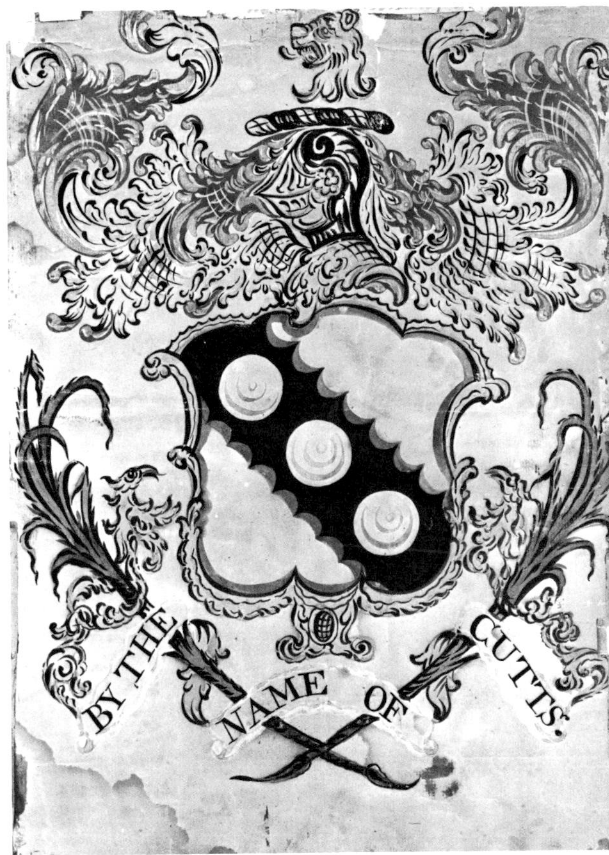

Cat. 142.1

embroider the scalloped edge of an engrailed bend than the straight sides of the fess or horizontal band.

An unfinished coat of arms begun by Jerusha Pitkin (1736–1800), probably in Boston in the 1750s, reveals an outline drawn in white paint on a black satin ground. The drawing is very simple and demonstrates that no special skill was involved in sketching coats of arms. Any artist with an understanding of heraldry, or a coat of arms to work from, was able to prepare the ground for a young woman to embroider.[5] It is likely that Samuel Gore provided the same service for Elizabeth Cutts: "to get the coat Arms prepared for working." It was her expertise, however, that dictated the choice of stitches to fill in a simple outline with brightly colored silk threads skillfully shaded, and embellished the whole with metal-wrapped threads and spangles (sequins).
CSP

1 See Ethel Stanwood Bolton and Eva Johnston Coe, *American Samplers* (1921; reprint, New York: Dover Publications, 1973), plate 121 for an illustration of the Boyd hatchment.
2 Elizabeth Cutts to Thomas Cutts, April 22, 1783, cited in George Addison Emery, *Colonel Thomas Cutts* (Saco, Me., 1917), 15.
3 Charles A. Hammond and Stephen A. Wilbur, *Gay and Graceful Style:*

A Catalogue of Objects associated with Christopher and Rebecca Gore (Waltham, Mass.: Gore Place Society, 1982), 7, 76.
4 John Guillim, *A Display of Heraldry*, 6th ed. (London: printed by T. W. for R. and J. Benwicke and R. Wilkin and J. Walthoe and Tho. Ward, 1724), 356. John Guillim, *A Display of Heraldrie*, 2nd ed. (London: Ralph Mae, 1638), 297–298. These arms also appear in the 1724 edition.
5 Jane C. Nylander, "Coat of Arms," in *The Great River*, 404, 407.

Cat. 142.1 Attributed to John Coles, Sr. (1749–1809), *By the Name of Cutts*, Boston, Massachusetts, ca. 1800. Pen and ink and watercolor on paper; H 12⅝ (32.0), W 9¹⁄₁₆ (23.0). Dyer Library, Saco.

143

Attributed to Thomas Dodds and Christian Claus
(w. 1791–1793)
English guitar
New York City, 1791–1793
Spruce, maple, ebony, ivory
Branded (on back) "DODDS, / & / CLAUS. / N.-YORK"
L 29⅛ (74.0)
York Institute Museum; Gift of George Addison Emery

On June 19, 1797, fifteen-year-old Eunice Cutts bought a guitar and case from William Selby of Boston for $25. This English guitar descended in her family and is believed to be the instrument she purchased. For music instruction from June 19 to November 16, 1797, Eunice's father, Thomas, paid Selby $21.17.[1] During this period, Eunice was a student at a Boston academy and her study of the guitar is presumed to have been part of the educational program; Selby was one of the foremost musicians of Boston until his death in 1798.

Maine residents seem to have enjoyed musical entertainments, and mention of a guitar often appears in correspondence and diaries, as do references to the pianoforte, violin, clarinet, and flute. "Laura Sanford play[ed] delightfully on the guitar," recorded Abigail May in the summer of 1796. When accompanied by a flute, "such music I could have listen[ed] all night."[2]

The English guitar is the common name for a type of cittern popular in Great Britain between 1750 and 1820. The use of this musical instrument increased as members of upper-class families sought instruments that were relatively easy to play, and less expensive than pianofortes. Instruments of this type are known to have been imported to America.[3]

Thomas Dodds and Christian Claus were importers and retailers, as well as makers, of musical instruments in New York City and this guitar bears their brand. Claus advertised in 1793 that he "intends to manufacture piano fortes and

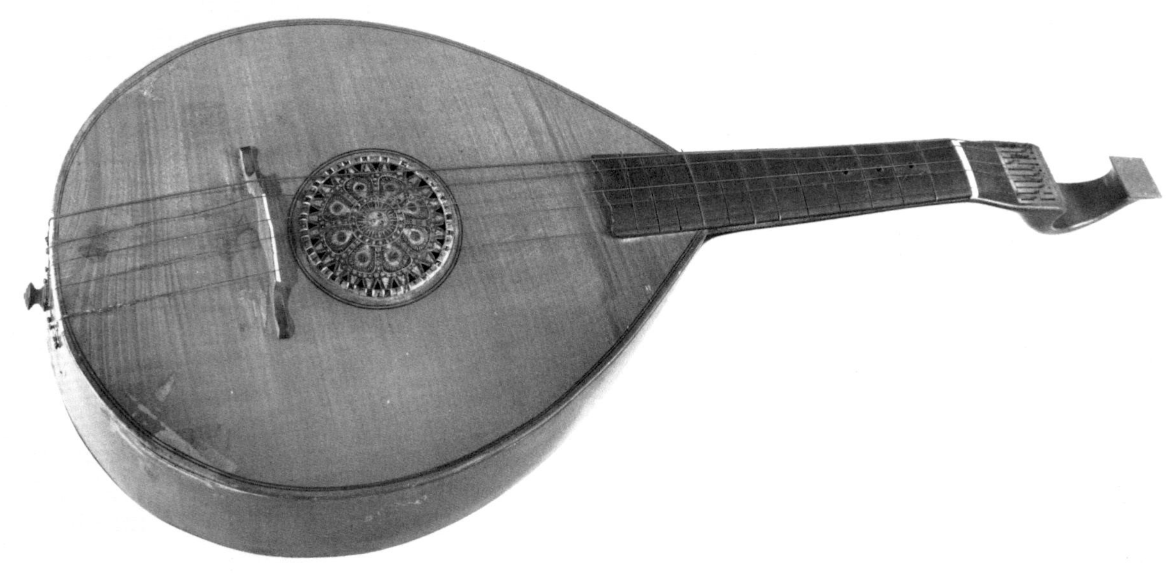

Cat. 143

common guittars *the same as he used to do in London*," and this
guitar can reasonably be attributed to the firm. The term
"common" is believed to have been used to distinguish the
cittern from the waisted or "Spanish" guitar which was not
as popular in America during this period.[4] Made of a
handsomely striped wood, the instrument is highlighted with
ebony and ivory. A disk of enameled peacock feathers
around a sun face decorates the soundhole.

Guitars continued to be acquired by Maine residents into
the nineteenth century. In 1814 a guitar described as
"elegant" was among the prize goods sold at auction in Portland.[5]   LFS

1 Two bills, William Selby to Thomas Cutts, June 19, 1797, and
  November 16, 1797, Cutts Family Papers, YIS.
2 Abigail May, diary, MEHS.
3 Stanley Sadie, ed., *The New Grove Dictionary of Music and Musicians*, 20
  vols. (London: Macmillan Publishers Ltd., 1980), 6:199–200. D.
  Samuel Quigley kindly assisted in the identification of this instrument.
4 Rita Susswein Gottesman, comp., *The Arts and Crafts in New York,
  1779–1799* (New York: New-York Historical Society, 1954), 361–362.
  Martha Gandy Fales kindly brought this to my attention. I would like
  to thank Laurence Libin for his assistance with the attribution. For
  more on Dodds and Claus, see Laurence Libin, *American Musical
  Instruments in The Metropolitan Museum of Art* (New York: Metropolitan
  Museum of Art and W. W. Norton, 1985), 162–163.
5 *Portland Gazette* (July 2, 1814).

144A

Mary Cleaves (1803–1871)
Oakhampton Castle, Devonshire
Biddeford, Maine, or Dorchester, Massachusetts, ca. 1818
Pen and ink and watercolor on paper
Inscribed "Painted by Mary Cleaves"
H 9 (22.9); w. 11¹¹⁄₁₆ (29.7) sight
The Brick Store Museum; William E. Barry estate
through Edith Cleaves Barry, 1936

144B

Mary Cleaves (1803–1871)
View near Liston
Biddeford, Maine, or Dorchester, Massachusetts, ca. 1818
Pen and ink and watercolor on paper
Inscribed "Drawn and painted by Mary Cleaves"
H 14 (35.6); w 9¹⁵⁄₁₆ (25.3)
The Brick Store Museum; William E. Barry estate
through Edith Cleaves Barry, 1936

These watercolor drawings of English landscapes were the
work of Mary Cleaves, probably while a student at Mrs.

Saunders's and Miss Beach's Academy in Dorchester, Massachusetts. The views recall a description of the English countryside found in Jedediah Morse's *The American Universal Geography*, a copy of which was in the library at the Cleaves house:

the pleasing vicissitudes of gently rising hills and bending vales . . . offer the most delightful landscapes of rural opulance and beauty. Some tracts abound with prospects of the more romantic kind; lofty mountains, craggy rock, deep narrow dells, and tumbling torrents; nor are there wanting, as a constrast to so many agreeable scenes, the gloomy features of black barren moors and wide uncultivated heaths.[1]

Copying prints was part of the academy education of many young women during the federal period and the sources for such scenes were found in numerous publications. Henry Boswell's *Pictorial Views of the Antiquities of England and Wales* contained a view of Oakhampton Castle with the note that "at present it may truly be styled a pile of ruins." Rendering picturesque buildings such as those in *View near Liston* challenged the skill of young artists, as Samuel Prout explained in his *Rudiments of Landscape in Progressive Studies*: "The varieties of thatch, slate, and tile upon the roofs of buildings,—of stone, brick, plaster, or boards, that compose walls of the same,—all require a particular execution, which characterizes their surfaces."[2]

Traveling to Washington with the "Misses Cleaves" about 1825, Josiah Quincy recalled that "being fresh from boarding school [they were] somewhat romantic." European landscapes were particularly evocative of this spirit and were prominently featured in works of visual art as well as in narratives like the Gothic novels of Sarah Wood. In *Tales of the Night*, Wood alluded to the American preferences for European literature: "I dare say [your grandmother] can tell you some story almost as good as those you find in the volumes that cross the Atlantic; many of which are more indebted to the distance from which they come, than to any intrinsic merit for the eagerness with which they are sought after."[3]   KDM

1 Jedediah Morse, *The American Universal Geography*, 2d ed. (Boston: Isaiah Thomas and Ebenezer T. Andrews, 1796), 100. A similar watercolor of a rural landscape was painted by Elizabeth Bass Hinckley of Boston in 1809 at the Saunders and Beach Academy. See Betty Ring, "Mrs. Saunders' and Miss Beach's Academy, Dorchester," *Antiques* 110, no. 2 (August 1976): 311.
2 Henry Boswell, *Pictorial Views of the Antiquities of England and Wales* (London: Alexander Hogg, ca. 1786), n.p. The view of Oakhampton published here is not the same as Mary drew. However, a search of publications from 1786–1817 containing English views revealed no other prints of Oakhampton castle and none of the *View near Liston*. Samuel Prout, *Rudiments of Landscape in Progressive Studies Drawn, and Etched in Imitation of Chalk* (London: R. Ackerman, 1813), B.
3 Josiah Quincy, *Figures of the Past* (Boston: Little Brown & Co., 1926), 165–166. Wood, *Tales*, 3–4.

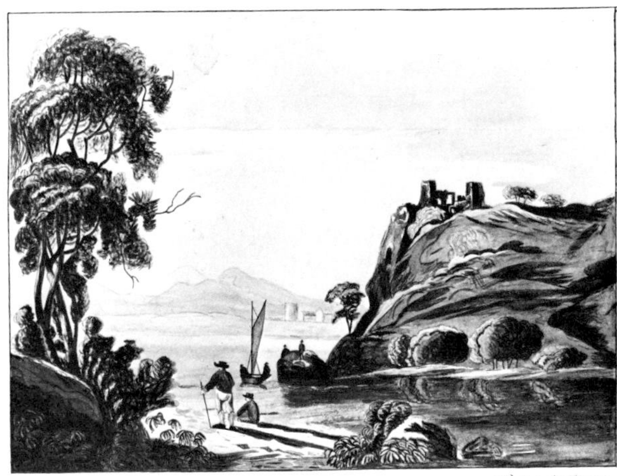

Cat. 144A

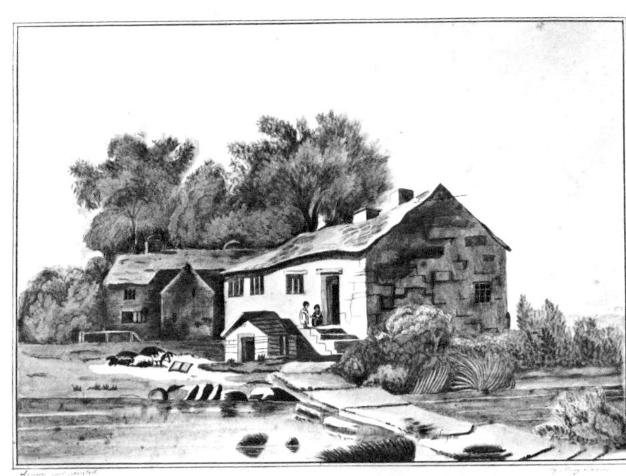

Cat. 144B

145

Joanna Poole (1794–1864)
Family register
Portland, Maine, 1807
Silk on linen
Inscribed "JOANNA POOLE AEt 12 Portland / July 29 1807"
H 20¹⁵⁄₁₆ (53.2); W 16¹⁵⁄₁₆ (43.0)
Maine Historical Society; Gift of Mrs. Alfred Haskell, 1936

Twelve-year-old Joanna Poole, the daughter of a bricklayer, stitched this family register with a geometric border of vines and flowers. When she signed it, she included the date and her place of residence. Its three-part arrangement is similar to one worked by Mary Ann Twombly ten years later (cat. 148). Joanna combined genealogical information with mourning elements; two urns at the bottom bear the stitched initials "s. p." for two brothers named Samuel who had died in 1793 and 1802.

Joanna Poole's family register bears a striking resemblance to "The Genealogy of Rufus and Abigail Horton" worked the same year, and the samplers with alphabets, verses, and dwelling houses worked by Lydia Dutch in 1805, Amelia Lowell in 1806, and Mary Richards in 1808. All bear the inscription "Portland."[1] The houses on the Horton and Richards needlework are similar to those worked by Sophia Dyer in 1817 (cat. 147).

This Portland group documents an increase in schools for girls. At least fifteen schools for both boarders and day students advertised during the 1820s, and although some appear to have lasted for only a few terms, others, including those of the Misses Mayo, Miss Alma Cross, and Abigail Murray operated for at least five years. [2]

One of the most highly regarded Portland schools was the Misses Martins', which Penelope and Catharine Martin conducted from 1804 until 1829. They taught day and boarding pupils in a large three-story house with a garden on India Street.[3] Sarah Mellen, a daughter of Prentiss (cat. 30), wrote to her brother in 1816, "I attended Miss Martin's School as usual, and am very much pleased with their manner of instructing."[4] Others, however, were less satisfied (see cat. 133).

The few Portland samplers attributed to specific schools (cat. 150) reveal a strong similarity in arrangement, choice of stitches, and motifs that may one day be documented.[5] AAE

1 The Horton sampler is illustrated in Glee Krueger, *A Gallery of American Samplers* (New York: E.P. Dutton, 1978), 44. Amelia Lowell's sampler is in the Baxter House Museum in Gorham and Mary Richard's is illustrated in Glee Krueger, *New England Samplers to 1840* (Sturbridge, Mass.: Old Sturbridge Village, 1978), fig. 74. Lydia Dutch married William Hackett (cat. 93); her sampler is privately owned.
2 For Portland schools, see the Jordan Newspaper Index, Portland Public Library, and Edward H. Elwell, *The Schools of Portland* (Portland: William M. Marks, 1888).
3 Elwell, *The Schools of Portland*, 33.
4 Sarah Mellen to Grenville Mellen, May 7, 1816, Mellen Papers, MEHS.
5 A sampler at the Pejepscot Historical Society in Brunswick, Maine, worked before 1832 by Sarah Ann Bonney and attributed to Miss Hall's Portland school is illustrated in Krueger, *New England Samplers to 1840*, fig. 75. For others attributed to Portland schools, see 154–155. The MEHS owns an elaborate 1838 needlework picture by Sarah Jane Moore who attended Miss Rea's School. I would like to thank Sheila Rideout for her assistance with Portland samplers.

146

Frances Leighton (1801–1889)
Sampler
Eliot, Maine, 1813
Silk on linen
Inscribed "Frances Leighton . . . eliot . . . / AE
12 Dec 1813"
H 12 (30.5); W 11½ (29.2)
The Brick Store Museum

This sampler from Eliot, Maine, resembles others from the Piscataqua River area.[1] A basket containing alternating colored berries, twig-like and stepped trees, and birds facing each other bearing angular swags are among the motifs they have in common. The verse she chose, "Frances Leighton is my name and america is my nation eliot is my / dwelling place and christ is my salvation," is recorded on many samplers.

More than twenty years after Frances Leighton completed her sampler, Mary Elizabeth Wentworth of Eliot worked one that retained the basket of colored berries, stepped trees, and birds with v-like swags.[2]

Frances Leighton was the daughter of Frances Usher Parsons (1778–1865) and General Samuel Leighton. Although she was born in Alfred, her parents had moved to Eliot by 1810. Frances may have attended school at nearby Berwick Academy, founded in 1791. She married Benjamin Emerson of Pittsfield, New Hampshire, in 1847. A sampler worked by Frances Leighton's mother survives at The Brick

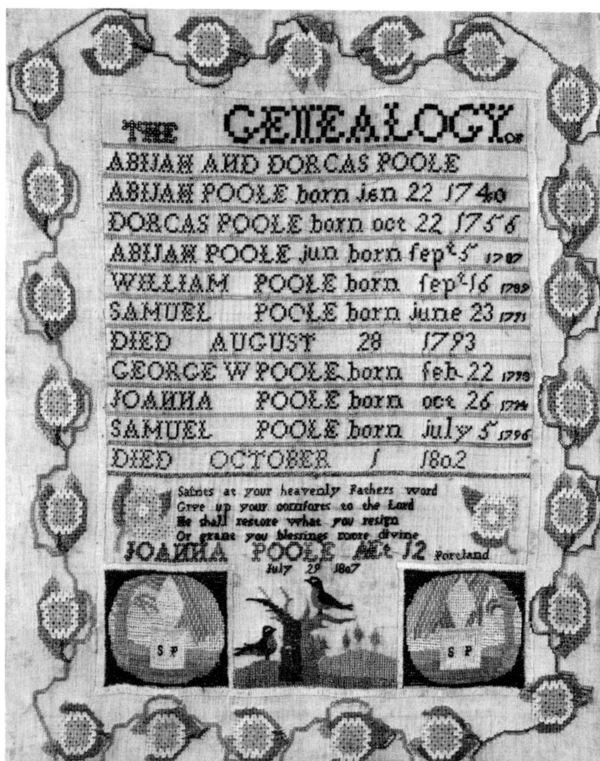

Cat. 145

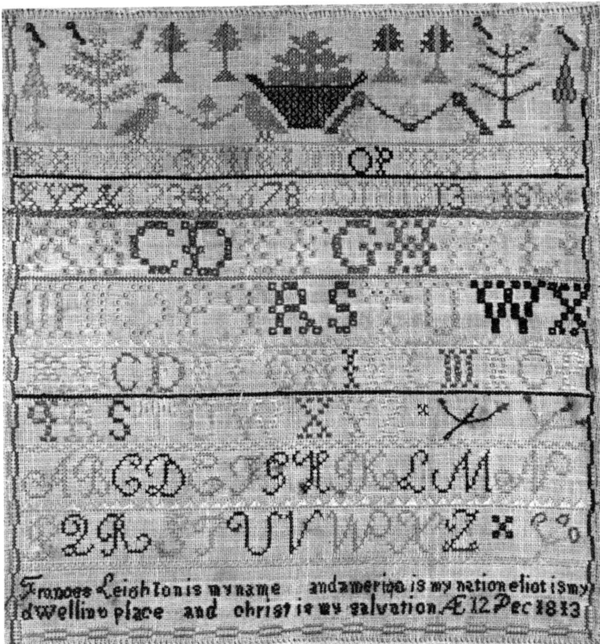

Cat. 146

Store Museum. Of simple and straightforward design, it is embroidered "Frances Usher Parsons," "Fanny," and "Alfred." An Eliot native, the mother worked this after her family removed to the inland community of Alfred. AAE

1 Glee Krueger, *New England Samplers to 1840* (Sturbridge, Mass.: Old Sturbridge Village, 1978), fig. 71. A sampler executed by Portsmouth's Margaret Jane Ball in 1837, now at Strawbery Banke, also bears the local motif of a basket containing alternating colored berries.
2 Mary Elizabeth Wentworth's sampler is at the Maine State Museum.

147

Sophia Dyer (b. 1804)
Sampler
Cape Elizabeth, Maine, 1817
Silk on linen
Inscribed "Sophia Dyer . . . / CAPEELIZABETH /
July the 14 1817"
H 16⁷⁄₁₆ (41.8); W 10¼ (26.0)
Maine Historical Society
Gift of Mrs. Adolph A. Gatheman, 1937

This sampler worked by Sophia Dyer of Cape Elizabeth is one of two signed and dated Cape Elizabeth samplers that must have been worked in the same school or academy. The other is signed by Caroline Woodbury.[1] Although it is

possible that a school was located in Cape Elizabeth, none has been identified.

Both illustrate two standard building types of the period. The two-and-one-half-story house with central chimney on the right is distinguished by a red front with white sides, perhaps suggesting a brick facade with wooden ends; it also features a fanlight over the door. The three-story house on the left has a light-colored balustrade and arched doorway.

The youngest of the thirteen children of Mary and shipwright Caleb Dyer of Cape Elizabeth, Sophia completed her sampler when she was thirteen years old. Pictorial needlework like this example was sometimes framed and hung in homes, where it was meant to be admired by family and friends. Fancy needlework, like that executed by Elizabeth Cutts, was hung in the parlor (cat. 142), but simpler works also appeared, such as the "2 samplers" valued at ten cents in William Moore's 1804 Berwick estate.[2] AAE

1 The Woodbury sampler is illustrated in F.O. Bailey Antiquarians, *The Americana Collection of David C. Morse* (Portland, Me.: F.O. Bailey Antiquarians, 1986), lot 9.
2 YCRP; 19:482.

148

Mary Ann Twombly (1802–1843)
Family register
Portland, Maine, 1817
Silk on linen
Inscribed "Mary A Twombly / AEt 12 years
Portld / July 3 1817"
H 16¹⁵⁄₁₆ (43.0); W 16¾ (42.5)
Maine Historical Society

Mary Ann Twombly's work relates closely to the family register Joanna Poole worked ten years earlier (cat. 145). Both have similar arrangements; the genealogy is followed by a verse and a three-part scene. Within these segments, the girls employed solid cross stitches in the lower scenes and the Holbein or double running stitch in black for lettering. Mary Ann, the daughter of a trader in Portland, left the memorial urns in the lower corners of her register blank. Although both works are enclosed in wide floral borders, the designs differ. With its roses and bows, Mary Ann's is more similar (and closer in date) to that worked by Mary Anne Morton in Portland in 1820.[1] The holes along the edge were caused by the linen being nailed to a stretcher.

Family information replaced alphabets and numbers. The content and arrangement suggest the teacher's preference and that the genealogical design had become fashionable. AAE

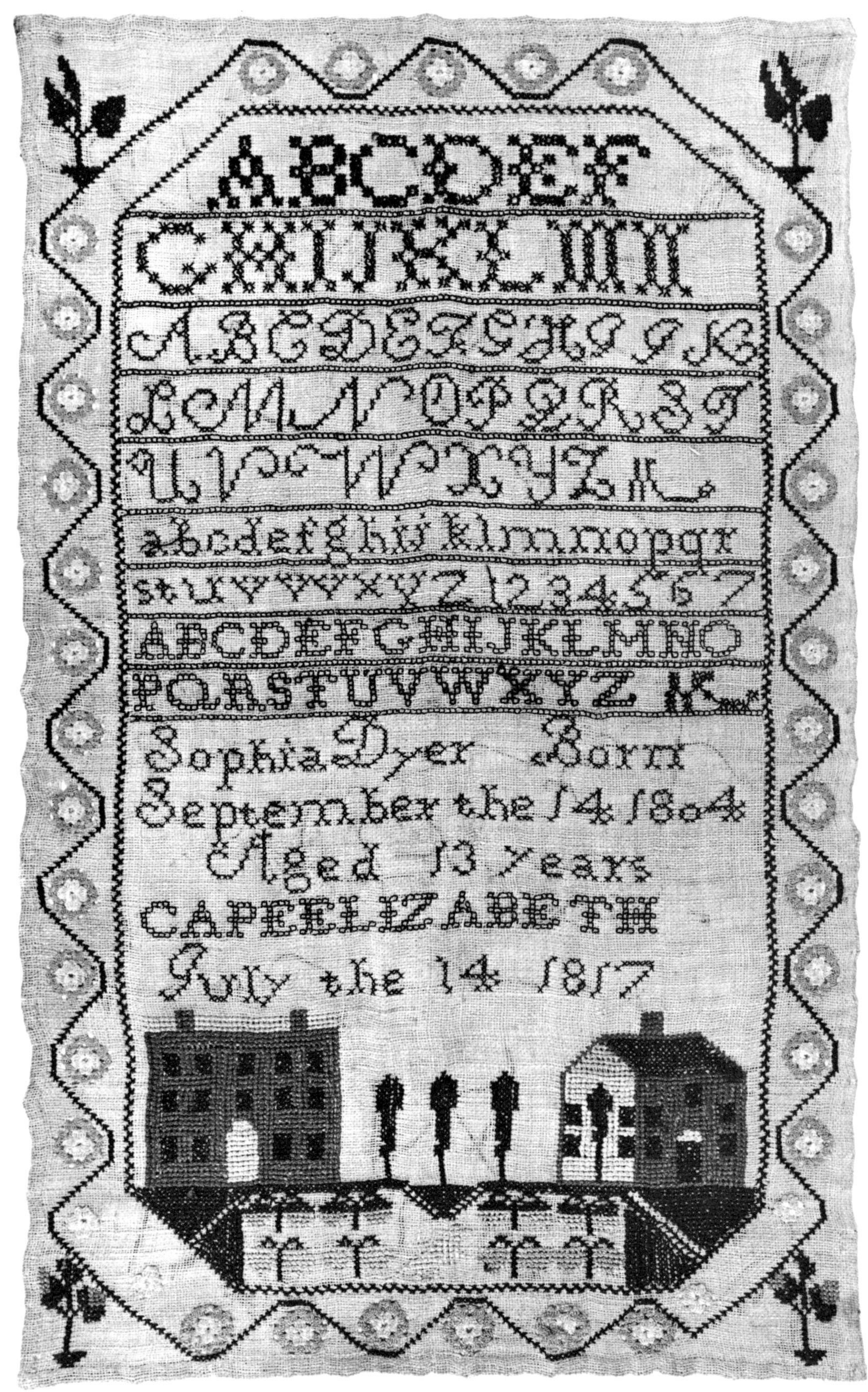

Cat. 147

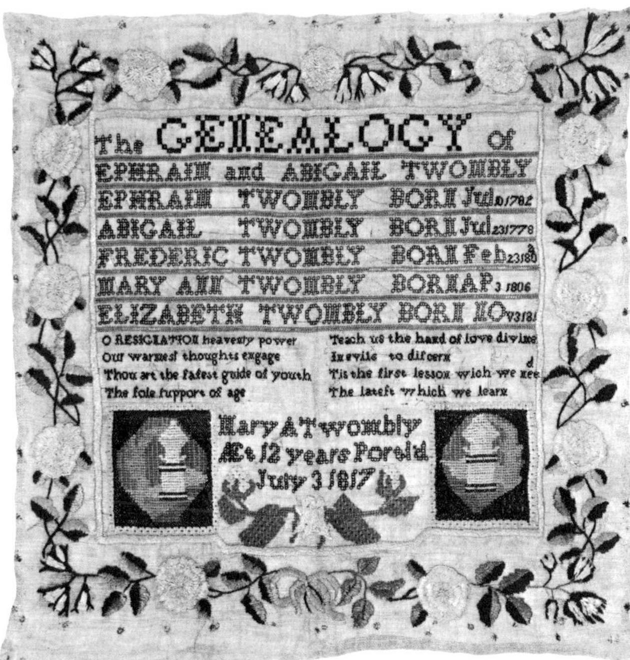

Cat. 148

1 Glee Krueger, *A Gallery of American Samplers* (New York: E.P. Dutton, 1978), 59.

149

Sarah Ann Minott (1814–1881)
Sampler
Portland, Maine, 1824
Silk on linen
Inscribed "Wrought by Sarah Ann Minott Portland.
Oct : 1824 / AE 9"
H 16⁹⁄₁₆ (42.1); W 12¹³⁄₁₆ (32.5)
Maine Historical Society; Gift of Sarah Wilder Allen, 1950

A Sketch of the Tour of General Lafayette, published in Portland in 1824, traced Lafayette's reception during the early part of his American tour and provided a brief biography. The *Sketches* and the *Memoirs of General Lafayette*, published in Boston the same year, both contain the same verse stitched by Sarah Ann Minott, age nine, on her sampler.[1]

This verse is the same one that "several hundred little girls" chanted to Lafayette when he visited their school in New York.[2] Except for its Lafayette verse, this sampler is conventional in all respects. It is stitched in black silk thread with a geometric border of leaves and berries enclosing the verse and alphabets. The verse reads: "Welcome Hero to the West To the land thy sword hath blest / To the country of the Free Welcome Friend of Liberty / Grateful millions Guard

thy fame Age and youth revere thy name / Beauty twines the wreath for thee Glorious son of Liberty / Tears shall Speak a nation's love Where soe'er thy footstep move / By the choral Paen met Welcome Welcome Lafayette."

Sarah Ann Minott's history has been difficult to determine. Probably the daughter of cooper John W. Minott, she was born in Riverside (now Westbrook) and lived with her family there and in Portland. In 1835 she married Gideon Stickney and moved to Eastport, Maine.[3]   AAE

1 *Memoirs of General Lafayette. With an Account of his Visit to America, and of his Reception by the People of the United States; from his arrival, August 15, to the celebration at Yorktown, October 19th 1824* (Boston: E. G. House, 1824), 203.
2 John Foster, *A Sketch of the Tour of General Lafayette* (Portland, Me.: A. W. Thayer, 1824), 50.
3 Accession records, MEHS.

150

Narcissa Lyman (1813–1873)
Sampler
York or Portland, Maine, 1827
Silk on linen or linsey woolsey
Inscribed "Wrought by Narcissa Lyman
November 8th 1827"
H 17¼ (43.8); W 16⁵⁄₁₆ (41.4)
Old York Historical Society

For many Americans children were the hope of the new nation, and teaching them to work samplers was one way of preparing them for a productive and virtuous adulthood. An early nineteenth-century textbook said children were "like soft wax, that will take any stamp we put upon it."[1] Samplers echo this sentiment in the often stitched phrase of Alexander Pope, "Just as the twig is bent the tree's inclin'd." In addition, another contemporary thought, "usefulness is happiness," was expressed in samplers, as well as in letters and diaries (see Chapter 5).[2]

Practicing and perfecting cross-stitched alphabets on a sampler enabled a girl to mark linens, blankets, other household textiles, and personal garments (cat. 163). Even as late as the mid-nineteenth century, a guide to sewing advised, "It is of essential importance that clothes should be marked and numbered. . . . The shapes of the letters or figures can be learned from an inspection of any common sampler."[3]

Narcissa Lyman attended the Misses Martins' school in Portland and may have worked this sampler under their supervision.[4] On greenish-black linen she combined the traditional lines of alphabets with a border of interlocking hearts, mourning motifs, and family history. The verse, "The Orphan," is followed by the death dates of both her parents. Although the sampler is dated November 8, 1827, its

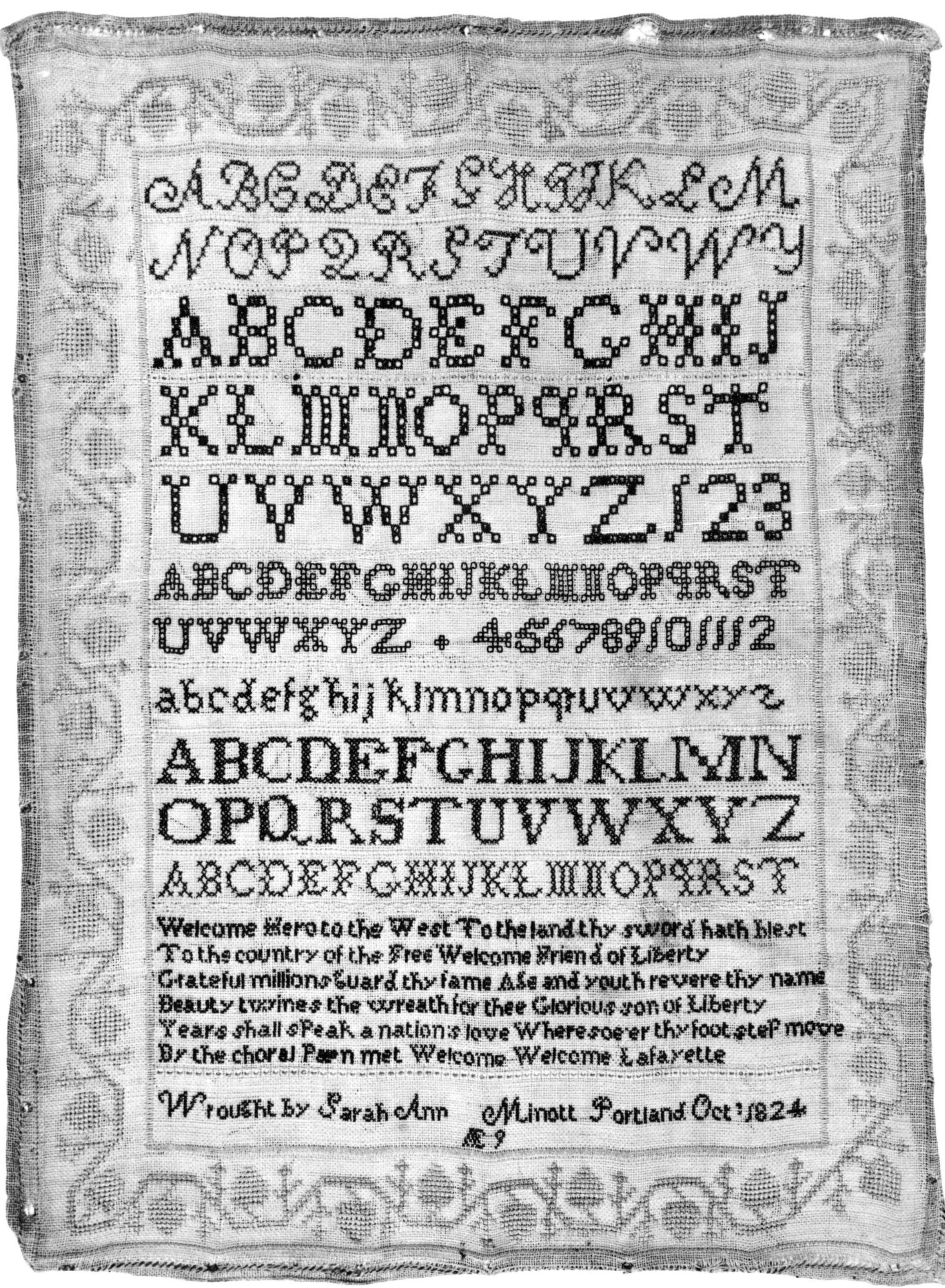

Cat. 149

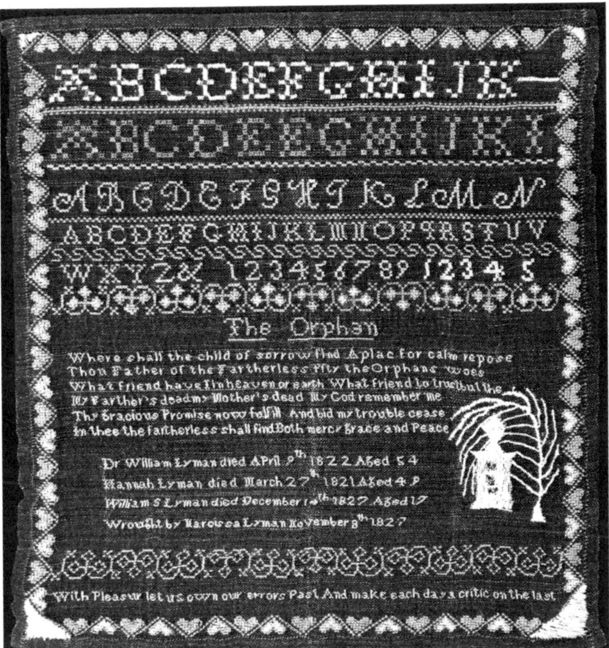

Cat. 150

completion did not stop Narcissa from adding the date of her brother's death a month later.   AAE

1 Ephraim Goodale, Esq., *The New Pleasing Spelling Book, or Child's Guide* (Hallowell, Me.: Glazier and Co. and C. Spaulding, 1826), 31.
2 Lydia Maria Child, *The American Frugal Housewife* (Boston: Carter, Hendee, and Co., 1832), 92.
3 *The Lady's Self-Instructor in Milliner, Mantua Making and all Branches of Plain Sewing, with particular directions for cutting our dresses* (Philadelphia: J. & L. Gihon, n.d.), 16.
4 Narcissa is included in *List of Young Ladies who Attended Misses Martins' School 1804–1829* (Portland, Me.: n.p., n.d.), 8 (copy at MEHS).

151A

Elizabeth Wadsworth (1779–1802)
Pocket
Portland, Maine, 1790–1800
Silk satin, silk brocade, silver threads
H 4½ (11.4); W 4½ (11.4)
Maine Historical Society; Wadsworth-Longfellow House

151B

Thimble
Probably New England, possibly Maine, 1800–1820
Silver
Unmarked
H 13/16 (2.0); Diam. 5/8 (1.6)
The Brick Store Museum; William E. Barry estate through Edith Cleaves Barry, 1936

151C

Needle sheath
Probably Maine, 1800–1816
Silver
Unmarked
H 1⅞ (4.8); W 1¼ (3.2)
The Brick Store Museum; Gift of Mrs. George C. Lord, 1946

Sewing accessories used by the women in Maine's prominent families survive to document the extent to which silver served commonplace functions. All three of these sewing accoutrements have been personalized for the owner. The blue satin pocket (cat. 151A) bears two sets of initials for Eliza Wadsworth in coiled silver resembling French knots. Its central pear-shaped section is covered with white silk brocade and functions as a pin cushion. This pocket was made to hang from the waist, so the initials appeared right-side up to the user. A casing around the opening could be drawn closed. Eliza Wadsworth (cat. 42) died at the age of twenty-three and the pocket she used has survived among the furnishings of the house she lived in, probably saved by her sister Zilpah.

The thimble (cat. 151B) bears the initials "M C" in script; they are thought to be those of Mary Cleaves, who worked a silk embroidered dress (cat. 168) included here. Similarly, the needle sheath (cat. 151C) is engraved with the decorative initials of Olive Jefferds (1793–1879) of Kennebunk. This may have been used to hold knitting on the needle and prevent it from slipping off. Fashioned in the form of a twisted heart, the obverse is bisected by the needle cover. It dates prior to her marriage in 1816. The wigglework borders are characteristic of Maine silver of this period and are used in a delightful and uninhibited way.[1]

Advertisements of Maine silversmiths suggest that a significant number of these small silver items were kept in stock. In 1813 Kennebunk watchmaker and jeweler Phineas Stevens advertised silver thimbles among the range of small silver items he sold. Two years later, Joshua Tolford, also of Kennebunk, included silver thimbles, hair combs, and elastic and common knitting needles in his advertisement. Although some local silversmiths manufactured these small articles, they often relied heavily on imported examples.[2] However, special orders such as initials required an engraver's individual attention.

Occasionally, small sewing items were recorded in household inventories. When William Moore died, his Berwick estate contained many small items belonging to a woman, including "1 sattin pocket book and two pin balls" valued at $1.50.[3] Thimble cases, and needle cases in fanciful shapes such as a tricorn hat, swans, and baskets survive at the Wadsworth-Longfellow house; some may date to the

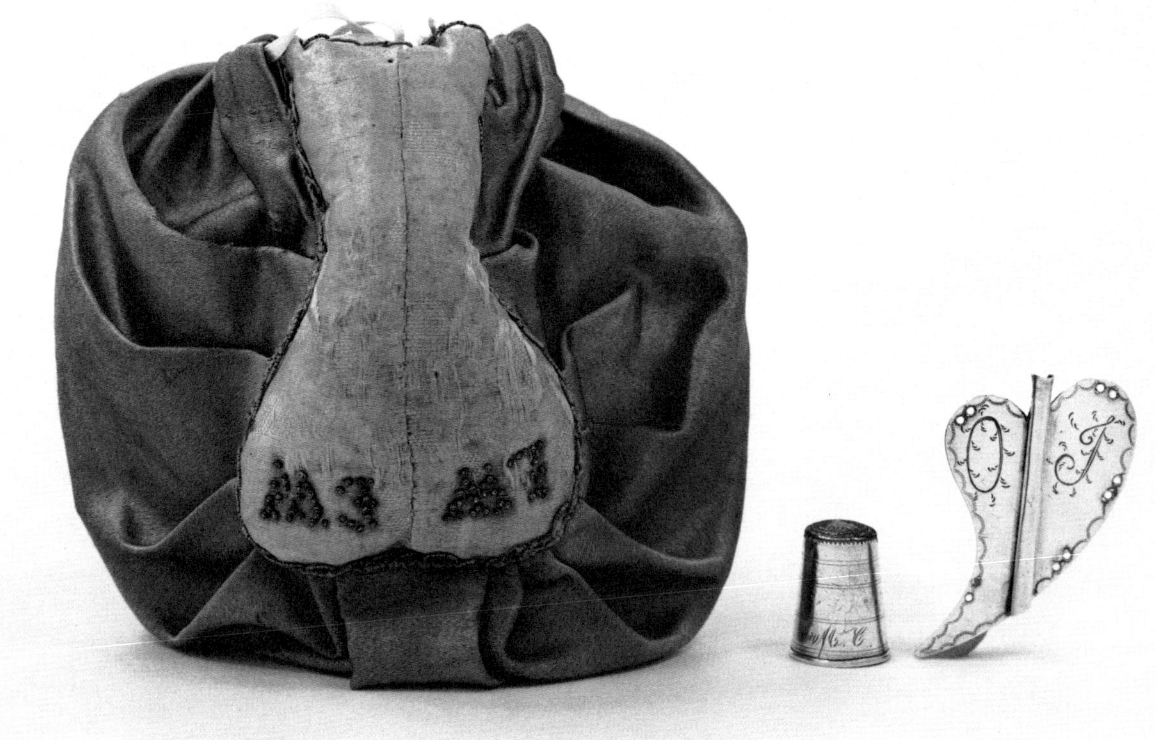

Cat. 151A, Cat. 151B and Cat. 151C

early nineteenth century, such as the "Nelson" sewing case
(cat. 152).   AAE

1 Conversation with Martha Gandy Fales, October 14, 1986.
2 *Weekly Visiter* (April 17, 1813; July 22, 1815); Churchill, "Crafts in
   Transition," 302, 307.
3 YCRP; 19:482.

152

Sewing case
England, possibly Birmingham, ca. 1805
Leather trimmed with silver and enamel;
silk lining; silver bindings; silver bodkin, steel
scissors and tweezers
Bodkin marked "SP" in circle
H closed 3 (7.6); W 4⅛ (10.4)
Maine Historical Society; Wadsworth-Longfellow House

This red leather sewing case with its engraved silver binding
and blue enamel clasp is a wonderful example of the decorative nature of utilitarian objects. The case unfolds several
times with running stitches along the length of the case used

to secure straight pins. On the inside, a small pocket with a
silver clasp opens to reveal white wool needle holders
trimmed in silver thread; below is a small looking glass. On
the opposite side of the pocket, flaps covered with blue silk
open to reveal slots that hold a pair of steel scissors, tweezers,
and a silver bodkin. The latter was used to run tapes through
casings. It bears the mark of a Birmingham silversmith,
Samuel Pemberton (1738–1803). Pemberton is known to
have produced small objects. [1]

   The enamel clasp, featuring an inlaid silver ship inscribed
"Victory" in a ribbon, commemorates Admiral Horatio
Nelson, his flagship, and probably the Battle of Trafalgar,
when Nelson was victorious over Napoleon's fleet. Nelson
died during the engagement. This case has a history in the
Wadsworth-Longfellow family, revealing the interest
Americans had in the great British hero.   LFS

1 Charles James Jackson, *English Goldsmiths and their Marks: A History of
   the Goldsmiths and Plate Workers of England, Scotland and Ireland*, 2d ed.
   (Los Angeles: Borden Publishing Co., 1921), 223, 408. Other sewing
   implements such as needle cases, bodkin cases, and scissors sheaths
   bear his mark; Estelle Horowitz, letter to author, August 20, 1986. See
   also Kenneth Crisp Jones, ed., *The Silversmiths of Birmingham and their
   Marks, 1750–1980* (London: N.A.G. Press, 1981), 53.

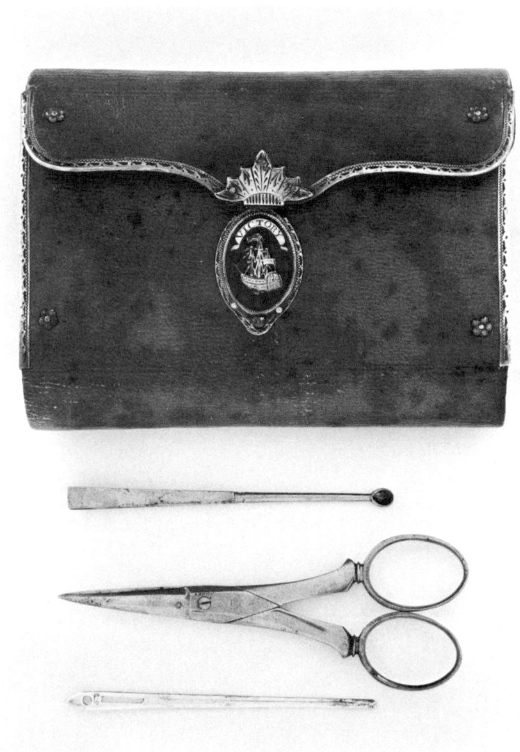

Cat. 152

Indian Wars strengthened her tribe's ties with the French. Molly Ocket had arrived in Canada by 1759. She probably learned the art of moosehair embroidery from the French nuns at this time.[2]

By 1766 she was living in Fryeburg, Maine, and after 1772 moved to Bethel. Local tradition there relates that she gave the moosehair embroidery to Eli Twitchell (1759–1845), clerk, selectman, and justice of the peace in Bethel. It was made into a pocketbook, lined with green wool, and fastened with a silver clasp engraved with bright-cut decoration and the date 1778.[3]

Molly Ocket was highly regarded in the Bethel area, and oral history retains stories of her generosity, healing skill, and friendship with the local inhabitants. The Maine Historical Society owns a birch box decorated with the pervasive double-curve motif that is attributed to her (see cat. 121). Baskets and other objects said to be made by her survive in Bethel families.[4]   AAE

1   Bruce Trigger and William Sturtevant, eds., *Handbook of North American Indians* (Washington, D. C.: Smithsonian Institution, 1978), 15: 155; Margaret Swain, "Moose-hair Embroidery on Birch Bark," *Antiques* 107, no. 4 (April 1975): 726–729.
2   Catherine S-C. Newell, *Molly Ocket* (Bethel, Me.: Bethel Historical Society, 1981), 2–4.
3   Newell, *Molly Ocket*, 5; William B. Lapham, *History of Bethel* (Augusta, Me.: Press of the Maine Farmer, 1891), 150.
4   Newell, *Molly Ocket*, 17.

153

Molly Ocket (ca. 1735–1816)
Pocketbook
Probably Cumberland County, Maine, 1778
Moosehair over twined bast foundation, wool, silver
H 4⅝ (11.8); w 6³⁄₁₆ (15.7)
Maine Historical Society; Gift of Lucia Kimball, 1863

This pocketbook made of embroidered moosehair shows the relationship between Indian and European customs and the culture of late eighteenth-century Maine. Stitched by the Abnaki Indian Molly Ocket, it illustrates a technique first practiced by Ursuline nuns in Canada. Moosehair was traditionally used by the Indians as ornamentation; here it is stitched using European embroidery techniques. Its transformation from a flat piece of embroidery into a pocketbook comparable to wool Irish-stitched pocketbooks produced in the American and European tradition further illustrates the melding of different cultures.[1]

Born in the Saco area in the 1730s, Molly Ocket was christened Marie Agathe due to the strong influence of the French Catholic missionaries. She lived with a group of Indians who traveled frequently between Plymouth, Massachusetts, and southwestern Maine. The French and

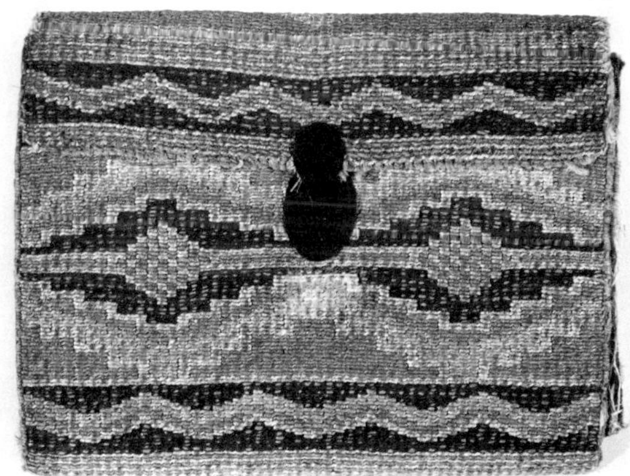

Cat. 153

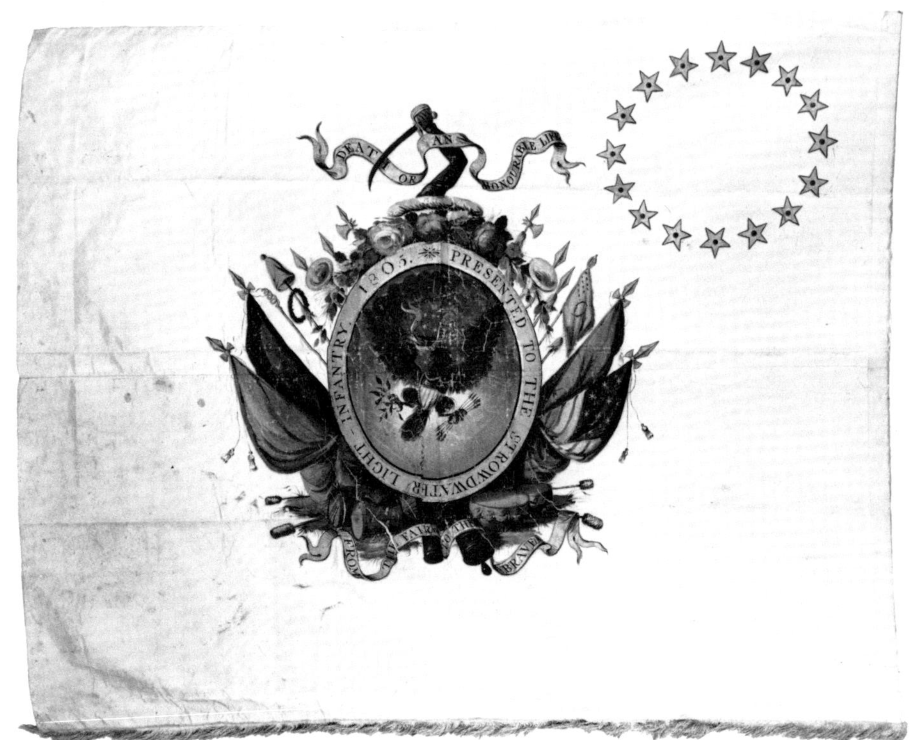

Cat. 154

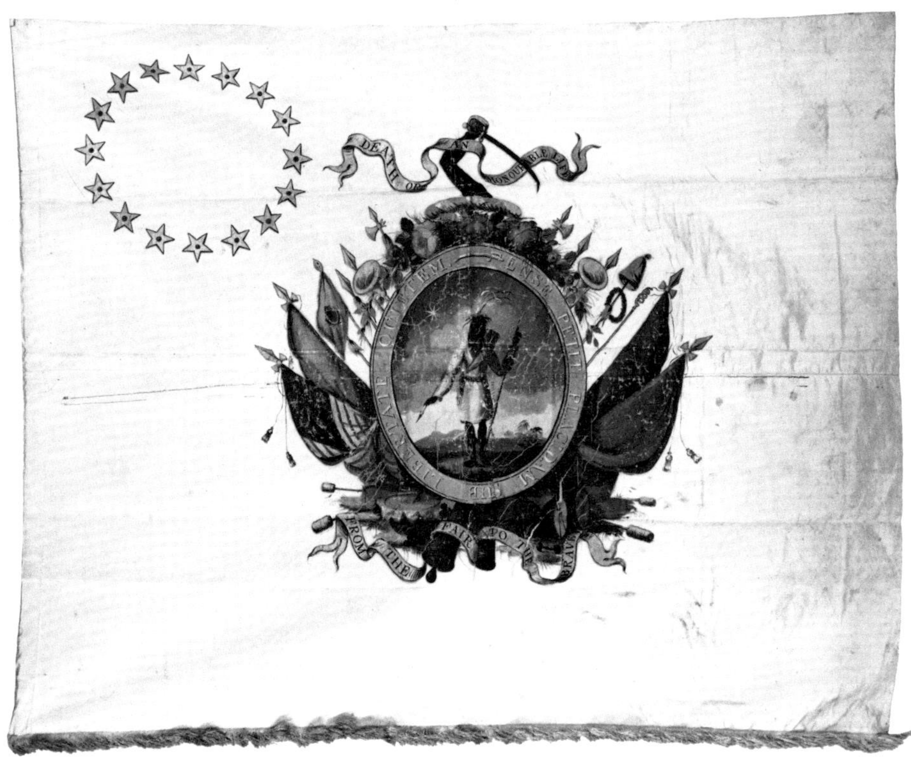

Cat. 154

Unidentified artist
Stroudwater Light Infantry banner
Boston or Newburyport, Massachusetts, 1805
Painted silk
H 57⁵/₁₆ (146.4); W 71⅞ (182.5)
Maine Historical Society; Gift of Almira Ann Broad, 1892
Color plate on page 255

The Stroudwater Light Infantry was one of the volunteer militia companies organized in Portland during the federal period. Its silk banner is a rare survival. The earliest example of Maine militia banners in the Maine Historical Society's collections, it may also be the earliest Maine example extant.[1] During the late nineteenth century, this banner was displayed at the Broad Tavern in Stroudwater along with other "Interesting Relics of 'Ye Olden Tyme'" (see cat. 156). Portland historian William Goold described it in 1880 as "the most attractive feature to any one interested in military affairs."[2]

Stroudwater is a district within Portland's town limits. Up the Fore River from the harbor, it had played an important role in the colonial mast trade. During the early nineteenth century, it was the site of the southernmost toll on the Cumberland-Oxford Canal.

Almira Ann Broad (1820–1902), the donor, was the daughter of Amos (1785–1864), and granddaughter of Thaddeus Broad (1744–1824), builder of the house that was the Broad Tavern, and the niece of William (1772–1846) and Silas Broad (1795–1873). William was the last ensign of the Stroudwater Light Infantry Company. During his early years, Broad's Tavern was the scene of muster gatherings. Traditionally, the company would assemble there to take refreshment after drill exercises. On their departure, the men would proceed across the Fore River to another tavern, the Frost-Brewer house. After the death of his father, Silas ran the Broad Tavern until 1832.[3]

Banners were often presented to militia companies by public-spirited young ladies but were not necessarily made by them. This banner was presented by Eunice (1783–1862), the oldest child of Eunice (Freeman) and John Quinby of Stroudwater (cat. 31).[4] With painted decoration on both sides, this banner depicts the seal of Massachusetts enclosed by the inscription *Ense Petit Placidam Sub Libertate Quietem*, the state motto. Freely translated, it means "By the sword we seek peace, but peace only under liberty."[5] On the reverse is a soaring eagle with shield, clutching arrows and an olive branch in its talons. Around the eagle medallion is the inscription "Presented to the Stroudwater Light Infantry 1805" with "From the Fair to the Brave" inscribed on a ribbon. Both the state seal and eagle medallions are surrounded by colorful flags, symbols of liberty, and trophies of war. A raised arm above the scenes carries a ribbon inscribed "Death or an Honorable Life."

Eagles are found in the decoration of other militia banners, including Portland's "Train of Artillery" of 1802 which is painted on the company's creamware pitcher (cat. 155). In 1799 Zilpah Wadsworth presented a banner to the Portland Federal Volunteers, the first uniformed volunteer company in Maine. In this banner, the eagle figured prominently in the arms of the United States. A letter written by Zilpah's sister, Eliza, in 1799 documents in detail this early banner. When ordering it to be made, she enlisted the assistance of "Mr. [Daniel] Davis" of Portland. He was requested to deliver the silk to "Mr. Gore, unless he knows of one who can paint it more elegantly." Samuel Gore was a heraldry painter in Newburyport (cats. 73, 142).[6] "The figure proposed, is the arms of the United States" in an oval surrounded with the inscription, "*Presented to the first company of federal volunteers of Portland*. The motto to be, *Defend the Laws*, or *The laws of our Country* whichever Mr. Davis chooses. We *must* name one." Eliza continued:

These directions are not to be attended to exactly, but room is left for the taste of the painter to be exercised, or the more refined taste of Mr. Davis. It is wished that the whole should be executed elegantly.[7]

Although the painter of the Stroudwater banner has not been identified, Eliza's correspondence indicates that a skilled Boston or Newburyport artist, like Gore, was probably responsible. In 1811 John Ritto Penniman of Boston painted a "Stand of Colours" for the Portland Rifle Corps, described in a newspaper account as "superior to any thing of the kind ever exhibited in this state." Other artists painted militia company banners in Portland. Henry Williams was in Portland by 1803 and advertised that he painted "draughts of every kind. Likewise, painting upon . . . silk and satin." However, Williams is not thought to have been old or competent enough to be credited with this banner of high quality. Another Portland artist, Charles Codman, was able to compete with the Boston artisans at least by 1830. In that year, the Portland Rifle Corps turned to him for a new banner.[8] LFS

1 Although there is a reference in the Society's files to a ca. 1810 Portland Rifle Corps banner, its whereabouts are not known.
2 William Goold, Scrapbook, 2.
3 Madeleine Wilkinson, comp., *Hezekiah Broad of Needham, Mass., and Some of His Descendants* (Montpelier, Vt., 1976), 4–6 (typescript, MEHS); Lovejoy, *This was Stroudwater*, 127–128.
4 Henry Cole Quinby, *Genealogical History of the Quinby (Quimby) Family* (New York, 1915), 218.
5 Allan Forbes and Ralph M. Eastman, *Town and City Seals of Massachusetts*, 2 vols. (Boston: State Street Trust Co., 1950), 1:2.
6 George C. Groce and David H. Wallace, *The New-York Historical Society's Dictionary of Artists in America 1564–1860* (New Haven, Conn.: Yale University Press, 1957), 267; Harold Bowditch, "Early Water-Color Paintings of New England Coats of Arms," *Publications of the Colonial Society of Massachusetts* 35 (1944): 181.

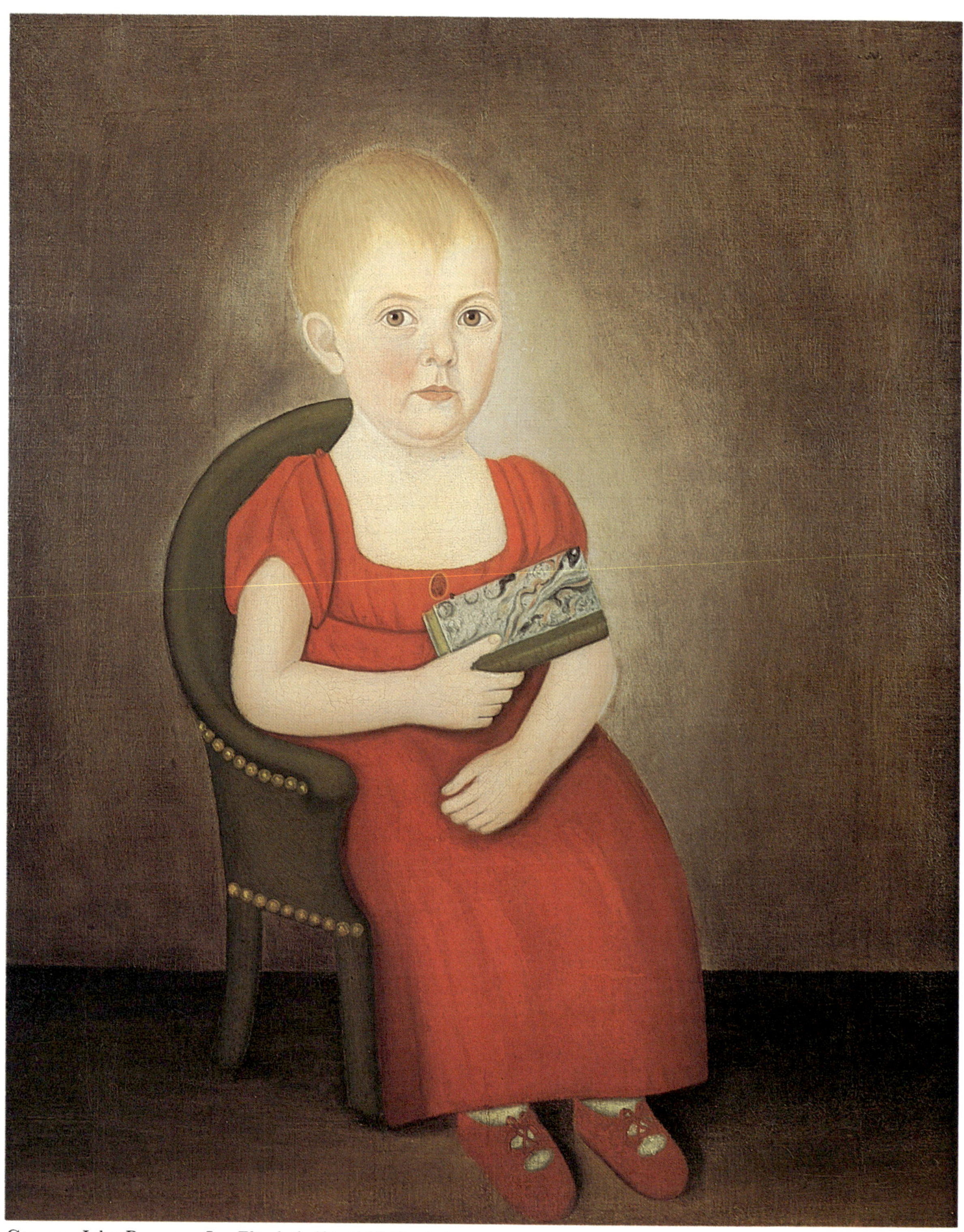

Cat. 41 John Brewster, Jr., *Elizabeth Abigail Wallingford*,
Kennebunk, Maine, 1808.

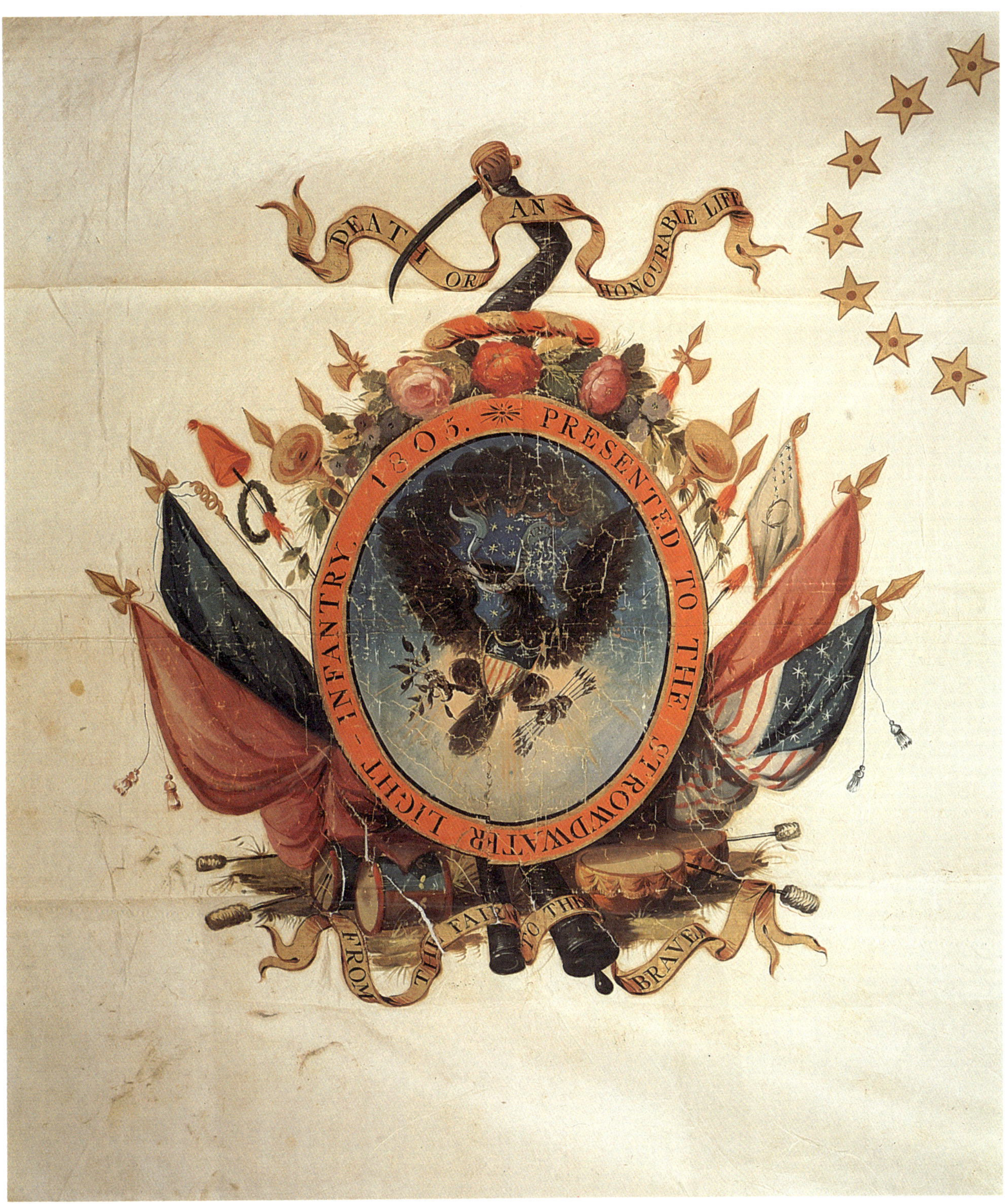

Cat. 154 Unidentified artist, Stroudwater Light Infantry Company banner,
Boston or Newburyport, Massachusetts, 1805.

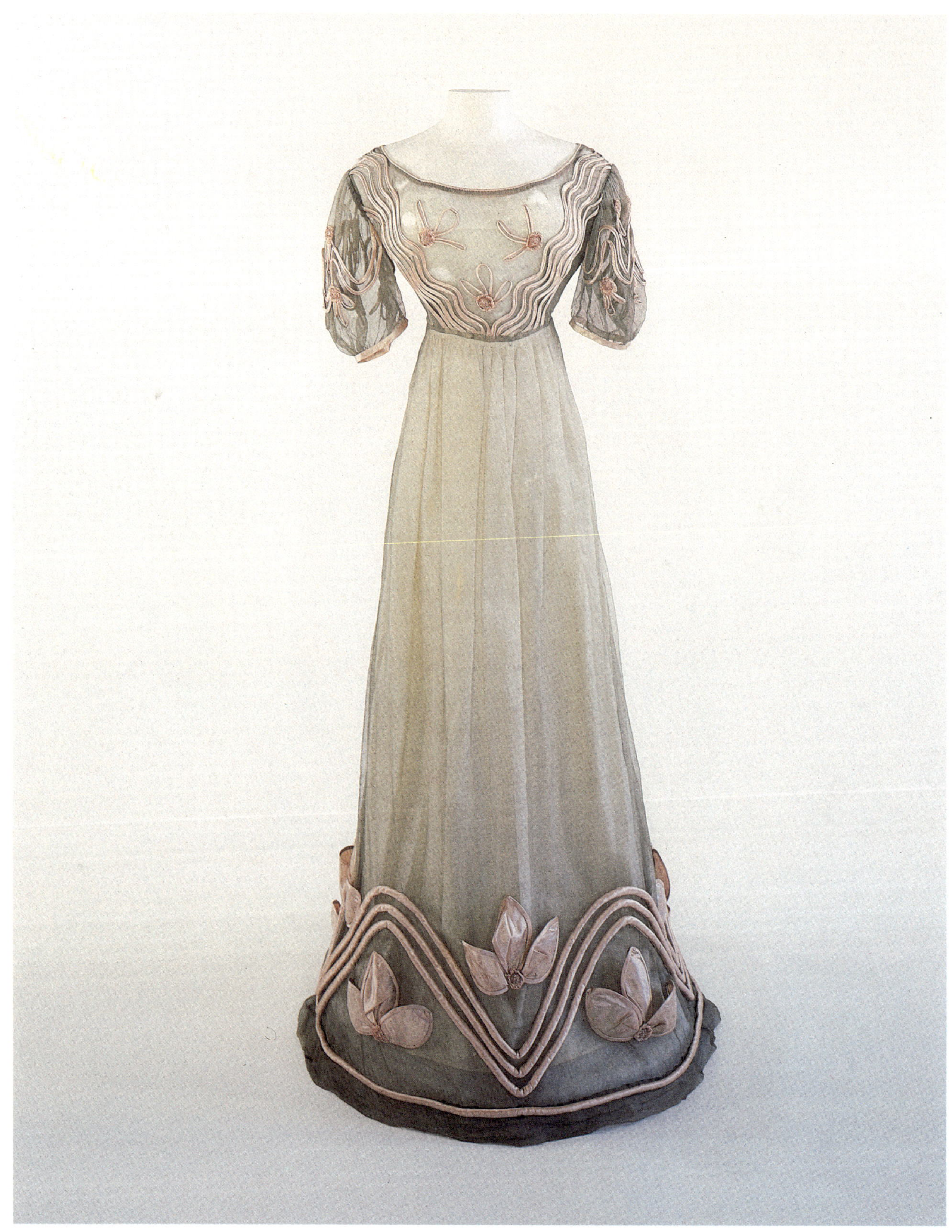

Cat. 167 Dress, Possibly Biddeford, Maine, 1815–1820.

7 Zilpah Wadsworth to Nancy Doane, letter journal, September 1799 (filed with 1797), Wadsworth-Longfellow Papers, LNHS. Joyce Butler kindly brought this to my attention.

8 *Portland Gazette and Maine Advertiser* (June 10, 1811); *Eastern Argus* (November 25, 1803). William D. Barry brought the Penniman ad to my attention and kindly assisted with the identification of Williams. The Codman banner is in MEHS.

155

Probably Herculaneum Pottery (1796–1840)
Pitcher
Liverpool, England, 1802
Creamware with hand-enamel painting in green, red, yellow, blue, and black, and transfer-printing in black
H 14¾ (37.5)
Maine Historical Society
Gift of Portland Society of Natural History, 1915

The Portland Train of Artillery was one of the earliest volunteer militia companies in federal-period Portland. Membership was by election and candidates had to meet military as well as social requirements. Members of the merchant class were those most likely to join since they had the financial means to absorb the cost of the uniforms, equipment, and dinners. Social events and special community activities were an integral part of the volunteer militia life. Some of their events surrounded the death of George Washington, although attempts to honor the "Father of our Country" did not always receive praise. On January 7, 1800, the Reverend Caleb Bradley of Westbrook "spent the day in Portland. The volunteer company undertook to bury General Washington, and such an irregular, confused and erratic piece of business, I believe no man ever saw before harum scarum."[1] The Portland Train of Artillery paraded, hopefully with greater skill, in the funeral procession of Commodore Preble in 1805.

This very large pitcher, held together by an old wire repair, was ordered by the Portland Train of Artillery in 1802. It depicts a scene of a militia company firing a cannon. Decoration of this type is rare in American historical wares. The inscriptions painted on the body and a contemporary source aid in its documentation. The soldiers are clad in uniforms that were chosen in October 1792, according to the minutes kept by the secretary of the company:

Voted that the company furnish themselves as soon as possible with a uniform dress as follows — Viz — A blue coat with scarlet faceings & lineing & yellow buttons. — Buff coloured waistcot & breaches. — Half gaiters. — Black kneebands. — A black cockade & a black plume tiped with red.[2]

In the foreground a soldier carries the company banner emblazoned with an eagle. Eagles are known to have been

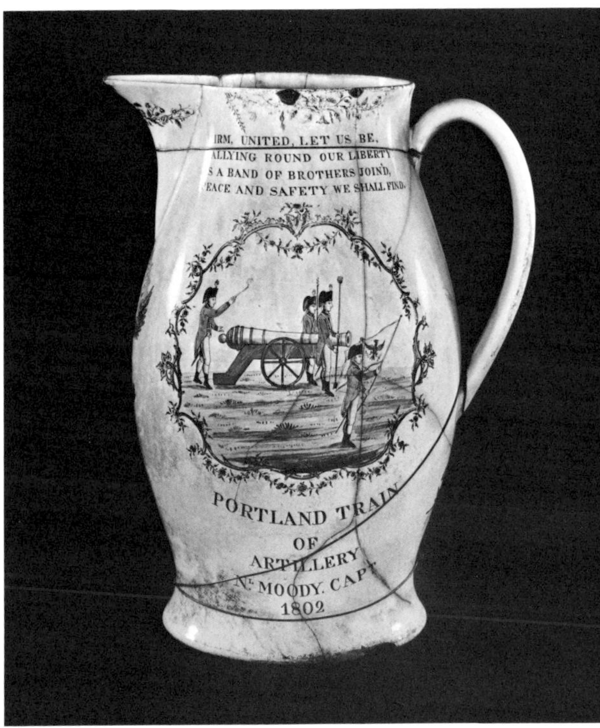

Cat. 155

included on other militia banners for Portland companies (cat. 154).[3]

In October 1791 Lemuel Weeks was elected captain of the company. Daniel Tucker was made captain lieutenant, and Nathaniel Moody, Sr., second lieutenant. Moody was made captain by 1802 as indicated by the inscription painted below the scene. Both ship owners and importers, Weeks and Tucker were active in the transatlantic trade. As one historian noted, "they were almost as well known in Liverpool as in Portland." In 1799 Weeks and Tucker received sixteen crates of "Liverpool ware" shipped on board the *Columbia*.[4] Below the spout of this pitcher is inscribed the name of the purchaser, "Captain Thrasher." Like the painted militia scene, this is a form of documentation rarely found on historical wares made for the American market. Captain Joseph Thrasher does not appear in the militia company roster; he probably commanded the vessel which carried the pitcher from Liverpool.   L F S

1 In January 1822, Daniel Walker Lord attended a "splendid military ball" in Kennebunk. He "did not leave the Hall until 3 o'clock in the morning & . . . did not return until next day at 12 o'clock. Had a complete good time"; journal, MEHS. Bradley as cited in William Goold, Scrapbook, 102.

2 Artillery book, First Company, 1791, MEHS.

3 The banner of a forerunner of this company depicted a phoenix and was described in the *Cumberland Gazette* (October 25, 1790). William D. Barry kindly brought this reference to my attention.

4 Willis, *History*, 845. Asa Clapp, account book, 1796–1799, MEHS.

156

Box
Portland, Maine, 1818
Paper
H 2⅝ (6.6); W 3 9/16 (9.0); D 2 9/16 (6.5)
Maine Historical Society; Gift of Mrs. George Hunt, 1927

This box is constructed of paper tickets used for admission to an anniversary dinner held at Broad's Tavern in Stroudwater for the Mechanic Blues. Whole and partial tickets are sewn together to form the bottom, sides, and cover.

Organized in 1807, the Mechanic Blues, a militia company, assisted in the defense of Portland during the War of 1812 and remained in existence until 1890.[1] In 1818 Thomas Osgood, captain of the company, ordered the members of the company "to appear at the usual place of parade near the Court House in complete uniform on thursday the 11th day of June . . . at eight o clock in the fore noon."[2] In celebration of their eleventh anniversary, the militia presented a display of drills, paraded through the town, and held a target shooting match. The *Eastern Argus* reported the actitivies which culminated in the dinner at the tavern.

As soon as the firing was ended, the company repaired to Mr. Broad's Tavern, where they partook of a sumptuous repast, prepared with elegance and taste by that gentleman. After enjoying a few hours in festive recreation, they returned to town — and by their maneuvering, &c. gave evident demonstration of their ability to endure fatigue.[3]

Broad's Tavern, the site of their dinner, was built in 1782 about two miles from Portland. A stop for the Portland and Boston stage, it was a popular gathering place. The attractions of the tavern included a bowling alley, a chained bear, and a famous bar built into a huge tree in front of the tavern. A set of steps led up to an enclosed platform that encircled the large elm, which was called the "barroom tree."[4] President Monroe visited the tavern in 1817, and after Lafayette's visit, the tree came to be called the Lafayette Elm. The tavern operated until about 1840, when it became a private residence of the Broad family.

In 1880, Almira Ann Broad, a great-niece of the original proprietor, Thaddeus Broad, opened the building as a museum to those interested in viewing the "mementoes of the past."[5] It remained standing until the late 1940s when it was demolished during the expansion of the Portland Jetport.

Augusta Barstow Hunt gave this box to the Maine Historical Society in 1927. She and Miss Mary Longfellow were the first women elected to the Society in 1909.[6]   AAE

1 Leonard Bond Chapman, comp., Scrapbook relating to Portland and Deering history, 1890–1915, 3 vols., 1:7.
2 Portland Mechanic Blues orderly book, 1807–1825, MEHS.
3 *Eastern Argus* (June 16, 1818).
4 Dr. Allston F. Hunt, Stroudwater Scrapbook, 1940, 43, MEHS.
5 William Goold, Scrapbook, 2.
6 *Proceedings of the Maine Historical Society* (Portland, Me.: Smith and Sale, 1910), 13.

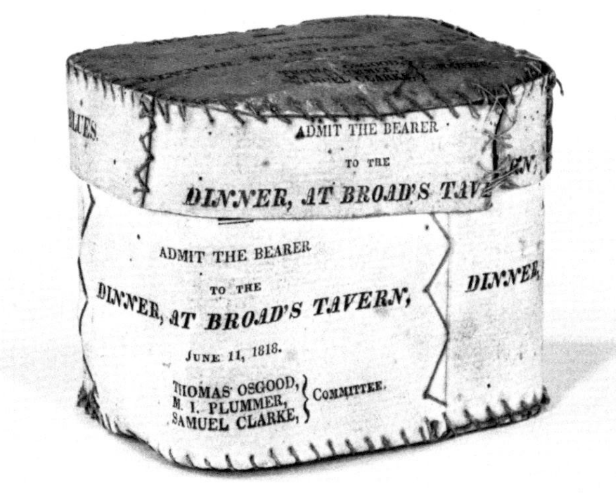

Cat. 156

157

Waistcoat
Probably Portland, Maine, ca. 1786
Silk embroidered with silk and metallic threads and spangles; linen
L 28 (71.2); Circum. hem 42½ (108.0)
Maine Historical Society

Waistcoats, often embroidered or striped, figured prominently in the wardrobes of New England gentlemen. Because the most expensive material was used only for the front, with the back and lining of less costly fabric, fashionable waistcoats or vests were within the reach of many men and were an economical way to present the desired image.

This waistcoat is an excellent example of the style popular after the Revolution. The hip-length garment with a round neck and two front pockets with flaps is embellished with elaborate silk embroidery, metal-wrapped threads, and buttons covered with embroidered silk. All the pieces—the front section, pocket flaps, and button coverings—were pre-embroidered and sold commercially. On the lower back edges of this vest, the pattern is visible. Local tailors would assemble the garment at the customer's request using, as in this example, a linen back for economy and durability. The prosperous and civic-minded Samuel Freeman (1743–1831) of Portland wore this vest at his marriage to Mrs. Betty Ilsley Jones on February 7, 1786. Attached to the waistcoat is a fragment of the blue silk coat said to have been worn at the same time.

Probate inventory references indicate that throughout the period men owned several waistcoats each. Cyrus King owned seventeen vests, two of silk, four of flannel, "5 thin vests," and six of unspecified fabric. The silk vests were valued at $1 and $2; the unspecified vests from $.75 to $4; the "thin vests" at $3; and all four flannel vests at $3.[1] A variety of fabrics were recorded in other probate inventories. Joseph Frye of Fryeburg owned a nankeen waistcoat worth five shillings. Nankeen was a plain woven cloth originally made from a yellow variety of cotton and sold in Nankin in China. By the mid-eighteenth century it was also produced in the West using ordinary cotton dyed yellow.[2] To wear with "sattin jackets" and "sattin breeches," Israel Wildes of Arundel had waistcoats of white wool, "spotted jean" (a linen/cotton twilled cloth), and calico, the latter of significantly less value than the other two. Saco mariner James Witherbee owned a white marseilles vest in 1804. Loom-woven marseilles imitated the earlier marseilles work composed of two layers of cloth with patterned areas closely stitched by hand and accentuated by stuffing forced through a coarser backing. Loom-woven "Marseilles Vesting" was available in Portland.[3]

Samuel Freeman was a leading citizen and public servant of Portland. In 1774 he was a member of the Committee of Correspondence and the following year he was elected as the town's delegate to the Provincial Congress. For forty-six years he was clerk of courts for Cumberland County, thirty-six years register of probate, and after 1804, judge of probate. Freeman was highly regarded by his contemporaries and Portland historian William Willis wrote in 1849:

We believe no other man ever held so many responsible trusts, at one time, and none was ever more faithful in the discharge of his duties; it is difficult to conceive the versatility of talent and capacity of endurance, which would enable him to go through the routine of these various offices. At the same time he was employed in preparing works for publication, which had a great value in their day; we refer to his Town Officer, Clerk's Magazine, and Probate Directory.[4]

For nearly half a century he was a deacon of the First Parish Church. Early in the nineteenth century, the diary of the Reverend Thomas Smith (1702–1795) came into Freeman's possession. When nearly eighty years old, Freeman's last work was the preparation of Smith's journal for publication in 1821.[5]

Judge Freeman was a founding member of the Portland

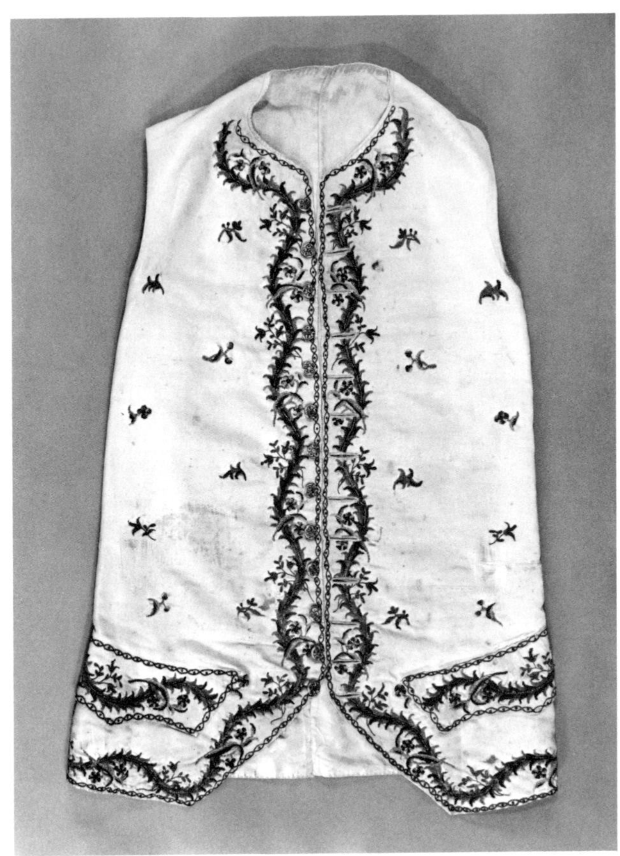

Cat. 157

Academy and a trustee of Bowdoin College. The list of other charitable, moral, and religious societies which he founded or to which he belonged is long and ranged from the Portland Benevolent Society to the society in Portland for suppressing vice and immorality. Freeman and his wife lived in a two-story hipped-roof house set back from Middle Street by a series of terraces. His two-storied office was located just off to the side, on the street.[6] CSP

1 YCRP; 27:317.
2 YCRP; 16:555. For a description of the manufacture and uses of nankeen, see Florence Montgomery, *Textiles in America 1650–1870* (New York: W. W. Norton, 1984), 308.
3 YCRP; 16:512; 20:227, Montgomery, *Textiles in America*, 289–292, and *Portland Gazette* (July 2, 1814).
4 Willis, *Journals*, 423.
5 Extracts of the Smith diary were published with extracts from Deane's diary as one volume in 1849; see Willis, *Journals*.
6 William Freeman, "Samuel Freeman—His Life and Service," *Collections and Proceedings of the Maine Historical Society*, 2d ser., 5 (1894):27–28; Shettleworth and Barry, *Mr. Goodhue*, no. 17.

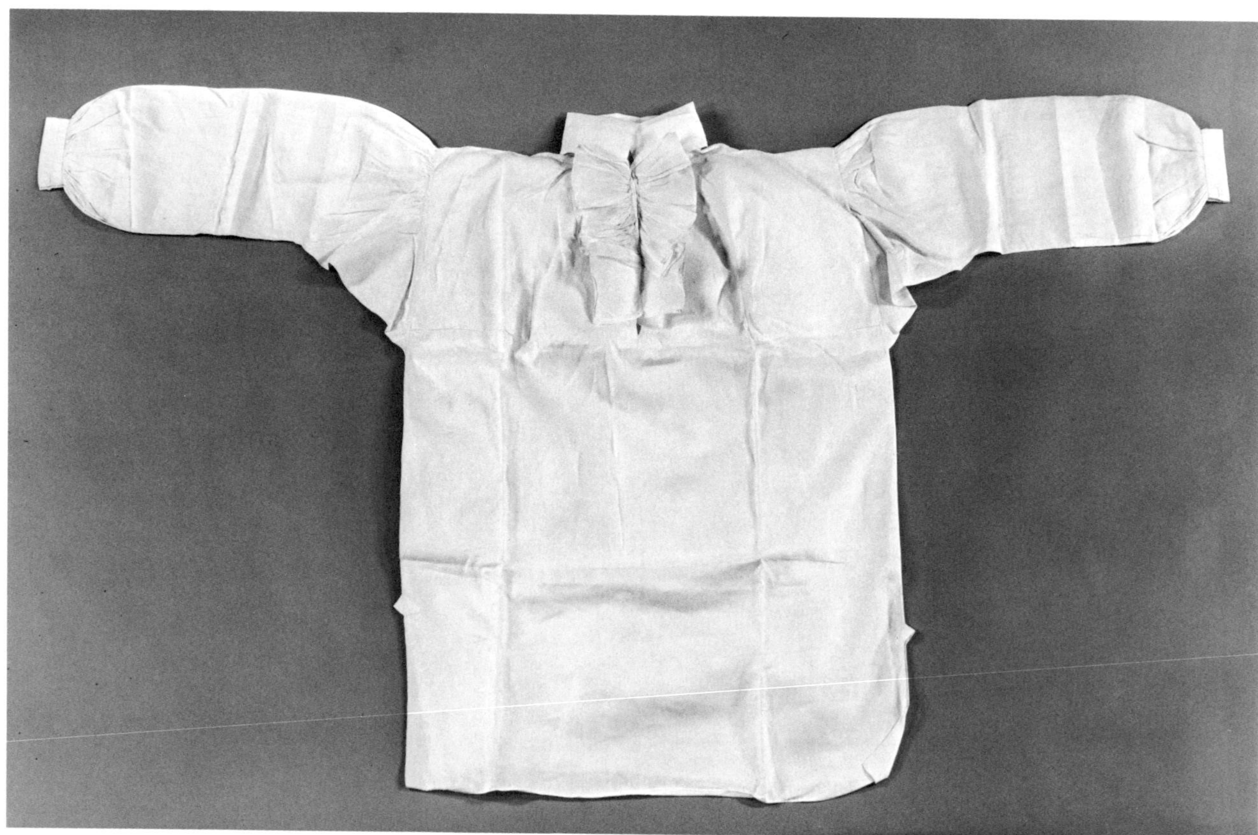

Cat. 158

158

Shirt
Probably Saco, Maine, 1810–1821
Linen
H 35⅛ (89.3); Circum. hem 54½ (138.4)
York Institute Museum

Two items of clothing with histories of ownership by Thomas Cutts survive in the York Institute: this linen shirt and a night cap (cat. 159). This shirt, one of the "31 shirts [valued at $] 9.50" listed in Cutts's inventory, is typical of early nineteenth-century construction. Due to the expense of purchasing fabric or the time involved in producing it, patterns were not used when cutting out shirts. Instead, they were constructed out of a series of rectangles and squares that fit into the selvage-to-selvage width of the fabric. The bulk of the yardage was taken up by the shirt's length. The underarm gussets and those at the top of the side slits allowed for a maximum of room with no waste of material.

Shirts constructed in this manner were immune to fashion changes well into the nineteenth century. The addition of lining in the shoulder area extended the length of time the shirts could be serviceable; small firm stitching and finished seams enabled them to withstand the stress of vigorous laundering. It was common practice for men to sleep in the shirt they had worn during the day, hence the need to make them durable. In 1844 great-grandson George was seen "strutting about in one of Col. Cutts's old waistcoats," demonstrating the longevity of garments that were carefully constructed of high quality materials.[1] Cutts's shirt is further embellished with decorative hem-stitching on the collar, shoulder gussets, and cuffs, and a fine ruffle down the front of the neck opening.

Women were responsible for the unending task of clothing their family and a great deal of effort was spent on "plain" sewing—shirts, shifts, other undergarments, and household linens—before marriage as well as after. In 1812 Eliza Southgate recorded that she had completed a dozen shirts for her father.[2] Another man's shirt, signed and dated by its maker, "A T Cunningham No 3 / 1822," is also in the York Institute. Made by Anne Cunningham prior to her marriage to Joseph Shepley, the garment features a heart-shaped piece of fabric reinforcing the neck opening, a romantic touch in an otherwise standard garment.

Along with boots, shoes, socks, and four hats listed in

Cutts's probate inventory were "11 black & other Vests & Jacket"; fifteen pairs of black and other small clothes or breeches; five coats; twenty-one pairs of hose (six of silk, five of cotton, and ten woolen); four handkerchiefs; thirteen stocks for around the neck; "1 Callico gown" for use at home; "2 Surtouts" or overcoats; a pair of pantaloons; a great coat; one-and-one-half yards of broadcloth; and "a lot of buckles & spoons & 2 old watches."[3] Cutts's wardrobe contained all the articles of clothing essential for a well-dressed man of federal-period New England. The numbers of various items—multiple changes of clothing—demonstrate the opportunity for personal cleanliness that money could buy. CSP

1 Jane C. Nylander, "Shirt," in *The Great River*, 392. John Fairfield to Anna Payne Thornton, March 10, 1844, in Arthur G. Staples, ed., *The Letters of John Fairfield* (Lewiston, Me.: Lewiston Journal, 1922), 326.
2 Cited in Elisabeth McClellan, *History of American Costume* (New York: Tudor Publishing Co., 1937), 565.
3 YCRP; 29:260.

America by 1773, but home production was not eliminated. Women could choose which items to buy and which to continue to knit at home. Ann Smith recorded in the same diary entry that she had "Bought a neat knitt petticoat" and "finished my husband another pair of good woolen hose and began a third pair."[4] CSP

1 Cotton yarn was not commonly used for knitting until after the Revolution. Susan Burrows Swan, *A Winterthur Guide to American Needlework* (New York: Crown Publishers, 1976), 124.
2 Susan Burrows Swan, *Plain and Fancy: American Women and their Needlework, 1700–1850* (New York: Holt Rinehart and Winston, 1977), 12, 24; Sarah Anna Emery, *Reminiscences of a Nonogenarian* (1879), cited in Mirra Bank, *Anonymous was a Woman* (New York: St. Martin's Press, 1979), 42.
3 Abigail May, diary, MEHS.
4 Swan, *Winterthur Guide*, 124. Ann Smith, diary, March 16, 1807, MEHS. The entry for January 20, 1806, records that she was "Making my good man and self some flannel night caps," sewing rather than knitting.

159

Night cap
Possibly Saco, Maine, 1800–1821
Cotton
H 10⅛ (51.1); Circum. 17⅛ (43.5)
York Institute Museum

Like the linen shirt (cat. 158), this night cap came to the York Institute with a history of ownership by Thomas Cutts (cat. 33). It is cotton, knitted rather than woven.[1] Knitting was practiced in most American homes as a basic method of textile construction. It was particularly suitable for producing articles of clothing that needed to fit well and could, if necessary, be seamless (socks, stockings, mittens, gloves, and caps). Knitting was an adjunct of "plain" sewing, the construction of essential forms. All women had to do plain sewing or arrange to have it done for them. Girls, and often boys, learned at a young age to knit and thus contributed to the family's plain sewing. Female schools taught knitting and plain sewing in addition to ornamental forms of needlework.[2]

A technique based on interlocking loops of yarn, knitting required little in the way of equipment and because it was simple and mechanical in nature, it did not involve the knitter's total concentration. For the same reason, it was easy to work in dimly lit rooms and its portability allowed women to engage in conversation and still "improve" the time. Abigail May wrote that she and her aunt "spent a charming social afternoon talking over our excursion and at our needles."[3]

Commercial knitting machines were operating in

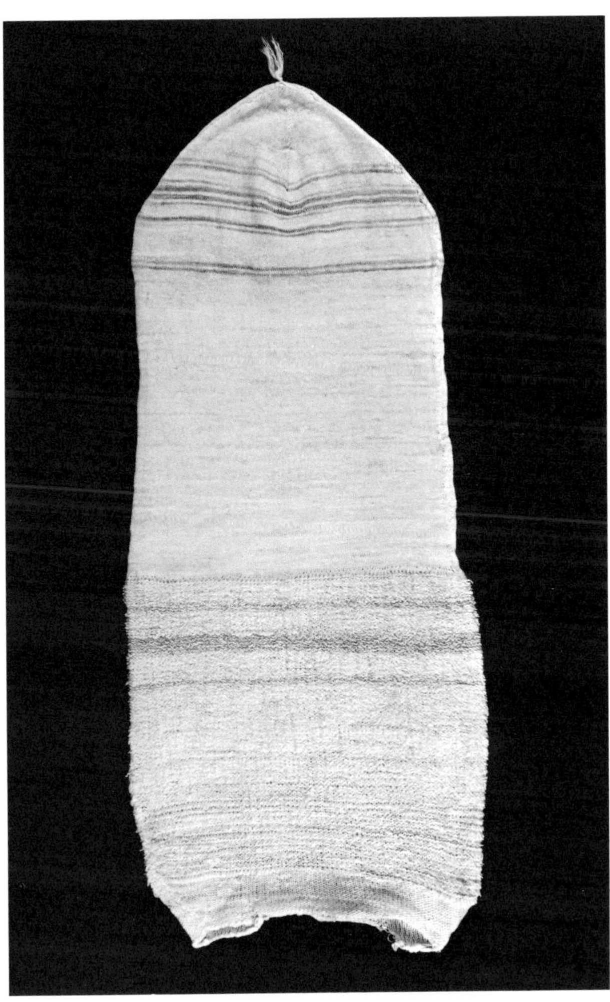

Cat. 159

Samuel Brimblecom (1767–1850)
Pair of dancing pumps
Lynn, Massachusetts, ca. 1820
Linen and leather uppers, linen lining and silk ties
Paper label (pasted to one insole) "SHO[ES]/ Made
and Warranted/ Samuel B[rim]blecom /LYNN"
L 10½ (27.0); W 2¹⁵⁄₁₆ (7.5)
Old York Historical Society

Pumps, flat thin shoes, were popular footwear for men and
women from 1790 to 1830. This is a particularly fancy man's
pair, as men generally wore pumps of black leather.[1] They
were owned by William W. Rollins.

The shaped uppers of the shoes are of white linen and
sage green leather; the top edge of the leather portion is
trimmed with a line of gold chain stitch, ending in an
embroidered bow at the toe. The pumps are lined with linen
and have silk ribbon ties. The flat leather soles are shaped for
the right and left foot, unlike the lady's silk slippers (cat. 173).
Right and left soles were developed in Philadelphia in 1800,
but were not used consistently until well into the nineteenth
century.[2]

These pumps were made at Lynn, Massachusetts, a city
known for high quality footwear since the 1670s. The
shoemaker, Colonel Samuel Brimblecom, was one of the two
principal shoe manufacturers in Lynn in 1800, and through
the first decades of the nineteenth century, he made advances
in the shoemaking process. "Before his time the whole trade
was so loosely conducted that few realized anything beyond a
bare maintenance from unremitted toil and perplexity; but
many of his suggestions tended greatly to systematize the
business and render it profitable."[3] KAO

1 Doreen Yarwood, *Costume of the Western World* (New York: St. Martin's
  Press, 1980).
2 Alice Morse Earle, *Customs and Fashions in Old New England* (1893;
  reprint, Rutland, Vt.: Charles E. Tuttle and Co., 1980), 756.
3 Alonzo Lewis and James R. Newhall, *History of Lynn, 1629–1864*
  (Lynn, Mass.: George C. Herbert), 91, 424.

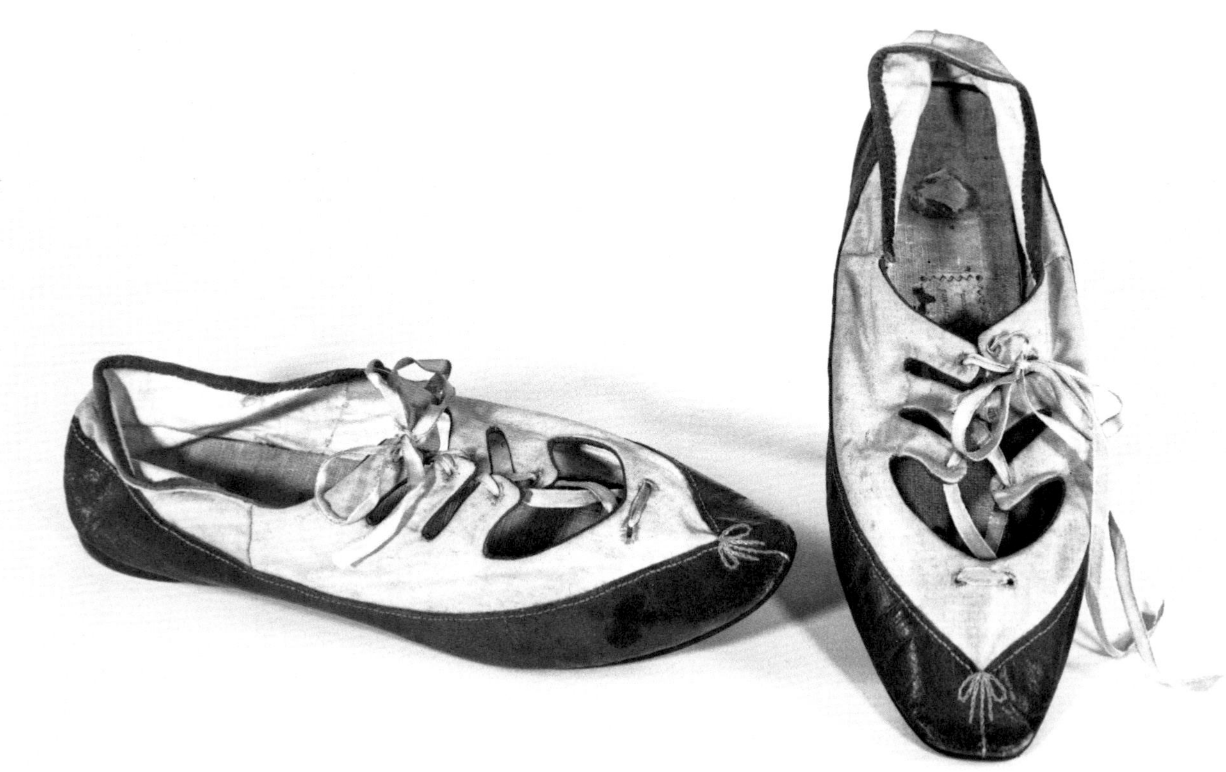

Cat. 160

161

Cloak and hood
Probably Saco, Maine, 1780–1800
Wool, silk binding
H 48⅜ (124.0); Circum. hem 209 (535.8);
H hood 17½ (44.9); L neckband 15½ (39.8)
York Institute Museum; Gift of Mrs. Robert M. Lord

Wool cloaks were worn by both men and women during the eighteenth century. The popular scarlet models were called "cardinals" because of their resemblance to ecclesiastical garb. Women's versions were also known as "red riding hoods" and "French hoods."[1]

This unlined cloak of dense red wool broadcloth is gathered into a rounded standing collar. A capelet is attached at the shoulders, scalloped around the sides and ending in a point at the center back. The collar, bottom edge of the capelet, and front opening of the cloak are bound with narrow red silk cording. An unlined hood of the same fabric is shaped with concentric pleats at the back. The neckband, faced with maroon silk satin, is sewn to a circular flounce. The hood could be gathered around the face with a linen drawstring.

Tradition links this cloak with Parson John Fairfield (1737–1819), first minister of the First Congregational Church of Saco. A graduate of Harvard College in 1757, Fairfield "got along unusually well with his parishioners, among whom he moved, a fair, blue-eyed man, customarily wearing a prominent red cloak."[2] Though worn by ministers, red cloaks, particularly hooded ones, were worn more frequently by women. The length and small shoulder size of this example suggest that it belonged to a woman, possibly a member of the Fairfield family.

Cloaks, mantles, coats, riding habits, and pelisses were indispensable outergarments for both men and women braving the cold Maine winters. In a letter to her mother in 1797, Eliza Southgate requested a loose, belted coat, and said she was unprepared for a trip to Wiscasset, Maine, in 1800: "I shall go by horseback,—how I wish I had my habit."[3] In 1822 George Wallingford of Kennebunk wrote to his daughter, Abigail (cat. 41), in Eastport, Maine: "Your Uncle you say is going to Boston and you want a new garment—what has become of your *grand mothers red cloak*—is *not that Smart enought* for Quoddy [Eastport]."[4] Perhaps Abigail shared the sentiments of this early nineteenth-century fashion editor:

Red cloaks are at length completely abandoned, and we congratulate our lovely readers on their emancipation from the most despotic dress that ever was introduced by the whimsical and arbitrary goddess of fashion. The writer of this article predicted, on their first appearance, that a color so disadvantageous to beauty could never become prevalent.[5]   KAO

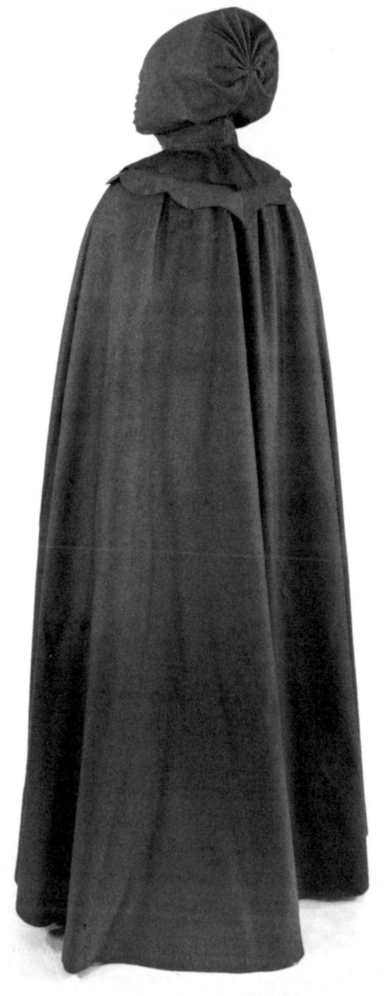

Cat. 161

1 Ruth Turner Wilcox, *The Mode in Hats and Headdress* (New York: Charles S. Scribner's Sons, 1945), 157; see also Jane C. Nylander, "Hooded Cloak," *The Great River*, 387–388.
2 Clifford K. Shipton, *Biographical Sketches of Those Who Attended Harvard College in the Classes 1756–1760 with Bibliographical and Other Notes*, Sibley's Harvard Graduates, vol. 14 (Boston: Massachusetts Historical Society, 1968), 159.
3 Bowne, *A Girl's Life*, 11, 28.
4 George Wallingford to Abigail Wallingford, March 13, 1822, Wallingford Papers, BSM.
5 Quoted in Elisabeth McClellan, *Historic Dress in America* (Philadelphia: George W. Jacobs & Co., 1910), 83–84.

162

Dress and petticoat (back)
Possibly Portland, Maine, 1775–1785
Silk brocade, bodice lined with linen;
alterations to sleeves, bodice, and petticoat
H 56½ (143.5); L skirt 44 (111.8); Circum.
waist 26 (66.0); Circum. skirt hem 130¼ (330.8);
w fabric 17 (43.2)
Maine Historical Society; Gift of Martha Pike Conant, 1925

In the 1770s and 1780s, figured silks were popular fabrics for
fancy dresses. The large patterns of silk brocades lent
themselves well to the voluminous skirts and petticoats of the
period. The brocade of this dress, probably Continental in
origin, features orange and maroon flowers, and white and
green leaves on a bright bottle-green ground. The dress is an
"open gown" typical of the 1770s, with a fitted bodice,

three-quarter sleeves, and a half skirt pleated into the back of
the bodice. A matching petticoat was worn under the dress,
though many open gowns were worn with petticoats of
contrasting fabric.[1] The bodice has a square neckline and a
front closure; shaped seams in the back join in a point below
the waistline. The brocade flounces on the sleeves were
probably added in 1825; in the eighteenth century detachable lace or embroidered ruffles would have been worn.

Women wore elaborate foundations to straighten the
torso and contract the waist when wearing this style. Many
open gowns were boned along the bodice seams. Stays of
heavy linen stiffened with boning, busks of bone, or wood
were also worn. Hip pads, cushions, and heavy petticoats
made the sides and backs of skirts full.

According to the donor, the dress was worn by a member
of the Jewett family in 1825, to "a ball" held in honor of the
Marquis de Lafayette during his visit to Portland.[2] The
"ball" may have been a reception held at Daniel Cobb's
house or a social call Lafayette made on Portland ladies at
the Ebenezer Thatcher residence.[3] The dress would have
been at least fifty years old at the time, and was probably
already considered a family heirloom. To wear such a dress
during the festivities for the Revolutionary War hero may be
considered a very early expression of the colonial revival
spirit, a fascination with history and "colonial curiosities"
which was to consume the nation fifty years later during the
Centennial in 1876.   KAO

1 The petticoat is pieced together and has been cut and sewn to the
  dress so that it opens in the front. It was probably remade ca. 1825.
2 Martha Pike Conant, a Jewett descendant, to MEHS, 1924, accession
  records, MEHS.
3 *Eastern Argus* (June 27, 1825); Lafayette was in Portland June 25 and
  26; see cat. 128 for other material relating to Lafayette's visit.

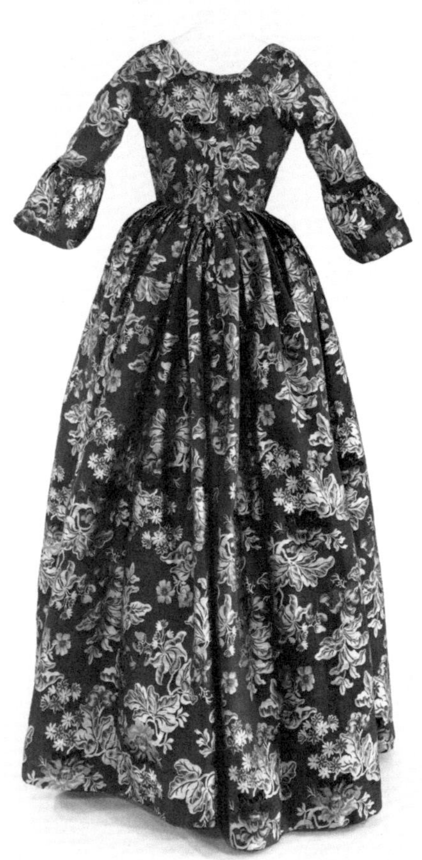

Cat. 162

163

Probably by Sarah Cutts Thornton (1774–1845)
Shift
Saco, Maine, 1790–1795
Linen
Marked (center front neckline) "SC / 10" in brown linen
H 34½ (87.0); Circum. hem 71 (180.3); w fabric 30 (76.2)
York Institute Museum

Of the garments featured in this volume, the most basic and
universally worn by women of all walks of life was the linen
shift. For centuries this was the standard body covering for
women, serving as an undergarment and sleeping gown as
well. The shift was worn under dresses or short gowns;
longer sleeved examples were worn with sleeveless waistcoats.
Ball gowns often had individual shifts or slips constructed

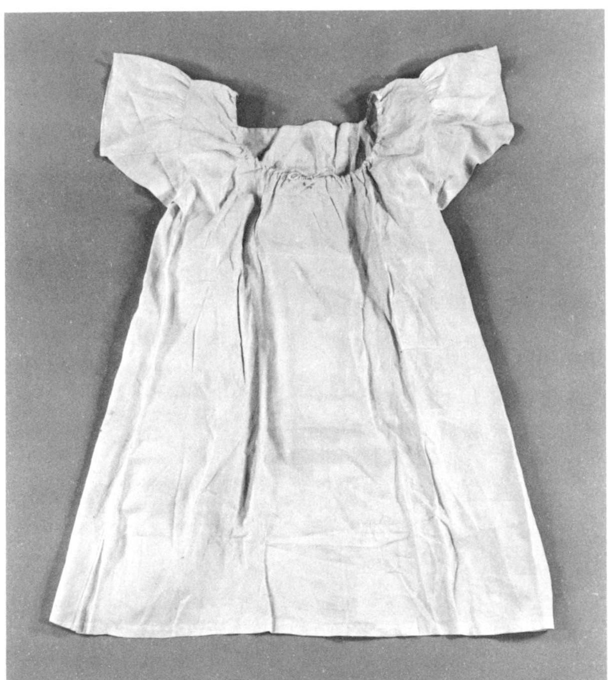

Cat. 163

especially for them. Stays, corsets, bustles, buns, and
petticoats were worn over the shift to create the preferred
silhouette for outerwear.

Made of linen, the most readily available locally produced material, this shift is typical of those made in the
eighteenth century. It is carefully sewn but unembellished,
save Sarah Cutts's initials, cross-stitched at the neckline in
brown linen.[1] The construction is simple and economical.
The full thirty-inch width of the linen was used, and the
calculated piecing of the square and triangular gussets at the
sleeves and sides left no fabric to waste (see cat. 158).

Sarah Cutts's shift is no different than one which may
have been worn by a farm girl or the wife of a struggling
fisherman. It is the cross-stitched numeral "10" beneath her
initials, however, that reveals her station because it indicates
that Sarah owned at least that number of shifts; women of
lesser means would undoubtedly have owned fewer.

Shifts, eventually known as chemises, were worn throughout the nineteenth century. After about 1840, however, they
were more commonly made of cotton, as it supplanted linen
as the least expensive fabric. Mid-nineteenth-century
chemises were often elaborately decorated with ruffles,
ribbons, tucks, and whitework embroidery, as the fancy
embellishment of undergarments became increasingly
fashionable.[2] KAO

1 Marking bed linens, undergarments, and stockings was a common
   practice, often the task of young girls who had mastered their lettering

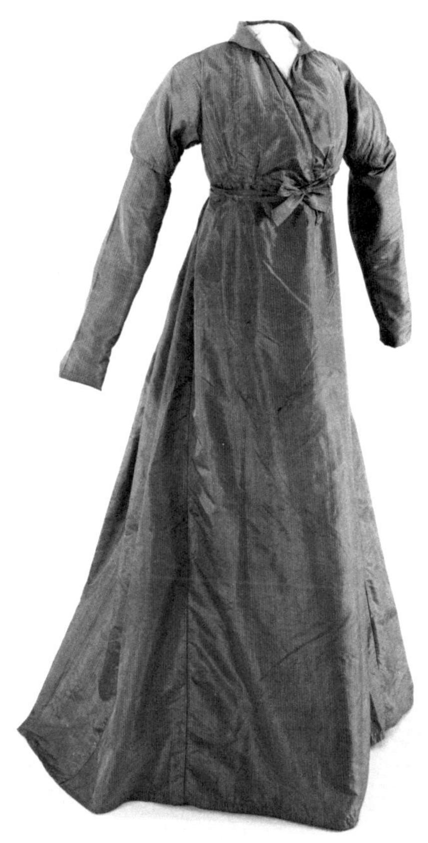

Cat. 164

skills by working samplers; Susan Burrows Swan, *Plain and Fancy:
American Women and Their Needlework, 1700–1850* (New York: Holt
Rinehart, and Winston, 1977), 52.
2 An example of a linen shift ca. 1830 is at YIS.

164

Dress
Possibly Biddeford, Maine, 1790–1810
Silk, bodice and oversleeves lined with linen
H 60 (152.4); L skirt front 44½ (113.0); L skirt
back 48¼ (122.6); Circum. original waist 25 (63.5);
Circum. hem 98 (248.9); W fabric 26 (66.0)
The Brick Store Museum; William E. Barry estate
through Edith Cleaves Barry, 1936

This dress of blue-gray and brown striped silk represents the
transitional period in women's fashions at the end of the
eighteenth century. The shaped waistlines of the open gowns
of the 1770s (see cat. 162) were replaced in the 1780s by
round gowns with natural waistlines and long fitted sleeves.

In the next decade, the waists were worn a bit higher, fitted around the rib cage. Silver-gray, mauve, beige, taupe, and blue were popular colors for dresses of this style made of silk. Plain or printed cotton calicoes were used for day dresses. Fichus, or neckerchiefs, which had been worn puffed over the bosom in the 1780s, were now less overstated, wrapped simply around the neck (see cat. 35). Narrower skirts required fewer hip cushions, and petticoats and trains became popular. Dress in the mid 1790s was less studied and formal, and more comfortable, as women shed some of the stays that they needed to squeeze into the gowns of the 1770s. By the 1800s, the style became more exaggerated, with very high waists, sheer fabrics, and virtually no foundations (see cat. 165).

Like many dresses of the 1790s, this example has a high shawl collar and a wrapped front closure. The linen lining is sewn to the back of the bodice but closes separately in the front. The long sleeves are capped with short lined over-sleeves, similar to those described by Eliza Southgate Bowne in 1803: "I am very glad you like your gown. Long sleeves are very much worn, made like mitts; crosswise, only one seam and that in the back of the arms, and a half drawn sleeve over and a close, very short one up high drawn up with a cord."[1] Typical of the period, the sleeves are cut deeply into the shoulders and back of the bodice. The skirt, which has a short train, is gathered into the bodice at the center back. The skirt closure is formed by a slit at either side of the gathered gores, joined to the bodice with buttons. Ties of silk, sewn to the back, are wrapped around the front and tied.

The dress was probably owned by a member of the Cleaves family of Biddeford. Its construction and lack of fancy pipings and trims would suggest that it was of home manufacture. A fragment of a similar silk fabric of green and taupe stripes descended to Edith Barry with a note that it was from a dress owned by Abigail Cleaves, Daniel's sister. These silks were the type of fabric that Cleaves could have imported and illustrate the variety available for sale in Maine. KAO

1 Bowne, *A Girl's Life*, 167.

165

Possibly by Lucia Wadsworth (1783–1864)
Assembly dress
Portland, Maine, ca. 1799
Cotton muslin, embroidered with cotton; bodice lined with linen; muslin shift
H 75¼ (191.1); L skirt front 44½ (113.0);
L skirt back 69½ (176.5); Circum. original waist 30 (76.2);
Circum. hem 132½ (336.6); W fabric 50 (127.0)
Maine Historical Society; Wadsworth-Longfellow House

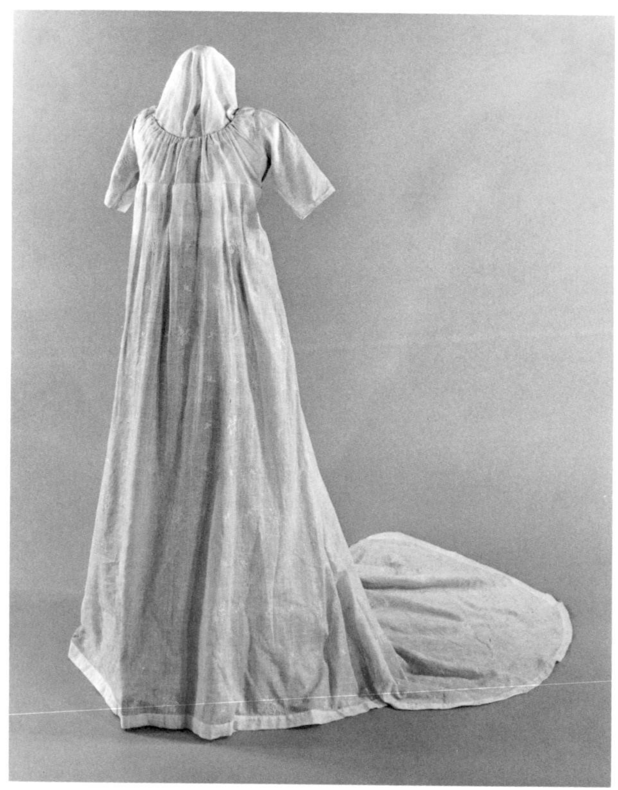

Cat. 165

Such was the advice of Lord Chesterfield in 1786. Chances are that he would not have approved of Lucia Wadsworth's transparent muslin dress, which she wore to an assembly in 1799. Lucia was following the latest fashion, imported from England and France, and inspired by the slender clinging gowns of Greek statuary. Classical dress at the turn of the century represented a radical break from tradition. Young girls cast off the heavy brocades, boning, and foundations of eighteenth-century apparel in favor of diaphanous sheaths in white or pastel shades. Older women continued to dress in the previous style; Elizabeth Scamman Cutts wore a dark, long-waisted, long-sleeved gown with a handkerchief when John Brewster, Jr., painted her portrait about 1800 (cat. 33). Eliza Southgate described a Mrs. Lowell of Bath, Maine, in 1800 as "a fine ladylike woman, yet her manners are such as would have been admired fifty years ago, there is too much appearance of whalebone and buckram to please the depraved taste of the present age."[2]

Lucia would not have been unusually dressed among the girls of her own generation, however. Plain and figured muslins were sold everywhere. There are numerous references to girls in Maine sporting muslin gowns, among them Eliza Southgate, who wrote anxiously in 1800: "so long a visit in Wiscasset [Maine] will oblige me to muster all my muslins, for I am informed they are so monstrous smart as to take no notice of any lady that can condescend to wear a calico gown, therefore, dear mother, to ensure me a favorable reception, pray send my spotted muslin by the next mail."[3]

Lucia's dress is of fine white cotton imported from India and embroidered with white floral sprays in the delicate chain stitch of tambour work. The extremely high waist, low neckline, and straight skirt pleated at the back with a train created a long, narrow silhouette. The bodice is lined with linen; a thin, plain muslin shift which now accompanies the dress may have been the original undergarment. A petticoat was also probably worn under the dress.   KAO

1 Lord Chesterfield, with additions by the Reverend Dr. John Trusler, *Principles of Politeness and of Knowing the World* (Portsmouth, N.H.: Melcher and Osborne, 1786), 113–114.
2 Bowne, *A Girl's Life*, 33.
3 Bowne, *A Girl's Life*, 28.

166

Dress
Probably Saco, Maine, ca 1815
Silk, bodice lined with linen; silk ribbon trim
H 53½ (135.9); L skirt 46 (116.8); Circum. altered
waist 28 (71.1); Circum. hem 81⅛ (208.0);
W fabric 29½ (74.9)
York Institute Museum

Immediately on the receipt of the gratifying news of Peace, the Inhabitants of Kennebunk and Kennebunkport assembled as if were by instinct — the Bell rang, the Cannon roared, Flags were displayed and Huzzars rent the welkin. In the evening Washington Hall and several other buildings were illuminated.[1]

News of the peace negotiated at Ghent in 1814, marking the end of the War of 1812, inspired celebration throughout the nation and gave hope to those families whose privateer men where still incarcerated in dreaded Dartmoor prison. Locally, a Peace Ball was organized in Kennebunk in February 1815.[2] The residents of Saco celebrated with a Peace Ball at Cleaves Tavern on the first of April 1815. For that event, Hannah Scamman Tucker, wife of merchant Jonathan Tucker, wore this dress of oyster-colored silk twill.

The high-waisted dress has a round collar, underlined in fine taupe silk, and a front bodice closure, caught with hooks and eyes on silk tape.[3] The collar, closure, and cuffs are trimmed with ruched white silk ribbon. The skirt, with side gores, has extra fullness at the back, in the fashionable shape of the day. The bottom of the skirt is decorated with an elaborate border of silk threads, woven into the fabric in a tree-and-shell motif. The hemline trim, of pieced silk ribbons box-pleated like the bodice trim, may not be original.

Another dress, of nearly identical design, but in yellow silk, was owned during the same period by Sarah Cutts Thornton (cat. 36), also of Saco, thus suggesting that both dresses were made locally. It was evidently not unusual for more than one lady to appear in the same popular dress pattern. Eliza Southgate Bowne often remarked about trading cherished patterns in her letters, and in 1796 Abigail May wrote:

Engaged to General W[adsworth]'s we assembled to the number of thirty had a charming visit. Matty [Robison] has got a fine theme for pestering me; Prentiss (she says,) mistook her for me (our dresses were

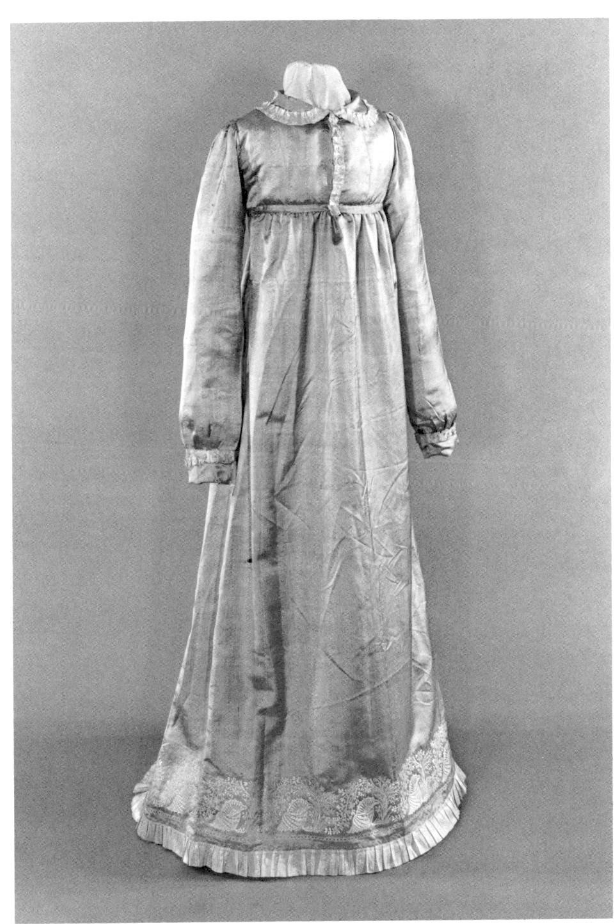

Cat. 166

1 *Weekly Visiter* (February 18, 1815).
2 *Weekly Visiter* (February 18, 1815).
3 The bodice has been made smaller.
4 The dress is at the Maine State Museum; Bowne, *A Girl's Life*, 10, 11, 2. Abigail May, diary, 1796, MEHS.

167

Dress
Possibly Biddeford, Maine, 1815–1820
Silk gauze; silk satin appliqué
H 47¼ (120.0); L skirt 39 (99.1); Circum.
original waist 21 (53.3); Circum. hem 80 (203.2)
The Brick Store Museum; William E. Barry estate
through Edith Cleaves Barry, 1936
Color plate on page 256

The beauty of many early nineteenth-century dresses lies in their simple form and meticulous surface design. This high-waisted dress is made of delicate, transparent pea-green silk gauze. The unstructured bodice has a shallow, rounded neckline, short sleeves, slightly gathered at the shoulders, and a simple back opening which would have been fastened at the neck and waistline. The narrow, straight skirt is gathered to the bodice, with more fullness at the center back. Edith Barry added a white linen lining to the skirt. Originally, the sheer dress was probably worn over a silk slip of the same color.

The dress is embellished with pale pink silk satin piping, in meandering lines on the bodice front and around the back neckline. Petal-like sprays appliquéd to the bodice and sleeves are formed of looped piping and buttons covered with coiled pink thread. Thicker corded *roleaux* and piped pink satin leaves are applied to the skirt border.

Trimming gauze or net dresses with piping and piped shapes, often flowers decorated with pearls and beads, became popular after about 1815.[1] Mrs. Bell, the famous London couturiere, exported her ideas in *Bells' Court and Fashionable Magazine* from 1806 until 1832. In 1820 she described new ball dresses, including one "of fine white net over white satin . . . finished by two flounces of net, richly embossed with fancy flowers and foliage in white satin."[2]

This green gauze dress was worn by Sarah Cleaves (b. 1799) of Biddeford, probably to a ball or an assembly, where young ladies, "elegantly dressed," drew lots for dances with beaux.[3] Sarah may have worn silk or kid elbow-length gloves with her dress, and flat slippers, perhaps of pink kid. She may have worn a scarf or shawl, and carried an indispensable

or reticule, the small drawstring handbags which became fashionable in the early nineteenth century, when skirts were too narrow for pockets to be worn under dresses.   KAO

1 Talbot Hughes, *Dress Design: An Account of Costume for Artists and Dressmakers* (London: Sir Isaac Pitman and Sons, Ltd., 1913), 238.
2 Cited in Elisabeth McClellan, *Historic Dress in America, 1800–1870* (Philadelphia: George W. Jacobs and Co., 1910), 141.
3 For descriptions of assemblies in Maine, see Abigail May, diary, 1796, MEHS, and Bowne, *A Girl's Life*, 20–21, 23, 27.

168

Embroidered by Mary Cleaves (1803–1871)
Dress
Biddeford, Maine, or Dorchester, Massachusetts, 1818–1820
Silk with cotton embroidery, cotton lining, linen waistband
H 49 (124.5); L skirt 41 (104.1); Circum. original waist 19 (48.3); Circum. hem 80 (203.2)
The Brick Store Museum; William E. Barry estate through Edith Cleaves Barry, 1936

This high-waisted dress is fashioned in the style of transparent muslin gowns (see cat. 165), but is made of fine, soft white silk. The bodice is of simple construction with a shallow rounded neckline and a plain closure at the center back, fastened with flat brass hooks.[1] The long sleeves are gathered at the shoulder and narrow cuffs. The gored skirt is slightly gathered at the center front and more fully at the back. The most striking feature of the gown is the openwork embroidery, worked in white cotton on the bodice, cuffs, and skirt. The flowered vine pattern on the bodice cleverly conceals the darts; the neckline is trimmed with a thin silk border, scalloped and embroidered. More elaborate openwork in floral motifs embellishes the shaped border of the hemline.

Family tradition maintains that the dress was embroidered by Mary Cleaves of Biddeford. Mary no doubt learned her fancy needlework skills while she was a student at Mrs. Saunders's and Miss Beach's Academy, a boarding school for girls in Dorchester, Massachusetts. The preceptresses, two ladies from Gloucester, Massachusetts, established their school in 1803 and held classes for more than thirty years in the Boston area. The curriculum included: "Reading, Writing, English Grammar, Arithmetic, Plain Sewing, Embroidery, Tambour, French Language, Painting, Geography, including the use of Globes," as well as dancing and music.[2]

Mary may have made the dress at home or while at the academy, perhaps for her older sister, Sarah, who married

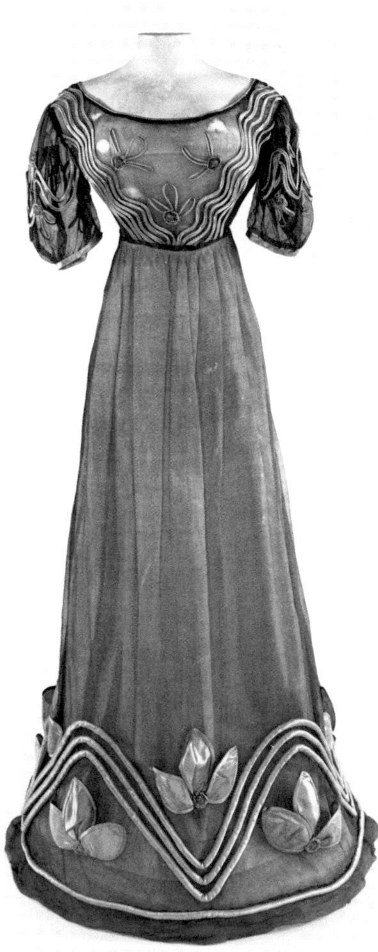

Cat. 167

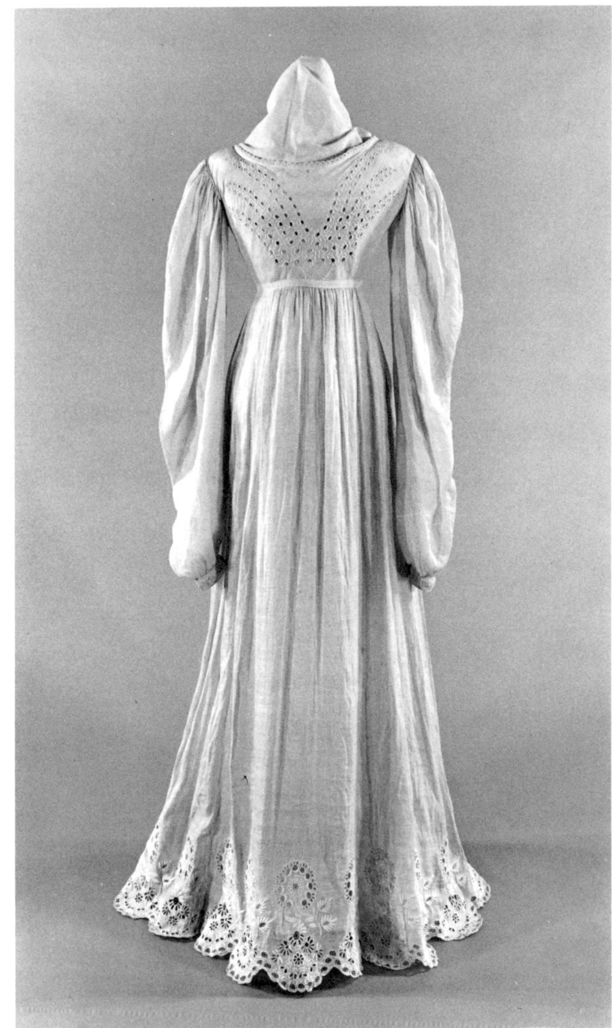

Cat. 168

William Lord of Kennebunk in 1820. In 1818 she wrote to her sister, Sarah, "Please tell Mama that if she wishes me very much to attend to Needlework I can do it, as all kinds of fine work are taught here. Much attention is paid to the Solid as well as the Ornamental Branches."[3] Indeed, a substantial group of fine silk needlework pictures survives, wrought by the students of Mrs. Saunders and Miss Beach.

Like many daughters of coastal Maine's wealthy citizens, Mary was sent to Boston as a teenager to study academics and learn the "accomplishments" of a genteel lady. Betsy Sewall of York attended an academy in Newton, Massachusetts, where she embroidered a sophisticated mourning picture (cat. 132), and Eliza Southgate of Scarborough became "an Accomplished Miss" under the tutelage of the famous Mrs. Rowson of Boston, of whom she wrote in 1798:

I am again placed at school under the tuition of an amiable lady, so mild, so good, no one can help loving her; she treats all her scholars with such a tenderness as would win the affection of the most savage brute. . . . I learn Embroidery and Geography at present and wish your permission to learn Musick.[4]   KAO & KDM

1 The brass hooks may be original since such fasteners came into use in the 1820s; see Naomi Tarrant, *Collecting Costume* (London: George Allen and Urwin, 1983), 90.
2 Betty Ring, "Mrs. Saunders' and Miss Beach's Academy, Dorchester," *Antiques* 110, no. 2 (August 1976): 302–312.
3 Mary Cleaves to Sarah Cleaves, July 17, 1818, William Lord Papers, BSM.
4 Bowne, *A Girl's Life*, 13, 16.

169

Dress
Possibly Biddeford, Maine, 1820–1825
Silk, cotton and linen lining, silk gauze trim
H pelisse 44 (111.8); L skirt 39½ (100.3); Circum.
pelisse waist 22 (55.9); Circum. skirt hem 98 (248.9)
The Brick Store Museum; William E. Barry estate
through Edith Cleaves Barry, 1936

This three-piece ensemble of thin aqua silk, worn by Mary
Cleaves, is a fine example of a fancy dress of the early 1820s.
The dress has a very small, high-waisted bodice and separate
skirt. [1] The bodice, lined with muslin, has a shallow v-neck-
line edged with lace. Tufts of silk trimmed with net form
small cap sleeves over the top of the armholes. The narrow

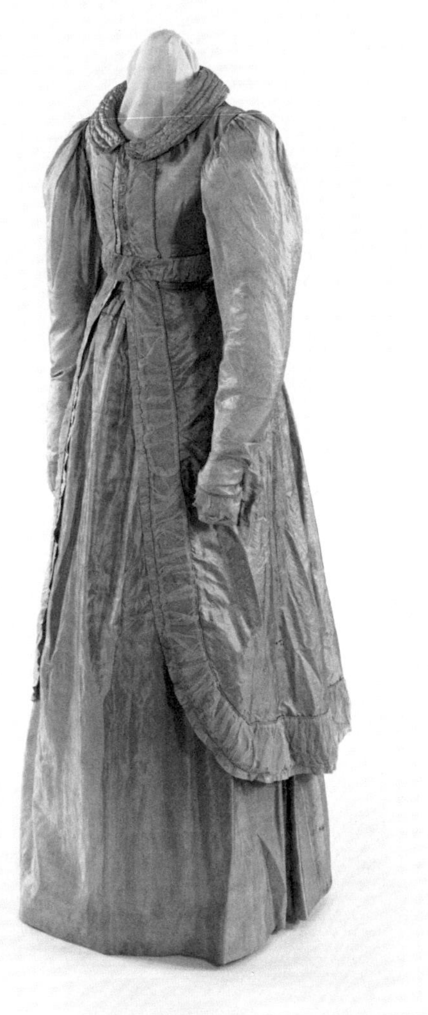

Cat. 169

waistband is lined with linen. The gored skirt with a full hem
is gathered only in the back.

The matching pelisse, a below-the-knee jacket, is
carefully constructed. With a lower waistline than the dress,
the bodice of the pelisse has a high neck and rounded collar
trimmed with decorative topstitching and with silk piping.
The collar is lined with gathered white silk gauze. To either
side of the front opening are bands of gathered gauze edged
with piping. This trim is also applied to the waistband, cuffs,
and shaped hem of the pelisse skirt. The long sleeves are full
at the shoulders and fitted at the cuffs, *en gigot*, a term used
by French fashion editors to describe the leg-of-mutton
sleeves which would become such an exaggerated feature of
dresses in the 1830s.

The fitted bodices of the 1820s demanded the return of
the corsets and stays which had been abandoned by young
women twenty years earlier. Such apparatus of feminine
vanity met with considerable ridicule in the newspapers. A
notice in the *Eastern Argus* described Russian officers in
France who "wear Corsets, 'to make their waists as small as
possible!'—we mention this for the consolation of the
AMERICAN FAIR who use these uncomfortable and unhealthy
machines—as 'misery loves company.'" Health was indeed
an issue; the *Argus* also related the "melancholy event" in
which a fifteen-year-old girl from Boston collapsed and
expired while dancing. "This distressing event is supposed to
have been occasinned [*sic*] by the tightness of her dress. It
cannot fail of inspiring a salutary caution against the excess
of a too prevalent fashion."[2]   KAO

1 The dress has been extensively altered, patched, and taken in. Some
  of the netting on the sleeves has been replaced. A coarse linen lining
  was added to the skirt by Miss Barry.
2 *Eastern Argus* (January 3, 1816; December 5, 1815).

170

"A French Modiste"
Dress (back)
New York City, 1822
Silk, bodice and upper sleeves lined with fine linen,
silk appliqué, silk cord trim
H 51¾ (131.4); L skirt 42⅝ (108.3); Circum.
altered waist 26 (66.0); Circum. hem 90¾ (230.5);
w fabric 23 (58.4)
Maine Historical Society; Wadsworth-Longfellow House

Members of well-to-do families in Maine had the mobility
and the means to purchase clothing in large urban centers
such as Boston or New York. In the 1790s Zilpah Wadsworth
wrote her father requesting that he bring dresses from Boston
for her and her sisters. A cousin in Boston was dispatched to

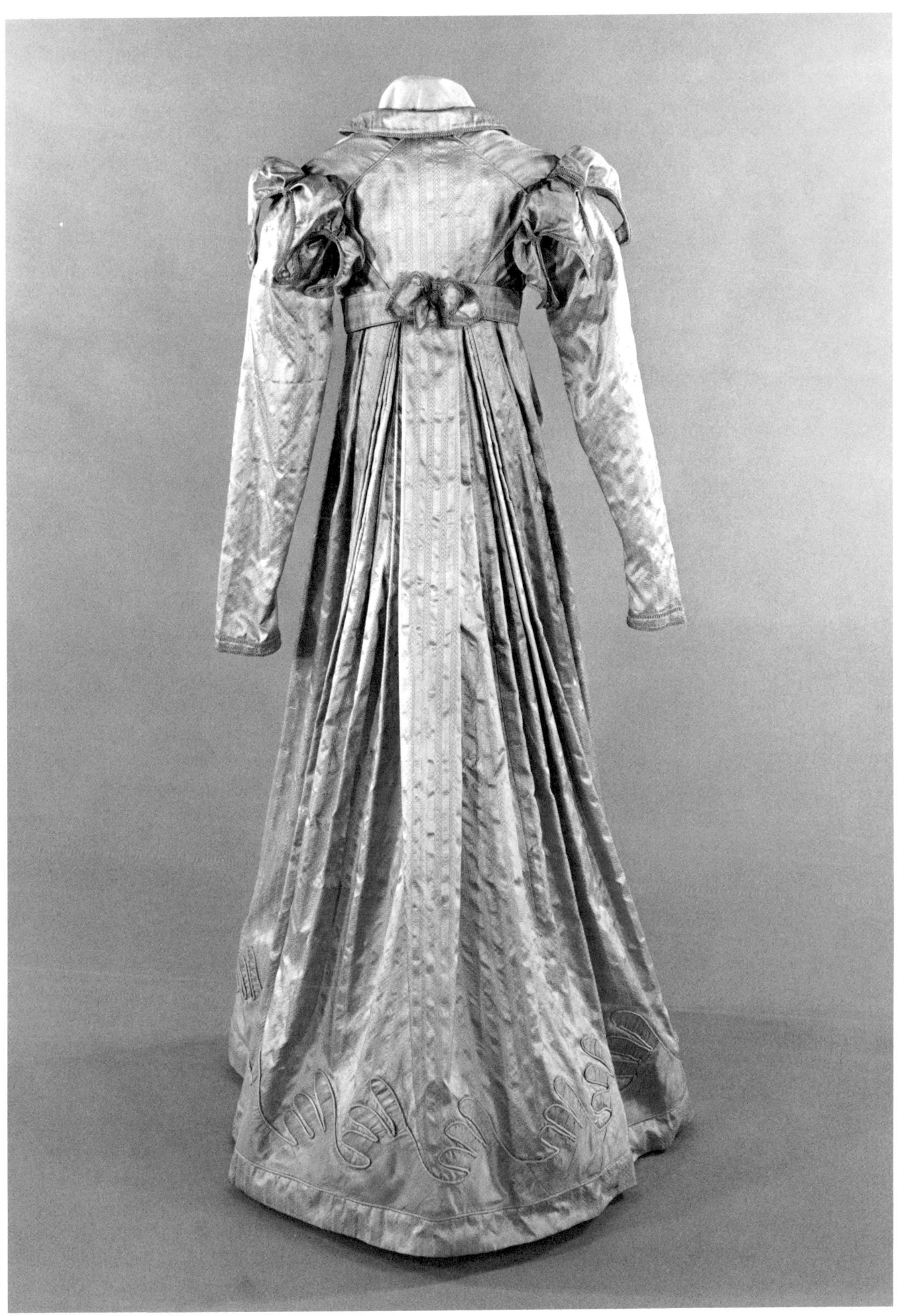

Cat. 170

aid in their selection. Eliza Southgate Bowne wrote from New York to her sister in Scarborough in 1803: "I have a mantua-maker here making you a gown which I hope to have finished to send by Mrs. Rodman." Ann Bryant Smith of Portland had gowns made while on a shopping trip to Boston in 1806.[1]

In the spring of 1822 Zilpah's husband, Stephen Longfellow, became ill. To hasten his recuperation, the couple made a trip to New Haven and several locations in New York, including "the Springs."[2] During that sojourn Zilpah purchased this silk dress, made by "A French Modiste," a professional dress designer and seamstress who made gowns, coats, riding habits, and possibly millinery.[3]

This dress is of the latest style for the 1820s, with a high neckline, longer waistline, and fuller skirt than dresses made a decade earlier. The fabric is a fine figured silk originally a pale pink-lilac hue, but now faded to silver-gray. The fitted bodice has a plain front closure with a round collar and a piped belt of the same fabric. The long sleeves are capped with *mancherons*, gathered and shaped oversleeves which were popular during the period.[4] The collar, *mancherons*, and cuffs are edged with coiled beige silk cording. The skirt, fastened with a drawstring, is made full at the back with four deep double pleats. A border of beige silk is appliquéd in a wave pattern at the hemline.   KAO

1 Zilpah Wadworth to Nancy Doane, letter journal, November 18, 1796, Wadsworth-Longfellow Papers, LNHS. Bowne, *A Girl's Life*, 157; Ann Smith, diary, MEHS.
2 Zilpah Longfellow to Lucia Wadsworth, June 28, 1822, Wadsworth-Longfellow Papers, LNHS. Joyce Butler kindly brought the Longfellow references to my attention.
3 Charlotte Green, a Portland mantua maker, advertised fabrics, trimmings and cords, hats, and bonnets in the *Eastern Argus* (February 5, 1807).
4 *Mancherons* shaped in three strawberry leaves and trimmed with lace are described in an excerpt from the fashion magazine *La Belle Assemblée*, in "London Female Fashions," *Eastern Argus* (September 28, 1827).

171

Dress
Possibly Biddeford, Maine, or Boston, Massachusetts, 1825–1835
Silk satin, linen lining
L skirt 39⅝ (100.6); Circum. altered waist 21 (53.3);
Circum. hem 88 (233.5); w fabric 19 (48.3)
The Brick Store Museum; William E. Barry estate through Edith Cleaves Barry, 1936

Through the 1820s, women's dresses became more fitted and skirts and sleeves fuller. By the 1830s, the natural waistline returned in day dresses, but many fancy dresses were still

high-waisted in the Empire style. The most prominent characteristic of this decade was the shoulder line. Wide, shallow necklines and pronounced shoulders extending over full sleeves created a broad, sloping silhouette which would remain popular into the early 1840s.

This elegant two-piece dress of ivory silk satin has a bias-cut bodice, lined in linen, with a bateau neckline trimmed with three layers of bias pleats. Diagonal pleated bands laid over the bodice from the center of the waistband to the shoulders accentuate the width of the shoulder line. Narrow loops of folded satin join the neckband and sleeve caps. The deeply gathered sleeves are lined with stiffened linen to maintain a wide, full shape. The armbands are trimmed with bows of satin. The piped belt has a large satin bow applied at the center back.

The separate, gored skirt is straight in the front and gathered at the center back. The skirt has been remade, probably when Edith Barry added a linen lining in the early twentieth century. One or more petticoats were probably worn under the skirts to broaden the hemline.

The dress was worn by Almira Cleaves (1806–1872) of Biddeford. She probably had the dress hemmed just above the ankle and wore flat, square-toed slippers of silk or kid (cat. 173). The dress may have been brought to Almira from Boston, or made by a dressmaker in Biddeford. In 1818, Sarah Cleaves wrote to her daughter Almira in Danvers, "you may have a new gown[.] ask your aunt to get you one and I will satisfye her for her trouble." Local merchants, such as William Lord of Kennebunk, carried fancy yard goods including silks, sinshaws, crapes, and sarsnets.[2]   KAO

1 A similar dress, with a diagonally pleated bodice and full sleeves, is illustrated in an 1820s lithograph reproduced in Elizabeth Sage, *A Study of Costume* (New York: Charles S. Scribner's Sons, 1926), 178.
2 Sarah Cleaves to Almira Cleaves, August 6, 1818, facsimile, William Lord Papers, BSM. *Weekly Visiter* (April 21, 1821).

172

Probably by Ruth Sewall Putnam (1791–1860)
Dress
York, Maine, ca. 1827
Silk, bodice and hemline lined with linen
H 49⅞ (126.7); L skirt 39⅝ (100.6);
Circum. altered waist 30 (76.2); Circum. hem 90⅛ (228.9);
w fabric 20¼ (51.4)
Old York Historical Society; Gift of Ruth Moore

This high-waisted gown of pattern-woven ivory silk is simple and unsophisticated in design. It was most likely of home manufacture rather than the work of a professional dressmaker. The shallow, square neckline of the dress is edged in piping and the bodice is gathered into the neckband

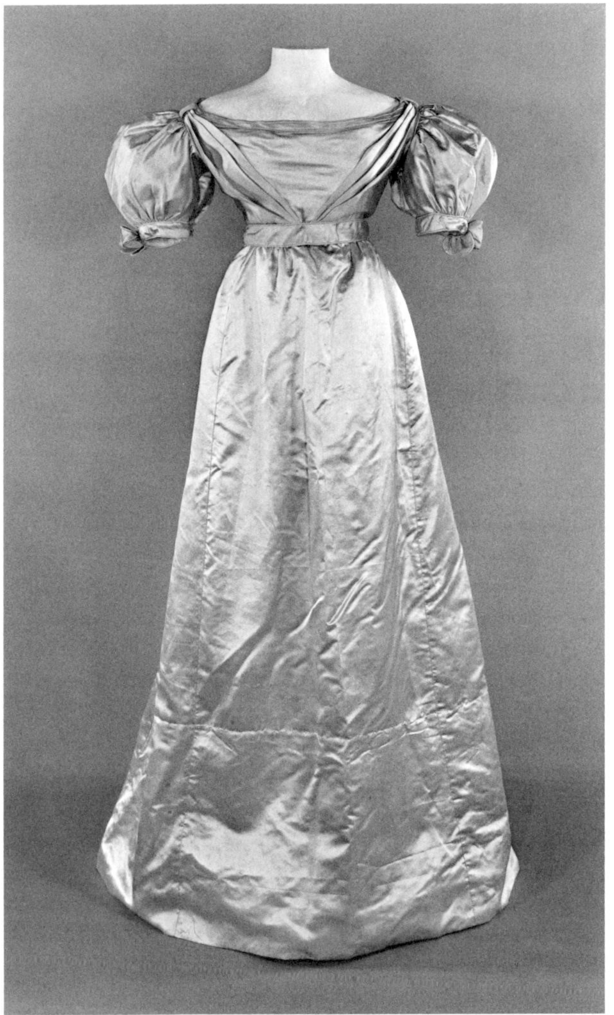

Cat. 171

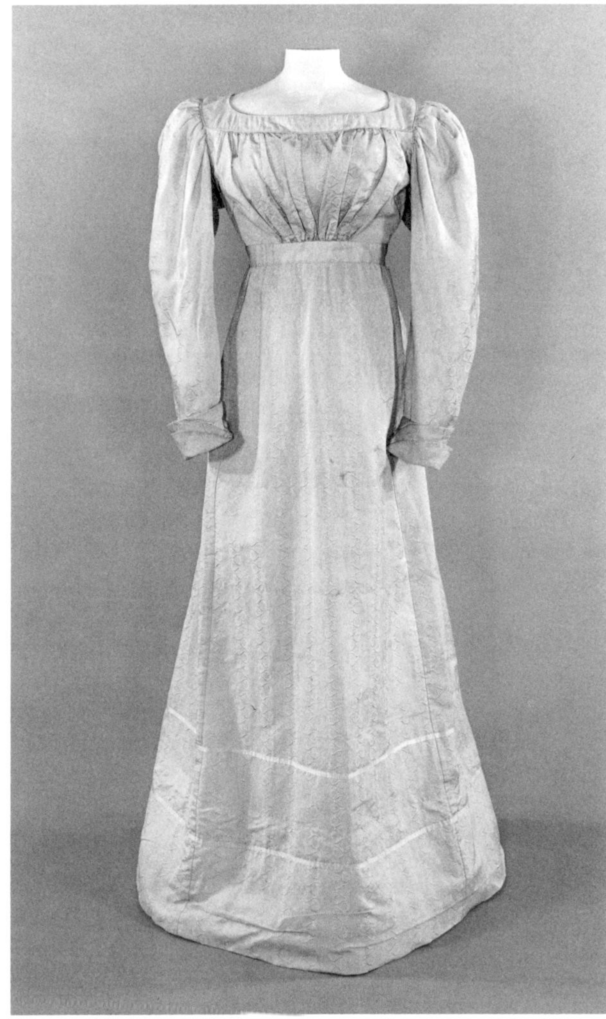

Cat. 172

and waistband to create the effect of diagonal pleats or tucks. The full gathered sleeves are long, the double cuffs designed to cover half the hands. The five-gore skirt, trimmed with silk ribbon, is gathered amply at the back of the dress.[1]

The fabric is as elegant as the dress design is simple. A pattern of meandering ribbons is created by a combination of plain, twill, and satin weaves. The crisp silk is probably of Chinese origin. There is no doubt that such imports were available in York, Portsmouth, and other ports. Bulkeley Emerson, a York merchant, left a shop inventory at the time of his death in 1815 which included yard goods such as blue silk plush, white and blue sarsnet, silk satin, black Italian crape, nankinette, satinett, cashmere, and bombazette.[2]

According to family history, this dress was the wedding gown of Ruth Sewall Putnam of York. The daughter of Captain Samuel Sewall, a mariner, and Hannah Moulton Sewall, Ruth married James Brown Thornton of Saco in

1816. He was a brother of Thomas Thornton (cat. 36). The couple settled in Saco, where Ruth continued to live after her husband's death in 1823. In 1827 she returned to York to marry Dr. Jeremiah Putnam, a Bowdoin College graduate who practiced homeopathic medicine in York for many years. A family anecdote chronicled Ruth's marriage to the young Dr. Putnam: "Nancy [Ruth's sister] beseeched widow Ruth to come back to York and set her cap for the highly eligible Dr. No reply from Ruth appears. Finally one day Ruth marches back to York from Saco and announces her engagement to Dr. Putnam."[3]

The white color of Ruth's dress does not in itself indicate that it was a wedding gown. In the nineteenth century, women were married in dresses of a variety of colors, including striped and plaid fabrics. If it is indeed a wedding dress, the style suggests that is was made for Ruth's second marriage in 1827.   KAO

1 The dress had been remade to enlarge the waistband.
2 YCRP; 25:373–381.
3 George Ernst, "Sewall Family Genealogy" (typescript, OYHS).

173

Viault Esté
Pair of slippers
Paris, France, 1820–1840
Silk satin, kid lining, silk binding, leather
Paper label (pasted to one insole) "VIAULT ESTÉ / PARIS /
Nº 17, Rue de la Paix / Fournisseur Brévelé de S. M.
l'Imperatrice des Français / THIERRY & SONS /
Regent Street 278 / LONDON."
Marked (on other insole) "MADE EXPRESSLY FOR / JOHN H.
ROGERS / BOSTON"
L 8⅞ (22.5); W 1⅞ (4.8)
Maine Historical Society

Throughout the 1820s and 1830s, women's dresses became
increasingly full at the hemline and skirts were worn shorter.
The exposed ankle and foot were adorned with fine stockings
and thin, flat slippers like this pair of white silk satin.
Square-toed with a very thin leather sole, the shoes are lined
with kid and trimmed with a tiny silk binding. Thin silk ties
at the vamp were tied over the arch, though some slippers
had longer ties, designed to be crisscrossed around the ankle.[1]

Such delicate, and for the Maine climate, impractical
shoes became popular at the beginning of the nineteenth
century with the introduction of equally scanty muslin
gowns.[2] Slippers were often of bright colors which contrasted

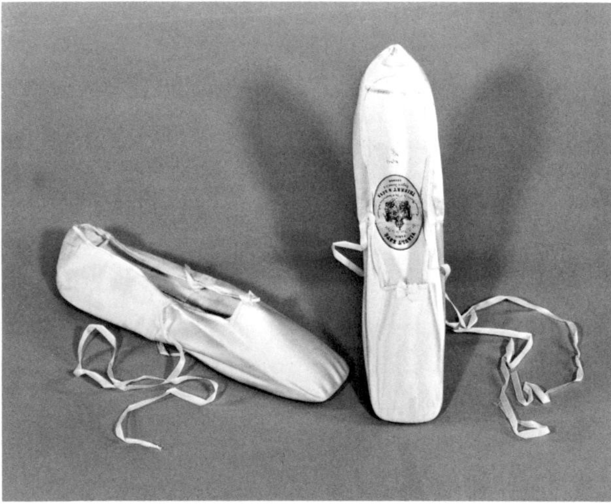

Cat. 173

with the garment. An 1827 report in a Portland newspaper
on "London Female Fashions," excerpted from *La Belle
Assemblèe*, a London fashion magazine, described a white
dress with an Indian red shawl and light blue kid slippers.[3]
During the 1830s, ankle-high boots which laced at the side
became fashionable. They were often made of a more
durable fabric called prunella, a twilled cotton.[4]

These slippers were made in Paris by Viault Esté and
bear the stamp of the Boston merchant, John H. Rogers. A
similar pair, of bronzed kid, also made by Esté is in the
collection of the Old York Historical Society.   KAO

1 Doreen Yarwood, *Costume of the Western World* (New York: St. Martin's
   Press, 1980).
2 A similar pair of silk slippers at MEHS was worn by Sarah Thompson
   at a Portland assembly in 1812.
3 *Eastern Argus* (September 28, 1827).
4 Elizabeth Sage, *A Study of Costume* (New York: Charles S. Scribner's
   Sons, 1926), 180.

174

Bonnet and veil
Possibly Portland, Maine, ca. 1804
Wool felt napped with beaver, silk ribbons, white silk
lining; black lace veil
H bonnet 8 (20.3); W bonnet 7¼ (18.4); D bonnet 9¼ (23.5);
L veil 52 (132.1); W veil 45 (114.3)
Maine Historical Society; Wadsworth-Longfellow House

As a close relative, Zilpah Wadsworth Longfellow went into
full mourning following the untimely death of her brother,
Henry, in 1804.[1] Zilpah most likely outfitted her existing
beaver bonnet with the ribbons and veil necessary to make it
proper mourning attire. The deep-brimmed black bonnet is
trimmed with gathered and pleated white silk ribbons with
black stripes.[2] A deep ruffle of black silk is applied around
the neckline of the bonnet. A detachable black lace veil is
tied around the crown with a drawstring, and would have
hung almost to the knees.[3] It could be swept off the face to
hang in back.

Formal mourning had been a common practice in the
eighteenth century, but became increasingly fashionable at
the end of the century. With the death of George Washington
in 1799, the entire nation mourned (cats. 75, 136–138). His
death inspired a rigid mourning etiquette which was closely
followed for the next one hundred years.

A sudden death would require that mourning dress be
made in great haste, with many hands at work to complete
the ensemble. Often clothing was modified with black
trimming for mourning. Black was the color for full mourning; the fabric generally had a dull finish.[4] Italian crape was

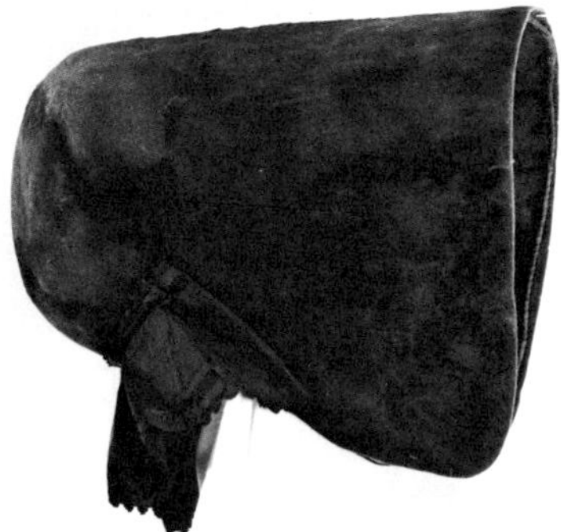

Cat. 174

the most common mourning fabric in the early nineteenth century, but bombazine (a matt, twilled wool or silk-and-wool-blend), wool broadcloth, velvet, silk gauze, and gossamer were also used. Merchants, aware of the potential profit in mourning customs, offered a wide variety of black fabrics and other mourning materials. Frequently more than half the stock advertised by Portland merchants was intended for mourning. J. Sawyer advertised "Broad and narow Black Bombazines . . . Press Crapes, Mantles and Shawls in great variety—Nankin Crapes—Black Sinshaw and Sarnetts." "Bombazines and Crapes" was the headline of Bradley and Dow's advertisement; C.F. Lyford offered "Mourning Articles" exclusively, including black silks, levantines, crapes, silk and kid gloves, hosiery, shawls, and vesting fabric.[5]

Somber dress was only one facet of the mourning tradition. Mourning jewelry was immensely popular throughout the period (cats. 134, 135). Many of the samplers, needlework pictures, and watercolors that have survived from female seminaries are memorials to lost loved ones or have man's mortality as their theme (see Chapter 5 and cats. 132, 133).   KAO

1 Henry was killed at age nineteen while serving under Commodore Preble in the Mediterranean when his fireboat, *Intrepid*, exploded prematurely at Tripoli (see cat. 2).
2 The "poke Bonnet" form is usually associated with the period of its greatest popularity, the 1840s. The style, however, appeared in London fashion plates around 1800, and was fashionable throughout the first half of the nineteenth century.
3 Veils of all types were fashionable in the early nineteenth century. They are found in advertisements in Portland, Kennebunk, and York. For a receipt for a white lace veil purchased in Boston by Samuel Nye, see Nye Papers, Dyer Library, Saco.
4 Gray with black or white accents was appropriate for second mourning, the period between full mourning and the return to normal dress; see Phillis Cunnington and Catherine Lucas, *Costume for Births, Marriages, and Deaths* (London: Adam and Charles Black, 1972), 244–250.
5 *Eastern Argus* (July 13, 1824; August 10, 1824).

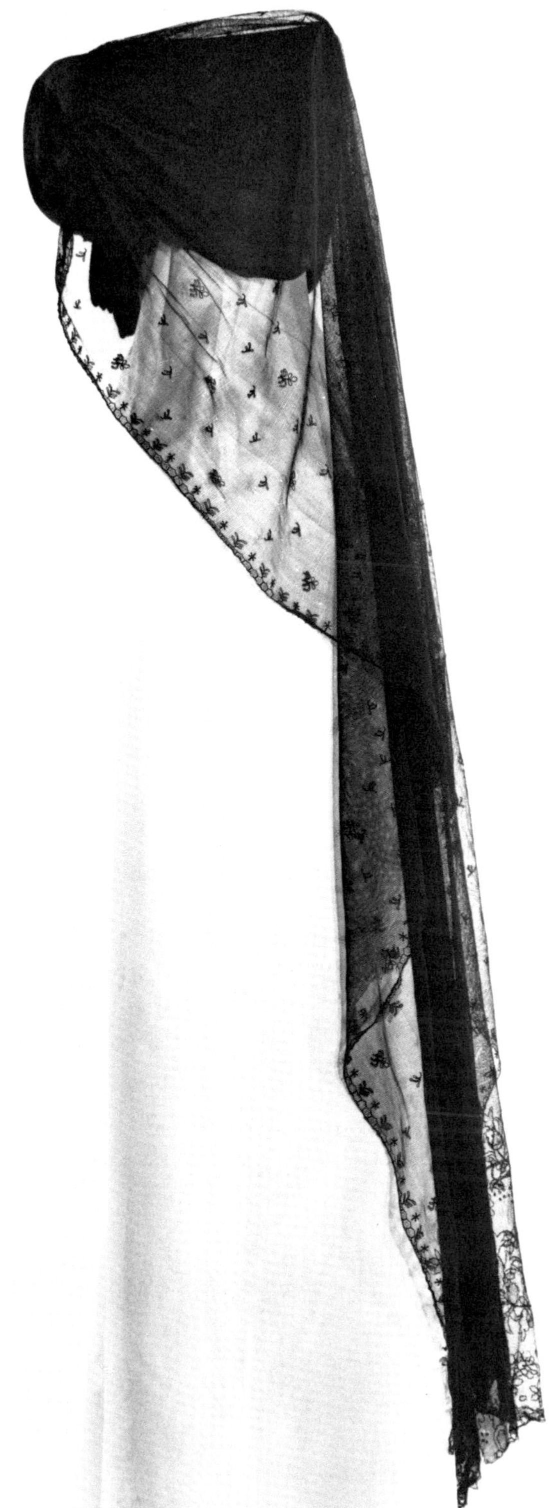

Cat. 174

Calash
Probably York County, Maine, or Portsmouth,
New Hampshire, ca. 1830
Green silk on reed and steel ribs, silk ribbon
H 16½ (42.3); W 13⅜ (34.2); D 13⅝ (35.0)
Old York Historical Society; Lent by Mrs. E. L. Paul,
1901; converted to gift by Florence Paul, 1960

*Her hair in front is craped at least a foot high much in the form of a
churn bottom upward and topped off with a wire skeleton in the same
form covered with black gauze which hangs in streamers down her back.
Her hair behind is in a large braid turned up and confined with a
monstrous comb.*[1]

So nonplussed was the Reverend Mannasseh Cutler by the
hair of Mrs. Knox, wife of General Henry Knox of Thomaston, Maine, that he penned this description in 1787. Mrs.
Knox was adhering to the fashions of the 1780s, which saw
oversized hairdos, pouter pigeon bosoms draped with yards
of sheer fabric "a la Buffont," and skirts made full with
bustles and petticoats. During this period of exaggeration in
women's dress, the preference was for long hair, which was
curled, stuffed, upturned, lengthened, and thickened with
hairpieces, and bedecked with flowers, beads, ribbons, and
feathers.

To avoid crushing the carefully sculpted coiffure, a calash
could be worn when traveling. This ample hood, resembling
the retractable roof of a carriage, was constructed of green
silk and shirred onto alternating ribs of reed and wire.[2] The
bonnet could be pulled up to protect the wearer from the
wind or the sun, and let down when out of the elements. This
calash is edged around the neck with a deep piped flounce
and has ties of yellow silk ribbon. It was owned by Sarah
Bradbury (1811–1890) of York.[3]

While huge calashes were most popular during the last
two decades of the eighteenth century, more moderated
examples were worn by some women through the 1840s and
1850s. Portsmouth milliner Eliza Ann Wilson advertised
calashes in 1834, and a list of "my best wearing apparel" in
the will of Abigail Emerson (1765–1836) of York included a
calash in 1836.[4] During this period, calashes were often worn
over elaborately trimmed caps rather than oversized
hair-styles.

The waning popularity of the large bonnet in the 1820s
was precipitated by the radical changes in women's fashion
in the first decades of the nineteenth century. The slender
and simple gowns of about 1800 were based on Greek
statuary (see cat. 165). The classical image inspired new
short haircuts or close-cropped wigs. In 1800, only thirteen
years after the comments prompted by Mrs. Knox's foot-high
coiffure, Eliza Southgate of Scarborough wrote home: "Now,

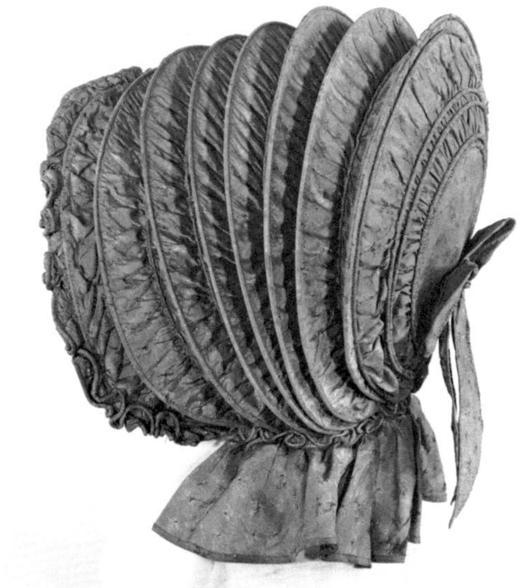

Cat. 175

Mamma, what do you think I am going to ask for?—a wig.
. . . I must either cut my hair or have one, I cannot dress it at
all *stylish* . . . how much time it will save—in one year we
could save it in pins and paper, besides the *trouble*. At the
assembly I was quite ashamed of my hair, for nobody has
long hair."[5]   KAO

1 Reverend Mannasseh Cutler, as quoted in Alice Morse Earle, *Customs
  and Fashions in Old New England* (1893; reprint, Rutland, Vt.: Charles
  E. Tuttle and Co., 1980), 294.
2 Although calashes were made in many colors, the most popular hue
  was green. C. C. Collins, a Portland merchant, advertised "Green
  Bonnet Silks" in the *Eastern Argus* (July 13, 1824).
3 George Ernst, "Bradbury Family Genealogy" (typescript, OYHS).
  Sarah Bradbury was the daughter of Joseph (1770–1854) and
  Jerusha Harmon Bradbury (1773–1846). Sarah's grandfather was
  York joiner Cotton Bradbury (1722–1806).
4 Advertised in *Edmund's Town Directory, Portsmouth* (Portsmouth, N.H.:
  Joseph Edmonds, 1834), 110; will of Abigail Emerson, cited in
  Edward Emerson, "The Emerson Family," OYHS, 2:196.
5 Bowne, *A Girl's Life*, 23.

Selected Bibliography

For a more complete list of titles concerning Maine in the new republic, see Ronald F. Banks, comp., *Maine During the Federal and Jeffersonian Period: A Bibliographical Guide* (Portland: Maine Historical Society, 1974).

Albion, Robert G., and Jennie B. Pope. *Sea Lanes in Wartime: The American Experience, 1775–1945.* 2d ed. Hamden, Conn.: Archon Books, 1968.

[Ayer, Sarah Connell.] *Diary of Sarah Connell Ayer.* Portland, Me.: Lefavour-Tower Co., 1910.

Banks, Charles Edward. *History of York, Maine, successively known as Bristol (1632), Agamenticus (1641), Gorgeana (1642), and York (1652).* 2 vols. 1931. Reprint. Baltimore, Md.: Regional Publishing Co., 1967.

Barry, William David, and John Holverson. "The Revolutionary McLellans." Manuscript prepared for the Portland Museum of Art, Portland, Me., 1976.

Barry, William David, with Frances W. Peabody. *Tate House: Crown of the Maine Mast Trade.* Portland, Me.: National Society of Colonial Dames of America in the State of Maine, 1982.

Barry, William E. *Pen Sketches of Old Houses.* Boston: James R. Osgood, [1874].

Baxter, James Phinney, ed. "Documentary History of the State of Maine." *Collections of the Maine Historical Society.* 2d ser., vols. 3–24. 1884–1916.

Bentley, William. *The Diary of William Bentley, D.D.* 4 vols. Salem, Mass.: Essex Institute, 1905–1914.

Bradbury, Charles. *History of Kennebunk Port, from its first discovery by Bartholomew Gosnold, May 14, 1602, to A. D. 1837.* 1837. Reprint. Kennebunkport, Me.: Durrell Publications, 1967.

Bourne, Edward E. *The History of Wells and Kennebunk from the earliest settlement to the year 1820.* Portland, Me.: B. Thurston & Co., 1875.

[Bowne, Eliza Southgate.] *A Girl's Life Eighty Years Ago: Selections from the Letters of Eliza Southgate Bowne.* New York: Charles Scribner's Sons, 1888.

Churchill, Edwin A. *Simple Forms and Vivid Colors: An Exhibition of Maine Painted Furniture, 1800–1850.* Augusta: Maine State Museum, 1983.

——."Crafts in Transition: A Case Study of Two Portland Silversmiths in the Early Nineteenth Century." *Maine Historical Society Quarterly* 24, no. 3 (Winter 1985): 298–337.

Clark, Charles E., and James S. Leamon, eds. *Maine in the Early Republic, 1783–1820: From Revolution to Statehood.* Hanover, N.H.: University Press of New England, forthcoming.

Cooney, Alice Knotts Bossert. "Ornamental Painting in Boston, 1790–1830." M.A. thesis, University of Delaware, 1978.

Cummings, Asa. *A Memoir of the Rev. Edward Payson, D.D., late of Portland, Maine.* New York: American Tract Society, 1830.

Dickson, Harold Edward, ed. "Observations of American Art, Selections from the Writings of John Neal (1793–1876)." The Pennsylvania State College Studies, No. 12. State College, Penn.: Pennsylvania State College, 1943.

Dwight, Timothy. *Travels in New-England and New York.* 4 vols. 1821. Reprint. Cambridge, Mass.: Belknap Press of Harvard University Press, 1969.

Fairfield, Roy P. *Sands, Spindles, and Steeples.* Portland, Me.: House of Falmouth, 1956.

Fairburn, William Armstrong. *Merchant Sail.* 6 vols. Center Lovell, Me.: Fairburn Marine Educational Foundation, 1945–1955.

Fales, Martha Gandy. "Benjamin Ilsley, Cabinetmaker in Federal Portland." *Antiques* 105, no. 5 (May 1974): 1066–1067.

——."Early Maine Silver." *Maine Historical Society Quarterly* 24, no. 3 (Winter 1985): 338–343.

Folsom, George. *History of Saco and Biddeford.* 1830. Reprint. Somersworth, N. H.: New Hampshire Publishing Co., 1975.

Garvin, James L. "Academic Architecture and the Building Trades in the Piscataqua Region of New Hampshire and Maine, 1715–1815." Ph.D. dissertation, Boston University, 1983.

Goold, William. Scrapbook. 1885–1890.

Maine Historical Society.

The Great River: Art and Society of the Connecticut Valley, 1635–1820. Hartford, Conn.: Wadsworth Atheneum, 1985.

Greenleaf, Moses. *A Survey of the State of Maine, in reference to its geographical features, statistics and political economy.* Portland, Me.: Shirley and Hyde, 1829.

Hepplewhite, George. *The Cabinet-Maker and Upholsterer's Guide.* 1794. Reprint. New York: Dover Publications, 1969.

Hilen, Andrew, ed. *The Letters of Henry Wadsworth Longfellow.* 6 vols. Cambridge, Mass.: Belknap Press of Harvard University Press, 1966.

Hülswitt, Ignatz. *Tagebuch einer Reise nach den bereinigten Staaten und der Nordwestküste bon America.* (Journals of a Trip to the United States and the North-West Coast of America.) Munster: Berlag der Coppenrathschen Buch und Runsthandlung, 1828.

Jobe, Brock, and Myrna Kaye. *New England Furniture: The Colonial Era, Selections from the Society for the Preservation of New England Antiquities.* Boston: Houghton Mifflin Co., 1984.

Kendall, Edward Augustus. *Travels through the Northern Parts of the United States in the years 1807 and 1808.* 3 vols. New York: I. Riley, 1809.

La Rochefoucault-Liancourt, Duc de. *Travels through the United States of North America . . . in the Years 1795, 1796, and 1797.* 2 vols. London, 1799.

Little, Nina Fletcher. "John Brewster, Jr., 1766–1854, Deaf-Mute Portrait Painter of Connecticut and Maine." *Connecticut Historical Society Bulletin* 25, no. 4 (October 1960): 97–129.

Lovejoy, Myrtle Kittridge. *This was Stroudwater, 1727–1860.* Portland, Me.: National Society of Colonial Dames of America in the State of Maine, 1985.

Lynn, Catharine. *Wallpaper in America.* New York: W. W. Norton, 1980.

McCauley, Robert H. *Liverpool Transfer Designs on Anglo-American Pottery.* Portland, Me.: Southworth-Anthoensen Press, 1942.

Marston, Doris. "A Lady of Maine: Sally Sayward Barrell Keating Wood, 1759–1855." M.A. thesis, University of New Hampshire, 1970.

Mellon, Gertrud A., and Elizabeth F. Wilder, eds. *Maine and its Role in American Art, 1740–1963.* New York: Viking Press, 1963.

Montgomery, Charles F. *American Furniture: The Federal Period in the Henry Francis du Pont Winterthur Museum.* New York: Viking Press, 1966.

Morris, Hobart L., Jr., ed. "Charlemagne Tower—His Journey through Maine in the Summer of 1829." *Down East* 16, no. 9 (June 1970): 46–49, 73, 75–76, 80, 84.

Myers, Denys Peter, comp. *Maine Catalog, Historic American Buildings Survey.* Augusta: Maine State Museum, 1974.

Nelson, Christina H. "Transfer-printed Creamware and Pearlware for the American Market." *Winterthur Portfolio* 15, no. 2 (Summer 1980): 93–115.

Nylander, Richard C. "The Jonathan Sayward House, York, Maine." *Antiques* 116, no. 3 (September 1979): 567–577.

Nylander, Richard C., Elizabeth Redmond, and Penny J. Sander. *Wallpaper in New England, Selections from the Society for the Preservation of New England Antiquities.* Boston: Society for the Preservation of New England Antiquities, 1986.

Old Houses of Kennebunk and Kennebunkport. 1939. Reprint. Kennebunk, Me.: The Brick Store Museum, 1962.

Owen, Daniel E. *Old Times in Saco; a brief monograph on local events.* Saco, Me.: Biddeford Times Print, 1891.

Remich, Daniel. *History of Kennebunk from Its earliest settlement to 1890.* Kennebunk, Me., 1911.

Rowe, William Hutchinson. *The Maritime History of Maine: Three Centuries of Shipbuilding, and Seafaring.* New York: W. W. Norton, 1948.

———. *Shipbuilding Days in Casco Bay, 1727–1890.* Yarmouth, Me., 1929.

Royall, Anne Newport. *The Black Book; or, A Continuation of Travels, in the United States, 1826–1827.* 3 vols. Washington, D.C.: Printed for the author, 1828.

Sadik, Marvin S. *Colonial and Federal Portraits at Bowdoin College.* Brunswick, Me.: Bowdoin College Museum of Art, 1966.

Sewall, David. "Topographical Description of York." *Collections of the Massachusetts Historical Society for the year 1794.* Vol. 3, 1794. Reprint. Boston: Massachusetts Historical Society, 1810.

Shettleworth, Earle G., Jr. "A Check-List of Portland, Maine, Cabinetmakers, 1785–1825." Graduate paper, Boston University, 1972.

———. "Portland Cabinetmakers of the Federal Period." *Antiques* 106, no. 2 (August 1974): 285–289.

———. "Portland, Maine, Engravers of the 1820s." Parts 1, 2. *Old-Time New England* 61, no. 3 (January-March 1971): 59–65; 61, no. 4 (April-June 1971): 105–110.

Shettleworth, Earle G., Jr., and William David Barry. *Mr. Goodhue Remembers Portland: Scenes from the Mid Nineteenth Century.* Augusta: Maine Historic Preservation Commission, 1981.

Sprague, Laura Fecych. "Glass in Maine 1630–1820." *Glass Club Bulletin*, no. 135 (Fall 1981): 3–7.

———. "Liverpool-type Pitchers Decorated for Portland." *American Ceramic Circle Bulletin* 5 (1986): 26–41.

———. "John Seymour in Portland, Maine." *Antiques* 131, no. 2 (February 1987): 444–449.

Thompson, Deborah, ed. *Maine Forms of American Architecture.* Camden, Me.: Down East Magazine, 1976.

Williamson, William D. *The History of the State of Maine; from its first discovery, A. D. 1602, to the separation, A. D. 1820, inclusive.*

Willis, William. *The History of Portland, from 1632 to 1864: with a notice of previous settlements, colonial grants, and changes of government in Maine.* 2d ed. Portland, Me.: Bailey & Noyes, 1865.

Willis, William, ed. *Journals of the Rev. Thomas Smith, and Rev. Samuel Deane, Pastors of the First Church in Portland: with notes and biographical notices; and a summary history of Portland.* Portland, Me.: Joseph S. Bailey, 1849.

[Wood, Sarah Sayward Barrell Keating.] *Julia and the Illuminated Baron.* Portsmouth, N.H., 1800.

———. *Tales of the Night.* 1827. Reprint. Somersworth, N.H.: New England History Press, 1982.

Zimmer, Edward Francis. "The Architectural Career of Alexander Parris (1780–1832)." Ph.D. dissertation, Boston University, 1984.

Manuscripts

American Antiquarian Society, Worcester, Massachusetts.
    Jonathan Sayward Journals, 1760–1799.
Baker Library, Harvard University School of Business Administration.
    Tristam Scammon Papers.
Bowdoin College, Special Collections, Brunswick, Maine.
    Hale-King Papers.
The Brick Store Museum, Kennebunk, Maine.
    Barry Family Collection.
    Bourne Family Papers.
    Oliver Keating and Co., Account Books.
    Lord Family Papers.
    Lyman Family Papers.
    George W. Wallingford Family Papers.
Columbia University, Rare Book and Manuscript Library, New York, New York.
    Cyrus King Papers.
Library of Congress, Manuscripts Division, Washington, D.C.
    Edward Preble Papers.
Longfellow National Historic Site, Cambridge, Massachusetts.
    Wadsworth-Longfellow Papers.
McArthur Library, Biddeford, Maine.
    Samuel Merrill Diary.
Maine Historical Society, Portland, Maine.
    Asa Clapp Papers.
    Cutts-Thornton Family Papers.
    Deering Family Papers.
    District of Kennebunk, Kennebunk Imports, Impost Book, 1800–1867.
    John Fox Papers.
    Andrew Hawes Papers.
    Cyrus King Papers.
    William King Papers.
    Nathaniel Knowlton Account Books, 1812–1859.
    Stephen Longfellow Family Papers.
    Daniel Walker Lord Journal.
    Abigail May Diary, 1796.
    Thomas Oxnard Journals, 1775–1786.
    Enoch Preble Expense Book, 1800–1804.
    Thomas Robison Papers.
    Ann Bryant Smith Diary, 1807.
    Wadsworth Family Papers.
    Elizabeth Perkins Wildes Diary.
Maine State Archives, Augusta, Maine.
    Records of the Cumberland County Court of Common Pleas.
Maine State Library, Augusta, Maine.
    Susanna Hovey Emerson Journal.
    William King Papers.
Massachusetts Historical Society, Boston, Massachusetts.
    District of Portland and Falmouth, Measurer's Return Book, No. 1, 1804–1807.
    Port of Portland, Exports and Imports, ca. 1827–1830.
    Portland, Maine, Custom House, Oaths and Registry of Vessels at Portland, Maine, April-June, 1813.
National Archives and Records Administration, National Archives-Boston Branch, Waltham, Massachusetts.
    United States District Court, Maine Records, 1789–1802.
New England Historic Genealogical Society, Boston, Massachusetts.
    Sheppard Family Papers.
    Southgate Papers.
    Thomas G. Thornton Collection.
New-York Historical Society, New York, New York.
    Erving-King Family Papers.
New York Public Library, New York, New York.
    Dennett Family Papers.
Old York Historical Society, York, Maine.
    Emerson Family Papers.
    William Frost Papers.
    Timothy Lyman Diary and General Store Ledger.
    Sewall Family Papers.
York Institute Museum (and Dyer Library), Saco, Maine.
    Abbott Family Papers.
    Cleaves Family Papers.
    Cutts Family Papers.
    John Haley, "Historical Notes on Saco."
    Samuel Nye Papers.
The Henry Francis du Pont Winterthur Museum, Winterthur, Delaware.
    John Doggett Account Books, 1802–1809; and Letter Book, 1829.

Index

Designed by Catherine Waters
Printer's negatives made by Robert Hennessey
Composed in Baskerville types,
Printed and bound by Meriden-Stinehour Press